Augsburger Rechtsstudien

Herausgegeben im Auftrag der
Juristischen Fakultät der Universität Augsburg von

Professor Dr. Arnd Koch
Professor Dr. Thomas M.J. Möllers
Professor Dr. Matthias Rossi

Band 86

Charl Hugo/Thomas M.J. Möllers (eds.)

Transnational Impacts on Law: Perspectives from South Africa and Germany

Nomos

JUTA

The Deutsche Nationalbibliothek lists this publication in the Deutsche Nationalbibliografie; detailed bibliographic data are available on the Internet at http://dnb.d-nb.de

ISBN: HB (Nomos) 978-3-8487-4611-8
ePDF (Nomos) 978-3-8452-8777-5

British Library Cataloguing-in-Publication Data
A catalogue record for this book is available from the British Library.

ISBN: Juta and Company (PTY) 978-1-4851-2604-1

Library of Congress Cataloging-in-Publication Data
Hugo, Charl / Möllers, Thomas M.J.
Transnational impacts on law: perspectives from South Africa and Germany
Charl Hugo / Thomas M.J. Möllers (eds.)
549 p.
Includes bibliographic references and index.

ISBN 978-1-4851-2604-1 (hardcover Juta and Company (PTY))

1st Edition 2017

Preface

"It happened on 5 March 2001. It was bluebell time in Johannesburg" (freely adapted from Lord Denning, in: *Hinz v Berry* [1970] 2 QB 40 42). On that day, a delegation from four faculties visited the Rand Afrikaans University in Johannesburg for the first time. The merger that led to the founding of the University of Johannesburg had not yet taken place. Under the auspices of Professor Helmut Koopmann (German literature), a cooperation agreement was concluded on the university level. (In 1998, the RAU had conferred an honorary doctorate on Koopmann in recognition of his work.) In 2006, the return visit took place at the University of Augsburg and in November 2008, another delegation travelled to Johannesburg. Once again, several faculties participated, represented on the Augsburg side by Professor Koopmann, Professor Juliane Alders (communication sciences), Professor Martin Middeke (English studies), as well as Professor Thomas MJ Möllers (law) and Vice President Professor Horst Hanusch (economics). In 2008, a partnership agreement was eventually concluded on the university level between the University of Augsburg and the University of Johannesburg. In 2009, Professor Möllers was invited to participate in the Annual Banking Law Update arranged by the Centre for Banking Law of the University of Johannesburg. In 2011, the deans of the Law Faculties of the Universities of Augsburg and Johannesburg signed a "Memorandum of Understanding in respect of Academic Cooperation". In 2012, Professor Möllers visited South Africa again to speak at the Goethe society in Johannesburg and to visit the University of Stellenbosch. In 2015, he again participated in the Annual Banking Law Update. In 2016, the ongoing cooperation and collaboration between the two Law Faculties eventually led to this publication, *Transnational Impacts on Law: Perspectives from South Africa and Germany.*

Professor Charl Hugo and Professor Thomas MJ Möllers met on numerous occasions during the last 15 years, several times in Stellenbosch, but also in Johannesburg. As emerges strongly from the number of contributions to the publication, this *Transnational Impacts* collaboration is without doubt a high point of the relationship to date. The cooperation of senior and junior researchers as well as the combination of paper and comment from a comparative law perspective present innovations. The parallels that can be detected between Germany and South Africa are impressive: various areas of commercial law (company, banking, insurance, social and labour law) and of public and criminal law led to numerous elucidating findings.

This volume is the result of our collaborative research. Fittingly, the German-South-African collaboration is also reflected by two publishers Nomos (in Germany) and Juta (in South Africa) joining hands. It is also the intention of both faculties that this should not be a once-off project, and, we are happy to say, planning for a second project focusing mainly on aspects of constitutional and public law, is far advanced.

We would also like to place on record that, in accordance with academic practice in South Africa, the contributions of all South African authors were subjected to a rigorous double blind peer-review process by reviewers who are experts in the fields of the contributions they were called upon to review, and who understand the importance of proper academic ethical standards. Their material recommendations led to the adjustment of the original contributions of the authors and assisted the editors in making editorial decisions. We would like to thank the reviewers for their efforts that have contributed positively towards the original and systematic analyses of the transnational impacts on law contained in this publication. It has been the aim of those involved (authors, editors, reviewers and publishers) to create a work that will contribute meaningfully to post-graduate research in comparative law.

The editors

Prof. Dr. Thomas M.J. Möllers (University of Augsburg) and
Prof Dr Charl Hugo (University of Johannesburg)

October 2017

Contents

Introduction

I

2016, in Europe, was the year of Brexit; in the US, it was the year that saw Donald Trump elected as president; and, in South Africa, it was the year in which the Government (in the wake of the Al Bashir drama described in detail below in Strydom's contribution) almost broke its bonds with the International Criminal Court. South African universities are also currently attempting to deal with strong demands for the de-colonialization of the curriculum. Debates arising from these events often contain elements of a mentality of keeping out what is not well-known and close to you – what Afrikaners term *laertrek* (a term that originated in the time of the Great Trek when the Trekkers formed a circle of ox-wagons to protect those inside from attack from outside).

It would be a sad day indeed if this type of mentality were to transcend into science – almost unthinkable. Law, however, containing elements or forming part of what Savigny termed the *Volksgeist*, is perhaps more vulnerable than most other disciplines in this regard. In the foreword of Tony Weir's translation of Franz Wieacker's seminal *Privatrechtsgeschichte der Neuzeit (A History of Private Law in Europe)* Reinhard Zimmermann points to a time when nationalism had led to "an ever increasing particularisation of law and legal science". "French professors at French universities", he states, "have started to write textbooks on French law to be read by French students, German professors at German universities to write textbooks on German law to be read by German students." Jhering was right when he complained that "science has been reduced to national jurisprudence".

Happily, however, this "nationalistic isolation of law" is in the process of being reversed. Internationally the harmonisation of law has become the focus point of many institutions that feature in the contributions below. Moreover, despite Brexit, the European Union is a reality, and, so too, the Southern African Development Community. In some areas, perhaps most notably international commerce, resistance to globalisation is in any event almost inconceivable. Moreover, it is suggested that the call for de-colonialization of the curriculum in South Africa, properly regarded, is a call for greater inclusion of African science rather than for the exclusion of foreign science.

It is further noteworthy, against this background, that South African courts are obliged by the Constitution, when interpreting the Bill of Rights, to consider "international law" and are expressly authorised to consider "foreign law".

As reflected by the first part of its title, "Transnational impacts on law", this publication attempts to contribute towards the breaking out from any "nationalistic isolation of law", and to open up the *laer*. However, as reflected by the second part of the title, "Perspectives from South Africa and Germany", the focus is specifically on these two countries. From the perspective of the South African contingent this must be seen as recognition of the major impact of German law, in particular, in South Africa. Not only do the two countries share civilian roots (despite the fact that the South African legal system is more accurately described as "mixed"), interesting parallels in their history, and, currently, very similar constitutional values, but, on a practical level Germany has been a prime destination for South African legal scholars over many years. The support by Germany of South African legal academics by means of stipends and scholarships, and especially the Von Humboldt scholarships, has been immense, and has led to highly valued academic friendships and ties. South Africa, too, however, has much to offer to international legal scholarship – especially in the context of breaking out from nationalistic attitudes towards law. The country has produced, over many years, a fine body of internationally recognised legal scholars, who, due to their "mixed" legal background, are able to move more comfortably in both the common-law and civil-law world than many others.

II

The volume starts with the contribution of *Van der Linde* and *Adams* on the movement of companies from their state of origin to a different destination state. The emigration and immigration of companies is, of course, at its very heart, a transnational issue. This issue is of central relevance especially for the European Union, because the seat theory clearly complicates transferring the seat from one member state to another and hence is opposed to the idea of a common market. The foundation theory, however, allows for a transfer without difficulties. Different manifestations of the movement of companies (the transfer of the real and statutory seat) both inbound and outbound are investigated. The authors review the position in the EU, Germany, the SADC and South Africa. They conclude that the SADC, though still in an embryonic phase in this context, will do well to integrate lessons learnt in the EU (which now allows restrictions on the emigration of companies but not on immigration). *Koch*, in commenting on the paper, sketches the "long journey" in Germany in this regard (associated with the question whether the place of incorporation or real seat should determine the *lex societas*) which culminated in the recognition of the free immigration of companies in the EU and Germany. He cautions that for the European position to serve as a model for the SADC it needs to be a convincing model and the disparities between the EU and the SADC as regional bodies must not be such as to preclude application of the EU model to the SADC. He suggests further that a supranational corporate form comparable to the *Societas Europaea* (European company) might also be considered for the SADC. Essentially the authors and commentator are in agreement that the globalisation of markets demands the relaxation of barriers in national company law and that lessons from the EU, carefully adapted, may be highly beneficial to the SADC.

The globalisation of markets extends, of course, also to insurance. The papers of *Millard* and *Möllers* provide, respectively, perspectives from South Africa and Germany regarding questions of fairness in advice and intermediary services in the insurance and financial markets industry. Millard sketches the manner in which insurance is, and has been, marketed and distributed in South Africa, starting with the Roman-Dutch background, the law of agency and mandate (governed by the legal principles that the mandatary must act in good faith and with care and skill), subsequent interventions by the legislature by means of the Financial Advisory and Intermediary Services Act 37 of 2002 (which moved from a principles approach towards a plethora of rules), and, finally, recommendations relating to market conduct published by the South African Insurance Regulator (the Financial Services Board) recently under the name of the *Retail Distribution Review (RDR)*. This she compares to the position in German law, which distinguishes between insurance intermediaries and those selling other financial products. Möllers, who in his paper concentrates more on the latter, explains the "overwhelming complexity" of the regulatory environment in this regard in Europe and Germany as it emerges from the *Wertpapierhandelsgesetzbuch (WpHG)*, *Versicherungsvertragsgesetz (VVG)* and, on the European level, the two *Markets in Financial Instruments Directives (MiFID 1 and 2)*, and the *Markets in Financial Instruments Regulation (MiFIR)*. Both authors identify a similar movement from a principles approach to a detailed-rules approach, especially after the 2008 financial crisis. Although both authors recognise that there are shortcomings in the rules-based approach, they are carefully optimistic that it will be beneficial and, if enforced rigorously, ensure a fairer dispensation for the consumers of financial services. Millard, moreover, points to the fact that the *RDR* recommendations are largely on a par with developments in Germany and the EU.

The financial crisis of 2008 emphasised the need for countries to have an effective and sound corporate rescue framework. Restructuring plays an important role in this context. The impact of restructuring proceedings on executory contracts of the company forms the specific subject-matter of the contribution of *Calitz* and *Lawrenson.* In a comparative analysis of South African and German law the authors indicate that international best practice, as recognised in the UNCITRAL Legislative Guide on Insolvency Law may involve the ability to take advantage of some such contracts (the beneficial ones) and to reject others (the burdensome ones). They indicate that both South Africa and Germany have struggled with similar questions in this regard (inter alia as to the rights of creditors when an executory contract of a debtor company is cancelled, and how ipso facto cancellation clauses should be dealt with). They conclude that the South African legislature can borrow beneficially from the German approach towards executory contracts in some respects – such as the principle that the business rescue practitioner or office holder must choose between being fully bound by the contract or cancelling it. Partial performance should not be an option.

The contribution of *Marxen* and *Hugo* relating to the independence principle that governs autonomous (abstract) instruments of payment and guarantee that are prevalent in international commercial contracts provides evidence of a transnational convergence of law as opposed, perhaps, to a direct impact. They demonstrate that the doctrinal basis of exceptions to the independence principle in South African law is public policy, and that this has, to date, led to the clear recognition of only one exception namely fraud by the beneficiary. In Germany, on the other hand, the doctrinal basis for exceptions to the independence principle has been the absence of good faith in the guise of *Rechtsmissbrauch* derived from paragraph 242 of the *BGB.* This has led to the recognition of a wider group of exceptions to the independence principle. Dicta from two recent cases in South Africa, however, are indicative of support for the absence of good faith (akin to the position in Germany but without reference to it) providing a basis for departing from the independence principle.

There are no less than three contributions from the South African authors dealing with aspects of private international law. *Neels* reflects on the transnational impact of German private international law in South Africa in relation to questions regarding the proprietary consequences of marriage. He concludes that the South African courts appear likely to adopt an approach at least partially inspired by the provisions of the *Gesetz zur Neuregelung des Internationalen Privatrechts* of 1986. *Fredericks*, in dealing with contractual capacity in German and South African private international law, points out that German law favours the *lex patriae* in this regard, and South African law the *lex domicilii*, *lex loci contractus*, *lex situs* and, possibly the putative objective proper law of the contract. Some transnational impact is evident in German law in so far as the *Einführungsgesetz zum Bürgerlichen Gesetzbuch (EGBGB)* has recognised the so-called *Lizardi* rule (derived from French case law) which, subject to certain exceptions, applies the *lex loci contractus*. Finally, as regards the international private law contributions, *Bouwers* reflects on the inferring of a tacit choice of law in international commercial contracts. He emphasises the importance of the private international law of different countries being in conformity with one another. Regarding tacit choice of law transnational impact is clearly discernible: the Rome I Regulation applicable in the EU (with the single exception of Denmark) requires a "clear demonstration" on the basis of "the terms of the contract" or the "circumstances of the case". The relevant South African case law, on the other hand, is to the effect that a tacit choice of law will not be "readily implied" but can be inferred on the basis of "the provisions of the contract and the circumstances of the case". Commenting on the paper of Bouwers from a German perspective, *Wurmnest* refers to the fact that the Rome I Regulation does not in this respect allow recourse to the "hypothetical will" of the parties, and, in this sense, changed the German law existing prior to the Rome I Regulation. Regarding the "clear demonstration" requirement he further refers to disputes between commentators arising from the terms used in different European languages for the English "clear demonstration" and opts for the interpretation that "clear demonstration" – the correct criterion, requires more than "demonstrated with reasonable certainty". Regarding the demonstrators of a tacit choice of law against this background both papers contain a wealth of examples.

Migrant work, of course, is by definition transnational. It is a social phenomenon of the modern world that poses many difficult questions in law. In their contribution from a South African perspective, *Fourie* and *Bowles* explore specifically the labour and social protection of migrant domestic workers. Their analysis takes account of various international instruments applicable to such workers as well as the position within the SADC. It is especially by means of these international instruments that a transnational impact on South African law is discernible. South Africa, for example, has ratified all the so-called core conventions required by the ILO Declaration on Fundamental Principles and Rights at Work. This, however, has not been enough to provide adequate protection to migrant domestic workers in South Africa. The authors expose the fact that such workers, due inter alia to their precarious immigration status as well as the fact that they often live in the home of their employers, are particularly vulnerable in South Africa (in comparison to Germany and the EU). They point out that while the South African courts are taking progressive steps to improve the legal and social position of these workers, significant and urgent changes in legislation are required. Commenting on this paper from the German perspective, *Benecke* points out that while it cannot be doubted that the typical domestic worker in Germany is indeed well-protected (most are EU citizens and accordingly have an unproblematic immigration status, and they seldom live in the homes of their employers), there is a specific group the members of which are employed to care for elderly or frail people requiring 24 hour on-call assistance. They face a de facto similar vulnerability. This is due to the fact that the combined effect of the German *Arbeitszeitgesetz* (limiting the maximum working hours to 48 per week) and the *Mindestlohngesetz* (imposing a minimum wage of EUR 8.50 per hour; 2017: EUR 8.84) effectively places the legal employment of such persons outside the financial means of most families.

The superior social protection offered by German law features also in the contribution of *Mpedi* and *Nyenti* on social insurance. Writing from the South African perspective they identify the three social security strategies in South Africa namely social insurance, social assistance and social allowance, as well as the plethora of legislation relating to them. They make the telling point that this multiplicity of laws leads to many persons who should be benefiting from them being excluded due to ignorance or an inability to find their way through the maze of legislation. Hence they argue for the systemisation and consolidation of all social-security law in a single more-accessible code, akin to Germany's *Sozialgesetzbuch* (which covers both social assistance and social insurance and is not dominated by the concept of compensation). The financing of social security, as well as adjudication and enforcement in both South Africa and Germany are dealt with, as well as the complications emerging from private schemes existing side-by-side with state schemes. Commenting on the paper from a German perspective, *Gassner* provides an overview of the development of the German social-security legislative framework and concludes that the planned reforms in South Africa may at least find partial inspiration from the long-lasting German experience. He points out, however, that there is a danger of creating a "paternalistic nanny state" if individual choice is unduly restricted – while acknowledging that the South African quest of protecting a large number of people with limited education may be a more important consideration.

Turning towards criminal law, and more specifically cybercrime, the paper of *De Villiers* provides a comprehensive oversight of the South African common-law background (the crimes of fraud, theft, malicious damage to property and forgery and uttering) and cyber-crime legislation (the Regulation of Interception of Communications and Provision of Communication Related Information Act 70 of 2002 (RICA), the Electronic Communications and Transactions Act 25 of 2002 (ECT) and the Cybercrimes and Cybersecurity Bill, 2016 (CCB)) in South Africa. He categorises the many different relevant statutory offences into three main groups: the unlawful securing of access and related issues; the expansion of the common-law crimes; and, finally, hate speech and related issues. This is compared with cybercrime in the German *Strafgesetzbuch (StGB)* and the EU's Convention on Cybercrime, 2001. The role of the EU's Area of Freedom and Justice in fighting financial crime is also emphasised. He concludes by pointing out that the common-law background of South African criminal law is significantly closer to that of Germany than that of England or America and that the German codification of these offences shows marked similarities, but also some differences, to those emerging from the CCB. Writing from the German perspective *Kaspar* deals with the difficulty in defining cybercrime, shares some empirical research (indicating that computer fraud, and fraud through access to communication devices, were the most common offences in Germany in 2014), strategic transnational and domestic measures relating to cybersecurity, and, finally, the development of German substantive criminal law relating to cybercrime (which, essentially, took the form of the introduction of new offences into the *StGB* – rather than, as was the case in some respects in South Africa, the adaptation of existing offences). He concludes with the point that this has resulted in a rather disjointed treatment and argues for a coherent and comprehensive new cybercrime act combining the offences, or at least a specific section within the *StGB* dealing with cybercrime.

There is, of course, a strong link between cybercrime and data (or privacy) protection. The latter forms the subject-matter of the contribution by *Watney* and *Cupido*. Their paper contains a comparative synopsis of the law of privacy and personal-information protection with reference to common law, constitutional law, legislation, and international treaty law. The role of privacy policies in relation to the online protection of personal information is also considered. In general terms the authors indicate how the internet, mobile phones and the social media (which are all transnational in nature) have created significant risks in relation to personal and financial information. The protection of this information against unlawful access has become very important. Hence, South Africa is in the process of implementing privacy legislation (the Protection of Personal Information Act 4 of 2013) based to a significant extent on the EU Data Protection Directive - the EU having taken the lead on an international level in this regard. It accordingly seems likely that the South African courts will look towards EU case law when called upon to interpret this legislation.

In the contribution of *Bilchitz* and *Heleba* the focus shifts to constitutional and administrative law. The authors explore, from a South African perspective, two fundamental concepts in constitutional law namely public participation and reasonableness. They investigate the manner in which the principle of public participation in relation to legislative processes, eviction cases and procedural fairness in administrative law has been developed by the constitutional court and has been linked to reasonableness. They further identify three rationales for, or approaches to, public participation (instrumentalist, dignitarian and relational) in this context. Commenting from a German perspective, *Wollenschläger* identifies a parallel development in Germany where constitutional law has also had a profound influence on administrative law. In his view, however, the salient distinction between reasonableness (as substantive standard for assessing actions of public authorities) and the procedural requirement of public participation may be diluted by some of the approaches identified by Bilchitz and Heleba. One difference between German and South African administrative law emerging from the respective papers is that in German administrative law substantive requirements (such as reasonableness) has been super ordinated over procedural correctness. Hence, an infringement of the right to a hearing, for example, does not necessarily imply, in German law, that the administrative decision is illegal. The potential for further interesting comparative research emerges clearly from the respective papers.

Turning to public international law, *Strydom*, in a thought provoking paper, traces the trends and principles that have emerged from the South African executive and the courts over the past two decades. He points out that despite the post-constitutional (post-1996) openness for international law to co-determine the future content of the law and the country's foreign trade-relations policies, the conduct of the executive in this regard has not been encouraging. On the other hand, the South African courts, when given the opportunity, have contributed much in this regard. This is demonstrated with reference to a number of cases relating to diplomatic protection, South Africa's Rome Statute obligations (including in relation to the recent Al

Bashir case), the national enforcement of decisions of the SADC Tribunal and selected extradition issues. In the process he deals also with the difficult question of the proper role of parliament in treaty-making. Responding from a German perspective *Lorenzmeier* deals also with the role of parliament which is further complicated as a result of Germany being a member of the EU. Regarding treaty-making he makes the point that the executive is bound by constitutional constraints and especially by the human-rights provisions which operate extra-territorially. Human-rights treaties have the status of federal statutory law in Germany. He points out that Germany has similar rules to South Africa as regards immunity and diplomatic protection, but has not as yet had to deal with extradition to the ICC (like South Africa in the Al Bashir case). It is, however, under a statutory obligation to do so if the Court so wishes.

The volume concludes with a demanding, legal philosophical consideration of transconstitutionalism (in the sense of the cross-scaling of constitutions at a regional/international level) and democratic legitimacy as dilemmas of regionalism (the European Union and the Southern African Development Community) in Germany and South Africa by *Lenong*.

III

As mentioned in our preface above, in November 2011 the then deans of the Law Faculties of the Universities of Augsburg and Johannesburg, respectively (Professors *Gassner* and *O'Brien*), signed a "Memorandum of Understanding in respect of Academic Cooperation". The aim was, inter alia, "to provide for cooperation on academic activities ... that will strengthen mutual understanding, foster friendly cooperation and promote sustainable and productive academic collaboration ... between faculty [and] ... researchers". The scope was expressed as including "joint research" and "joint publications". The envisaged activities include "[r]esearch collaboration, including joint research projects in areas of mutual interest".

South African universities are experiencing a strong drive towards "internationalisation". Within this context many agreements akin to that between UJ and Uni-Augsburg have been concluded. Unfortunately, however, they too often go no further than a signed document in a filing cabinet. This volume bears testimony to the fact that this one is a working agreement – it is in perfect harmony with the aim, scope and envisaged activities quoted above. It has produced quality research and fostered friendship.

The project received strong financial support from both Universities. From the South African side, many papers were co-authored by a senior and more junior colleague. As such it was a valuable capacity-building exercise that should bear fruit in future. And, while reflecting on the future, a follow-up publication is in the process of being conceived: hopefully we will one day be able to look back on a series, or, if the German is to be preferred, a *Augsburger-Johannesburger-Schriftenreihe*.

The editors

Prof Dr Charl Hugo (University of Johannesburg) and
Prof. Dr. Thomas M.J. Möllers (University of Augsburg)

October 2017

Towards free movement of companies – the European position as a model for the SADC

*Kathleen van der Linde**
*Faadhil Adams***

* Professor of Company Law, University of Johannesburg.
** Lecturer, Department of Mercantile Law, University of Johannesburg; Doctoral candidate, University of Johannesburg.

I. Introduction

An ever globalising world goes hand in hand with an increase in trade between nations.[1] Regional communities have been founded, throughout the world, with the understanding that the relaxation of trade barriers will increase commerce between them.[2] In pursuit of an integrated market they regularly look towards the facilitation of the free movement of, among others, goods, services, capital and persons.[3] The free movement of companies forms a natural corollary of this initiative. While it can be read into the movement of capital, goods or even services, it is primarily embodied in the freedom of establishment. A person (natural or juristic) will be "estab-

---

1 See http://www.worldbank.org/depweb/beyond/beyondco/beg_12.pdf; Kathleen van der Linde "Freedom of Establishment and Movement of Companies – Does South Africa Live Up to the Challenge of a Globalised Economy?" 2011 (unpublished) UNISA conference paper.

2 See Southern African Development Community (SADC) http://www.sadc.int/files/5314/4559/5701/Consolidated_Text_of_the_SADC_Treaty_-_scanned_21_October_2015.pdf (15-09-2017); East African Community (EAC) http://www.eac.int/sites/default/files/docs/treaty_eac_amended-2006_1999.pdf (15-09-2017); Association of South East Asian Nations (ASEAN) http://www.asean.org/storage/2016/02/The_ASEAN_Charter.pdf (10-04-2016); European Union (EU) the Treaty on the Functioning of the European Union [TFEU] http://eur-lex.europa.eu/legal-content/EN/TXT/PDF/?uri=CELEX:12012E/TXT&from=EN (15-09-2017).

3 See the SADC treaty (n 2) art 5(2)*(d)*; See the EAC treaty (n 2) art 7(1)*(c)*; ASEAN charter (n 2) art 1(5); the Treaty on the Functioning of the European Union (n 2) title II and IV. All of the charters and treaties of these respective communities identify the movement of goods, persons, capital and services as crucial to the development of the economic community.

lished" in a foreign state when it carries on economic activities of a permanent (stable or continuous) nature in that state.[4] Freedom of establishment necessarily involves cross-border situations.[5] A distinction can be made between primary and secondary establishment.[6] Primary establishment refers to the transfer of a company's central management and control (its real seat) or its legal seat (registered office) to another state.[7] Freedom of secondary establishment refers to the ability to conduct permanent economic activities in more than one state. In the case of a company, this could be done through a branch, subsidiary or agency in another state.

Free movement of companies within a regional community implies that the substantive law of the state of origin and the host or destination state must be tested for any barriers to emigration and immigration that do not accord with freedom of establishment. Unless secondary regional legislation or instruments regulate the methods and procedures for emigration and immigration, consideration should also be given to introducing domestic provisions that can give effect to the demands of corporate mobility.

In addition, conflict of law rules might impact on the freedom of establishment if they lead to the non-recognition of a company establishing itself in the host state. The connecting factors used by the home and host countries must be considered in order to determine whether the company will be recognised in the host state and also to ascertain the *lex societas* (applicable law) of the company once it has moved. The *lex societas* refers to what can

---

4 See European Commission *Guide to the case law of the European Court of Justice on Articles 43 et seq. EC Treaty. Freedom of Establishment* 1/1/2001 paras 2.1 and 2.2. In relation to the concept under the EU Treaty, see European Court of Justice Case C-2/74 21.6.1974 *Reyners v Belgium* ECLI:EU:C:1974:68 para 21: "the concept of establishment within the meaning of the Treaty is therefore a very broad one, allowing a Community national to participate, on a stable and continuous basis, in the economic life of a Member State other than his State of origin and to profit therefrom". See further Case C-378/10 12.7.2012 *Vale Építési kft* ECLI:EU:C:2012:440 para 34: "the court notes that the concept of establishment within the meaning of the treaty provisions on the freedom of establishment involves the actual pursuit of an economic activity through a fixed establishment in the host member state for an indefinite period."

5 EC *Freedom of Establishment* (n 4) para 2.4.

6 EC *Freedom of Establishment* (n 4) para 3.

7 EC *Freedom of Establishment* (n 4) para 3.1.2 makes reference to the central administration only.

be termed the internal law of the company or the law of the company's formation, life, and liquidation (death).[8] The *lex societas* is determined by means of two theories: the incorporation theory and the real seat theory. The incorporation theory states that the law of the place where the company is initially formed (incorporated) constitutes the *lex societas* of the company, regardless of where the company actually does business or where the actual management of the company is situated.[9] The real seat theory, on the other

---

8 Ebke "The real seat doctrine in the conflict of corporate laws" 2002 *The International Lawyer (Int. Lawyer)* 1015 1023. This is in keeping with the definition of the *lex societas* in many countries throughout the world for instance the Australian Foreign Corporations (Application of Law) Act 1989 which states that any of the following will be referred to the law of the *lex societas*: the status of a foreign corporation; the membership of a foreign corporation; the shareholders of a foreign corporation having a share capital; the officers of a foreign corporation; the rights and liabilities of the members or officers of a foreign corporation, or the shareholders of a foreign corporation having a share capital, in relation to the corporation; or the existence, nature or extent of any other interest in a foreign corporation; the internal management and proceedings of a foreign corporation or the validity of foreign corporations' dealings otherwise than with outsiders; see further Davies, Bell and Brereton *Nygh's Conflict of Laws in Australia* (2010) 719–724 for a further exposition on the Australian position. The position in the majority of common law countries is based on the English law position and is almost identical with reference to the issues that will be governed by the *lex societas*. For an exposition of these rules, see Collins (gen ed) *Dicey, Morris and Collins on the Conflict of Laws* (2012) 1527–1557. For a summary of the position in Canada and India, see Setalvad *Conflict of Laws* (2009) 22.3 and 22.4 who identifies the same subjects as falling to the *lex societas* both in Canada and India. Regulation (EC) No 593/2008 on the law applicable to contractual obligations (Rome I) (2008) art 1(2)*(f)* specifically excludes all of these aspects from its material scope (http://eur-lex.europa.eu/legal-content/EN/TXT/PDF/?uri=CELEX:32008R0593&from=EN (15-09-2017)). The Brussels I Regulation leaves all internal issues to the courts of the member state in which the company has its seat. The seat is determined by the private international law rules of the company – Regulation (EC) No 44/2001 on jurisdiction and the recognition and enforcement of judgments in civil and commercial matters (Brussels I) (http://eur-lex.europa.eu/legal-content/EN/TXT/PDF/?uri=CELEX:32001R0044&rid=1 (15-09-2017)).

9 This is generally accepted, see Rabel *The Conflict of Laws: A Comparative Study. Volume II: Foreign Corporations: Torts: Contracts in General* (1947) 31; Myszke-Nowakowska *The Role of Choice of Law in Shaping Free Movement of Companies* (2014) 63; Rammeloo *Companies in Private International Law* (2001) 16; Paschalidis *Freedom of Establishment and Private International Law for Corporations* (2012) 12. From the countries mentioned in this paper the following apply the incorporation theory: the United Kingdom (Collins *et al* (n 8)); the Netherlands (*Uitvoeringswet Europees Vestigingsverdrag* of 25 July 1959, *Staatsblad* 1959, 256 and see Rammeloo (n 9) 98–127); Italy (see the private international

hand, is generally interpreted to mean that the law of the place where the central management of the company is situated would apply as the *lex societas*.[10] This would be the place from which the company makes its decisions on a day-to-day basis.[11]

---

law code of 1995 ch 25 which states: "Companies, associations, foundations and other bodies, both public and private, even though not having the characteristics of an association, shall be governed by the law of the state in whose territory their incorporation was completed." Nevertheless, Italian law shall apply if the seat of management is in Italy. See further Rammeloo (n 9) 222 for the translated provisions); Hungary (Hungary has converted its connecting factor from the real seat doctrine to the incorporation doctrine. The previous position in Hungary under the private international law code of 1989 at art 18 of the decree law No 13 of 1979 states that: "If a legal person has been lawfully registered in accordance with the laws of several states or if, under the rules applicable in the place where the seat designated in its articles of association is situated, registration is not required, its personal law shall be that applicable in the State of the seat." This was with the proviso that the real seat and registered seat had to be located in the same place, which is usually a consequence of the real seat doctrine. The position has, however, been amended by law LXI of 2007 which allows the real seat of the company to be situated separately from the registered seat, but allows the company to continue being governed by the law of its place of incorporation. *Contra* Gerner-Beuerle and Schillig "The mysteries of freedom of establishment after Cartesio" 2010 *International and Comparative Law Quarterly (Int'l. Comp LQ)* 313 317–318 where they state that Hungary never subscribed to the real seat theory as "the provisions of the Company Act and the Commercial Register that refer to the real seat restrict the scope of application of Hungarian company law in cases that have a certain connecting factor (the location of the real seat) with another country; they do not determine the applicable law").

10 See further Myszke-Nowakowska (n 9) 55. In addition to the centre of decision-making and the main place of establishment there are also other variants that could be used in the determination of the real seat. These include the actual place of the general meetings of the shareholders and/or board of directors and the criterion of control (*critere du controle*) which refers to the nationality of the shareholders of the company and imputes the governing law of the place of their nationality.

11 This would be in line with the French interpretation. Traditionally French law appeared to favour the central place of business where it referred to the *lieu d'explotation* (business centre). The conflict between the *lieu d'explotation* and the *siege social* (registered seat, which also referred to nationality) was a long-standing source of friction under French law. This position was eventually resolved in favour of a connecting factor that in all essence appears to be the same as the actual centre of administration, see further Rammeloo (n 9) 203–205 in this regard. Also see Garcia-Riestra "The transfer of seat of the European Company v Free establishment case-law" 2004 *European Business Law Review (EBLR)* 1295 1309 where he states that the default position under French law is to look to the registered seat and only if there is an element of fraud, the court will refer to the real

The incorporation theory is widely recognised as being the approach better suited to establishing free movement of companies.[12]

We discuss the meaning and scope of freedom of establishment under three sub-headings: (a) recognition, (b) emigration, and (c) immigration. While emigration and immigration represent sides of the same coin, it is useful to deal separately with the rules imposed by the state of origin (in respect of emigration or outbound transfers) and those imposed by the host or destination state (in respect of immigration or inbound transfers). We consider two types of cross-border transfers: (a) the transfer of a company's real seat or centre of administration (*Verwaltungssitz*) and (b) the transfer of a company's registered office or statutory seat (*Satzungssitz*). Our focus is on the cross-border transfer of the seat and as such the scope of this paper does not extend to other structural changes such as cross-border mergers, divisions or takeovers. We also refrain from dealing with the *Societas Europaea* (SE), a company form subject to European Union (EU) law.[13] The fact that such companies are ideally positioned to move freely within the EU does not detract from the need to facilitate the movement of companies incorporated under the laws of individual member states.

First, we set out the legal position in the EU based on the Treaty on the Functioning of the European Union (TFEU) and important ECJ decisions on its interpretation of freedom of establishment.[14] We then consider how

---

seat as the connecting factor. See Ebke (n 5) 1015. When Germany still adhered to the real seat theory (*Sitztheorie*) the connecting factor was definitively stated as the place from which the company was managed or controlled; see further Rammeloo (n 9) 176 for the cases of the Supreme Court of Germany; Drury "The regulation and recognition of foreign corporations: response to the Delaware syndrome" 1998 *Cambridge Law Journal (Cambridge L.J.)* 165 175; Erk "The cross-border transfer of seat in European Company Law: a deliberation about the status quo and the fate of the real seat doctrine" 2010 *European Business Law Review (EBLR)* 413 416.

12 See Schmidt *Cross-border mergers and divisions: is there a need to legislate?* (2016) 34 (http://www.europarl.europa.eu/RegData/etudes/STUD/2016/556960/IPOL_STU(2016)556960_EN.pdf (15-09-2017)).

13 Introduced by Council Regulation (EC) No 2157/2001 on the Statute for a European Company.

14 See arts 49 and 54 of the Treaty on the Functioning of the European Union (2012) [TFEU]; http://eur-lex.europa.eu/legal-content/EN/TXT/PDF/?uri=CELEX:12012E/TXT&from=EN (15-09-2017). European Court of Justice Case C-81/87 27.9.1988 *The Queen v Treasury and Commissioners of Inland Revenue, ex parte Daily Mail and General Trust PLC* ECLI:EU:C:1988:456; Case C-212/97

German company law accommodates freedom of establishment in its various forms. A brief overview of freedom of establishment in the SADC follows. In view of the embryonic development in the SADC, we evaluate how South African company law would measure up to freedom of establishment should this concept be given the same content in the SADC as in the EU. We conclude that the SADC could learn much from the EU experience.

II. Freedom of establishment in the European Union

The free movement of companies can be read into most of the fundamental freedoms of the EU but it is principally based on the freedom of establishment as contained in the following two articles of the TFEU:[15]

> "Article 49
>
> Within the framework of the provisions set out below, restrictions on the freedom of establishment of nationals of a Member State in the territory of another Member State shall be prohibited. Such prohibition shall also apply to restrictions on the setting-up of agencies, branches or subsidiaries by nationals of any Member State established in the territory of any Member State.[16]
>
> Freedom of establishment shall include the right to take up and pursue activities as self-employed persons and to set up and manage undertakings, in particular companies or firms within the meaning of the second paragraph of Article 54, under the conditions laid down for its own nationals by the law of the country where such

---

9.3.1999 *Centros Ltd* ECLI:EU:C:1999:126; Case C-208/00 5.11.2002 *Überseering* v *NCC Nordic Construction Baumanagement GmbH* ECLI:EU:C:2002:632; Case C-167/01 30.9.2003 *Inspire Art Ltd* ECLI:EU:C:2003:512; Case C-411/03 13.12.2005 *Sevic Systems Aktiengesellschaft v Amtsgericht Neuwied* ECLI:EU:C:2005:762; Case C-210/06 16.12.2008 *Cartesio* ECLI:EU:C:2008:723 and *Vale* case (n 4).

15 The fundamental freedoms of the EU are the same as those of other regional communities see n 3 above. These articles of the TFEU are derived from arts 43 and 48 of the Treaty Establishing the European Union (2002) (consolidated version) (commonly referred to as the EC Treaty); http://eur-lex.europa.eu/legal-content/EN/TXT/PDF/?uri=CELEX:12002E/TXT&from=EN (15-09-2017).

16 This is referred to as secondary establishment. The term subsidiary is often interpreted to mean a legally independent company that is subject to the economic decisions of a parent company. In the context of art 49 the subsidiary is formed in a foreign jurisdiction. Branches and agencies can be interpreted in a different manner. Unlike subsidiaries, branches and agencies are not autonomous legal persons but extensions of their parent body, see further Myszke-Nowakowska (n 9) 26–27 for a more thorough understanding of the differences between primary and secondary establishment. For examples of case law where the secondary establishment of a branch has been raised, see the *Inspire Art* and *Centros* cases (n 14).

> establishment is effected, subject to the provisions of the Chapter relating to capital."
>
> "Article 54
>
> Companies or firms formed in accordance with the law of a Member State and having their registered office, central administration or principal place of business within the Union shall, for the purposes of this Chapter, be treated in the same way as natural persons who are nationals of Member States.
>
> 'Companies or firms' means companies or firms constituted under civil or commercial law, including cooperative societies, and other legal persons governed by public or private law, save for those which are non-profit-making."

1. Recognition of a foreign company in the EU

Recognition refers to the acknowledgement, in a foreign jurisdiction, of the legal personality bestowed on a company. Recognition must always be the first step in any type of free movement, as without it, a company has no legal standing, no ability to contract and does not offer the critical advantage of limited liability to its shareholders.[17] In this sense, according to Rammeloo, recognition can be construed in both a narrow and a broad sense.[18] In the narrow sense recognition refers only to a company being acknowledged as a legal subject, the bearer of rights and duties, which can be involved in transactions in the host state. The issue of recognition at this point does not take cognisance of the law applicable to the company; this would still need to be ascertained.[19] Sequentially speaking, determining the proper law of the company must come after its "recognition".[20] Recognition in the broad sense, on the other hand, "encompasses the ultimate outcome of the process of finding the proper law of the company",[21] the determination of the *lex societas* with all that it entails.[22] Recognition, in a narrow sense,

---

17 See the *Überseering* case (n 14) where the failure by the German court to recognise a Dutch company would have resulted in the loss of legal personality.
18 Rammeloo (n 9) 10.
19 Rammeloo (n 9) 10.
20 Rammeloo (n 9) 10.
21 Rammeloo (n 9) 10.
22 See n 5 above for a comprehensive illustration.

should be regarded as the minimum characteristic necessary for the free movement of companies.[23]

The need for cross-border recognition was already considered in 1929 by the League of Nations.[24] There have also been various attempts by the European Community to accede to a convention or treaty on mutual recognition. The Hague Conference on Private International Law drafted a convention on the recognition of legal personality in 1956. [25] Although it was signed by a number of member states of the Hague Conference, it never entered into force. A treaty on the mutual recognition of companies was drafted by the European Commission during the same period, but it also never came to fruition.[26]

The struggle for recognition within the EU has with a sense of finality been resolved by the European Court of Justice (ECJ).[27] The court has now definitively ruled that a company validly incorporated or formed in accordance with the laws of any EU member state must be recognised by all the other Member States.[28] A company formed in accordance with the laws of a Member State would usually have its centre of administration, principal place of business or registered seat within the EU as envisioned in article 54. The recognition conferred by the court in *Überseering* is, however, not all encompassing; it appears to be restricted only to recognition in the narrow sense. This is clear in both paragraphs 94 and 95 of the judgment where the courts states that freedom of establishment requires the recognition of " legal capacity and, consequently, the capacity to be a party to legal proceedings which the company enjoys under the law of its state of incorporation".[29] This position may, of course, lead to the application of two different laws to a company: one law dealing with the rights and duties as well as the capacity of a company in line with its place of incorporation and another covering the other aspects forming part of the *lex societas*.

---

23 See Rammeloo (n 9) 10, where he states that the recognition of a company as a legal being is now hardly ever contested.

24 Drury (n 11) 181.

25 Convention of 1 June 1956 concerning the recognition of the legal personality of foreign companies associations and institutions, available at https://www.hcch.net/en/instruments/conventions/full-text/?cid=36 (15-09-2017).

26 See the 1968 draft treaty on the mutual recognition of companies available at http://aei.pitt.edu/29885/1/P_14_68.pdf (15-09-2017).

27 *Überseering* (n 14) para 94.

28 *Überseering* (n 14) para 94.

29 *Überseering* (n 14) paras 94 and 95.

2. Emigration

a) Transfer of the real seat

In order to understand the ECJ's jurisprudence on the emigration of companies, one must begin with this statement:

> "...companies are creatures of the law, in the present state of Community law, creatures of national law. They exist only by virtue of the varying national legislation which determines their incorporation and functioning".[30]

One could argue that it is from this statement that the entirety of the jurisprudence restricting emigration is derived. It sets out the so-called European creation theory (*europäische Gründungstheorie*).[31] At the outset, in the absence of any secondary law, the court placed at the forefront the ability of the member state of incorporation to determine the conditions for the incorporation and continued recognition of companies. These requirements or conditions are sometimes referred to as "connecting factors", but should not be confused with connecting factors as understood in conflicts law.[32] The jurisprudence of the court indicates that a restriction on a company's ability to move will not violate its freedom of establishment. The restriction involved in *Daily Mail* is a clear indication of this. In this case, the restriction on movement stemmed from the United Kingdom (UK) Income and Corporation Taxes Act of 1970, which required a company to obtain permission from the treasury before moving its real seat out of the UK. The implication is that even though the UK subscribed to the incorporation theory,[33] which would in general allow a company to move its central place of administration while retaining its governing law, a restriction contained in its tax law prevented this type of movement. The court does not consider restrictions on outbound transfers as being in conflict with the freedom of establishment, categorically stating that the freedom of establishment conferred by the treaty cannot be construed as giving "a right to a company incorporated

30 *Daily Mail* (n 14) para 19.

31 Bayer and Schmidt "Grenzüberschreitende Sitzverlegung und grenzüberschreitende Restrukturierungen nach MoMiG, Cartesio und Trabrennbahn: Europäischer Rahmen, deutsche lex lata und rechtspolitische Desiderata" 173 (2009) *Zeitschrift für das gesamte Handelsrecht und Wirtschaftsrecht* (*ZHR*) 735 739.

32 This is clear from the reference to national legislation which determines "incorporation and functioning". See also Gerner-Beuerle and Schillig (n 9) 313 316–317.

33 See n 9 above.

under the legislation of a Member State and having its registered office there to transfer its central management and control to another Member State".[34]

Cartesio, decided 20 years later, is consistent with *Daily Mail* and evinces the intent of the ECJ to regard freedom of establishment as predominantly a matter of immigration that is imposing a duty on the destination state only.[35] The court in *Cartesio* was charged with determining whether a substantive law rule requiring the dissolution of a company wishing to emigrate amounted to an infringement on the freedom of establishment. The question was thus cast along the same lines as the one in *Daily Mail*, except that while in *Daily Mail* the company was not at risk of being dissolved, in *Cartesio* dissolution would function as a complete bar to emigration. Nevertheless, both cases involved companies wishing to move their real seat to another country, while retaining the law of the state of incorporation. The court again affirms the power of a state to select the "connecting factor" to which it subscribes.[36] The court, however, goes one step further in this case. It states that this power includes the right of a member state to restrict a company from making use of that law if there is a "breaking of the connecting factor".[37] The justification of the court for disallowing such movement appears to be clear. Referring back to the quote from *Daily Mail* at paragraph 19 the court consistently maintains that the national law of the member state of incorporation will determine whether or not a company is allowed to move its seat out of that state while maintaining its status as a company under its law.[38]

---

34 *Daily Mail* (n 14) para 25.

35 See *Daily Mail* (n 14) paras 21–23; *Überseering* (n 14) paras 69–70 and *Cartesio* (n 14) paras 107–109.

36 *Cartesio* (n 14) para 110 as well as *Daily Mail* (n 14) para 20. In order to understand the concept of a connecting factor as the court uses it here one must again consider it in the wider sense as referred to above. See Gerner-Beuerle and Schillig (n 9) 313 316–317 who argue that the reason behind the apparent contradiction in paras 109–113 in *Cartesio* is that at para 110 the court was not referring to a connecting factor as it is understood in private international law but was rather referring to a connecting factor in domestic terms.

37 *Cartesio* (n 14) para 110.

38 *Cartesio* (n 14) para 124.

b) Transfer of the statutory seat with a change in the applicable law (cross-border conversion)

The court in *Cartesio*, in the *obiter* part of its judgment, proceeds to distinguish between cases where a move will result in the change of the applicable law from cases where it does not.[39] Where there is a change of the applicable law, which requires the company to convert into a form of the host state, national legislation of the home state that requires dissolution does not enjoy any protection under the freedom of establishment.[40] The *obiter* remarks serve to inform the court's interpretation of "breaking" the connecting factor. It indicates that there is an exception to a member state's absolute right to bar emigration. It introduces a purposive element into the enquiry. If the purpose of the company's move is to convert into a corporate form of the host state, the company may "break the connecting factor" with the state of incorporation. Dissolution or winding-up, in such an instance, will result in an infringement of article 49. Returning to the *ratio decidendi*, the court concludes that under European Community law "legislation of a Member State under which a company incorporated under the law of that Member State may not transfer its seat to another Member State whilst retaining its status as a company governed by the law of the Member State of incorporation" is compatible with freedom of establishment.[41] Clearly, in the *obiter* situation, it is decisive that the converting company will indeed forfeit its status as a company of the home state – the law of the state of incorporation will not remain applicable. Apparently, the state of incorporation is thus merely obliged to keep the company on "life support" until the conversion is complete. A temporal requirement is introduced into the enquiry. Universal succession or transmission cannot ensue if the legal personality of the entity is already lost. In *Vale* the fact that the company had been deregistered in its home state, before re-registration in the host state, was viewed

39 *Cartesio* (n 14) para 111.

40 *Cartesio* (n 14) para 112: "…the EC treaty on freedom of establishment, cannot, in particular, justify the member state of incorporation, by requiring the winding-up or liquidation of the company, in preventing that company from converting itself into a company governed by the law of the other Member State to the extent that it is permitted under that law to do so." See further Schmidt (n 12) 35 who in her proposal for a legislative instrument argues that a cross-border conversion should always be an identity preserving conversion.

41 *Cartesio* (n 14) para 124.

as potentially fatal to its application for conversion.[42] The law of the home state, however, provided for resuscitation. In the view of the advocate general, if the company had remained deregistered in its home state, conversion in the host state would not have been possible. After conversion, there would be no obstacle to removing the company from the register in the original state of incorporation. According to Schmidt freedom of establishment should encompass a situation where the statutory seat is moved in isolation, without the simultaneous movement of the real seat or head office of the company.[43] She points out, however, that a company converting to a host state that requires the head office of a company to be located in its territory cannot make the law of the host state applicable to it unless it also moves its real seat.[44] This is because the rules determining the applicable law of companies have not been harmonized.

3. Immigration (inbound transfer)

The ECJ has on a number of occasions held that any provisions that obstruct the application of fundamental freedoms must be justified in the public interest. A justification would mean that the restrictions are "applied in a non-discriminatory manner; are justified by imperative requirements in the public interest; are suitable for obtaining the objective which they pursue; and do not go beyond what is necessary in order to attain it."[45]

a) Secondary establishment

The right to secondary establishment falls within the ambit of article 49 of the TFEU. In the *Inspire Art* case, the Dutch *Wet op de Formeel Buitelandse Vennootschappen* (law on formally foreign companies, WFBV) applied as mandatory provisions of the forum and had the effect of requiring an English company establishing a branch in the Netherlands to comply with certain provisions of the act.[46] The WFBV required the company, or the branch

---

42 Opinion of the Advocate General Jääskinen in the *Vale* case (n 4) para 79.

43 See Schmidt (n 12) 35.

44 See Schmidt (n 12) 35.

45 *Inspire Art* (n 14) para 111, *Centros* (n 14) para 34.

46 See Hansen "The free movement of companies" 2003 *Scandinavian Studies in Law (Sc St L)* 147 161; see also Nygh *Autonomy in International Contracts* (1999)

in this case, to comply with the rules on minimum capital. It also provided for the joint and several liability of directors in cases where the minimum capital fell below the prescribed minimum. This had the effect of rendering the establishment more difficult, and served to restrict the freedom of establishment. The provisions on minimum capital were justified by the Dutch government as falling under the umbrella of protection of creditors, as well as protecting both effective tax inspections and fairness in business dealings.[47] The requirements pertaining to minimum capital could not be attacked by relying on the principle of equivalence, as Dutch companies were required to have the same minimum levels of capital.[48] The provisions relating to the directors were, however, held to be in contravention of the principle of equivalence as directors of Dutch companies were not held liable in the same way.[49] The court held that any provisions that hindered the application of fundamental freedoms must be justified. Justification would mean that they are "applied in a non-discriminatory manner; they must be justified by imperative requirements, in the public interest; they must be suitable for obtaining the objective which they pursue; and they must not go beyond what is necessary in order to attain it."[50] The reasons behind the provisions of the WFBV were thus not justifiable, according to the ECJ.[51] With regard to the protection of creditors it was clear that *Inspire Art* held itself out as a company governed by the law of England and Wales and not as a Netherlands company.[52] Its potential creditors were thereby given sufficient notice that it was governed by legislation other than the legislation of the Netherlands. On the grounds of efficiency of tax inspection and fairness in business dealings the court held that the Netherlands government did not produce any evidence that showed that the measure satisfied the criteria of proportionality and non-discrimination. The provisions of the WFBV therefore constituted an unjustified restriction on the freedom of establishment. The ECJ in the *Centros* case came to a similar conclusion, on

---

199–209 for a further explanation on mandatory rules and their effect on the applicable law.

47 *Inspire Art* (n 14) para 123.

48 *Inspire Art* (n 14) paras 82, 114.

49 *Inspire Art* (n 14) para 128.

50 *Inspire Art* (n 14) para 133; *Centros* (n 14) para 34.

51 *Inspire Art* (n 14) paras 135–142.

52 *Inspire Art* (n 14) para 135.

the same basis.[53] Any mandatory provisions of a state which will have the effect of an unjustifiable restriction on the establishment of a branch will constitute an infringement on the freedom of establishment.[54]

b) Transfer of the real seat

There is a clear line of reasoning on the part of the ECJ that stipulates that if the home state allows the company to emigrate to the host state by moving its real seat, then the host state must accept this immigration. If the home state allows the continued application of its law, there is no breaking of the connecting factor, the onus on accepting the transfer then falls to the host state. The circumstances in which the host state can prevent the transfer of the real seat are limited by the same considerations as the section above, namely, they must be justified by overriding requirements in the public interest. The *Überseering* case provides a clear illustration of this. In *Überseering* the court found that the laws applied to an incoming company fall squarely within the freedom of establishment.[55] The court reasoned that by virtue of *Überseering* being incorporated within the European community it could avail itself of the freedom of establishment in another member state. The court was at pains to differentiate this transfer of the real seat from the transfer of the real seat in *Daily Mail.* The court reasoned that *Daily Mail* was a matter between a domestic company and its state of incorporation, while the case of *Überseering* was a matter between a foreign company and a host state.[56] The case thus involved the continued application of the law of the state of incorporation in another member state, as under the law of the state of incorporation the company did not cease to be validly incorporated.[57] "Thus unlike the case before the national court in this instance (*Überseering*), *Daily Mail* ...did not concern the way in which one member state treats a company which is validly incorporated in another member state".[58] The ECJ's interpretation could perhaps be further distilled from

53 The *Centros* case (n. 14) involved an English company seeking to establish a branch in Denmark. The minimum capital requirements of Danish law functioned as an impediment to secondary establishment.

54 See *Centros* (n 14) paras 34–39.

55 *Überseering* (n 14) para 52.

56 *Überseering* (n 14) para 62.

57 *Überseering* (n 14) para 63.

58 *Überseering* (n 14) para 66.

paragraph 72 where the court states that the decision in *Daily Mail* could not be construed as giving a host state the power to subject a company's right to the freedom of establishment to its own domestic laws. This position is later confirmed in *Inspire Art* where the court was asked whether the laws of the member state in which the company actually carries out its activities could be applied to a company when it was formed under the laws of another member state.[59]

The essence of the court's reasoning appears to be clear. A company incorporated in another member state is allowed to exercise its right to the freedom of establishment by moving its real seat to the host member state. The host member state may not apply its domestic law to the company in a manner that would restrict the exercise of this right.

c) Transfer of the statutory seat (inbound conversion)

The *Vale* case considered the transfer of the registered or statutory seat of the company. A conversion in this manner will lead to a re-incorporation of the entity in the host state and the law of the host state becoming the *lex societas* of the company.[60] It is the situation contemplated in the *obiter* remarks in *Cartesio*. The absence of statutory provisions of the host state posed an obstacle to the cross-border conversion of the company. In response to this, the court in *Vale* once again refers to the power of a member state to define the connecting factor required for the company to be incorporated in its jurisdiction as well as to maintain that status.[61] The reference to the connecting factor, on this occasion, is not referring to the power that the home member state enjoys but rather the power that the host member state enjoys. The natural consequence of a cross-border conversion is re-incorporation in the host state. The connecting factors that now apply must thus be those of the host state, as the new state of incorporation. It is clear that this is what the ECJ envisioned in referring to these statements again. As to whether the host state may deny the company this re-incorporation, the ECJ declares "that any obligation under articles 49 and 54 to permit a

59 *Inspire Art* (n 14) para 103.

60 *Vale* (n 4) para 51; see further the opinion of the Advocate General Jääskinen in the *Vale* case paras 74–78. Roth "From Centros to Überseering: free movement of companies, private international law, and community law" 2003 *International and Comparative Law Quarterly (Int'l. Comp LQ)* 177 198.

61 *Vale* (n 4) para 29.

cross-border conversion neither infringes the power…of the host member state (to select it's connecting factor) nor the state's determination of the rules governing the incorporation and functioning of the company resulting from a cross-border conversion."[62] The inferences that can be drawn from these statements are that a cross-border conversion inherently falls within the ambit of the freedom of establishment.[63] The references to discrimination, equivalence and effectiveness should therefore be seen as supplementing this initial conclusion reached by the court. The view of Advocate General Jääskinen would also appear to support this position. In his view the right to transfer the registered seat is a right that is inherently protected by the freedom of establishment.[64] Having identified it as falling within the provisions of article 49 and 54, he proceeds to answer the question whether a host country can deny a company the power to convert. Both the court and the advocate general answer this question with reference to paragraph 112 of *Cartesio* where the court refers to the possibility of a company converting into a company governed by the law of another member state "to the extent that it is permitted under that law to do so".[65] The reference to the law of the host state permitting the company to do so cannot be construed in a manner that gives the host state an unlimited discretion to restrict the conversion.[66] The statement in *Cartesio* should rather be viewed as indicating that the law of the host state will now apply to the company, indicating that the conversion can only proceed in line with domestic law requirements.[67] There are two aspects of the host state's law that would apply.[68] The first would deal with the normal rules for the conversion of domestic entities, which must be applied to the cross-border context: this would ensure that the converted company is seen as the legal successor of the entity in the home state.[69] The second aspect concerns the requirements for incorporation into a form of the host state, and this would require that the converting

---

62 *Vale* (n 4) paras 30, 49.

63 Rammeloo "Freedom of establishment: cross-border transfer of company seat – the last piece of the puzzle?" 2012 *Maastricht Journal of European and Comparative Law (MJECL)* 563 567.

64 Opinion of the Advocate General Jääskinen in the *Vale* case (n 4) para 69.

65 *Vale* (n 4) para 32.

66 Opinion of the Advocate General Jääskinen in the *Vale* case (n 4) para 70. See Rammeloo (n 63) 578, where he supports this position.

67 *Vale* (n 4) para 74.

68 Opinion of the Advocate General Jääskinen in the *Vale* case (n 4) para 74.

69 Opinion of the Advocate General Jääskinen in the *Vale* case (n 4) para 75 where he states that these provisions would include aspects such as the making up of

company complies with the normal rules for the formation of the particular type of entity.[70]

Referring to the destination state's rules for domestic conversions, the court discusses the principle of equivalence.[71] This principle entails that the rules of a domestic legal order must not be less favourable to persons who acquire their rights under European Union law, than they would be to persons who acquire their rights under the domestic law of a member state.[72] The principle goes hand in hand with the principle of effectiveness, which prevents a member state from applying laws that would render the rights granted by European Union law "impossible in practice or excessively difficult to exercise".[73] The court's decision is based, in principle, on the fact that while the law of the host state allowed for domestic conversions it did not allow for cross-border conversions. The application of the principle of equivalence thus rendered such an impediment contrary to the freedom of establishment.[74] There are indeed circumstances in which a host state could justifiably restrict the freedom of establishment, but this would be limited to instances where it was in the public interest, "such as the protection of interests of creditors, minority shareholders and employees, the preservation of the effectiveness of fiscal supervision and the fairness of commercial transactions".[75] The measures taken by the host state must thus not go further than what is necessary to protect the public interest. In *Vale* the absolute prevention of cross-border conversions was deemed to go beyond what is

---

accounts ensuring that the opening balance sheet of the company to be formed corresponds with the closing balance sheet of the predecessor company.

70 Opinion of the Advocate General Jääskinen in the *Vale* case (n 4) para 75. The provisions imposed by the national law of the host state would include aspects such as the share capital, shareholders and terms of the articles of association. See also *Vale* (n 4) para 40. See further Schmidt (n 12) 35 where she states that the procedural elements should be considered in line with the framework set out in the cross-border merger directive, the key elements of which would include the draft terms of the conversion, publication of the draft terms and additional information, report of the management or administrative organ, an independent expert report, approval by the general meeting, and two-step legal scrutiny in line with articles 10 and 11 of the cross-border merger directive.

71 *Vale* (n 4) para 48.

72 *Vale* (n 4) para 48.

73 *Vale* (n 4) para 48.

74 *Vale* (n 4) paras 54, 56, 57 and 62. See also paras 24 and 25 where the court refers to the *Sevic Systems* case (n 14), as a cross-border merger being of the same nature as a cross-border conversion. See further Schmidt (n 12) 12.

75 *Vale* (n 4) para 39.

necessary to protect the public interest. If a bar to cross-border conversion is considered in this light, it would be no different to domestic legislation such as the WFBV provisions referred to above. The interpretation of *Vale* could then be extended to situations in which domestic legislation does not cater for any type of conversion.

4. An evaluation of the EU approach to transfers

The dichotomy between the treatment of companies by the home state they are exiting and the host state they are entering, which begun in the *Daily Mail* case, has permeated the entire jurisprudence of the ECJ on the freedom of establishment of companies. At each juncture along the way, up until *Vale*,[76] where it was hoped that the court would remove this distinction, the court has, instead, further entrenched it. The position as it stands allows the home state to place restrictions on the emigration of a company. A host state, however, may not prevent a company from immigrating to it.[77]
One may question why the ECJ does not consider a restriction on the company's ability to emigrate as an infringement on the freedom of establishment.[78] A possible explanation for this could be the formulation of article 49: "Within the framework of the provisions set out below, restrictions on the freedom of establishment of nationals of a Member State *in the territory of another Member State* shall be prohibited."[79] The inference that can be drawn from this article is that the TFEU confers no right on a company to leave its Member State of incorporation but that only host Member States are required to grant a company the right of establishment. This interpretation is, however, criticised by Ringe, who argues that it would result in the freedom of establishment not conferring any right on a company to apply the freedom of establishment against its home state.[80] This interpretation

76 See the cases mentioned in n 14.

77 See Koch and Eickmann "Gründungs- oder Sitztheorie? Eine 'never ending story'?" 2009 *Die Aktiengesellschaft (AG)* 73 74.

78 See Gerner-Beuerle and Schillig (n 9) 304; Myszke-Nowakowska (n 9) 113 and sources there quoted, and Paschalidis (n 9) 76.

79 Emphasis added.

80 Ringe "No freedom of emigration for companies?" 2005 *European Business Law Review (EBLR)* 621 633 639.

would not be in keeping with the other fundamental freedoms of the EU.[81] The ECJ itself at paragraph 16 of the *Daily Mail* judgment, referring to the provisions on freedom of establishment, states that these provisions "would be rendered meaningless if the member state of origin could prohibit undertakings from leaving in order to establish themselves in another member state."[82] The court in *Daily Mail*, however, consistently adopts the position that a directive would be imperative for the case of emigration. The court thus accepts that while the right to establishment as it applies to natural persons includes both the right to exit and enter, this position arises solely by virtue of the directive allowing natural persons to leave their member states.[83] In the case of legal persons there is no directive and thus no right to exit.[84]

This explanation of the ECJ is problematic for various reasons. First, in *Überseering* the court remarked that freedom of establishment could not be made dependent upon directives and conventions.[85] Similarly, in the *Vale* case the court said that the absence of rules laid down in secondary European Union law could not justify restrictions on establishment – in this instance a cross-border conversion.[86]

Secondly, if the directive is indeed necessary in order to give effect to the freedom of establishment of natural persons, the question arises whether article 54 does not imply that a directive aimed at juristic persons should have been adopted alongside the one for natural persons. If juristic persons

---

81 See Ringe (n 80) 638 where he refers to the movement of workers as including both exit and entry; Wymeersch "The transfer of a company's seat in European company law" 2003 *Common Market Law Review (CML Rev.)* 661 677 where he refers to the free movement of capital as not being differentiated on whether it is exiting or entering a country.

82 Ringe (n 80) 633.

83 Council Directive 73/148/EEC of 21 May 1973 on the abolition of restrictions on movement and residence within the community for nationals of member states with regard to the establishment and the provision of services 1973 OJ L172/14, available at http://eur-lex.europa.eu/legal-content/EN/TXT/PDF/?uri=CELEX:31973L0148&from=EN (15-09-2017). See *Daily Mail* (n 14) paras 21–23 and *Überseering* (n 14) para 69.

84 *Daily Mail* (n 14) para 28.

85 *Überseering* (n 14) para 55. See further Ringe (n 80) 633 for an analysis of this position. He states that the *Überseering* judgment expressly points out that the use of fundamental freedoms cannot be dependent on the existence of secondary legislation such as directives.

86 *Vale* (n 4) para 38.

have to be treated in the same way as natural persons, and a directive facilitates freedom of establishment for natural persons, then one for companies appears to be necessary. This is all the more so if the existence of the directive results in different treatment of natural persons and companies. Alternatively, if the absence of a directive is the only explanation for the difference in treatment between natural persons and juristic persons, the question arises whether the directive goes beyond the scope of the treaty instead of merely giving effect to it.[87]

The proposed 14th company law directive was intended to deal specifically with issues relating to the transfer of a company's seat. Although the directive has been put on hold,[88] the cross-border transfer of a company's registered seat is one of the types of movement that was to be specifically addressed and made available to companies. Allowing cross-border conversions was justified as catering to the need of companies to select the law which best suited their needs. A report conducted by the European Parliament found that the only way in which a company could currently change the applicable law and move to another jurisdiction whilst retaining its legal persona was through the use of the cross-border merger directive. The facilitation of conversions by means of a directive would thus save the company start-up costs and simplify procedural steps.[89]

III. Germany

1. Recognition

Traditionally, the real seat doctrine underpinned German conflicts law. A foreign company would be recognised only if its real seat was in its state of

---

87 Art 54 of the TFEU states that "Companies formed in accordance with the laws of a Member State…shall for the purposes of this Chapter be treated in the same way as *natural persons* who are nationals of Member States" (emphasis added).

88 See the full report of the European Parliament: European Added Value Assessment (EAVA): Directive on the cross-border transfer of a company's registered office (14th Company Law Directive) http://www.europarl.europa.eu/RegData/etudes/etudes/join/2013/494460/IPOL-JOIN_ET(2013)494460_EN.pdf (15-09-2017); see further Schmidt (n 12) 15.

89 See the report of the European Parliament: European Added Value Assessment (EAVA): Directive on the cross-border transfer of a company's registered office (14th Company Law Directive) (n 88).

incorporation. In view of the ECJ case law on freedom of establishment,[90] Germany could no longer apply the real seat as connecting factor in conflicts of law matters involving companies that are treated as nationals of EU member states. It thus effectively adopted the incorporation theory in this regard.[91] In relation to non-EU companies, the real seat is still used as the connecting factor to determine the *lex societas*.[92] This has resulted in a "peaceful co-existence" of the incorporation and real seat approaches.[93]

A proposal was made in 2008 for the amendment of chapter 2 of the Introductory Act to the Civil Code (*Einführungsgesetz zum Bürgerlichen Gesetzbuche* or *EGBGB*).[94] This chapter deals with private international law and the proposal entailed introducing provisions aimed specifically at companies and other juristic persons. It would apply to EU and non-EU situations alike. Under the proposed new article 10(1) a company would be subject to the law of the country in whose official register it had been entered.[95] The particular matters to be governed by the *lex societas* would be set out in article 10(2). Article 10a would determine the law applicable to mergers, conversions and similar reorganisations. Changing the applicable law would be possible under article 10b when a company is entered into the official register of another country. This would be possible only if both the state of origin and the destination state allowed such a change of applicable law without dissolution in the original state and a new incorporation in the

90 Particularly *Überseering* (n 14).

91 See Behrens "From 'Real Seat' to 'Legal Seat': Germany's Private International Company Law Revolution" in *Resolving International Conflicts: Liber Amicorum Tibor Varady* (2009) 46–50 and Teichman "Report from Germany" in 2008 *European Company Law (ECL)* 189.

92 Kieninger in Leible and Reichert (eds) *Münchener Handbuch des Gesellschaftsrechts Band 6* (2013) § 52 para 9; Jasper and Wollbrink in Priester and Mayer (eds) *Münchener Handbuch des Gesellschaftsrechts Band 3* (2009) § 75 para 26; Dauner-Lieb in Zöllner and Noack (eds) *Kölner Kommentar zum Aktiengesetz Band 1* (2010) § 5 para 28.

93 Jasper and Wollbrink (n 92) § 75 para 33; Dauner-Lieb (n 92) § 5 para 29; Koch and Eickmann (n 77) 74. See BGH 27-10-2008 – II ZR 158/06 – *Die Aktiengesellschaft (AG)* 2009, 84.

94 See Referentenentwurf Gesetz zum Internationalen Privatrecht der Gesellschaften, Vereine und juristische Personen of 7 January 2008, available at http://www.rwi.uzh.ch/oe/stiftungsrecht/rechtsentwicklungen/Referentenentwurf-IGR_120417.pdf (15-09-2017).

95 Companies and other entities not (yet) appearing in the commercial register would be governed by the law according to which they have been organised.

destination state and provided the respective requirements of each state had been satisfied. This proposal appears to have been abandoned.[96]

A foreign company establishing itself in Germany through an independent branch (*Zweigniederlassung*) must be registered in the commercial register.[97] An operational location (*Betriebsstätte*) is not required to enter in the commercial register, but might have to register with a local trade office.

2. Emigration (outbound transfers)

a) Transfer of the real seat

Given the dichotomy between emigration and immigration in EU law, Germany could have continued requiring that companies incorporated under its laws have some physical nexus with their statutory seat.[98] This would have prevented companies from moving their real seats out of Germany while still being governed by German law.[99] Faced with the competitive pressure of incorporation states that made their corporate forms available regardless of the location of the real seat, Germany instead opted to amend its legislation by removing the requirement that the statutory and real seat should coincide.[100] This not only made German corporate forms available as vehicles for off-shore business operations, but also facilitated emigration by allowing German companies to move their real seats to other countries.[101]

---

96 See Dauner-Lieb (n 92) § 5 para 28.

97 secs 13 et seqq of the *Handelsgesetzbuch (HGB)*. An independent branch is basically a branch that could function without its headquarter company and must have its own share of the company's assets and its own accounts.

98 See Bayer and Schmidt (n 31) 735. A company had to determine its statutory seat as a place where business was carried on, management took place or administration was seated, see sec 5 *Aktiengesetz (AktG)* and sec 4 *Gesetz betreffend die Gesellschaften mit beschränkter Haftung (GmbHG)* prior to their amendment by *Gesetz zur Modernisierung des GmbH-Rechts und zur Bekämpfung von Missbrächen (MoMiG)* of 28.10.2008, BGBl. I 2026.

99 The resolution to move would be void or would be regarded as dissolving the company, see Dauner-Lieb (n 92) 63 21.

100 Sec 4 *GmbHG* was amended in 1998 by *Handelsrechtsreformgesetz* (*HRefG)* of 22.6.1998, BGBl. I 1474 which brought its provisions into line with sec 5 AktG.

101 Dauner-Lieb (n 92) § 5 para 29.

b) Transfer of the statutory seat (*Herausformwechsel*)

A German company must have its statutory seat in Germany.[102] An attempt to move its statutory seat to another country, whilst still being governed by German law, would be void.[103] However, the emigration of a company intending to convert into a corporate form of a host state within the EU, and to be governed by the law of the host state, must be allowed. In particular, it was established in *Vale* that the company may not be wound up or dissolved in the home state before the completion of its conversion.

The procedure for outbound conversions is not expressly regulated by German statutory provisions,[104] but such conversions must be accommodated with due regard for the requirements of equivalence and effectiveness. It has been suggested that the rules on domestic conversions,[105] as well as aspects of the requirements applicable to cross-border mergers,[106] should be adapted. In order to protect the interests of minority shareholders, employees and creditors, which could support justifiable restrictions on freedom of establishment, the provisions of the Conversion Law (*Umwandlungsgesetz, UmwG*) pertaining to cross-border mergers should be applied by analogy.[107] The protection mechanisms of the *UmwG* include the right of minority shareholders to attack the validity of the shareholder resolution approving the transfer,[108] the right to be compensated for inadequate consideration received in respect of shares or ownership rights,[109] and the right of creditors to insist on security where the recovery of outstanding debts is endangered by the transfer.[110] In addition, guidance should be derived from the regulation of "conversions", in the sense of changes in the applicable law, pertaining to the *Societas Europea* (SE), which among other things sets out the

---

102 sec 4 *GmbHG*; sec 5 *AktG*.

103 The shareholder resolution to change the seat would be void, see OLG Düsseldorf 26.3.2001 – 3 Wx 88/01 – 2001 *Neue Juristische Wochenschrift (NJW)* 2184.

104 Hoffmann in Leible and Reichert (eds) *Münchener Handbuch des Gesellschaftsrechts Band 6 (2013)* §54 paras 11 et seqq.

105 In particular sec 190 and sec 192 *Umwandlungsgesetz (UmwG)*.

106 secs 122 et seqq *UmwG*.

107 See Hoffmann (n 104) §54 paras 6 and 11.

108 sec 195 *UmwG*. See Hoffmann (n 104) § 54 para 12.

109 sec 196 *UmwG*.

110 Either by analogy to sec 22 or sec 122j *UmwG*, see Hoffmann (n 104) § 5 para 16.

requirements pertaining to register entries in the two states.[111] Ideally, in order to promote legal certainty, legislation should be introduced.[112]

3. Immigration

a) Transfer of the real seat

The right of primary establishment enjoyed by companies under the TFEU implies that Germany must allow an EU company to move its real seat into Germany while remaining subject to the *lex societas* of the state of origin.[113]

No specific provisions have been introduced to facilitate or justifiably restrict such transfers.

b) Transfer of the statutory seat (*Hereinformwechsel*)

The *Vale* case made it clear that cross-border conversions within the EU resorted under the freedom of establishment. That Germany had to allow foreign companies to convert into companies governed by German law was confirmed by the OLG Nürnberg in a decision of 19 June 2013.[114] The court explained that this was based on the principle of equivalence and that since Germany provided for domestic conversions, it could not prevent the conversion of foreign EU companies. The court made it clear that the company would remain the same entity before and after the conversion – its identity would be preserved.

As in the *case* of outbound conversions, specific statutory provisions are lacking and the provisions on domestic conversions will have to be adapted and supplemented by relevant requirements pertaining to cross-border mergers.

---

111 Council Regulation (EC) No 2157/2001 of 8 October 2001 on the Statute for a European company (SE) (SE-VO) and the SE executive law (*Gesetz zur Ausführung der Verordnung (EG)* Nr. 2157/2001 des Rates vom 8. Oktober 2001 über das Statut der Europäischen Gesellschaft (SE) (*SE-Ausführungsgesetz – SEAG*)).

112 Hoffmann (n 104) § 54 para 6.

113 See the *Überseering* case (n 14).

114 OLG Nürnberg 19.6.2013 – 12 W 520/13 –2014 *Zeitschrift für Wirtschaftsrecht (ZIP)* 128.

IV. The Southern African Development Community (SADC)

This topic of free movement of companies is especially relevant to Southern Africa and Africa as a whole, as many countries in the different African economic blocs have committed themselves to a free trade area which it is hoped will eventually lead to an economic organisation, cast in the same mould as the EU. Although the SADC[115] is in its infancy, it is likely that this economic union will face many of the same hurdles that the EU experienced in its formative years. As the EU already has vast experience on these matters it is hoped that EU law can be used as a model which can be adapted to suit African circumstances. The SADC, in its current form, was established by treaty in 1992.[116] South Africa became a member of the SADC in 1994.[117]

Article 5 of the SADC treaty stipulates the objectives, which among others, includes the promotion of sustainable and equitable economic growth. The manner by which the SADC hopes to achieve this economic growth is through the development of regional integration and eventually, a single market. The development of a single market is dependent on the development of policies which will eliminate obstacles to the free movement of capital, labour, goods, services and of the people of the SADC generally.[118] In line with these policies, the SADC has developed a protocol on the free movement of persons which contains within it an article calling for the right of establishment for natural persons as well as the harmonisation of national laws.[119] The position is thus similar to that in the EU where a specific instrument facilitates free movement of natural persons, but not of companies.

---

115 The SADC, established by the SADC treaty (n 2) above, has 15 member states: Angola, Botswana, the DRC, Lesotho, Malawi, Mauritius, Mozambique, Namibia, South Africa, Swaziland, Tanzania, Zambia and Zimbabwe.

116 SADC treaty (n 2).

117 Essop "The role of SADC in boosting domestic, regional, continental and international trade" 2015 *Commonwealth Youth and Development* 88 89.

118 SADC treaty (n 2) art 5(2)*(d)*.

119 See arts 18–20 of the SADC Protocol on the facilitation of movement of persons (2005) http://www.sadc.int/files/9513/5292/8363/Protocol_on_Facilitation_of_Movement_of_Persons2005.pdf (15-09-2017); art 18 states: "Establishment shall mean permission or authority granted by a State Party in terms of its national laws to a citizen of another State Party, for: (a) Exercise of economic activity either as an employee or a self-employed person; (b) Establishing and managing a profession, trade, business or calling. This article could provide a basis for the free movement of companies within the SADC." The article is comparable to art 4 of the

The SADC treaty also calls for the development of a tribunal.[120] The envisioned function of the tribunal will be similar to that of the ECJ, in interpreting the treaty and protocols to the treaty.[121] The decisions of the tribunal will be final and binding.[122] The tribunal will thus have to determine the precise scope of freedom of establishment of companies in the SADC.

V. South Africa

The South African Companies Act[123] makes provision for, and differentiates between, three types of foreign companies, namely foreign companies, external companies and domesticated companies.[124] The term "foreign company" refers to a company incorporated outside South Africa, irrespective of whether it is a profit or non-profit company or whether it is carrying on business in South Africa or non-profit activities within South Africa.[125] An "external company" is a foreign company that carries on business activities or non-profit activities within South Africa.[126] A "domesticated company" is a foreign company whose registration has been transferred to South Africa.[127]

1. Recognition in South Africa

A foreign company in terms of the act therefore refers to any company that is not a company incorporated in terms of South African law. The Companies Act, without expressly stipulating it, seems to support the incorporation

first EU directive on the abolition of restrictions on movement and residence within the Community for nationals of Member States with regard to establishment and the provision of services (Council Directive 73/148/EEC of 21 May 1973) http://eur-lex.europa.eu/legal-content/EN/TXT/PDF/?uri=CELEX:31973L0148&from=EN (15-09-2017). Protocols are developed under art 22 of the SADC treaty.

120 SADC Treaty (n 2) art 16.

121 SADC Treaty (n 2) art 16(4).

122 SADC Treaty (n 2) art 16(5).

123 71 of 2008, which came into operation on 1 May 2011.

124 The act refers to foreign, external and domesticated companies.

125 Companies Act of 2008, sec 1.

126 Companies Act (n. 123) sec 1 sv "external company".

127 Companies Act (n. 123) sec 1 sv "domesticated company".

theory. This is perhaps more clearly seen when the definition of a "juristic person" is further analysed. In terms of section 1, a juristic person is deemed to include a foreign company. The common understanding of a juristic person in South African law is a separate legal entity with the ability to be the holder of rights and the bearer of duties.[128] The indication seems to be that, even though foreign and external companies do not fall within the definition of a "company",[129] if a company is validly incorporated in its state of incorporation it will be recognised in South Africa as having juristic personality and the competence to be a party to legal proceedings.

2. Freedom of establishment: foreign and external companies

The Companies Act implicitly recognises the freedom of foreign companies to establish themselves in South Africa. The consequences of such establishment are set out in the act.

a) The obligation to register as external company

The Companies Act requires registration as external company when a foreign company is "conducting business" in South Africa. But the ambit of "conducting business" is limited in two ways. First, there is a list of activities that may take place in South Africa without being regarded as the carrying on of business.[130] Secondly, a company will generally be regarded as conducting business in South Africa only if it is reasonable to conclude, based on a course of conduct extending over some time, that it intended to

---

128 See Cassim et al *Contemporary Company Law* (2012) 31. See further *Dadoo Ltd v Krugersdorp Municipal Council* 1920 AD 530 550–551 and *Ebrahim v Airport Cold Storage v (Pty) Ltd* 2009 1 All SA 330 (SCA) where the court upholds a company as a separate legal person which owns assets in its own right and is liable to pay its own debts.

129 "Company" refers to juristic persons incorporated under the Companies Act, domesticated companies, and pre-existing companies registered under repealed legislation, see Companies Act (n. 123) sec 1 sv "company".

130 Companies Act (n. 123) sec 23(2A).

do so on a continuous basis.[131] There is thus a temporal and qualitative aspect.[132] The list of activities that can be undertaken in South Africa without triggering the obligation to register as external company[133] includes the holding of board or shareholder meetings or otherwise conducting the internal affairs of the company; having bank or other financial accounts; having a securities registration or transfer office; creating or acquiring (becoming entitled to) debts, mortgages or security interests in property situated in South Africa; securing or collecting debts and enforcing mortgages and security interests; and acquiring any interest in property within South Africa.

Within 20 business days of first beginning to conduct business within South Africa, an external company must register with the commission as an external profit company.[134] The meaning of "conducting business" is set out in section 23(2) and (2A). The first of these subsections identify two instances when a foreign company must be regarded as conducting business. The first is when it is a party to one or more employment contracts within South Africa.[135] The second instance is where the company is engaged in a course of conduct or pattern of activities over a period of at least six months in a way that would lead a person to reasonably conclude that the company intended to continually engage in business or non-profit activities within South Africa.[136]

The six month requirement limits the ambit of the duty to register. Read with section 23(1) the implication is that the foreign company "first begins to conduct business" only if its conduct or activities have been going on for six months or more. If, at the end of the six month period, one can conclude

---

131 This is the general rule, but a company must also be regarded as conducting business in South Africa when it is a party to an employment contract in South Africa, Companies Act (n. 123) sec 23(2).

132 The previous Companies Act 61 of 1973 relied on physical presence through the establishment of a place of business, sec 332(1).

133 Companies Act (n. 123) sec 23(2A).

134 An external company that in its country of incorporation meets requirements similar to those for non-profit companies under the Act, must register as an external non-profit company within 21 business days of commencing non-profit activities in South Africa, Companies Act (n. 123) sec 23(1)*(a)*. The procedural requirements for registration are set out in regulation 17.

135 This, of course, raises the question when an employment contract will be 'within the Republic'. Is it when the services have to be rendered in South Africa or would it suffice if the contract was concluded here? This inclusion was likely motivated by tax considerations as the external company would then become liable to withhold employees' tax.

136 Companies Act (n. 123) sec 23(2)*(b)*.

that the company intends to continually conduct business here, the company has to register within 20 business days. But if that conclusion regarding the company's intention is justified only at a later stage, the time period for registration will start running at this later stage.

An external company that does not register within three months of commencing its activities can be directed in a compliance notice to do so within 20 business days of receiving the notice.[137] The compliance notice can require the external company to cease carrying on business in South Africa if it fails to register.[138]

b) Procedure and consequences of registration

In addition to prescribing the form to be used for notification of the Commission, the regulations require the filing of certified copies of the company's memorandum of incorporation or similar document and its certificate of incorporation or comparable document.[139] The Commission must also be informed of the address of the company's principal office outside South Africa, the names of its directors, the address of its registered office in South Africa and the details of the person within South Africa who has been appointed by the company and has consented to accept service on behalf of it.[140]

An external company is required to continuously maintain at least one office in South Africa. The address of this office, or of its principal office within South Africa if it has more than one office, must be provided to the Commission.[141] An external company has to file an annual return.[142]

Although the above stated provisions may make registration as an external company more difficult in South Africa or could be construed as not

137 Companies Act (n. 123) sec 23(6)*(a)*. Failure to comply with the notice can lead to a criminal prosecution or the imposition of an administrative fine, see sec 171(7).

138 Companies Act (n. 123) sec 23(6)*(b)*.

139 reg 20(1)*(b)*. A translation is required if the document is not in one of the official languages.

140 reg 20(1)*(c)–(e)*.

141 Companies Act (n. 123) sec 23(3).

142 Companies Act (n. 123) sec 33(2).

favourable to the external company they would still comply with the principle of equivalence as there are provisions of a similar nature required for the registration as a domestic company in South Africa.[143]

The only other provisions of the act dealing with external companies are sec 11(2)*(a)*, providing that an external company using its foreign registration number as its name must insert the name of the country of incorporation into its name if this is not already included in its name (sec 23(5)*(d)*); sec 32(1), which provides that an external company must disclose its full name and registration number to anyone requesting it and must not misstate its name and registration number in a way that can mislead or deceive others; and sec 159(3)*(b)* which protects whistle-blowers who provide information pertaining to external companies.

These provisions would be classified as provisions that relate only to external companies and not to domestic companies. When viewed in this light they may appear to discriminate against foreign companies as there is a differentiation between foreign and domestic companies. They would, however, appear to still be justifiable in terms of the EU's criteria of justifiability in the public interest.[144]

3. Company immigration: domesticated companies

A foreign company can become domesticated by applying to transfer its incorporation to South Africa.[145] As a domesticated company it will then be subject to the act as if it had originally been incorporated and registered under the act.[146] Domestication neither establishes a new juristic person nor affects the identity and continuity of the juristic person.[147]

The prerequisites for a transfer of registration focus on the interests of different stakeholders. First, the interests of the country of registration are recognised in that the transfer must be allowed by its law and any applicable requirements set by it must be met.[148] The company's registration in the

---

143 Companies Act (n. 123) sec 13(1)–(2).

144 See para II.3 above.

145 Companies Act (n. 123) sec 13(5)–(11).

146 Companies Act (n. 123) sec 13(5).

147 Companies Act (n. 123) sec 13(11)*(a)–(b)*. The rights of others are not prejudiced, the property, rights and obligations of the company are not affected (sec 13(11)*(c)*), and legal proceedings remain effective (sec 13(11)*(d)*).

148 Companies Act (n. 123) sec 13(6)*(a)*.

other jurisdiction must be terminated.[149] Shareholders are also protected as they must have approved the transfer, either in accordance with the law of the jurisdiction of registration, or, if that law does not impose a shareholder approval requirement, by the equivalent of a special resolution under the Act.[150] Finally, the interests of creditors and potential creditors are protected in that the company must immediately after the transfer satisfy the solvency and liquidity test.[151]

The foreign company is required to have a significant nexus with South Africa: the whole or the greater part of the company's assets and undertaking must be in South Africa;[152] the majority of its shareholders must be resident in South Africa;[153] and the majority of its directors must be South African citizens.[154]

Even if they satisfy the above requirements, certain foreign companies are prohibited from transferring their registration to South Africa. The prohibitions can be divided into two groups, namely companies who are allowed to issue bearer shares or who have issued bearer shares that remain issued[155] and companies who are under various forms of financial distress ranging from liquidation, the appointment of a receiver or manager in respect of its property, business rescue and similar mechanisms in other jurisdictions to compromises or arrangements that "are in force"[156] or in respect of which applications pertaining to any of the above have been made.[157]

While the South African legislature might be commended for expressly regulating the cross-border conversion of foreign companies, it is debatable whether its requirements would meet the demands of equivalent treatment

149 Companies Act (n. 123) sec 13(6)*(f)*(ii).

150 Companies Act (n. 123) sec 13(6)*(b)* read with sec 4. S 1 of the act defines a "special resolution" in relation to juristic persons other than domestic companies, as "a decision by the owner or owners of that person, or by another authorised person, that requires the highest level of support in order to be adopted, in terms of the relevant law under which that juristic person was incorporated".

151 Companies Act (n. 123) sec 13(6)*(f)*(i).

152 Companies Act (n. 123) sec 13(6)*(c)*. The assets and undertaking of a foreign subsidiary are excluded from this calculation.

153 Companies Act (n. 123) sec 13(6)*(d)*. This seems to refer to the majority in number of shareholders.

154 Companies Act (n. 123) sec 13(6)*(e)*. It is not clear why the directors are required to be SA citizens as opposed to being resident in South Africa.

155 Companies Act (n. 123) sec 13(7)*(a)*.

156 This probably means that the compromise or arrangement has not yet been fully executed or implemented.

157 Companies Act (n. 123) sec 13(5)*(b)*–*(e)*.

of domestic and foreign entities which would be implied by the SADC treaty.

If the freedom of establishment in the SADC develops along similar lines to the concept in the EU, the first question would have to be whether South Africa provides for domestic conversions. The act impliedly recognises the "transformation"[158] of one category of profit company into another category of profit company through a simple amendment of the memorandum of incorporation resulting in it no longer satisfying "the criteria for its particular category of profit company".[159] The act makes no mention of the fact that the company is the same juristic person and no provision is made for transfer of rights and obligations[160] or for universal succession. The entire conversion is seen as a simple change of the memorandum which results in a change of the company's name to reflect the appropriate ending for the category of company.[161]

The only additional requirement applies to the transformation of a personal liability company[162] into another category of company. Creditors and potential creditors have to be notified, as they clearly have an interest in the removal of the personal liability of the directors of such a company.[163]

---

158 This word is used in Companies Act (n. 123) sec 16(10) in relation to a personal liability company that amends its memorandum in a way that results in it becoming another category of company.

159 Companies Act (n. 123) sec 16(6). The categories of company under the act are: non-profit companies, state-owned companies, public companies (comparable to the *AG*) and private companies (comparable to the *GmbH*), see sec 8(2). Non-profit companies cannot convert into profit companies as their assets must always be applied exclusively for non-profit objectives.

160 Delport (ed) *Henochsberg on the Companies Act 71 of 2008* 67.

161 The act also provides for the "conversion" of close corporations into profit companies, sch 2 and reg 18. The reference to "shareholders" implies that a close corporation cannot be converted into a non-profit company. It can also not be converted into a state-owned company, as the members of a close corporation have to be individuals, Conversion of companies into close corporations is no longer possible, a rule that supports the discontinuance of close corporations. Since 1 May 2011, no further close corporations may be incorporated.

162 The directors and former directors of such a company are jointly and severally liable for the debts and liabilities of the company contracted during their periods of office, Companies Act (n. 123) sec 19(3).

163 Companies Act (n. 123) sec 16(10)*(b)*. In addition, any relevant industry regulator must be notified, sec 16(10)*(a)*. Personal liability companies are most often used by members of organised professions, *eg* attorneys, hence the need to recognise regulatory interests.

On the assumption that the "transformation" of a domestic profit company into a different category of profit company amounts to a "conversion", the principles of justifiability and equivalence would then have to be considered. The act imposes rather strict nexus requirements for domestication (or cross-border inbound conversion). Firstly, the requirements go beyond what could be classified as embodying the requirement of some physical presence or economic activity[164] in order to avoid letter-box conversions. They rather amount to requiring the company's real seat to be in South Africa. It is questionable whether these requirements could be justified on the basis of preventing abuse, as they are not aimed at the protection of creditors, for instance. No similar nexus requirements are imposed when a company is originally incorporated in South Africa, which raises concerns regarding equivalence.

The shareholder approval requirement does not appear to be problematic. Arguably the solvency and liquidity requirement and the restriction on immigration of companies in insolvency and reorganisation proceedings could be seen as justifiable creditor protection mechanisms.

4. Company emigration

The Companies Act provides for the emigration of a company that is transferring its registration to a foreign jurisdiction.[165] A company may apply for its deregistration with the approval, by special resolution, of its shareholders.[166] It must satisfy the prescribed requirements.[167] The requirements currently prescribed by the minister are that a copy of the special resolution approving the transfer should accompany the application, that satisfactory evidence must be submitted that the company complies with the requirements for registration in the host state, and that the prescribed fee must be paid.[168]

164 See *Cartesio* (n 14) and *Vale* (n 4).
165 Companies Act (n. 123) sec 82(3)–(6) and see sec 83(1).
166 Companies Act (n. 123) sec 82(5)*(a)*.
167 Companies Act (n. 123) sec 82(5)*(b)*.
168 reg 40(8)*(a)–(c)*.

VI. Conclusion

The principles of the freedom of establishment have, to a certain extent, been clearly distilled in the European Union. The freedom of establishment in the European Union consists of three elements: recognition, emigration and immigration. Recognition is the foundation stone on which the other two are built. The ECJ in *Überseering* has, for the first time, granted a universal recognition to EU companies.[169] A company, formed anywhere in the EU, will be recognised as a legal person and thus have legal standing in a court, in any state within the EU. This insight can serve SADC in the development of a protocol for legal persons. SADC will, from the outset, appreciate that the recognition of legal personality must be built into any protocol, despite the connecting factor that a state subscribes to at a private international law level.

In relation to emigration and immigration it is apparent that the EU takes a one sided approach. The state of incorporation is entitled to "lock in" a company, by restricting the exit of that company, except in circumstances where the company intends to reorganise in another state. The consistent approach taken by the ECJ in these matters would appear to indicate that it is a policy decision. The freedom of establishment in the EU is thus only partial. SADC could again look to this position as an example. Based on SADC's own policies would SADC apply the freedom of establishment in this one sided manner?

The EU also clarifies the position with regard to restrictions that a host state can place on an incoming company. The ECJ demonstrates that secondary establishment, as well as primary establishment in the form of the movement of the real seat and the registered seat, will qualify as falling under the right to establishment. The host state's rights to restrict this entry into their borders are severely curtailed. Only in instances in which there would be a clear violation of a matter that falls within the public interest could the host state impose such a restriction. The manner in which these purported restrictions were dealt with by the ECJ could perhaps be the most enlightening to SADC. That court has blazed a clear path illustrating what form these restrictions could take and has developed a clear set of principles that can be applied to novel cases. Armed with this knowledge, and before the advent of any protocol, the SADC member states could thus perform an introspection of their domestic company laws. This introspection could

169 EU companies are companies that have their registered seat, central place of administration or central place of business within the EU.

ward off the protracted litigation that was necessary to establish free movement in the EU and therefore promote legal certainty. An investigation into the provisions of the South African Companies Act has already revealed possible impediments to the development of freedom of establishment as it exists in the EU. In addition to companies legislation one would have to consider treasury and tax restrictions on free movement, particularly in the case of outbound conversions.

When Germany amended its domestic laws to enhance the competitiveness of its corporate vehicles, it simultaneously facilitated the emigration of German companies. There is no specific legislation on the implementation of and requirements for immigration and emigration. It has no specific requirements for inbound transfers of the real seat of EU or non-EU companies and does not prevent German companies from moving their real seat out of Germany. In satisfying the demands of EU law in relation to cross-border conversions or transfers of the statutory seat, it relies on the analogy of rules applicable to domestic conversions and cross-border mergers.

South Africa, on the other hand, has always followed the incorporation doctrine. It consequently does not regulate the transfer of a South African company's real seat. Any foreign company commencing business operations in South Africa, whether through a primary or secondary establishment, would have to register and must maintain at least one office in the country. In contrast with German law, the South African Companies Act expressly regulates the cross-border conversion of companies. Inbound conversions (domestication of companies) are, perhaps curiously, regulated far more strictly than outbound conversions. We have argued that the substantial physical nexus requirements, particularly pertaining to the residence or nationality of stakeholders and the requirement that the greater part of the assets or undertaking be situated in South Africa, would infringe on freedom of establishment in the SADC if the concept were to be given a similar content as in the EU. It in effect requires a company's real seat to be in South Africa before allowing it to convert into a South African company. On the other hand, outbound conversions may be under-regulated in South Africa. While there is a shareholder approval requirement, the protection of shareholders and creditors falls short of that provided by Germany in comparable situations. The current South African approach should be revisited.

The EU is undoubtedly a pioneer in its regional integration exercise. The building blocks of the freedom of establishment have begun to fall in place. The SADC, although still in an embryonic phase, can integrate the many lessons learnt by the EU into its development. Some of these can be adopted as is, while others can be expanded on and adapted to suit the community's own needs. The contribution of Germany to the development of the SADC over more than 20 years must be acknowleged. In this period, Germany has contributed over €300 million to the SADC and has assisted the SADC in the development of regional integration through a new programme, Cooperation for the Enhancement of SADC Regional Economic Integration (CESARE),[170] which commenced in 2015.[171]

170 See SADC news/events http://www.sadc.int/news-events/news/sadc-and-germany-agree-jointly-support-deepening-regional/ (15-09-2017).

171 The relationship between Germany and the SADC spans more than 20 years. Germany has in the ensuing period contributed over €300 million to the SADC and has assisted the SADC in the development of regional integration through a new programme, Cooperation for the Enhancement of SADC Regional Economic Integration (CESARE), which commenced in 2015, see the newsletter: German Development Cooperation SADC http://www.sadc.int/files/2514/6099/0959/Newsletter_German_Development_Cooperation_SADC.pdf (15-09-2017).

Bibliography

Bayer W and Schmidt J "Grenzüberschreitende Sitzverlegung und grenzüberschreitende Restrukturierungen nach MoMiG, Cartesio und Trabrennbahn. Europäischer Rahmen, deutsche lex lata und rechtspolitische Desiderata" 173 (2009) *Zeitschrift für das gesamte Handelsrecht und Wirtschaftsrecht* (*ZHR*) 735.

Behrens P "From 'Real Seat' to 'Legal Seat': Germany's Private International Company Law Revolution" in Hay P, Lajos V, Elkana Y and Dimitrijevic N (eds) *Resolving International Conflicts: Liber Amicorum Tibor Varady* (Central European University Press, Budapest 2009) 46.

Cassim FHI, Cassim MF, Cassim R, Jooste R, Shev J and Yeats JL *Contemporary Company Law* (2nd Edition, Juta, Claremont 2012).

Collins L (gen ed) *Dicey, Morris and Collins on the Conflict of Laws* (15th Edition, Sweet & Maxwell, London 2012).

Davies M, Bell AS and Brereton P *Nygh's Conflict of Laws in Australia* (8th Edition, LexisNexis, Sydney 2010).

Drury RR "The regulation and recognition of foreign corporations: response to the Delaware syndrome" 57 (1998) *Cambridge Law Journal (Cambridge LJ)* 165.

Ebke WF "The real seat doctrine in the conflict of corporate law" 2002 *The International Lawyer (Int-Lawyer)* 1015.

Erk NK "The cross-border transfer of seat in European Company Law: a deliberation about the status quo and the fate of the real seat doctrine" 2010 *European Business Law Review (EBLR)* 413.

Essop GB "The role of SADC in boosting domestic, regional, continental and international trade" 2015 *Commonwealth Youth and Development* 88.

Garcia-Riestra M "The transfer of seat of the European Company v Free establishment case-law" 2004 *European Business Law Review (EBLR)* 1295.

Gerner-Beuerle C and Schillig M "The mysteries of freedom of establishment after Cartesio" 2 (2010) *International and Comparative Law Quarterly (Int'l Comp LQ)* 313.

Hansen SF "The free movement of companies" 2003 *Scandinavian Studies in Law* 147.

Koch R and Eickmann M "Gründungs- oder Sitztheorie? Eine 'never ending story'?" 2009 *Die Aktiengesellschaft (AG)* 73.

Münchener Handbuch des Geschaftsrechts, Stefan Leible and Jochem Reichert (eds), Volume 6 (4th Edition, CH Beck, Munich 2013).

Münchener Handbuch des Gesellschafsrechts, Hans-Joachim Priester and Dieter Mayer (eds), Volume 3 (3rd Edition, CH Beck, Munich 2009).

Myszke-Nowakowska M *The Role of Choice of Law in Shaping Free Movement of Companies* (Intersentia, Cambridge 2014).

Nygh PE *Autonomy in International Contracts* (Clarendon Press, Oxford 1999).

Paschlidis P *Freedom of Establishment and Private International Law for Corporations* (Oxford University Press, Oxford 2012).

Rabel *The Conflict of Laws: A Comparative Study. Volume II: Foreign Corporations: Torts: Contracts in General* (Callaghan & Company, Chicago 1947).

Rammeloo S "Freedom of establishment: cross-border transfer of company seat – the last piece of the puzzle?" 2012 *Maastricht Journal of European and Comparative Law (MJECL)* 563.

Rammeloo S *Corporations in Private International Law* (Oxford University Press, Oxford 2001).

Ringe WG "No freedom of emigration for companies?" 2005 *European Business Law Review (EBLR)* 621.

Roth WH "From Centros to Überseering: free movement of companies, private international law, and community law" 2003 *International and Comparative Law Quarterly (Int'l Comp LQ)* 177.

Schaper M "Grenzüberschreitender Formwechsel und Sitzverlegung: Die Umsetzung der Vale-Rechtsprechung des EuGH" 2014 *Zeitschrift für Wirtschaftsrecht (ZIP)* 810.

Setalvad AM *Conflict of Laws* (LexisNexis Butterworths, New Delhi 2009).

Soubbotina TM and Sheram K *Beyond Economic Growth: Meeting the Challenges of Global Development* World Bank Learning Resource Series (World Bank, Washington, DC 2000).

Teichman C "Report from Germany 2008" 5 (2008) *European Company Law (ECL)* 189.

Wymeersch E "The transfer of a company's seat in European company law" 40 (2003) *Common Market Law Review (CML Rev)* 661.

Zöllner W and Noack U (eds) *Kölner Kommentar zum Aktiengesetz Band 1* (3rd Edition, Carl Heymanns, Cologne 2010).

Case Law

European Court of Justice

Case C-2/74 21.6.1974 *Reyners v Belgium* ECLI:EU:C:1974:68.

Case C-81/87 27.9.1988 *The Queen v Treasury and Commissioners of Inland Revenue, ex parte Daily Mail and General Trust PLC* ECLI:EU:C:1988:456.

Case C-212/97 9.3.1999 *Centros Ltd* v Erhvervs ECLI:EU:C:1999:126.

Case C-208/00 5.11.2002 *Überseering* v *NCC Nordic Construction Baumanagement GmbH* ECLI:EU:C:2002:632.

Case C-167/01 30.9.2003 *Kamer van Koophandel en Fabrieken voor Amsterdam v Inspire Art Ltd* ECLI:EU:C:2003:512.

Case C-411/03 13.12.2005 *Sevic Systems Aktiengesellschaft v Amtsgericht Neuwied* ECLI:EU:C:2005:762.

Case C-210/06 16.12.2008 *Cartesio* ECLI:EU:C:2008:723.

Case C-378/10 12.7.2012 *Vale Építési kft* ECLI:EU:C:2012:440.

Germany

OLG Düsseldorf 26.3.2001 – 3 Wx 88/01 – 2001 *Neue Juristische Wochenschrift (NJW)* 2184.

OLG Nürnberg 19.6.2013 – 12 W 520/13 – 2014 *Zeitschrift für Wirtschaftsrecht* (*ZIP)* 128.

South Africa

Dadoo Ltd v Krugersdorp Municipal Council 1920 AD 530

Ebrahim v Airport Cold Storage v (Pty) Ltd 2009 1 All SA 330 (SCA)

Comment: Towards free movement of companies – the European position as a model for the SADC

*Raphael Koch**

I. Introduction

Globalisation of markets demands international unification of the law and relaxation of trade barriers. Disparities in national laws governing international trade create obstacles to the flow of trade. Free movement of companies is a key issue in order to overcome trade barriers. It is a complex topic. The reason for the complexity is easily identified: companies are embedded in national law and they are incorporated in national law. However, free movement of companies refers to cross-border situations and consequently we are touching – on the European level – the freedom of establishment, laid down in Articles 49 and 54 of the Treaty on the Functioning of the European Union (TFEU): primary establishment on the one hand and secondary establishment on the other hand. There are even more levels to pay attention to: the law of the state of origin and the law of the host (or destination) state. Conflict-of-law rules might be relevant, too. In the end, it can be decisive which law is applicable. Thus, ascertaining the lex societas is a crucial point.

---

* Raphael Koch, *Dr. iur. habil., LL.M. (Cambridge), EMBA*; Professor, University of Augsburg, Faculty of Law. Chair for Civil Law, Law of Civil Procedure, Corporate and Company Law, European Private Law and International Procedural Law.

"Towards free movement of companies – the European position as a model for the SADC" – the title of this comment provides the modus operandi: the European and German positions are starting points, analysing whether these positions can serve as a model for the Southern African Development Community (SADC) is the next step. It appears that the European position can be used as a reference because both the European Union and the SADC are regional communities. Hence, it is a comparison of situations and legal questions which are, at least at first glance, identical in their point of origin. If one takes a closer look, one can formulate, to the absolute minimum, two preconditions in order to use the European position as a model for the SADC: First, the European model has to be convincing. Second, there must not be such disparities between the European Union and the SADC that preclude the transfer of the European position on the SADC.

This paper will examine two aspects: the European – especially the German – position regarding free movement of companies (section II.); and one type of legal form for European enterprises, namely the European Company (Societas Europaea – SE), in particular with its advantages and disadvantages (section III.).

II. A long way: milestones of the European and German position

In Germany, it has been a long journey towards free movement of companies, and the journey has been driven by the courts, mostly the European Court of Justice (ECJ) and subsequently by legislation. Questions and problems that have arisen have centred around the two possible means for the determination of the lex societas: the incorporation theory and the real seat theory. Under the incorporation theory the law of the place where the company is initially incorporated constitutes the lex societas. Contrary to this, under the real seat theory the law of the place where the central management of the company is situated dictates the lex societas to be applied.

Until 2002, the real seat theory had serious legal and economic impacts on foreign companies incorporated in a Member State of the European Union when they moved the central management of the company (their real seat) to Germany. They were denied their legal capacity because they were not recognised. Therefore, they could not sue in German courts even though they could themselves be sued pursuant to section 50 paragraph 2 of the Code of Civil Procedure (*Zivilprozessordnung* – ZPO) in an analogous manner.[1] This approach had deep impacts on a foreign company – for example, on the shareholders who were no longer financially protected because the limited liability concept was not applied.

In 1988, the ECJ held in the case of *Daily Mail*[2] that

> "the Treaty regards the differences in national legislation concerning the required connecting factor and the question whether – and if so how – the registered office or real head office of a company incorporated under national law may be transferred from one Member State to another as problems which are not resolved by the rules concerning the right of establishment but must be dealt with by future legislation or conventions."

The right to leave, in concrete the

> "right to transfer their central management and control and their central administration to another Member State while retaining their status as companies incorporated under the legislation of the first Member State"

was not regarded as an essential component of the right of establishment.

In *Centros*[3], the ECJ held that

> "a situation in which a company formed in accordance with the law of a Member State in which it has its registered office desires to set up a branch in another Member State falls within the scope of Community law."

The consequence of this ruling was that a corporation which is validly incorporated in an EU Member State enjoys the freedom of establishment guaranteed by Article 43 (Article 49 TFEU) and Article 48 EC (Article 54 TFEU) even if it never intended to do any business in its state of incorporation but was formed in one Member State "only for the purpose of establishing itself in a second, where its main, or indeed entire, business is to be

---

1 Ingo Saenger, *Gesellschaftsrecht* (3rd Edition, 2015), para. 441.

2 European Court of Justice, Case 81/87, 27.9.1988, *The Queen v H. M. Treasury and Commissioners of Inland Revenue, ex p Daily Mail and General Trust plc.*, ECR 5483, para. 23 et seq.

3 European Court of Justice, Case 212/97, 9.3.1999, *Centros Ltd v Erhvervs*, ECR I-1459, para. 17.

conducted"[4]. *Centros* has to be seen as a turning point in favour of the incorporation doctrine. In *Überseering*[5] and *Inspire Art*[6] the ruling was concretised. The *Überseering* judgment denied Germany the strict application of the real seat theory in matters of European relations. Hence, freedom of establishment led to the recognition of the incorporation doctrine in cases of taking up residence.

In 2005, the ECJ was questioned in *SEVIC*[7] whether Articles 43 and 48 EC (Articles 49 and 54 TFEU) are

> "to be interpreted as meaning that it is contrary to freedom of establishment for companies if a foreign European company is refused registration of its proposed merger with a German company in the German register of companies under (…) the Umwandlungsgesetz (Law on Transformations – UmwG), on the ground that paragraph 1(1) sentence 1 of that law provides only for transformation of legal entities established in Germany."

It was held that the general refusal to register a merger between companies in the commercial register where one is established in another Member State is contrary to Articles 43 and 48 EC (Articles 49 and 54 TFEU). It is worth noting that the reasoning was based not predominantly on a restriction of mobility but rather on the discrimination in comparison to a domestic conversion. The ECJ decided that "German law establishes a difference in treatment between companies according to the internal or cross-border nature of the merger (…)".[8]

Shortly after the decision in *SEVIC* a European directive was introduced for the cross-border mergers of limited liability companies.[9] German legislation implemented sections 122a–122l into the UmwG.[10] By virtue of the

4 European Court of Justice, Case 212/97, 9.3.1999, *Centros Ltd v Erhvervs*, ECR I-1459, para. 17.

5 European Court of Justice, Case 208/00, 5.11.2002, *Überseering BV v Nordic Construction Company Baumanagement GmbH*, ECR I-9919.

6 European Court of Justice, Case 167/01, 30.9.2003, *Kamer van Koophandel en Fabrieken voor Amsterdam v Inspire Art Ltd.*, ECR I-10155.

7 European Court of Justice, Case 411/03, 13.12.2005, *SEVIC Systems AG*, ECR I-10805, para. 10.

8 ibid, para. 22.

9 Council Directive 2005/56/EC of the European Parliament and of the Council of 26 October 2005 on cross-border mergers of limited liability companies.

10 Jochen Hoffmann in *Münchener Handbuch des Gesellschaftsrechts*, Vol. 6 (4th Edition, 2013), § 53, para. 20.

cross-reference in section 122a para 2 of UmwG, its other provisions are applicable to cross-border conversions.

However, quite surprisingly, in *Cartesio*, the ECJ held that

> "as Community law now stands, Articles 43 EC and 48 EC (Articles 49 and 54 TFEU) are to be interpreted as not precluding legislation of a Member State under which a company incorporated under the law of that Member State may not transfer its seat to another Member State whilst retaining its status as a company governed by the law of the Member State of incorporation."[11]

As a consequence of this ruling, the German legislature reacted with significant amendments to the law: the Act on Companies with Limited Liability (*Gesetz betreffend die Gesellschaften mit beschränkter Haftung* – GmbHG) and the Stock Corporation Act (*Aktiengesetz* – AktG), in the version after the Law for the Modernisation of the German Limited Liability Company Law and the Prevention of Misuse was implemented, now state that the place of the company's registered office shall be that place in Germany as specified in the articles of association. Hence, the place where the company has its central administration (so-called real seat) can be outside Germany. Therefore, a German company with limited liability (GmbH) or a Stock Corporation (AG) can transfer its real seat to another Member State whilst retaining its status as a company governed by German law (that is, the law of the Member State of incorporation).

As stated above, it has been a long journey. But it has been worthwhile. Free movement of companies is established in the European Union and in Germany, at least in a case of taking up residence, because the ECJ regards the freedom of establishment predominantly as a guarantee for immigration, imposing a duty on the destination state.

III. Forms of European companies

Companies fulfilling some preconditions can opt to take the legal form of the European Company (Societas Europaea – SE). The European Company can operate on a European-wide basis and is governed by Community law directly applicable in all Member States. The European Company Statute is established by two pieces of legislation, namely, a Regulation (directly applicable in the Member States) establishing the company law rules, and a

---

11 European Court of Justice, Case 210/06, 16.12.2008, *CARTESIO Oktató és Szolgáltató bt*, ECR I-9641, para. 124.

Directive on worker involvement (which must be implemented into national law in all Member States). The legal basis for the European Company is the Council Regulation (EC) No 2157/2001 of October 8, 2001.[12] With its authorisation, German legislation introduced the Law implementing the European Company (*SE-Ausführungsgesetz* – SEAG). Also, the Council Directive 2001/86/EC of October 8, 2001[13] supplementing the Statute for a European company with regard to the involvement of employees and the German Act transposing the Directive into the Act regarding the involvement of employees in the European Company (*SE-Beteiligungsgesetz* – SEBG) have to be taken into account.

Some of the biggest German companies (inter alia, Allianz, BASF, Fresenius and Porsche), have been transformed into European Companies. Thus, significant and key features of this legal form are noteworthy. The advantages of the legal form of a European Company are manifold. Companies established in more than one Member State are able to merge and operate throughout the EU on the basis of a single set of rules and a unified management and reporting system. A company can avoid the need to set up a financially costly and administratively time-consuming complex network of subsidiaries governed by different national laws. Significant reductions in administrative and legal costs, a single legal structure, and unified management and reporting systems are the consequence. Trading opportunities offered by the Internal Market can be taken by the company more easily. It has to be recognised as another key advantage that a company can choose between a single-tier system (Chairman and Board of Directors) and a two-tier system (Executive Board and Supervisory Board). There is separate regulation for employee participation, the number of Supervisory Board members can be reduced and the employee side can be composed internationally.[14] As a supranational company, it can register its seat in any Member State of the European Union which defines its applicable law. A beneficial factor is the flexibility in transferring its seat in another Member State while retaining its status.

It is seen as a disadvantage that the company's share capital is set at EUR 120,000, as this may discourage smaller companies. For that reason

12 Council Regulation (EC) No 2157/2001 of 8 October 2001 on the Statute for a European company (SE).

13 Council Directive 2001/86/EC supplementing the Statute for a European company with regard to the involvement of employees.

14 Christoph Teichmann in *Münchener Handbuch des Gesellschaftsrechts*, Vol. 6 (4th Edition, 2013), § 49, para. 2.

the European Private Company (Societas Privata Europaea – SPE) was supposed to be introduced on 1 July 2010. However, due to opposition from different Member States, mostly because of concerns to create competition for their own legal forms[15], the European Commission eliminated the European Private Company on 2 October 2013 in favour of a new proposal, the single-member private limited liability company (Societas Unius Personae – SUP).[16]

IV. Summary

It is nearly 30 years ago that the ECJ delivered its ruling in the *Daily Mail* case. The judgment generated a great deal of important discussion; it certainly did not induce legal certainty. The EU acted as a pioneer for freedom of establishment and free movement of companies. From other regional communities' perspective such as the SADC the decisions of the ECJ should be reviewed carefully. The European position on freedom of establishment, especially on free movement of companies, should serve as a role model for other regional communities such as the SADC. Globalisation of markets demands the relaxation of barriers in national company law. Free movement of companies is a key precondition.

In addition: The advantages of the European Company which have been highlighted lead to the conclusion that such a company can also be a model for the SADC. It is a relatively new entity and legal problems may still arise. Any adaptation must bear this in mind. Difficulties with the implementation of such a legal form are not to be underestimated. Nonetheless, balancing chance and risk, it should serve as a model.

---

15 Jürgen Tiedje in *Europäisches Unionsrecht*, Vol. 1 (7th Edition, 2015), Art. 50, para. 76.

16 Proposal for a Directive of the European Parliament and of the Council on single-member private limited liability companies: http://eur-lex.europa.eu.

Bibliography

Münchener Handbuch des Geschaftsrechts, Stefan Leible and Jochem Reichert (eds), Volume 6 (4th Edition, C.H.Beck, Munich 2013).

Ingo Saenger, *Gesellschaftsrecht*, (3rd Edition, Vahlen, Munich 2015).

Hans von der Groeben, Jürgen Schwarze and Armin Hatje (eds), *Europäisches Unionsrecht*, Volume 1 (7th Edition, Nomos, Baden-Baden 2015).

Case Law

European Court of Justice, Case 81/87, 27.9.1988, *The Queen v H. M. Treasury and Commissioners of Inland Revenue, ex p Daily Mail and General Trust plc.*, ECR 5483.

European Court of Justice, Case 212/97, 9.3.1999, *Centros Ltd v Erhvervs*, ECR I-1459.

European Court of Justice, Case 208/00, 5.11.2002, *Überseering BV v Nordic Construction Company Baumanagement GmbH*, ECR I-9919.

European Court of Justice, Case 167/01, 30.9.2003, *Kamer van Koophandel en Fabrieken voor Amsterdam v Inspire Art Ltd.*, ECR I-10155.

European Court of Justice, Case 411/03, 13.12.2005, *SEVIC Systems AG*, ECR I-10805.

European Court of Justice, Case 210/06, 16.12.2008, *CARTESIO Oktató és Szolgáltató bt*, ECR I-9641

Tacit choice of law in international commercial contracts – the position in South African law and under the Rome I Regulation

*Garth J. Bouwers**

I. Introduction

As cross-border trade continues to grow, an important issue in private international law that deserves consideration is the law applicable to international commercial contracts. As Lord Diplock put it:

> "[c]ontracts are incapable of existing in a legal vacuum. They are mere pieces of paper devoid of all legal effect unless they were made by reference to some system of private law which defines the obligations assumed by the parties to the contract by their use of particular forms of words and prescribes the remedies enforceable in a court of justice for failure to perform any of those obligations."[1]

---

* Lecturer, Department of Procedural Law, and Research Associate at the Research Centre for Private International Law in Emerging Countries at the University of Johannesburg.

1 *Amin Rasheed Shipping Corporation v Kuwait Insurance Co* 1984 AC 50 65.

Given the vast problems that could occur in international commercial transactions, parties are advised to take the necessary precaution in selecting the law applicable to the contract.[2] However, this does not always take place in practice. Where individuals entering into agreements fail to select a law to govern their contract expressly, it is left to the court to determine the proper law of the contract.[3] First the court will attempt to determine the parties' unexpressed or tacit choice of law.[4] In the absence of a tacit choice, the court must assign an objective proper law to the contract.[5]

---

2 Van Niekerk and Schulze *The South African Law of International Trade: Selected Topics* (2016) 59. The law applicable to the contract is also referred to as the "proper law" or "governing law" and under the Rome Convention on the Law Applicable to Contractual Obligations (1980) and the Regulation on the Law Applicable to Contractual Obligations (Rome I) (2008) as the "applicable law". See, also, McClean and Beevers *The Conflict of Laws* (2009) 353: "In the common law approach developed by English judges, the 'proper law of the contract' was the system of law by reference to which the contract was made...." It is almost universally recognised that, within certain limitations, the law chosen by the parties will govern the contract. See Schwenzer, Hachem and Kee *Global Sales and Contract Law* (2012) 52–53: the notable exceptions to this rule are found in the law of Brazil, Saudi Arabia and Uruguay, in terms of which parties are prevented from choosing the applicable law in their contract. However, see De Araujo "Recent developments and current trends on Brazilian private international law concerning international contracts" 2013 *Panorama of Brazilian Law (PBL)* 73 on the developments in Brazilian law in this regard.

3 Collins (gen ed) *Dicey, Morris and Collins on The Conflict of Laws II* (2012) 1809; Davies, Bell and Brereton *Nygh's Conflict of Laws in Australia* (2014) 442; Forsyth "Enforcement of foreign arbitral awards, choice of law in contract, characterization and a new attitude to private international law" 104 (1987) *South African Law Journal (SALJ)* 4 14; Forsyth *Private International Law. The Modern Roman-Dutch Law including the Jurisdiction of the High Courts* (2012) 326–327; North *Private International Law Problems in Common Law Jurisdictions* (1993) 105; North and Fawcett *Cheshire and North's Private International Law* (1987) 444; and Nygh *Conflict of Laws in Australia* (1991) 277.

4 Collins (gen ed) (n 3) 1809; North (n 3) 105; Nygh (n 3) 277; Nygh *Autonomy in International Contracts* (1999) 108–109. See, also, Neels and Fredericks "Tacit choice of law in the Hague Principles on Choice of Law in International Contracts" 2011 *De Jure* 101 104: some legal systems refer to tacit choice of law while others refer to an implied choice of law. See, also, Van Niekerk and Schulze (n 2) 61. The terms "tacit", "implied" and "presumed" have been used interchangeably in private international law.

5 Bogdan *Private International Law in Sweden* (2012) 66; Bonomi "Rome I Regulation – some general remarks" in Bonomi and Volken (eds) *Yearbook of Private International Law Volume X – 2008* 165 173–174; Davies, Bell and Brereton (n 3) 442 and 453; Forsyth (n 3) 329; Marshall "Reconsidering the proper law of the

Although falling short of an express choice by the parties, a tacit choice still amounts to a true or real choice of law.[6] However, the notion of inferring an actual intention is based upon making assumptions that may or may not be correct.[7] This may have undesirable consequences for the parties to the contract, as their reasonable expectations will not necessarily be portrayed in the inferences drawn by the court. Nevertheless, most legal systems around the world recognise the possibility of a tacit (or implied) choice of law.[8]

This paper will focus on the determination of tacit choice of law in South African law. Attention will be devoted to the level of strictness of the criterion for inferring a choice of law and the factors that have been relied upon, as well as the weight that has been attached to these factors. The legal position will be compared to that under the Regulation on the Law Applicable to Contractual Obligations,[9] which applies in the European Union Countries, apart from Denmark.[10]

---

contract" 13 (2012) *Melbourne Journal of International Law (Mel. J. Int. Law)* 501 526–527; North (n 3) 105; Schoeman, Roodt and Wethmar-Lemmer *Private International Law in South Africa* (2014) 53; and Van Niekerk and Schulze (n 2) 63.

6 Collins (gen ed) (n 3) 1809; Forsyth (n 3) 326–327; Marshall (n 5) 512–513; Neels and Fredericks (n 4) 104; and Nygh (n 4) 108–109. See, also, Bogdan (n 5) 66: "[T]he choice must be a real choice, so that a hypothetical reasoning about which law the parties would probably have chosen if they had made a choice is not sufficient". See the Official Commentary para 4.6 in Hague Conference on Private International Law *Principles of Choice of Law in International Commercial Contracts* (2015).

7 North and Fawcett (n 3) 461.

8 Nygh (n 4) 109; and Schwenzer, Hachem and Kee (n 2) 55.

9 Council Regulation (EC) No 593/2008 of the European Parliament and of the Council of 17 June 2008 on the law applicable to contractual obligations (Rome I) (hereinafter referred to as the "the Rome I Regulation").

10 Member States of the European Union refer to Austria, Belgium, Bulgaria, Croatia, Cyprus, the Czech Republic, Denmark, Estonia, Finland, France, Germany, Greece, Hungry, Ireland, Italy, Latvia, Lithuania, Luxembourg, Malta, the Netherlands, Poland, Portugal, Romania, Slovakia, Slovenia, Spain, Sweden, and the United Kingdom. However, Denmark is the only country that continues to apply the Rome Convention (n 2).

II. Party autonomy

The Rome I Regulation constitutes a set of uniform conflict rules, replacing the private international law of contract of member states in certain types of contractual obligations.[11] Subject to certain limitations,[12] the Regulation recognises the principle of party autonomy.[13] Recital 11 of the Rome I Regulation provides that "[t]he parties' freedom to choose the applicable law should be one of the cornerstones of the system of conflict-of-law rules in matters of contractual obligations". The principle of party autonomy is enunciated in article 3(1) of the Regulation (the basic provision on choice of law): "A contract shall be governed by the law chosen by the parties. The choice shall be made expressly or clearly demonstrated by the terms of the contract or the circumstances of the case…." Parties may exercise their choice by stating expressly the law applicable to their contract, or the court can find that they had tacitly agreed on the applicable law.

Generally, South African private international law also recognises party autonomy in respect of choice of law in a contract.[14] In *Laconian Maritime Enterprises Ltd v Agromar Lineas Ltd*,[15] Booysen J stated: "That our law

---

11 art 1 of the Rome I Regulation (n 9). The reach that the Rome I Regulation, together with its predecessor, the Rome Convention has had, is noteworthy. See, for example, Neels "Rome in the Far East" (unpublished lecture at the University of Amsterdam, the University of British Columbia and the University of Johannesburg) (2011–2012) 1: the basic provisions of codifications in many states are in principle based on the Rome model, including non-EU European countries such as Liechtenstein, Macedonia, Russia, Switzerland and the Ukraine; countries in the Far East, including China, Japan, Mongolia and South Korea; as well as countries in the Middle East such as Azerbaijan, Turkey and Uzbekistan.

12 See, for example, art 9 (overriding mandatory provisions) and art 21 (public policy of the forum) of the Rome I Regulation. See, in general, Symeonides "Party autonomy in Rome I and II: an outsider's perspective" 2010 *Nederlands Internationaal Privaatrecht (NIPR)* 191 194–200. A discussion of the limitations are beyond the scope of this article.

13 See, for example, Bogdan (n 5) 66; Bonomi (n 5) 169; Collins (gen ed) (n 3) 1798; Schwenzer, Hachem and Kee (n 2) 53; and Symeonides (n 12) 194.

14 Forsyth (n 3) 321; Schoeman, Roodt and Wethmar-Lemmer (n 5) 50; and Van Niekerk and Schulze (n 2) 59. See, for example, *Guggenheim v Rosenbaum (2)* 1961 4 SA 21 (W) 31A: "[t]he proper law of the contract is the law of the country which the parties have agreed or intended or presumed to have intended shall govern it". See, also, *Standard Bank of South Africa Ltd v Efroiken and Newman* 1924 AD 171 185; and *Improvair (Cape) (Pty) Ltd v Establissements Neu* 1983 2 SA 138 (C) 145A.

15 1986 3 SA 509 (D).

recognises party autonomy in respect of the proper law of a contract seems clear. Thus where the parties have expressly or impliedly (or tacitly) agreed upon a governing law our Courts would give effect to the intention of the parties."[16] Parties may exercise their autonomy by agreeing expressly[17] upon a governing law, or a court may find that a tacit choice of law exists.[18] In *Improvair (Cape) (Pty) Ltd v Establissements Neu*,[19] it was said that where there is an express choice "there is usually no difficulty in finding that the agreed system constitutes the proper law of the contract".[20] However, problems may arise when the parties fail to record their intention. In such a situation the court is given the task to determine whether there is a tacit (or implied) choice of law, failing which a court must assign a proper law to the contract.

III. Tacit choice of law

Where the parties express a choice of law, it is unproblematic to give effect to that choice under the Rome I Regulation.[21] It is significantly more difficult to infer a choice of law when the parties have failed to record their intention in the contract.[22] The court must be satisfied that the deduced tacit (or implied) choice of law reflects the real intention of the parties.[23] In other words, the court must find the parties' choice of law to be "clearly demonstrated", despite falling short of an actual expression.[24]

---

16 525.

17 Forsyth (n 3) 325; Fredericks and Neels "The proper law of a documentary letter of credit" (part 1) 2003 *South African Mercantile Law Journal (SA Merc LJ)* 63 64; Schoeman, Roodt and Wethmar-Lemmer (n 5) 50; and Van Rooyen *Die Kontrak in die Suid-Afrikaanse Internasionale Privaatreg* (1972) 99–100.

18 Forsyth (n 3) 325; Fredericks and Neels (n 17) 64; Schoeman, Roodt and Wethmar-Lemmer (n 5) 50; and Van Rooyen (n 17) 99–100.

19 1983 2 SA 138 (C).

20 145B. See, also, Schoeman, Roodt and Wethmar-Lemmer (n 5) 51: an express choice of law is the most concrete expression of party autonomy and is usually easy to identify.

21 Collins (gen ed) (n 3) 1802; and Marshall (n 5) 510–511.

22 Marshall (n 5) 511.

23 Bogdan (n 5) 66; Collins (gen ed) (n 3) 1809; Forsyth (n 3) 326–327; Marshall (n 5) 512–513; Neels and Fredericks (n 4) 104; and Nygh (n 4) 108–109.

24 See Neels and Fredericks (n 4) 106: the authors are of the opinion that the word "demonstrated" has a procedural connotation which does not seem warranted in a choice-of-law context. They recommend that one should rather use the phrases

In South African case law,[25] the line between a real "tacit choice" and an "assignment of law" is often blurred.[26] The reason for this is that the assignment of the proper law (where there is no real choice) is often justified on the ground that the assigned law is the legal system that the parties may be presumed to have chosen.[27] In *Standard Bank of South Africa Ltd v Efroiken and Newman*,[28] for instance, despite the fact that the parties clearly lacked any intention in respect of the governing law, the court still presumed that they must have had some legal system in mind.[29] Thus tacit choice of law and the assignment of law are treated in a similar manner, and frequently it is unclear whether a case falls into one category or the other.[30] Forsyth correctly states that it is artificial to refer to the parties' presumed intention, which the court knows to be absent.[31]

IV. Level of strictness of the criterion for a tacit choice of law

To give effect to the real or true intention of the parties, the criteria for identifying a tacit (or implied) choice of law must be articulated clearly and stringently.[32] The level of strictness of the criterion under the Rome I Regulation requires the tacit choice to be "clearly demonstrated",[33] while the formulation under the predecessor of the Rome I Regulation, the Rome

"evident from", "appear clearly from" or "manifestly clear from". See, also, Giuliano and Lagarde "Report on the Convention on the Law Applicable to Contractual Obligations by Mario Giuliano and Paul Lagarde" 1980 *Official Journal of the European Communities (O.J.)* C-282/01 15-17 (hereinafter referred to as "Giuliano and Lagarde Report") in respect of the Rome Convention.

25 See, for example, *Improvair (Cape) (Pty) Ltd v Establissements Neu* 1983 2 SA 138 (C) 145–146.

26 For a discussion and further references, see Forsyth (n 3) 326–327; Fredericks and Neels (n 17) 66–67; and Schoeman, Roodt and Wethmar-Lemmer (n 5) 53–54.

27 Forsyth (n 3) 326; Fredericks and Neels (n 17) 66; Schoeman, Roodt and Wethmar-Lemmer (n 5) 53; and Van Niekerk and Schulze (n 2) 63.

28 1924 AD 171.

29 185. See Fredericks and Neels (n 17) 66.

30 Forsyth (n 3) 326–327.

31 Forsyth (n 3) 326 n 67.

32 Marshall (n 5) 216; and Nygh (n 4) 111.

33 Art 3(1): "A contract shall be governed by the law chosen by the parties. The choice shall be made expressly or clearly demonstrated by the terms of the contract or the circumstances of the case…".

Convention on the Law Applicable to Contractual Obligations,[34] required that the tacit choice of law be "demonstrated with reasonable certainty".[35] It can be argued that the formulation under the Rome Convention did not necessarily go far enough in the pursuance of legal determinability.[36] To allow readily deduced tacit agreements may leave too much to the discretion of the individual judge, and, accordingly, could result in unpredictability of decision.[37] The test under the Rome I Regulation requiring a tacit choice to be "clearly demonstrated" ensures a far greater measure of legal certainty and predictability of decision.[38]

There is very little guidance in South African private international law with regard to the level of strictness of the criterion for inferring a tacit choice of law. In *Improvair (Cape) (Pty) Ltd v Establissements Neu*,[39]

---

34 Rome I Regulation (n 9). The convention continues to apply to contracts concluded before 17 December 2009.

35 Art 3(1): "A contract shall be governed by the law chosen by the parties. The choice must be expressed or demonstrated with reasonable certainty by the terms of the contract or the circumstances of the case...."

36 Neels and Fredericks "Revision of the Rome Convention on the Law Applicable to Contractual Obligations (1980): perspectives from international commercial and financial law" 2004 *Revue européene de droit bancaire et financier / European Banking and Financial Law Journal (EUREDIA)* 173 179, reprinted in 2006 *Tydskrif vir die Suid-Afrikaanse Reg (TSAR)* 121 125.

37 Neels and Fredericks (n 4) 106; Neels and Fredericks (n 36) 125. See, also, Marshall (n 5) 517. See the Official Commentary (n 6) paras 4.8–4.14.

38 See, for example, Marshall (n 5) 518 n 87: "The revision from the 'reasonable certainty' test under the *Rome Convention* to the 'clearly demonstrated' test under the *Rome I Regulation* was an attempt by the European Commission to quash the practice of the English and German courts in readily discerning a tacit choice where their French counterparts would not.... The French language version of the test, which requires that the choice of law result 'de façon certaine des dispositions du contrat ou des circonstances de la cause', remained unchanged in the transition from the *Rome Convention* to the *Rome I Regulation*." For a different view, see Plender and Wilderspin *The European Private International Law of Obligations* (2015) 148: "At first sight, this change of wording might be thought to require stronger evidence of the parties' intention than was the case under the Rome Convention. However, it is thought that that was not the intention of the legislature.... [T]here was a discrepancy between the French and English texts of the Convention.... The most likely explanation is that the change of wording in both language versions is simply prompted by a wish to align the different language versions while leaving the substantive meaning unchanged."

39 1983 2 SA 138 (C).

Grosskopf J held that "it is clear that such a term should not readily be implied".[40] The phrase "should not readily be implied" suggests a more stringent test than the "reasonable certainty" criterion of the Rome Convention, but would seem to correspond with the revised threshold in the Rome I Regulation.

The recently adopted Hague Principles on Choice of Law in International Commercial Contracts[41] set forth general principles concerning choice of law in international commercial contracts.[42] They may be used as a model for national, regional, supranational or international instruments.[43] Although the Hague Principles constitute a non-binding instrument, they are also intended to be used in the interpretation, supplementation and development of rules of private international law by courts and arbitral tribunals.[44] The Hague Principles were drafted by experts from many countries and may be considered as a code of best practice in respect of choice of law in international commercial contracts.[45] In providing more clarity on the level of strictness of the criterion for a tacit choice of law, a South African court could refer to the Hague Principles; it is suggested that they may provide valuable guidance within the South African context. Article 4 of the Hague Principles uses the phrase "appear clearly" to indicate the level of strictness in determining a tacit choice of law,[46] which, one may argue, in any event

---

40 145B–C: "Difficulties arise, however, where there is no express agreement. In such event there may be cases in which a court may conclude that the contract contains a tacit term concerning the law to be applied.... It is clear that such a term should not readily be implied."

41 The Principles were approved by the Member States of the Hague Conference on Private International Law on 19 March 2015 (see https://www.hcch.net/en/instruments/conventions/full-text/?cid=135 (15-09-2017)). See the Principles and the Official Commentary in Hague Conference on Private International Law *Principles on Choice of Law in International Commercial Contracts* (2015).

42 para 1 of the preamble.

43 para 2 of the preamble.

44 paras 3–4 of the preamble. See, generally, Neels "The Nature, Objective and Purposes of the Hague Principles on Choice of Law in International Contracts" in Bonomi and Romano (eds) *Yearbook of Private International Law Volume XV – 2013/2014* 45 50–56.

45 Neels (n 44) 56.

46 Art 4 of the Hague Principles: "A choice of law, or any modification of a choice of law, must be made expressly or appear clearly from the provisions of the contract or the circumstances...." See the Official Commentary (n 6) para 4.14: "A tacit choice of law must appear clearly from the provisions of the contract or the circumstances. This means that the choice must be evident as a result of the existence of strong indications for such a choice."

resembles the court in *Improvair's* instruction not to readily imply a tacit choice of law.[47] A tacit choice of law must appear clearly (from the provisions of the contract or the circumstances)[48] and will therefore not readily be implied.[49]

V. Indicators of a tacit choice

The Rome I Regulation allows a tacit choice to be inferred by "the terms of the contract" or "the circumstances of the case".[50] This means that a court, in deciding whether or not the parties have made a tacit choice of law, is not confined to the written agreement, but may take account of considerations surrounding the contract.[51]

The Giuliano and Lagarde Report,[52] which accompanied the Rome Convention, lists some of the factors from which a tacit choice of law may be inferred.[53] Some notable examples include the use of a standard form which is known to be drafted with reference to a particular system of law,[54] where there has been an express choice of law in related transactions between the

47 *Improvair (Cape) (Pty) Ltd v Establissements Neu* 1983 2 SA 138 (C) 145B–C.

48 Art 4 of the Hague Principles.

49 *Improvair (Cape) (Pty) Ltd v Establissements Neu* 1983 2 SA 138 (C) 145B–C.

50 Art 3(1).

51 Bogdan (n 5) 66; Collins (gen ed) (n 3) 1809; Marshall (n 5) 518; McClean and Beevers (n 2) 360; Neels and Fredericks (n 4) 106–107; Plender and Wilderspin (n 38) 148; and Schwenzer, Hachem and Kee (n 2) 55.

52 Giuliano and Lagarde Report (n 24) 17.

53 Giuliano and Lagarde Report (n 24) 17.

54 Giuliano and Lagarde Report (n 24) 17. See, for example, Collins (gen ed) (n 3) 1810; Nygh (n 4) 115; and Plender and Wilderspin (n 38) 154. See, also, Briggs *Private International Law in English Courts* (2014) 540: "[T]he retort that if the parties had chosen a law they would have said so may be rebutted by the equally simplistic observation that it is possible for parties to make a choice which they do not write into a contract which is presented as a standard form."

parties,[55] and the inclusion of specific provisions of a particular legal system in the contract.[56]

After providing a list of examples from which a tacit choice of law may be inferred, the Giuliano and Lagarde Report states that article 3 of the Rome Convention does not permit a court to infer a choice of law where there is no clear indication of such choice.[57] Although the report was written as a guide to the Rome Convention, nothing suggests that the position would have changed under the Rome I Regulation. The existence of any of the abovementioned factors as such should therefore not automatically be conclusive. They are mere indicators that a court must consider to determine whether it is clear that the parties intended to make a choice of law.[58]

In searching for indicators of a tacit (or implied) choice of the law, a South African court will examine not only the provisions of the contract but also all the circumstances surrounding the agreement.[59] The position in South Africa therefore corresponds with the European position in this regard.[60] Although some conflicts codes in this context refer to the provisions of the contract only,[61] there seems to be no reason to limit the search for a tacit choice of law to the provisions of the contract without taking note of the surrounding circumstances.[62]

---

55 Giuliano and Lagarde Report (n 24) 17: "[A] previous course of dealing between the parties under contracts containing an express choice of law may leave the court in no doubt that the contract in question is to be governed by the law previously chosen where the choice of law clause has been omitted in circumstances which do not indicate a deliberate change of policy by the parties." See Collins (gen ed) (n 3) 1810; Nygh (n 4) 116; and Plender and Wilderspin (n 38) 156.

56 Giuliano and Lagarde Report (n 24) 17. See, also, Collins (gen ed) (n 3) 1813–1814.

57 Giuliano and Lagarde Report (n 24) 17.

58 Collins (gen ed) (n 3) 1809.

59 Forsyth (n 3) 327; and Van Niekerk and Schulze (n 2) 61. See *Standard Bank of South Africa v Efroiken and Newman* 1924 AD 171 185: "[W]here parties did not give the matter a thought, courts of law have of necessity to fall back upon what ought, reading the contract by the light of the subject-matter and of the surrounding circumstances, to be presumed to have been the intention of the parties."

60 Art 3(1) of the Rome I Regulation (n 9).

61 Neels and Fredericks (n 4) 106 refer to art 2 of the Hague Convention on the Law Applicable to International Sale of Goods (1955); sec 7 of the Oregon Conflicts Law Applicable to Contracts of 2001; and art 3111 of the Quebec Civil Code of 1994.

62 Neels and Fredericks (n 4) 107: the phrase "circumstances" will encompass the conduct of the parties. See, also, art 4 of the Hague Principles; and Schwenzer,

There are a number of factors that South African courts have considered in the search for a tacit choice of law.[63] In *Improvair (Cape) Pty Ltd v Establissements Neu*, it was held: "There may nevertheless be circumstances, e.g., where the contract deals with concepts peculiar to a particular system, in which the parties may be held to have agreed tacitly that their contract should be governed by a particular legal system."[64] Similarly, a reference to the legislation of a particular country has also been taken as evidence of a tacit choice of that country's law.[65] However, one must be mindful to draw a distinction between a choice of law, and the incorporation of certain statutory measures of a foreign legal system to govern a particular aspect of the contract.[66] In *Ex Parte Spinazze*,[67] the use of a standard form was considered as a factor that may indicate a tacit choice of law.[68]

The South African authors are of the opinion that factors such as the use of technical terms, references to legislation or the use of a standard form are mere indications of a tacit choice of law and not automatically conclusive

---

Hachem and Kee (n 2) 55: most legal systems refer to the contract and/or the circumstances of the case. See, also, Davies, Bell and Brereton (n 3) 451; and Symeonides *Codifying Choice of Law Around the World* (2014) 121.

63 Forsyth (n 3) 328; Schoeman, Roodt and Wethmar-Lemmer (n 5) 51–52; and Van Niekerk and Schulze (n 2) 61–62.

64 145D–E. Grosskopf J did, however, acknowledge that such cases would be rare.

65 *Stretton v Union Steamship Company Ltd* (1881) 1 EDC 315 323.

66 Schoeman, Roodt and Wethmar-Lemmer (n 5) 52; Van Niekerk and Schulze (n 2) 62: "Thus, where parties to an international sale agree that the rules of English law relating to the rejection of defective goods will apply to their relationship, that is not necessarily a (tacit) choice of English law generally to govern as the proper law; in fact, their express specification of a particular aspect of the foreign legal system would seem to contradict any such intention…." See, also, Forsyth (n 3) 328.

67 1985 3 SA 650 (A).

68 665E–H: "Reverting to the facts of this case, I am of the opinion that the proper law or *lex causae* of the antenuptial contract in issue was unquestionably South African law. The contract was in South African form; it was entered into in order to avoid a matrimonial property regime, viz community of property, which obtained in South Africa at the time, but not in Italy (according to the expert evidence, in 1957 marriages governed by Italian law were out of community of property); at the time when the contract was executed the deceased was domiciled and resident in South Africa; and the parties to the contract obviously intended South Africa to be their matrimonial home and the country where the contract was to operate. These factors may be taken either as indicating a tacit choice of South African law or, at any rate, as showing that South African law was the system with which the contract had its closest and most real connection."

of such a choice.[69] This is particularly relevant when the question arises whether a choice of forum constitutes a choice of law, which is discussed in more detail in paragraph VI.

VI. Choice of forum and tacit choice of law

The legal systems of the world provide highly divergent views in respect of the relationship between choice of forum and tacit choice of law by the parties.[70] This diversity extends to the member states of the Rome I Regulation.[71] Notably, the English and German courts have been liberal in inferring a choice of law from the presence of a jurisdiction or localised arbitration clause, while French courts were reluctant to draw this conclusion.[72]

The Giuliano and Lagarde Report addressed this issue by proving that "[t]he choice of a particular forum may show in no uncertain manner that the parties intend the contract to be governed by the law of that forum, but this must always be subject to the other terms of the contract and all the circumstances of the case".[73] However, Lagarde has since indicated that a jurisdiction clause is merely a factor to be considered, and may not, without more, be interpreted as establishing the unexpressed will of the parties.[74]

---

69 Forsyth (n 3) 326; Schoeman, Roodt and Wethmar-Lemmer (n 5) 52; and Van Niekerk and Schulze (n 2) 62–63.

70 For an overview and references, see Neels "Choice of forum and tacit choice of law: the Supreme Court of India and the Hague Principles on Choice of Law in International Commercial Contracts (an appeal for an inclusive comparative approach to private international law)" in International Institute for the Unification of Private Law (UNIDROIT) (ed) *Eppur Si Muove – The Age of Uniform Law. Festschrift for Prof MJ Bonell* (2016) 358.

71 Marshall (n 5) 519 n 95; Neels (n 70); and Plender and Wilderspin (n 38) 152–153.

72 Plender and Wilderspin (n 38) 152–153. See, also, Marshall (n 5) 519 n 95: "Under the auspices of the *Giuliano-Lagarde Report* ... English courts continued to conform to the common law belief that a forum clause was a 'weighty indicator' when ascertaining tacit choice pursuant to the Rome Convention. While the German courts followed a similar trajectory, other contracting states, notably France, were loath to draw the inference."

73 Giuliano and Lagarde Report (n 24) 17.

74 See Lagarde "Le nouveau droit international privé des contrats" 80 (1991) *Revue critique de droit international privé (Rev. crit. d.i.p.)* 287 303 as referred to in Nygh (n 4) 117 and Plender and Wilderspin (n 38) 151.

The European Group of Private International Law (GEDIP)[75] is also of the opinion that the choice of a court of a given state shall not in itself be equivalent to a choice of the law of that state.[76]

While article 3 of the Rome I Regulation is silent on the matter, recital 12 attempts to clarify the issue by stating: "An agreement between the parties to confer on one or more courts or tribunals of a Member State exclusive jurisdiction to determine disputes under the contract should be one of the factors to be taken into account in determining whether a choice of law has been clearly demonstrated." However, it does not appear that recital 12 provides much clarity. On the one hand, it may be read as support for the idea that a choice of forum is not sufficient to indicate a choice of law but may be a factor to be taken into account,[77] and, on the other, that a choice of forum may on its own indicate a choice of law.[78] The divergent practices of the member states of the Rome I Regulation will undoubtedly continue as long as the fora in these states are free to determine how much weight is to be attached to a choice of forum clause as evidence of the parties' intention in respect of the applicable law.[79]

The role of choice of forum clauses in South African private international law is not settled.[80] Based on the maxim *qui elegit iudecem elegit ius*,[81] it is sometimes suggested that a choice of court or localised arbitration clause may be taken as an implied choice of the law of the relevant country as the

---

75 European Group of Private International Law or *Groupe européen de droit international privé (GEDIP)* (see http://www.gedip-egpil.eu).

76 GEDIP "Third consolidated version of a proposal to amend articles 1, 3, 4, 5, 6, 7, 9, 10*bis*, 12 and 13 of the Rome Convention of 19 June 1980 on the Law Applicable to Contractual Obligations, and article 15 of the Regulation 44/2001/EC (Brussels I)" (Vienna 2003) *per* http://www.gedip-egpil.eu/documents/gedip-documents-13vce.html (15-09-2017): "In particular, the choice of a court or the courts of a given State shall not in itself be equivalent to a choice of law of that State."

77 Marshall (n 5) 519; and Neels (n 70). Briggs (n 54) 541–542 suggests that a choice of arbitral tribunal is completely irrelevant in respect of choice of law.

78 For a discussion in this regard, see Neels (n 70) and Plender and Wilderspin (n 38) 154. Recital 12 is limited to exclusive choice of forum clauses in respect of court or tribunals "of a Member State".

79 Briggs (n 54) 542; Marshall (n 5) 520; and Plender and Wilderspin (n 38) 154.

80 Although a South African court (*Reiss Engineering Co Ltd v Isamcor* 1983 1 SA 1033 (W) 1039 A–B) has pronounced that a choice of a proper law does not constitute submission to jurisdiction, the opposite has yet to be clarified. See Neels and Fredericks (n 36) 126 n 29.

81 See Schoeman, Roodt and Wethmar-Lemmer (n 5) 51: he who chooses the judge, chooses the law. See, also, Forsyth (n 3) 328.

proper law of the contract.[82] However, in *Benidai Trading Co Ltd v Gouws and Gouws*[83] the court held:

> "In the international commercial world it has almost become a universal practice to select London as the seat for arbitration proceedings, not because the parties to an international mercantile transaction necessarily have confidence in English law, but for purposes of convenience, because London is an important commercial centre and because of the expertise of London arbitrators. And if they do so they do not, unless there is an express indication in the contract or other circumstances which point in that direction, submit to the jurisdiction of the English Courts. Not only do the parties not submit to the jurisdiction of the English law, but, unless a clear inference is to be drawn to the contrary, they do not even accept English law as the proper law of the contract…."[84]

Although it is generally accepted that a choice of forum should be a factor in the determination of a tacit choice of law,[85] choice of law and choice of forum are, in principle, separate issues and must be distinguished.[86] A forum may be chosen for its neutrality, experience or expertise and not necessarily for the application of its domestic law.[87] Furthermore, the forum will determine the law of the contract in terms of the applicable rules of

82 Forsyth (n 3) 328; Schoeman, Roodt and Wethmar-Lemmer (n 5) 51; Van Niekerk and Schulze (n 2) 61; and Van Rooyen (n 17) 44: "Oor die algemeen word 'n jurisdiksie-klousule nie beskou as 'n stilswyende regskeuse nie. Aan die ander kant word dit as praktiese reëling aanvaar dat die aanwysing van 'n arbiter wel ook 'n aanwysing van sy regstelsel inhou – die rede: arbiters, in teenstelling met regters, is gewoonlik leke wat die reg betref!"

83 1977 3 SA 1020 (T).

84 1028H–1029A. The court referred to the English case of *Compagnie d' Armement SA v Compagnie Tunisienne de Navigation SA* [1970] 3 WLR 389, where the House of Lords concluded that an arbitration clause was not necessarily conclusive of a choice of law. See, also, Forsyth (n 3) 328 fn 76: "And this is as it should be: no rule of law can provide a conclusive guide to the parties' actual intention."

85 See McClean and Beevers (n 2) 361; Neels (n 70); Neels and Fredericks (n 4) 108; and Schwenzer, Hachem and Kee (n 2) 56. See, also, the Official Commentary on the Hague Principles (n 6) para 4.11.

86 Briggs (n 54) 66; Neels (n 70); and Neels and Fredericks (n 4) 108. See, also, the Official Commentary on the Hague Principles (n 37) para 4.11. See, also, Nygh (n 4) 117; Plender and Wilderspin (n 38) 151; and GEDIP (n 76): "In particular, the choice of a court or the courts of a given State shall not in itself be equivalent to a choice of law of that State."

87 Neels (n 70); and Neels and Fredericks (n 4) 108. See, also, the Official Commentary on the Hague Principles (n 37) paras 4.11–4.12.

private international law.[88] Parties who submit to a court or tribunal's jurisdiction do not intend thereby that the forum should abandon its choice of law process and mechanically apply the *lex fori*.[89] A choice of court or localised arbitral tribunal should therefore not on its own be taken to indicate a choice of law by the parties. The second sentence of article 4 of the Hague Principles therefore states that: "An agreement between the parties to confer jurisdiction on a court or an arbitral tribunal to determine disputes under the contract is not in itself equivalent to a choice of law."[90]

VII. Conclusion

The determination of a tacit choice of law under the Rome I Regulation and in South African private international law is not dissimilar. The level of strictness of the criterion under the Rome I Regulation requires the choice to be "clearly demonstrated",[91] while in the South African case of *Improvair (Cape) (Pty) Ltd v Establissements Neu*[92] the phrase "should not readily be implied" is used.[93] The latter threshold would seem to correspond to that of the Rome I Regulation.[94]

The position both under the Regulation and in South Africa is that a court must examine the provisions of the contract and the circumstances of the case in searching for indicators of a tacit choice of law.[95] The Giuliano and Lagarde Report lists various examples from which a tacit choice of law may be inferred.[96] As is the position under the report, the South African courts have taken references to national legislation[97] and the use of a standard form[98] as evidence of a tacit choice of the relevant country's law.

88 Neels (n 70). See, also, the Official Commentary on the Hague Principles (n 37) para 4.11.
89 Forsyth (n 3) 328; and Van Rooyen (n 17) 99–100.
90 Art 4.
91 Art 3(1).
92 1983 2 SA 138 (C).
93 145 B–C.
94 See para IV.
95 See para V.
96 Giuliano and Lagarde Report (n 24) 17.
97 See para V.
98 See para V.

The Rome I Regulation is not clear on the role of choice of forum clauses. Recital 12 in its present form is ambiguous and allows for different interpretations.[99] The intention behind recital 12 should be made clear by stating whether a choice of forum is not sufficient to indicate a choice of law but may be a factor to be taken into account, or whether a choice of forum clause may on its own indicate a choice of law. This would curb the divergent practices of the member states of the Rome I Regulation in this regard. A South African court, when given the opportunity, should also clarify the position in this regard, with reference to article 4 of the Hague Principles.[100]

99 See para VI.
100 See art 4.

Bibliography

Bogdan M *Private International Law in Sweden* (Wolters Kluwer, The Hague 2012).

Bonomi A "Rome I Regulation on the law applicable to contractual obligations– some general remarks" in Bonomi A and Volken P (eds) *Yearbook of Private International Law Volume X – 2008* (Sellier, Munich 2009) 165.

Briggs A *Private International Law in English Courts* (Oxford University Press, Oxford 2014).

Collins L (gen ed) *Dicey, Morris and Collins on The Conflict of Laws II* (15th Edition, Sweet & Maxwell, London 2012).

Davies M, Bell A and Brereton P *Nygh's Conflict of Laws in Australia* (9th Edition, LexisNexis Butterworths, Chatswood 2014).

De Araujo N "Recent developments and current trends on Brazilian private international law concerning international contracts" 2013 *Panorama of Brazilian Law (PBL)* 73 (available at http://panoramaofbrazilianlaw.com/index.php/BrLaw/article/viewFile/20/4).

Forsyth CF "Enforcement of foreign arbitral awards, choice of law in contract, characterization and a new attitude to private international law" 104 (1987) *South African Law Journal (SALJ)* 4.

Forsyth CF *Private International Law. The Modern Roman-Dutch Law including the Jurisdiction of the High Courts* (5th Edition, Juta, Cape Town 2012).

Fredericks EA and Neels JL "The proper law of a documentary letter of credit" (part 1) 15 (2003) *South African Mercantile Law Journal (SA Merc LJ)* 63.

GEDIP (European Group of Private International Law/*Groupe européen de droit international privé*) "Third consolidated version of a proposal to amend articles 1, 3, 4, 5, 6, 7, 9, 10*bis*, 12 and 13 of the Rome Convention of 19 June 1980 on the Law Applicable to Contractual Obligations, and article 15 of the Regulation 44/2001/EC (Brussels I)" (Vienna, 2003) (available at http://www.gedip-egpil.eu/documents/gedip-documents-13vce.html (15-09-2017)).

Giuliano M and Lagarde P "Report on the Convention on the Law Applicable to Contractual Obligations by Mario Giuliano and Paul Lagarde" 1980 *Official Journal of the European Communities (OJ)* C-282/01 15.

Marshall BA "Reconsidering the proper law of the contract" 2012 *Melbourne Journal of International Law (Mel J Int Law)* 501.

McClean JD and Beevers K *The Conflict of Laws* (7th Edition, Sweet & Maxwell, London 2009).

Neels JL "Choice of forum and tacit choice of law: the Supreme Court of India and the Hague Principles on Choice of Law in International Commercial Contracts (an appeal for an inclusive comparative approach to private international law)" in in International Institute for the Unification of Private Law (UNIDROIT) (ed) *Eppur Si Muove – The Age of Uniform Law. Festschrift for Prof MJ Bonell* (Unidroit, Rome 2016).

Neels JL "Rome in the Far East" (unpublished lecture at the University of Amsterdam, the University of British Columbia and the University of Johannesburg, 2011–2012).

Neels JL "The Nature, Objective and Purposes of the Hague Principles on Choice of Law in International Contracts" in Bonomi A and Romano GP (eds) *Yearbook of Private International Law Volume XV – 2013/2014* (Sellier, Berlin 2014) 45.

Neels JL and Fredericks EA "Revision of the Rome Convention on the Law Applicable to Contractual Obligations (1980): perspectives from international commercial and financial law" 2004 *Revue européene de droit bancaire et financier / European Banking and Financial Law Journal (EUREDIA)* 173, reprinted in 2006 *Tydskrif vir die Suid-Afrikaanse Reg (TSAR)* 121.

Neels JL and Fredericks EA "Tacit choice of law in the Hague Principles on Choice of Law in International Contracts" 2011 *De Jure* 101.

North PM and Fawcett J *Cheshire and North's Private International Law* (11th Edition, Butterworths, London 1987).

North PM *Private International Law Problems in Common Law Jurisdictions* (Nijhoff Publishers, Dordrecht 1993).

Nygh PE *Autonomy in International Contracts* (Oxford University Press, Oxford 1999).

Nygh PE *Conflict of Laws in Australia* (5th Edition, Butterworths, Sydney 1991).

Plender M and Wilderspin R *The European Private International Law of Obligations* (4th Edition, Sweet & Maxwell, London 2015).

Schoeman E, Roodt C and Wethmar-Lemmer M *Private International Law in South Africa* (Wolter Kluwer, The Hague 2014).

Schwenzer IH, Hachem P and Kee C *Global Sales and Contract Law* (Oxford University Press, Oxford 2012).

Symeonides S "Party autonomy in Rome I and II: an outsider's perspective" 2010 *Nederlands Internationaal Privaatrecht (NIPR)* 191.

Symeonides S *Codifying Choice of Law Around the World. An International Comparative Analysis* (Oxford University Press, New York 2014).

Van Niekerk JP and Schulze WG *The South African Law of International Trade: Selected Topics* (4th Edition, SAGA Legal Publications, Pretoria 2016).

Van Rooyen JCW *Die Kontrak in die Suid-Afrikaanse Internasionale Privaatreg* (Juta, Cape Town 1972).

Case Law

South Africa

Benidai Trading Co Ltd v Gouws and Gouws 1977 3 SA 1020 (T)

Ex Parte Spinazze 1985 3 SA 650 (A)

Guggenheim v Rosembaum (2) 1961 4 SA 21 (W)

Improvair (Cape) (Pty) Ltd v Establissements Neu 1983 2 SA 138 (C)

Reiss Engineering Co Ltd v Isamcor 1983 1 SA 1033 (W)

Standard Bank of South Africa Ltd v Efroiken and Newman 1924 AD 171

Stretton v Union Steamship Company Ltd (1881) 1 EDC 315

United Kingdom

Amin Rasheed Shipping Corporation v Kuwait Insurance Co 1984 AC 50

Compagnie d' Armement SA v Compagnie Tunisienne de Navigation SA 1970 3 WLR 389

Comment on "Tacit Choice of Law in International Commercial Contracts"

*Wolfgang Wurmnest**

I. Some general considerations about Article 3 Rome I Regulation

In his paper, Bouwers analyses the conditions for a tacit choice of law under the South African rules of private international law. In addition, he compares South African law with the standards set forth by the Rome I Regulation, i.e. the rules of European private international law which apply in all EU countries except Denmark.

Under EU law, the freedom of the parties to choose the law that shall apply to their contractual relationship is laid down in Article 3(1) Rome I Regulation. According to this provision, a "contract shall be governed by the law chosen by the parties. The choice shall be made expressly or clearly demonstrated by the terms of the contract or the circumstances of the case". A tacit choice of law is a real (not hypothetical) choice of law requiring a meeting of minds of the parties even though the parties have not expressly stated that choice in their contract, as Bouwers correctly points out.[1] The

* Wolfgang Wurmnest, *Dr. iur. habil., LL.M. (Berkeley)*; Professor, University of Augsburg, Faculty of Law. Chair for Civil Law, Economic Law, International Private Law, Civil Procedure and Comparative Law.

1 Garth Bouwers, p. 72 in this publication.

1980 report of Giuliano and Lagarde on the Rome Convention on the law applicable to contractual obligations[2] (i.e. the forerunner of the Rome I Regulation) stated that the rule on tacit choice of law "does not permit the court to infer a choice of law that the parties might have made where they had no clear intention of making a choice."[3]

It is thus not allowed under Article 3 Rome I Regulation to make recourse to the "hypothetical will" of the contracting parties, as assumed by German courts under the German rules of private international law before the implementation of the Rome Convention.[4] It seems that similar attempts as made by German courts under the old rules of private international law can be traced in the case law of South African courts. Bouwers states that courts sometimes refer to the hypothetical will of the contracting parties and apply the law that the parties may have presumably chosen.[5]

Reliance on the presumed will of the parties is not allowed under EU law and this approach makes sense. Courts cannot know, and do not need to know, what reasonable parties would have done. Where the parties have not chosen the applicable law expressly or tacitly, the Rome I Regulation contains a full set of statutory rules for the determination of the law applicable in the absence of a choice of law (Articles 4 et seq. Rome I Regulation). These rules mirror the expectations of reasonable parties as the European approach to private international law is largely based on the concept of predictability.[6]

II. Level of strictness

In his paper, Bouwers devotes much attention to the level of strictness that is required to assume tacit choice of law by the parties. He correctly observes that the criterion of European law was altered when the Rome Convention was transferred into the Rome I Regulation. Under the Rome Con-

---

2 O.J. C 282, 31.10.1980, 1.

3 Report of Mario Giuliano and Paul Lagarde, Art. 3 para. 3, O.J. C 282, 31.10.1980, 17.

4 BGH 22.11.1955 – I ZR 218/53 – NJW 1956, 377; BGH 7.3.1962 – VIII ZR 9/61 – NJW 1962, 1005. Also BGH 30.9.1987 – IV a ZR 22/86 – NJW-RR 1988, 159 (160), refers to this maxim but in the end assumes a tacit choice of law.

5 Garth Bouwers, p. 74 in this publication.

6 Cf. Regulation (EC) No 593/2008 of the European Parliament and the Council of 17 June 2008 on the law applicable to contractual obligations (Rome I), Recital 6.

vention, a treaty between the Member States of the then European Community, the various language versions were not congruent. Under the English, German and Italian versions, a tacit choice had to be demonstrated "with reasonable certainty" ("*mit hinreichender Sicherheit*", "*in modo ragionevolmente certo*"). The French and the Spanish versions contained a stricter criterion as the choice had to be "certain" ("*de façon certaine*", "*de manera cierta*").

When drafting the Rome I Regulation the European legislature aligned these different versions and used the French and Spanish versions as a yardstick. The Rome I Regulation, therefore, states in the English version that a tacit choice must be "clearly demonstrated". Correspondingly, the German and Italian language versions demand that the choice must be "*eindeutig*" or "*chiaramente*". The French version uses the same wording as the Rome Convention ("*de façon certaine*"), whereas the Spanish version reads "*de manera inequívoca*" (instead of "*de manera cierta*") which is a purely linguistic change.

There is a dispute among commentators in Europe whether the alignment of the English, German and Italian versions with the French version means that the legislature intended to set forth a stricter standard for the determination of a tacit choice of law to avoid an unwarranted "*Heimwärtsstreben*".[7] Bouwers takes the view that this change "ensures a far

---

7 That the European legislature imposed a stricter standard is advocated by Ole Lando and Peter Arnt Nielsen, *Common Market Law Review (CML Rev.)* 45 (2008), 1687 (1698); Gerhard Hohloch in Harm Peter Westermann, Barbara Grunewald and Georg Maier-Reimer (eds) *Erman, BGB* (14th Edition 2014), Art. 3 Rom I-VO, para. 11; Kathrin Kroll-Ludwigs, *Die Rolle der Parteiautonomie im europäischen Kollisionsrecht* (2013), 49; Stefan Leible and Matthias Lehmann, *Recht der Internationalen Wirtschaft (RIW)* 2008, 528 (532); Ulrich Magnus, *Praxis des Internationalen Privat- und Verfahrensrechts (IPRax)* 2010, 27 (33); Dieter Martiny in Franz Säcker, Roland Rixecker, Hartmut Oetker et al (eds) *Münchener Kommentar zum BGB, Vol. 10* (6th Edition 2015), Art. 3 Rom I-VO, para. 47; Thomas Pfeiffer, *Europäische Zeitschrift für Wirtschaftsrecht (EuZW)* 2008, 622 (624); Giesela Rühl, *Statut und Effizienz* (2011), 470; Ringe in Martin Herberger, Michael Martinek, Helmut Rüßmann et al (eds) *juris PraxisKommentar-BGB* (7th Edition 2014), Art. 3 Rom I-VO, para. 17; Sandra Wandt, *Rechtswahlregelungen im Europäischen Kollisionsrecht* (2014), 125–126; Matthias Wendland in Beate Gsell, Wolfgang Krüger, Stephan Lorenz et al (eds) *beck-online Großkommentar zum Zivilrecht* (15.2.2016), Art. 3 Rom I-VO, para. 132; contra (no changes): Dorothee Einsele, *Wertpapier-Mitteilungen (WM)* 2009, 289 (290); Franco Ferrari in Franco Ferrari, Eva-Maria Kieninger and Peter Mankowski et al (eds), *Internationales Verfahrensrecht* (2nd Edition, 2012), Art. 3 Rom I-VO, para.

greater measure of legal certainty and predictability of decision".[8] If this also means that under the Rome I Regulation there is a more demanding test than under the German and English versions of the Rome Convention, I agree. In my point of view, there can be no doubt that the legislature wanted to avoid courts assuming too readily a tacit choice of law. A choice of law to be "clearly demonstrated", requires more than a choice of law "demonstrated with reasonable certainty", and one cannot qualify this change as being solely of an editorial nature.[9] Also, the genesis of Article 3 Rome I Regulation implies that the legislature intended to impose a stricter standard on the courts.[10]

III. Indicators of a tacit choice of law

Bouwers moves on to analyse the indicators from which a tacit choice of law can be inferred. Under European law, the choice can be either inferred from the contractual stipulations or of the circumstances of the case. A court has to look at the case as a whole and weigh all relevant indications. There is no "closed catalogue" of factors that can be taken into account by a court to infer the will of the parties. The wording of Article 3 Rome I Regulation, however, does give some indications. The court must first examine the contract and identify whether the contractual stipulations indicate a choice of law. It must then look at other factors surrounding the contract to see whether they give evidence of a tacit choice of law.[11]

27; Richard Plender and Michael Wilderspin, *The European Private International Law of Obligations* (4th Edition, 2015), para. 6-026; Thomas Tiede, 'Die Rechtswahl in den Römischen Verordnungen' in Bea Verschraegen (ed), *Rechtswahl – Grenzen und Chancen* (2010), 51 (52–53).

8 Garth Bouwers, p. 75 in this publication.

9 Jan v. Hein in Thomas Rauscher (ed), *Europäisches Zivilprozess- und Kollisionsrecht, Vol. 3* (4th Edition, 2015), Art. 3 Rom I-VO, para. 14; contra: Francisco Garcimartín Alférez, *European Law Forum (EuLF)* 2008, I-61 (I-66); Thomas Thiede, 'Die Rechtswahl in den Römischen Verordnungen' in Bea Verschraegen (ed), *Rechtswahl – Grenzen und Chancen* (2010), 51 (53).

10 Jan v. Hein in Thomas Rauscher (ed), *Europäisches Zivilprozess- und Kollisionsrecht, Vol. 3* (4th Edition, 2015), Art. 3 Rom I-VO, para. 14; Ole Lando and Peter Arnt Nielsen, *Common Market Law Review (CML Rev.)* 45 (2008), 1687 (1698).

11 Jan v. Hein in Thomas Rauscher (ed), *Europäisches Zivilprozess- und Kollisionsrecht, Vol. 3* (4th Edition, 2015), Art. 3 Rom I-VO, para. 14.

Bouwers reports the practice of South African courts. I would like to add some thoughts on German case law. Looking at more recent cases, it appears that the tighter standard imposed by the Rome I Regulation does not prevent German courts from pursuing their liberal approach, which often leads to the application of German law. For example, the Amtsgericht Frankfurt, in a case involving a contract for the carriage of passengers, inferred a tacit choice in favour of German law from the fact that the plaintiff had purchased the flight ticket from the defendant in Germany and that the flight to (presumably) South America left from a German airport.[12] These factors are, in my point of view, not very strong to indicate the will of the parties to choose German law.[13]

Another example concerns the tendency of German courts to infer a choice of German law from parties' communications on the dispute during or before the court proceedings. Often parties analyse a claim based on German law in their communications between each other. German courts tend to assume a tacit choice of German law from such communications. For example, the Oberlandesgericht Stuttgart assumed that the parties to an international contract for the carriage of goods had chosen German law simply by the fact that both parties had discussed the conclusion of the carriage contract based on German legal provisions.[14] Such practice by courts was common under the Rome Convention[15] (and prior to that convention under the German conflict rules) and was criticised by many commentators.[16] In my opinion, this critique is correct. Inferring a choice of the lex

12 AG Frankfurt 25.10.2013 – 30 C 1377/13 (47) – BeckRS 2014, 12196.

13 Despite the weak basis for a tacit choice of law, the application of German law was correct. The Amtsgericht pointed out that even if no choice of law is assumed German law applies by virtue of Article 5(1)sentence 2 Rome I Regulation. According to this provision the law applicable to a contract for the carriage of passengers "shall be the law of the country where the passenger has his habitual residence, provided that either the place of departure or the place of destination is situated in that country." As the passenger had her habitual residence in Germany and the place of departure was an airport in Germany, it was proper to apply German law.

14 OLG Stuttgart 24.4.2013 – 3 U 184/12 – BeckRS 2014, 19218 para. 46.

15 BGH 12.12.1990 – VIII ZR 332/89 – NJW 1991, 1292 (1293); BGH 19.1.2000 – VIII ZR 275/98 – NJW-RR 2000, 1002 (1004); BGH 26.7.2004 – VIII ZR 273/03 – NJW-RR 2005, 206 (208); OLG Düsseldorf 29.12.2009 – 6 U 9/09 – NJW-RR 2009, 1380 (1381).

16 Peter Mankowski, 'Stillschweigende Rechtswahl und wählbares Recht' in: Stefan Leible (ed), *Das Grünbuch zum Internationalen Vertragsrecht* (2004), 63 (71); Haimo Schack, *Neue Juristische Wochenschrift (NJW)* 1984, 2736 (2737 et

fori from the communications between parties before or during a court trial presupposes that the parties were aware of the fact that the contract might be governed by foreign law. Otherwise, the parties did not act with the necessary will to choose the applicable law. In situations involving a conflict of laws it is, therefore, not proper, in my eyes, to infer a tacit choice of the lex fori from the simple fact that the parties basing their legal arguments on the lex fori. This holds true even if these arguments are voiced by legal representatives, as many legal representatives do not possess sufficient knowledge of private international law matters.[17] The situation is different if the parties realise that their contract is governed by a foreign law – for example, after the judge has indicated so – but still continue to rely on the lex fori.[18] In such a case, the assumption of a choice of law is proper.

IV. Choice of forum and choice of law

In the last part of his paper, Bouwers analyses the disputed relationship between the choice of forum and a tacit choice of law. He points out that German and English courts have been rather liberal in inferring a tacit choice of law from an exclusive jurisdiction agreement in the past, whereas French courts separate the two issues strictly. The European Commission included a presumption in its proposal to the Rome I Regulation according to which the choice of a court in the EU Member State presumes that the parties have also chosen the law of that Member State (Article 3(1) sentence 3 Commission Proposal 2005).[19] This proposal was not adopted for good reasons. Parties choose a court for a variety of reasons (for example, its geographic location, neutrality or expertise in certain matters) and not necessarily for the application of the lex fori. Consequently, the "soft" Recital 12 was included in the Regulation which states that clauses conferring exclusive jurisdiction on courts of an EU Member State to determine disputes under the contract

seq).

17 Ulrich Magnus, *Praxis des Internationalen Privat- und Verfahrensrechts (IPRax)* 2010, 27 (33).

18 Stefan Leible and Matthias Lehmann, *Recht der internationalen Wirtschaft (RIW)* 2008, 528 (532); Ulrich Magnus, *Praxis des Internationalen Privat- und Verfahrensrechts (IPRax)* 2010, 27 (33).

19 Proposal for a Regulation of the European Parliament and the Council on the law applicable to contractual obligations (Rome I), COM (2005) 650 final.

can be taken into account in determining whether a choice of law has been established.[20]

I agree with Bouwers that this recital does not add much clarity. The recital is, however, of helpful for the courts, as they are reminded that they should have a closer look at the issue of choice of law.[21] In this context, it has to be noted that only an exclusive jurisdiction agreement, i.e. an agreement that confers jurisdiction upon one court (or courts in one country), can be used as indicator to assume a tacit choice of law. Agreements conferring jurisdiction on a court in addition to the courts that have otherwise jurisdiction to hear the case ("*fakultative Gerichtsstandsvereinbarungen*")[22] or agreements that confer jurisdictions to courts at the respective seat of the defendant are not proper indicators from which a court may infer a tacit choice of law.

Moreover, it must be emphasised that even German courts do not automatically infer a choice of law from an exclusive jurisdiction agreement and have not done so in the past. Rather, they look at the contract as a whole to evaluate whether a tacit choice of law can be assumed. Usually, German courts do not rely on the jurisdiction agreement alone but assume a choice of the lex fori only if other factors also point towards German law – for example, the domicile or seat of the parties, references to statutory provisions of German law in the contract or the language of the contract.[23] This interpretation makes sense and should be maintained under the Rome I Regulation.

20 The fact that the parties confer exclusive jurisdiction on a court in a third state is also relevant to the analysis. In such a case the court in the third state would, however, decide the question whether the parties have tacitly chosen the law of the third state according to the lex fori and not the Rome I Regulation, see Ulrich Magnus, *Praxis des Internationalen Privat- und Verfahrensrechts (IPRax)*2010, 27 (33 fn 81).

21 Thomas Pfeiffer, *Europäische Zeitschrift für Wirtschaftsrecht (EuZW)* 2008, 622 (624) ("Merkposten").

22 Peter Mankowski, *Internationales Handelsrecht (IHR)* 2008, 133 (135).

23 BGH 26.10.1989 – VII ZR 153/88 – NJW-RR 1990, 183–184 (exclusive jurisdiction clause in favour of German courts, both parties had their seat in Germany, building contract to be performed in Switzerland, payment in Swiss currency); BGH, 13.9.2004 – II ZR 276/02 – NJW 2004, 3706 (3708) (exclusive jurisdiction clause in favour of German courts, contract was written in German language and references to legal terms of German corporation law) (both judgments interpret the German implementation rule of the Rome Convention).

Bibliography

Dorothee Einsele, Auswirkungen der Rom I-Verordnung auf Finanzdienstleistungen, *Wertpapier-Mitteilungen (WM)* 2009, 289.

Erman, Kommentar zum Bürgerlichen Gesetzbuch, Harm Peter Westermann, Barbara Grunewald, and Georg Maier-Reimer (eds), Volume 1 (14th Edition, Otto Schmidt, Cologne 2014).

Franco Ferrari, Eva-Maria Kieninger, Peter Mankowski et al. (eds), *Internationales Vertragsrecht* (2nd Edition, C.H. Beck, Munich 2012).

Francisco Garcimartín Alférez, The Rome I Regulation: Much ado about nothing?, *European Law Forum (EuLF)* 2008, I-61.

beck-online Großkommentar zum Zivilrecht, Beate Gsell, Wolfgang Krüger, Stephan Lorenz and Jörg Mayer (eds) (C.H. Beck, Munich 2016).

juris PraxisKommentar BGB, Martin Herberger, Michael Martinek, Helmut Rüßmann and Stephan Weth (eds), Volume 6 (7th Edition, juris, Saarbrücken 2014).

Kathrin Kroll-Ludwigs, *Die Rolle der Parteiautonomie im europäischen Kollisionsrecht* (Mohr Siebeck, Tübingen 2013).

Ole Lando and Peter Arnt Nielsen, The Rome I Regulation, *Common Market Law Review (CML Rev.)* 45 (2008), 1687.

Stefan Leible and Matthias Lehmann, Die Verordnung über das auf vertragliche Schuldverhältnisse anzuwendende Recht („Rom I"), *Recht der Internationalen Wirtschaft (RIW)* 2008, 528.

Ulrich Magnus, Die Rom I-Verordnung, *Praxis des Internationalen Privat- und Verfahrensrechts (IPRax)* 2010, 27.

Peter Mankowski, "Stillschweigende Rechtswahl und wählbares Recht" in Stefan Leible (ed), *Das Grünbuch zum Internationalen Vertragsrecht. Beiträge zur Fortentwicklung des Europäischen Kollisionsrechts der vertraglichen Schuldverhältnisse* (Sellier, Munich 2004), 63.

Peter Mankowski, Die Rom I-Verordnung – Änderungen im europäischen IPR für Schuldverträge, *Internationales Handelsrecht (IHR)* 2008, 133.

Münchner Kommentar zum Bürgerlichen Gesetzbuch, Franz Jürgen Säcker, Roland Rixecker, Hartmut Oetker and Bettina Limperg (eds), Volume 10 (6th Edition, C.H. Beck, Munich 2015).

Thomas Pfeiffer, Neues Internationales Vertragsrecht. Zur Rom I-Verordnung, *Europäische Zeitschrift für Wirtschaftsrecht (EuZW)* 2008, 622.

Richard Plender and Michael Wilderspin, *The European Private International Law of Obligations* (4th Edition, Sweet & Maxwell, London 2015).

Thomas Rauscher (ed), *Europäisches Zivilprozess- und Kollisionsrecht (EuZPR/EuIPR)*, Volume 3 (4th Edition, Otto Schmidt, Cologne 2015).

Giesela Rühl, *Statut und Effizienz. Ökonomische Grundlagen des Internationalen Privatrechts* (Mohr Siebeck, Tübingen 2011).

Haimo Schack, Rechtswahl im Prozess?, *Neue Juristische Wochenschrift (NJW)* 1984, 2736.

Thomas Tiede, "Die Rechtswahl in den Römischen Verordnungen" in Bea Verschraegen (ed), *Rechtswahl – Grenzen und Chancen* (Sramek, Vienna 2010), 51.

Sandra Wandt, *Rechtswahlregelungen im Europäischen Kollisionsrecht* (PL Acad. Research, Frankfurt am Main 2014).

Case Law

BGH 22.11.1955 – I ZR 218/53 – NJW 1956, 377.

BGH 7.3.1962 – VIII ZR 9/61 – NJW 1962, 1005.

BGH 30.9.1987 – IV a ZR 22/86 – NJW-RR 1988, 159.

BGH 26.10.1989 – VII ZR 153/88 – NJW-RR 1990, 183.

BGH 12.12.1990 – VIII ZR 332/89 – NJW 1991, 1292.

BGH 19.1.2000 – VIII ZR 275/98 – NJW-RR 2000, 1002.

BGH 26.7.2004 – VIII ZR 273/03 – NJW-RR 2005, 206.

BGH 13.9.2004 – II ZR 276/02 – NJW 2004, 3706.

OLG Düsseldorf 29.12.2009 – 6 U 9/09 – NJW-RR 2009, 1380.

OLG Stuttgart 24.4.2013 – 3 U 184/12 – BeckRS 2014, 19218.

AG Frankfurt 25.10.2013 – 30 C 1377/13 (47) – BeckRS 2014, 12196.

Contractual capacity in German and South African private international law: a comparative study

*Eesa Allie Fredericks**

I. Introduction

This contribution contains a comparative study of the contractual capacity of natural persons in German and South African private international law. The investigation therefore deals with the law applicable to the competence of a natural person to create rights and duties by concluding a contract with another (natural or juristic) person or persons. The focus is on positive law and not, in detail, on the suggestions for legal development found in doctrine.

Sometimes it is implied that contractual capacity is no longer such an important issue in private international law due to, for instance, the emancipation of married women. However, it is suggested that this development indeed increases the relevance of the topic, as today a husband's contractual capacity could be dependent on the consent of his spouse, while a century

* Senior lecturer in the Department of Mercantile Law, Deputy Director of the Research Centre for Private International Law in Emerging Countries and HOD: Practical Business Law at the University of Johannesburg.

ago this was invariably the position only in respect of the wife's contractual capacity.[1] In any event, there may be many non-Western legal systems where a married women's contractual capacity remains limited. In respect of the age of majority, it is true that many legal systems now accept 18 years as the legal age. Nevertheless, a substantial minority of legal systems adhere to ages above or below.[2] Contractual capacity may also be affected by mental illness, curatorship (for instance, in the case of prodigality and insolvency) or emancipation.[3] It is therefore clear that contractual capacity continues to play an important role in private international law.

---

1 Sonnekus "Handelingsbevoegdheid van getroudes en die norme van die internasionale privaatreg" 2002 *Tydskrif vir Regswetenskap (TRW)* 145. In South African law, the husband, in marriages concluded in community of property before 1 November 1984, was the sole administrator of the estate and was entitled to manage and alienate all the assets. In terms of the Matrimonial Property Act 88 of 1984, spouses married in community of property since 1 November 1984, have equal capacity to manage the joint estate and equal powers regarding the estate (s 14). Sec 15 of the act requires that consent of the other spouse must in specified circumstances be obtained before a juristic act which binds the estate can be performed. Three forms of consent are distinguished: consent without any formalities; written consent; and written consent attested by two witnesses. The patrimonial consequences of civil marriages entered into by people of African origin were brought into line with those of other population groups in terms of the Marriage and Matrimonial Property Law Amendment Act 3 of 1988. See Skelton, Carnelley, Human et al (eds) *Family Law in South Africa* (2010) 14 in this regard. *Cf* sec 6 of the Recognition of Customary Marriages Act 120 of 1998 and cl 3 of the Muslim Marriages Bill of 2010. See, on the constitutionality of the Muslim Marriages Bill, Neels "Constitutional aspects of the Muslim Marriages Bill" 2012 *Tydskrif vir die Suid-Afrikaanse Reg (TSAR)* 486 and, on the recognition of foreign Muslim marriages in South Africa, Neels "The positive role of public policy in private international law and the recognition of foreign Muslim marriages" 2012 *South African Journal of Human Rights (SAJHR)* 219.

2 Hausmann in *J von Staudingers Kommentar zum Bürgerlichen Gesetzbuch mit Einführungsgesetz und Nebengesetzen. Internationales Recht der natürlichen Personen und der Rechtsgeschäfte* (2013) art 7 EGBGB Anhang para 1–5; Hausmann in Reithmann and Martiny (eds) *Internationales Vertragsrecht. Das internationale Privatrecht der Schuldverträge* (2010) 1878–1880; and Schwenzer, Hachem and Kee *Global Sales and Contract Law* (2012) 204–205 and 211. However, the age of majority in South Africa is now 18 years (Children's Act 38 of 2005) and no longer 21 (as in Hausmann (*op cit*) art 7 EGBGB Anhang para 4).

3 Hutchison, Pretorius and Du Plessis (eds) *The Law of Contract in South Africa* (2009) 149; and Nagel *Commercial Law* (2011) 73.

II. German private international law

The provisions relevant to contractual capacity are found in art 7 and art 12 of the *Einführungsgesetz zum Bürgerlichen Gesetzbuch*.[4] These rules also apply to limited capacity.[5] Relevant issues in this context are minority and mental illness.[6] However, in German law, whether or not the consent of a spouse is necessary for the valid conclusion of a contract depends on the applicable matrimonial property regime. This question consequently forms part of matrimonial property law and is regulated by the legal system that governs the proprietary consequences of marriage.[7]

In terms of the first sentence of art 7(1), contractual capacity is in general governed by the *lex patriae* (the law of the country of nationality): "Die Rechtsfähigkeit und die Geschäftsfähigkeit einer Person unterliegen dem Recht des Staates, dem die Person angehört."[8] The second sentence provides that the same rule applies where capacity is expanded through the

4 Introductory Act to the Civil Code (*Einführungsgesetz zum Bürgerlichen Gesetzbuche, EGBGB*). For the German text, see http://bundesrecht.juris.de/bgbeg/BJNR006049896.html (15-09-2017) For a translation in English, see www.gesetze-im-internet.de/englisch_bgbeg/index.html (15-09-2017). The German term for contractual capacity in art 7 is *Geschäftsfähigkeit*. Art 12, in addition, utilises the concept of *Handlungsfähigkeit*. Hausmann in Staudinger (n 2) art 12 EGBGB para 27 suggest that the latter notion is otherwise unknown and of no particular use in German law and should therefore be ignored.

5 Spellenberg in Säcker and Rixecker (eds) *Münchener Kommentar zum Bürgerlichen Gesetzbuch X Internationales Privatrecht* (2010) art 13 Rom I-VO paras 30, 33 and art 12 EGBGB para 22; Birk in Säcker and Rixecker (eds) *Münchener Kommentar zum Bürgerlichen Gesetzbuch X Internationales Privatrecht* (2010) art 7 EGBGB para 29 and Hausmann in Staudinger (n 2) art 7 EGBGB para 45 and art 12 para 26.

6 See, for example, Kropholler *Internationales Privatrecht* (2006) 317–321.

7 See Spellenberg (n 5) art 13 Rom I-VO para 32; Reinhartz *Derdenbescherming in het Huwelijksvermogensrecht* (1997) 397 and 529; and Hausmann in Staudinger (n 2) art 7 EGBGB paras 40, 75–77, art 12 EGBGB paras 5, 44–46. See arts 14–15 of the *EGBGB* for the applicable legal system.

8 Translated at www.gesetze-im-internet.de/englisch_bgbeg/index.html (15-09-2017) as "The legal capacity and capacity to contract of a person are governed by the law of the country of which the person is a national." *Cf* art 5(1). The title of art 7 is "Rechtsfähigkeit und Geschäftsfähigkeit" ("Legal capacity and capacity to contract").

conclusion of marriage: "Dies gilt auch, soweit die Geschäftsfähigkeit durch Eheschließung erweitert wird."[9]

A leading commentary provides a number of examples of the application of art 7(1) in respect of minority from which the following statements may be deduced: A minor of 17 years old who is a citizen of country A (which maintains the majority age of 21) and who acquires the nationality of country B (where the majority age is 18) will become a major at age 18. A minor of 19 years old who is a citizen of country A (majority age of 21) and who acquires the nationality of country B (majority age 18) will become a major immediately at the moment of naturalisation. A minor of 17 years old who is a citizen of country A (majority age 18) and who acquires the nationality of country B (majority age 21) will become a major only at age 21.[10]

Article 7(2) states that, once capacity is acquired, it shall not lapse as a result of a subsequent acquisition or loss of German citizenship: "Eine einmal erlangte Rechtsfähigkeit oder Geschäftsfähigkeit wird durch Erwerb oder Verlust der Rechtsstellung als Deutscher nicht beeinträchtigt."[11] The Latin *adagium* referred to in this regard is *semel maior, semper maior*.[12] Therefore a German citizen aged 19 who acquires the nationality of a country where 21 is the age of majority, will remain a major for the purposes of German private international law.[13]

Article 7(2) is an incomplete conflicts rule as it only refers to German citizenship. The German commentators are of the opinion that the rule should also be applied in the context of other nationalities. Once a contractant has acquired capacity, it should not lapse as a result of a subsequent

9 Translated at www.gesetze-im-internet.de/englisch_bgbeg/index.html (15-09-2017) as "This is also applicable where the capacity to contract is extended by marriage." See, for instance, Birk (n 5) art 7 EGBGB paras 33 et seq, 76 et seq.

10 Hausmann in Staudinger (n 2) art 7 EGBGB para 107 et seq. On dual citizenship in this context, see Hausmann in Staudinger (n 2) art 7 EGBGB para 108.

11 Translated at www.gesetze-im-internet.de/englisch_bgbeg/index.html (15-09-2017) as "The once acquired legal capacity or capacity to contract shall not be lost or restricted by the acquisition or loss of legal status as a German national."

12 Birk (n 5) art 7 EGBGB para 72; Hausmann in Reithmann and Martiny (eds) (n 2) 1877; and Hausmann in Staudinger (n 2) art 7 EGBGB paras 110 et seqq.

13 Hausmann in Staudinger (n 2) art 7 EGBGB para 111. The majority age in Germany is 18 years (see, for example, Hausmann in Staudinger (n 2) art 7 EGBGB Anhang no 10).

acquisition or loss of any nationality.[14] Therefore, a South African citizen of 19 years old, who acquires the nationality of a country where 21 is the age of majority, should remain a major for the purposes of German private international law.[15]

The application of the *lex patriae* is limited by the provision in the first sentence of art 12 of the *EGBGB*:

> "Wird ein Vertrag zwischen Personen geschlossen, die sich in demselben Staat befinden, so kann sich eine natürliche Person, die nach den Sachvorschriften des Rechts dieses Staates rechts-, geschäfts- und handlungsfähig wäre, nur dann auf ihre aus den Sachvorschriften des Rechts eines anderen Staates abgeleitete Rechts-, Geschäfts- und Handlungsunfähigkeit berufen, wenn der andere Vertragsteil bei Vertragsabschluß diese Rechts-, Geschäfts- und Handlungsunfähigkeit kannte oder kennen musste."[16]

The provision in art 12 is substantially based on art 11 of the Rome Convention[17] (which is again inspired by the French decision in *Lizardi v Chaize*).[18] Article 12 must therefore be interpreted in the light of European law. The provision applies[19] when the contract is governed by neither art 11 of the Rome Convention nor art 13 of the Rome I Regulation.[20]

Article 12 ("the *Lizardi* rule") in effect provides that when a contractant, lacking capacity in terms of his or her *lex patriae*, concludes a contract in a country where he or she would have possessed capacity, and the counterpart

---

14 Kegel and Schurig *Internationales Privatrecht* (2000) 493; Kropholler (n 6) 318; Hausmann in Reithmann and Martiny (eds) (n 2) 1877; and Hausmann in Staudinger (n 2) art 7 EGBGB paras 105, 113.

15 The majority age in South Africa is 18 years: see n 2 above.

16 Translated at www.gesetze-im-internet.de/englisch_bgbeg/index.html (15-09-2017) as "In a contract concluded between persons who are in the same country, a natural person who would have capacity under the substantive provisions of the law of that country may invoke his incapacity resulting from the substantive provisions of another law only if the other party to the contract was aware or should have been aware of this incapacity at the time of the conclusion of the contract."

17 Convention 80/934/EEC on the Law Applicable to Contractual Obligations opened for signature in Rome on 19 June 1980 (Rome Convention).

18 Cass req 16 janv 1861 Sirey 1861 (1) 305 DP 1861 (1) 193.

19 Spellenberg (n 5) art 13 Rom I-VO para 1, art 12 EGBGB para 3; and Hausmann in Staudinger (n 2) Vorbemerkung para 2, art 7 EGBGB para 27 and art 12 paras 4–8.

20 Regulation (EC) No 593/2008 of the European Parliament and of the Council of 17 June 2008 on the Law Applicable to Contractual Obligations (Rome I). See, in general, on art 13 of the Rome I Regulation: Collins (gen ed) *Dicey, Morris and Collins on the Conflict of Laws II* (2012) 1865.

is also physically present in the same country at the conclusion of the contract, the *lex loci contractus* (the law of the country where the contract was concluded) shall apply to determine the capacity of the first-mentioned contractant. This exception to the application of the *lex patriae* by virtue of art 7 shall not apply if the counterpart was aware of the incapacity in terms of the *lex patriae* at the moment of concluding the contract, or was unaware thereof as a result of negligence. Although art 12 neither directly refers to the law of the country where the contract was concluded nor the law of the presence of the parties, the German commentators are unanimous that application of the *lex loci contractus* is implied.[21]

Application of the *lex patriae* is limited by art 12 as the indiscriminate use of this legal system would be very onerous for the local legal traffic: creditors would have to inform themselves of the content of the law of the nationality of every possible contractant. The protection of normal legal interaction, specifically daily commercial activities, and the aim of legal certainty both indicate the need for an exception to the application of the *lex patriae*.[22] The application of the *lex loci contractus* is preferred on the following basis: the *locus contractus* is *ab initio* known; the application of the *lex loci contractus* is foreseeable; the *lex loci contractus* is geographically the best system to govern; both contractants intentionally participated in legal interaction in the *locus contractus*; and application of the *lex loci contractus* protects trust in the law of the country of contracting.[23] The intention of art 12 is clearly the protection of the *bona fide* counterpart[24] who is also not negligent. This is already clear from the title of the provision: "Schutz des anderen Vertragsteils".[25]

21 Spellenberg (n 5) art 12 EGBGB paras 22, 24; Hausmann in Reithmann and Martiny (eds) (n 2) 1913; and Hausmann in Staudinger (n 2) art 12 EGBGB paras 10–12, 59–61 and 70 et seq. See, however, sec 22(2) and sec 23(c) of the South African Electronic Communications and Transactions Act 25 of 2002: the law of presence will not necessarily coincide with the law of conclusion of the contract.

22 Hausmann in Staudinger (n 2) art 7 EGBGB para 27, art 12 EGBGB paras 1, 6, 11 et seq, 26 et seq.

23 Hausmann in Staudinger (n 2) art 12 EGBGB para 12.

24 Spellenberg (n 5) art 12 EGBGB para 17; Hausmann in Reithmann and Martiny (eds) (n 2) 1913; and Hausmann in Staudinger (n 2) art 12 EGBGB paras 6 and 73 et seqq.

25 Translated at www.gesetze-im-internet.de/englisch_bgbeg/index.html (13-04-2016) as "Protection of the other party".

For art 12 to be applicable, the incapable person must be a natural person. The capable party may either be a natural or a juristic person.[26] However, the *Bundesgerichtshof*, in a decision in 1998, refers to the possibility of the analogous application of art 12 to incapable juristic persons.[27] The court did not find it necessary to decide this point as the requirements for art 12 were in any event not complied with.

Article 12 is an "allseitige Kollisionsregel" in that it applies irrespective in which country the contract was concluded.[28] The parties must be present in the same country at the conclusion of the contract. Their nationality, domicile and habitual residence are irrelevant.[29] Short-term presence, including presence on "verkehrstechnische Gründen" (for instance, meeting at an airport) and even coincidental presence will be sufficient.[30] The parties must be present in the same country, not necessarily in the same town or in each other's presence.[31] The relevant moment in time is the conclusion of the contract.[32]

Article 12 is an alternative reference rule in the sense that, in the circumstances as described, the party invoking incapacity will nevertheless be held to possess capacity if he or she has such in terms of either the *lex patriae* or the *lex loci contractus*.[33] The relevant party cannot at will invoke either the *lex patriae* or the *lex loci contractus* as the governing legal system.[34] Article 12 does not play a role when the incapable party has no capacity in terms of both the *lex patriae* and the *lex loci contractus* (the relevant party will then not be bound to the contract). Article 12 is also not applicable when the relevant party has capacity in terms of the *lex patriae*, whether or not

---

26 Hausmann in Staudinger (n 2) art 12 EGBGB paras 16 et seqq.

27 BGH 23.4.1998 – III ZR 194/96 – 1999 IPRax 104 = 1998 NJW 2452.

28 Kegel and Schurig (n 14) 493.

29 Kegel and Schurig (n 14) 480; and Hausmann in Staudinger (n 2) art 12 EGBGB paras 61, 79.

30 Hausmann in Staudinger (n 2) art 12 EGBGB para 60.

31 Hausmann in Staudinger (n 2) art 12 EGBGB para 59. Error in respect of the presence of the parties at the time of conclusion is irrelevant: Hausmann in Staudinger (n 2) art 12 EGBGB para 69. See Hausmann in Reithmann and Martiny (eds) (n 2) 1913–1914 and Hausmann in Staudinger (n 2) art 12 EGBGB para 62–66 on distance contracts and the position where the parties make use of agents.

32 Hausmann in Staudinger (n 2) art 7 EGBGB paras 57, 106, art 12 EGBGB para 67 et seq.

33 Hausmann in Staudinger (n 2) art 12 EGBGB paras 13, 85 .

34 Hausmann in Staudinger (n 2) art 12 EGBGB para 86.

capacity exists in terms of the *lex loci contractus* (the party invoking incapacity will be bound to the contract). However, art 12 will be relevant if the party invoking incapacity has no capacity in terms of the *lex patriae* but would have such in terms of the *lex loci contractus*, provided that the requirements of this paragraph are satisfied.[35] It follows that art 12 is irrelevant when the *lex patriae* and the *lex loci contractus* are the same law. This indeed happened in a case which came before the *Bundesgerichtshof* in 2004, resulting in two related decisions,[36] both dealing with the one factual scenario of a mentally incapable German director of a Swiss company. The court did not even refer to art 12 *EGBGB* as German law was both the *lex patriae* and the *lex loci contractus*.[37] The issue was held to be governed by the *lex patriae* in terms of the first sentence of art 7(1).

The *lex loci contractus* does not apply (and therefore only the *lex patriae* will govern) when the capable party was aware of the incapacity in terms of the *lex patriae* or should have been aware thereof. The onus to prove that the capable party had knowledge of the incapacity or was negligent in not being aware of the incapacity rests on the incapable party.[38] The *Oberlandesgericht* of Hamm decided in 1995 that the capable party would clearly not be able to invoke art 12 as the minor's date of birth was included in the contract.[39] In the circumstances, the capable party was deemed to have been aware of the incapacity in terms of the *lex patriae*.[40]

Some commentators are of the opinion that the content of negligence in this regard should be determined by German law[41] but others argue that art 12 should be interpreted along the lines of art 13 of the Rome I Regulation.[42]

---

35 *Cf* Hausmann in Staudinger (n 2) art 12 EGBGB paras 85 et seqq.

36 BGH 3.2.2004 – XI ZR 125/03 – NJW 2004 1315; BGH 30.3.2004 – XI ZR 145/03 – openJur 2012 56548, www.openjur.de/u/344496.html (15-09-2017).

37 *Cf* Spellenberg (n 5) art 13 Rom I-VO para 19 n 35. German law was also the law applicable to the contract.

38 Hausmann in Staudinger (n 2) art 12 EGBGB para 84.

39 OLG Hamm 23.11.1995 – 22 U 227/94 – IPRspr 1995 7 = NJW-RR 1996 1144. See Hausmann in Staudinger (n 2) art 12 EGBGB para 73.

40 However, it seems that the minor would have lacked capacity in terms of both relevant legal systems as Germany and Spain adhere to the majority age of 18. See Hausmann in Staudinger (n 2) art 7 EGBGB Anhang paras 10, 46.

41 Hausmann in Staudinger (n 2) art 12 EGBGB para 80. But see Hausmann in Staudinger (n 2) art 12 EGBGB para 5, arguing in favour of a European-oriented interpretation of art 12 of the EGBGB.

42 Hausmann in Reithmann and Martiny (eds) (n 2) 1913. *Cf* Spellenberg (n 5) art 12 Rom I-VO paras 11–16.

In any event, negligence will be readily found to be present in respect of important transactions and when valuable goods are involved (for instance, buying and selling immovable property versus goods for daily living) and also when a merchant, rather than a private person, concludes a contract.[43] The *Bundesgerichtshof* found in 1998 that even slight negligence[44] would be sufficient to exclude the protection of the capable party in art 12.[45] This case concerned a German company which neglected to obtain legal advice on whether a Yugoslavian company[46] would have capacity to conclude a transnational contract;[47] the German company could therefore not invoke art 12.[48]

The alternative application of the *lex loci contractus* does not apply to contracts concerning family and succession law, nor to these involving immovable property situated outside of Germany. This is provided for in the last sentence of art 12:

> "Dies gilt nicht für familienrechtliche und erbrechtliche Rechtsgeschäfte sowie für Verfügungen über ein in einem anderen Staat belegenes Grundstück."[49]

In summary it may be stated that in German private international law, the *lex patriae* and, in certain circumstances, the *lex loci contractus* are applied to contractual capacity. The law (putatively) applicable to the contract is not a relevant legal system. In particular, the law chosen by the parties to govern their contract does not play any role. For instance, a minor cannot choose another law that would have been applicable to provide him or her with

---

43 Hausmann in Reithmann and Martiny (eds) (n 2) 1880 and 1915; and Hausmann in Staudinger (n 2) art 12 EGBGB paras 10, 43 and 80 et seqq.

44 "leichte Fahrlässigkeit". Also see Hausmann in Reithmann and Martiny (eds) (n 2) 1914–1915.

45 BGH 23.4.1998 – III ZR 194/96 – 1999 IPRax 104 = 1998 NJW 2452.

46 See the text at n 27 on the possible analogous interpretation of art 12 to incapable juristic persons.

47 The court takes a rather optimistic view of public bodies being able and willing to provide expeditious expert opinions on intricate legal questions: the capable party should have telephonically contacted the German ministry of trade, the Yugoslavian mission in Germany, the German mission in Yugoslavia or the chamber of commerce in Croatia.

48 It is unclear whether mere knowledge of the foreign nationality of the counterpart is sufficient to require the capable party to be alert: see Hausmann in Staudinger (n 2) art 12 EGBGB para 82.

49 translated at www.gesetze-im-internet.de/englisch_bgbeg/index.html (15-09-2017) as "This does not apply to legal transactions under family law and the law of succession neither to dispositions relating to immovable property situated in another country."

capacity.[50] This is also clear from the decision of the *Oberlandesgericht* of Hamm in 1995,[51] where a German minor had agreed to Spanish law governing the contract. The choice of law was held to be ineffective and German law applied as the *lex patriae*.[52]

The doctrine of public policy may be utilised to exclude an otherwise applicable legal system; this also applies in the context of contractual capacity. If, for instance, the *lex patriae* or the *lex loci contractus* were to consider a 10 year old as an adult, the law of nationality would be excluded. Of course, the fact that there is a different age of majority in the applicable legal system compared to that in the *lex fori* is no reason to exclude the foreign law. It is probably also not against public policy to have a (slightly) different age of majority for boys and girls.[53] However, having different rules in respect of capacity for clearly adult women compared to these for men, or different rules for people of minority religions, may indeed infringe the *ordre public*.[54]

III. South African private international law

The Roman-Dutch authors suggested application of the *lex domicilii* (the law of the country of domicile of the alleged incapable party) or the *lex loci contractus* to the contractual capacity of natural persons with some flexibility, taking into account the need for an equitable outcome in the particular case.[55] Some authors argued in favour of the application of the *lex situs* (the law of the country where the property is situated) in respect of immovable property.[56]

The application of the *lex domicilii*, the *lex loci contractus* and the *lex situs* were all received into South African law. There is no binding judicial

---

50 Hausmann in Staudinger (n 2) art 7 EGBGB para 60.

51 OLG Hamm 23.11.1995 – 22 U 227/94 – IPRspr 1995 7 = NJW-RR 1996 1144.

52 German law was also the *lex loci contractus*. See n 40.

53 In some Latin American countries the majority age for girls is 12 and for boys 14. See Hausmann in Staudinger (n 2) art 7 EGBGB para 44.

54 See Birk (n 5) art 7 EGBGB para 26; and Hausmann in Staudinger (n 2) art 7 EGBGB para 28 and art 12 EGBGB para 96.

55 See Forsyth *Private International Law. The Modern Roman-Dutch Law including the Jurisdiction of the High Courts* (2012) 338.

56 See Forsyth (n 55) 338 and Fredericks "The common-law authors on contractual capacity in private international law" 2015 *Obiter* 762 for an overview of the opinions of the Roman-Dutch authors in this regard.

authority in South Africa in respect of the law applicable to contractual capacity, as no decisions from the Supreme Court of Appeal (or the Constitutional Court) exist.

The court in *Hulscher v Voorschotkas voor Zuid Afrika*[57] refers to the *lex domicilii* and the *lex loci contractus* as possible systems to govern contractual capacity, without choosing between them – they coincided *in casu*.[58] *Kent v Salmon*[59] is clear authority in favour of the *lex loci contractus*[60] and *Powell v Powell*[61] should be read as support for the *lex domicilii*.[62] The court in *Guggenheim v Rosenbaum (2)*[63] refers to authority in favour of the *lex loci contractus* and the *lex domicilii*[64] but it is clear that the *lex domicilii* would have been favoured if the two did not coincide *in casu*.[65] *Ferraz v d'Inhaca*[66] is the only case dealing with immovable property; here it was decided that the *lex situs* should apply.[67]

There is emerging support in South African private international law for the application of the proper law of the contract in the context of contractual capacity. The court in *Tesoriero v Bhyjo Investments Share Block (Pty) Ltd*[68] is critical about the application of the *lex loci contractus* and clearly favours the proper law of the contract to govern capacity.[69] *In casu* no choice had to be made as these legal systems were the same on the facts.[70] Various authors support the application of the proper law of the contract as an alternatively applicable legal system.[71] For instance, Van Rooyen argues

---

57 1908 TS 542.

58 545–546.

59 1910 TPD 637.

60 640.

61 1953 4 SA 380 (W).

62 383H–384A. See Fredericks "Contractual capacity in private international law: interpreting the *Powell* case" 69 (2006) *Tydskrif vir Hedendaagse Romeins-Hollandse Reg (THRHR)* 279. Some support for the application of the objective putative proper law to contractual capacity may also be found in the decision (see 383C–D).

63 1961 4 SA 21 (W).

64 33D–E.

65 Fredericks (n 62) 281.

66 1904 TH 137.

67 142–143.

68 2000 1 SA 167 (W).

69 172A–B and 172B–C.

70 172G–H.

71 Kahn "Conflict of laws" 2000 *Annual Survey of South African Law* 871 876; Kahn "International contracts – V. The general rule in South Africa, and the issue of

in favour of the alternative application of the *lex domicilii* and the objective proper law – but the proper law should not be applied where the contract assertor knew, or reasonably should have known, of his counterpart's incapacity under the *lex domicilii.*[72] The *lex situs* will usually be applied in respect of immovable property.[73]

Van Rooyen correctly refers to the objective proper law of the contract, as the parties should not be allowed to choose a legal system to confer capacity on them – this is generally accepted by the South African authors.[74] When referred to in the context of contractual capacity, the proper law of the contract must invariably refer to the putative proper law, as in the absence of contractual capacity no contract comes into existence. The putative proper law is the law that would have been the proper law of the contract if a contract were indeed concluded.[75] The author will therefore below refer to the objective putative proper law in this regard.

The decisions in *Ferraz,*[76] *Hulscher,*[77] *Kent*[78] and *Tesoriero*[79] all dealt with the contractual capacity of married women who concluded contracts without the consent of their husbands. *Powell*[80] concerned the capacity of spouses to conclude a contract of donation between them and *Guggenheim*[81] involved the capacity to conclude a contract of engagement.

---

capacity" 1991 *Businessman's Law* 126 128; Sonnekus (n 1) 147–148; and Van Rooyen *Die Kontrak in die Suid-Afrikaanse Internasionale Privaatreg* (1972) 126. Schoeman, Roodt and Wethmar-Lemmer *Private International Law in South Africa* (2014) para 115 merely refer to the approach.

72 Van Rooyen (n 71) 126. *Cf Kent v Salmon* (n 59) 639–640, Forsyth (n 55) 340 n 145 and Sonnekus (n 1) 146 in respect of the *lex loci contractus.*

73 Van Rooyen (n 71) 126. Also see Forsyth (n 55) 338; Kahn "Jurisdiction and conflict of laws" in Hahlo *The South African Law of Husband and Wife* (1975) 577 625; and Schoeman, Roodt and Wethmar-Lemmer (n 71) para 114.

74 See, for example, Forsyth (n 55) 340; Schoeman, Roodt and Wethmar-Lemmer (n 71) para 107; and Van Rooyen (n 71) 126.

75 See Edwards and Kahn "Conflict of laws" in Joubert, Faris and Harms (eds) II.2 *The Law of South Africa* (2003) para 333; *cf* Forsyth (n 55) 337, 338, 340 and 343; Kahn (n 71 (1991)) 128; Schoeman, Roodt and Wethmar-Lemmer (n 71) paras 102 and 108; and Van Rooyen (n 71) 126.

76 *Ferraz v d'Inhaca* (n 66).

77 *Hulscher v Voorschotkas voor Zuid Afrika* (n 57).

78 *Kent v Salmon* (n 59).

79 *Tesoriero v Bhyjo Investments Share Block (Pty) Ltd* (n 68).

80 *Powell v Powell* (n 61).

81 *Guggenheim v Rosenbaum (2)* (n 63).

South African private international law recognises the fact that the application of foreign law may be excluded on the basis of public policy.[82] This would also apply to foreign rules in respect of contractual capacity.

IV. A short comparison

The *lex patriae* is the primary legal system in German private international law in respect of the contractual capacity of natural persons.[83] In South African private international law, the primary legal systems could be the *lex domicilii*[84] or the *lex loci contractus*[85] and, for immovables, the *lex situs*.[86] The *Tesoriero* case supports the application of the (objective putative) proper law of the contract to contractual capacity;[87] so do various authors, within the context of an alternative reference rule.[88]

The *lex loci contractus* applies in German private international law as an alternatively applicable legal system when the parties were present in the same country at the conclusion of the contract. The *lex loci contractus* does not apply in addition to the *lex patriae* if the capable contractant was aware of the incapacity in terms of the *lex patriae* at the moment of concluding the contract, or was unaware thereof as a result of negligence ("the *Lizardi* rule").[89] In contrast, as indicated above,[90] in positive South African private international law, the *lex loci contractus* could be the primary applicable legal system.[91] The author Van Rooyen supports the application of the *Lizardi* rule in a proposed alternative reference rule consisting of the *lex domicilii* and the objective (putative) proper law of the contract: the proper law

82 See Forsyth (n 55) 12 and 120–127; Schoeman, Roodt and Wethmar-Lemmer (n 71) paras 20, 53, 54, 70, 71, 72, 116 and 122; and Schulze "Conflict of laws" in Heaton (ed) *The Law of Divorce and Dissolution of Life Partnerships* (2014) 631 646.

83 art 7(1) EGBGB.

84 See the *Powell* case (n 61). Also see the *Guggenheim* case (n 63).

85 See the *Kent* case (n 59).

86 See the *Ferraz* case (n 66).

87 *Tesoriero v Bhyjo Investments Share Block (Pty) Ltd* (n 68).

88 See n 71.

89 art 12 EGBGB.

90 See the text at n 57–60 and n 63–64.

91 *Hulscher v Voorschotkas voor Zuid Afrika* (n 57) 545–546; *Kent v Salmon* (n 59) 640; and *Guggenheim v Rosenbaum (2)* (n 63) 33D–E.

should not apply (in other words: only the law of domicile must be employed) where the contract assertor knew, or reasonably should have known, of his counterpart's incapacity under the *lex domicilii*.[92]

In German private international law, whether or not the consent of a spouse is necessary for the valid conclusion of a contract, depends on the law applicable to the proprietary consequences of marriage.[93] In South Africa, there is strong authority in case law that this issue (whether or not consent is required) is governed by the law applicable to the capacity of the contracting spouse.[94]

The *semel maior, semper maior* rule from German private international law[95] could be adapted for the purposes of South African private international law, provided it is reformulated in a bilateral form and with reference to the connecting factor of domicile rather than nationality, for instance: "The contractual capacity of a natural person that has previously been acquired shall not be affected by a subsequent change in the individual's domicile."

Of course, both conflicts systems may exclude the application of foreign law where this would be contrary to public policy.[96]

---

92 Van Rooyen (n 71) 126.

93 Spellenberg (n 5) art 13 Rom I-VO, para 32; Reinhartz (n 7) 397 and 529; and Hausmann in Staudinger (n 2) art 7 EGBGB paras 40, 75–77 and art 12 EGBGB paras 5, 44–46. See arts 14–15 of the EGBGB for the applicable legal system.

94 *Ferraz v d'Inhaca* (n 66); *Hulscher v Voorschotkas voor Zuid Afrika* (n 57); *Kent v Salmon* (n 59); and *Tesoriero v Bhyjo Investments Share Block (Pty) Ltd* (n 68).

95 Birk (n 5) art 7 EGBGB para 72; Hausmann in Reithmann and Martiny (eds) (n 2) 1877; and Hausmann in Staudinger (n 2) art 7 EGBGB para 110 et seqq.

96 See the text at n 50–54 and n 82.

Bibliography

Collins L (gen ed) *Dicey, Morris and Collins on the Conflict of Laws II* (15th Edition, Sweet & Maxwell, London 2012).

Edwards AB and Kahn E "Conflict of laws" in Joubert WA, Harms LT and Faris JA (eds) *The Law of South Africa II.2* (2nd Edition, LexisNexis, Durban 2003).

Forsyth CF *Private International Law. The Modern Roman-Dutch Law including the Jurisdiction of the High Courts* (5th Edition, Juta, Cape Town 2012).

Fredericks EA "Contractual capacity in private international law: interpreting the *Powell* case" 69 (2006) *Tydskrif vir Hedendaagse Romeins-Hollandse Reg* (*THRHR*) 279.

Fredericks EA "The common-law authors on contractual capacity in private international law" 2015 *Obiter* 762.

Hutchison D, Pretorius CJ and Du Plessis JE (eds) *The Law of Contract in South Africa* (2nd Edition, Oxford University Press Southern Africa, Cape Town 2009).

Kahn E "Conflict of laws" 6 (2000) *Annual Survey of South African Law* 871.

Kahn E "International contracts – V. The general rule in South Africa, and the issue of capacity" 1991 *Businessman's Law* 126.

Kahn E "Jurisdiction and conflict of laws" in Hahlo HR (ed) *The South African Law of Husband and Wife* (4th Edition, Juta, Cape Town 1975).

Kegel G and Schurig K *Internationales Privatrecht* (8th Edition, C.H.Beck, Munich 2000).

Kropholler J *Internationales Privatrecht* (6th Edition, Mohr Siebeck, Tübingen 2006).

Münchener Kommentar zum Bürgerlichen Gesetzbuch, Säcker FJ, Rixecker R (eds), Volume X, Internationales Privatrecht (5th Edition, C.H.Beck, Munich 2010).

Nagel CJ (ed) *Commercial Law* (4th Edition, LexisNexis, Durban 2011).

Neels JL "Constitutional aspects of the Muslim Marriages Bill" 2012 *Tydskrif vir die Suid-Afrikaanse Reg (TSAR)* 486.

Neels JL "The positive role of public policy in private international law and the recognition of foreign Muslim marriages" 28 (2012) *South African Journal on Human Rights (SAJHR)* 219.

Reinhartz B *Derdenbescherming in het Huwelijksvermogensrecht* (Kluwer, Deventer 1997).

Reithmann C and Martiny D (eds) *Internationales Vertragsrecht. Das internationale Privatrecht der Schuldverträge* (7th Edition, Otto Schmidt, Cologne 2010).

Schoeman E, Roodt C and Wethmar-Lemmer MM *Private International Law in South Africa* (Kluwer Law International, Alphen aan den Rijn 2014).

Schulze C "Conflict of laws" in Heaton J (ed) *The Law of Divorce and Dissolution of Life Partnerships* (Juta, Cape Town 2014).

Schwenzer IH, Hachem P and Kee C *Global Sales and Contract Law* (Oxford University Press, New York 2012).

Skelton A, Carnelly M, Human S et al (eds) *Family Law in South Africa* (Oxford University Press Southern Africa, Cape Town 2010).

Sonnekus JC "Handelingsbevoegdheid van getroudes en die norme van die internasionale privaatreg" 2002 *Tydskrif vir Regswetenskap (TRW)* 145.

Van Rooyen JCW *Die Kontrak in die Suid-Afrikaanse Internasionale Privaatreg* (Juta, Cape Town 1972).

von Staudinger J *Kommentar zum Bürgerlichen Gesetzbuch mit Einführungsgesetz und Nebengesetzen. Internationales Recht der natürlichen Personen und der Rechtsgeschäfte* (Sellier, de Gruyter, Berlin 2013).

Case Law

France

Lizardi v Chaize Cass req 16 janv 1861 Sirey 1861 (1) 305 DP 1861 (1) 193

Germany

BGH 23.4.1998 – III ZR 194/96 – 1999 IPRax 104 = 1998 NJW 2452.

BGH 3.2.2004 – XI ZR 125/03 – 2004 NJW 1315.

BGH 30.3.2004 – XI ZR 145/03 – 2012 openJur 56548.

OLG Hamm 23.11.1995 – 22 U 227/94 – 1995 IPRspr 7 = 1996 NJW-RR 1144.

South Africa

Ferraz v d'Inhaca 1904 TH 137

Guggenheim v Rosenbaum (2) 1961 4 SA 21 (W)

Hulscher v Voorschotkas voor Zuid Afrika 1908 TS 542

Kent v Salmon 1910 TPD 637

Powell v Powell 1953 4 SA 380 (W)

Tesoriero v Bhyjo Investments Share Block (Pty) Ltd 2000 1 SA 167 (W)

The law applicable to the proprietary consequences of marriage in South Africa – the influence of German private international law

*Jan L. Neels**

South African private international law was primarily received from the Roman-Dutch conflict of laws, although English law also had a substantial influence on its development.[1] In Roman-Dutch law the proprietary consequences of marriage were, in the absence of a choice of law in an antenuptial contract, governed by the law of the country of matrimonial domicile (the *lex domicilii matrimonii*), which was interpreted to be the law of the country of the domicile of the husband at the time of the marriage. This rule applied to immovable and all other forms of property. The applicable legal system governed the proprietary consequences of the marriage once and for all; a change in domicile at a later stage did not affect the governing legal system.[2] The Roman-Dutch rules in this regard were confirmed to be part of South African law in *inter alia* the leading decisions of *Frankel's Estate v The*

* Professor of Private International Law and Director of the Research Centre for Private International Law in Emerging Countries at the University of Johannesburg.

1 Schoeman "The South African conflict rule for proprietary consequences of marriage: learning from the German experience" 2004 *Tydskrif vir die Suid-Afrikaanse Reg (TSAR)* 115 117–119; and Schoeman, Roodt and Wethmar-Lemmer *Private International Law in South Africa* (2014) 13–14. Also see Forsyth "The provenance and future of private international law in Southern Africa" 2002 *Tydskrif vir die Suid-Afrikaanse Reg (TSAR)* 60.

2 See the references in Forsyth *Private International Law. The Modern Roman-Dutch Law including the Jurisdiction of the High Courts* (2012) 295–299; Schoeman, Roodt and Wethmar-Lemmer (n 1) 83–86; and Schulze "Conflict of laws" in Heaton (ed) *The Law of Divorce and Dissolution of Life Partnerships in South Africa* (2014) 631 647–650 and 658–661.

Master[3] and *Sperling v Sperling*.[4] However, under the new constitutional dispensation, the rule became untenable due to two reasons.

First, the rule is in conflict with the principle of gender equality, as protected in section 9(3) of the Constitution of the Republic of South Africa, 1996.[5] Of course, it depends on the content of the relevant legal systems whether the application of the law of the country of the domicile of the husband or the law of the country of the domicile of the wife at marriage would be beneficial to the latter,[6] but the rule as such, on a formal or abstract level,[7] constitutes discrimination on the basis of gender and therefore has to change. The South African courts have indeed expressed doubt about the constitutionality of the Roman-Dutch rule. In *Sadiku v Sadiku*,[8] Van Rooyen AJ questioned "whether a categorical application of the *lex domicilii* of the husband is still acceptable within a gender equal society as ours".[9] In *AS v CS*,[10] Gamble J was of the opinion that the current position "is likely to fall foul of the equality provisions entrenched in sec 9 of the

---

3 1950 1 SA 220 (A). This case also determined that the intention of the parties at the time of marriage to obtain another domicile, is not relevant: see 239–240. Also see n 58.

4 1975 3 SA 707 (A). The law of East Germany was the *lex domicilii matrimonii.*

5 "The state may not unfairly discriminate directly or indirectly against anyone on one or more grounds, including … gender, [and] sex…."

6 Forsyth (n 2) 295–296 n 115 and 300; Neels and Fredericks "The proper law of the proprietary consequences of marriage: Mauritian law in the South African Supreme Court of Appeal" 2015 *Tydskrif vir die Suid-Afrikaanse Reg (TSAR)* 918 920; Neels and Wethmar-Lemmer "Constitutional values and the proprietary consequences of marriage in private international law – introducing the *lex causae proprietatis matrimonii*" 2008 *Tydskrif vir die Suid-Afrikaanse Reg (TSAR)* 587 587–588; Schoeman, Roodt and Wethmar-Lemmer (n 1) 84. Also see Mankowski in *J von Staudingers Kommentar zum Bürgerlichen Gesetzbuch mit Einführungsgesetz und Nebengesetzen. Internationales Eherecht* (2011) Vorbem. zu Art 13–17b EGBGB para 9.

7 *Cf* Schulze (n 2) 658–659.

8 (30498/06) 2007 ZAGHPC 1 (26 Jan 2007) (available at www.saflii.org). See the discussion by Neels and Wethmar-Lemmer (n 6).

9 para 10.

10 2011 2 SA 360 (WCC).

Constitution".[11] In *Lenferna v Lenferna*,[12] Zondi AJA, on behalf of the Supreme Court of Appeal, doubted whether the current situation "can still be regarded as acceptable in our Constitutional democracy".[13]
Secondly, the received rule does not provide for same-sex marriages, which are now recognised in terms of the Civil Union Act.[14] This fact has been noted by both the Supreme Court of Appeal[15] and the Constitutional Court of South Africa.[16]

Which rule should replace the received one? The courts have not yet needed to provide a solution in this regard as, in the cases referred to, the issue had not pertinently come up for decision. For instance, in the *Sadiku*[17] and *Lenferna*[18] decisions the parties were domiciled in the same country (Nigeria and Mauritius, respectively) at the time of marriage.[19] However, it is clear from the relevant case law that, in the absence of a choice of law in an antenuptial contract, the law of the country of common domicile of the parties would govern.[20] Nevertheless, it is not clear which law applies if the parties did not have the same domicile at the time of the marriage.

---

11 para 55.

12 (120/13) 2013 ZASCA 204 (2 Dec 2013) (available at www.saflii.org; www.supremecourtofappeal.gov.za; 2013 JDR 2705 (SCA)).

13 para 10. In the meantime, at least two courts, in electronically reported decisions, merely applied the common-law rule without reference to constitutional issues, which were apparently not pleaded: see *Hillard v Hillard* (1464/2007) 2008 ZAFSHC 135 (4 Dec 2008) para 5.1; and *B v B* (10019/2014) 2014 ZAWCHC 178 (2 Dec 2014) para 6 (both available at www.saflii.org).

14 17 of 2006. See sec 9(3) of the Constitution of the Republic of South Africa, 1996: "The state may not unfairly discriminate directly or indirectly against anyone on one or more grounds, including … sexual orientation …" and the decisions referred to in n 15 and 16.

15 *Fourie v Minister of Home Affairs* 2005 1 All SA 273 (SCA) 315d–g.

16 *Minister of Home Affairs v Fourie (Doctors for Life International); Lesbian and Gay Equality Project v Minister of Home Affairs* 2006 1 SA 524 (CC) 536–537 n 24. Also see *AS v CS* (n 10) para 55.

17 (n 8) paras 9–10.

18 (n 12) paras 8–10.

19 The parties in *AS v CS* (n 10) entered into a (same-sex) civil partnership agreement in the United Kingdom while resident there (paras 2–3) but domiciled in South Africa (para 54). See para 57: "To the extent that the parties *in casu* resolved the proprietary consequences of their relationship by concluding a written deed of settlement, it was not necessary to make any determination on the applicable proprietary regime. However, practitioners would be advised to plead the applicable regime with the necessary degree of accuracy in order that a court may properly adjudicate the proprietary claims before it."

20 Neels and Fredericks (n 6) 921.

The late authors Stoll and Visser were the first (in 1989) to propose a solution.[21] Hans Stoll was a professor of private international law at the Albert Ludwig University of Freiburg im Breisgau; P J (Hans) Visser was a professor of law at the University of Pretoria. Their proposal for South African private international law is based on the *Gesetz zur Neuregelung des Internationalen Privatrechts* of 1986,[22] which revised the provisions on German private international law in the *Einführungsgesetz zum Bürgerlichen Gesetzbuche*.[23] The act was necessitated *inter alia* by certain decisions of the German courts prohibiting the priority of the application of the husband's national law on the basis of the principles of Gender Equality (*Gleichberechtigung von Mann und Frau*) in article 3 of the *Grundgesetz für die Bundesrepublik Deutschland*.[24]

The authors[25] in this regard referred to the so-called *Spanierentscheidung* of the *Bundesverfassungsgericht* in 1971, where the court found that German private international law is subject to the human rights provisions in the German Constitution:

> "Als nationales, innerstaatliches Recht … sind die Vorschriften des deutschen Internationalen Privatrechts in vollem Umfang an den Grundrechten zu messen."[26]

The decision concerned the freedom of entering a valid marriage, which is based on article 6(1) of the *Grundgesetz*.[27]

---

21 Stoll and Visser "Aspects of the reform of German (and South African) private international family law" 1989 *De Jure (DJ)* 330.

22 The IPRNG is dated 25 July 1986; it entered into force on 1 September 1986. For discussions of the legislation, see Basedow "Die Neuregelung des Internationalen Privat- und Prozeßrechts" 1986 *Neue Juristische Wochenschrift (NJW)* 2971; and Böhmer "Das deutsche Gesetz zur Neuregelung des Internationalen Privatrechts von 1986. Struktur, Entstehung und Schwerpunkte" 1986 *Rabels Zeitschrift für ausländisches und internationales Privatrecht (RabelsZ)* 646.

23 The EGBGB was originally promulgated together with the *Bürgerliches Gesetzbuch* in 1896. See *eg* Kropholler *Internationales Privatrecht* (2006) 4.

24 art 3(2) sentence 1: "Männer und Frauen sind gleichberechtigt"; art 3(3) sentence 1: "Niemand darf wegen seines Geschlechtes … benachteiligt oder bevorzugt werden." See Kegel and Schurig *Internationales Privatrecht* (2004) 205; Kropholler (n 23) 4; and Mankowski (n 6) Vorbem. zu Art 13–17b EGBGB paras 4 et seqq and Art. 15 para 5.

25 (n 21) 330.

26 German Constitutional Court (*Bundesverfassungsgericht*, BVerfG) 4.5.1971 – 1 BvR 636/68 – BVerfGE 31, 58. See *eg* Kropholler (n 23) 34–35 and 251–254 on the role of constitutional values in private international law.

27 "Ehe und Familie stehen unter dem besonderen Schutze der staatlichen Ordnung."

A later decision of the same court, in 1983, specifically dealt with the proprietary consequences of marriage, which were previously, in the absence of a choice of law by the parties, governed by the law of the country of nationality of the husband. The court declared the relevant provision of the EGBGB[28] to be unconstitutional, being in conflict with article 3(2) of the *Grundgesetz*,[29] thereby initiating its reform in 1986.[30]

The reform legislation, as still contained in the current text of the EGBGB, allows for a limited possibility of a choice of law by the parties in respect of the proprietary consequences of marriage.[31] If there is no valid choice of law, article 15 refers the determination of the proprietary consequences of marriage to the *Familienrechtliche Anknüpfungsleiter*[32] in article 14. The proprietary consequences of marriage must be determined by the law of the country of the common nationality of the parties at the time of the conclusion of the marriage. If the parties did not have a common nationality, the law of the country of their common habitual residence at marriage applies. If the parties did not have a common habitual residence, the law with which the parties were most closely connected at the time of the conclusion of the marriage will apply.[33]

For the purposes of South African private international law, Stoll and Visser proposed, in the advancement of the legal position of women, that the then South African Law Commission[34] investigates "the possible introduction of legal rules accommodating the following principles":

---

28 former version of art 15 EGBGB (alte Fassung).

29 German Constitutional Court (*Bundesverfassungsgericht*, BVerfG) 22.2.1983 – 1 BvL 17/81 – BVerfG 63, 181. Stoll and Visser (n 21) do not refer to this decision.

30 See the current version of art 15 EGBGB (neue Fassung).

31 art 15(2) EGBGB. The choice of law must be contained in an "Ehevertrag": art 15(3) EGBGB referring to art 14(4) EGBGB.

32 Kropholler (n 23) 347–348. Also see 143 and 171.

33 art 15(1) EGBGB referring to art 14(1) sentences 1–3 EGBGB. As art 15(1) EGBGB refers to the relevant law at the conclusion of the marriage, the references to the last shared law of nationality or habitual residence in art 14(1) sentences 1–2 EGBGB are not relevant. See Kropholler (n 23) 354; Looschelders *Internationales Privatrecht – Art 3–46 EGBGB* (2004) 235 and 237–238; Mankowski (n 6) Art 15 EGBGB paras 1–2, 23–24, 28; Schoeman (n 1) 129; and Siehr in Säcker, Rixecker, Oetker et al (eds) *Münchener Kommentar zum Bürgerlichen Gesetzbuch X Internationales Privatrecht I* (2015) Art 15 EGBGB para 50. Also see Kegel and Schurig (n 24) 846.

34 now the South African Law Reform Commission.

> "In the absence of any express or implied[35] choice by the parties to the contrary, all the proprietary consequences of marriage shall be determined by the *lex domicilii* of both parties at marriage, or the law of the habitual residence of both parties at marriage, or the law of the state of which they are both nationals at marriage, or the law of the state with which both spouses are most closely connected at marriage."[36]

The proposal is clearly inspired by the model in the German reform legislation. However, the authors do not provide reasons for their specific design, for instance, the recognition and the order of the relevant connecting factors.

Elsabe Schoeman was the third author on South African private international law to engage with the issue under discussion. She first suggested that, in the absence of a choice of law in an antenuptial contract, the law of the country of common domicile of the parties at the conclusion of the marriage applies; if there was no such common domicile, the law of closest connection should govern.[37] She added that it is possible that "connecting factors, such as habitual residence, may develop to lend more certainty to the notion of 'most significant connection'".[38] In a later article, which contains a detailed study of German private international law in this regard, Schoeman proposed "a thorough investigation into the viability of habitual residence as a connecting factor for the proprietary consequences of marriage, probably as a second option to domicile".[39] The latter suggestion by Schoeman was referred to by Farlam JA in the decision of the Supreme Court of Appeal in *Fourie v Minister of Home Affairs*[40] as "a possible solution to the problem" of the inappropriateness of the common-law rule to same-sex marriages.[41]

A fourth author supported the view of Stoll and Visser[42] on the ground that the extra two steps in this model (with the express reference to habitual

---

35 read: tacit. See Forsyth (n 2) 325–329; and Neels and Fredericks "Tacit choice of law in the Hague Principles on Choice of Law in International Contracts" 2011 *De Jure (DJ)* 101.

36 Stoll and Visser (n 21) 335.

37 Schoeman "The connecting factor for the proprietary consequences of marriage" 2001 *Tydskrif vir die Suid-Afrikaanse Reg (TSAR)* 72 80–81.

38 Schoeman (n 37) 81.

39 Schoeman (n 1) 133. Also see Schoeman "The South African conflict rule for proprietary consequences of marriages: the need for reform" 2004 *Praxis des Internationalen Privat- und Verfahrensrecht (IPRax)* 54.

40 (n 15).

41 para 125 n 112.

42 (n 21) 335.

residence and also to nationality) provide far more certainty. This was, in his view, a more important consideration than the fact that the connecting factors of nationality and, to a lesser extent, habitual residence, did not traditionally play an important role in South African private international law.[43]

In any event, habitual residence and nationality are increasingly employed as connecting factors in the South African conflict of laws, often under the influence of international conventions.[44] Habitual residence already plays a role in respect of the formal validity of wills[45] and the determination of the proper law of a contract;[46] it also plays a role in the context of the Hague conventions on the civil aspects of child abduction[47] and intercountry adoption,[48] as incorporated in the Children's Act.[49] Nationality today plays a role in the context of the formal validity of wills,[50] the recognition and enforcement of foreign divorce orders,[51] an application in terms of section 21(1) of the Matrimonial Property Act[52] and the determination of the proper law of a contract.[53]

The order of the connecting factors as proposed by Stoll and Visser was supported on the following grounds: (i) The principle of party autonomy is generally accepted in South African private international law of contract.[54] (ii) Domicile is the most important connecting factor in personal-law issues

---

43 Neels "The revocation of wills in South African private international law" 2007 *International and Comparative Law Quarterly (Int'l Comp. L.Q.)* 613 620.

44 Neels and Wethmar-Lemmer (n 6) 588.

45 sec 3*bis* (1)*(a)*(ii) of the Wills Act 7 of 1953.

46 Fredericks and Neels "The proper law of a documentary letter of credit" (part 1) 2003 *South African Mercantile Law Journal (SA Merc LJ)* 63 68.

47 Hague Convention on the Civil Aspects of International Child Abduction (1980).

48 Hague Convention on Protection of Children and Co-operation in Respect of Intercountry Adoption (1993).

49 38 of 2005. *Cf* sec 13(1)*(b)* of the Divorce Act 70 of 1979.

50 secs 3*bis* (1)*(a)*(iii) and 3*bis* (4)*(a)* of the Wills Act 7 of 1953.

51 sec 13(1)*(c)* of the Divorce Act 70 of 1979.

52 88 of 1984. See *Ex Parte Senekal* 1989 1 SA 38 (T) 39–40.

53 Forsyth (n 2) 332; Fredericks and Neels (n 46) 68; and Van Rooyen *Die Kontrak in die Suid-Afrikaanse Internasionale Privaatreg* (1972) 98.

54 The courts may take guidance in the interpretation, supplementation and development of rules of private international law in this regard from the recently adopted Hague Principles on Choice of Law in International Commercial Contracts (2015). See, in general, Neels "The nature, objective and purposes of the Hague Principles on Choice of Law in International Contracts" 2013/2014 *Yearbook of Private International Law* 45.

in South African private international law. (iii) Habitual residence is the concept that is most closely related to that of domicile.[55]

The proposal by Stoll and Visser may be reformulated as a five-step model[56] for the purposes of greater clarity:

- Step 1: The proprietary consequences of marriage are governed by the law chosen by the parties in an antenuptial contract.[57]
- Step 2: In the absence of a choice of law in an antenuptial contract, the proprietary consequences of marriage are governed by the law of the country of the common domicile of the parties at the time of the marriage.[58]

---

55 Neels and Wethmar-Lemmer (n 6) 589. *Cf* art 26(1) of the European Commission Proposal for a Council Regulation on Jurisdiction, Applicable Law and the Recognition and Enforcement of Decisions in Matters of Matrimonial Property Regimes COM (2016) 106 final 2016/0059 (CNS) (2 March 2016).

56 The German authors refer to the three-step model in art 14(1) sentences 1–3 EGBGB as a so-called *Anknüpfungsleiter*: see *eg* Kropholler (n 23) 347, Mankowski (n 6) Art 14 EGBGB paras 27–28, Art 15 EGBGB para 1 and Siehr (n 33) Art 14 EGBGB para 12.

57 Under current South African law and under the proposals it remains unclear whether a tacit choice of law in an antenuptial contract or a choice of law in an informal antenuptial contract would be sufficient in this regard. There is also uncertainty in respect of the legal system to govern the material validity (and effect) of (a choice of law in) an antenuptial contract. See for references Neels and Fredericks (n 6) 921–922. A declaration to a Mauritian marriage officer that the parties intended to marry in terms of a certain local matrimonial property regime, was found to be insufficient for the purposes of step 1 (the *Lenferna* decision (n 12) para 10; see Neels and Fredericks (n 6) 922) but is indeed sufficient for the purposes of a claim for redistribution in terms of sec 7(3) of the Divorce Act 70 of 1979 (*Lagesse v Lagesse* 1992 1 SA 173 (D); see Forsyth (n 2) 309; Vrancken "Foreign informal antenuptial contracts and sec 7(3) of the Divorce Act 70 of 1979" 1993 *Tydskrif vir die Suid-Afrikaanse Reg (TSAR)* 180; *cf Mathabathe v Mathabathe* 1987 3 SA 45 (W)).

58 In 1950 it was authoritatively decided that the relevant domicile is that at the moment of conclusion of the marriage; the intention to obtain a foreign domicile at that stage, or any other, is not relevant. See the *Frankel's Estate* case (n 3) 239–240. Also see the decision of the court *a quo* in *Frankel's Estate* (n 3) 230 and the *Sadiku* case (n 8) para 7. Today, therefore, the intention, at the conclusion of the marriage (or any other stage), of the parties to acquire a foreign domicile, habitual residence or nationality should likewise not be taken into account in determining the legal system applicable to the proprietary consequences of marriage. See Neels and Fredericks (n 6) 924; *cf* Neels and Wethmar-Lemmer (n 6) 593. On the ques-

- Step 3: If the parties did not have such a common domicile, the law of the country of the common habitual residence of the parties at the time of the marriage applies.[59]
- Step 4: If the parties did not have such a common habitual residence, the law of the country of the common nationality of the parties at the time of the marriage applies.[60]
- Step 5: If the parties did not have such a common nationality, the law of the country applies to which both spouses were most closely connected at the time of the marriage.[61]

Today there seems to be general acceptance amongst the South African authors of, at least, the first three[62] but predominantly the first four[63] or even all five steps of the model.[64] However, Christopher Forsyth, the author of the leading text book on Southern African private international law,[65] ten-

---

tion whether the intention to obtain a foreign domicile, habitual residence or nationality could play a role in respect of step 5 of the proposed model, contrast Schoeman (n 1) 134 with Neels and Wethmar-Lemmer (n 6) 593.

59 See n 58.

60 See n 58.

61 Neels and Fredericks (n 6) 920–921 (also see Neels and Wethmar-Lemmer (n 6) 588). See n 58 and n 81. The proposed rule is intended for all types of property. The received Roman-Dutch rule also applied to movable and immovable property. Some doubt was cast on the latter rule in the *Sadiku* case (n 8) para 10 (see Neels and Wethmar-Lemmer (n 6) 593–596) but after the *Lenferna* decision (n 12) it is clear that the traditional position remains (see Neels and Fredericks (n 6) 922–923). On the legal system applicable to redistribution at divorce (secs 7(3) and 7(9) of the Divorce Act), see Neels and Fredericks (n 6) 926–929, with detailed references.

62 Schoeman (n 1) 133 (tentative support in respect of step 3). *Cf* Schoeman (n 37) 80–81. Schoeman also supports the law of closest connection as the final step: Schoeman (n 37) 80–81; and Schoeman (n 1) 133.

63 Forsyth (n 2) 302; Schulze (n 2) 660–661.

64 Neels (n 43) 619–620; Neels and Fredericks (n 6) 920–921; Neels and Wethmar-Lemmer (n 6) 588; and Stoll and Visser (n 21) 335.

65 Roman-Dutch private international law applies in Botswana, Lesotho, Namibia, South Africa, Swaziland and Zimbabwe. See Forsyth (n 1) 68. Roman-Dutch law (including its private international law branch) also applies in Sri Lanka. See, in general, Amerasinghe "The Dutch influence on the legal system of Sri Lanka" in Kelegama and Madawela (eds) *400 Years of Dutch–Sri Lanka Relations 1602–2002* (2002) 287; Cooray "Sri Lanka: oriental and occidental laws in harmony" in Örücü, Attwool and Cyle (eds) *Studies in Legal Systems: Mixed and Mixing* (1996)

tatively suggests that, if the parties did not have a common domicile, habitual residence or nationality at the time of marriage, the law of the country where the marriage was concluded must be applied.[66]

On the one hand, the place of the conclusion of the marriage may be totally unrelated to the parties. On the other hand, the law of closest connection will be difficult to determine if there was no common domicile, habitual residence or nationality.[67] Nevertheless, in some instances the facts of the case may clearly indicate the law of the closest connection. The following scenario may be considered in this regard:

> "The wife was habitually resident and domiciled in country Q at the time of the marriage. She was a citizen of state R but never resided in, or even visited, that country. The husband had the nationality of country Q. Some time before the conclusion of the marriage, he had become lawfully and habitually resident in country S, with the intention of settling there for an indefinite period of time for work purposes; he was therefore domiciled in country S at the time of the marriage....[68] The parties owned a business, as well as immovable property, in country Q at the time of the marriage and, before the wedding, executed a joint and mutual will in country Q, attested to by a notary in Q and registered in the central registry for wills in the same country. Both parties had their closest cultural, linguistic, religious and social links to country Q. Although the parties married on an exotic island forming part of country T, the law of country Q was clearly closer connected to the parties."[69]

The majority of the South African authors support application of the law of the country of the closest connection rather than the *lex loci celebrationis* as the ultimate step.[70] As indicated, German private international law (on which all the current South African proposals are based) also utilises the law of closest connection in this regard.[71] The same solution is found in the

---

71; and Goonesekere "The Roman Dutch law in the plural legal system of Sri Lanka" 1995 *Colombo Law Review (CLR)* 1.

66 Forsyth (n 2) 302; *cf* Schulze (n 2) 661.

67 Forsyth (n 2) 302; Neels and Fredericks (n 6) 921; and Schulze (n 2) 661.

68 See sec 1(2) of the Domicile Act 3 of 1992.

69 Neels and Fredericks (n 6) 921. In another factual scenario, the place of the conclusion of the marriage may be a factor to be taken into account in determining the law of closest connection. See, in general, on relevant factors in this regard: Kegel and Schurig (n 24) 348; and Schoeman (n 1) 131–132 and 134.

70 Neels (n 43) 619–620; Neels and Fredericks (n 6) 920–921; Neels and Wethmar-Lemmer (n 6) 588; Schoeman (n 37) 80–81; Schoeman (n 1) 133; and Stoll and Visser (n 21) 335.

71 art 15(1) EGBGB referring to art 14(1) sentence 3 EGBGB.

Hague Convention on the Law Applicable to Matrimonial Property Regimes of 1978[72] and in the recently published European Commission Proposal for a Council Regulation on Jurisdiction, Applicable Law and the Recognition and Enforcement of Decisions in Matters of Matrimonial Property Regimes,[73] referring, as the final step, to, respectively, "the … law of the State with which, taking all circumstances into account, [the matrimonial property regime of the parties] is most closely connected"[74] and "the law of the State … with which the spouses jointly have the closest connection at the time of the celebration of the marriage, taking into account all the circumstances".[75]

To summarise: the proposal by Stoll and Visser[76] is fully supported by three other South African authors (a total of five),[77] steps 1–3 and 5 by Schoeman,[78] and steps 1–4 by Forsyth[79] and Schulze,[80] and therefore seems to be the leading model for the reform of international matrimonial property law in South Africa.[81]

---

72 See art 4. The Convention is in force since 1 September 1992 in France, Luxembourg and the Netherlands. See the status table for the Convention at www.hcch.net. For discussions of the Convention, see Reinhartz *Derdenbescherming in het Huwelijksvermogensrecht* (1997) 335–358; and Strikwerda *Inleiding tot het Nederlandse Internationaal Privaatrecht* (2012) 135–139.

73 (n 55). See art 26(1). Germany and sixteen other European Union member countries requested the drafting of the proposed Regulation – recital 11.

74 art 4 (last sentence).

75 art 26(1)*(c)*.

76 (n 21) 335.

77 Neels (n 43) 619–620; Neels and Fredericks (n 6) 920–921; and Neels and Wethmar-Lemmer (n 6) 588.

78 Schoeman (n 1) 133 (tentative support in respect of step 3); *cf* Schoeman (n 37) 80–81. Schoeman, Roodt and Wethmar-Lemmer (n 1) 84 do not express support for any particular model.

79 (n 2) 302.

80 (n 2) 661.

81 The proposal may be compared to art 15(1) referring to art 14(1) sentences 1–3 of the EGBGB; art 4 of the Hague Convention on the Law Applicable to Matrimonial Property Regimes of 1978; and art 26(1) of the European Commission Proposal for a Council Regulation on Jurisdiction, Applicable Law and the Recognition and Enforcement of Decisions in Matters of Matrimonial Property Regimes (n 55). *Cf* art 26 of the European Commission Proposal for a Council Regulation on Jurisdiction, Applicable Law and the Recognition and Enforcement of Decisions in Matters of the Property Consequences of Registered Partnerships COM (2016) 107 final 2016/0060 (CNS) (2 March 2016); also see *AS v CS* (n 10).

As the proposed models for the reform of South African private international law use connecting factors other than domicile, the common-law term *lex domicilii matrimonii* is no longer appropriate to refer to the legal system governing the proprietary consequences of marriage. The expressions *lex causae proprietatis matrimonii* or the proper law of the proprietary consequences of marriage were therefore proposed to replace the traditional concept.[82] In the *Lenferna* case,[83] the Supreme Court of Appeal indeed employed the notion of the proper law – in the phrase "the proper law of the marriage".[84] The use of the concept of the proper law is supported but the courts should specifically refer to the proper law of the proprietary consequences of marriage in this context as other aspects of marriage (for instance, the formal validity, the material validity and the personal consequences of marriage) may be governed by other legal systems.[85]

The current academic proposals for the reform of the received Roman-Dutch rule reveal a decidedly German influence. This comes as no surprise as, "[o]n the particular issue of the proprietary consequences of marriage, German private international law presents itself as an excellent system for comparative reference, since exactly the same issue was dealt with [in that conflict-of-laws system] some time ago",[86] although the relevant personal-law system in Germany was the law of nationality, whereas the law of domicile plays the dominant role in South Africa.[87] The leading proposal today,[88] as inspired by German reform legislation of 1986,[89] adjusted for the purposes of South African private international law by German and South

82 Neels and Wethmar-Lemmer (n 6) 589–592.
83 (n 12).
84 para 1.
85 Neels and Fredericks (n 6) 920. See, in general, Forsyth (n 2) 278–311; Schoeman, Roodt and Wethmar-Lemmer (n 1) 78–92; and Schulze (n 2) 642–661.
86 Schoeman (n 1) 119.
87 Schoeman (n 1) 123.
88 the proposal by Stoll and Visser (n 21) 335.
89 See the text at n 22 et seqq .

African academics[90] and widely accepted by local authors,[91] is likely to become positive law in the near future through endorsement by the courts,[92] in particular the Supreme Court of Appeal and the Constitutional Court.[93]

90 Stoll and Visser (n 21) 335. Also see Forsyth (n 2) 300–303; Neels (n 43) 619–620; Neels and Fredericks (n 6) 920–921; Neels and Wethmar-Lemmer (n 6) 588; Schoeman (n 37) 80–81; Schoeman (n 1) 133; and Schulze (n 2) 658–661.

91 See the text at n 62 et seqq and n 76 et seqq. Also see n 81.

92 Indications that reform is imminent may be found in the case law referred to in (the text at) n 8–13, 15–16 and 40–41.

93 See the following sections of the Constitution: "When applying a provision of the Bill of Rights to a natural or juristic person in terms of subsection (2), a court (a) in order to give effect to a right in the Bill, must apply, or if necessary develop, the common law to the extent that legislation does not give effect to that right" (sec 8(3)); "When interpreting any legislation, and when developing the common law or customary law, every court, tribunal or forum must promote the spirit, purport and objects of the Bill of Rights" (sec 39(2)); and "The Constitutional Court, Supreme Court of Appeal and High Courts have the inherit power … to develop the common law, taking into account the interests of justice" (sec 173). However, Forsyth (n 2) 302–303 is of the opinion that the legislature should preferably address the issue, especially to be able to deal with transitional arrangements. Also see *AS v CS* (n 10) para 56 and Schulze (n 2) 661.

Bibliography

Amerasinghe HS "The Dutch influence on the legal system of Sri Lanka" in Kelegama S and Madawela R (eds) *400 Years of Dutch–Sri Lanka Relations 1602–2002* (Institute of Policy Studies, Colombo 2002) 287.

Basedow J "Die Neuregelung des Internationalen Privat- und Prozeßrechts" 1986 *Neue Juristische Wochenschrift (NJW)* 2971.

Böhmer C "Das deutsche Gesetz zur Neuregelung des Internationalen Privatrechts von 1986. Struktur, Entstehung und Schwerpunkte" 1986 *Rabels Zeitschrift für ausländisches und internationales Privatrecht (RabelsZ)* 646.

Cooray A "Sri Lanka: oriental and occidental laws in harmony" in Örücü E, Attwool E and Cyle S (eds) *Studies in Legal Systems: Mixed and Mixing* (Kluwer Law International, The Hague 1996) 71.

Forsyth CF "The provenance and future of private international law in Southern Africa" 2002 *Tydskrif vir die Suid-Afrikaanse Reg (TSAR)* 60.

Forsyth CF *Private International Law. The Modern Roman-Dutch Law including the Jurisdiction of the High Courts* (5th Edition, Juta, Cape Town 2012).

Fredericks EA and Neels JL "The proper law of a documentary letter of credit" (part 1) 2003 *South African Mercantile Law Journal (SA Merc LJ)* 63.

Goonesekere S "The Roman Dutch law in the plural legal system of Sri Lanka" 1995 *Colombo Law Review (CLR)* 1.

Kegel G and Schurig K *Internationales Privatrecht* (9th Edition, Mohr Siebeck, Tübingen 2004).

Kropholler J *Internationales Privatrecht* (6th Edition, Mohr Siebeck, Tübingen 2006).

Looschelders D *Internationales Privatrecht – Art 3–46 EGBGB* (Springer, Berlin 2004).

Münchener Kommentar zum Bürgerlichen Gesetzbuch, Säcker FJ, Rixecker R, Oetker H et al (eds), Volume X, Internationales Privatrecht I (6th Edition, CH Beck, Munich 2015).

Neels JL "The nature, objective and purposes of the Hague Principles on Choice of Law in International Contracts" 2013/2014 *Yearbook of Private International Law* 45.

Neels JL "The revocation of wills in South African private international law" 2007 *International and Comparative Law Quarterly (Int'l Comp. L.Q.)* 613.

Neels JL and Fredericks EA "Tacit choice of law in the Hague Principles on Choice of Law in International Contracts" 2011 *De Jure (DJ)* 101.

Neels JL and Fredericks EA "The proper law of the proprietary consequences of marriage: Mauritian law in the South African Supreme Court of Appeal" 2015 *Tydskrif vir die Suid-Afrikaanse Reg (TSAR)* 918.

Neels JL and Wethmar-Lemmer MM "Constitutional values and the proprietary consequences of marriage in private international law – introducing the *lex causae proprietatis matrimonii*" 2008 *Tydskrif vir die Suid-Afrikaanse Reg (TSAR)* 587.

Reinhartz BE *Derdenbescherming in het Huwelijksvermogensrecht* (Kluwer, Deventer 1997).

Schoeman E "The connecting factor for the proprietary consequences of marriage" 2001 *Tydskrif vir die Suid-Afrikaanse Reg (TSAR)* 72.

Schoeman E "The South African conflict rule for proprietary consequences of marriages: the need for reform" 2004 *Praxis des Internationalen Privat- und Verfahrensrecht (IPRax)* 54.

Schoeman E "The South African conflict rule for proprietary consequences of marriage: learning from the German experience" 2004 *Tydskrif vir die Suid-Afrikaanse Reg (TSAR)* 115.

Schoeman E, Roodt C and Wethmar-Lemmer MM *Private International Law in South Africa* (Kluwer Law International, Alphen aan den Rijn 2014).

Schulze HCAW "Conflict of laws" in Heaton J (ed) *The Law of Divorce and Dissolution of Life Partnerships in South Africa* (Juta, Cape Town 2014) 631–668.

Stoll H and Visser PJ "Aspects of the reform of German (and South African) private international family law" 1989 *De Jure (DJ)* 330.

Strikwerda L *Inleiding tot het Nederlandse Internationaal Privaatrecht* (10th Edition, Kluwer, Deventer 2012).

Van Rooyen JCW *Die Kontrak in die Suid-Afrikaanse Internasionale Privaatreg* (Juta, Cape Town 1972).

von Staudinger J *Kommentar zum Bürgerlichen Gesetzbuch mit Einführungsgesetz und Nebengesetzen. Internationales Eherecht* (Sellier, de Gruyter, Berlin 2011).

Vrancken PHG "Foreign informal antenuptial contracts and s 7(3) of the Divorce Act 70 of 1979" 1993 *Tydskrif vir die Suid-Afrikaanse Reg (TSAR)* 180.

Case Law

Germany

BVerfG 4.5.1971 – 1 BvR 636/66 – BVerfGE 31, 58 = 1971 *Neue Juristische Wochenschrift* 1509.

BVerfG 22.2.1983 – 1 BvL 17/81 – BVerfGE 63, 181 = 1983 *Neue Juristische Wochenschrift* 1968.

South Africa

AS v CS 2011 2 SA 360 (WCC)

B v B (10019/2014) 2014 ZAWCHC 178 (2 Dec 2014) (available at www.saflii.org)

Ex Parte Senekal 1989 1 SA 38 (T)

Fourie v Minister of Home Affairs 2005 1 All SA 273 (SCA)

Frankel's Estate v The Master 1950 1 SA 220 (A)

Hillard v Hillard (1464/2007) 2008 ZAFSHC 135 (4 Dec 2008) (available at www.saflii.org)

Lagesse v Lagesse 1992 1 SA 173 (D)

Lenferna v Lenferna (120/13) 2013 ZASCA 204 (2 Dec 2013) (available at www.saflii.org; www.supremecourtofappeal.gov.za; and 2013 JDR 2705 (SCA))

Mathabathe v Mathabathe 1987 3 SA 45 (W)

Minister of Home Affairs v Fourie (Doctors for Life International); Lesbian and Gay Equality Project v Minister of Home Affairs 2006 1 SA 524 (CC)

Sadiku v Sadiku (30498/06) 2007 ZAGHPC 1 (26 Jan 2007) (available at www.saflii.org)

Sperling v Sperling 1975 3 SA 707 (A)

Exceptions to the independence of autonomous instruments of payment and security: the growing emergence of good faith

*Karl Marxen**
*Charl Hugo***

* Doctoral student, University of Johannesburg.
** Professor of Banking Law and Director of the Centre for Banking Law, University of Johannesburg.

I. Introduction

Letters of credit (*Dokumentenakkreditiv*)[1] and independent guarantees payable on demand (*abstrakte Bankgarantie/Garantie auf erstes Anfordern*)[2] are employed regularly in commercial transactions and international trade.[3] The success of these two instruments is founded on the principle of independence (*Unabhängigkeit*) and the principle of strict compliance (*Dokumentenstrenge*). Strict compliance means that in order to obtain payment under a letter of credit or an independent guarantee, the beneficiary must submit documents which comply strictly with the stipulations in the instrument.[4] The principle of independence, on the other hand, detaches the obli-

---

1 Letters of credit are also referred to as, inter alia, documentary credits, documentary letters of credit, or bankers' (irrevocable) credits. In Germany the terms *Akkreditiv* or *Dokumentenakkreditiv* are used. The International Chamber of Commerce das drafted the so-called *Uniform Customs and Practice for Documentary Credits (UCP)* that are almost invariably incorporated by the parties and as such govern those aspects of letters of credit dealt with in the *UCP*. The current revision is the *UCP 600* (2007).

2 Independent guarantees are known by many different names. The most widespread are abstract or autonomous guarantees, demand guarantees, (bank) guarantees payable on first demand, performance bonds, guarantee bonds, and standby letters of credit. In Germany such guarantees are known as *(abstrakte) Bankgarantie*, *Garantie auf erstes Anfordern* and also *selbstständige Garantie*. The International Chamber of Commerce has drafted the co-called *Uniform Rules on Demand Guarantees (URDG)* that resemble strongly the *UCP*, and are supposed to do for demand guarantees what the *UCP* does for letters of credit. Its market penetration, however, has been significantly less. The current revision is the *URDG 758* (2007).

3 Horowitz *Letters of Credit and Demand Guarantees* (2010) 2 paras 1.05–1.06.

4 Proctor *The Law and Practice of International Banking* (2010) 452 para 24.32; Rüßmann and Britz "Die Auswirkung des Grundsatzes der formellen Garantiestrenge auf die Geltenmachung einer befristeten Garantie auf erstes Anfordern" 1995 *Wertpapier Mitteilungen (WM)* 1825; Mahler *Rechtsmißbrauch und einstweiliger Rechtsschutz bei Dokumentenakkreditiven und Akkreditiven auf erstes Anfordern* (1986) 59. Letters of credit mostly require transport documents (such as a bill of lading), insurance documents, commercial invoices, and any of various certificates. Independent guarantees require a written demand by the beneficiary and usually a declaration that the underlying contract has been breached or terminated. It should be noted that the required level of strictness of a documentary presentation for independent guarantees has not been clearly established under South African law. See in this regard Kelly-Louw and Marxen "General update on the law of demand guarantees and letters of credit" 2015 *Annual Banking Law*

gation arising under the instrument from the underlying contracts and relationships; hence they are independent of one another.[5] Independence in this context means that the liability of the issuer of the instrument is determined solely with regard to the instrument itself.[6] If the beneficiary is able to submit conforming documents (in accordance with the principle of strict compliance), the issuer or guarantor must honour the claim and pay.[7] Disputes relating to questions of performance (whether it is satisfactory or defective) and the beneficiary's material entitlement to the monies requested under the instrument are to be argued later, and only after payment has been made.[8] This is a direct consequence of the principle of independence in letters of credit and independent guarantees, and commonly described as the rule of "pay first – argue later".[9] A beneficiary of such an abstract instrument of

---

Update (ABLU) 276 285–286. See also Kelly-Louw "The doctrine of strict compliance in the context of demand guarantees" 2016 *Comparative and International Law Journal of Southern Africa (CILSA)* 85 91. See further arts 5, 14, 15 & 16 of the *UCP 600* and arts 6, 15, 19 & 20 of the *URDG 758*, which, although not the only rules relating to compliance in the respective instruments, reflect the essence.

5 Ellinger and Neo *The Law and Practice of Documentary Letters of Credit* (2010) 138 and 316 para i; Bertrams *Bank Guarantees in International Trade* (2013) 11; Byrne *Standby and Demand Guarantee Practice* (2014) 5–7 para 1.1.2.2; Proctor (n 4) 439 para 24.10 and 449–450 paras 24.24–24.25. See further arts 4 & 5 of the *UCP 600* and arts 5 & 6 of the *URDG 758.* It should be noted that although the *UCP 600* and the *URDG 758* contain provisions stating in essence the independence principle, they do not deal with exceptions to the independence principle – which forms the main topic of this contribution. This aspect is clearly left to the different national legal systems to regulate.

6 See, for example, *Lombard Insurance Co Ltd v Landmark Holdings (Pty) Ltd* 2010 2 SA 86 (SCA), and Proctor (n 4) 461 para 24.61.

7 Byrne (n 5) 4 para 1.1.2.1; Graf von Westphalen and Zöchling-Jud *Die Bankgarantie im internationalen Handelsverkehr* (2014) 626 para 83.

8 *Cf* Malek and Quest *Jack: Documentary Credits* (2009) 366 para 12.68; Lwowski, Fischer and Langenbucher *Das Recht der Kreditsicherung* (2011) 344–345 para 219; Mülbert *Mißbrauch von Bankgarantien und einstweiliger Rechtsschutz* (1985) 10 ("Jeder Streit über den Eintritt des Sicherungsfalles soll auf einen späteren Zeitpunkt verschoben werden."); and Bertrams (n 5) 75 paras 6–3 and 347–351 paras 13–44.

9 Bertrams (n 5) 73 ("universally adopted expression"); Dunham "The use and abuse of first demand guarantees in international construction projects" 2008 *The International Construction Law Review (ICLR)* 273 290. See also Wood *International Loans, Bonds, Guarantees, Legal Opinions* (2007) 317 para 17. In German law the expression "erst zahlen, dann klagen/prozessieren" is used to describe this process of initial payment and only subsequent material determination and repayment (see BGH 16.03.1987 – II ZR 127/86 – BGHZ 101, 84 91); Schütze and

payment or security can therefore rest assured that it will receive the money once conforming documents are tendered, irrespective of objections by the other parties (the issuer/guarantor or the applicant for the instrument) relating to its material entitlement (or lack thereof). This contributes to legal certainty, which is of utmost significance to commercial law.

II. Exceptions to independence

1. The South African approach to fraud

Legal certainty, however, cannot prevail unconditionally, but must be balanced against notions of fairness and justice.[10] Therefore, it is necessary that under exceptional circumstances the independence principle in letters of credit and independent guarantees may be infringed upon. South African law, in this regard, closely follows the English common-law approach, and accepts that fraud by the beneficiary can form an exception to the independence principle. In *Phillips v Standard Bank of South Africa Ltd*[11] the Witwatersrand Local Division suggested that the fraud exception may be part of South African law.[12] A definite stance was later expressed by the Appellate Division in *Loomcraft Fabrics CC v Nedbank Ltd*[13] when Scott AJA held:

> "Nonetheless, it is now well established that a court will grant an interdict restraining a bank from paying the beneficiary under a credit in the event of it being established that the beneficiary was a party to fraud in relation to the documents presented to the bank for payment. [...] But the fraud on the part of the beneficiary will have to be clearly established."[14]

Edelmann *Bankgarantien* (2011) 122; Derleder, Knops and Bamberger *Handbuch zum deutschen und europäischen Bankrecht* (2009) 1868 para 44; and Wielandt *Die einseitig verpflichtende Schuldzusage* (2010) 61.

10 See Marxen "Abstrakte Garantie und Dokumentenakkreditiv in Südafrika" 2015 *Internationales Handelsrecht* (IHR) 137 145 para III.

11 1985 3 SA 301 (W).

12 *Cf* the dicta by Goldstone J at 304.

13 1996 1 SA 812 (A).

14 At 817 (our omission). Whilst the *Phillips* and *Loomcraft* cases both dealt with a situation in which an applicant attempted to interdict the bank from paying, in *Ex Parte Sapan Trading (Pty) Ltd* 1995 1 SA 218 (W) (a case involving a South African buyer and German seller) the court had to contend with an application by the buyer to attach the claims of the seller against the South African bank that had

With the South African law's clear appreciation of the fraud exception to the autonomy of letters of credit in *Loomcraft*,[15] its position was aligned, to a large extent, with the English common-law approach.

Due to the similarity of the legal principles governing letters of credit and independent guarantees,[16] exceptions to independence based on beneficiary fraud in letters of credit can also be applied to independent guarantees. While the South African law is aware of the need to support legal certainty, and thus the right of a beneficiary under letters of credit and demand guarantees to obtain payment in accordance with the terms of the instrument concerned alone, public policy necessitates the recognition of the fraud exception to curb unacceptable calls on the instruments. If the fraud exception is successfully raised, the applicant can obtain interdictory relief barring the issuer of the letter of credit or guarantee from paying, or the beneficiary from submitting a demand.

Fraud by the beneficiary, therefore, allows for the principle of independence to be disregarded and for effect to be given to considerations of public policy in support of equitable results by denying payment in exceptional circumstances. In relation to *documentary letters of credit*, fraud is usually understood as (i) the presentation of documents which have been forged or falsified by the beneficiary or obtained through fraud (the *narrow fraud exception*), or (ii) the presentation of documents which, despite formally conforming and being genuine, relate to goods which are, to the knowledge of the beneficiary, of defective quality (the *wide fraud exception*).

Although some dicta in South African case law appear to support the narrow fraud exception with its exclusive focus on the documents,[17] others apply the wider fraud approach which takes into account the underlying transaction and the beneficiary's fraudulent behaviour relating thereto.[18]

In regards to the fraud exception in *independent guarantees*, South African case law has shown further development and legal refinement. In recent

---

issued the letter of credit. The attachment was to have served to found or confirm jurisdiction on the South African court to determine a dispute arising from the contract of sale. Due to the independence principle and the absence of fraud, the application was unsuccessful.

15 Kelly-Louw *Selective Legal Aspects of Bank Demand Guarantees* (2009) 325–328.

16 See the remarks in the *Lombard Insurance* case (n 6) at 20.

17 As proposed in the *Loomcraft* case (n 13) paras 10 and 27–28.

18 See, for example, *Union Carriage and Wagon Company Ltd v Nedcor Bank Ltd* 1996 CLR 724 (W) 735; and the case comment by Oelofse "Developments in the law of documentary letters of credit" 1997 *Annual Banking Law Update (ABLU)* 6–7.

times, courts have operated with concepts based on the beneficiary's knowledge of the absence of material entitlement in order to interfere with the payment obligations of the guarantor. Moreover, as becomes evident below, it has been suggested that the absence of good faith may provide an exception to the principle of independence in demand guarantees.

2. Knowledge of absence of material entitlement and bad faith

Demand guarantees are utilised to provide fast and certain access to funds in commercial transactions without having to prove material entitlement to the monies under the guarantee.[19] These readily available funds serve to enable the beneficiary to rectify poor performance and mitigate damages, or recover any advance payments made.[20] In order to fulfil such expectations, the guarantee must be independent of the underlying relationships; in general any defences stemming from the underlying contract have to be disregarded when assessing the demand for payment. As was explained above, however, in extraordinary situations of reprehensible conduct by the beneficiary the law must offer a remedy to prevent payment. South African courts have explored new approaches as to what may constitute reprehensible behaviour which is serious enough to warrant judicial intervention.

---

19 Blesch and Lange *Bankgeschäfte mit Auslandsbezug* (2007) 130 para 505.

20 The exact purpose of the guarantee depends on the particular type of guarantee, for example a construction guarantee (covering the completion of the construction works), warranty guarantee (ensuring the rectification of defects during the warranty period), advance payment guarantee (provide for repayment of frustrated advance payments), or a retention money guarantee (securing the prematurely released monies).

In *Dormell Properties 282 CC v Renasa Insurance Ltd*[21] the Supreme Court of Appeal decided on the validity of a call on an independent guarantee.[22] In this case, the beneficiary had made a call on a guarantee after an alleged breach of the underlying construction contract by the applicant and subsequent cancellation by the beneficiary. Before the demand on the guarantee was honoured, however, the dispute between the parties on the underlying contract was finally determined in an arbitral award to the effect that the underlying contract had not been breached by the applicant and the beneficiary had not been entitled to cancel the contract. The Supreme Court of Appeal was now faced with the challenge to ascertain the legal consequences, if any, of the arbitral award on the guarantee. Without discussing the merits of this very interesting judgment, it is important to take note of the minority judgment by Cloete JA.[23] Although he was in favour of allowing the call on the guarantee, he made reference to conduct of bad faith in independent guarantee transactions. He suggested, by implication, in the following words, that bad faith may constitute a proper justification for departing from the principle of independence:

> "For these reasons, it is not in my view *bad faith* for an employer, who has made a proper demand in terms of a construction guarantee, to continue to insist on payment of the proceeds of the guarantee, when the basis upon which the guarantee was called up has subsequently been found in arbitration proceedings between the building owner and the contractor to have been unjustified. I would add that the fact that the arbitrator's award is final as between the appellant and the second respondent does not mean that it is correct, or that the appellant would have to set it aside

---

21 2011 1 SA 70 (SCA).

22 For a case discussion see Hugo "Construction guarantees and the supreme court of appeal (2010–2013)" in Visser, Pretorius and Koekemoer (eds) *Essays in Honour of Frans Malan* (2014) 159 171–172; and Hugo "Protecting the lifeblood of commerce: a critical assessment of recent judgments of the South African supreme court of appeal relating to demand guarantees" 2014 *Tydskrif vir die Suid-Afrikaanse Reg (TSAR)* 661 663–666.

23 It is important to note that the majority judgment was later overturned in *Coface South Africa Insurance Co Ltd v East London Own Haven t/a Own Haven Housing Association* 2014 1 All SA 536 (SCA), and preference was given to the minority judgment by Cloete JA After strong obiter criticism by the SCA in *Firstrand Bank Ltd v Brera Investments CC* 2013 5 SA 556 (SCA) paras 10 & 11. See in this regard Marxen (n 10) 141–144; Hugo "Independent guarantees and letters of credit" 2014 *Annual Banking Law Update (ABLU)* 49 49–52; Hugo (n 22 *Essays*) 173; and Hugo (n 22 *TSAR*) 665.

before calling up the guarantee, much less that the appellant is acting in *bad faith* in seeking to enforce payment under the guarantee against the first respondent."[24]

Unfortunately, Cloete JA did not provide additional guidance in respect of the suggestion that conduct of bad faith may constitute an exception to the independence principle. Neither the requirements of bad faith, nor the ambit of such an exception, if any, was considered by the court.

Furthermore, litigation before the High Court (Gauteng Division, Pretoria) in *Sulzer Pumps v Covec-MC Joint Venture*[25] led to remarks suggesting that "unconscionable conduct" by the beneficiary may constitute an exception to independence. In this case the applicant for an independent guarantee argued that the beneficiary had bound itself not to draw on the guarantee in a *pactum de non petendo*. When a call on the guarantee was made, in contravention of the agreement not to do so, an urgent interdict was granted prohibiting the imminent call. The High Court had to decide whether the interim interdict must be made final. Jansen J held:

> "What the old authorities do demonstrate though, is that not only fraud may prohibit the calling up of a construction guarantee, but also *unconscionable conduct* and also when a contract to the contrary has been entered into between the relevant parties (in this instance, including the bank)."[26]

She continued as follows:

> "[T]he court holds that it is clear that when it is *unconscionable* to rely on the literal wording of a contract without reading such wording within the context of the background facts, the surrounding circumstances and the purpose of the agreement, then a *construction guarantee cannot be called up*."[27]

Regrettably the court did not divulge on what particular legal basis the case was decided, or what constitutes "unconscionable conduct" sufficient to override the principle of independence. What can be inferred from the judgment, however, is the growing readiness by South African courts to consider general notions of justice and fairness, good faith and the imperative to act conscionably. How these imprecise abstract and flexible terms and concepts are to be interpreted and applied, on the other hand, is not properly explained.

---

24 para 65 of the *Dormell* case (n 21) (emphasis added).

25 *Sulzer Pumps (South Africa) (Proprietary) Limited v Covec-MC Joint Venture* 2014 ZAGPPHC (2 September 2014). For a discussion of the case see Kelly-Louw and Marxen (n 4) 287 et seq.

26 para 115 (our emphasis).

27 para 125 (our alteration and emphasis).

In *Guardrisk Insurance Company Ltd v Kentz (Pty) Ltd*[28] the Supreme Court of Appeal defined the fraud exception with specific reference to independent guarantees. Theron JA held:

> "It would be useful to briefly consider the legal position in relation to the fraud exception. It is trite that where a beneficiary who makes a call on a guarantee does so with *knowledge that it is not entitled to payment*, our courts will step in to protect the bank and decline enforcement of the guarantee in question."[29]

This judgment follows an interpretation of the fraud exception which puts emphasis on the state of mind of the beneficiary. The focus is not exclusively on the document presented under the instrument and its status (whether it is genuine or forged or whether it contains true statements or misrepresentations); instead the Court's approach inquires whether the beneficiary knew that it was in fact not entitled to the money called up in the demand. Thus, the approach of "lack of entitlement" in this context must mean that the Court went beyond the sphere of documentary presentations and the immediate terms of the independent guarantee. It is submitted that the test in the *Guardrisk Insurance* case comprises of an assessment of (1) the underlying relationship between the applicant and beneficiary, (2) the mutual obligations arising thereunder (whether payment was due or not), and, finally, (3) an evaluation of the beneficiary's knowledge in this respect. Regarding the last point, the crucial question revolves around the beneficiary's positive knowledge of its lack of entitlement. If it is supported by strong evidence to prove that, at the time of the demand, the beneficiary was aware of the material *dis*entitlement to monies, the fraud test is satisfied. Referring to the judgment in *Loomcraft* with approval, Theron JA continued as follows:

> "Mere error, misunderstanding or oversight, however unreasonable, would not amount to fraud. Nor was it enough to show that the beneficiary's contentions were incorrect. A party had to go further and show that the beneficiary knew it to be incorrect and that the contention was advanced in *bad faith*."[30]

The court stressed the need to assume fraud only in exceptional cases, and the importance of the knowledge of the beneficiary relating to his lack of entitlement. Even if the beneficiary's demand relied on incorrect assumptions and faulty contentions, it cannot be deemed to be fraudulent *per se*. Instead, the decisive question is whether the beneficiary thought it to be correct or at least possible. Should it, however, have had positive

28 2014 1 All SA 307 (SCA).
29 para 17 (our emphasis).
30 para 18 (our emphasis).

knowledge of the lack of entitlement at the time of the demand, the fraud exception would apply. This is a sound approach to the fraud exception, as it preserves the independence in abstract guarantees as much as reasonably possible. Simple disputes and differences in opinion between the parties to the underlying construction contract are still irrelevant to the payment obligation under the guarantee. The fraud defence is only available if it can be proved with certainty that the beneficiary was positively aware of the disentitlement. Lastly, this judgment in the *Guardrisk Insurance* case seems to suggest that "bad faith" in the context of independent guarantees could simply describe conduct whereby the beneficiary submits a demand which rests on statements of fact which, to its own positive knowledge, are incorrect or contain misrepresentations. Should this be a correct interpretation of the bad-faith remarks in the judgment, it is respectfully submitted that "bad faith" may well be a mere reformulation of the fraud exception as discussed above.

The High Court (Western Cape Division) subsequently had the opportunity of applying the reasoning in the *Guardrisk Insurance* case relating to the knowledge of lack of entitlement. In *Scatec Solar SA 163 Ltd v Terrafix Suedafrika Ltd*[31] the court was concerned with a case involving several independent guarantees (standby letters of credit). The guarantees were issued by a Japanese bank (Sumitomo) at the behest of the applicant (Scatec Solar) to the beneficiary (Terrafix). During the execution of the underlying contract Terrafix, through its director Mr Reisch, made several demands on the instruments. The applicant alleged Terrafix's lack of entitlement to the monies, contested the validity of the calls, and sought a declaratory order to this effect against the beneficiary. Cloete J explained the applicable test for the fraud defence:

> "[23] At the risk of repetition, the question is whether Reisch *knew* when he presented the demands for payment to Sumitomo that Terrafix was in fact *not entitled to payment* in terms of the relevant invoices, but he nonetheless intentionally went ahead and deliberately represented to Sumitomo that the amounts were due. Linked to this is whether Reisch took positive steps to inform himself that the amounts were in fact not due, or whether he deliberately refrained from acquainting himself with the true position so as to relieve himself of knowledge of the true facts."[32]

Moreover, the court elaborated as follows:

> "[40] Of course the possibility exists that Reisch has opportunistically seized upon the objective facts to which I have referred and found himself an escape hatch. The

31 2014 ZAWCHC 63 (25 April 2014).
32 para 23 (our emphasis).

> fact remains however that on the probabilities as they stand there is just not enough to find fraudulent intent on his part. He might have been wrong, he might even have been negligent, but I cannot find that he knew that he was wrong and that he presented the demand under the [guarantee] to Sumitomo in *bad faith.*
>
> [41] Accordingly, and although Reisch made a misrepresentation in the presentation of the demand under the [guarantee] to Sumitomo, the applicants have failed to show, on a balance of probabilities, that such misrepresentation was fraudulent, whether deliberate or as a result of fraudulent diligence in ignorance."[33]

Akin to the decision in the *Guardrisk* case, this judgment operates with the "knowledge of lack of entitlement" formula, but also makes reference to "bad faith". The classic forgery of documents, on the other hand, does not play a role.

A similar interpretation was once more supported in *Group Five Construction Ltd v Member of the Executive Council for Public Transport Roads and Works Gauteng*[34] in the High Court (Gauteng Local Division). The litigation referred to a construction guarantee which was available upon cancellation of the underlying contract.[35] The court observed in its judgment, that the *"[a]bsence* of *good faith* as ground for declining enforcement of a guarantee has received support from the Supreme Court of Appeal".[36] Absence of good faith, according to this decision, can therefore be seen as essentially the same as knowledge of lack of entitlement. It is simply another way of saying the same thing.

In conclusion, the analysis of the most recent case law emanating from the courts in South Africa proves the recognition of the fraud exception in independent instruments such as letters of credit and demand guarantees. The fraud approach favoured in respect of independent guarantees seems to be increasingly influenced by considerations of fairness and bad/good faith. The central aspect of the knowledge of the beneficiary to its material entitlement has gained ground in order to ascertain whether a demand if fraudulent or not.

---

33 paras 40–41 (per Cloete J, our emphasis and alterations).

34 *Group Five Construction Ltd v Member of the Executive Council for Public Transport Roads and Works Gauteng* 2015 2 All SA 716 (GJ).

35 See Kelly-Louw and Marxen (n 4) 294.

36 para 50, per Satchwell J (our emphasis). She made reference to the *Dormell Properties* case and the *Scatec Solar* case as well as the English case of *Cargill International SA v Bangladesh Sugar and Food Industries* Corp 1996 4 All ER 563 (QBD).

III. German law

The principle of independence, both in letters of credit and abstract guarantees, is well-established in German law. The independent nature of such instruments is nevertheless considered to be subject to notions of good faith.[37] Abusive demands on letters of credit or independent guarantees are approached by invoking the doctrine of abuse of rights (*Rechtsmissbrauch)*. The concept of *Rechtsmissbrauch* is derived from paragraph 242 of the German civil code (*Bürgerliches Gesetzbuch* (*BGB*)),[38] containing the central good faith provision (*Treu und Glauben*).[39] The beneficiary under a letter of credit or independent guarantee will be denied payment, if it is abusing its *formal* position (*mißbräuchliche Ausnutzung einer formalen Rechtsstellung*) under the instrument.[40] For example, if the documents presented under the letter of credit or independent guarantee would *formally* comply and thus enable the beneficiary to claim under the instrument, it remains conceivable that it may not be entitled to the monies from a *material* perspective (for example because the goods were clearly of grossly defective quality (in the case of a letter of credit), or absolutely no breach of contract had occurred (in the case of an independent guarantee)).[41] In such a situation the beneficiary, by demanding payment, would be acting abusively (*rechtsmissbräuchlich*).

However, the abuse of an abstract instrument is not inferred lightly, but only in exceptional circumstances.[42] The abuse must be obvious and clear

---

37 See BGH 12.03.1984 – II ZR 198/82 – BGHZ 90 287 291–292 ("Das Berufungsgericht geht zutreffend davon aus, [...] daß aber auch dieser Einwendungsausschluß den Maßstäben von Treu und Glauben unterliegt." – omission by the authors); similar also OLG Saarbrücken 06.07.2001 – 1 U 55/99 – 13, 1 U 55/99 – WM 2001, 2055 2061 para III.

38 Blesch and Lange (n 19) 228 para 788; Graf von Westphalen and Zöchling-Jud (n 7) 205–206; Mülbert (n 8) 51 et seq; and Mahler (n 4) 77.

39 Sec 242 BGB reads: "Der Schuldner ist verpflichtet, die Leistung so zu bewirken, wie Treu und Glauben mit Rücksicht auf die Verkehrssitte es erfordern." This has been translated as "An obligor has a duty to perform according to the requirements of good faith, taking customary practice into consideration." (Langenscheidt Translation Service).

40 See, for example, BGH 10.10.2000 – XI ZR 344/99 – BGHZ 145, 286 291.

41 OLG Saarbrücken 06.07.2001 – 1 U 55/99 – 13, 1 U 55/99 – WM 2001, 2055; OLG Celle 18.03.2009 – 3 U 167/08 – WM 2009, 1408; and Graf von Westphalen and Zöchling-Jud (n 7) 200 para 195.

42 As is evident, for instance, from BGH 16.03.1987 – II ZR 127/86 – BGHZ 101, 84 92 ("Dabei ist ein strenger Maßstab anzulegen."); OLG Celle 18.03.2009 – 3

(*offensichtlich oder liquide beweisbar*) from available evidence.[43] According to the *Bundesgerichtshof*,[44] payment under letters of credit and abstract guarantees will only be blocked in extraordinary circumstances if there remains no doubt as to the abusive nature of the beneficiary's conduct:

> "Für die Garantie auf erstes Anfordern vertritt der Bundesgerichtshof in ständiger Rechtsprechung den Grundsatz, daß Einwendungen gegen die materielle Berechtigung der Ansprüche des Begünstigten erst nach Zahlung durch Rückforderungsklage gegen den Begünstigten geltend gemacht werden können. Nur in Fällen, in denen die *mißbräuchliche Ausnutzung einer formalen Rechtsstellung klar erkennbar*, d.h. *offensichtlich oder liquide beweißbar* ist, entfällt die Zahlungspflicht des Garantiegebers."[45]

German courts impose a high threshold for acceptable evidence of the alleged abuse of rights. In order to satisfy the high evidentiary burden the applicant is required to submit evidence from which the abuse is obvious and beyond doubt – documentary proof is therefore usually necessary.[46] Subject to appropriate evidence, the courts would be able to deny payment with reference to the *Rechtsmissbrauch* principle, and disregard the autonomy of the instrument.

From a comparative perspective, it is interesting to note that the German law engages with grossly unfair conduct by the beneficiary in a way which differs from the South African law. The German doctrine of *Rechtsmissbrauch* views discrepancies of *formal* entitlement as opposed to *material* entitlement as the central aspect. If such a discrepancy (that is the *formal entitlement* through a conforming demand under the instrument stands in stark contrast to the actual, *material disentitlement* of the beneficiary) can be proved convincingly, the courts will step in and deny enforcement of the guarantee. It must be emphasised again, however, that German law recognises and strongly protects the independence principle in letters of credit

---

U 167/08 – WM 2009, 1408 1410 ("Dabei sind die Voraussetzungen, die für die Bejahung eines Rechtsmissbrauchs gegeben sein müssen, streng."); and Canaris *Bankvertragsrecht* (1988) 694 para 1016 ("Der Einwand des Rechtsmißbrauchs kann nur unter Anlegung strengster Maßstäbe in äußerst seltenen Ausnahmefällen zugelassen werden" – emphasis omitted).

43 BGH 12.03.1984 – II ZR 198/82 – BGHZ 90, 287 292; BGH 21.04.1988 – IX ZR 113/87 – NJW 1988, 2610; BGH 16.03.1987 – II ZR 127/86 – BGHZ 101, 84 91–93; BGH 10.10.2000 – XI ZR 344/99 – BGHZ 145, 286 290–291.

44 The German court akin to the Supreme Court of Appeal.

45 BGH 10.10.2000 – XI ZR 344/99 – BGHZ 145, 286 291 (our emphasis).

46 Graf von Westphalen and Zöchling-Jud (n 7) 202 paras 200–201.

and abstract guarantees; the *Rechtsmissbrauch* defence will therefore only succeed in very obvious and compelling situations of abuse.

IV. Comparative conclusion: indications of alignment and similarity in result

Although the outcomes of cases relating to exceptions to the independence principle are mostly remarkably similar in South African and German law, from a conceptual point of view the approaches of the two legal systems differ notably.[47] The law in South Africa is currently firmly based on the fraud exception as initially established in relation to letters of credit and then extended to independent guarantees. Despite its civilian roots, South African law does not recognise the *Rechtsmissbrauch* doctrine of German law. This doctrine arose in German law from the centrality and importance of the good faith provision (paragraph 242 *BGB*) in the German private-law system with its statutory imperative of *Treu und Glauben*. Although often encountered in many contexts in the South African law of contract, it would be fair to say that the role of good faith has not been as strong in South African law, but it seems to be growing. In a comparatively recent and prominent judgment of the supreme court of appeal, *Brisley v Drotsky*,[48] the majority of the court in a split decision, put it thus:

> "[22] Regarding the role of good faith we agree in essence with the view of prof Hutchison[49] ... in accordance with which good faith is not an independent, or 'free-floating', basis for the rescission or non-application of contractual terms. Good faith is a fundamental principle that underlies the law of contract in general and finds expression in specific rules and principles thereof. Or, as he puts it:
>
> > 'What emerges quite clearly from recent academic writing and from some of the leading cases, is that good faith may be regarded as an ethical value or controlling principle based on community standards of decency and fairness that underlies and informs the substantive law of contract. It finds expression in various technical rules and doctrines, defines their form, content and field of application and provides them with a moral and theoretical foundation. Good faith thus has a creative, a controlling and a legitimating or explanatory function. It is not,

---

47 See also Marxen (n 10) 146 para IV.

48 2002 4 SA 1 (SCA) 15.

49 Hutchison "Non-variation clauses in contract: any escape from the *Shifren* straightjacket?" 2001 *South African Law Journal (SALJ)* 720 743–4 (our footnote).

however, the only value or principle that underlies the law of contract; nor, perhaps, even the most important one.'"[50]

In the same case, in a minority judgment, Olivier JA stated that in recent times

"reasonableness and equity in the form of *bona fides* has become more prominent. It is clear that our law is in a phase of development where *contractual justice* has emerged stronger than ever before as a moral and juridical norm. This tendency will in all probability ... be strengthened by constitutional values."[51]

This dictum was undoubtedly prophetic. As in the *Brisley* case, the battle in subsequent cases was the tension between *pacta sunt servanda* and "[n]otions of fairness, justice and equity, and reasonableness" which, in *Barkhuizen v Napier*,[52] the constitutional court stated "cannot be separated from public policy", which "takes into account the necessity to do simple justice between individuals" and "is informed by the concept of ubuntu".[53] More recently the constitutional court, in dealing with the question whether parties who have undertaken to negotiate with one another were constitutionally obliged to do so in good faith, stated:

"Good faith is a matter of considerable importance in our contract law and the extent to which our courts enforce the good faith requirement in contract law is a matter of considerable public and constitutional importance. The question whether the

---

50 *Brisley* case (n 15). The judgment was written in Afrikaans and the translation is ours. The Afrikaans reads: "Wat die rol van goeie trou betref, stem ons in wese saam met die siening van prof Hutchison ... waarvolgens goeie trou nie 'n onafhanklike, oftewel 'free-floating', basis vir die tersydestelling of die nie-toepassing van kontraktuele bepalings bied nie. Goeie trou is 'n grondbeginsel wat in die algemeen onderliggend is aan die kontraktereg en wat uiting vind in die besondere reëls en beginsels daarvan. Of, soos hy dit ter aangehaalde plaatse stel:"

51 para 25. The translation is ours. The Afrikaans reads: "redelikheid en billikheid in die vorm van die *bona fides* al hoe meer op die voorgrond getree. Dit is duidelik dat ons reg in 'n ontwikkelingsfase is waar *kontraktuele geregtigheid* meer as ooit tevore as 'n morele en juridiese norm van groot belang op die voorgrond tree. Hierdie tendens sal na alle waarskynlikheid ... deur grondwetlike waardes versterk word."

52 2007 5 SA 323 (CC).

53 para 51. "Ubuntu" is a concept derived from (South) African culture and is commonly linked to, or translated as – inter alia – human dignity, humaneness, compassion, personhood and solidarity; see *S v Makwanyane* 1995 3 SA 391 (CC) (paras 307–308, 310, per Mokgoro J); and Malan "The suitability and unsuitability of ubuntu in constitutional law" 2014 *De Jure* 231 231–232. However, in Bennett "Ubuntu: an African equity" 2011 *Potchefstroom Electronic Law Journal (PELJ)* 351 352, such attempts of translation were criticised as that they "cannot convey the many connotations in ubuntu nor, of course, its cultural implications".

spirit, purport and objects of the Constitution require courts to encourage good faith in contractual dealings and whether our Constitution insists that good faith requirements are enforceable should be determined sooner rather than later. Many people enter into contracts daily and every contract has the potential not to be performed in good faith. The issue of good faith in contract touches the lives of many ordinary people in our country."[54]

The dicta in recent South African case law relating to bad faith providing a basis for escaping from the independence of a demand guarantee or letter of credit, must be viewed against the background of this development in the general law of contract. It is suggested that the movement in South African law regarding the position of good faith is well-aligned with the German thinking from which the *Rechtsmissbrauch* doctrine was developed. Terminologically the South African "good faith" relates to the German "*Treu und Glauben*". Growth of the substantive impact of good faith in South African law brings it closer to playing a similar role to that of paragraph 242 of the *BGB* in German law.

Moreover, when considering the material results of cases in South Africa and Germany, an increasing similarity can be detected. The test for fraud employed in recent demand guarantee cases in South Africa focuses on the beneficiary's lack of confidence in its own statement, its own demand, and its own entitlement to the monies called up. This test, it is suggested, may well go wider than traditional notions of fraud in South African law. It could, for example, also include a situation where the beneficiary is well-aware of the illegality of the underlying transaction,[55] or of the fact that the underlying dispute has been completely and finally determined against the beneficiary before payment is demanded[56] – two situations which are recognised manifestations of *Rechtsmissbrauch* in German law.[57]

In conclusion, however, it must be stressed that we are not hereby advocating that a significantly wider inroad into the autonomous or independent

54 *Everfresh Market Virginia (Pty) Ltd v Shoprite Checkers (Pty) Ltd* 2012 1 SA 256 (CC) 264 para 22.

55 *Mahonia Ltd v JP Morgan Chase Bank* 2003 EWHC 1927 (Comm); and *Group Josi Re Co SA v Walbrook Insurance Co Ltd* 1996 1 WLR 1152. Further, see the in-depth discussion in Horowitz (n 3) 173–225.

56 See the discussion of the *Dormell Properties* case (n 21) and *Coface* case (n 23) in Hugo (n 22 *TSAR*) 663–6.

57 BGH 24.04.1958 – II ZR 38/57 – WM 1958, 696 697; Canaris (n 42) paras 1018–1019; Lücke *Das Dokumentenakkreditiv in Deutschland, Frankreich und der Schweiz* (1976) 184–185.

nature of letters of credit and/or demand guarantees can be justified. Certainty of payment of these types of instruments has often been described, with reason, as the "lifeblood of international commerce".[58] Interference with such payment must be kept to a minimum. Where on considerations of public policy, however, it is necessary to intervene, it is our contention that the growing impact of good faith in South African law may lead to the possibility of such interventions in particular instances being based on the absence of good faith instead of trying to force them into the mould of fraud.

58 See Hugo (n 22 *TSAR*) 661, with reference to *RD Harbottle (Mercantile) Ltd v National Westminster Bank Ltd* 1977 2 All ER 862 (QB) 870 and *Edward Owen Engineering Ltd v Barclays Bank International Ltd* 1978 1 All ER 976 (CA) 983.

Bibliography

Bennett TW "Ubuntu: an African equity" 2011 *Potchefstroom Electronic Law Journal (PELJ)* 351.

Bertrams RF *Bank Guarantees in International Trade* (4th Edition, Wolters Kluwer, The Hague 2013).

Blesch G and Lange C *Bankgeschäfte mit Auslandsbezug* (Bank-Verlag, Cologne 2007).

Byrne JE *Standby and Demand Guarantee Practice* (Institute of Banking Law and Practice, Montgomery Village 2014).

Canaris CW *Bankvertragsrecht* (3rd Edition, de Gruyter, Berlin 1988).

Derleder P, Knops KO and Bamberger HG *Handbuch zum deutschen und europäischen Bankrecht* (2nd Edition, Springer, Berlin 2009).

Dunham P "The use and abuse of first demand guarantees in international construction projects" 2008 *The International Construction Law Review (ICLR)* 273.

Ellinger EP and Neo DSS *The Law and Practice of Documentary Letters of Credit* (Hart Publishing, Oxford 2010).

Graf von Westphalen F and Zöchling-Jud B *Die Bankgarantie im internationalen Handelsverkehr* (4th Edition, Deutscher Fachverlag, Frankfurt/Main 2014).

Horowitz D *Letters of Credit and Demand Guarantees* (Oxford University Press, Oxford 2010).

Hugo C "Construction guarantees and the supreme court of appeal (2010–2013)" in Visser C, Pretorius TT and Koekemoer MM (eds) *Essays in Honour of Frans Malan* (LexisNexis, Durban 2014) 159.

Hugo C "Independent guarantees and letters of credit" 2014 *Annual Banking Law Update (ABLU)* 49.

Hugo C "Protecting the lifeblood of commerce: a critical assessment of recent judgments of the South African supreme court of appeal relating to demand guarantees" 2014 *Tydskrif vir die Suid-Afrikaanse Reg (TSAR)* 661.

Hutchison D "Non-variation clauses in contract: any escape from the *Shifren* straight-jacket?" 2001 *(South African Law Journal) SALJ* 720.

International Chamber of Commerce *Uniform Customs and Practice for Docmentary Credits* (ICC Publication 600, Paris, 2007).

International Chamber of Commerce *Uniform Rules on Demand Guarantees* (ICC Publication 758, Paris, 2010).

Jack R, Malek A and Quest D *Documentary Credits* (4th Edition, Tottel Publications, London 2009).

Kelly-Louw M "The doctrine of strict compliance in the context of demand guarantees" 2016 *Comparative & International Law Journal of Southern Africa (CILSA)* 85.

Kelly-Louw M and Marxen K "General update on the law of demand guarantees and letters of credit" 2015 *Annual Banking Law Update (ABLU)* 276.

Kelly-Louw M *Selective Legal Aspects of Bank Demand Guarantees* (VDM Verlag Dr. Müller, Saarbrücken 2009).

Lücke G *Das Dokumentenakkreditiv in Deutschland, Frankreich und der Schweiz* (Dissertation, Kiel 1976).

Lwowski HJ, Fischer G and Langenbucher K *Das Recht der Kreditsicherung* (9th Edition, Verlag Erich Schmidt, Berlin 2011).

Mahler DH *Rechtsmißbrauch und einstweiliger Rechtsschutz bei Dokumentenakkreditiven und "Akkreditiven auf erstes Anfordern"* (Verlag Peter Lang, Frankfurt/Main 1986).

Malan K "The suitability and unsuitability of ubuntu in constitutional law" 2014 *De Jure* 231.

Marxen K "Abstrakte Garantie und Dokumentenakkreditiv in Südafrika" 2015 Internationales Handelsrecht *(IHR)* 137.

Mülbert PO *Mißbrauch von Bankgarantien und einstweiliger Rechtsschutz* (Mohr Siebeck, Tübingen 1985).

Oelofse "Developments in the law of documentary letters of credit" 1997 *Annual Banking Law Update (ABLU)* 1.

Proctor C *The Law and Practice of International Banking* (Oxford University Press, Oxford 2010).

Rüßmann H and Britz J "Die Auswirkung des Grundsatzes der formellen Garantiestrenge auf die Geltenmachung einer befristeten Garantie auf erstes Anfordern" 1995 *Zeitschrift für Wirtschafts- und Bankrecht (WM)* 1825.

Schütze RA and Edelmann H *Bankgarantien* (Bank-Verlag, Cologne 2011).

Wielandt N *Die einseitig verpflichtende Schuldzusage* (Verlag Peter Lang, Frankfurt/Main 2010).

Wood P *International Loans, Bonds, Guarantees, Legal Opinions* (Sweet & Maxwell, London 2007).

Case Law

Germany

BGH 24.4.1958 – II ZR 38/57 – WM 1958, 696.

BGH 12.3.1984 – II ZR 198/82 – BGHZ 90, 287.

BGH 16.3.1987 – II ZR 127/86 – BGHZ 101, 84.

BGH 21.4.1988 – IX ZR 113/87 – NJW 1988, 2610.

BGH 10.10.2000 – XI ZR 344/99 – BGHZ 145, 286.

OLG Saarbrücken 6.7.2001 – 1 U 55/99 – 13, 1 U 55/99 – WM 2001, 2055.

OLG Celle 18.3.2009 – 3 U 167/08 – WM 2009, 1408.

South Africa

Barkhuizen v Napier 2007 5 SA 323 CC

Brisley v Drotsky 2002 4 SA 1 (SCA)

Coface South Africa Insurance Co Ltd v East London Own Haven t/a Own Haven Housing Association 2014 1 All SA 536 (SCA)

Dormell Properties 282 CC v Renasa Insurance Company Ltd 2011 1 SA 70 (SCA)

Everfresh Market Virginia (Pty) Ltd v Shoprite Checkers (Pty) Ltd 2012 1 SA 256 (CC)

Firstrand Bank Ltd v Brera Investments CC 2013 5 SA 556 (SCA)

Group Five Construction Ltd v Member of the Executive Council for Public Transport Roads and Works Gauteng 2015 2 All SA 716 (GJ)

Guardrisk Insurance Company Ltd v Kentz (Pty) Ltd 2014 1 All SA 307 (SCA)

Lombard Insurance Co Ltd v Landmark Holdings (Pty) Ltd 2010 2 SA 86 (SCA)

Loomcraft Fabrics CC v Nedbank Ltd 1996 1 SA 812 (A)

Phillips v Standard Bank of South Africa Ltd 1985 3 SA 301 (W)

S v Makwanyane 1995 (3) SA 391 (CC)

Sapan Trading (Pty) Ltd, Ex Parte 1995 1 SA 218 (W)

Scatec Solar SA 163 Ltd v Terrafix Suedafrika Ltd 2014 ZAWCHC 63 (25 April 2014)

Sulzer Pumps (South Africa) (Proprietary) Limited v Covec-MC Joint Venture 2014 ZAGPPHC (2 September 2014)

Union Carriage and Wagon Company Ltd v Nedcor Bank Ltd 1996 CLR 724 (W)

United Kingdom

Cargill International SA and Another v Bangladesh Sugar and Food Industries Corp 1996 4 All ER 563 (QBD).

Edward Owen Engineering Ltd v Barclays Bank International Ltd 1978 1 All ER 976 (CA).

Group Josi Re Co SA v Walbrook Insurance Co Ltd 1996 1 WLR 1152.

Mahonia Ltd v JP Morgan Chase Bank 2003 EWHC 1927 (Comm).

RD Harbottle (Mercantile) Ltd v National Westminster Bank Ltd 1977 2 All ER 862 (QB).

Lessons to be learnt from Germany regarding the treatment of executory contracts when a debtor company is being restructured: a South African perspective

*Juanitta Calitz**
*Sanrie Lawrenson***

* Associate Professor, University of Johannesburg.
** Lecturer, University of Johannesburg.

> "Efficient, reliable and transparent creditor rights and insolvency systems are of key importance for the reallocation of productive resources in the corporate sector, for investor confidence and forward-looking corporate restructuring. These systems also play a pivotal role in times of crisis to enable a country and stakeholders to promptly respond to and resolve matters of corporate financial distress on systemic scales."[1]

I. Introduction

The recent global economic crisis has emphasised the need for countries to have an effective and sound corporate-rescue framework. Restructuring proceedings play an important role in the economic well-being of a country and its society, as it aims, amongst other things, to trade a company back to a solvent status in order to enable a company to continue with its operations.[2]

---

1 The World Bank *Principles for Effective Insolvency and Creditor Rights Systems* (revised 2015) available at http://siteresources.worldbank.org/EXTGILD/Resources/5807554-1357753926066/2015_Revised_ICR_Principles(3).pdf (15-09-2017).

2 For ease of reference, it should be noted that in practice "restructuring" and "reorganisation" are used rather interchangeably. "Restructuring" often simply means the restructuring of liabilities – financial rather than operational changes – and "reorganisation" often refers to the operational changes of the company itself. In German there is an umbrella term for both – *Sanierung*. (Bork *Rescuing Companies in England and Germany* (2012) 19). For consistency, this paper will make us of the term "restructuring".

At a time when a company is placed under or initiates restructuring proceedings, chances are that the company is party to a contract in terms whereof performance by either the company itself, or the counterparty, or both, it still outstanding. This is known as an executory contract, which is described as a contract under which "one or the other, or all the obligations remain unfulfilled".[3] In practice the term tends to be reserved for contracts under which the debtor has one or more unperformed obligations under a contract that is not usually terminated by bankruptcy or insolvency (or restructuring) while reciprocal obligations of the other contract party may or may not be outstanding.[4] International best practice as indicated in the *UNCITRAL Legislative Guide on Insolvency Law* also notes that:

> "Achieving the objectives of maximizing the value of the estate and reducing liabilities and, in reorganization, enabling the debtor to survive and continue its affairs to the maximum extent possible in an uninterrupted manner may involve taking advantage of those contracts which are beneficial and contribute value to the estate (including contracts that will enable the continued use of crucial property that may be owned by a third party) and rejecting those which are burdensome or those where the ongoing costs of performance exceed the benefit to be derived from the contract."[5]

Due to the important role of contracts in the commercial sphere, it is imperative that legal certainty be had in relation to the treatment of executory contracts when a debtor company is placed under restructuring. Paulus and Berberich that

> "[a] living business is entangled in a web of contracts with varying significance; for instance, ordinary sales contracts seen as a whole may sustain a significant customer base, but regarded individually may not be crucial in making the choice between shutting down or continuing a business. Yet other contracts, such as rental, leasing or licensing contracts, may be indispensable for the use of important production

---

3 *Nedcor Investment Bank v Pretoria Belgrave Hotel (Pty) Ltd* 2003 5 SA 189 (SCA) 192, which sets out the South African position. The German position in this regard is slightly more complex. See the discussion in para 3.2 below.

4 Van der Linde "National report for South Africa" in Faber, Vermunt, Kilborn and Van der Linde (eds) *Treatment of Contracts in Insolvency* (2013) 365, which sets out the South African position. For a full discussion on the treatment of contracts in insolvency under South African law, see chapter 14. The German position in this regard is slightly more complex. See the discussion in para III.2 below.

5 *UNCITRAL Legislative Guide on Insolvency Law* (2005) available at http://www.uncitral.org/pdf/english/texts/insolven/05-80722_Ebook.pdf (15-09-2017).

assets, and therefore may be of the utmost importance for any restructuring efforts."[6]

In what follows the South African case of *Cloete Murray NO v FirstRand Bank Ltd*[7] and some cases which followed afterwards, as well as a discussion on the enforceability of *ipso facto* cancellation clauses (termination and acceleration clauses) will be employed as point of reference to illustrate the position of a creditor in relation to uncompleted or executory contracts of a company placed under restructuring proceedings.

II. A South African perspective

1. General overview of business rescue

The Companies Act[8] was enacted in May 2011 and introduced the corporate restructuring system of business rescue into South African law, thereby replacing the judicial management system found under the previous Companies Act.[9] The preamble to the Companies Act defines its purpose as, *inter alia*, "to provide for efficient rescue of financially distressed companies" and also mentions that one of the main purposes of the Companies Act is to, among other things, provide for this efficient rescue and recovery in a manner that balances the rights and interests of all relevant stakeholders.[10] The business-rescue regime represents a significant deviation from the previously creditor-friendly regime as the provisions now explicitly attempt to balance the rights and interests of all interested parties within the company's sphere.[11]

6 Paulus and Berberich "National Report for Germany" in Faber et al (n 4) 199 199–200..

7 2015 3 SA 438 (SCA).

8 Companies Act 71 of 2008.

9 Companies Act 61 of 1973. South Africa was one of the first countries actually to introduce a business rescue regime in the form of judicial management. See Rajak and Henning "Business Rescue for South Africa" 1999 *South African Law Journal (SALJ)* 262.

10 Companies Act (n 8) sec 7(k).

11 *African Banking Corporation of Botswana v Kariba Furniture Manufacturers* 2015 SA 192 (SCA) para 42.

Business-rescue is the primary formal restructuring procedure available means to restructure a corporate entity under South African law.[12] The procedure is intended to facilitate the rehabilitation of a distressed company and has as affect, *inter alia*, a general moratorium on legal proceedings, including enforcement action, against the company under business rescue.[13] As business-rescue proceedings are still relatively new in South African law there has been some uncertainty regarding the interpretation of some of the provisions concerned, which can mainly be attributed to the fact that key concepts and terms have not been adequately defined.[14] This uncertainty has extended to the provisions dealing with the rights of a creditor and the role of the business-rescue practitioner,[15] *inter alia*, in relation to uncompleted or executory contracts. This position is unlike the position under general insolvency proceedings where the rights of a creditor and the role of the liquidator have over the years been well established *via* common law principles, statutory provisions and precedent.[16]

The Companies Act defines business rescue as follows:

> "...proceedings to facilitate the rehabilitation of a company that is financially distressed by providing for-
>
> (i) the temporary supervision of the company, and of the management of its affairs, business and property;
>
> (ii) a temporary moratorium on the rights of claimants against the company or in respect of property in its possession; and

---

12 Compare this to the German position discussed in para III.1 below, where the restructuring of a debtor company may be initiated in one of three ways. The compromise mechanism, contained in sec 155 of Companies Act (n 8) allows for a company to propose a compromise or arrangement to its creditors.

13 Companies Act (n 8) sec 133. See *Cloete Murray NNO v FirstRand Bank Ltd t/a Wesbank* 2015 3 SA 438 (SCA) para 28–33 for a discussion of the concept of the moratorium.

14 Prins *Priority issues in business rescue* (2015, LLM dissertation, UCT) 3. See in this regard also Bradstreet "The new business rescue: will creditors sink or swim?" 2011 *South African Law Journal (SALJ)* 352, and "The leak in the lifeboat: inadequate regulation of business rescue practitioners may adversely affect lenders' willingness and the growth of the economy" 2010 *South African Mercantile Law Journal (SA Merc LJ)* 195. Also see *African Banking Corporation of Botswana v Kariba Furniture Manufacturers* 2015 5 SA 192 (SCA) para 43 and *Panamo Properties (Pty) Ltd v Nel* 2015 5 SA 63 (SCA) para 1 in this regard.

15 For the role of the business rescue practitioner, see para II.2 below.

16 Van der Linde (n 4) 365.

(iii) the development and implementation, if approved, or a plan to rescue the company by restructuring its affairs, business, property, debt and other liabilities, and equity in a manner that maximizes the likelihood of the company continuing in existence on a solvent basis or, if it is not possible for the company to so continue in existence, results in a better return for the company's creditors or shareholders than would result from the immediate liquidation of the company…"[17]

With regard to the definition and interpretation of the concept of "business rescue" the courts have likewise stated that:

> "Business rescue, as the definition proclaims or explains, is a regime which is largely self-administered by the company, under independent supervision within the constraints set out in Chapter 6 of the Act, and subject to court intervention at any time on application by any of its stakeholders. This is an important difference or aspect that differentiate [sic] business rescue from its counterpart in the old Companies Act, 1973, namely, judicial management. Business rescue is geared at saving significant costs, thus among others enabling financially distressed small (and big) companies to opt for it as a viable alternative to "*last resort*" liquidation."[18]

Once a company is placed under business rescue, the Companies Act provides for the appointment of a business-rescue practitioner to oversee the business-rescue proceedings.[19] The company is placed under the temporary supervision of the business-rescue practitioner, and the business-rescue practitioner has full management control of the company in substitution for its board and pre-existing management.[20]

17 Companies Act (n 8) sec 128(b).

18 *Merchant West Working Capital Solutions (Pty) Ltd v Advanced Technologies and Engineering Company (Pty) Ltd* (13/12406) 2013 ZAGPJHC 109 (10 May 2013) para 3.

19 Companies Act (n 8) sec 129(3)*(b)* or sec 131(5), depending on whether the company was placed under voluntary business rescue or compulsory business rescue.

20 Companies Act (n 8) sec 140. Compare this to the German position under standard insolvency and insolvency-plan proceedings discussed in paras III.1.a) and III.1.b) below, as well as to debtor-in-possession proceedings discussed in para III.1.c) below.

2. Provisions of the Companies Act relating to executory contracts

Executory contracts are not automatically terminated upon the commencement of business-rescue proceedings.[21] Insolvency legislation makes specific provision for, and sets out the treatment of, certain classes of executory contracts (specifically employment contracts,[22] transactions on exchanges[23] and market agreements on informal markets[24]), and there is no legal uncertainty in this regard.[25]

The Companies Act provides for the following rights of the business-rescue practitioner as a general rule in relation to executory contracts:

> "...despite any provision of an agreement to the contrary, during business rescue proceedings, the practitioner may –
> (a) entirely, partially or conditionally suspend, for the duration of the business recue proceedings, any obligation of the company that –
> (i) arises under an agreement to which the company was a party at the commencement of the business rescue proceedings; and
> (ii) would otherwise become due during those proceedings; or
> (b) apply urgently to a court to entirely, partially or conditionally cancel, on any terms that are just and reasonable under the circumstances, any obligation of the company contemplated in paragraph (a)."[26]

Subsections (a) and (b) of section 136(2) of the Companies Act respectively grant a discretion to the business-rescue practitioner to *suspend* an executory contract and requires a court order should the business-rescue practitioner wish to *cancel* an executory contract. It is clear from the aforementioned that the business-rescue practitioner has no power to cancel any executory contract to which the debtor company is a party without obtaining a court order in this regard.

The business-rescue practitioner may not, however, suspend employment contracts, transactions on exchanges and market agreements on informal markets.[27]

---

21 Van der Linde (n 4) 371. Compare this to the German position discussed in para III.2 below.
22 Companies Act (n 8) sec 136.
23 Insolvency Act 24 of 1936 sec 35A.
24 Insolvency Act 24 of 1936 sec 35B.
25 Under South African law insolvency is dealt with in the Insolvency Act 24 of 1936 and business rescue is dealt with in the Companies Act 71 of 2008.
26 Companies Act (n 8) sec 136(2)*(a)* and *(b)*.
27 See the discussion above.

The business-rescue practitioner need not obtain the instructions of creditors prior to suspending obligations, but it is imperative that the business-rescue practitioner takes a stand in relation to all executory contracts to which the company is a party, as part B of the business-rescue plan[28] requires the business-rescue practitioner to include information on the treatment of any existing contracts to which the company is a party.[29]

3. The rights of a creditor of the company under business rescue in relation to the cancellation of executory contracts and *ipso facto* clauses

The Companies Act only makes provision for the right of the business-rescue practitioner to cancel an executory contract (which cancellation may only be done by way of a court order),[30] but makes no reference to any such rights afforded to a creditor, and therefore the question as to the rights of a creditor to an executory contract has arisen.[31] To date there have only been a few judgments handed down which deal with the rights of creditors in the context of executory contracts.

In *178 Stamfordhill CC v Velvet Star Entertainment CC*[32] the court held that in the case of an executory lease agreement a landlord would be able rightfully to cancel the lease during business rescue and to seek the ejectment of the tenant where the tenant did not honour its obligations in terms of the lease incurred prior to commencement of the business rescue. The court also held that the position of the business-rescue practitioner *vis-à-vis* the contract is similar to that of a liquidator of a company in liquidation or a trustee in insolvency and he would therefore be obliged to perform whatever is required of the company including unfulfilled past obligations.[33]

---

28 A business-rescue plan is compulsory under business-rescue proceedings. Compare this to the German position relating to the standard insolvency procedure discussed in para III.1.a) below.

29 Companies Act (n 8) sec 150(2)*(b)*(iii).

30 Companies Act (n 8) sec 136(2)*(b)*.

31 The court only, and not the business-rescue practitioner, is empowered to consent to the enforcement against a company of claims based on guarantees and suretyships. See *Investec Bank Ltd v Bruyns* 2012 5 SA 430 WCC.

32 (1506/15) 2015 ZAKZDHC 34 (1 April 2015).

33 In para 27 of the judgment the court held that the lease survives the *concursus creditorum* and the rights and obligations of both parties to the contract remain in existence, and insofar as the obligations of the insolvent in terms of the contract are concerned; the trustee steps into the insolvent's shoes. The trustee is obliged to

The court has thus drawn a clear analogy between the position of a creditor of a company under liquidation and in the case of business-rescue proceedings. As such the basic common-law principle that specific performance will not be ordered against an insolvent estate, and should the liquidator of a company refuse to render performance under an uncompleted contract, the other party will have merely a concurrent claim for damages based on breach of contract as well as the right to cancellation for breach of contract, would also apply to the business-rescue scenario.[34] With regard to the position of the liquidator the court held in *Ellerine Brothers (Pty) Ltd v McCarthy Ltd*[35] that at commencement of insolvency proceedings, the liquidator in office will take over all uncompleted contracts, including leases, in their entirety. The creation of the *concursus creditorum* does not terminate the continuous operation of a lease to which the insolvent was a party but rather the liquidator, as the universal successor, steps into the shoes of the insolvent and must, on its election to abide by such contract, perform whatever is required of the insolvent in terms of the agreement.[36] In *Goodricke & Son v Auto Protection Insurance Co Ltd*[37] the court also held:

> "that a trustee who elects to abide by an executory contract entered into prior to insolvency cannot demand performance of any remaining obligations under the contract from the other party unless the trustee is prepared to perform in full and tenders complete performance of all the insolvent's obligations, including unfulfilled past ones, under the contract."[38]

---

perform whatever is required of the insolvent in terms of the contract, including unfulfilled past obligations of the insolvent. The contract is neither terminated nor modified nor in any way altered by the insolvency of one of the parties, except in one respect, and that is because of the supervening *concursus creditorum* the trustee cannot be compelled by the other party to perform the contract. See also *Ellerine Brothers (Pty) Ltd v McCarthy Ltd* 2014 4 SA 22 (SCA).

34 Loubser *Some Comparative Aspects of Corporate Rescue in South African Company Law* (2010 thesis University of South Africa) 89; see also Bertelsmann et al *Mars – The Law of Insolvency in South Africa* (2008) 222. Van der Linde submits that business-rescue proceedings do not establish a *concursus creditorum* and is of the opinion that specific performance can be ordered against the company under business rescue (see Van der Linde (n 4) 367 and 373).

35 2014 4 SA 22 (SCA).

36 para 13 of the judgment (n 35).

37 1968 1 SA 717 (A).

38 723G–H. See *Thomas Construction (Pty) Ltd (in liquidation) v Grafton Furniture Manufacturers (Pty) Ltd* 1988 2 SA 546 (A). See also *De Wet NO v Uys* 1998 4 SA 694 (T) as discussed in O'Brien "Cancellation, restitution and forfeiture

a) The moratorium

In order to be able to organise the restructuring (including developing a business-rescue plan), the company needs protection from its creditors made nervous by the crisis in which the company finds itself.[39] Kloppers also aptly described the moratorium as the "cornerstone of all business rescue procedures".[40]

The Companies Act provides that:

> "[d]uring business rescue proceedings, no legal proceeding, including enforcement action, against the company, or in relation to any property belonging to the company, or lawfully in its possession, may be commenced or proceeded with in any forum, except –
> (a) with the written consent of the practitioner;
> (b) with the leave of the court and in accordance with any terms the court considers suitable…".[41]

Once the company is placed under business rescue, the section 133 of the Companies Act moratorium takes immediate effect, and there is an automatic and general moratorium (or stay) on legal proceedings or executions against the company, its property, its assets and on the exercise of the rights of creditors of the company.[42]

Although no definition of the terms "legal proceeding" or "enforcement action" is provided in the Companies Act, it is clear that the main objective of the provision is to cover as wide a range as possible in order to include

against the background of section 35 of the Insolvency Act" 1999 (3) *Tydskrif vir die Suid-Afrikaanse Reg (TSAR)* 534.

39 Bork *Rescuing Companies in England and Germany* (2012) 38.

40 Kloppers "Judicial management – a corporate rescue mechanism in need of reform?" 1999 *Stellenbosch Law Review (Stellenbosch L Rev)* 417 429. Also see *Booysen v Jonkheer Boerewynmakery (Pty) Ltd (in business rescue)* 2017 1 All SA 862 (WCC) para 49 in this regard.

41 sec 133(1)*(a)* and *(b)*.

42 Cassim et al *Contemporary Company Law* (2012) 878. Compare this to the German position discussed in para 3.3.4 below, where there is no automatic moratorium upon the filing of insolvency proceedings, but only upon opening of insolvency proceedings. Under protective-shield proceedings the moratorium is also not *ex lege*. See also *Investec Bank Ltd v Bruyns* 2012 5 SA 430 (WCC) paras 17–22.

any conceivable type of action against the company.[43] In *Chetty v Hart*[44] the court confirmed:

> "To conclude this analysis, the phrase legal proceeding may, depending on the context within which it is used, be interpreted restrictively, to mean court proceedings or more broadly, to include proceedings before other tribunals including arbitral tribunals. The language employed in s 133(1) itself suggests that a broader interpretation commends itself, an approach with which academic commentators concur. ... And finally, the purpose of the provision, which is to give breathing space to the practitioner to get the company's financial affairs in order, also requires it to be construed widely because arbitrations, like court proceedings also involve diversion of resources – both time and money – that may hinder the effectiveness of business rescue proceedings. To construe it narrowly, as the court *a quo* did, and as the respondent contends we should, would be at odds with its language, defeat its purpose and lead to insensible and impractical consequences."[45]

b) Case discussions on the right of a creditor to cancel an executory contract

There has been some debate as to whether the moratorium imposed by section 133 of the Companies Act aims to preclude the cancellation of an executory contract by a creditor, and the courts have been tasked with deciding whether the cancellation of an executory contract by a creditor, after a debtor company has been placed under business rescue, amounts to "legal proceeding" or "enforcement action", as provided for in section 133(1).[46] After three high court judgments (one on appeal to a full bench), the Supreme Court of Appeal has provided clarity on this matter in the recent case of *Cloete Murray NNO v FirstRand Bank Limited t/a Wesbank*.[47] In this matter the relevant facts included that the debtor company was already in

---

43 *Blue Star Holdings (Pty) Ltd v West Coast Oyster Growers CC* 2013 6 SA 540 (WCC) para 14; Delport et al *Henochsberg on the Companies Act 71 of 2008* (loose-leaf publication).

44 (20323/2014) 2015 ZASCA 112 (4 September 2015).

45 para 35 of the judgment (n 44).

46 In *LA Sport 4x4 Outdoor CC v Broadsword Trading 20 (Pty) Ltd* 2013 JDR 1215 (GNP) the court held that the cancellation of an agreement during business rescue constituted legal process, which falls under the moratorium in section 133(1). The judgment was later overturned on appeal in *LA Sport 4x4 Outdoor CC v Broadsword Trading 20 (Pty) Ltd* (A513/2013) 2015 ZAGPPHC 78 (26 February 2015) and it was confirmed that section 133(1) does not limit the performance of juristic acts and that a cancellation is therefore valid.

47 2015 3 SA 438 (SCA).

breach of the executory contract with its creditor in question at the time that the creditor purported to cancel the executory contract.[48] The Supreme Court of Appeal held that the Companies Act does not provide definitions for "legal proceeding" or "enforcement action", but that the term "legal proceeding" is well-known in South-African law and usually means a lawsuit, and not the cancellation of an agreement.[49] Therefore, cancellation of an executory contract by a creditor does not resort under "enforcement action" or "legal proceedings" as per the wording of the section 133 moratorium, and such a cancellation will indeed be valid. Following the decision in the *Cloete*[50] case, various divisions of the high court have now handed down judgements relating to cancellation, and some of these jedgments will be briefly dicussed below with reference to the *Cloete* case.

Suspension of an agreement[51] has as effect that obligations will not become due and enforceable until the cessation of business-rescue proceedings, and as a result no contractual stipulations based on default by the debtor company in respect of the suspended obligations will take effect. Contract terms rendered ineffective would include, among others, cancellation.[52] In the recent judgment of *BP Southern Africa (Pty) Ltd v Intertrans Oil SA (Pty) Ltd*[53] the court held that the remedy of cancellation will, however, be at the disposal of a creditor under such circumstances where the business rescue practitioner still expected the creditor to perform its reciprocal obligations even though the company's obligations (under business rescue) had been suspended.

---

48 para 3 of the judgment (n 47). In a subsequent case of *Schickerling NO v Chickenland (Pty) Ltd t/a Nando's* (22712/2016) 2016 ZAGPPHC 208 (15 April 2016) the court held that breach of an executory contract that took place after the commencement of business rescue proceedings still entitled the creditor to the right of cancellation.

49 para 31 of the judgment (n 47). Also see *Van Zyl v Euodia Trust (Edms) Bpk* 1983 3 SA 394 (T) 399C–D.

50 (n 47) above.

51 For the right of the business rescue practitioner to suspend obligations, see the discussion in para 2.2 above.

52 *Kythera Court v Le Rendez-Vous Cafē CC T/A Newscafe Bedfordview (in Business Rescue)* 2016 6 SA 63 (GJ) para 15. Also see Van der Linde (n 4) 375.

53 (34716/2016) 2016 ZAGPJHC 310 (25 November 2016) para 40.

Further, in *Kythera Court v Le Rendez-Vous Cafē CC T/A Newscafe Bedfordview (in Business Rescue)*[54] the court held that should the debtor company fail to perform under an unsuspended obligation, the creditor counterparty will be able to rely on the general remedies for breach of contract and invoke any contractually stipulated remedies (including cancellation of the contract in question). Upon the suspension or cancellation of an executory contract by the business-rescue practitioner as per section 136(2)*(a)* and *(b)* of the Companies Act, the creditor's only right of recourse is a claim for damages.[55]

Although the *Cloete*[56] case brought about certainty with regard to whether a creditor may cancel an agreement with a company in business rescue, Van der Linde is of the opinion that some of the court's *obiter* remarks must be read with caution.[57] In response to the liquidators' argument that the cancellation of contracts would result in the inevitable demise of the company in business rescue, the court referred to certain safeguards in that by invoking the right in section 136(2)*(a)* of the Companies Act to suspend the company's obligations under a contract, the practitioner could prevent a creditor from instituting action and repossessing or attaching property.[58] In the *BP Southern Africa*[59] case the high court, however, held that the company under business rescue will only be safe from such action and repossession or attachment as long as the company continues to perform, as suspension of obligations in terms of section 136(2)*(a)* and *(b)* of the Companies Act entitles the creditor to withhold performance and even cancel the

54 2016 6 SA 63 (GJ). Also see Van der Linde (n 4) 373, *Cloete Murray NNO v FirstRand Bank Limited t/a Wesbank* 2015 3 SA 438 (SCA) (n 47) and *BP Southern Africa (Pty) Ltd v Intertrans Oil SA (Pty) Ltd* (34716/2016) 2016 ZAGPJHC 310 (25 November 2016) in this regard.

55 Companies Act (n 8) sec 136(3).

56 (n 47) above.

57 See discussion by Van der Linde "An overview of recent company law cases: a mixed bag of emerging clarity, lingering doubt and deepening confusion" 2015 *Annual Banking Law Update (ABLU)* 60.

58 para 35 of the judgment (n 47). Also see para 39. Also see *Kythera Court v Le Rendez-Vous Cafē CC T/A Newscafe Bedfordview (in Business Rescue)* 2016 6 SA 63 (GJ) para 15; *Southern Value Consortium v Tresso Trading 102 (Pty) Ltd* 2016 6 SA 501 (WCC) and *JVJ Logistics (Pty) Ltd v Standard Bank of South Africa Ltd* 2016 6 SA 448 (KZD) in this regard.

59 (n 53) above at paras 40 and 56.

contract in question.[60] Van der Linde also mentions that as such a suspension can relate only to the obligations becoming due during business-rescue proceedings; it will not prevent a creditor from cancelling on the basis of pre-commencement breaches. Suspension of the company's obligations also cannot force the other contract party to continue performing under a contract with continuing or periodic obligations.[61] The court in the *BP Southern Africa*[62] case also held that a creditor may elect to equally suspend its reciprocal obligations once the business rescue practitioner had suspended the company's obligations in terms of section136(2)*(a)* and *(b)* of the Companies Act. The court held that the creditor was therefore entitled to withhold performance under these circumstances, and even cancel the contract in question.[63]

The conclusion of this judgment is therefore that a creditor can lawfully cancel a contract concluded with a company prior to the company being placed under business rescue proceedings. What is also quite significant about this case is that the court emphasised that the aim of the legislation has always been to allow the company in distress the necessary breathing space by placing a moratorium on legal proceedings and enforcement action in any forum, but confirmed that the motive was not to interfere with the contractual rights and obligations of the parties to an agreement.[64] As emphasised by Rushworth the wording of section 133(3) of the Companies Act is on par with the general principle of a temporary moratorium on the rights of a creditor to institute claims, rather than a greater restriction on creditors' rights.[65]

---

60 See the discussion of the relevant principle of this case in para II.3.b) below.

61 para 35 of the judgment (n 47). Also see para 39.

62 (n 53) above at para 40.

63 See the discussion in para II.3.b) above.

64 para 40 of the judgment (n 47). Also see *Kythera Court v Le Rendez-Vous Cafẽ CC T/A Newscafe Bedfordview (in Business Rescue)* 2016 6 SA 63 (GJ) and *BP Southern Africa (Pty) Ltd v Intertrans Oil SA (Pty) Ltd* (34716/2016) 2016 ZAGPJHC 310 (25 November 2016) in this regard.

65 Rushworth "A critical analysis of the business rescue regime in the Companies Act 71 of 2008" 2010 *Acta Juridica* 375 384.

c) *Ipso facto* cancellation clauses

Under liquidation proceedings, the rules relating to *ipso facto* clauses have been well established, and such clauses are not effective as they deprive the liquidator of the election right to continue with the executory contract in question.[66] Section 37(5) of the Insolvency Act[67] strengthens this position by providing that a "stipulation in a lease that the lease shall terminate or be varied upon the sequestration of the estate of either party shall be null and void". A further consideration in this regard is that only a completed accrued right of cancellation can survive the *concursus creditorum*.[68]

Under business-rescue proceedings, in contrast to insolvency proceedings, there is no establishment of a *concursus creditorum*[69] and consequently contractual remedies stipulated by the parties will in principle be enforceable during business-rescue proceeding[70] – subject only to the general moratorium and the possibility of suspension or cancellation of a company's unperformed obligations.[71] In *BP Southern Africa (Pty) Ltd v Intertrans Oil SA (Pty) Ltd and Others*[72] the court held that a creditor has available "the residual Law of Contract" in a scenario where a section is silent on its effect on a contractual obligation, as the legislature is aware of such "residual Law of Contract". The enforcement of such *ipso facto* clauses under business rescue proceedings has, however, not yet been tested by the South African courts, but there have been some recent judgments from which, based on *obiter* remarks, the conclusion may be drawn that such clauses will be enforceable under business rescue.[73]

66 *Bryant & Flanagan (Pty) Ltd v Muller and Another NNO* 1978 2 SA 807 (A) at 812 to 813.
67 Insolvency Act 24 of 1936.
68 *Roering NNO v Nedbank Ltd* 2013 3 SA 160 (GSJ) para 7.
69 See the discussion on the opinion of Van der Linde in n 34 above.
70 Faber (n 4) 399.
71 See the discussion in paras II.2. and II.3.a) above.
72 (34716/2016) [2016] ZAGPJHC 310 (25 November 2016) para 38.
73 See *Homez Trailers and Bodies (Pty) Ltd v Standard Bank of South Africa Ltd* (35201/2013) 2013 ZAGPPHC 465 (27 September 2013) and *Firstrand Bank Ltd v Singh* (4273/2012) 2015 ZAGPJHC 279 (30 October 2015) in this regard. Compare this to the German position discussed in para III.3.c) below.

III. A German perspective

1. General overview of restructuring in terms of the *Insolvenzordnung*

Apart from out-of-court debt restructuring to avert insolvency (often undertaken in terms of German company law),[74] German insolvency law does not provide for a general restructuring scheme or other mechanisms without formal insolvency proceedings.[75] For the purpose of this paper only restructuring within the context of insolvency proceedings shall be discussed, as it is the only form of restructuring that deals with the relationship between a debtor and a creditor.[76]

German insolvency law is regulated by the comprehensive Insolvency Code (*Insolvenzordnung*) (InsO) which came into force on 1 January 1999 and replaced the Bankruptcy Code (*Konkursordnung*) (KO), the Settlement Statute (*Vergleichsordnung*) (VerglO) (in the West German States) and the Act on Collective Enforcement (*Gesamtvollstreckungsordnung*) (GesO) (in the East German States). The Insolvency Code was amended on 1 March 2012 by the Act for Further Facilitation of the Restructuring of Companies (*Gesetz zur weiteren Erleichterung der Sanierung vor Unternehmen*) (ESUG), and introduced two new proceedings at a pre-insolvency stage.[77] The aim of this amendment was to improve restructuring and recapitalisation opportunities and thereby bring Germany's legislation broadly in line with other jurisdictions,[78] and further to make insolvency proceedings in

74 Bork (n 39) 46.

75 See Gantenberg's jurisdictional comparison of German law in Henrot, Borch, Petersen and Varrenti (eds) *Debt Restructuring: an alternative to insolvency proceedings (jurisdictional comparisons)* (2014) 91. Also see Paulus and Berberich (n 6) 235.

76 Bork (n 39) 47.

77 Hess, Oberhammer and Pfeiffer *European Insolvency Law: Heidelberg-Luxembourg-Vienna Report* (2014) 36.

78 To bring Germany's insolvency legislation in line with other jurisdictions, InsO had already at the time of its adoption included some provisions similar to Chapter 11 of the Bankruptcy Code of the United States of America. See Ehlers "Statutory Corporate Rescue Proceedings in Germany: The *Insolvenzplan* Procedure" in Broc and Parry (eds) *Corporate Rescue: An Overview of Recent Developments* (2006) 151 161. Also see para III.1.b) below.

Germany more predictable and introduce a "rescue culture"[79] by significantly promoting debtor-in-possession proceedings.[80]

In terms of the Insolvency Code, the restructuring of a debtor company under German law may take one of three forms:

- standard insolvency procedure with the appointment of a preliminary and final insolvency administrator; or
- insolvency plan (*Insolvenzplan*) and insolvency plan proceedings (*Insolvenzplanverfahren*) with the appointment of a preliminary and final insolvency administrator;[81] or
- debtor-in-possession proceedings (*Eigenverwaltung*) with the appointment of a preliminary and final insolvency trustee.[82]

The above procedures are divided into preliminary and final insolvency proceedings – preliminary insolvency proceedings being commenced upon the filing of an insolvency petition, and final insolvency proceedings upon the opening thereof by a competent insolvency court.[83]

a) Standard insolvency procedure

When making use of the standard insolvency procedure, the court appoints a preliminary insolvency administrator to evaluate the chances of a successful restructuring as early as the insolvency filing stage, and the preliminary insolvency administrator may also initiate restructuring measures at this

79 Ehlers (n 78) 185 sets out that it became apparent that law reform in Germany had been necessary not even long after InsO had been adopted. Also see Wolf A "Sense of Modesty: Germany's Progress towards Corporate Rescue" (2016) 4(2) *Nottingham Insolvency and Business Law eJournal (NIBLeJ)* 163 166, 171 and 173.

80 Gantenberg (n 78) 93 and Wolf (n 79). Debtor-in-possession proceedings are discussed in para III(1)(c) below.

81 sec 217 InsO.

82 secs 270 et seqq InsO.

83 The aim of debtor-in-possession proceedings is, however, to not proceed to the final insolvency proceedings stage. See the discussion in para III.1.b) below. Further, in order to avoid confusion as to the type of insolvency practitioner appointed, and for ease of reference when referring to certain principles in general, this paper refers to the "office holder", which term will refer to either the preliminary or final insolvency administrator, or the preliminary or final insolvency trustee, depending on the type of restructuring procedure initiated and the stage of such restructuring procedure.

early stage. This procedure is more commonly used when dealing with natural rather than juristic persons.[84]

Under this type of proceedings the management of the company is replaced by the insolvency administrator,[85] and the filing of an insolvency plan is not a prerequisite.

b) Insolvency-plan proceedings (*Insolvenzplanverfahren*)

Insolvency plan (*Insolvenzplan*) and insolvency-plan proceedings (*Insolvenzplanverfahren*)[86] aim at preserving the business of the debtor company as a going concern[87] and may be initiated if the economic evaluation of the debtor's business leads to the conclusion that it can if fact be restructured.[88] The insolvency-plan proceedings are mainly based on Chapter 11 of the Bankruptcy Code of the United States of America.[89]

Insolvency-plan proceedings include the preparing and filing of an insolvency plan, which may be initiated by the debtor company, the insolvency administrator or the creditors.[90] Such an insolvency plan may take various forms, depending on the restructuring needs of the debtor company.

c) Debtor-in-possession proceedings (*Eigenverwaltung*)

Additional protection available to a debtor company wanting to make use of insolvency-plan proceedings is to combine an early filing for insolvency with a motion for the ordering of debtor-in-possession proceedings[91] (also known as personal management or self-administration) (*Eigenverwaltung*).[92] Under these circumstances the insolvency court may, upon the application of the debtor company indicating that (i) it is over-indebted but

84 Bork (n 39) 48.
85 This is similar to the provisions under South African law relating to the business-rescue practitioner. See para II.2. above.
86 sec 217 InsO.
87 sec 1 InsO.
88 Ehlers (n 78) 164.
89 Lobo *World Insolvency Systems: A Comparative Study* (2009) 319. Also see Ehlers (n 78) in this regard.
90 sec 218 InsO.
91 secs 270 et seqq InsO.
92 Hess (n 77).

not insolvent and (ii) that the envisaged restructuring has prospects of success, order a stay on individual enforcement measures against the debtor company[93] known as protective-shield proceedings (*Schutzschirmverfahren*),[94] which proceedings may not be in excess of three months. Under the protection of the protective shield proceedings, the debtor company may prepare for the restructuring and prepare an insolvency plan, in order for it to be executed speedily upon the opening of insolvency proceedings.[95]

Under debtor-in-possession proceedings, there is no appointment of an insolvency administrator, and the debtor company remains in control of its business and of the restructuring process, albeit under the supervision of a court officer (*Sachverwalter*).[96] German courts have in the past been reluctant to order debtor-in-possession proceedings, as the courts generally mistrust the business sense of the debtor company, and this type of proceeding was more typical in extraordinary cases where the debtor company had taken on special professional advisors (who could have served as administrators in an ordinary insolvency procedure).[97] The Act for Further Facilitation of the Restructuring of Companies (ESUG) has significantly narrowed the grounds upon which a creditor or the court may veto a debtor company's application for debtor-in-possession proceedings.[98]

Should debtor-in-possession proceedings be granted by the court, the aim thereof, once the court has approved the insolvency plan, is to suspend the provisional proceedings and allow the debtor company to implement the insolvency plan in an out-of-court scenario, thus without having to open official insolvency proceedings.[99] Should the court, however, decide to open insolvency proceedings, it may order that the proceedings take the form of standard insolvency proceedings or insolvency-plan proceedings. Protective-shield proceedings can also be converted to standard insolvency proceedings before the proposed date to open insolvency proceedings in

---

93 sec 89 InsO.

94 sec 270b InsO.

95 Bork (n 39) 139.

96 Bork (n 39) 49. Compare this to the position under South African law and the role of the business rescue practitioner, as discussed in para II.2. above.

97 Bork (n 39) 49. Also see Ehlers (n 78) 173–176 in this regard.

98 One of the purposes of ESUG being to make German insolvency law more "rescue friendly". See the discussion in para III.1. above.

99 Hess (n 77).

certain instances, among others when the prospect of success for the proposed restructuring becomes futile during the restructuring planning process.[100]

2. The rights of the office-holder and provisions of the Insolvency Code relating to executory contracts

Since contracts concluded by the debtor company prior to restructuring proceedings may constitute either an economic burden or a benefit for the estate, it is generally accepted that the debtor company should only be bound to those contracts that are beneficial, and seek relief from detrimental executory contracts (provided certain conditions are fulfilled).[101] German law therefore sets out specific provisions for the treatment of various types of executory contracts under restructuring proceedings.

Important to note is that under German law, the distinction between "executory contracts" and "executed contracts" (which is in reference to the state of performance of such contract) is important as it determines the treatment of such a contract under restructuring proceedings. An "executory contract" is a mutual contract in terms whereof both the debtor company and the creditor have not fully performed at the time of commencement of the restructuring proceedings. An "executed contract", on the other hand, is a contract in terms whereof one or both parties have fully performed at the time of commencement of the restructuring proceedings.[102] The Insolvency Code only affords a choice to an office-holder to be bound to or cancel an executory contract, and other ordinary rules apply to executed contracts.

In summary, as regards executed contracts, it provides that if the creditor has fully performed in terms of a contract prior to the opening of restructuring proceedings and without receiving full consideration from the debtor company, this type of performance is deemed to be equivalent to the grant-

100 sec 272 InsO.
101 Paulus and Berberich (n 6) 199.
102 Paulus and Berberich (n 6) 202. Compare this to the South African position discussed in para I above. "Executory contracts" and "executed contracts" (except full performance by both parties covered under this definition) under German law would thus both resort under "executory contracts" under South African law.

ing of credit, and the performance claim against the debtor company (converted into a monetary claim[103]), or any claim for damages will rank as ordinary insolvency claims. With the opening of restructuring proceedings, any unfulfilled performance claims become unenforceable.

Regarding executory contracts it provides that certain types: (a) are automatically dissolved upon the opening of insolvency proceedings;[104] (b) may be renegotiated on more favourable terms for the company or be terminated should this not be possible;[105] or (c) may be terminated or continued with at the option of the insolvency administrator.[106] This right to terminate or continue with a contract extends primarily to executory contracts not subject to other special regulation, such as contracts with energy providers, sale or delivery contracts, licenses and rental agreements or leasing contracts over movable assets.[107] The decision as to continue with or terminate the executory contract is usually not subject to approval by the court.[108]

3. The rights of a creditor of the company under restructuring in relation to the cancellation of executory contracts and *ipso facto* clauses

a) Cancellation of an executory contract by a creditor of a debtor company being restructured

Should the office holder elect to remain bound to, and abides by the terms of, an executory contract, the counterparty creditor is not afforded any special termination rights and is usually bound to such a contract. Whether a creditor may cancel the executory contract in question is regulated by the

---

103 sec 45 InsO.

104 sec 115 and sec 116 InsO. Compare this to the position under South African law, as discussed in para II.2. above.

105 sec 108 and sec 109 InsO. This termination may take place at the discretion of the insolvency administrator. Compare this to the position under South African law, as discussed in para II.2. above.

106 sec 103 InsO. Also see Ahrendt in Schmidt *Hamburger Kommentar zum Insolvenzrecht* (2012) § 103 no 2. Compare this to the position under South African law, as discussed in para II.2. above. Further also see Robert-Tissot F "The Effects of a Reorganization on (Executory) Contracts: A Comparative Law and Policy Study [United States, France, Germany and Switzerland]" *International Insolvency Law Review* (*IILR*) Vol 3, No 2 (2012) 234 263 in this regard.

107 Borl (n 39) 183.

108 Paulus and Berberich (n 6) 205.

principles of the general law of contract.[109] Should the debtor company, however, default in terms of the assumed contract, the creditor may rely on all remedies provided in terms of general law of contract, including cancellation of the contract.[110]

b) Specific executory contracts: operational lease and rental contracts

For a lease over immovable property where the debtor company is the lessee, the creditor landlord has no right of cancellation, as such a contract simply continues to operate by force of law to the benefit of the estate.[111] As a result, such a creditor's only other recourse is general contractual and statutory termination rights (which rights will not become applicable as long as the office-holder abides by the contract in question).[112]

In a recent judgment of the Federal Court of Justice (Bundesgerichtshof) the court held that under certain circumstances the office holder of a licensor is barred from exercising the right whether to assume or reject an executory contract relating to licensing agreements and intellectual property.[113] The court further held that such license agreements should be treated in terms of sec 108 and sec 112 of the Insolvency Code, and not in terms of sec 103,[114] and such a contract thus continues to operate on the same basis as a lease over immovable property.

c) The enforceability of *ipso facto* clauses

In general, German law does not prevent creditors from exercising contractual termination rights triggered by the opening of insolvency proceedings or the use of insolvency-plan proceedings, subject to the case discussions below.[115]

109 Bork (n 39) 185.
110 Paulus and Berberich (n 6) 209.
111 sec 108 and sec 112 InsO.
112 Bork (n 39) 185. See the discussion in para III.3.a).
113 BGH 21.10.2015 – I ZR 173/14.
114 See the discussion in para III(2) above.
115 Also see Huber in *Münchener Kommentar zum Insolvenzordnung* (2013) § 119.

Recently the Federal Court of Justice (*Bundesgerichtshof*) had to decide on the validity of a contractual clause in a long-term power-supply agreement providing for a right of termination upon the occurrence of insolvency.[116] The matter came on appeal before the court after both the Regional Court (*Landgericht*) of Hannover and the Higher Regional Court (*Oberlandesgericht*) of Celle held that such a clause was valid. The English translation of the clause in question reads as follows –

> "The agreement terminates automatically and without notice if the customer files a petition for the opening of insolvency proceedings (Insolvenztrag) or if, following the filing of an insolvency petition by a creditor, preliminary insolvency proceedings (vorläufiges Insolvenzverfahren) are initiated or opened."

The court held that the Insolvency Code affords the office holder an election whether to terminate or abide by certain contracts,[117] and the purpose of the office holder election right is to protect and enhance the estate of the debtor company for the benefit of an equal distribution to its creditors. This purpose is defeated if a solvent counterparty could terminate a contract which is beneficial for the insolvent estate, thereby undermining the office holder's election right. The court held that the clause in question precluded the office holder from exercising this statutory right, and ruled that the early-termination clause was invalid on the basis of sec 119 of the Insolvency Code, which provides that "*[a]greements that exclude or restrict the applicability of sections 103 to 118 in advance are invalid*".[118]

Parties to a contract may, however, insert termination clauses based on grounds other than insolvency, for example default or other forms of breach of contract, which termination clauses will be valid and enforceable by a creditor against a debtor company under restructuring proceedings.

This decision of the Federal Court of Justice is, however, not applicable in all instances. Should the insolvency-related termination clause in question be supported in terms of statute, such a termination clause will be valid. The court *in casu* referred to one of its previous decisions, where it held that an insolvency-related termination clause corresponding to a termination right in terms of the German Insurance Act (*Versicherungsvertragsgesetz*) was valid.[119]

---

116 BGH 15.11.2012 – IX ZR 169/11 – BGHZ 195, 348.

117 Sec 103 InsO. See the discussion in para III.2. above on the election rights of the office-holder.

118 Also see Hess *Insolvenzrecht Großkommentar in zwei Bänden I* (2013) § 119 no 11 and no 12 in this regard.

119 BGH of 14.12.2006 – IX ZR 194/05 – BGHZ 170, 206 para 11.

More recently the Federal Court of Justice was once again faced with deciding on the validity of an insolvency-related termination clause, and the clause in question pertained to a clause in the Standard German Building Contract Terms B (*Allgemeine Vertragsbedingungen für die Ausführung von Bauleistungen*) (VOB/B) which had been incorporated into the contract between the parties.[120] The clause in question entitles a client to cancel a building contract when the contractor enters insolvency proceedings. The matter came on appeal before the court after the Higher Regional Court (OLG) of Frankfurt held that such an insolvency-related termination clause was null and void with reference to sec 119 of the Insolvency Code.[121]

The Federal Court of Justice however held that the insolvency-related termination clause in question was indeed enforceable, as the skills of, and trust in, the building contractor is of great importance in building contracts. The court further held that its previous judgment[122] relates only to the continued supply of goods or electricity.

The Insolvency Code also provides for instances of early termination in terms whereof such clauses would be valid.[123]

IV. Comparative conclusion

South African and German provisions on company restructuring have certain similarities. To a certain extent both procedures were implemented within the last few years[124] and neither country has a separate restructuring act.[125] Although the procedures in both countries are relatively new,[126] the countries do not face similar issues in relation to restructuring structures and procedures – exept perhaps some uncertainty in relation to and the en-

120 BGH 07.04.2016 – VII ZR 56/15.

121 See the discussion in para III.3.c) above.

122 BGH 15.11.2012 – IX ZR 169/11.

123 sec 104 InsO.

124 The German procedure has been implemented since 1999 when the Insolvency Code was enacted, but only in 2012 with the enactment of ESUG did the Insolvency Code become more geared towards restructuring introducing, among other things, protective shield proceedings. See the discussion in para III.1. above.

125 In South Africa the relevant provisions are contained in the Companies Act 71 of 2008, and in Germany the relevant provisions are contained in the Insolvency Code (Insolvenzordnung – InsO).

126 Debtor-in-possession proceedings and the protective shield in Germany.

forceability of *ipso facto* cancellation clauses. It would seem that the provisions of the German Insolvency Code is more in line with international best practice than the provisions of the South African Companies Act.[127]

1. The rights of the business-rescue practitioner and office holder

The German Insolvency Code is much more detailed in relation to the rights of the office holder regarding the treatment of executory contracts than South African law. On the one hand, German law is more restrictive than South African law as the law prescribes the treatment of specific agreements (such as an automatic termination) over which the office holder has no choice, where in terms of South African law the business-rescue practitioner may choose which contracts to suspend or cancel by means of a court order. On the other hand, German law is less restrictive than South African law as the office bearer is free to exercise his choice (where this choice is afforded to him) without obtaining a court order.

2. The cancellation right of a creditor

Under South African law, a creditor is allowed to cancel an executory contract with a debtor company placed under business-rescue, subject to certain conditions.

The Supreme Court of Appeal has held that the moratorium imposed by the Companies Act[128] does not preclude a creditor from cancelling an executory contract with a debtor company once such company has been placed under business rescue.[129] On the facts before the court, the debtor company was already in breach of the agreement at the time that it was placed under business rescue.[130]

127 See para V. below.
128 sec 133.
129 *Cloete Murray NNO v FirstRand Bank Limited t/a Wesbank* 2015 3 SA 438 (SCA).
130 Also see *Schickerling NO v Chickenland (Pty) Ltd t/a Nando's* (n 48) above in this regard.

Suspension of an agreement[131] has as effect that obligations will not become due and enforceable until the cessation of business-rescue proceedings, and as a result no contractual stipulations based on default by the debtor company in respect of the suspended obligations will take effect. Contract terms rendered ineffective would include, among others, cancellation.[132] The position before the *BP Southern Africa*[133] case was that a creditor was not allowed to cancel an agreement with the debtor company had the business-rescue practitioner chosen to suspend the executory contract in question, and had the debtor company not been in breach of the contract at the time that it was placed under business rescue. The current position thus makes it clear that the suspension right provided to the business rescue practitioner is of no real practical effect as a creditor may still cancel such a contract.

Further, should the debtor company fail to perform under an unsuspended obligation,[134] the creditor counterparty will be able to rely on the general remedies for breach of contract and invoke any contractually stipulated remedies (including cancellation of the contract in question).[135]

Under German law, should the office holder elect to remain bound to, and abides by the terms of, an executory contract, the counterparty creditor is not afforded any special termination rights and is usually bound to such a contract. Should the debtor company, however, default in terms of the assumed contract, the creditor may rely on all remedies provided in terms of general law of contract, including cancellation of the contract.[136]

3. The enforceability of *ipso facto* clauses

Under South African law, contractual remedies stipulated by the parties will in principle be enforceable during business-rescue proceedings.[137]

---

131 For the right of the business-rescue practitioner to suspend obligations, see the discussion in para II.2. above.

132 Van der Linde (n 4) 375.

133 (n 53) above.

134 For the right of the business-rescue practitioner to suspend obligations, see the discussion in para II.2. above.

135 See *Kythera Court v Le Rendez-Vous Cafē CC T/A Newscafe Bedfordview (in Business Rescue)* (n 54). Also see Van der Linde (n 4) 373 in this regard.

136 Paulus and Berberich (n 6) 209.

137 See *Homez Trailers and Bodies (Pty) Ltd v Standard Bank of South Africa Ltd* (n 73) and *Firstrand Bank Ltd v Singh* (n 73) in this regard, Also see Van der Linde (n 4) 399.

Under German law, the Federal Court of Justice has held on once case that insolvency-related termination clauses are invalid.[138] The reasoning of the court was not based on the principle of a moratorium or a stay in proceedings, but was based on the election right afforded to an office holder in terms of the Insolvency Code,[139] and that cancellation by a creditor would deprive the office-holder of this statutory right.[140]

In a later case the Federal Court of Justice held that such a clause is however valid in a building contract, as in such a contract the skill and trustworthiness of the building contractor is of great importance and the office holder's statutory election right[141] may be excluded under such circumstances.[142] The court further held that its previous judgment[143] relates only to the continued supply of goods or electricity. The position under German law may therefore still be unclear in certain instances.

Parties to a contract may, however, insert termination clauses based on grounds other than insolvency, for example default or other forms of breach of contract, which termination clauses will be valid and enforceable by a creditor against a debtor company under restructuring proceedings.

V. Conclusion

An effective insolvency and creditor-rights system should ensure that the restructuring proceedings relevant to companies in financial distress maximises the total value received by all interested parties. It is essential that such proceedings aim to balance clarity and flexibility as well as contain sufficient measures of protection of the rights of creditors.[144] Not only is the ability of creditors to provide credit and capital essential to the growth of a

---

138 BGH 15.11.2012 – IX ZR 169/11 – BGHZ 195, 348.

139 sec 103 InsO. See the discussion in para III.2. above on the election rights of the office holder.

140 sec 119 InsO.

141 sec 119 InsO.

142 BGH 07.04.2016 – VII ZR 56/15.

143 BGH 15.11.2012 – IX ZR 169/11.

144 Burdette and Calitz "4:3:2:1... Fair distribution of appointments or countdown to catastrophe? South Africa's ministerial policy for the appointment of liquidators under the spotlight" 3 (2015) *Nottingham Insolvency and Business Law eJournal (NIBLeJ)* 437 460.

market economy, but they would also require a certain level of certainty to incentivise their participation in a restructuring process.[145]

In *Oakdene Square Properties (Pty) Ltd v Farm Bothasfontein (Kyalami (Pty) Ltd*,[146] Claassen J states "the power of a business rescue practitioner to suspend any obligation of a company that arises under an agreement is highly contentious. It may lead to 'cherry picking' where the practitioner selects certain obligations best suited to the company for suspension."[147] In allowing the business-rescue practitioner to "cherry pick" which obligations should be suspended, essentially signifies a unilateral amendment of a contract by the business-rescue practitioner, which is contrary to South African common law and could affect the sanctity of contracts in South Africa.[148] It is also submitted that in light of the *BP Southern Africa*[149] case the suspension right of the business-rescue practitioner is not of much practical effect.[150]

The *UNCITRAL Legislative Guide on Insolvency Law* is designed to provide guidance to states on how to develop and improve administration during restructuring and subsequently includes the following range of legislative recommendations on the treatment of contracts:

> "72. The insolvency law should specify that the insolvency representative may decide to continue the performance of a contract of which it is aware where continuation would be beneficial to the insolvency estate. The insolvency law should specify that:
>
> (a) The right to continue applies to the contract as a whole; and
>
> (b) The effect of continuation is that all terms of the contract are enforceable.
>
> 73. The insolvency law may permit the insolvency representative to decide to reject a contract. The insolvency law should specify that the right to reject applies to the contract as a whole."[151]

---

145 Cirmizi, "The challenges of bankruptcy reform" 2012 *The World Bank Research Observer* 185 199.

146 *Oakdene Square Properties (Pty) Ltd v Farm Bothasfontein (Kyalami) (Pty) Ltd, Farm Bothasfontein (Kyalami) (Pty) Ltd v Kyalami Events and Exhibitions (Pty) Ltd* (2011/35199, 2011/24545) 2012 ZAGPJHC 12; 2012 (3) SA 273 (GSJ); 2012 2 All SA 433 (GSJ) (17 February 2012) para 17.

147 See Loubser "The Business Rescue Proceedings in the Companies Act of 2008: Concerns and Questions (part 2)" 2010 *Tydskrif vir die Suid-Afrikaanse Reg (TSAR)* 689 691.

148 Loubser (n 147) 690.

149 (n 53) above.

150 See para IV.2. above.

151 UNCITRAL *Legislative Guide on Insolvency Law recommendations* 72–73.

From the discussion above it becomes clear that according to international guidelines the restructuring representative (the business-rescue practitioner or the office holder *in casu*) ought to be given the right to choose between fulfilment or not of uncompleted contracts, but should not acquire the right to decide on partial performance, or suspension of only part of the agreement. German insolvency law provides for specific rules relating to specific types of executory contracts, and only affords a choice to an office holder to be bound to or cancel an executory contract (where specific treatment is not prescribed).[152] South African law should follow suit and it is submitted that section 136[153] should be amended according to the accepted principles of the South African common law, in particular the law of contract, in order to preserve pre-insolvency creditor rights and priorities inside of insolvency.[154]

---

152 See the discussion in para III.2. above.
153 of the Companies Act.
154 Loubser (n 34) 90.

Bibliography

Bertelsmann E, Evans RG, Harris A et al *Mars – The Law of Insolvency in South Africa* (9th Edition, Juta Law, Cape Town 2008).

Bork R *Rescuing Companies in England and Germany* (Oxford University Press, Oxford 2012).

Bradstreet R "The leak in the lifeboat: Inadequate regulation of business-rescue practitioners may adversely affect lenders willingness and the growth of the economy" 2010 *South African Mercantile Law Journal (SA Merc LJ)* 195.

Bradstreet R "The new business-rescue: will creditors sink or swim?" 2011 *South African Law Journal (SALJ)* 352.

Burdette O and Calitz J "4:3:2:1... Fair distribution of appointments or countdown to catastrophe? South Africa's ministerial policy for the appointment of liquidators under the spotlight" 3 (2015) *Nottingham Insolvency and Business Law eJournal (NIBLeJ)* 437.

Cassim FHI et al *Contemporary Company Law* (2nd Edition, Juta Law, Cape Town 2012).

Cirmizi E "The challenges of bankruptcy reform" 2012 *The World Bank Research Observer (World Bank Res Obs)* 185.

Delport PA, Vorster Q, Burdette D, Esser IM and Lombard S *Henochsberg on the Companies Act 71 of 2008* (loose leaf, Lexis Nexis South Africa, Durban).

Ehlers E "Statutory Corporate Rescue Proceedings in Germany: The *Insolvenzplan* Procedure" in Broc and Parry (eds) *Corporate Rescue: An Overview of Recent Developments* (Kluwer Law International 2006) 151.

Faber D, Vermunt N, Kilborn J and van der Linde K *Treatment of Contracts in Insolvency. Oxford International & Comparative Insolvency Law Series* Vol 2 (Oxford University Press, Oxford 2013).

Gantenberg F's jurisdictional comparison of German law in Henrot, Borch, Petersen and Varrenti (eds) *Debt Restructuring: an alternative to insolvency proceedings (jurisdictional comparisons)* (1st Edition, Thomson Reuters 2014) 91.

Hamburger Kommentar zum Insolvenzrecht, Schmidt Andreas (ed) (4th Edition 2012).

Hess B, *Insolvenzrecht Großkommentar in zwei Bänden I* (2013) § 119.

Hess B, Oberhammer P and Pfeiffer T *European Insolvency Law: Heidelberg-Luxembourg-Vienna Report* (CH Beck Hart Nomos 2014).

Münchener Kommentar zur Insolvenzordnung, Hans-Peter Kirchhof, Horst Eidenmüller, and Rolf Stürner, Volume 2 (3rd Edition, 2013).

Kloppers P "Judicial management – a corporate rescue mechanism in need of reform?" 1999 *Stellenbosch Law Review (Stellenbosch L Rev)* 417.

Lobo OEF *World Insolvency Systems: A Comparative Study* (Carswell, Toronto 2009).

Loubser A "The business-rescue proceedings in the Companies Act of 2008: concerns and questions (part 2)" 2010 *Tydskrif vir die Suid-Afrikaanse Reg (TSAR)* 689.

Loubser A *Some Comparative Aspects of Corporate Rescue in South African Company Law* (2010 thesis University of South Africa).

O'Brien P "Cancellation, restitution and forfeiture against the background of section 35 of the Insolvency Act" 1999 *Tydskrif vir die Suid-Afrikaanse Reg (TSAR)* 534.

Prins D "Priority issues in business-rescue" (2015 LLM dissertation UCT).

Rajak H and Henning J "Business-rescue for South Africa" 1999 *South African Law Journal (SALJ)* 262.

Robert-Tissot F "The Effects of a Reorganization on (Executory) Contracts: A Comparative Law and Policy Study [United States, France, Germany and Switzerland]" *International Insolvency Law Review* (*IILR*) Vol. 3, No. 2 (2012) 234.

Rushworth J "A critical analysis of the business-rescue regime in the Companies Act 71 of 2008" (2010) *Acta Juridica* 375.

UNCITRAL (ed) *Legislative Guide on Insolvency Law (2005)* available at http://www.uncitral.org/pdf/english/texts/insolven/05-80722_Ebook.pdf (15-09-2017).

Van der Linde K "An overview of recent company law cases: a mixed bag of emerging clarity, lingering doubt and deepening confusion" *Annual Banking Law Update (ABLU)*, conference Johannesburg 15 May 2015 60.

Wolf A "Sense of Modesty: Germany's Progress towards Corporate Rescue" (2016) 4(2) *Nottingham Insolvency and Business Law eJournal (NIBLeJ)* 163.

World Bank (ed) *Principles for Effective Insolvency and Creditor Rights Systems (revised 2015)* available at http://siteresources.worldbank.org/EXTGILD/Resources/5807554-1357753926066/2015_Revised_ICR_Principles(3).pdf (15-09-2017).

Case Law

Germany

BGH 14.12.2006 – IX ZR 194/5 – BGHZ 170, 206.

BGH 15.11.2012 – IX ZR 169/11 – BGHZ 195, 348.

BGH 21.10.2015 – I ZR 173/14.

BGH 07.04.2016 – VII ZR 56/15.

South Africa

178 Stamfordhill CC v Velvet Star Entertainment CC (1506/15) 2015 ZAKZDHC 34 (1 April 2015)

African Banking Corporation of Botswana v Kariba Furniture Manufacturers 2015 5 SA 192

Blue Star Holdings (Pty) Ltd v West Coast Oyster Growers CC 2013 6 SA 540 (WCC)

Booysen v Jonkheer Boerewynmakery (Pty) Ltd (in business rescue) 2017 1 All SA 862 (WCC)

BP Southern Africa (Pty) Ltd v Intertrans Oil SA (Pty) Ltd (34716/2016) 2016 ZAGPJHC 310 (25 November 2016)

Bryant & Flanagan (Pty) Ltd v Muller NNO 1978 2 SA 807 (A)

Chetty v Hart (20323/2014) 2015 ZASCA 112 (4 September 2015)

Cloete Murray NNO v FirstRand Bank Limited t/a Wesbank 2015 3 SA 438 (SCA)

Ellerine Brothers (Pty) Ltd v McCarthy Ltd 2014 4 SA 22 (SCA)

Firstrand Bank Ltd v Singh (4273/2012) 2015 ZAGPJHC 279 (30 October 2015)

Goodricke & Son v Auto Protection Insurance Co Ltd 1968 1 SA 717 (A)

Homez Trailers and Bodies (Pty) Ltd v Standard Bank of South Africa Ltd (35201/2013) 2013 ZAGPPHC 465 (27 September 2013)

Investec Bank Ltd v Bruyns 2012 5 SA 430 WCC

JVJ Logistics (Pty) Ltd v Standard Bank of South Africa Ltd 2016 6 SA 448 (KZD)

Kythera Court v Le Rendez-Vous Cafẽ CC T/A Newscafe Bedfordview (in Business Rescue) 2016 6 SA 63 (GJ)

LA Sport 4x4 Outdoor CC v Broadsword Trading 20 (Pty) Ltd 2013 JDR 1215 (GNP)

LA Sport 4x4 Outdoor CC v Broadsword Trading 20 (Pty) Ltd (A513/2013) 2015 ZAGPPHC 78 (26 February 2015)

Merchant West Working Capital Solutions (Pty) Ltd v Advanced Technologies and Engineering Company (Pty) Ltd (13/12406) 2013 ZAGPJHC 109 (10 May 2013)

Nedcor Investment Bank v Pretoria Belgrave Hotel (Pty) Ltd 2003 5 SA 189 (SCA)

Oakdene Square Properties (Pty) Ltd v Farm Bothasfontein (Kyalami) (Pty) Ltd, Farm Bothasfontein (Kyalami) (Pty) Ltd v Kyalami Events and Exhibitions (Pty) Ltd (2011/35199, 2011/24545) 2012 ZAGPJHC 12; 2012 3 SA 273 (GSJ); 2012 2 All SA 433 (GSJ) (17 February 2012)

Panamo Properties (Pty) Ltd v Nel 2015 5 SA 63 (SCA)

Roering NO v Nedbank Ltd 2013 3 SA 160 (GSJ)

Schickerling NO v Chickenland (Pty) Ltd t/a Nando's (22712/2016) 2016 ZAGPPHC 208 (15 April 2016)

Southern Value Consortium v Tresso Trading 102 (Pty) Ltd 2016 6 SA 501 (WCC)

Thomas Construction (Pty) Ltd (in liquidation) v Grafton Furniture Manufacturers (Pty) Ltd 1988 2 SA 546 (A)

Van Zyl v Euodia Trust (Edms) Bpk 1983 3 SA 394 (T)

The quest for fairness in the rendering of financial advice and intermediary services in light of the retail distribution review

*Daleen Millard**

* BIur LLB LLM (UP) LLD (UJ). Professor of private law, University of Johannesburg.

I. Introduction

In South Africa, advice and intermediary services regarding financial products have always been regulated by the law of agency and mandate.[1] That means that a number of Roman-Dutch principles dictated the standards to which the conduct of financial advisers and intermediaries were held.[2] These included the fact that the mandatory had to act with care and skill and with good faith.[3] The recent promulgation of the Financial Advisory and Intermediary Services Act 37 of 2002 (FAIS Act) introduced a number of very detailed rules for financial advisers and intermediaries These minimum standards not only prescribe the qualifications and characteristics of honesty and integrity that an adviser had to conform to,[4] but also stipulate in detail what an adviser must do when rendering advice.

---

1 Havenga *The Law of Insurance Intermediaries* (2001) 1.

2 Havenga (n 1) 3–4.

3 Havenga (n 1) 2, 4; *Durr v Absa Bank Ltd* 1997 3 SA 448 (SCA); *Ries v Boland Bank PKS Ltd* 2000 4 SA 955 C; *Stander v Raubenheimer* 1996 2 SA 670 (O); *David Trust v Aegis Insurance Co Ltd* 2000 3 SA 289 (SCA).

4 Board Notice 106 of 2008 "Determination of Fit and Proper requirements for Financial Services Providers, 2008". Sec 6A of the FAIS Act, reads as follows: (1) The registrar, for purposes of this Act, by notice on the official web site — (a) must — (i) classify financial services providers into different categories; (ii) determine fit and proper requirements for each category of providers; and (iii) in each category of providers determine fit and proper requirements for — (aa) key individuals of providers; (bb) representatives of providers; (cc) key individuals of representatives of providers; and (dd) compliance officers; and (b) may determine fit and proper requirements for providers, key individuals, representatives, key individuals of representatives and compliance officers in general. (2) Fit and proper requirements may include, but are not limited to, appropriate standards relating to— (a) personal character qualities of honesty and integrity; (b) competence, including— (i) experience; (ii) qualifications; and (iii) knowledge tested through examinations determined by the registrar; (c) operational ability; (d) financial soundness; and (e) continuous professional development. (3) Different fit and proper requirements may be determined for providers, representatives and compliance officers that are natural persons and for those that are partnerships, trusts or corporate or unincorporated bodies. (4) The registrar may amend the fit and proper requirements from time to time and a provider, key individual, representative, key individual of a representative and compliance officer must comply therewith within such period as determined by the registrar." The new definition and the very specific content of the new section 6A does not alter the content of the fit and proper requirements, as these have always pertained to financial soundness, honesty and integrity and competency requirement (Reinecke, Van Niekerk and Nienaber *South African Insurance Law* (2013) 511). However, it is suggested that

Although there is a good argument to be made for the view that the FAIS Act simply enhanced the existing Roman-Dutch law principles and that these were inherently fair,[5] it is also true that the FAIS Act complicated matters by moving away from principles to rules. Instead of giving effect to the principles that underpin the rules, the very detailed rules became a tick-box exercise for advisers and this inevitably led to cosmetic compliance, where a long list of duties is ticked off. Despite the best intentions of the legislature to regulate every single aspect of advice, mistakes were still made by intermediaries and advisers and clients still suffered the consequences of ill-conceived advice. The *Retail Distribution Review* (RDR) was therefore initiated by the Regulator, the *Financial Services Board* (FSB), in an attempt to ensure that customers receive fair outcomes when purchasing financial products. The review is focused on the distribution and compensation practices within the retail financial services industry and has been conducted under the market conduct peak of the "Twin Peaks" approach, which is informed by the Treating Customers Fairly (TCF) principles. RDR is most directly related to TCF outcome 4, which provides as follows: "Where advice is given, it is suitable and takes account of customer circumstance". RDR contained no less than 55 specific proposals that were out for comment until 2 March 2015.

This paper asks whether RDR does not present an over-exaggeration of the difficulties with and the cost of advice. In addition, it evaluates whether this review should be seen as a step towards the abolition of the FAIS Act, whether customer circumstances are the only consideration in evaluating whether customer treatment was fair and whether there is not perhaps the danger of creating new imbalances by over-emphasising customer needs. More specifically, it analyses the first phase of the implementation of the RDR recommendations that specifically focuses on commissions payable to advisers who render assistance with the purchase of financial services. It evaluates these recommendations in light of recent decisions that dealt with faulty advice, mis-selling and mis-buying. In the final instance, this paper will compare the legal structure for financial advisers in South Africa to the current position in Germany with a view to evaluating the true contribution

this definition conceptualises "fit and proper" and that it should have been included in the FAIS Act from the start as it deals with one of the key concepts in the FAIS Act. Furthermore, an individual's being fit and proper is key to the functioning of a financial-services provider or representative's activities and these minimum standards for being fit and proper as set out by the FAIS Act ensure that members of the public deal with suitably qualified individuals.

5 Hattingh and Millard *The FAIS Act Explained* (2010) 77–78.

of the RDR in measuring fairness in the rendering of advice and intermediary services.

The paper progresses by first considering the position of advisers before the FAIS Act. It next provides a brief exposition of the meaning of advice in terms of the current FAIS Act and the way in which principles of agency and representation were embedded in this statute and in subsequent legislation. In order to place the RDR in perspective, an overview of the Twin Peaks legislation and TCF is provided. This will be followed by a discussion of the RDR, comments on the new proposals pertaining to advice and a critical review of these. In the final instance, the position of advisers in Germany will be discussed.

II. Advice pre-FAIS

As was alluded to in paragraph 1 above, the rendering of advice for purposes of procuring a financial product was simply categorised as representation, as it happened more often than not that the adviser also concluded the agreement.[6] As Roman-Dutch law was significantly influenced by English law, the term "agency" can be used to denote two situations.[7] In its restricted sense, it refers to a person who has authority to conclude a juristic act in the name of his principal, such as the conclusion of an insurance contract, the payment of a premium, or the payment of a claim. In the wider sense, agency refers to any person who is mandated to perform a task on behalf of his mandator and this may include the situation where someone is authorised to carry out a certain task for his mandatory.[8] It will depend on the facts of a particular matter whether someone in fact acted as an agent and furthermore, for whom such a person acted, as the agent could either be an agent for the client or for the financial services provider. For years, agents and representatives rendered advice within this legal framework and because financial services providers are all companies and therefore juristic persons, they can only act through natural persons who are in some way affiliated with that company.

---

6 Reinecke, Van Niekerk and Nienaber (n 4) 507–508; Havenga (n 1) 1.
7 Reinecke, Van Niekerk and Nienaber (n 4) 509.
8 Reinecke, Van Niekerk and Nienaber (n 4) 509.

Insurance brokers, for example, had a long list of duties, which included *inter alia* the duty to act with reasonable care and skill,[9] the duty to act in good faith,[10] to obtain insurance cover,[11] to prepare the policy wording,[12] not to insure with an unregistered or insolvent insurer,[13] to deliver the policy, to advise the insured as to the meaning of the policy and to assist the insured to disclose material information.[14] As was alluded to in paragraph 1, it became evident that these broad rules were inadequate for the rendering of advice in a modern-day commercial market as many problems were experienced with financial advice and the FSB as the regulator introduced a new statutory regime with the enactment of the FAIS Act.[15]

III. Salient features of the FAIS Act

1. Fit and proper requirements

As was alluded to in the introduction, the main legislative functions of the FAIS Act were to supervise the control of any activities relating to financial services rendered by financial institutions.[16] The very first point of departure of the FAIS Act was that nobody could render financial services in any capacity, whether as an insurance company, a brokerage, an investor or any other such service unless that person was in fact issued with a licence to do so.[17] This licensing process is in fact referred to as the authorisation of financial services providers and as from 30 September 2004, any person who was not exempted from the FAIS Act had to be duly authorised to render services.[18] Apart from categorising financial services providers according

9 This is in fact a *naturale* of the agreement. See *Stander v Raubenheimer* 1996 2 SA 70 (O).
10 Reinecke, Van Niekerk and Nienaber (n 4) 519.
11 Havenga (n 1) 24–25.
12 *Kliptown Clothing Industries (Pty) Ltd v Marine and Trade Insurance Co of SA Ltd* 1961 1 SA 103 (A).
13 Havenga (n 1) 33–35.
14 Havenga (n 1) 35; *Rabinowitz NNO v Ned-Equity Insurance Co Ltd* 1980 1 SA 403 (W) 407H.
15 Van Zyl *Financial Advisory and Intermediary Services Manual* (2004) 1–9.
16 Hattingh and Millard (n 5) 3.
17 Reinecke, Van Niekerk and Nienaber (n 4) 511.
18 sec 7(1) of the FAIS Act.

to the type of business they conducted,[19] the FAIS Act also stipulates that any provider who seeks to render financial services should comply with the fit-and-proper requirements and in a sense, these requirements grouped together those rules that underpinned the Roman-Dutch law of agency. The Fit-and-proper Requirements in terms of the FAIS Act contain detailed rules pertaining to honesty and integrity, competency, operational ability and financial soundness.[20] Although the FAIS Act did not initially contain a definition of the fit-and-proper requirements, this was in fact changed when the Financial Services Laws General Amendment Act[21] inserted the following definition into section 1 of the FAISA:

> "[F]it and proper requirements' means the requirements published under section 6A'. Section 6A reads as follows:
>
> (1) The registrar, for purposes of this Act, by notice on the official web site—
>   (a) must—
>   (i) classify financial services providers into different categories;
>   (ii) determine fit and proper requirements for each category of providers; and
>   (iii) in each category of providers determine fit and proper requirements for—
>   (aa) key individuals of providers;
>   (bb) representatives of providers;
>   (cc) key individuals of representatives of providers; and
>   (dd) compliance officers; and
>   (b) may determine fit and proper requirements for providers, key individuals, representatives, key individuals of representatives and compliance officers in general.
>
> (2) Fit and proper requirements may include, but are not limited to, appropriate standards relating to—
>   (a) personal character qualities of honesty and integrity;
>   (b) competence, including—
>   (i) experience;
>   (ii) qualifications; and
>   (iii) knowledge tested through examinations determined by the registrar;
>   (c) operational ability;
>   (d) financial soundness; and
>   (e) continuous professional development.

---

19 For example, a category II FSP could provide advice and render intermediary services as a discretionary FSP, which meant that it was authorised to manage clients' investments on a discretionary basis.

20 See Board Notice 106 of 2008 "Determination of Fit and Proper Requirements for Financial Services Providers".

21 45 of 2014.

(3) Different fit and proper requirements may be determined for providers, representatives and compliance officers that are natural persons and for those that are partnerships, trusts or corporate or unincorporated bodies.

(4) The registrar may amend the fit and proper requirements from time to time and a provider, key individual, representative, key individual of a representative and compliance officer must comply therewith within such period as determined by the registrar."

The new definition, and the very specific content of the new section 6A, do not alter the content of the fit-and-proper requirements but rather conceptualises "fit and proper". Most importantly, an individual's being fit and proper is key to the functioning of a financial services provider or the representative's activities and these minimum standards for fit and proper as set out by the FAISA ensure that members of the public deal with *suitably qualified individuals*. In fact, the whole driver behind the FAIS Act was to ensure that the rendering of financial services were professionalised.

2. Key definitions

Apart from ensuring that only licensed financial services providers who were suitably qualified could render financial services, the FAIS Act also introduced an extensive range of definitions. For purposes of the present discussion, it is only necessary to take cognisance of the meaning of "financial product" and "advice". The FAIS Act defines a financial product as follows:

"'financial product' means, subject to subsection (2) –

(a) securities and instruments, including —
   (i) shares in a company other than a "share block company" as defined in the Share Blocks Control Act, 1980 (Act No. 59 of 1980);
   (ii) debentures and securitised debt;
   (iii) any money-market instrument;
   (iv) any warrant, certificate, and other instrument acknowledging, conferring or creating rights to subscribe to, acquire, dispose of, or convert securities and instruments referred to in subparagraphs (i), (ii) and (iii);
   (v) any "securities" as defined in section 1 of the Financial Markets Act, 2012 (Act No. 19 of 2012);

(b) a participatory interest in one or more collective investment schemes;

(c) a long-term or a short-term insurance contract or policy, referred to in the Long-term Insurance Act, 1998 (Act No. 52 of 1998), and the Short-term Insurance Act, 1998 (Act No. 53 of 1998), respectively;

(d) a benefit provided by —

(i) a pension fund organisation as defined in section 1(1) of the Pension Funds Act, 1956 (Act No. 24 of 1956), to the members of the organisation by virtue of membership; or

(ii) a friendly society referred to in the Friendly Societies Act, 1956 (Act No. 25 of 1956), to the members of the society by virtue of membership;

(e) a foreign currency denominated investment instrument, including a foreign currency deposit;

(f) a deposit as defined in section 1(1) of the Banks Act, 1990 (Act No. 94 of 1990);

(g) a health service benefit provided by a medical scheme as defined in section 1(1) of the Medical Schemes Act, 1998 (Act No. 131 of 1998);

(h) any other product similar in nature to any financial product referred to in paragraphs (a) to (g), inclusive, declared by the registrar by notice in the Gazette to be a financial product for the purposes of this Act;

(i) any combined product containing one or more of the financial products referred to in paragraphs (a) to (h), inclusive;

(j) any financial product issued by any foreign product supplier and marketed in the Republic and which in nature and character is essentially similar or corresponding to a financial product referred to in paragraphs (a) to (i), inclusive[.]"[22]

From this extensive definition it can be deduced that it is the intention of the legislature to ensure that as many products as possible should be included in the FAIS Act and with that, the consumer protection rules that bind services providers are extended to a wide range of consumers. "Advice" is defined as:

"any recommendation, guidance or proposal of a financial nature furnished, by any means or medium, to any client or group of clients —

(a) in respect of the purchase of any financial product; or

(b) in respect of the investment in any financial product: or

(c) on the conclusion of any other transaction, including a loan or cession, aimed at the incurring of any liability or the acquisition of any right or benefit in respect of any financial product; or

(d) on the variation of any term or condition applying to a financial product, on the replacement of any such product, or on the termination of any purchase of or investment in any such product, and irrespective of whether or not such advice —

(i) is furnished in the course of or incidental to financial planning in connection with the affairs of the client; or

(ii) results in any such purchase, investment, transaction, variation, replacement or termination, as the case may be, being effected [.]"[23]

---

22 sec 1(1) of the FAIS Act, *sv* "financial product".

23 sec 1(1) of the FAIS Act, *sv* "advice".

In short, it means recommendations, guidance or proposals of a financial nature and it further encompasses assistance to a consumer in the weighing up of alternatives on which a consumer must make a final decision.[24] Advice may indeed be rendered in the course of financial planning and it will be classified as such, regardless of whether it eventually results in a purchase, transaction, investment, variation or replacement of an existing product.[25]

3. The General Code of Conduct for Authorised FSPs and Representatives

As was mentioned in paragraph 1 above, the FAIS Act introduced detailed rules on the exact way in which advice should be rendered. These rules are contained in the General Code of Conduct for Authorised FSPs and Representatives (GCC) and it is essential to this argument to scrutinise these rules to demonstrate that although very detailed, advisers still need to do more to avoid being unfair to the consumer.[26]

Accordingly, section 2 of the GCC stipulates that a provider must at all times render financial services honestly, fairly, with due skill, care and diligence, and in the interests of clients and the integrity of the financial services industry. In fact, this section is probably the one that is frequently the subject of complaints before the Financial Advisory and Intermediary Services Ombud (FAIS Ombud).[27] In addition, section 3 of the GCC lists a number of very specific provisions. It stipulates that when a provider renders a financial service (such as the rendering of advice), representations made and information provided must be factually correct;[28] must be pro-

---

24 Reinecke, Van Niekerk and Nienaber (n 4) 511–512.

25 Reinecke, Van Niekerk and Nienaber (n 4) 512 n 36.

26 See *Gary le Vatte v Rosspen Financial Services* (Case no FOC/600/05 EC) and *Johan Adriaan Steenkamp v Old Mutual Life Assurance Company (South Africa) Limited* (Case no FOC 1343/05 FS).

27 Over the past two years, a number of financial services providers have been found guilty of a contravention of this section. See, for example, the enforcement committee cases of *The Registrar of Financial Services Providers v Talksure Trading (Pty) Ltd* (Case no 20/2014); *The Registrar of Financial Services Providers v Clifford Mey* (Case no 11/2014); *The Registrar of Financial Services Providers v Jacobus Gouws* (Case no 16/2014) and *The Registrar of Financial Services Providers v Rowe Hooper Insurance and Investment Brokers CC* (Case no 27/2015).

28 sec 3(1)*(a)*(i) of the GCC.

vided in plain language, avoid uncertainty and confusion and not be misleading;[29] must be adequate and appropriate in the particular circumstances, taking into account the client's level of understanding;[30] must be provided timeously; may be provided orally unless the client wants it in writing and where it is provided in writing, must be in a clear and readable print size, spacing and format.[31] Furthermore, where representations are made regarding amounts, sums, charges, values, fees, remuneration or monetary obligations, the basis of calculation of these must be adequately described.[32] In addition, a services provider must at all times avoid a conflict of interest between himself and a client.[33] There are many examples of conflicts of interest but an obvious one is where a broker advises a client to procure a product that is more expensive than a comparable one simply because the broker will earn a bigger commission.[34]

The GCC further stipulates that services should be rendered in accordance with the contractual relationship between the parties and reasonable requests or instructions of the client. [35]

What really requires skill is the way in which an adviser must provide information about the financial service.[36] Section 7 stipulates that a provider, other than a direct marketer, has the obligation to provide a reasonable and appropriate general explanation of the nature and material terms of the relevant contract or transaction to a client, and should generally make full and frank disclosure of any information that would reasonably be expected to enable the client to make an informed decision.[37] The provisions

---

29 sec 3(1)*(a)*(ii) of the GCC.

30 sec 3(1)*(a)*(iii) of the GCC.

31 sec 3(1)*(a)*(vi) of the GCC.

32 sec 3(1)*(a)*(vii) of the GCC. In *Charles Spencer Griffiths v Alwyn Smith Finansiële Dienste BK and Alwyn Bernardus Smith* (Case no FAIS 05659/11-12/WCI) the respondent failed to explain properly to the client the charges and fees that were included in investments sold to him. The Ombud ordered the respondent to pay to the complainant an amount which represented the respondent's damages, calculated as the sum of two penalties the respondent had to pay because he was forced to make the product paid-up as a result of the fact that it was unaffordable.

33 sec 3(1)*(c)* of the GCC.

34 See *Charles Spencer Griffiths v Alwyn Smit Finansiële Dienste BK and Alwyn Bernardus Smit* (Case No FAIS 05659/11-12/WC1).

35 sec 3(1)*(d)* of the GCC.

36 sec 7 of the GCC.

37 sec 7(1)*(a)* of the GCC. The remainder of sec 7 stipulates *inter alia* that a financial services provider should, at the earliest reasonably possible opportunity, provide full and appropriate information of the name, class or type of financial product

of section 7 are very detailed and it is apparent that the pre-FAIS, common-law duties of acting in good faith and with reasonable care and skill have been developed into finely detailed rules. Unfortunately, section 7 does not prevent advisers from earning fees for services where they in actual fact present the client with a standard application form. Once the client completes this application form , a cover letter is issued and the financial product will in fact have been purchased, and that without the advisor having given advice. Although section 7 of the GCC contains onerous obligations and one may accept that not all the sub-sections will apply to all financial products, it remains unfair for a services provider to circumvent section 7 and still charge a fee for the rendering of professional services. In *Fliptrans CC v S & P Insurance Advisors (Pty) Ltd t/a McCrystal and Partners and E Solms*[38] a motor vehicle dealer sold a motorcycle and also arranged insurance on behalf of the purchaser. The insurance agent was nowhere to be found when the insurance was sold but earned a commission regardless. When it transpired that nobody provided the policyholder (owner of the motorcycle) with information regarding certain onerous clauses in the policy, the FAIS Ombud ruled that the services provider had acted in contravention of section 7 of the GCC.[39]

Perhaps one of the most spectacular failures of the GCC, if the Retail Distribution Review can be believed, is Part VII, "Furnishing of Advice". Section 8 details the suitability of advice on a financial product to a client. Furthermore, section 8 stipulates that a provider is obliged to take reasonable steps to seek from the client appropriate and available information regarding the client's financial situation, financial product experience and objectives to enable the provider to advise the client properly.[40] Following this analysis, the adviser must conduct an analysis and identify the product that will be appropriate to the client's risk profile and financial needs, subject to

concerned, the nature and extent of benefits to be provided (sec 7(1)*(c)*(i)–(ii)). Where the product is an investment or has an investment component, the client should be provided with concise details of the manner in which the value of the investment is determined, including concise details of any underlying assets or other financial instruments (sec 7(1)*(c)*(iii)*(aa)*).

38 Case no FAIS 07987/11-12/GP3.

39 See also sec 7(3) of the GCC.

40 sec 8(1)*(a)*.

"the limitations imposed on the provider under the [FAIS] Act or any contractual arrangement".[41] For replacement products, there are additional arrangements, namely that all fees, charges, special terms and conditions, exclusions of liability, waiting periods, loadings, penalties, excesses, restrictions or circumstances in which benefits will not be applicable to the replacement product should be disclosed to the client.[42]

Perhaps the most important disclosure that should be made to a client where a replacement product is sold, is contained in section 8(1)*(d)*(ix) with stipulates that the provider must advise the client on the following:

> "Any incentive, remuneration, consideration, commission, fee or brokerages received, directly or indirectly, by the provider on the terminated product and any incentive, remuneration, consideration, commission, fee or brokerages payable, directly or indirectly, to the provider on the replacement product where the provider rendered financial services on both the terminated and replacement product."

It is in actual fact not surprising then that section 8 is often not complied with, especially where replacement products are concerned.[43] Therefore, despite these very detailed obligations regarding advice, it seems that advisers still hoodwink clients. It is therefore perhaps no wonder that the regulator decided to move away from these detailed rules and back to a more values-based approach. The next paragraph explains this in more detail.

IV. Treating Customers Fairly

Advice pertaining to financial products is governed by the FAIS Act. However, recently government has started to move away from the so-called practice of "silo" regulation and supervision, that focuses on supervision ac-

---

41 sec 8(1)*(c)*.

42 sec 8(1)*(d)*(i)–(ii). For insurance replacement products, the impact of age and health changes on the premium payable should be disclosed (sec 8(1)*(d)*(iii)). There should also be disclosures regarding tax implications, penalties for unrecovered expenses, and the extent to which the replacement product is readily realizable (sec 8(1)*(d)*(iv)–(vii)).

43 See *Marc Rupert Hughes v Mariette Jolene Slippens and Gen-Assist Insurance Brokers (Pty) Ltd* (Case no FAIS 05470/13-14/GP (3)); *David Marthinus Adlen v Herman Coertzen Brokers CC and Herman Bernardus Coertzen* (Case no FAIS 05054/12-14/GP2); *Johannes Cornelis Bothma Bester v Louise Lee T/A Louise Lee Finansiële Adviseurs* (Case no FAIS 0091-13/14 G 3); *Lizelle Franca Botha v Anna Mathilda Ackermann* (Case no FAIS 04766/14-15/GP 3).

cording to industry (such as banking and insurance), to a model which regulates according to function, for example systemic risk management and consumer treatment (the so-called "Twin Peaks" model).[44]

The Financial Sector Regulation Bill (FSR Bill) is the first step towards the implementation of the Twin Peaks model. Clause 2 of the second draft of the FSR Bill defines a financial product as follows:

> "(a) a participatory interest in a collective investment scheme;
> (b) an interest, subscription, contribution, or commitment in a pooled fund;
> (c) a long-term or a short-term policy, as defined in section 1(1) of the Long-term Insurance Act and section 1(1) of the Short-term Insurance Act, respectively;
> (d) a benefit provided by—
> (i) a pension fund organisation as defined in section 1(1) of the Pension Funds Act, to the members of the organisation by virtue of membership; or
> (ii) a friendly society as defined in section 1(1) of the Friendly Societies Act, to the members of the society by virtue of membership;
> (e) a deposit as defined in section 1(1) of the Banks Act;
> (f) a health service benefit provided by a medical scheme as defined in section 1(1) of the Medical Schemes Act, 1998 (Act No. 131 of 1998);
> (g) a credit agreement;
> (h) a facility, arrangement or system that is designated by the Minister in terms of subsection (2) in Regulations as being a "financial product";
> (i) any combined product containing one or more of the financial products referred to in paragraphs (a) to (h)."

This definition corresponds with the current definition of "financial product" in the FAIS Act.[45] The Prudential Authority will henceforth be respon-

---

44 Gilmour "South Africa 2014's twin peaks – no, it's not next year's Play Boy calendar…" *Moneyweb* 5 May 2015, www.moneyweb.co.za/archive/2014s-twin-peaks/ (15-09-2017). After publication of the first draft bill, a period was allowed for comment from 13 December 2013 to 7 March 2014. Several comments were received on various aspects of the draft bill, and on matters pertaining to insurance and intermediaries. The Association for Savings and Investment South Africa (ASISA), the Financial Intermediaries Association of Southern Africa (FIA) and the South African Insurance Association (SAIA) made submissions on a number of issues, such as the definition of "financial crisis" in the draft bill. The revised version still does not contain a definition of "financial crisis" but now defines "systemic event" and "systemic risk" and chapter 2 of the Bill explains the Reserve Bank's powers and responsibilities in managing systemic risk and systemic events.

45 sec 1(1), *sv* "financial product".

sible for supervising safety and soundness of financial institutions that provide financial products, market infrastructures or payment systems.[46] Prudential oversight is aimed to ensure that institutions meet financial obligations to customers.[47]

The other peak, the Financial Sector Conduct Authority, is expected to be responsible for fair treatment, integrity and education, and will supervise services performed in relation to financial products, foreign financial products, securities, market infrastructure or the payment system.[48] What is important to note is that the definition of "financial service" is quite comprehensive and differs markedly from the current definition of "financial service" in the FAIS Act.[49] "Financial service" in the FSR Bill means—

> "(a) in relation to a financial product, foreign financial product, securities, market infrastructure or the payment system as applicable—
> (i) promotion, marketing or distribution;
> (ii) providing advice, recommendations or guidance;
> (iii) dealing or making a market;
> (iv) operating or managing, or providing administration services;
> (v) services provided in relation to credit agreements, including legal services;
> (vi) services provided by payment system participants;
> (b) providing an intermediary service as defined in section 1(1) of the Financial Advisory and Intermediary Services Act;
> (c) securities services provided by a regulated person as defined in section 1(1) of the Financial Markets Act;
> (d) providing credit rating services as defined in section 1(1) of the Credit Rating Services Act, 2012 (Act No. 24 of 2012);
> (e) the calculation of a financial benchmark;
> (f) services related to an interest, subscription, contribution, or commitment in a pooled fund;
> (g) services related to the buying and selling of foreign exchange;

---

46 cl 27–29 of the FSR Bill.

47 The FSR Bill also allows the Minister in terms of sec 215 and in accordance with sec 231(3) to designate in Regulations as a "financial product", a category or type of facility, arrangement, or system that is not already regulated in terms of a financial sector law, and cannot be designated in Regulations in terms of another financial sector law to be regulated in terms of that financial sector law. This designation is aimed at furthering the objectives of the FSR Bill.

48 cl 3 of the FSR Bill.

49 The current definition in sec 1(1) of the FAIS Act stipulates that a financial service "means any service contemplated in paragraph *(a)*, *(b)* or *(c)* of the definition of 'financial services provider', including any category of such services."

(h) dealing with trust property, as defined in section 1 of the Financial Institutions (Protection of Funds) Act, 2001 (Act No. 23 of 2001), as a regular feature of business;

(i) a service that is designated by the Minister in terms of subsection (2) in Regulations as a financial service."

Whether consumers will be better off after the implementation of the FSR Bill is an open question. What is evident is that the new dispensation will regulate market conduct via the Financial Sector Conduct Authority. Because market conduct refers to the way in which financial services providers conduct their business, design and price their products and treat their customers, this function is primarily concerned with the relationship between financial services providers (such as insurance companies) and clients and it is in this context that matters pertaining to advertising, compliance with product features and standards, claims handling and dispute resolution becomes relevant.

Although there is no specific clause that states that there will be such a thing as TCF, the TCF principles are embedded in the proposed legislation and there can be no doubt that the conduct of financial institutions will henceforth be measured against TCF principles. A perusal of a number of clauses of the FSR Bill makes this evident. For instance, clause 6 of the Bill postulates that it is the object of the proposed act

"to achieve a financial system that works in the interests of financial customers, and supports balanced and sustainable economic growth in the Republic, by establishing, in conjunction with the other financial sector laws, a regulatory and supervisory framework that promotes–

(a) financial stability;

(b) the safety and soundness of financial institutions;

(c) the fair treatment and protection of financial customers;

(d) the efficiency and integrity of the financial system;

(e) the prevention of financial crime;

(f) financial inclusion; and

(g) confidence in the financial system." (Own emphasis.)

In addition, clause 52(a) states that the objective of the new Financial Sector Conduct Authority (FSCA) will be to ensure that financial institutions treat customers fairly[50] and the functions of the FSCA are set out in accordance with these objectives.[51]

It is in fact clause 95(1)*(c)*(i) of the FSR Bill that authorises the FSCA to make conduct standards to ensure the protection and fair treatment of financial customers.

While the current legal status of TCF is debatable,[52] it is a fact that TCF is the new direction that will be followed in the financial services industry and that the new principles-based approach is one of the cornerstones of Twin Peaks. According to National Treasury, "the TCF framework is transforming the way in which the supervision of market conduct happens. Being implemented by the FSB, TCF is an activities-based, cross-cutting and outcomes-driven approach to regulation and supervision, designed to ensure that regulated financial institutions apply specific standards of fairness to all financial customers".[53] What is clear is that financial institutions must demonstrate that they deliver specified outcomes to their customers. These outcomes are the following, namely:

- Customers can be confident they are dealing with firms where TCF is central to the corporate culture;
- Products and services marketed and sold in the retail market are designed to meet the needs of identified customer groups and are targeted accordingly;
- Customers are provided with clear information and are kept appropriately informed before, during and after point of sale;
- Where advice is given, it is suitable and takes account of customer circumstances;

---

50 Other objectives include enhancing the efficiency and integrity of the financial system (cl 52 (b)) and providing financial customers and potential financial customers with financial education programs, promoting financial literacy and financial capability (cl 52(c)).

51 cl 52.

52 See Millard "Through the looking glass: fairness in insurance contracts – a caucus race?" 2014 *Tydskrif Vir Hedendaagse Romein-Hollandse Reg (THRHR)* 547–566.

53 National Treasury *Treating customers fairly in the financial sector: a draft market conduct policy for South Africa Discussion Document* (December 2014) http://www.treasury.gov.za/public%20comments/FSR2014/Treating%20Customers%20Fairly%20in%20the%20Financial%20Sector%20Draft%20MCP%20Framework%20Amended%20Jan2015%20WithAp6.pdf (15-09-2017) 50.

- Products perform as firms have led customers to expect, and service is of an acceptable standard and as they have been led to expect; and
- Customers do not face unreasonable post-sale barriers imposed by firms to change product, switch providers, submit a claim or make a complaint.[54]

It is in fact outcome three that deals with clear information before, during and after point of sale and outcome four that deals with the suitability of advice. Together, these outcomes aim to achieve a fair outcome for consumers.

It does seem as though section 8 of the GCC (para 3 above) and outcomes three and four have the same objectives but because section 8 did not have the effect of providing advice in a way which is fair, this paper now turns to the findings of the Retail Distribution Review (RDR).

V. Retail Distribution Review (RDR)

1. Background

The FSB published its Retail Distribution Review (RDR) discussion document in November 2014. Even though the TCF approach was at that stage not law (and in fact is still not), the thinking was that TCF is a better approach to regulating conduct of business in financial services.[55]

Comprising some 97 pages, the review has been undertaken against the background of the "Twin Peaks" approach.[56] Desired outcomes of the RDR include distribution models that do the following, namely: support the delivery of suitable products and provide fair access to suitable advice for financial customers; enable customers to understand and compare the nature, value and cost of advice and other services intermediaries provide; enhance standards of professionalism in financial advice and intermediary services to build consumer confidence and trust; enable customers and distributors

---

54 National Treasury (n 53) 51.

55 Financial Services Board *Retail Distribution Review (2014)*, https://www.fsb.org.uk/docs/default-source/Publications/reports/fsb-retail-distribution-review-2014.pdf?sfvrsn=1 (15-09-2017).

56 Financial Services Board (n 50) 1.

to benefit from fair competition for quality advice and intermediary services, at a price more closely aligned with the nature and quality of the service; and support sustainable business models for financial advice that enable adviser businesses viably to deliver fair customer outcomes over the long term.[57]

The RDR recognises that it builds on the "strong foundation already provided by the FAIS Act in terms of intermediary professionalism, disclosure to clients and mitigating certain conflicts of interest".[58] However, one of the focus areas of the review is to:

> "[G]ive special attention to achieving fair outcomes for low-income customers, through enabling distribution models that support financial inclusion combined with other measures to ensure that products marketed and sold are suitable and offer adequate value, including targeted product standards."[59]

The 55 specific regulatory proposals are to be implemented in phases over the next couple of years. After extensive consultation, the FSB released a follow-up document in which phase 1 is outlined. According to the *RDR Review Phase 1*,[60] the FAIS Act dealt only with *actual advice* and although this statute made great strides towards professionalising financial advice, the rest of the role players in the industry are not necessarily contributing towards the process of rendering proper advice. For instance, where advisers have those onerous duties as described in paragraph 4 above, product suppliers get off very lightly. Where a client purchased an inappropriate product, it was almost inevitably laid at the door of the adviser.[61] Product design was perhaps less important and the role of product suppliers easier as the blame was readily shifted from suppliers to advisers. Furthermore, as advisers are greatly dependent upon product suppliers for designing appropriate products and for commission, the *RDR Review Phase 1* suggests several interventions to re-balance the relationship between clients, product suppliers and providers.

---

57 Financial Services Board (n 50) 1.

58 Financial Services Board (n 50) 1.

59 Financial Services Board (n 50) 1.

60 Financial Services Board *Treating Customers Fairly. Status Update: Retail Distribution Review Phase 1: An update on the "Phase1" Proposals identified in the Retail Distribution Review* (2015), https://www.fsb.co.za/NewsLibrary/FSB%20Retail%20Distribution%20Review%20Phase%201%20Status%20Update%202015.pdf (15-09-2017) (*RDR Review Phase 1).*

61 *See Andrew Graham Stunden and Nicolaas Leon van der Walt t/a Investment v Insurance Brokers* (Case number FAIS 01993/11-12/WC3).

2. New dispensation for advisers

One of the biggest shifts envisaged by the *RDR Review Phase 1* is that instead of product suppliers paying advisers commission, the client should in fact be paying the commission. Although a client will still be able to instruct a product supplier to deduct the commission, the whole marketing strategy will henceforth be different as there can be no hidden fees. In addition, it will have to be abundantly clear whether the client will pay for advice, administration or business charges. These proposed interventions are in fact envisaged in order for a client to understand the value chain better because of so-called clean pricing. Advisers will therefore have to change their business models and this is in fact a challenge, especially on the long-term life side where commission is typically a mixture of up-front versus on-going commission. Further proposals also seek to introduce caps on the commission that may be earned by advisers.[62]

Another matter that is said to be confusing to clients is the actual status of the financial adviser. Independent advice should in fact be advice that takes into account all possible products, regardless of the commission that is payable to the adviser. A client should ideally benefit from such advice as a *bona fide*, independent adviser will present all options available to the client, regardless of the amount of commission payable. Unfortunately, a truly independent adviser's advice would actually come at a higher premium as such an adviser needs to have knowledge of a very wide range of products and should also stay abreast of all the latest developments. Where some products are in fact quite simple and should in fact be capable of being sold without advice, others require extensive advice.[63] Therefore, *RDR Review Phase 1* suggests that instead of calling an adviser "independent", it is perhaps more correct to speak of a "multi-tied" agent, as no adviser is in fact completely independent. Because the cost of advice constitutes a significant portion of the product cost, clients should in fact know what exactly they are paying for.

---

62 *RDR Review Phase 1* (n 60) 11, 16, 31, 37, 46.

63 Consider for example the difference between a funeral policy with a benefit of R10 000 and a life policy. Where a funeral policy may perhaps have a "no-claim period" of three months and no exclusions based on ill-health or even age, a life policy may require extensive disclosures. In addition, there is also a difference between a risk only policy and an endowment policy. See Reinecke and Nienaber *Life Insurance in South Africa* (2009) 74–75.

More specifically, the FSB's current thinking is to adopt a two-tier model for the categorisation of advisers. Notably, the main distinction between the two tiers will be whether the adviser is the agent of a product supplier, a licensed adviser in his or her own right (sole proprietor) or a representative of a licensed adviser firm that is not also a product supplier.[64] In addition, an adviser or adviser firm will only be permitted to provide advice in *one* capacity. Instead of referring to all advisers as "advisers", it seems that the idea is to refer to an adviser who is the agent of a product supplier as a "registered product supplier agent" and to a sole proprietor or a representative of a licensed adviser as a "registered financial adviser".[65]

As far as the actual activities of these advisers are concerned, product supplier agents (previously tied advisers) will be permitted to provide advice on the products of one product supplier or product-supplier group only and with investment or savings products, this will include allowing the agent also to advise on products of so-called external suppliers that are offered through an investment platform administered by the primary supplier or group.[66] This means that the disclosures that an adviser (or in future, agent), will have to make to a client will have to be re-considered. Another innovation is that in future, these product supplier agents will not be licensed advisers in their own right but will operate under the product supplier's licence.[67] As far as their remuneration is concerned, these agents will also, in the case of long-term insurance risk products, be subject to the principle of equivalence of reward. Exactly how the equivalence of reward will be implemented in future is not sure at present, as existing commission structures of so-called tied agents will have to be revised in substantial detail.[68]

All advisers that are not product supplier agents but registered financial advisers will be advisers that are either licensed to provide advice in their own right, as sole proprietors, or are registered representatives of a firm that is licensed to provide advice.[69] A registered financial adviser will only be allowed to describe itself or its advice as "independent" if such adviser has not entered into any binder agreement with any insurer, does not earn any

64 *RDR Review Phase 1* (n 60) 11.
65 *RDR Review Phase 1* (n 60) 11.
66 *RDR Review Phase 1* (n 60) 12.
67 *RDR Review Phase 1* (n 60) 13.
68 *RDR Review Phase 1* (n 60) 36.
69 *RDR Review Phase 1* (n 60) 13.

remuneration, directly or indirectly, from any product supplier and does not hold any ownership or similar interest in any product supplier.[70]

These proposals seem to support the principle that product-supplier responsibility for customer outcomes should be brought into balance with the extent of product-supplier influence over advice and product suppliers who have binders, outsourcing or ownership relationships with a registered financial adviser in relation to any advice provided on its (or its group's) products will have stricter responsibilities than those that rest on product suppliers who do not have these relationships.[71]

Against this exposition, the discussion now turns to financial advice in German law.

VI. Position of financial advisers in German law

1. General

In Germany, as in South Africa, financial services are highly regulated.[72] The Federal Financial Supervisory Authority *(Bundesanstalt für Finanzdienstleistungsaufsicht)* (BaFin) supervises financial services. However, where the rules pertaining to the activities of all advisers and intermediaries who render financial services are presently contained in the (generic) FAIS Act in South Africa, the German supervisory framework distinguishes between insurance intermediaries and those who sell other financial products. The local Chambers of Trade and Commerce *(Industrie- und Handelskammer)* are responsible for licensing and overseeing insurance intermediaries.

2. Insurance intermediaries

As far as insurance is concerned, the European Union's Insurance Mediation Directive (2002/92/EC) of 2002 is significant. This particular directive creates a duty for every intermediary (who is not an employee) to be registered. In addition, it sets minimum requirements pertaining to professional

---

70 *RDR Review Phase 1* (n 60) 13.
71 *RDR Review Phase 1* (n 60) 13.
72 Bähr *Handbuch des Versicherungsaufsichtsrechts* (2011) 2–24.

qualifications and personal characteristic to serve as requisites for registration. It also stipulates that intermediaries must have compulsory professional liability insurance. Furthermore, it sets out duties to inform, to advise and to document to which the insurance intermediary is subject. On the whole, this directive aims to ensure professionalism and competence among insurance intermediaries, the protection of customers' interests and that individuals and companies providing insurance or reinsurance mediation are registered in their home EU country (which allows them to do business elsewhere in the EU). In addition, it aims to ensure that there is respect for minimum professional requirements such as the appropriate knowledge and ability to sell insurance and sufficient financial capacity to protect customers. Furthermore, customers should be given clear explanations on the advice given and there should be appropriate and effective alternative dispute-resolution procedures.[73]

The German legislator implemented the directive through supervisory law in the Insurance Supervisory Act,[74] in the trade regulation (*GewO*)[75] and in the *German Insurance Contract Act (VVG)*.[76] In addition, there are the regulations covering insurance mediation and advice, insurance mediation regulations (*Versicherungsvermittlungsverordnungen*), and also the regulations governing obligations to provide information with insurance

73 "Distribution of insurance products and after-sale activities" accessed at http://ec.europa.eu/finance/insurance/consumer/mediation/index_en.htm (15-09-2017).

74 secs 80, 80a and 80b of the *Versicherungsaufsichtsgesetz (VAG)*.

75 sec 34d(1) of the *Gewerbeordnung (GewO)*. This section reads as follows: "Wer gewerbsmäßig als Versicherungsmakler oder als Versicherungsvertreter den Abschluss von Versicherungsverträgen vermitteln will (Versicherungsvermittler), bedarf der Erlaubnis der zuständigen Industrie- und Handelskammer. Die Erlaubnis kann inhaltlich beschränkt und mit Auflagen verbunden werden, soweit dies zum Schutze der Allgemeinheit oder der Versicherungsnehmer erforderlich ist; unter denselben Voraussetzungen sind auch die nachträgliche Aufnahme, Änderung und Ergänzung von Auflagen zulässig. In der Erlaubnis ist anzugeben, ob sie einem Versicherungsmakler oder einem Versicherungsvertreter erteilt wird. Die einem Versicherungsmakler erteilte Erlaubnis beinhaltet die Befugnis, Dritte, die nicht Verbraucher sind, bei der Vereinbarung, Änderung oder Prüfung von Versicherungsverträgen gegen gesondertes Entgelt rechtlich zu beraten; diese Befugnis zur Beratung erstreckt sich auch auf Beschäftigte von Unternehmen in den Fällen, in denen der Versicherungsmakler das Unternehmen berät. Bei der Wahrnehmung der Aufgaben nach den Sätzen 1 und 2 unterliegt die Industrie- und Handelskammer der Aufsicht der obersten Landesbehörde."

76 secs 59–73 of the *Versicherungsvertragsgesetz (VVG) of 23 November 2007.*

contracts (*VVG-InfoV*) which in fact are not directly aimed at the insurance mediators, but should also provide the customer with certain information.

Concerning insurance intermediation, the German Insurance Contract Act (*VVG*) mainly distinguishes between insurance agent and insurance broker.[77] In contrast to the insurance broker, the insurance agent is primarily a representative of the insurer and thus promotes the latter's interests.[78]

Another important regulatory aspect pertaining to intermediaries is that the insurer may only cooperate with mediators (brokers or agents) who either in the meaning of section 34d(1) of the *GewO* have a permit, are exempted from the permit[79] or are not subject to any permit.[80] Only a person who intends to mediate the conclusion of insurance contracts commercially as an insurance broker or insurance agent fall under section 34d *GewO* and thus can work as an insurance mediator of an insurer.

As far as the actual rendering of advice is concerned, section 11 of the insurance mediation regulations embodies the stipulations on information obligations for mediators as specified by section 12 of the EU Insurance Mediation Directive. Section 11 stipulates that as soon as an intermediary establishes contact with a client, that intermediary must inform a (prospective) policyholder in writing of his personal particulars, his business status and his commercial register data. For purposes of a possible conflict of interest, he must also disclose the direct or indirect participation of more than 10 % in an insurance company or similar concern. In addition, the address of the Ombudsman must be provided. Section 60 stipulates the basis upon which advice should be provided[81] and sections 61 and 62 of the VVG stipulate that an insurance broker has a duty to advise and to also document the

---

77 sec 59 VVG; Dörner in Prölss and Martin (eds) *Versicherungsvertragsgesetz* (29th Edition 2010) § 59 VVG paras 1–3, 9–12, 65–69, 111 et seqq.

78 sec 69 VVG; Dörner in Prölss and Martin (n 77) § 69 VVG paras 1–3.

79 sec 34d(3).

80 secs 34d(4) and 34d(5).

81 Sec 60 stipulates as follows: "(1) The insurance broker shall be obligated to base his advice on a sufficient number of contracts of insurance and insurers available on the market so that he is in a position to make his recommendation, based on professional criteria, regarding which contract of insurance is suited to meeting the needs of the person wishing to take out insurance. This shall not apply if he explicitly informs the person wishing to take out insurance in individual cases prior to contractual acceptance of the limited selection of insurers and contracts. (2) An insurance broker who informs a person wishing to take out insurance of the limited selection in accordance with para (1), second sentence, and an insurance agent must inform the person wishing to take out insurance on which market and

advice. Such advice should be based on a sufficient number of products available on the market and the adviser must then make a recommendation as to the suitability of a particular product.[82]

Breach of section 11 of the insurance mediation regulations has consequences. Section 18 of the Regulations, read with 144 of the *GewO* state that breach of any of these regulations is punishable as administrative offences. In addition, section 63 of the *VVG* regulates damages in those instances where the policyholder suffers damages through a breach of the intermediary's duty to provide information and advice and to properly document this. However, the intermediary will escape liability where he was not at fault.[83]The intermediary's duties to disclose will vary according to the legal classification of that intermediary.[84] In the case of an insurance agent, the policyholder will have further recourse against the insurance company. In fact, a prejudiced policyholder may hold the agent and the insurer liable, jointly and severally for damages.[85] However, if an insurance broker concludes the contract with the policyholder, the insurer's duties under section 6 *VVG* to advise and to document do not apply.

The most recent legislative amendments in insurance in the German Life Insurance Reform Act (*Lebensversicherungsreformgesetz, LVRG*) include the limitation of the policyholders' share of the valuation reserves, the limitation of the profits distributed to shareholders, multi-year projections, a lower maximum interest rate and extended notification obligations. The latter innovation is significant in the context of advice and it simply means that life insurers have a duty to inform their customers of the publication of additional information on the surplus participation in order to provide their customers with a clearer understanding of the value and composition of the minimum surplus participation which is required by law.[86]

---

information basis they are providing their services, and must state the names of the insurers on the basis of which they are giving advice. The insurance agent must also name the insurer on behalf of whom he is working and whether he is working exclusively for him. (3) The person wishing to take out insurance may waive the right to the notifications and information in accordance with para (2) by separate written declaration."

82 sec 60 of the VVG; Dörner in Prölss and Martin (n 77) § 60 para 1.

83 sec 63(1); Dörner in Prölss and Martin (n 77) § 63 paras 13–15.

84 secs 60 and 61 of the VVG.

85 See secs 280, 311 and 278 of the *Bürgerliches Gesetzbuch* (BGB) read together with sec 6 VVG. See also Rudy in Prölss and Martin (n 77) § 6 paras 54–68.

86 Elsner *The German Life Insurance Reform Act from the point of view of consumers* (17 February 2015) https://www.bafin.de/SharedDocs/Veroeffentlichungen/

For purposes of a proper comparison, it is perhaps handy to consider the content of section 6:

> "(1) Der Versicherer hat den Versicherungsnehmer, soweit nach der Schwierigkeit, die angebotene Versicherung zu beurteilen, oder der Person des Versicherungsnehmers und dessen Situation hierfür Anlass besteht, nach seinen Wünschen und Bedürfnissen zu befragen und, auch unter Berücksichtigung eines angemessenen Verhältnisses zwischen Beratungsaufwand und der vom Versicherungsnehmer zu zahlenden Prämien, zu beraten sowie die Gründe für jeden zu einer bestimmten Versicherung erteilten Rat anzugeben. Er hat dies unter Berücksichtigung der Komplexität des angebotenen Versicherungsvertrags zu dokumentieren.
>
> (2) Der Versicherer hat dem Versicherungsnehmer den erteilten Rat und die Gründe hierfür klar und verständlich vor dem Abschluss des Vertrags in Textform zu übermitteln. Die Angaben dürfen mündlich übermittelt werden, wenn der Versicherungsnehmer dies wünscht oder wenn und soweit der Versicherer vorläufige Deckung gewährt. In diesen Fällen sind die Angaben unverzüglich nach Vertragsschluss dem Versicherungsnehmer in Textform zu übermitteln; dies gilt nicht, wenn ein Vertrag nicht zustande kommt und für Verträge über vorläufige Deckung bei Pflichtversicherungen.
>
> (3) Der Versicherungsnehmer kann auf die Beratung und Dokumentation nach den Absätzen 1 und 2 durch eine gesonderte schriftliche Erklärung verzichten, in der er vom Versicherer ausdrücklich darauf hingewiesen wird, dass sich ein Verzicht nachteilig auf seine Möglichkeit auswirken kann, gegen den Versicherer einen Schadensersatzanspruch nach Absatz 5 geltend zu machen.
>
> (4) Die Verpflichtung nach Absatz 1 Satz 1 besteht auch nach Vertragsschluss während der Dauer des Versicherungsverhältnisses, soweit für den Versicherer ein Anlass für eine Nachfrage und Beratung des Versicherungsnehmers erkennbar ist. Der Versicherungsnehmer kann im Einzelfall auf eine Beratung durch schriftliche Erklärung verzichten.
>
> (5) Verletzt der Versicherer eine Verpflichtung nach Absatz 1, 2 oder 4, ist er dem Versicherungsnehmer zum Ersatz des hierdurch entstehenden Schadens verpflichtet. Dies gilt nicht, wenn der Versicherer die Pflichtverletzung nicht zu vertreten hat.
>
> (6) Die Absätze 1 bis 5 sind auf Versicherungsverträge über ein Großrisiko im Sinn des § 210 Absatz 2 nicht anzuwenden, ferner dann nicht, wenn der Vertrag mit dem Versicherungsnehmer von einem Versicherungsmakler vermittelt wird oder wenn es sich um einen Vertrag im Fernabsatz im Sinn des § 312c des Bürgerlichen Gesetzbuchs handelt."[87]

EN/Fachartikel/2015/fa_bj_1502_lebensversicherungsreformgesetz_en.html (15-09-2017).

87 The translation as taken from Wandt and Gal "German Report to the Questionnaire of AIDA on Transparency of Insurance Contract Terms and Conditions and Pre-

When considering this section, together with section 7 that deals with information that should be provided to the policyholder, it is evident that there are great similarities between the South African and German legislation as far as advice is concerned. Disclosures are of key importance, product advice should enable a client to make an informed decision and failure of an intermediary and/or insurer to provide proper advice not only attracts a penalty but is also actionable in civil law. However, it does seem as though there is a distinction between an insurance agent and an insurance broker. Once the South African legislation has been amended as envisaged by RDR, there will (once again) be this distinction in South African law.

Contractual Information" (unpublished paper 2014) 32 reads as follows: "(1) If the difficulty in assessing the insurance being offered or the policyholder himself and his situation gives occasion thereto, the insurer must ask him about his wishes and needs and, also bearing in mind an appropriate relation between the time and effort spent in providing this advice and the insurance premiums to be paid by the policyholder, the insurer shall advise the policyholder and state reasons for each of the pieces of advice in respect of a particular insurance. He shall document this, taking into account the complexity of the contract of insurance being offered. (2) Before the contract is concluded, the insurer shall provide the policyholder with the advice in writing, clearly and comprehensibly stating reasons. This information may be provided verbally if the policyholder so wishes or if and insofar as the insurer guarantees provisional cover. In such cases the information shall be provided in writing to the policyholder without undue delay as soon as the contract has been made; this shall not apply where a contract is not made and to contracts in respect of provisional cover in the case of compulsory insurances. (3) The policyholder may waive the right to advice and documentation thereof in accordance with paras (1) and (2) by a separate written declaration in which the insurer explicitly indicates that such waiving may have an unfavourable effect on his option for asserting a claim for damages against the insurer in accordance with para (5). (4) The obligation under para (1), first sentence, shall also apply after the contract has been made for the entire term of the insurance agreement insofar as it is clear that the insurer recognises that the policyholder requires information and advice. The policyholder may in individual cases waive the right to advice by written declaration. (5) If the insurer breaches an obligation under paras (1), (2) or (4), he shall be liable to indemnify the policyholder for any loss or damage resulting therefrom. This shall not apply if the insurer is not responsible for the breach of obligation. (6) Paras. (1) to (5) shall not apply to contracts of insurance covering a large risk within the meaning of section 210 para (2) or if the contract is negotiated with the policyholder by an insurance broker or if it is a distance contract within the meaning of section 312b (1) and (2) of the German Civil Code."

3. Investment funds

BaFin regulates domestic management companies (*Kapitalverwaltungsgesellschaften*) and investment funds offered by these companies in terms of the Investment Code (*Kapitalanlagegesetzbuch, KAGB*). As far as intermediary services are concerned, two key changes that directly affected sales of financial instruments were brought about by the Investor Protection and Capital Markets Improvement Act (*Anlegerschutz- und Funktionsverbesserungsgesetz*). These changes are included in part 6 of the Securities Trading Act (*Wertpapierhandelsgesetz, WpHG*) and stipulates inter alia that investment-services enterprises must design, implement and monitor policies and objectives that concern the turnover or volume of or the profit from the transactions recommended as part of the enterprises' investment advice.[88] These amendments stem from a dilemma that saw investment-services enterprises trying to act in the best interests of clients as well as in the interests of the enterprise to make and increase profits. The latter objective is achieved in various ways, such as incentives for employees, financial targets and bonuses and, however, good for enterprise profits, these measures run the risk of diverting the attention from the best interests of the clients, thereby creating an imbalance.[89] The new section 33(1) of the *Wertpapierhandelsgesetz* introduces a new term, namely *Vertriebsvorgaben*, which refers to sales policies and objectives. These include all policies that directly or indirectly concern the turnover or volume of, or the profit from, the transactions recommended by an investment adviser. Therefore, in addition to the existing rules that provided that advisers needed to be honest and forthcoming with information, these additional disclosures of potential conflicts of interest strengthen the focus on client interests.

The South African FAIS Act also contains extensive provisions on conflict of interests.[90] It is submitted that this particular aspect of advice has the potential to persuade advisers and intermediaries to market and sell investments in a particular way because they stand to gain something from the transaction. As this may affect their objectivity, it is submitted that more detailed disclosures in fact protect the interests of clients.

---

88 Rüsche *Financial instruments: sales policies and objectives for investment services enterprises* (17 November 2014), https://www.bafin.de/SharedDocs/Veroeffentlichungen/EN/Fachartikel/2014/fa_bj_1411_vertriebsvorgaben_fuer_wertpapierdienstleistungsunternehmen_en.html (15-09-2017).

89 Rüsche (n 89).

90 secs 3(1)*(c)* and 3A of the GCC in terms of the FAIS Act.

Another recent development in investment advice is the enactment of the Fee-Based Investment Advice Act (*Honoraranlageberatungsgesetz*), which came into force on 1 August 2014 and introduced this term into the Securities Trading Act for the first time.[91] The new rules are intended to increase transparency regarding fees or commissions paid for investment advice. In terms of the new legislation, investment advisers under this model who recommend products in return for a fee may receive payment only from clients, supporting the notion that fee-based investment advice should be given solely in the client's interests.[92] If one considers this rule, it seems that the South African RDR is not quite off the mark. In addition to the fee requirements, the legislation provides that investment advisers must base their recommendations on sufficient market knowledge and the product range offered must also be sufficiently diversified with regards to providers and issuers of financial instruments. This requirement in fact forces providers of fee-based investment advice to refrain from exclusively offering their own financial instruments, instruments from their own group of investment companies or instruments from providers or issuers with whom the advisers are closely connected. By doing so, they avoid a conflict between their own interests and those of their clients.[93]

In addition to these requirements, section 31 (4d) of the *Wertpapierhandelsgesetz* prohibits conducting recommended transactions on a fixed-price basis. An institution's intention to generate margin profits in fixed-price transactions acts, in principle, as an opposing force to the independence of fee-based investment advisers, who are supposed to act only in their clients' interests. The statutory sanction for continuous failure by an institution to comply with the special conduct of business obligations and organisational requirements for the provisions of fee-based investment advice is the banning by BaFin of the institution, which means that such institution will no longer be permitted to carry the legally protected designation "fee-based investment adviser".[94]

---

91 Begner *Fee-based investment advice: New rules to enter into force in August* (15 July 2014), https://www.bafin.de/SharedDocs/Veroeffentlichungen/EN/Fachartikel/2014/fa_bj_1407_honorar-anlageberatung_en.html (15-09-2017).

92 Begner (n 92) 1.

93 Begner (n 92) 2.

94 Begner (n 92) 2.

4. Comment

It is submitted that as far as insurance and investment intermediaries are concerned, the notions of payment by the client for advice, avoidance of conflict of interests and the difference between an agent and an independent intermediary already form part of the legislation. It is therefore fair to say that rigorous regulation of financial services aim to curb unfair treatment of customers both in South Africa.

VII. Conclusion

Opinion remains divided on the Regulator's obsession with advisers and those who subscribe to the notion that the devil makes work for idle hands, will argue that the actual difficulties experienced with advice in the current legal framework are in fact grossly exaggerated. If one considers the multitude of transactions that are concluded daily, it seems that those complaints that are in fact brought to the attention of the FAIS Ombud and the FSB are negligible. If one also considers that the *RDR* does not deal with the unregulated product space, the only conclusion that can be made is that the current issues regarding commission structures and violations of clients' rights is an unwarranted pre-occupation of the Regulator.

However the opposite view is that because clients are currently not fully aware of what exactly they pay and to whom, it is no wonder that there are relatively little complaints. It is in fact the Regulator who sees the full picture and that it is why action is required. There is perhaps a bit of truth in both these views.

Overall, although the implementation of some drastic changes to the legal position of advisers are no doubt aimed at creating a fairer dispensation for those who use financial services, it is submitted that it may also provide some relief for advisers. Currently, FAIS Ombud cases seem to suggest that very little has been done by product providers to create products that are appropriate and easy to understand and that the fall-out of this way of conducting business inevitably becomes part of bad product advice, placing advisers, and not suppliers, at risk. It is also doubtful whether product providers properly explain onerous clauses in their contracts and whether the effect of these clauses (such as forfeiture clauses, exclusionary clauses and clauses that place other obligations on clients) are ever drafted in plain language. However, the proposed new dispensation will clearly differentiate between those advisers who are in fact agents of product suppliers and those who are not. This means that product suppliers will in future have to shoulder more of the responsibility for inappropriate products, bad advice and inevitably, mis-selling and mis-buying. Whether this will restore the current imbalances is an open question. It can at least be said that if one considers that the new dispensation will also allow for registered financial advisers who are in fact independent, it is suggested that a client who wants to take the risk of using such advice will have proper recourse if the adviser did not advise him properly. That means that clients should have a better chance of knowing who they are dealing with and product suppliers cannot hide behind advisers any more.

The position in Germany pertaining to insurance and investment intermediaries respectively already seem to reflect some of the changes that are envisaged by *RDR*. For insurance intermediaries, there is a definite distinction between independent intermediaries and those who represent insurance companies. In addition, disclosure requirements are such that commission structures in Germany must be revealed to the client. As far as investments are concerned, advisers are forced to present clients with various options and the client also pays for the advice.

When the fairness of advice and the suitability thereof as viewed by *RDR* is cast in the international arena and compared to the situation in Germany, it becomes evident that although it seems superfluous at first glance, those changes that are envisaged by *RDR* are not so far-fetched. In fact, it seems to be on par with developments in Germany, which complies with EU regulations. Overall, it is suggested that those recommendations that aim to address aspects of advice pertaining to the categorisation of advice and most importantly, fees structures, will continue the good work that was started by the FAIS Act. It will most likely cement the solid foundations that already exist and will ensure a fairer dispensation for the consumers of financial services.

Bibliography

Bähr GW *Handbuch des Versicherungsaufsichtsrechts* (C.H. Beck, Munich 2011).

Begner J *Fee-based investment advice: New rules to enter into force in August* (2014), https://www.bafin.de/SharedDocs/Veroeffentlichungen/EN/Fachartikel/2014/fa_bj_1407_honorar-anlageberatung_en.html (15-09-2017).

Elsner D *The German Life Insurance Reform Act from the point of view of consumers* (17 February 2015), https://www.bafin.de/SharedDocs/Veroeffentlichungen/EN/Fachartikel/2015/fa_bj_1502_lebensversicherungsreformgesetz_en.html (15-09-2017).

European Commission (ed) *Distribution of insurance products and after-sale activities*, http://ec.europa.eu/finance/insurance/consumer/mediation/index_en.htm (15-09-2017).

Financial Services Board (ed) *Retail Distribution Review (2014)*, https://www.fsb.org.uk/docs/default-source/Publications/reports/fsb-retail-distribution-review-2014.pdf?sfvrsn=1 (15-09-2017).

Financial Services Board (ed) *Treating Customers Fairly Status Update: Retail Distribution Review Phase 1: An update on the "Phase1" Proposals identified in the Retail Distribution Review (2015)*, https://www.fsb.co.za/NewsLibrary/FSB%20Retail%20Distribution%20Review%20Phase%201%20Status%20Update%202015.pdf (15-09-2017).

Gilmour J *South Africa 2014's twin peaks – no, it's not next year's Play Boy calendar...* Moneyweb (2 December 2013), www.moneyweb.co.za/archive/2014s-twin-peaks/ (15-09-2017).

Hattingh W and Millard D *The FAIS Act Explained* (LexisNexis, Durban 2010).

Havenga P *The Law of Insurance Intermediaries* (Juta Law, Lansdowne 2001).

Millard D "Through the looking glass: Fairness in Insurance contracts – A caucus race?" 2014 *Tydskrif vir Hedendaagse Romeins-Hollandse Reg. (THRHR)* 547.

National Treasury "Treating customers fairly in the financial sector: a draft market conduct policy for South Africa" *Discussion Document* (December 2014) http://www.treasury.gov.za/public%20comments/FSR2014/Treating%20Customers%20Fairly%20in%20the%20Financial%20Sector%20Draft%20MCP%20Framework%20Amended%20Jan2015%20WithAp6.pdf (15-09-2017) 50.

Prölss J and Martin A *Versicherungsvertragsgesetz* (29th Edition, CH Beck, Munich 2015).

Reinecke MFB and Nienaber PM *Life Insurance in South Africa* (LexisNexis, Durban 2009).

Reinecke MFB, Van Niekerk JP and Nienaber PM *South African Insurance Law* (LexisNexis, Durban 2013).

Rüsche M *Financial instruments: sales policies and objectives for investment services enterprises* (2014), https://www.bafin.de/SharedDocs/Veroeffentlichungen/EN/Fachartikel/2014/fa_bj_1411_vertriebsvorgaben_fuer_wertpapierdienstleistungsunternehmen_en.html (15-09-2017).

Van Zyl FH *Financial Advisory and Intermediary Services Manual* (Juta Law, Lansdowne 2004).

Wandt M and Gal J *German Report to the Questionnaire of AIDA on Transparency of Insurance Contract Terms and Conditions and Pre-Contractual Information* (unpublished paper 2014).

Case Law

Stander v Raubenheimer 1996 2 SA 670 (O)

Durr v Absa Bank Ltd and Another 1997 3 SA 448 (SCA)

David Trust v Aegis Insurance Co Ltd 2000 3 SA 289 (SCA)

Ries v Boland Bank PKS Ltd 2000 4 SA 955 (C)

Ombud decisions

Andrew Graham Stunden and Nicolaas Leon van der Walt t/a Investment v Insurance Brokers (Case number FAIS 01993/11-12/WC3)

Charles Spencer Griffiths v Alwyn Smith Finansiële Dienste BK and Alwyn Bernardus Smith (Case no FAIS 05659/11-12/WCI)

David Marthinus Adlen v Herman Coertzen Brokers CC and Herman Bernardus Coertzen (Case no FAIS 05054/12-14/GP2)

Gary le Vatte v Rosspen Financial Services (Case no FOC/600/05 EC).

Johan Adriaan Steenkamp v Old Mutual Life Assurance Company (South Africa) Limited (Case no FOC 1343/05 FS)

Johannes Cornelis Bothma Bester v Louise Lee T/A Louise Lee Finansiële Adviseurs (Case no FAIS 0091-13/14 G3)

Lizelle Franca Botha v Anna Mathilda Ackermann (Case no FAIS 04766/14-15/GP3).

Marc Rupert Hughes v Mariette Jolene Slippens and Gen-Assist Insurance Brokers (Pty) Ltd (Case no FAIS 05470/13-14/GP3)

Masimdumise Gabriel Bengu v Outsurance Insurance Company Ltd (Case no FAIS 06001/14-15/KZN 3)

Enforcement Committee cases

The Registrar of Financial Services Providers v Clifford Mey (Case no 11/2014)

The Registrar of Financial Services Providers v Jacobus Gouws (Case no 16/2014)

The Registrar of Financial Services Providers v Talksure Trading (Pty) Ltd (Case no 20/2014)

The Registrar of Financial Services Providers v Rowe Hooper Insurance and Investment Brokers CC (Case no 27/2015)

Providing investment advice in light of MiFID I and II

*Thomas M.J. Möllers**
*Isabella Brosig***

---

* Thomas M.J. Möllers, *Dr. iur. habil.*; Professor, University of Augsburg, Faculty of Law. Managing Director of the Center for European Legal Studies. Chair for Civil Law, Economic Law, European Law, Private International Law and Comparative Law.

** Isabella Brosig, Academic Assistant, University of Augsburg, Faculty of Law, Chair for Civil Law, Economic Law, European Law, Private International Law and Comparative Law.

I. The regulation of financial intermediaries in the EU

1. Evolution of EU and German law

Securities law and the law governing financial intermediaries was harmonised on the European level for the first time by the Securities Investment Services Directive in 1993.[1] It was replaced in 2004 by the Markets in Financial Instruments Directive (MiFID I)[2]. Following the financial crisis in 2008, legislators across the world tightened up rules for financial intermediaries, including the EU and South Africa.[3] In 2014, the second Markets in Financial Instruments Directive (MiFID II) was passed,[4] supplemented by the Markets in Financial Instruments Regulation (MiFIR).[5] The provisions of both are presumably applicable in Member States as of 3 January 2018.[6] MiFID II can be seen as a "Single Rulebook" for all EU member states and is massive in scale.[7] Furthermore, it includes extensive delegations to the Commission and the European Securities and Markets Authority (ESMA). The delegated and implementing acts of ESMA and the Commission are

---

1 Council Directive 93/22/EEC of 10 May 1993 on investment services in the securities field (Securities Investment Services Directive).

2 Directive 2004/39/EC of the European Parliament and of the Council of 21 April 2004 on markets in financial instruments (MiFID I).

3 Financial Regulatory Reform Steering Committee, *Implementing a twin peaks model of financial regulation in South Africa* available at http://www.treasury.gov.za/twinpeaks/20131211%20-%20Item%203%20Roadmap.pdf (15-09-2017).

4 Directive 2014/65/EU of the European Parliament and of the Council of 15 May 2014 on markets in financial instruments and amending Directive 2002/92/EC and Directive 2011/61/EU (MiFID II); Martin Weber, *Neue Juristische Wochenschrift (NJW)* 2014, 2327 (2328).

5 Regulation (EU) No 600/2014 of the European Parliament and of the Council of 15 May 2014 on markets in financial instruments and amending Regulation (EU) No 648/2012 (MiFIR).

6 Art. 1 of the Proposal for a Directive of the European Parliament and of the Council amending Directive 2014/65/EU on markets in financial instruments as regards certain dates, 10.2.2016, COM(2016) 56 final.

7 Niamh Moloney, *EU Securities and Financial Markets Regulation* (3rd Edition, 2014), 339.

part of the Lamfalussy-II Process, which is deemed to align the application and interpretation of the legal framework (regulation of directives) in all Member States. The European provisions of MiFID I are implemented in the German Securities and Trading Act (*Wertpapierhandelsgesetzbuch*, WpHG), and changes through MiFID II will be implemented by the end of 2017.[8] Moreover, administrative regulations further substantiate the provisions of the WpHG. This leads to an overwhelming complexity on the European and German level.[9]

8 MiFID II will be implemented in a "Second Financial Market Amendment Act" (*Second FiMaNoG).* See Draft of the German Federal Government for a Second Financial Market Amendment Act, available at http://dipbt.bundestag.de/doc/btd/18/109/1810936.pdf (15-09-2017).

9 Thomas M.J. Möllers, 'Harmonisation of Capital Markets Law – MiFID II and PRIIP' 31 (2015) *Banking and Finance Law Review (B.F.L.R.)* 143–176.

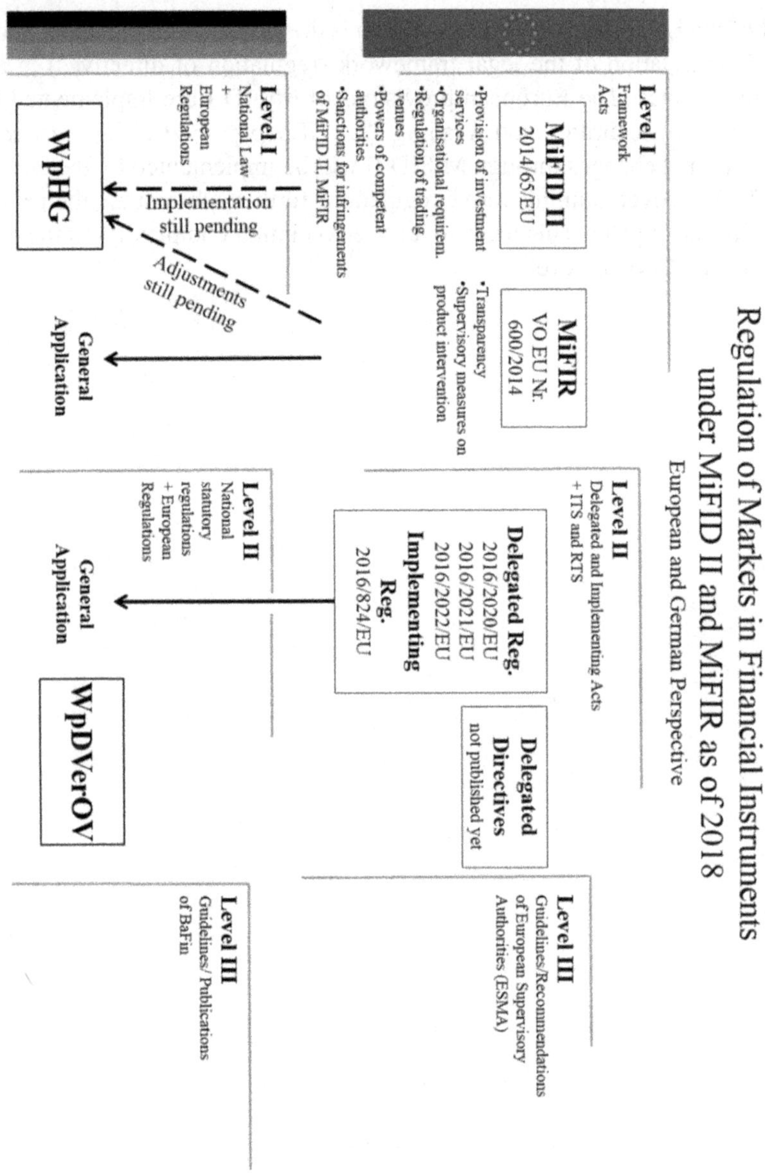

The Law Governing Investment Advice[10]

10 Authors' own diagram.

2. The law governing investment advice provided by investment firms

a) Scope

The European and German approach to the regulation of investment advice is different to the South African one: in Germany, it depends on the institution giving the advice, and not on the product alone. Moreover, different institutions may only give advice on specific products. In terms of scope, Section 31 et seq. of the WpHG only cover "investment firms"[11] when offering investment services including, inter alia, the provision of advice with respect to investments in "financial instruments"[12].

The WpHG or MiFID does not cover services in relation to insurance products.[13] Even though an inclusion of insurance firms providing advice or selling insurance products has been discussed in the preliminary negotiations about MiFID II,[14] it was dismissed in the final version.[15] In Germany, investment advice with respect to insurance products is regulated by the German Insurance Contract Act (*Versicherungsvertragsgesetz*, VVG). It uses very similar instruments as the WpHG, including information-based obligations.[16]

11 As defined in sec. 2(4) WpHG.

12 As defined in sec. 2(2b) WpHG.

13 See sec. 31 WpHG; Niamh Moloney, *EU Securities and Financial Markets Regulation* (3rd Edition, 2014), 341.

14 See Report on the proposal for a directive of the European Parliament and of the Council on markets in financial instruments, 5.10.2012, A7-0306/2012, Art. 3a, available at http://www.europarl.europa.eu/sides/getDoc.do?pubRef=-//EP//NONSGML+REPORT+A7-2012-0306+0+DOC+PDF+V0//EN (15-09-2017).

15 See Recital 87 of MiFID II: "their different market structures and product characteristics make it more appropriate that detailed requirements are set out in the ongoing review of Directive 2002/92/EC rather than setting them in this Directive".

16 For an overview of the different obligations, see Christian Armbrüster, *Privatversicherungsrecht* (2013), paras. 614 et seqq., 717 et seqq.

b) Obligations according to Section 31 WpHG

(i) General principle

When providing financial services, an investment firm must comply with the fiduciary-like obligation to act honestly, fairly and professionally in accordance with the best interests of its clients, and avoid conflicts of interest ("fair treatment" principle).[17]

(ii) Special obligations

The following duties prescribed in Section 31(2)–(11) are addressed to mitigate principal-agent risks associated with the distribution of investment products. Where private ordering by disclosure-based controls fails to reduce conflicts of interests, regulators tend to introduce more interventionist approaches in the form of suitability and appropriateness tests.[18]

First, every product offered to retail clients or demanded by retail clients must be accompanied by a standardised information form, which allows the client to fully understand the associated risks (Section 31(3) WpHG).[19]

Furthermore, Section 31 WpHG involves different levels of obligations depending on the provided service to the retail client. In case of execution-only transactions, the investment firm does not have to gather or provide more information than the above-mentioned (Section 31(7) WpHG). In case of unsolicited orders, the investment firm needs to inform itself about the client's knowledge and experience with respect to the recommended financial products or investment field, to assess whether the product is suitable for the client and to warn the client if it is not (Section 31(5) WpHG). If the investment firm provides investment advice or portfolio management (Section 31(4) WpHG), it has to inquire from the client about his knowledge and

---

17 Sec. 31(1) WpHG, Art. 24(1) MiFID I; see Thomas M.J. Möllers in Heribert Hirte and Thomas M.J. Möllers (eds), *KK-WpHG* (2nd Edition, 2014), § 31 paras. 82 et seqq.

18 Niamh Moloney, 'Regulating the Retail Markets' in Niamh Moloney, Eilís Ferran and Jennifer Payne (eds), *The Oxford Handbook of Financial Regulation* (2015), 736 (758).

19 Similar to the South African regulation in sec. 7(1)*(a)* of the GCC (General Code of Conduct for Authorised FSPs and Representatives); see Darleen Millard, p. 198 in this publication.

experience, his financial situation and his investment objectives including his risk tolerance ("know your customer"). This should enable the investment firm to recommend only products ("know your product") which are appropriate for the client's objectives.[20] If the product is not appropriate for the client, the investment firm may not recommend the product.

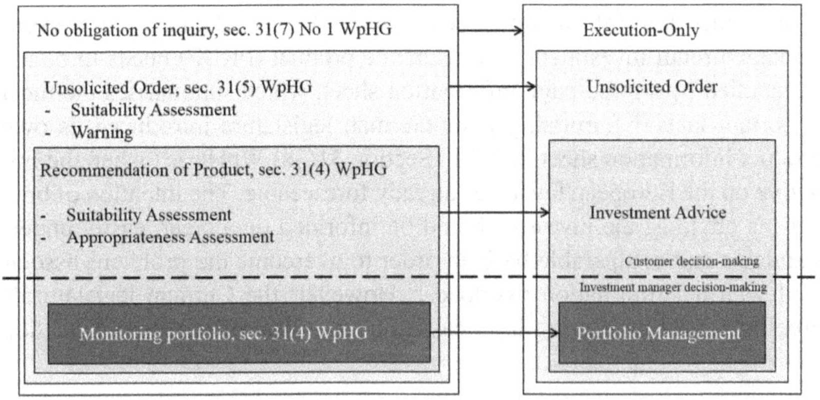

Different obligations depending on the provided service[21]

Most of these obligations are information-based.[22] The legislature abandons the principle that it rests solely on each contractor's responsibility to collect the necessary information.[23] It reduces informational asymmetries and is supposed to enable an investment decision on an informed basis.[24] So far, the European and national legislature has considered the investor to be able

20 Both principles were also developed by the Federal Court of Justice (*BGH*), BGH 6.7.1993 – XI ZR 12/93 – BGHZ 123, 126, 128 et seqq. – Bond; see Thomas M.J. Möllers in Heribert Hirte and Thomas M.J. Möllers (eds), *KK-WpHG* (2nd Edition, 2014), § 31 para. 338.

21 Authors' own diagram.

22 See Thomas M.J. Möllers and Mauritz Poppele, *Zeitschrift für Unternehmens- und Gesellschaftsrecht (ZGR)* 2013, 437 (448 et seqq.).

23 Thomas M.J. Möllers and Mauritz Poppele, *Zeitschrift für Unternehmens- und Gesellschaftsrecht (ZGR)* 2013, 437 (448).

24 Ingo Koller in Heinz-Dieter Assmann and Uwe H. Schneider (eds), *WpHG* (6th Edition, 2012), § 3, paras. 1–12; Thomas M.J. Möllers in Heribert Hirte and Thomas M.J. Möllers (eds), *KK-WpHG* (2nd Edition, 2014), § 31 para. 4.

to understand and process the provided information.[25] But behavioural scientists have shown significant evidence that there are limits to the ability of human beings to process and understand a certain quantity and complexity of information (bounded rationality theory). When surpassing this limit (information overload), human beings' behaviour tends to become confused and dysfunctional.[26] Therefore, the European legislature started an initiative to introduce key information documents.[27] As of 1 January 2018 every packaged retail investment and insurance product (PRIIP) needs to be accompanied by a three-page information sheet, which summarises the most important facts.[28] Surprisingly the German legislature introduced its own product information sheet in 2011 (Section 31(3a) WpHG),[29] when the initiative on the European level was already foreseeable. The intention of both laws is obvious: the investor should be informed on a clear, easily understandable and comparable basis in order to overcome the problems associated with an information overload.[30] However, the German legislature's pressing ahead by passing laws caused a great deal of criticism:[31] Section

---

25 Thomas M.J. Möllers and Mauritz Poppele, *Zeitschrift für Unternehmens- und Gesellschaftsrecht (ZGR)* 2013, 437 (456 et seqq.).

26 Jacob Jacoby, Donald E. Speller and Carol Kohn Berning, 'Brand Choice Behavior as a Function of Information Load: Replication and Extension' 1 (1974) *Journal of Consumer Research (JCR)*, 33 et seqq.; Thomas M.J. Möllers and Eva Kernchen, *Zeitschrift für Unternehmens- und Gesellschaftsrecht (ZGR)* 2011, 1 (10 et seqq. with further references).

27 Thomas M.J. Möllers, 'Harmonisation of Capital Markets Law – MiFID II and PRIIP' 31 (2015) *Banking and Finance Law Review (B.F.L.R.)* 143 (150).

28 Such as: How does risk arise? What costs will be incurred? How long should I hold the investment? How can I make a complaint? See Art. 8(3)*(d)* of Regulation (EU) No 1286/2014 of the European Parliament and of the Council of 26 November 2014 on key information documents for packaged retail and insurance-based investment products (PRIIPs) (PRIIP Regulation).

29 Introduced by Art. 1(6) of the Investor Protection and Capital Markets Improvement Act (AnsFuG) from 5 April 2011. Substantiated by Section 5a of the Regulation Specifying Rules of Conduct and Organisational Requirements for Investment Services Enterprises (WpDVerOV) from 20 July 2007; see Thomas M.J. Möllers and Thomas G. Wenninger, *Neue Juristische Wochenschrift (NJW)* 2011, 1697 (1698).

30 Recital 13 of the PRIIP Regulation.

31 Thomas M.J. Möllers and Mauritz Poppele, *Zeitschrift für Unternehmens- und Gesellschaftsrecht (ZGR)* 2013, 437 (459 et seq.); Thomas M.J. Möllers, 'Harmonisation of Capital Markets Law – MiFID II and PRIIP' 31 (2015) *Banking and Finance Law Review (B.F.L.R.)* 143 (150 et seqq.).

31(3a) WpHG differs in several aspects from the European PRIIP-Regulation.[32] Therefore, the German investment law and the whole industry must adapt to the new European rules again. As the scope of the German product information sheet is wider than the European scope, a combination of both laws will be relevant from 1 January 2018. The new Section 31(3a) WpHG, as introduced by the "First Financial Market Amendment Act"[33], states that where the PRIIP Regulation is not applicable, investment firms must still hand over the German product information sheet.[34] This "solution" contradicts the objective of information documents to provide a comparable summary among the different types of products. From next year, investment firms rendering investment advice must deal with three different categories of information sheets in Germany: key investor information sheets (KIIDs) for investment funds, key information documents (KIDs) for PRIIPs, and product information sheets (*Produktinformationsblatt*, PIBs) for all other financial instruments (for example, a simple share).[35]

	Key Information Document, PRIIP Regulation	**Product Information Sheet, sec. 31(3a) WpHG**
Material Scope of Application	– only PRIIPs	– *until 31.12.2017*: all financial instruments (e.g. shares) – *as of 1.1.2018*: all financial instruments except PRIIPs – only for investment advice
Personal Scope of Application	– PRIIP product manufacturers have to compile key information document – Provided to client by advisor or seller	– Provided to client by investment firm
Formal Requirements	– standardised	– Specified in Sec. 5a WpDVerOV

Key Information Document (PRIIP) v. Product Information Sheet (WpHG)[36]

32 See Thomas M.J. Möllers and Mauritz Poppele, *Zeitschrift für Unternehmens- und Gesellschaftsrecht (ZGR)* 2013, 437 (459 et seq.).

33 First Financial Market Amendment Act (*First FiMaNoG*) from 30 June 2016.

34 See Art. 2 No 5 of the First FiMaNoG (n 33).

35 For an overview over the different categories, see Jochen Seitz, Adrian Juhnke and Sven Seibold, *Zeitschrift für Bank- und Kapitalmarktrecht (BKR)* 2013, 1 et seqq.

36 Authors' own Diagram.

c) Conflict of interest: fee-based vs. commission-based advice

Giving investment advice is time- and cost-intensive, and investment advisors are subject to considerable commission pressure. It is not surprising that clients are often given recommendations for the product that generates the highest commission, even though it is not necessarily the one most suitable for their needs.[37]

Inducements[38] are therefore only permissible if they allow or are necessary for the provision of investment services (Section 31d(5) WpHG), if the inducement is from a third party commissioned by the client, or if the investment services enterprise grants such an inducement to such a third party (Section 31d(1) sentence 2 WpHG). Inducements are also permissible if they enhance the quality of the service to the client ("quality enhancement test"), if they do not impair the proper provision of the service in the interest of the client, and if the existence of the inducement is disclosed (Section 31d(1) sentence 1 Nos. 1–2 WpHG).[39]

In addition to regulatory rules, the Federal Court of Justice (BGH) has interpreted a civil law advisory contract to include a duty to disclose any kickbacks. This interpretation has been heavily criticised, as it is clear to business partners that a commercial service will only be provided for a fee.[40]

(i) Introduction of fee-based advice in Germany and the EU

MiFID II was the first law on the European level to distinguish between independent and non-independent investment advice. Fee-based advice can be found in the United Kingdom,[41] the Netherlands and the USA.[42] In Germany, traditional advice is usually given free of charge. MiFID II requires

---

37 Katharina Uffmann, *Juristenzeitung (JZ)* 2015, 282 et seqq.

38 Includes commissions, other fees or other cash, and any non-cash benefits: sec. 31d(2) WpHG.

39 See Ingo Koller in Heinz-Dieter Assmann and Uwe H. Schneider (eds), *WpHG* (6th Edition, 2012), § 31d para. 27 et seqq.

40 Hans Christoph Grigoleit, 177 (2013) *Zeitschrift für das gesamte Handels- und Wirtschaftsrecht (ZHR)*, 264 (291); previously, Matthias Habersack, *Wertpapier-Mitteilungen (WM)* 2010, 1245 (1251); Peter O. Mülbert, *Wertpapier-Mitteilungen (WM)* 2007, 1149 (1160).

41 Rules 6.2A.3, 6.2A.4A COBS, available at https://www.handbook.fca.org.uk/handbook/COBS/6/2A.html (15-09-2017).

42 Daniela Manzei, *Wertpapier-Mitteilungen (WM)* 2009, 393 (396).

advisors to disclose whether or not the advice is given on an independent basis.[43] Fee-based advice prohibits payment of fees by third parties[44] and requires a comprehensive market analysis. The fee-based advice may not be limited to financial instruments issued or provided by the investment firm itself.[45] Although MiFID II does not have to be implemented until 3 January 2018, the German legislature has already passed the Fee-Based Investment Advice Act (*Honoraranlageberatungsgesetz*)[46] in advance of the MiFID provisions. The new rules already take account of the MiFID II provisions, including the general prohibition of third-party fees (Section 31(4c) No 2 sentence 3 WpHG), and introduce a duty to disclose financial instruments issued or provided by the investment firm itself or by entities having direct links with the investment firm (Section 31(4d) sentence 1 WpHG).[47]

---

43 Art. 24(4) sentence 2(a)(ii) MiFID II (n 4).

44 Art. 24(7)(b) MiFID II (n 4).

45 Art. 24(7)(a) MiFID II (n 4).

46 Fee-Based Investment Advice Act (*Honoraranlageberatungsgesetz*) from 15 July 2013; re Sections 31(4b), (4c), Sections 33(1) paras. 3a, 36c, 36d WpHG; see Thomas M.J. Möllers in Heribert Hirte and Thomas M.J. Möllers (eds), *KK-WpHG* (2nd Edition, 2014), §§ 36c, 36d paras. 1 et seqq.

47 For another view on civil law duty, BGH 19.12.2006 – XI ZR 56/05 – BGHZ 170, 226, 233 para. 21 with comment, Thomas M.J. Möllers and Thomas G. Wenninger, *Lindenmaier-Möhring, Kommentierte BGH-Rechtsprechugn (LMK)* 2007, 220857.

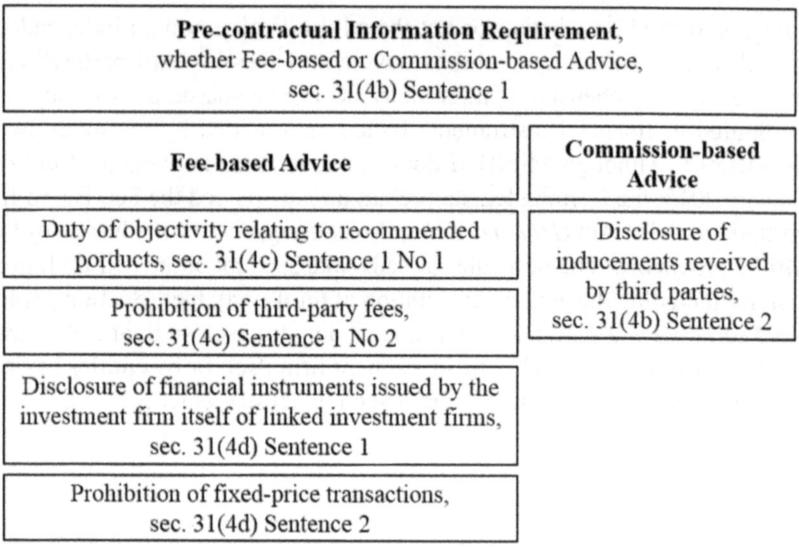

Fee-based Advice: Disclosure and Organisational Requirements[48]

(ii) Commission's delegated directive

During the legislative process, the EU Parliament had proposed to make it possible for Member States to entirely prohibit kickbacks for commission-based advice.[49] However, this rule was thrown out by the Economic and Monetary Affairs Committee of the European Parliament. Political discussions now turn on the issue of whether only fee-based advice should be permitted in the future. ESMA's Consultation Paper dated 22 May 2014 included a formulation of a prohibition on commissions.[50] After protests from

48 Authors' own Diagram.

49 Art. 24(5) of Amendments adopted by the European Parliament on 26 October 2012 on the proposal for a directive of the European Parliament and of the Council on markets in financial instruments repealing Directive 2004/39/EC of the European Parliament and of the Council (recast), P7_TA-PROV(2012), 0406; see Thomas M.J. Möllers and Mauritz Poppele, *Zeitschrift für Unternehmens- und Gesellschaftsrecht (ZGR)* 2013, 437 (465, 471 et seq.).

50 Commissions should not be permissible when they are only used to pay for or provide goods or services that are essential for the recipient firm in its ordinary course of business; see Consultation Paper ESMA/2014/549 dated 22.5.2014,

businesses, this prohibition was significantly watered down in the Final Report dated 19 December 2014.[51] The final draft for a delegated directive[52] was passed on 7 April 2016 by the Commission: Article 11 introduces several conditions which need to be met if the investment firm wishes to enhance the quality of the relevant service by receiving inducements ("quality enhancement test"[53]). Commission-based advice is therefore still permitted, but the standard of quality must be significantly higher than before.

d) The search for a suitable third way: robo advice

German influence to retain the present forms of commission-based advice was impossible to ignore. As long as commission-based advice remains free of charge, there is no protection against the investment firm recommending its own financial products instead of objectively searching the market for the most suitable products for the client. Therefore, fee-based advice is an important complement to commission-based advice. The positive aspect about fee-based advice is that the classic conflict of interest is no longer present. However, at EUR 150–350 per hour, fee-based advice does not come cheap. It normally does not make sense unless the investor has an investment sum of at least EUR 50,000. Fee-based advice is effectively excluded for large sections of the population. Although fee-based advice has

---

available at https://www.esma.europa.eu/sites/default/files/library/2015/11/2014-549_-_consultation_paper_mifid_ii_-_mifir.pdf (15-09-2017).

51 Commissions should be allowed if a client receives one of the following services: investment advice and access to a wide range of products, including third-party products, investment advice and regular appropriateness assessments, or other regular services, or access to a wide range of products, including third-party products, and regular reports about value increases and costs or other information tools; see Final Report ESMA/2014/1569, 19.12.2014, p. 127 ff., available at https://www.esma.europa.eu/sites/default/files/library/2015/11/2014-1569_final_report_-_esmas_technical_advice_to_the_commission_on_mifid_ii_and_mifir.pdf (15-09-2017).

52 Commission Delegated Directive (EU) of 7.4.2016 supplementing Directive 2014/65/EU of the European Parliament and of the Council with regard to safeguarding of financial instruments and funds belonging to clients, product governance obligations and the rules applicable to the provision or reception of fees, commissions or any monetary or non-monetary benefits, C(2016) 2031 final, available at http://ec.europa.eu/finance/docs/level-2-measures/mifid-delegated-regulation-2016-2031.pdf (15-09-2017).

53 Art. 24(9) MiFID II.

already been available in Germany for many years, it is not used much by investors.[54] Moreover, it would be overly paternalistic to allow for only one form of advice – each has its own advantages and disadvantages.

A third way is already being developed in the US – for example, robo advice, or computer algorithms that replace traditional investment advice.[55] Also in Germany, investment firms are starting to offer automated "assistants" via the Internet to support individuals in their investment decision.[56] Some banks offer automated advice as a cheaper alternative to a fee-based face-to-face advice.[57] Others do not regard this "assistance" or "guidance" as advice, but only as a provision of information to support the individual client in its own investment decision.[58] The referral to the "client's own investment decision" does not move "assistance" outside the scope of investment advice and its associated public law obligations in Section 31 et seqq. WpHG. In the case of investment advice, the final investment decision is also made by the client and not by the investment firm. Only in the case of portfolio management is the decision made by the investment firm and not by the individual client.[59] According to the German definition in Section 2(3)1 No 9 WpHG, investment advice "means the provision of personal

---

54 For arguments in favour and against, see Thomas M.J. Möllers in Heribert Hirte and Thomas M.J. Möllers (eds), *KK-WpHG* (2nd Edition, 2014), §§ 36c, 36d, paras. 9 et seqq.; Hans Christoph Grigoleit, 177 (2013) *Zeitschrift für das gesamte Handels- und Wirtschaftsrecht (ZHR)*, 264 (297); Mauritz Poppele, *Kapitalmarktinvestmentprodukte* (2015), 452.

55 On "robo advice" (offered in the US by Betterment, Wealthfront, Jemstep, and Personal Capital) see Gerald Braunberger, *Der Roboter als Anlageberater*, FAZ, 12.6.2014, available at http://www.faz.net/aktuell/finanzen/meine-finanzen/sparen-und-geld-anlegen/robo-advice-der-roboter-als-anlageberater-12969006.html (15-09-2017); Kim Bode, *Empfohlen vom Computer*, Die Zeit, 8.1.2015, 26 (13-02-2017).

56 See, for example, in Germany by comdirect, available at https://jetzt-besser-geld-anlegen.comdirect.de/start (15-09-2017).

57 Emma Dunkley, *RBS cuts face-to-face service and brings in 'robo-advisors'*, Financial Times, 13.3.2016, available at http://www.ft.com/cms/s/0/10df9f22-e90f-11e5-bb79-2303682345c8.html#axzz48KdWSNAp (13-02-2017).

58 Emma Dunkley, *RBS cuts face-to-face service and brings in 'robo-advisors'*, Financial Times, 13.3.2016; for an example, see the "disclaimer" provided by comdirect, avaiblate at https://jetzt-besser-geld-anlegen.comdirect.de/start. (15-09-2017).

59 For the distinction, see the definitions in sec. 2(3) No 9 WpHG (= investment advice) and sec. 2(3) No 7 WpHG (portfolio management); see Thomas M.J. Möllers in Heribert Hirte and Thomas M.J. Möllers (eds), *KK-WpHG* (2nd Edition, 2014), § 31, paras. 330 et seqq.

recommendations to a client […] in respect of one or more transactions relating to financial instruments […].” The definition is activity-based.[60] Therefore, a reference by the investment firm that the provided service is not deemed to be investment advice does not influence the legal qualification of the activity under the WpHG. As long as the service provided via the Internet leads to a recommendation relating to specific financial instruments which take into account the client's personal circumstances, or at least are presented as suitable for the person, the activity falls under the definition of investment advice.[61] Thus it depends on the specific questions asked on the “robo” homepage for the qualification as financial advice. Finally, as the investment advice needs to be made to “a client”, there must be some contractual relationship.[62] But the protection provided by the WpHG already starts earlier: it also covers “potential investors”.[63] Investment firms can in fact stray into an implicit personal recommendation even though there is no registration process and no contractual relationship.

It would be helpful to include such alternative forms of advice in the laws by way of example. Doing so would, on the one hand, encourage the development of alternative forms of advice; on the other hand, a legal qualification of “robo advice” by the legislator should help to navigate the boundary between providing guidance based on the customer's situation and to avoid inadvertently straying into an implicit personal recommendation without fulfilling all legal requirements. Banks remain reluctant to use such form of information provision because of these legal uncertainties.[64] A clarification may also prevent market participants from trying to circumvent obligations when providing “automated assistance” which looks like advice to the client but is not regarded as such by the investment firm.

---

60 See Petra Buck-Heeb, *Zeitschrift für Wirtschaftsrecht (ZIP)* 2013, 1401 (1409).

61 Sec. 2(3) sentence 1 No 9 WpHG; see also Art. 52 of the Directive 2006/73/EC of 10 August 2006 implementing Directive 2004/39/EG of the European Parliament and of the Council (MiFID I) as regards organizational requirements and operating conditions for investment firms and defined terms for the purpose of that Directive.

62 Petra Buck-Heeb, *Zeitschrift für Wirtschaftsrecht (ZIP)* 2013, 1401 (1409).

63 See Art. 52 of the Implementing Directive 2006/73/EC (n 61); Harald Baum in Heribert Hirte and Thomas M.J. Möllers (eds), *KK-WpHG* (2nd Edition, 2014, § 2, para. 189; Heinz-Dieter Assmann in Heinz-Dieter Assmann and Uwe H. Schneider (eds), *WpHG* (6th Edition, 2012), § 2, para. 114.

64 Financial Conduct Authority (FCA), *Financial Advice Market Review, Final Report* (March 2016), p. 28 et seq., available at https://www.fca.org.uk/static/fca/documents/famr-final-report.pdf (15-09-2017).

To foster this third way for investment advice or guidance, a joint committee on the European level published a discussion paper on automation in financial advice last year.[65] The Financial Conduct Authority and the Treasury in Great Britain already started a consultation[66] on possible benefits of robo advice, especially to those with small sums to invest. The results were published in a final report as part of the "Financial Advice Market Review". It recommended a clarification of the legal framework for robo advice by suggesting two different categories: one which is only "guidance" to the client without a personal recommendation,[67] and the other called "streamlined advice" for a limited range on simple customer needs.[68] All other forms of advice need to be personal and may not only use an automated process.[69] This should help market participants to avoid slipping unintentionally into advice and its associated liability risks.

It seems worthwhile to keep an eye on this new promising development, as "guidance" could help customers to choose a third way for investment decisions: an independent but, most importantly, nevertheless informed investment decision. This development fits also into today's changes: increasing use of technology, greater awareness of the cost of advice and a huge distrust in financial advisors.[70]

II. Law enforcement: principles vs. rules

1. Recent development: a shift from principles to rules

In the aftermath of the financial crisis, the European Union and legislators all over the world passed a "tsunami" of new provisions to eliminate conflicts of interest and unsound market behaviour which were key factors of the financial crisis. The subordinate goal was to "strengthen […] regulatory

---

65 Joint Committee of the European Supervisory Authorities, *Joint Committee Discussion Paper on automation in financial advice* (4.12.2015), available at https://www.eba.europa.eu/documents/10180/1299866/JC+2015+080+Discussion+Paper+on+automation+in+financial+advice.pdf (15-09-2017).

66 Financial Advice Market Review (n 64).

67 Financial Advice Market Review (n 64), 33 (Recommendation 3).

68 Financial Advice Market Review (n 64), 35 (Recommendation 4).

69 Financial Advice Market Review (n 64), 29.

70 Financial Advice Market Review (n 64), 3.

regimes, prudential oversight, and risk management, and ensure that all financial markets, products and participants are regulated or subject to oversight"[71]. It seems questionable whether a flood of detailed rules is the appropriate instrument to close all existing gaps and at the same time to constitute a legal framework anticipating also potential future developments in the financial industry. This development may also be observed in the law regulating investment advice. The German regulation in Section 31 WpHG originally consisted of two principles-based subsections in 1994.[72] More than 20 years later, it has increased to 16 subsections as of 3 July 2016;[73] and the implementation of the MiFID II is still pending![74] Closing every kind of legal loophole and regulating every imaginable situation has already failed in history: an illustrative example was the "Preußisches Landrecht" of 1794 with its 19,000 sections. A higher level of abstraction combined with the court's ability to interpret and develop the law is a more effective way to provide legal certainty and flexibility.

While rules are quite inflexible in their application, principles might serve this flexibility. Great Britain's financial system has traditionally been principles-based regulated (PBR) for a long time.[75] The Financial Conduct Authority's (FCA) Handbook of Rules and Guidelines is a plain-vanilla piece of PBR setting out the most important standards for firms in the financial industry. During its "Treating Customers Fairly" (TCF) initiative based on Principle 6 of the Handbook, the Financial Services Authority (FSA, predecessor of the FCA) published six approach-based requirements to a "product life cycle". In 2006, the FSA declared the initiative a "core

---

71 G20, Declaration of the Summit on Financial Markets and the World Economy, Washington 2008, 3, available at http://www.un.org/ga/president/63/commission/declarationG20.pdf (15-09-2017).

72 The third subsection prescribed the scope for foreign investment firms. See the old version of sec. 31 WpHG of the Securities Trading Act (*Wertpapierhandelsgesetz*) introduced by Art. 1 of the Second Act for the Promotion of Financial Markets (*Zweites Finanzmarktförderungsgesetz*) from 26 July 1994.

73 As implemented by the *First FiMaNoG* (n 33).

74 MiFID II will be implemented by the *Second FiMaNoG* by the end of 2017 (n 8).

75 Julia Black, Martyn Hopper and Christa Band, 'Making a success of Principles-based regulation' 1 (2007) *Law and Financial Markets Review (LFMR)*, 192; Julia Black, 'Regulatory Styles and Supervisory Strategies' in Niamh Moloney, Eilís Ferran and Jennifer Payne (eds), *The Oxford Handbook of Financial Regulation* (2015), 217 (228); Financial Services Authority (FSA), *Principles-based regulation, Focusing on the outcomes that matter* (April 2007), available at http://www.fsa.gov.uk/pubs/other/principles.pdf (15-09-2017).

part of our move to a more principles-based approach to regulation"[76]; later the development was interpreted as a shift from "principles-based" to "outcome-focused" regulation.[77] But times changed the trust in the success of the PBR. The experiences of regulators during the financial crisis led to the conclusion that a "principles-based approach does not work with individuals who have no principles"[78]. The FCA started to work on more prescriptive rules on how to achieve the intended outcome of the regulation. Pressure to abandon a predominantly purposive and principles-based system came also from the EU by introducing a "Single Rulebook" for capital requirements with its detailed rules.[79] One might describe the new system as a "principles-based regulation in rule design and operation"[80]. The South African regulation has gone through the same stages as Great Britain.[81]

2. Regulation

The Concept of PBR has several advantages but is still one of the most complex and controversial aspects of regulation.[82] Instead of using detailed,

76 Financial Services Authority (FSA), *Treating customers fairly – towards fair outcomes for consumers* (July 2006), 5, available at http://www.fca.org.uk/static/fca/documents/fsa-tcf-towards.pdf (15-09-2017).

77 Julia Black, 'Regulatory Styles and Supervisory Strategies' in Niamh Moloney, Eilís Ferran and Jennifer Payne (eds), *The Oxford Handbook of Financial Regulation* (2015), 217 (232).

78 Hector Sants, *Delivering Intensive Regulation and Credible Deterrence*, Speech delivered to the Reuters Newsmakers Event on 12.3.2009, available at http://www.fsa.gov.uk/pages/Library/Communication/Speeches/2009/0312_hs.shtml (15-09-2017).

79 Regulation (EU) No 575/2013 of the European Parliament and of the Council of 26 June 2013 on prudential requirements for credit institutions and investment firms; Directive 2013/36/EU of the European Parliament and of the Council of 26 June 2013 on access to the activity of credit institutions and the prudential supervision of credit institutions and investment firms.

80 See Julia Black, 'Regulatory Styles and Supervisory Strategies' in Niamh Moloney, Eilís Ferran and Jennifer Payne (eds), *The Oxford Handbook of Financial Regulation* (2015), 217 (238).

81 For a detailed description see Darleen Millard, p. 186 above.

82 Julia Black, 'Regulatory Styles and Supervisory Strategies' in Niamh Moloney, Eilís Ferran and Jennifer Payne (eds), *The Oxford Handbook of Financial Regulation* (2015), 217 (228).

prescriptive rules, principles are drafted with a high level of generality, being purposive and expressing the reason behind the regulation.[83] It enables the regulator to react flexibly to new developments or market circumstances in the financial sector, whereas detailed rules might not reflect or suit these new conditions. Moreover, it prohibits "creative compliance"[84], where market participants fulfil the detailed provision but the underlying objective might still be undermined. But principles also provide flexibility to market participants: by stating only the objective of the regulation, it is on the firm which processes and actions they want to implement to achieve the given outcome ("outcomes-based regulation"). It is based on the assumption that market participants have the expertise and best insight to find the most efficient steps to comply with the regulation.[85]

The most important concern is the principles' lack of transparency and the uncertainty they produce for market participants. Therefore, regulated entities and public authorities are in regular exchange about the application of the principles. This "informal communication" may lead to a non-transparent administration. Others raise the concern of "agency capture", where market participants attempt to influence illegitimately the regulatory agency's understanding of the principles.[86] A lack of transparency may even raise constitutional concerns: it might violate the principle of normative clarity (*Normklarheit*) which is applicable in all EU Member States via their constitutional traditions.[87]

---

83 Julia Black, Martyn Hopper and Christa Band, 'Making a success of Principles-based regulation' 1 (2007) *Law and Financial Markets Review (LFMR)*, 192 et seq.; Fabian Walla, 'Rechtssetzungsverfahren und Regulierungsstrategien' in Rüdiger Veil (ed), *Europäisches Kapitalmarktrecht* (2nd Edition, 2014), 38 (54 et seq.).

84 See the wording in Julia Black, Martyn Hopper and Christa Band, 'Making a success of Principles-based regulation' 1 (2007) *Law and Financial Markets Review (LFMR)*, 192, 204 n 7.

85 Julia Black, Martyn Hopper and Christa Band, 'Making a success of Principles-based regulation' 1 (2007) *Law and Financial Markets Review (LFMR)*, 192 et seq.; Fabian Walla, 'Rechtssetzungsverfahren und Regulierungsstrategien' in Rüdiger Veil (ed), *Europäisches Kapitalmarktrecht* (2nd Edition, 2014), 38 (54 et seq.).

86 Fabian Walla, 'Rechtssetzungsverfahren und Regulierungsstrategien' in Rüdiger Veil (ed), *Europäisches Kapitalmarktrecht* (2nd Edition, 2014), 38 (56 et seq.).

87 Originally developed by the European Court of Justice, Case 4/73, 14.5.1974 *J. Nold, Kohlen- und Baustoffgroßhandlung v Commission of the European Communities*, ECLI:EU:C:1974:51 , para. 13; today enacted in Art. 6 of the Treaty on the European Union (TEU); see Meinhard Hilf and Frank Schorkopf in Eberhard

Moreover, regulators tend to issue guidelines which represent their understanding of the principle at issue. But guidelines themselves produce further problems: they lead to a fragmented regulation depending on "special cases".[88] They may also raise constitutional concerns: it is the legislator's power to enact and substantiate the essential parts of laws and not the administration's power to do so.[89]

3. Public and private enforcement

The effectiveness of principles is dependent on the ability to enforce them. Where principles provide flexibility to supervisors by enabling them to react to new developments, flexibility may also weaken enforcement: regulators might develop a very conservative interpretation and practice of principles, especially where there is no political willingness for tough enforcement actions ("paradox of supervision and enforcement"[90]).

Most principles in the FSA's Handbook constitute only public obligations and no private rights.[91] Consequently, pressure to comply with the underlying principles can only come from public and not from private law enforcement. But this is a well-known problem not only with principles: jurisdictions in all of Europe are struggling whether rules and principles for market conduct only constitute public obligations or whether they may generate private liability.[92] In Germany, an investor may not automatically receive damages within the meaning of Section 823 (2) of the Civil Code (BGB) for losses he suffered due to the investment firm's violation of an

---

Grabitz, Meinhard Hilf and Martin Nettesheim (eds), *Das Recht der Europäischen Union* (40th Edition 2010), Art. 6 EUV, paras. 6 et seqq.; Fabian Walla, 'Rechtssetzungsverfahren und Regulierungsstrategien' in Rüdiger Veil (ed), *Europäisches Kapitalmarktrecht* (2nd Edition, 2014), 38 (56 et seq.).

88 Julia Black, Martyn Hopper and Christa Band, 'Making a success of Principles-based regulation' 1 (2007) *Law and Financial Markets Review (LFMR)*, 197.

89 According to the Principles of Materiality (*Wesentlichkeitsgrundsatz*) in Germany, Art. 80(1) sentence 2 of the German Constitution.

90 Julia Black, 'Forms and paradoxes of principles-based regulation' 3 (2008) *Common Markets Law Journal (CMLJ)*, 427, 450.

91 Julia Black, Martyn Hopper and Christa Band, 'Making a success of Principles-based regulation' 1 (2007) *Law and Financial Markets Review (LFMR)*, 192, 204 n 4.

92 See for a discussion of private liability under MiFID I and II: Thomas M.J. Möllers, 'Harmonisation of Capital Markets Law – MiFID II and PRIIP' 31 (2015) *Banking and Finance Law Review (B.F.L.R.)* 143 (163 et seqq.)..

obligation under the WpHG.[93] The results even differ between EU Member States: whereas there is no civil law enforcement of Section 20a WpHG (market manipulation) in Germany,[94] courts in Austria do award damages in this respect.[95]

However, the Market Abuse Regulation (MAR)[96] has imparted new impetus to the debate regarding the granting of damages according to Section 823(2) BGB for a violation of obligations under the European regulation in Germany.[97] The prohibition of market manipulation (Articles 12 and 15 MAR) as well as the obligation of public disclosure of inside information (Article 17 MAR) are now regulated on the European level. For the first time European market abuse law explicitly mentions the goal to "enhance investor protection and confidence in those markets" in Article 1 MAR, which is a strong point for the obligation of the German legislature to implement private enforcement of the above-mentioned two European rules via Section 823(2) BGB.[98] Others argue that a private liability needs to be

---

93 BGH 22.6.2010 – VI ZR 212/09 – BGHZ 186, 58 paras. 26 et seqq. re sec. 34a(1) sentence 1 WpHG; BGH 19.2.2008 – XI ZR 170/07 – BGHZ 175, 276 para. 18 with further evidence to sec. 32 (1) sentence 1 WpHG; BGH 13.12.2011 – XI ZR 51/10 – BGHZ 192, 91 paras. 20 et seqq. – IKB on sec. 20a WpHG.

94 BGH 13.12.2011 – XI ZR 51/10 – BGHZ 192, 91, 97 et seqq. – IKB; Sebastian Mock in Heribert Hirte and Thomas M.J. Möllers (eds), *KK-WpHG* (2nd Edition, 2014), § 20a, paras. 474 et seqq.; for private enforcement see Rüdiger Veil, 'Sanktionen' in Rüdiger Veil (ed), *Europäisches Kapitalmarktrecht* (2nd Edition, 2014), 163 (182 et seq.).

95 Susanne Kalss, Martin Oppitz and Johannes Zollner, *Kapitalmarktrecht – System* (2nd Edition, 2015), § 22, paras. 72 et. seqq.; see also OGH, 15.3.2012 – 6 Ob 28/12d – GES 2012, 230, 5.2 et seqq.

96 Regulation (EU) No 596/2014 of the European Parliament and of the Council of 16 April 2014 on market abuse (market abuse regulation) and repealing Directive 2003/6/EC of the European Parliament and of the Council and Commission Directives 2003/124/EC, 2003/125/EC and 2004/72/EC (MAR).

97 For an overview over the debate regarding private enforcement under MAR, see Alexander Hellgardt, *Die Aktiengesellschaft (AG)* 2012, 154 (163 et seqq.); Christoph H. Seibt, 177 (2013) *Zeitschrift für das gesamte Handels- und Wirtschaftrecht (ZHR)*, 388 (424 et seqq.); Lars Klöhn, 'Die private Durchsetzung des Marktmanipulationsverbots' in Susanne Kalss, Holger Fleischer and Hans-Ueli Vogt (eds), *Gesellschafts- und Kapitalmarktrecht in Deutschland, Österreich und der Schweiz 2013* (2013), 227–249; Hartmut Krause, *Corporate Compliance Zeitschrift (CCZ)* 2014, 248 (260).

98 Alexander Hellgardt, *Die Aktiengesellschaft (AG)* 2012, 154 (164 et seq.); Dörte Poelzig, *Zeitschrift für Unternehmens- und Gesellschaftsrecht (ZGR)* 2015, 801 (815).

granted as a matter of effectiveness and equivalence.[99] A specific argument for private enforcement in case of information-based market manipulation (Art. 12 (1) c) MAR) could be found in Recital 47 phrase 4 of the MAR, as this form of manipulation "is particularly harmful to investors because it causes them to base their investment decisions on incorrect or distorted information".[100] For liability under Art. 17 MAR, Recital 49 states that "the public disclosure of inside information […] is essential […] to ensure that investors are not misled". [101] Besides Section 37b, c WpHG, which already explicitly grants damages to investors who were misled by false or deferred ad-hoc disclosures in Germany, there would still be scope for Section 823 (2) BGB in connection with Art. 17 MAR, as slight and average negligence of the disclosing firm is sufficient for a liability under Section 823 (2) BGB. On the other hand, there would still be room for Section 37b, c WpHG besides Section 823 (2) BGB because it reverses the burden of proof for absence of negligence on the disclosing firm.[102] It will be interesting how German courts will deal with these new arguments in future decisions.

The same discussion can be expanded to the liability of investment firms in case of violating obligations under Section 31 WpHG. The German Federal Supreme Court (BGH) has rejected claims for damages under Section 823 (2) BGB so far.[103] According to the European Court of Justice, MiFID

---

99 Alexander Hellgardt, *Die Aktiengesellschaft (AG)* 2012, 154 (165); Christoph H. Seibt, 177 (2013) *Zeitschrift für das gesamte Handels- und Wirtschaftsrecht (ZHR)*, 388 (424); Christoph H. Seibt and Berward Wollenschläger, *Die Aktiengesellschaft (AG)* 2014, 593 (607); Dörte Poelzig, *Zeitschrift für Unternehmens- und Gesellschaftsrecht (ZGR)* 2015, 801 (816); for arguments against liability for market-based manipulation see Lars Klöhn, 'Die private Durchsetzung des Marktmanipulationsverbots' in Susanne Kalss, Holger Fleischer and Hans-Ueli Vogt (eds), *Gesellschafts- und Kapitalmarktrecht in Deutschland, Österreich und der Schweiz 2013* (2013), 227 (248 et seq.).

100 Alexander Hellgardt, *Die Aktiengesellschaft (AG)* 2012, 154 (165); Dörte Poelzig, *Zeitschrift für Unternehmens- und Gesellschaftsrecht (ZGR)* 2015, 801 (815).

101 Alexander Hellgardt, *Die Aktiengesellschaft (AG)* 2012, 154 (164); Christoph H. Seibt, 177 (2013) *Zeitschrift für das gesamte Handels- und Wirtschaftsrecht (ZHR)*, 388 (424); Christoph H. Seibt and Berward Wollenschläger, *Die Aktiengesellschaft (AG)* 2014, 593 (607).

102 Christoph H. Seibt, 177 (2013) *Zeitschrift für das gesamte Handels- und Wirtschaftsrecht (ZHR)*, 388 (425 et seq.).

103 BGH 19.12.2006 – XI ZR 56/05 – BGHZ 170, 226 paras. 17 et seqq. re Section 31(1) No 2 WpHG; BGH 13.12.2011 – XI ZR 51/10 – BGHZ 192, 91, para. 26 – IKB: WpHG only public law and therefore no qualification under sec. 823(2) BGB.

I does not oblige member states to implement civil law liability in case of a violation of Art. 19 MiFID I, which is the European background to Section 31 WpHG. It is up to the internal legal order of each Member State to determine the contractual consequences of non-compliance subject to observance of the principles of equivalence and effectiveness.[104] It is questionable whether this ruling under MiFID I is transferrable to MiFID II: Recital 70 of MiFID II states that "[t]he continuous relevance of personal recommendations for clients and the increasing complexity of services and instruments require enhancing the conduct of business obligations in order to strengthen the protection of investors". Recital 74 provides significant evidence that further restriction of inducements under Article 24(9) MiFID II was implemented to protect investors. Finally, one of the overall objectives of the directive is explicitly "to protect investors"[105]. Further, Recital 86 sentence 2 states: "in order to enhance the regulatory framework applicable to the provision of services […,] principles to act honestly, fairly and professionally and the obligation to be fair, clear and not misleading apply to the relationship with any clients". MiFID II is clearly referring to a contractual obligation which the investment firm owes to its client,[106] which is a strong argument for a "double nature" of Section 31 et seqq. WpHG: On the one hand, the national regulator enforces the obligation and on the other hand, the investment firm owes all obligations to the client.[107] These arguments, which indicate that the focus of the directive is increasingly shifting towards investor protection[108], might increase the pressure on national courts to enforce Section 31 et seqq. WpHG via civil law. Up until now, the

---

104 European Court of Justice Case 604/11, 30.5.2013, *Genil 48 SL, Comercial Hostelera de Grandes Vinos SL v Bankinter SA, Banco Bilbao Vizcaya Argentaria SA*, ECLI:EU:C:2013:344, para. 57 re Art. 19 MiFID I.

105 See Recital 86 sentence 1 MiFID II; see Dorothee Einsele, 180 (2016) *Zeitschrift für das gesant Handels- und Wirtschaftsrecht (ZHR)*, 233 (241, 244).

106 Dorothee Einsele, 180 (2016) *Zeitschrift für das gesant Handels- und Wirtschaftsrecht (ZHR)*, 233 (241).

107 Franz Clemens Leisch, *Informationspflichten nach § 31 WpHG* (2004), 44 et seqq.; Thomas M.J. Möllers in Heribert Hirte and Thomas M.J. Möllers (eds), *KK-WpHG* (2nd Edition, 2014), § 31 para. 15; Christoph Benicke, *Wertpapiervermögensverwaltung* (2006), 457 et seqq.; Tilman Weichert and Thomas G. Wenninger, *Wertpapier-Mitteilungen (WM)* 2007, 627 (635); for a different view see Andreas Fuchs in Andreas Fuchs (ed), *WpHG Kommentar* (2nd Edition, 2016), Vorbem §§ 31 ff. paras. 78 et seqq.; Dorothee Einsele, 180 (2016) *Zeitschrift für das gesant Handels- und Wirtschaftsrecht (ZHR)*, 233 (247 et seqq.).

108 Recitals under MiFID I stated "investor protection" only twice, whereas under MiFID it can be found 22 times.

BGH has been reluctant to do so, but the principles of equivalence and effectiveness might call for private enforcement in the future.[109]

European Competition Law is already one step ahead: The directive on actions for damages for infringements of national and EU competition adopted in 2014[110] will harmonise national private law enforcement from 27 December 2016 when member states shall have adopted measures to comply with the directive.[111]

4. Principles as a second layer of regulation and enforcement

Whereas there are several concerns regarding the regulation and enforcement via principles, a combination of rules and principles could be an adequate regulatory framework for markets with a high degree of innovation. These markets give rise to risks of circumvention and market abuse.[112] In particular the above-mentioned automation of investment advice could be regulated by principles as long as the legislature has not reacted to this new market development. A regulation via principles as a second layer has proven effective in cases in Great Britain, where supervisors were not able to sanction a specific behaviour under the Financial Services and Markets Act 2000 (FSMA), which implements the European rules, but under Principles of the FSA Handbook.[113] However, when drafting principles, the leg-

---

109 Dorothee Einsele, 180 (2016) *Zeitschrift für das gesant Handels- und Wirtschaftsrecht (ZHR)*, 233 (242 et seq.).

110 Directive 2014/104/EU of the European Parliament and of the Council of 26 November 2014 on certain rules governing actions for damages under national law for infringements of the competition law provisions of the Member States of the European Union; see Josef Drexel, 'The Interaction Between Private and Public Enforcement in European Competition Law' in Hans-Wolfgang Micklitz and Andrea Wechsler (eds), *The Transformation of Enforcement* (2016), 135–159.

111 For a comparison of civil law enforcement between competition, antitrust, company and capital markets law in Germany and Europe, see Thomas M.J. Möllers and Bernhard Pregler, 'Civil Law Enforcement and Collective Redress in Economic Law', 2013 *Diritti Nazionali e Comparazione*, 27–74.

112 Fabian Walla, 'Rechtssetzungsverfahren und Regulierungsstrategien' in Rüdiger Veil (ed), *Europäisches Kapitalmarktrecht* (2nd Edition, 2014), 38 (57 et seq.).

113 For an example, see Financial Services Authority (FSA), *Final Notice*, 20.11.2006, available at http://www.fca.org.uk/static/pubs/final/pignatelli.pdf (15-09-2017).

islature and the regulators should keep in mind the above-mentioned constitutional concerns.[114] In the end, "neither principles nor rules usually function particularly successfully without the other"[115].[116]

III. Concluding remarks

The period of deregulation in the 1980s and 1990s was blamed as one of the key factors of the last financial crisis. The activism and political willingness to draft new rules and ensure a gapless regulation is tremendous. Not only Britain[117] and South Africa[118], which have traditionally been principles-based regulated, but also Germany[119] and the whole European Union are currently shifting to a regulatory system which is characterised by an overwhelming complexity and amount of meticulously detailed rules. The intention of the European legislature to draft a Single Rulebook for a Capital Markets Union[120] is worthy of support. A uniform and strong framework to foster market integrity and decrease regulatory arbitrage and legal complexity arising from differing national rules are often cited goals of new European laws.[121]

Three notes on complexity: First, harmonisation of national laws via European directives and regulations may in fact reduce divergences among national laws. But seen from a national perspective, it adds three more layers of European law and guidelines via the Lamfalussy-Process to the existing national laws. In Germany, market participants now have to comply

114 Fabian Walla, 'Rechtssetzungsverfahren und Regulierungsstrategien' in Rüdiger Veil (ed), *Europäisches Kapitalmarktrecht* (2nd Edition, 2014), 38 (58).

115 Julia Black, 'The rise, fall and fate of principles-based regulation' in Kern Alexander and Niamh Moloney (eds), Law Reform and Financial Markets (2011), 3 (33).

116 John Braightwaite, 'Rules and Principles: A Theory of Legal Certainty' 27 (2002) *Australian Journal of Legal Philosophy (Aust. J. Leg. Phil.)*, 47.

117 Julia Black, 'Regulatory Styles and Supervisory Strategies' in Niamh Moloney, Eilís Ferran and Jennifer Payne (eds), *The Oxford Handbook of Financial Regulation* (2015), 217–253.

118 See Darleen Millard, p. 186 above.

119 Thomas M.J. Möllers, 'Harmonisation of Capital Markets Law – MiFID II and PRIIP' 31 (2015) *Banking and Finance Law Review (B.F.L.R.)* 143 (148 et seqq.).

120 European Commission, *Building a Capital Markets Union*, Green Paper COM(2015) 63 final, 18.2.2015.

121 See recital 4 of the MAR (n 96); similarly in recital 3 and 4 of the PRIIP Regulation (n 28).

with six relevant legal levels.[122] Second, the European laws tend to be excessive in size and fast-paced. Today it seems more important to find every applicable law than interpreting the law. Databases[123] which structure this complexity are becoming more and more important, whereas literature as German commentaries which try to interpret the law are already outdated on the day they are published.[124] Third, as the level of detail is impressive, the overall objectives and essential regulations get lost in the flood of applicable laws. For a long time, the US-American Capital Markets Law has served as a role model for legislators in continental Europe.[125] But the flood of European legislative initiatives after the financial crisis even overshadowed US-American initiatives. A way back to a more outcomes-based regulation seems desirable. Great Britain might have taken one step closer to this "way back" since 23 June 2016.

---

122 Thomas M.J. Möllers, 'Harmonisation of Capital Markets Law – MiFID II and PRIIP' 31 (2015) *Banking and Finance Law Review (B.F.L.R.)* 143 (163 et seq.).

123 See the author's database, available at kapitalmarktrecht-im-internt.eu or caplaw.eu.

124 See for example the preface of Andreas Fuchs (ed), *WpHG Kommentar* (2nd Edition, 2016), V; Ulrich Noack and Dirk Zetzsche, 'Kommentieren und Kommentare im europäisch-deutschen Wirtschaftsrecht' in Bettina Limperg, Jens Bormann, Axel C. Filges, Marie Luise Graf-Schlicker and Hanns Prütting, *Recht im Wandel europäischer und deutscher Rechtspolitik: Festschrift 200 Jahre Carl Heymanns Verlag* (2015), 213 (226).

125 For the development of European Capital Markets Law see Rüdiger Veil, 'Kapitalmarktrecht in Forschung und Lehre' in Rüdiger Veil (ed), *Europäisches Kapitalmarktrecht* (2nd Edition, 2014), 83 (84 et seq.).

Bibliography

Christian Armbrüster, *Privatversicherungsrecht* (Mohr Siebeck, Tübingen 2013).

Heinz-Dieter Assmann and Uwe H. Schneider, *Wertpapierhandelsgesetz* (6th Edition, Verlag Dr. Otto Schmidt, Cologne 2012).

Christoph Benicke, *Wertpapiervermögensverwaltung* (Mohr Siebeck, Tübingen 2006).

John Braightwaite, 'Rules and Principles: A Theory of Legal Certainty' 27 (2002) *Australian Journal of Legal Philosophy (Aust. J. Leg. Phil.)*, 47.

Petra Buck-Heeb, Die „Flucht" aus dem Anlageberatungsvertrag, *Zeitschrift für Wirtschaftsrecht (ZIP)* 2013, 1401.

Julia Black, Martyn Hopper and Christa Band, 'Making a success of Principles-based regulation' 1 (2007) *Law and Financial Markets Review (LFMR)*, 192.

Julia Black, 'Forms and paradoxes of principles-based regulation' 3 (2008) *Common Markets Law Journal (CMLJ)*, 427.

Julia Black, 'Regulatory Styles and Supervisory Strategies', in Niamh Moloney, Eilís Ferran and Jennifer Payne (eds), *The Oxford Handbook of Financial Regulation* (Oxford Handbooks, Oxford 2015), 217.

Josef Drexel, 'The Interaction Between Private and Public Enforcement in European Competition Law' in Hans-Wolfgang Micklitz and Andrea Wechsler (eds), *The transformation of enforcement* (Hart Publishing, Oxford 2016), 135.

Dorothee Einsele, Verhaltenspflichten im Bank- und Kapitalmarktrecht – öffentliches Recht oder Privatrecht? *Zeitschrift für das gesamte Handels- und Wirtschaftrecht (ZHR)* 180 (2016), 233.

Andreas Fuchs (ed), *Wertpapierhandelsgesetz (WpHG)* Commentary (2nd Edition, C.H. Beck, Munich 2016).

Eberhard Grabitz, Meinhard Hilf and Martin Nettesheim, *Das Recht der Europäischen Union* (40th Edition, C.H. Beck, Munich 2010).

Hans Christoph Grigoleit, Anlegerschutz – Produktinformationen und Produktverbote, *Zeitschrift für das gesamte Handels- und Wirtschaftrecht (ZHR)* 177 (2013), 264.

Matthias Habersack, Die Pflicht zur Aufklärung über Rückvergütungen und Innenprovisionen und ihre Grenzen, *Wertpapier-Mitteilungen (WM)* 2010, 1245.

Alexander Hellgardt, Europarechtliche Vorgaben für die Kapitalmarktinformationshaftung, *Die Aktiengesellschaft (AG)* 2012, 154.

Jacob Jacoby, Donald E. Speller and Carol Kohn Berning, 'Brand Choice Behavior as a Function of Information Load: Replication and Extension' 1 (1974) *Journal of Consumer Research (JCR)*, 33.

Susanne Kalss, Martin Oppitz and Johannes Zollner, *Kapitalmarktrecht – System* (2nd Edition, Linde Verlag, Vienna 2015).

Lars Klöhn, 'Die private Durchsetzung des Marktmanipulationsverbots', in Susanne Kalss, Holger Fleischer and Hans-Ueli Vogt (eds), *Gesellschafts- und Kapitalmarktrecht in Deutschland, Österreich und der Schweiz 2013* (Mohr Siebeck, Tübingen 2014), 227.

Kölner Kommentar zum WpHG, Heribert Hirte and Thomas M.J. Möllers (eds) (2nd Edition, Carl Heymanns Verlag, Cologne 2014).

Hartmut Krause, Kapitalmarktrechtliche Compliance: neue Pflichten und drastisch verschärfte Sanktionen nach der EU-Marktmissbrauchsverordnung, *Corporate Compliance Zeitschrift (CCZ)* 2014, 248.

Franz Clemens Leisch, *Informationspflichten nach § 31 WpHG* (C.H. Beck, Munich 2004).

Daniela Manzei, Rechtsvergleichende Betrachtung von Verhaltensregeln für Wertpapierdienstleistungsunternehmen im Privatkundengeschäft unter deutschem wie US-amerikanischem Aufsichtsrecht, *Wertpapier-Mitteilungen (WM)* 2009, 393.

Thomas M.J. Möllers, 'Harmonisation of Capital Markets Law – MiFID II and PRIIP' 31 (2015) *Banking and Finance Law Review (B.F.L.R.)*, 143.

Thomas M.J. Möllers and Eva Kernchen, Information Overload am Kapitalmarkt, *Zeitschrift für Unternehmens- und Gesellschaftsrecht (ZGR)* 2011, 1.

Thomas M.J. Möllers and Mauritz Poppele, Paradigmenwechsel durch MiFID II: divergierende Anlegerleitbilder und neue Instrumentarien wie Qualitätskontrolle und Verbote, *Zeitschrift für Unternehmens- und Gesellschaftsrecht (ZGR)* 2013, 437.

Thomas M.J. Möllers and Bernhard Pregler, 'Civil Law Enforcement and Collective Redress in Economic Law' *Diritti Nazionali e Comparazione* 2013, 27.

Thomas M.J. Möllers and Thomas G. Wenninger, BGH: Aufklärungspflichten der Bank über verdeckte Rückvergütungen (Retrozessionen/kick back-Provisionen) beim Vertrieb von Anteilen an Investmentfonds, *Lindenmaier-Möhring, Kommentierte BGH-Rechtsprechugn (LMK)* 2007, 220857.

Thomas M.J. Möllers and Thomas G. Wenninger, Das Anlegerschutz- und Funktionsverbesserungsgesetz, *Neue Juristische Wochenschrift (NJW)* 2011, 1697.

Niamh Moloney, *EU Securities and Financial Markets Regulation*, (3rd Edition, Oxford EU Law Library, Oxford 2014).

Niamh Moloney, 'Regulating the Retail Markets' in Niamh Moloney, Eilís Ferran and Jennifer Payne (eds*), The Oxford Handbook of Financial Regulation* (Oxford Handbooks, Oxford 2015), 736.

Peter O. Mülbert, Anlegerschutz bei Zertifikaten, *Wertpapier-Mitteilungen (WM)* 2007, 1149.

Ulrich Noack and Dirk Zetzsche, 'Kommentieren und Kommentare im europäisch-deutschen Wirtschaftsrecht', in Bettina Limperg, Jens Bormann, Axel C. Filges, Marie-Luise Graf-Schlicker and Hanns Prütting (eds), *Recht im Wandel deutscher und europäischer Rechtspolitik: Festschrift 200 Jahre Carl Heymanns Verlag* (Carl Heymanns Verlag, Cologne 2015) 213.

Dörte Poelzig, Private Enforcement im deutschen und europäischen Kapitalmarktrecht, *Zeitschrift für Unternehmens- und Gesellschaftsrecht (ZGR)* 2015, 801.

Mauritz Poppele, *Kapitalinvestmentprodukte* (Nomos, Baden-Baden 2015).

Christoph H. Seibt, Europäische Finanzmarktregulierung zu Insiderrecht und Ad hoc-Publizität, *Zeitschrift für das gesamte Handels- und Wirtschaftrecht (ZHR)* 177 (2013), 388.

Christoph H. Seibt and Bernward Wollenschläger, Revision des Marktmissbrauchsrechts durch Marktmissbrauchsverordnung und Richtlinie über strafrechtliche Sanktionen für Marktmanipulation, *Die Aktiengesellschaft (AG)* 2014, 593.

Jochen Seitz, Adrian Juhnke and Sven Seibold, PIBs, KIIDs und nun KIDs – Vorschlag der Europäischen Kommission für eine Verordnung über Basisinformationsblätter für Anlegerprodukte im Rahmen der PRIPs-Initiative, *Zeitschrift für Bank- und Kapitalmarktrecht (BKR)* 2013, 1.

Katharina Uffmann, Fehlanreize in der Anlageberatung durch interne Vertriebsvorgaben, *Juristenzeitung (JZ)* 2015, 282.

Rüdiger Veil, 'Kapitalmarktrecht in Forschung und Lehre', in Rüdiger Veil (ed), *Europäisches Kapitalmarktrecht* (2nd Edition, Mohr Siebeck, Tübingen 2014), 83.

Rüdiger Veil, 'Sanktionen', in Rüdiger Veil (ed), *Europäisches Kapitalmarktrecht* (2nd Edition, Mohr Siebeck, Tübingen 2014), 163.

Fabian Walla, 'Rechtssetzungsverfahren und Regulierungsstrategien', in Rüdiger Veil (ed), *Europäisches Kapitalmarktrecht* (2nd Edition, Mohr Siebeck, Tübingen 2014), 38.

Martin Weber, Die Entwicklung des Kapitalmarktrechts im ersten Halbjahr 2014, *Neue Juristische Wochenschrift (NJW)* 2014, 2327.

Tilman Weichert and Thomas Wenninger, Die Neuregelung der Erkundigungs- und Aufklärungspflichten von Wertpapierdienstleistungsunternehmen gem. Art. 19 RiL 2004/39/EG (MiFID) und Finanzmarkt-Richtlinie-Umsetzungsgesetz, *Wertpapier-Mitteilungen (WM)* 2007, 627.

Case Law

Germany

BGH 6.7.1993 – XI ZR 12/93 – BGHZ 123, 126 – Bond.

BGH 19.12.2006 – XI ZR 56/05 – BGHZ 170, 226.

BGH 19.2.2008 – XI ZR 170/07 – BGHZ 175, 276.

BGH 22.6.2010 – VI ZR 212/09 – BGHZ 186, 58.

BGH 13.12.2011 – XI ZR 51/10 – BGHZ 192, 91 – IKB.

European Court of Justice

European Court of Justice, Case 4/73, 14.5.1974, *J. Nold, Kohlen- und Baustoffgroßhandlung v Commission of the European Communities*, European Court Report 1974, 491.

European Court of Justice, Case 604/11, 30.5.2013, *Genil 48 SL, Comercial Hostelera de Grandes Vinos SL v Bankinter SA, Banco Bilbao Vizcaya Argentaria SA*, ECLI:EU:C:2013:344.

Austria

OGH, 15.3.2012 – 6 Ob 28/12d – GES 2012, 23

Treaty-making and select foreign policy matters under constitutional and judicial scrunity in South Africa

*Hennie Strydom**

I. Introduction

The process of democratic state formation in the late twentieth century has been influenced mainly by two ideas which exerted a powerful influence in giving shape to the post-war community of states. The first idea suggests that the model of the constitutional state provides the best framework for a post-conflict reconfiguration of state, government and society, while the

* National Research Foundation Chair in International Law, University of Johannesburg.

second requires a constitutionally recognised alignment with the commonly accepted rights and obligations of the international legal order.

Both these ideas were fundamental to the process that culminated in the first democratic elections in South Africa on 27 April 1994 and the subsequent adoption of the 1996 Constitution.[1] Apart from the obvious and much needed changes, the new constitutional dispensation envisaged in the areas of governance, the rule of law, the protection of human rights, and the international law "openness" of the Constitution provided an entirely new platform for international law to co-determine the future content of the law and the country's foreign relations policies. Other important factors that paved the way for this fundamental re-orientation are the number of South African scholars, exiled for political reasons, or not, who studied or practiced (international) law abroad and who later played a significant role in shaping the new constitutional dispensation; the success of the anti-apartheid movement in using international law to discredit the policies of the apartheid government in a growing number, over time, of General Assembly and Security Council resolutions[2]; and the protracted litigation in the International Court of Justice in the South West Africa cases.[3]

Already in the preamble to the 1996 Constitution the building of a "united and democratic South Africa able to take its rightful place as a sovereign state in the family of nations" was seen as one of the aims of the new Constitution. This statement positions the post-apartheid state as a respected member of the international community with the promise that it accepts and will act in accordance with the commonly accepted precepts of the international legal order. Building on this, a number of substantive provisions, which will feature later on in this chapter, bear further testimony to this outward vision of the drafters of the Constitution, a vision that was in no small part motivated by the years of isolation South Africans had to endure

1 Constitution of the Republic of South Africa, 1996. The 1996 Constitution was predicated on the Interim Constitution of 1993, the product of a constitution-writing effort by a multi-party Congress for a Democratic South Africa and formally adopted by Parliament in 1993.

2 On this see the seminal work of Dugard *The South West Africa/Namibia Dispute* (1973).

3 Of special significance was the ruling on the termination of South Africa's mandate over South West Africa/Namibia in *Legal Consequences for States of the Continued Presence of South Africa in Namibia (South West Africa) notwithstanding Security Council Resolution 276 (1970)*, 1971 ICJ Reports 16. For a comprehensive account of the controversy between South Africa and the United Nations on the issue of the administration of South West Africa/ Namibia see Dugard (n 2).

as a result of the minority government's universally discredited policies of apartheid.

The rest of this chapter is devoted to a selection of legal and political developments during the first twenty years since the advent of the new constitutional dispensation. However, at the outset it must be noted that the selection is varied and includes issues that may not strictly fall within the scope of the title but which may nevertheless contribute to an understanding of the tensions and legal disputes that have arisen in giving effect to the new constitutional dispensation.

II. Treaty-making: the uncertain role of parliament

The power to negotiate and sign international agreements is assigned to the national executive.[4] For the South African state to be bound internationally by an agreement concluded by the executive the agreement must be approved by resolution in both houses of parliament.[5] A domestic enactment is then required for the agreement to become law in the Republic.[6]

Besides the function of approval assigned to parliament, the provision is silent on any other potential role parliament may play in the treaty-making process. For instance, may parliament play an active role in co-determining the contents of a treaty still to be negotiated by the executive or determine in some other way the contents of a treaty or the scope of the negotiating powers of the executive with regard to a specific treaty? A potentially useful source for reflecting on these questions is the general constitutional provisions on the oversight role of parliament. For instance, the constitution ordains that parliament provides a "national forum for public consideration of issues by …scrutinising and overseeing executive action"[7], and further that the National Assembly (one of the Houses of Parliament) "must provide for mechanisms to (a) ensure that all executive organs of state in the national sphere of government are accountable to it; and (b) to maintain oversight of (i) the exercise of national executive authority …".[8]

---

4 Constitution sec 231(1).

5 sec 231(2).

6 sec 231(4). There are certain exceptions to the required procedures set out above. See sec 231(3) and (4).

7 sec 42(3).

8 sec 55(2).

These formulations are open-ended and contain no indication that parliament may be interdicted from interfering in the treaty-making process in the manner contemplated above. Naturally, when contemplating any such role, parliament will have to be guided by the separation of powers principle. Another potential source is chapter 5 of the 2006 Manual on Executive Acts of the President.[9] According to this document an agreement subject to parliamentary approval must be tabled in parliament and accompanied by, among others, an explanatory memorandum briefly setting out the history, objective and implications of the agreement; the recommendation of the executive; and the legal opinions of the state law advisors. An agreement tabled in this manner is then referred to the relevant parliamentary portfolio committees for *debate* and *consideration* and the reports of their *decisions* are then considered and decided upon by both Houses of Parliament sitting separately.

The way in which the powers in section 231 of the Constitution and the proceedings in the 2006 Manual have been understood and applied in practice is that parliament has no power to co-determine in some or other way the contents of a treaty. This is considered to fall within the exclusive powers of the executive and solely determined by the negotiating process which is the prerogative of the executive. Seemingly, the only action available to parliament once a negotiated treaty comes before it, is to approve or disapprove. It is not clear on what grounds disapproval can take place and whether the executive will then have to re-negotiate the treaty to accommodate parliament's concerns. Since parliamentary disapproval has never occurred, there is no emerging practice to rely on for an assessment of the situation in this regard.[10]

On average South Africa annualy concludes between fifty and seventy treaties and Memoranda of Understanding (MOU's) with other states.[11] Those of a bilateral nature often provide for the rendering of cooperation and services in various fields with the objective of furthering trade between and economic development in the two states parties. Whether these agreements are actually implemented and to what extent and result are matters that parliament has never exercised control over and no mechanism has been created to enable parliamentary oversight over the implementation of

---

9 available at www.dfa.gov.za/chiefstatelawadvicer/ratification.html (17-05-2016).

10 The position explained above has been confirmed in a telephonic enquiry with the Office of the Chief State Law Advisor (International Law) on 18 May 2016.

11 available at http://www.dirco.gov.za/chiefstatelawadvicer/treatysection.html (24-08-2017).

these agreements once they have been concluded by the executive and approved by parliament. It may be debatable whether this strict separation between executive and legislature is a healthy development, especially in view of the constitution's founding principles which include a "multi-party system of democratic government to ensure accountability, responsiveness and openness"[12] and in view of the fact that national treasury funds are often appropriated for the implementation of such agreements.

On this issue some valuable insights may be gained from other jurisdictions. For current purposes this will be restricted to developments under the American and German constitutions. In Federalist Paper No 75, George Hamilton commented on the treaty-making power of the executive[13] in response to an objection at the time against what was referred to as the "inter-mixture of powers". Seemingly a clear illustration of such "inter-mixture" was to be found in Article II, section 2 of the American Constitution, which, in part determines that the President shall have the power, "by and with the Advice and Consent of the Senate, to make Treaties…". In defending the "union of the Executive with the Senate", in this provision, Hamilton questioned (as being an arbitrary disposition) the views according to which treaty-making is a peculiar executive function and argued that the power of treaty-making "if we attend carefully to its operation, it will be found to partake more of the legislative than of the executive character, though it does not seem strictly to fall within the definition of either of them".[14] Given this dual character of the treaty-making process, Hamilton then concluded that the "joint possession of the power in question, by the President and Senate, would afford a greater prospect of security, than the separate possession of it by either of them".

The question then is what exactly is the function of Senate in the treaty-making process? Relying on the "advice and consent" part of the provision Fisher has argued that it "implies that the Senate will have an opportunity to shape the content of a treaty", since if the intention was merely to limit Senate's power to a yes or no vote, the word "advice" would be superfluous.[15] Fisher also points out that several US Presidents have followed this approach with the result that he questions the correctness of the *Curtiss-*

12 Constitution sec 1.

13 available at http://www.let.rug.nl/usa/documents/1786-1800/the-federalist-papers/the-federalist-75.php (15-09-2017).

14 *ibid.*

15 Fisher "Congressional participation in the treaty process" 1989 *University of Pennsylvania Law Review (U Pa L Rev)*) 1511 1512.

Wright ruling[16] that it is only the President that negotiates treaties.[17] On a more general note Fisher has defended the composite nature of treaty-making by arguing that the "ultimate objective of the treaty process is to enter into foreign commitments capable of being sustained. To honour those promises, especially those that commit the nation's economic and military sources, it is necessary for the President to develop a consensus with both branches of Congress by seeking their advice throughout the process of negotiating and making a treaty".[18]

According to Henkin, while the President's part seems clear – he appoints and instructs negotiators and follows their progress in the negotiations – it is Senate's part that has been more problematic. Originally conceived as a kind of Presidential Council affording the President advice throughout the treaty-making process and also determining the scope of negotiations, in time this was considered unworkable by Presidents; while Senate, rejecting it too "was more inclined to deliberate and pass judgement, rather than to advise".[19] Although all sorts of political controversies and tensions between President and Senate with regard to the giving of consent to and ratification of treaties have emerged from time to time, Henkin is of the view that "[n]egotiators have always kept clearly in mind that the treaties they produce will have to be acceptable to the Senate and meet its objections, political or constitutional, partisan or substantive, real or pretended".[20]

In German constitutional law the interaction between parliament and the executive with regard to foreign affairs has received considerable attention over the years. Arguments in favour of a shared responsibility to be exercised by parliament and the executive in matters involving the foreign relations of the German state[21] were informed by mainly two developments.

---

16 *United States v Curtiss-Wright* 299 US 304, 319 (1936).
17 Fisher (n 15) 1517–1518.
18 Fisher (n 15) 1522.
19 Henkin *Foreign Affairs and the Constitution* (1975) 131.
20 *ibid* 132, 133.
21 See Wolfrum "Kontrolle der auswärtigen Gewalt" (2. Bericht) in *Veröffentlichungen der Vereinigung der deutschen Staatsrechtlehrer* Vol 56 (1997) 38 40: "Die auswärtige Gewalt gehört wesensmäßig nicht grundsätzlich zu dem Bereich der Regierung und Verwaltung, sondern sie wird von Regierung und Parlament gemeinsam ausgeübt". Also Giegerich "Verfassungsgerichtliche Kontrolle der auswärtigen Gewalt im europäisch-atlantischen Verfassungsstaat: Vergleichende Be-

The one is the growing influence of international law on the interpretation and application of national law brought about by post-WWII developments in areas such as the protection of human rights, international criminal law, international environmental law and international commercial law which caused a sharp distinction between internal and external matters to become unrealistic.[22] In addition, commentators have drawn attention to the influence of globalisation in that states are increasingly forced to address a range of challenges within a transnational network comprising state and non-state entities alike, as well as international and regional organisations.[23] Consequently, state functions, in their growing diversity, have become the subject of international regulation with such domestic consequences that a well-defined distinction between external and internal affairs has become problematic in many instances.[24]

Apart from these developments and the inferences drawn from them, there are concrete examples in the German Constitution (*Grundgesetz*) that illustrate the need for and scope of parliamentary involvement in the treaty-making process. The one is article 59(2) which provides for a participatory role by the legislature in the form of a legislative enactment. This intervention is limited to treaties that regulate the political relations of the German state or relate to matters that may also be subject to federal laws. The German Constitutional Court (*Bundesverfassungsgericht*) has interpreted "treaties regulating the political relations of the German state" as referring to treaties creating alliances, political cooperation agreements, peace agreements, border agreements, disarmament treaties, etc.[25] Since treaties of this nature may affect the sovereignty, independence and territorial integrity of the state, as well as its power relations with other states, it stands to reason

---

standsaufnahme mit Ausblick auf die neuen Demokratien in Mittel- und Osteuropa" 57 (1997) *Zeitschrift für ausländisches öffentliches Recht und Völkerrecht (ZaöRV)* 409 415–416.

22 Wolfrum (n 21) 41, 42. See also Heun in Dreier (ed) *Grundgesetz Kommentar Bd II* (2015) Art 59 para 7.

23 See, for instance, Hingst *Auswirkungen der Globalisierung auf das Recht der völkerrechtlichen Verträge* (2001) 39 *et seq*.

24 Heun (n 22).

25 German Constitutional Court (*Bundesverfassungsgericht*, BVerfG) 29.7.1952 – 2 BvE 2/51 – BVerfGE 1, 372, 381 (German/French economic agreement); BVerfG 12.7.1994 – 2 BvE 3/92 – BVerfGE 90, 286, 359 (extraterritorial deployment of the armed forces).

that parliament cannot be denied a control and oversight function altogether.[26] In the case of treaties regulating subject-matters that may also be subject to domestic legal regulation, the purpose of parliament's legislative intervention is firstly to bring about conformity between international and national law,[27] and secondly to preserve parliament's final legislative discretion in such matters and to prevent executive interests to prejudice the domestic significance of the subject-matter.[28]

The other example is the constitutional amendment in 1992, following the establishment of the European Union, and which resulted in a new article 23 of the German Constitution providing, inter alia, for the transfer by law of sovereign powers to the Union in furtherance of a commitment to bring about the realisation of a united Europe.[29] Although article 23 entrenches this commitment in clear reference to the fundamental principles of the German constitutional order (social democracy, rule of law, federalism and subsidiarity[30]), their application and interpretation can hardly escape adaptation and modification as an integral part of a greater European legal order which, in order to be workable and effective, requires a certain level of homogeneity between the national and the supra-national legal orders. Most likely to be affected is the separation of powers principle. In this regard it is pointed out that a categorical and institutional separation between legislative and executive power is a foreign concept in the European Union and not realisable in such a supra-national structure where control (checks and balances) over and restraint of the exercise of power are achieved through a distribution of competencies between different organs.[31]

---

26 Nettesheim in Maunz and Dürig (eds) *Grundgesetz Kommentar Band V* (2009) Art 59 para 94.

27 See also *Grundgesetz* art 25: "Die allgemeinen Regeln des Völkerrechts sind Bestandteil des Bundesrechtes. Sie gehen den Gesetzen vor und erzeugen Rechte und Pflichten unmittelbar für die Bewohner des Bundesgebietes."

28 Nettesheim (n 26) Art 59 para 104. See also Heun (n 22) Art 59 paras 18, 27.

29 Art 23(1). See also Uerpmann-Wittzack in von Münch and Kunig (eds) *Grundgesetz Kommentar Bd I* (2012) Art 23 paras 2, 9.

30 *Grundgesetz* art 23(1).

31 Uerpmann-Wittzack (n 29) art 23 para 12. See also European Court of Justice Case C-70/88 22.5.1990 *European Parliament v Council of the European Communities* ECLI:EU:C:1990:217 paras 21, 22: "The Treaties set up a system for distributing powers among the different Community institutions, assigning to each institution its own role in the institutional structure of the Community and the accomplishment of the tasks entrusted to the Community. Observance of the institutional balance means that each of the institutions must exercise its powers with due regard for the powers of the other institutions."

Some provisions in article 23 deserve special reference. According to article 23(2) the federal parliament (*Bundestag*) is entitled to participate in matters concerning the European Union. To make this possible, the executive is instructed to comprehensively and at its earliest convenience inform[32] parliament about such matters. A similar participatory function is assigned to the states (*Länder*) which they exercise through the federal council (*Bundesrat*). From this it follows that the executive, by virtue of article 23(3), is constitutionally bound to give parliament an opportunity to make known its position before the executive participates in a law-making activity of the EU and to take that position into account in negotiations with the EU.

This mechanism aims at compensating, to a certain extent at least, for the loss of decision-making power by the legislature over European Union affairs and to somehow counteract the prevailing influence of European Union directives and regulations.[33] It is also important to note that the practice of article 23, namely to claim and protect by law the legislature's role in external affairs involving the EU, is not limited to Germany but has been adopted by a number of other EU member states to ensure that the democratic legitimation function of national legislatures is also realised at the regional level.[34]

In 2012, article 23 was subjected to legal scrutiny by the German Constitutional Court in a landmark decision involving the alleged failure of the executive to inform parliament, as required by article 23, about developments regarding the EU's financial stability mechanisms which the EU Council and the executive branches of EU member states started working on in 2010 in response to the financial crisis in the Euro zone area.[35] At the outset the Court acknowledged that foreign affairs, traditionally and as a matter of principle, fall within the executive's area of competence.[36] However, this does not mean that the exercise of this competency completely falls outside parliamentary control and oversight. Parliament, after all, is still constitutionally empowered to use its questions and debate mechanism as well as its resolutions to influence decisions of the executive.[37] A further

32 The German text uses the term "unterrichten" which literally means "to teach" or "to educate", but also "to inform of" or "to acquaint with".

33 Uerpmann-Wittzack (n 29) Art 23 para 71.

34 See Wollenschläger in Dreier (n 22) Art 23 paras 27, 33; Brand *Europapolitische Kommunikation zwischen Bundestag und Bundesregierung* (2015) 24 *et seq*.

35 German Constitutional Court (BVerfG) 19.6.2012 – 2 BvE 4/11 – BVerfGE 131, 152 (duty to inform parliament about EU matters).

36 *ibid* 195.

37 *ibid* 196.

example is parliament's power of intervention in case of certain treaties under article 59 referred to earlier on. In the case of the legislature's traditional oversight role over the external transactions of the executive, the extent and substance of that role in many countries are by no means clear and may even fluctuate depending on the applicable legal framework, circumstances and subject-matter. A clearer picture and stricter legal parameters seem to emerge when the situation falls under article 23, i.e. when a regional organisation and its individual members are closely integrated - legally, politically and economically – and cooperation between regional and national organs are essential for holding the structure and its founding principles together.[38] This also explains the rationale for a legislative measure such as article 23. As the Court pointed out, the transfer of sovereign and law-making powers to the EU, coupled with the direct applicability of EU law in member states and the concomitant creation of rights and duties for the citizens of EU member states, made it necessary for national parliaments to be given a meaningful say in EU affairs to compensate for their loss of influence over the decision-making processes of the European Council which is made up of Heads of State and Government and officials of different organs of the EU. By providing for the active cooperation of national parliaments in the law-making decisions of the executive in the EU Council, article 23 also ensures that there is a certain measure of democratic legitimation of the law-making processes at the supra-national level.[39]

Parliamentary participation in the sense of article 23(2) is only foreseen in "European Union matters" ("Angelegenheiten der Europaïschen Union"). This was understood by the Court to refer to the performance of all law-making functions of the EU as well as to international treaties that supplement EU law or are otherwise closely linked to EU law. In view of the open-ended character of the wording in article 23(2), the Court avoided an interpretation that would limit the scope of the article to specific acts of the EU. Instead it argued in favour of an extensive interpretation of the phrase "matters of the European Union", especially in view of the fact that the concept of European integration denotes a dynamic and progressive process that requires a high level of flexibility at the level of the member states.[40]

---

38 See also Giegerich (n 21) 422–425.

39 German Constitutional Court (BVerfG) 19.6.2012 – 2 BvE 4/11 – BVerfGE 131, 197, 198.

40 *ibid* 200–202.

The executive's duty to inform in article 23(2) has been approached by the Court to mean that the executive must ensure that its information, comments and explanation must be such that it places parliament in a position to timeously and effectively exert its influence on the will of the executive. Put differently, parliament's role must not be reduced to that of merely comprehending the situation.[41] Hence, the duty to inform cannot be restrictively interpreted, otherwise it will fail in its objective, namely to cancel out asymmetrical information levels between executive and legislature.[42] Moreover, Parliament's right to be informed as required by article 23(2) is also understood to be an integral part of the democratic principle which constitutes an immutable core of the democratic constitutional state.[43]

In 2013, the Federal Parliament gave further effect to the Constitutional Court's ruling in the form of a legislative enactment intended to regulate the cooperation between the executive and the legislature in European Union matters.[44] The Act states unequivocally that parliament has a right to take a position on EU matters and that the executive must inform parliament comprehensively and at its earliest convenience about such matters.[45] In complying with its duty to inform, the executive must ensure that the information enables parliament to effectively deal with the matter.[46] However, compliance with this duty does not affect the executive's core function and own responsibility in foreign relations.[47]

Of specific importance are the provisions on the timing of parliament's involvement. The Act determines that parliament must be given an opportunity to intervene in the matter *before* the executive takes part in an EU initiative with the result that the executive must provide parliament continuously with up to date information about the course of events and the point at which parliament's position on the matter will be required.[48] Once parliament's position has been made known, it will form part of the executive's negotiations and parliament must be informed how its position has been

---

41 *ibid* 202, 203.

42 *ibid* 203, 206 *et seq.*

43 See German *Grundgesetz* art 20; Brand (n 34) 62.

44 *Gesetz über die Zusammenarbeit von Bundesregierung und Deutschem Bundestag in Angelegenheiten der Europäischen Union* (4 July 2013, BGBI I S. 2170), hereinafter EUZBBG.

45 sec 1 EUZBBG.

46 sec 3(1) EUZBBG.

47 sec 3(4) EUZBBG.

48 sec 8(1) EUZBBG.

taken into account by the executive in the course of the negotiations.[49] While negotiations are under way, parliament may also supplement or amend its position.[50] Should it happen that parliament's position is not accepted in any of its essential elements, the executive must table a parliamentary reservation in the negotiations and inform parliament about it. This has the effect that before a final decision is taken on the matter in the negotiations, the executive must try and reach consensus with parliament. However, this does not affect the right of the executive to take a different position when important foreign affairs or EU integration issues are at stake.[51] Even when the matter has reached conclusion in the EU process, parliament needs to be informed about the acceptance or not of its position on the matter.[52]

The Act follows the broad interpretation of the Constitutional Court on what will constitute "matters of the European Union". According to the Act this will include EU treaty amendments and law-making activities of the EU as well as international treaties and inter-governmental agreements to the extent that they supplement EU law or are otherwise closely related to EU law.[53] The influence of the Court's ruling on this formulation is obvious. Further to this, the Act contains a non-exhaustive list of specific EU activities in respect of which parliament's participation and the executive's concomitant duty to inform will apply.[54]

It is with reference to the above developments at the international and regional levels that commentators have pointed to a blurring of the traditional separation between domestic and foreign policy as a result of the mutual penetration of both spheres of governmental activity.[55] This development, it is further argued, raises the expectation in favour of greater parliamentary participation in matters of foreign affairs to ensure its democratic legitimation[56], a claim that sits uncomfortably with the traditional view of the executive's unimpeded discretion in foreign relations. These developments raise a number of questions on the consequences of South Africa's membership in regional bodies such as the African Union and The Southern

49 sec 8(2) EUZBBG.
50 sec 8(3) EUZBBG.
51 sec 8(4) EUZBBG.
52 sec 8(5) EUZBBG.
53 sec 1(2) EUZBBG.
54 sec 5 EUZBBG.
55 Nettesheim (n 26) Art 59 paras 18 et seq.
56 Wolfrum (n 21) 43.

African Development Community regarding the relationship and communication between the executive and the legislature. At the AU level, for instance, executive bodies such as the Assembly of Heads of State and Government[57] and the Executive Council[58] are assigned decision-making powers over a wide range of subject-matters with domestic and external consequences without a legally binding framework regulating in clear terms the demarcation of powers and functions between the national organs (executive and legislature) and the regional institutions.

However, apart from emerging similarities between the AU/SADC and the EU integration processes suggesting the need for greater parliamentary control over the treaty-making process, for the moment there may be other, even more compelling reasons, why the hitherto strict separation in the South African practice between the executive and the legislature as far as treaty-making is concerned, should be reconsidered. Accountability for how and for what reason state revenues are spent is one such reason. Another is that cooperative governance may be necessary for the sustainable performance of a treaty; and yet another, the growing influence of international treaty law in an increasing number of areas with domestic effects which makes a sharp distinction between external and internal matters unsustainable.

III. Human rights as a priority in South Africa's foreign relations

In 1996, Alfred Nzo, the first Foreign Affairs Minister of post-apartheid South Africa announced that South Africa's foreign policy will be principled and "if consistently adhered to will render our foreign policy predictable and in line with our perception of the kind of nation we seek to be, and the kind of world we seek to live in". He then also explained that the principles in question will "serve as a yardstick by which the quality of our practical foreign policy decisions may be measured …".[59] In the same year, speaking at the 51st session of the UN General Assembly, the Minister made clear that a high premium will be placed on the promotion of human rights

57 Constitutive Act of the African Union (2000) art 3, 4, 7 and 9.

58 *ibid* art 13.

59 South African Foreign Policy Discussion Document available at https://www.gov.za/af/documents/foreign-policy-south-africa-discussion-document (15-09-2017).

and that the "South African government regards it as a priority to contribute to the efforts of the international community to combat the violation of human rights".[60] On this score he echoed Nelson Mandela, soon to be President, who wrote in 1993 that South Africa's future foreign relations will be based on our belief that human rights should be the core concern of international relations, and we are ready to play a role in fostering peace and prosperity in the world we share with the community of nations".[61]

Since the ruling party's decades long international campaign against the apartheid government was fundamentally built on human rights and democratic rule, it made perfect sense, not only at the time, but also in subsequent years, to invoke a commitment to human rights and democratic principles as the guiding light for the country's foreign policy. For instance, in an *aide-memoire* in support of South Africa's candidature for election to the newly established UN Human Rights Council, the South African delegation again referred to South Africa's commitment to the protection of human rights and the advancement of democracy as a "central consideration in South Africa's foreign policy".[62] This singling out of human rights as a strategic foreign relations theme even had some credibility to it that manifested in the country's ratification in time of all the major international human rights treaties.

In more recent times this exuberant allegiance to the human rights cause has become less prominent in official documentation of the Department of International Relations and Cooperation and in the public statements of its officials. A good illustration is the 2015–2020 Strategic Plan of the Department.[63] The dominant tone of this report is set by allusions to the "major shifts in political, economic, social and cultural dynamics" to which "South Africa must adapt and respond"; "environmental and developmental priorities"; the "alignment of South Africa's foreign policy to Africa's Agenda 2063"; the "priority of contributing to socio-economic development on the African continent"; and that "Africa continues to drive the vision of South

---

60 Press release on end of year report on the activities of the Department of Foreign Affairs 30 December 1996 available at http://www.info.gov.za/speeches/a998/98903_2329810870.htm (21-05-2016).

61 Mandela "South Africa's future foreign policy" 72 (1993) *Foreign Affairs* 85–97.

62 UN Doc A/61/889 (2007).

63 Department of International Relations and Cooperation (ed) Strategic Plan 2015–2020 available at http://www.dirco.gov.za/department/strategic_plan_2015_2018/strategic_plan2015_2020.pdf (15-09-2017).

Africa's foreign policy". Although these foreign policy issues received attention from the beginning, over the years they have become defining elements of the direction the country was taking after its re-entry into the community of states. Another emerging strategic theme was South-South relations, another cause which the country took upon itself and which seemingly coincided with South Africa's membership of the Non-Aligned Movement which it joined in 1994.[64]

But even at the time when the human rights agenda was still flying high as a strategic theme, the actual voting conduct of South Africa in the United Nations told a different story. In a 2007 report on the assessment of the voting record on key human rights issues of the UN Human Rights Council's members, South Africa, together with fifteen other developing states with membership in the Council, received the lowest score.[65] Based on this negative voting record, South Africa was classified as a questionable member of the Council in 2010 in a joint analysis by Freedom House and UN Watch.[66] South Africa's record in the UN General Assembly's Third Committee, where country-specific resolutions on human rights issues are dealt with, is equally disappointing. Between 1994 and 2008, it has consistently abstained from voting on condemnatory resolutions against countries such as Belarus, North Korea, Myanmar, DRC, Kosovo, Iraq, Iran, Turkmenistan, and Uzbekistan; or has voted against such resolutions in the case of Cuba, Iran and Belarus.[67] The general mood on South Africa's foreign policy regarding human rights is perhaps best summed up by the perceptions of participants in a 2010 workshop on the issue, namely that over the years human rights concerns have been deprioritised in the country's performance at the UN and that the reasons sometimes given for its voting conduct were not convincing.[68]

---

64 Graham *South Africa's Voting Behaviour in the United Nations: 1994 – 2008* (PhD Thesis University of Johannesburg 2013) 180 *et seq*.

65 UN Watch (ed) *Dawn of a New Era: Assessment of the UN Human Rights Council and its Year of Reform* (2007) 26, 27.

66 Freedom House and UN Watch (eds) *Evaluation of 2007–2010 UN Human Rights Council Candidates: Joint Analysis by Freedom House and UN Watch* (2007) available at http://www.unwatch.org/wp-content/uploads/2016/01/UNW__FH_ASSESSMENT_OF_HRC_CANDIDATES1.pdf (15-09-2016).

67 Graham (n 64) 78.

68 Corrigan *South Africa's Foreign Engagement: Whither Human Rights? Workshop Report, South African Institute of International Affairs* (2009) 10 (http://www.saiia.org.za/images/stories/research/aprm/2009_hr_workshop/aprm_rpt_corrigan_human_rights_safp_20090827.pdf (15-09-2017)).

Whether this is the result of shifting alliances, historical relationships, or the triumph of realism over idealism, is beside the point. The real irony is that while the government in matters of foreign affairs has reneged on its earlier commitments regarding the human rights agenda, the courts have not forgotten about it. The result is that in legal proceedings involving human rights and a foreign relations element, the judiciary has not shied away from reminding the government of its human rights-infused foreign policy commitments. This is dealt with in the next section.

IV. Judicial interventions ins select foreign policy matters

1. Diplomatic protection

It is a well-established rule in international law that a state whose national has been injured by another state, is entitled to take up the case of the injured person by resorting to diplomatic action or judicial proceedings.[69] Between 1995 and 2006, the matter of diplomatic protection has been on the agenda of the International Law Commission as a topic that was identified as appropriate for codification and progressive development. One of the controversial issues relating to this topic was whether the state of nationality is under a *duty* to provide diplomatic protection or whether it was merely a *right* of that state. The option of a duty entered the debate in the work of the then Special Rapporteur, John Dugard, as a result of a growing number of judicial decisions in domestic law supporting the view that there is some form of obligation on a state to protect its citizens abroad when facing serious violations of their human rights.[70]

Since opinions remain divided, the 2006 report, which contains a set of Draft Articles on Diplomatic Protection, opted for a compromise position. Draft Article 2 states unequivocally that a state "has a right to exercise diplomatic protection" and in the commentary to this article it is made clear

---

69 *Mavrommatis Palestine Concessions* Case PCIJ Reports Series A No 2 (1924) 12. The traditional view that in doing so the state is exerting its own rights to ensure respect for international law – as opposed to acting on behalf of the national – is questionable. See Dugard, Du Plessis, Katz et al *International Law: A South African Perspective* (2011) 281, 282.

70 International Law Commission *Report on the Work of the 58th Session (2006)* UN Doc A/61/10 Chapter IV 28 para (3), hereinafter ILC Report.

that although the internal law of a state may oblige a state to exercise diplomatic protection in certain circumstances, there is no such obligation in international law.[71] Thus, the position in the *Barcelona Traction* case prevailed, namely that the "[s]tate must be viewed as the sole judge to decide whether its protection will be granted, to what extent it is granted, and when it will cease. It retains in this respect a discretionary power the exercise of which may be determined by considerations of a political or other nature, unrelated to the particular case".[72] However, the ILC Report also contains a Draft Article 19 under the title "Recommended practice", which determines, in relevant part, that a state entitled to exercise diplomatic protection *should* (a) give due consideration to the possibility of exercising diplomatic protection, especially when a significant injury has occurred; and (b) take into account, wherever feasible, the views of injured persons with regard to resort to diplomatic protection and the reparation to be sought …". In the commentary to this provision, these recommendations were considered "desirable practices, constituting necessary features of diplomatic protection that add strength to diplomatic protection as a means for the protection of human rights and foreign investment".[73]

In 2005 these issues came before the South African constitutional court in the *Kaunda* case.[74] The applicants were a group of mercenaries made up of ex-South African soldiers contracted for a military *coup* against the President of Equatorial Guinea. Their plans went sour when they were arrested and detained in Zimbabwe when their plane, *en route* from Johannesburg, landed in Harare to pick up a consignment of weapons destined for the *coup*. When their extradition from Zimbabwe to Equatorial Guinea for purposes of a criminal trial loomed large, they petitioned the South African High Court for an order compelling the government to intervene on their behalf and to take steps to prevent their extradition to Equatorial Guinea, where, according to the particulars of their claims, they would not receive a fair trial, and if convicted, could face the death penalty. They also sought an intervention from the government that would ensure at all times their rights to dignity, freedom and security of the person, as well as fair conditions of detention and trial. When their application was dismissed by the High

---

71 *ibid* para (2).

72 *Barcelona Traction, Light and Power Company, Ltd (2nd Phase)* Judgement ICJ Reports 1970 3 44.

73 ILC Report (n 70) art 19 para (1) of commentary.

74 *Kaunda and Others v President of the Republic of South Africa and Others* 2005 4 SA 235 (CC).

Court, they successfully applied for direct leave to appeal to the Constitutional Court. In this Court the issues raised questions about the constitutional obligations of the state to take steps to protect its citizens in such circumstances, the reach of the Constitution and the relationship between the judiciary and the executive.

By word of Chaskalson CJ, the Court, relying on the ILC study on diplomatic protection and the *Barcelona Traction* case, followed traditional wisdom and concluded that in international law there is no duty to provide diplomatic protection, but only a right to do so.[75] The Court then turned to consider whether South African law provided an answer to the question of diplomatic protection for the applicants. Two constitutional provisions played a part in this enquiry. The one is section 7(2) which requires the state to "respect, protect, promote and fulfil the rights in the Bill of Rights". The applicants contended that this provision placed a positive obligation on the state to act in accordance with what the provision stipulates and, in the case of the applicants, can only do so by resorting to diplomatic protection on their behalf. This raised the question whether the section 7(2) obligations apply extra-territorially, a proposition the court was prepared to entertain provided that such an application does not interfere with the sovereignty of another state, which was the case here since what the applicants asked for was for the South African government to prevent the two foreign states involved in the matter to apply and enforce their national laws in respect of the impugned conduct of the applicants.[76]

The second and more interesting section the applicants relied on is section 3 of the constitution which entrenches what is called a "common South African citizenship" and which entitles South African citizens to claim the rights, privileges and benefits of citizenship on the basis of equality.[77] The Court had no problem in reading into these entitlements the entitlement to request the government to provide diplomatic protection to a citizen in need in a foreign country.[78] According to the Court, this entitlement has the consequence that if, as was held, a citizen has a right to request diplomatic protection, then government must have a corresponding duty to at least consider the request and how to respond to it.[79] Of further importance though,

75 *ibid* paras 23–29.
76 paras 31–44, 57.
77 Constitution sec 3(2)*(a)*.
78 Kaunda (n 74) paras 60–63.
79 para 67.

is the statement that in the case of a gross violation of international human rights norms, the government may have a duty to act in a manner that is consistent with its obligations under international law. In case there is a refusal by government to act in such circumstances, the refusal would be reviewable and the court could order government to take appropriate action.[80] Exactly what action is to be taken, however, is a foreign policy matter that is best left to the discretion of the executive.[81] Intervention by the judiciary, the Court pointed out, is reserved for those instances where government has acted irrationally or in bad faith or has refused to consider a legitimate request.[82]

Although in substantial agreement with the above conclusion, Ngcobo J followed a different approach to the claims made by the applicants. While Chaskalson CJ rejected the argument in favour of the extraterritorial application of the constitution in view of the Bill of Rights, and especially section 7(2) as indicated earlier on, Ngcobo J defended the position that sections 7(2) and 3 must be read together in determining the obligations of the South African government *vis-à-vis* its citizens.[83] This resulted in a much stronger emphasis on the human rights elements that should guide our foreign policy in matters of this kind and which should inform the duty government owes to its citizens.[84] Further support for such an approach, Ncgobo J derived from the state's ratification of international human rights instruments which, according to him must not only inform the government's foreign policy but also forms the foundation of the state's obligation to take steps when a serious violation of a citizen's human rights has been committed abroad and the citizen exercises his or her section 3 right to request diplomatic protection.[85]

O'Regan J, relying also on section 3 of the Constitution and on South Africa's constitutional and international law obligations with regard to the protection of human rights, in confirming that the South African government had an obligation to provide diplomatic protection to the applicants[86], took the matter a step further on the issue of what would constitute appropriate relief in the circumstances. Based on information placed before the

---

80 paras 69, 70.
81 paras 73–77.
82 paras 79, 80.
83 paras 176.
84 paras 159.
85 paras 159–188.
86 paras 237–242.

Court, the honourable justice was of the view that the pending extradition application gave rise to an "appreciable risk" that the applicants will be extradited to Equatorial Guinea and could face unfair trial proceedings. In such circumstances, she concluded, the Court is entitled to make a declaratory order with regard to the obligations of government to the effect that the Court declares that government is "under a constitutional obligation to take appropriate steps to provide diplomatic protection to the applicants to seek to prevent the egregious violation of international human rights norms".[87]

In *Von Abo v Government of the RSA*,[88] the applicant, a South African national and owner of agricultural land and related enterprises in Zimbabwe suffered considerable financial losses as a result of the expropriation without compensation of his farmland by the Zimbabwean government. When all his attempts to obtain redress in the Zimbabwean courts failed, he turned to the South African government for assistance. An intransigent attitude by the government finally persuaded him to apply for a court order to the effect that he had a right to diplomatic protection and that the South African government had failed to consider his requests rationally and in good faith. In finding that the South African government had "done absolutely nothing to assist the applicant, despite diligent and continued requests for diplomatic protection",[89] Prinsloo J, relying on *Kaunda*, ruled that the applicant had a "right to apply for diplomatic protection" and that the respondents (the South African government) "were under a constitutional duty at the very least to properly (that is rationally) apply their minds to the request for diplomatic protection".[90] The government, having failed to comply with its constitutional duty in this regard, was then ordered to forthwith take all necessary steps to have the violation of the applicant's rights by the Zimbabwean government remedied and to report to the court within 60 days on the steps it has taken in this regard.[91]

A claim for damages against the government, subject to compliance with the court's order, was postponed, and in the follow-up hearing on this matter,[92] the court found that there was once again "abject failure … to demonstrate any visible sign of even taking notice of these orders"[93] and that the

87 paras 268–271.
88 2009 2 SA 526 (T).
89 para 91.
90 para 141. See also paras 137–40.
91 para 161.
92 *Von Abo v Government of the Republic of South Africa* 2010 3 SA 269 (GNP).
93 para 27. See also para 28.

respondents showed "no interest whatsoever in attempting to comply with the orders of this court ...".[94] In the circumstances, the court decided on the payment of damages as appropriate relief arising from the violation of the applicant's rights by the Zimbabwean government.[95] In effect, this meant that the damages suffered by the applicant as a result of the expropriation of his property by the Zimbabwean government became the responsibility of the South African government as a result of the latter's failure to afford the applicant appropriate and effective relief in response to his request for diplomatic protection. On appeal by the South African government, this order was set aside by the Supreme Court of Appeal.[96] The latter reasoned that the order against the South African government to pay damages to the applicant for a breach committed by another government is akin to vicarious liability and a foreign concept in this instance; a state cannot attract liability in terms of its domestic law (the constitutional law basis of the alleged duty to provide diplomatic protection) *vis-à-vis* its own national for wrongs committed by another state against that same individual.[97]

The only breach that could have occurred, according to the Supreme Court of Appeal, was that the South African government had failed to comply with its duty to consider the applicant's request for diplomatic protection appropriately.[98] But, the court pointed out, even if there was a constitutional breach in the sense of a failure to respond appropriately to the request, the result of such a breach is not causally linked to the loss suffered, which was a result of the expropriation by the Zimbabwean government.[99] Apart from declaring the order made in the High Court legally untenable for the above reasons, the Supreme Court of Appeal was also of the view that it was unrealistic and impractical to expect the respondents (appellants before the SCA) to remedy the situation within 60 days; the respondents were set an impossible task, given the complexities of diplomatic negotiations, which are dependent on the responses and co-operation of the foreign government and the known uncompromising attitude of the Zimbabwean government in matters of this nature.[100] By prescribing in this manner the result the government's efforts should achieve and the time frame within

---

94 para 56.
95 para 68.
96 *Government of the Republic of South Africa v Von Abo* 2011 5 SA 262 (SCA).
97 para 31.
98 *ibid.*
99 para 33.
100 paras 26, 27.

which it was supposed to do so, the High Court had violated the rule on the separation of powers and encroached on the functions of the executive.[101]

The Supreme Court of Appeal was also critical of Prinsloo J's reading of the *Kaunda* case on the issue of the *right* to diplomatic protection. Instead of following the majority judgment, Prinsloo J, according to the Supreme Court of Appeal, seemed to have been influenced by the "broader … and less precise views" expressed by Ngcobo J in his concurring minority judgment, resulting in an incorrect approach.[102] In support of the discretionary nature of the exercise of diplomatic protection followed by the majority in *Kaunda*, the Supreme Court of Appeal in this instance also invoked the judgment of Harms DP in the *Van Zyl* case.[103] There it was stated:[104]

> "The appellants' request was premised on a 'right' to diplomatic protection and not on a right to have a request considered. It was further based on the duty of government to provide a particular type of diplomatic protection. These demands were, in the light of the constitutional court's judgment, ill-founded."[105]

The approach followed by the Supreme Court of Appeal in *Von Abo* does not correspond well with the court's own concessions in regard to the nature of the violation suffered by the applicant in the initial proceedings, and the conduct of the South African government in response to the request for diplomatic protection. With regard to the former, the court, in setting out the facts of the case, stated that "[i]t is common cause" that the loss suffered by the applicant as a result of the expropriation "was suffered as a result of a gross violation of international human rights standards".[106] And in noting the frustration of the court a quo in trying to establish the reasonableness or appropriateness of the government's conduct, the Supreme Court of Appeal made the following telling conclusion:[107]

> "This case is an example of how a government, founded on a constitutional dispensation and a culture of human rights, is not supposed to treat its citizens and its courts."

---

101 para 29.

102 para 23. See also Tladi "The right to diplomatic protection, the *Von Abo* decision, and the one big can of worms: eroding the clarity of *Kaunda*" 20 (2009) *Stellenbosch Law Review (Stellenbosch L Rev)* 14 22.

103 *Van Zyl v Government of the Republic of South Africa* 2008 3 SA 294 (SCA).

104 para 52.

105 See also *Kaunda* (n 74) para 144.

106 *Von Abo* (n 96) para 1.

107 *ibid* para 39.

Given these circumstances, one should be reminded of the majority judgment in *Kaunda* where Chaskalson CJ, pointed out that there:

> "may be a duty on government, consistent with its obligations under international law, to take action to protect one of its citizens against a gross abuse of international human rights norms. A request to the government for assistance in such circumstances where the evidence is clear would be difficult, and in extreme cases possibly impossible to refuse. It is unlikely that such a request would ever be refused by government, but if it were, the decision would be justiciable, and a court could order the government to take appropriate action."[108]

But intervention by a court in such circumstances is by no means limited to a *refusal* by government to respond to a request for diplomatic protection. Irrational or inappropriate responses are equally subject to judicial review, as will be a failure to properly consider a request and to act upon it.[109] Even so, it remains within the discretion of the executive to decide upon the manner and form of the diplomatic intervention; it is for intervening in this sphere of decision-making that the *Von Abo* judgment in the High Court has specifically been criticised. Thus, it has been suggested that the correct approach would have been an order directing the South African government to properly re-consider the request for diplomatic protection and to re-apply its mind as to what would be an appropriate form of intervention in the circumstances.[110]

In international law, diplomatic intervention is an obligation of conduct and not of result. Since the co-operation of the foreign state is essential in remedying the wrong done to the national of the intervening state, the latter cannot guarantee that the intervention will have a positive outcome. But this does not place the intervening state's considered options for intervention beyond judicial scrutiny. The intervening state must be able to show why the measures chosen are best suited to obtain a remedy in the circumstances of each case, and that those measures, compared to others, have the greatest potential for success.

108 *Kaunda* (n 74) para 69.
109 *ibid* paras 78–80.
110 Tladi (n 102) 25.

2. Rome Statute obligations

The different rulings of the South African courts in what is popularly referred to as the *Torture Docket* case[111] have received much acclaim nationally and internationally and may be viewed as constituting the most exciting piece of jurisprudence yet on post-apartheid South Africa's treaty obligations. What lies at the heart of this matter is South Africa's Rome Statute duty to investigate crimes against humanity committed in a neighbouring state (Zimbabwe) when there is probable evidence that the perpetrators may foray into South Africa, as they have done in the past. Here the emphasis will be on the judgment of the Constitutional Court which in all salient respects confirmed the judgements in the High Court and the Supreme Court of Appeal in the matter.

In brief the case arose out of a police raid on the headquarters of the opposition party in 2007, a year before national elections in Zimbabwe. In the raid, which allegedly took place on the instructions of the ruling ZANU-PF party, over a hundred people were arrested and detained and those affiliated to the opposition party were subsequently severely and continuously tortured over several days. Acting on behalf of the torture victims, an NGO, the Southern African Litigation Centre (SALC), submitted a dossier in 2008 to the South African Priority Crimes Litigation Unit (PCLU) containing statements and other evidence of the raid and the subsequent torture acts. At the time, the PCLU was the government agency responsible for the investigation and prosecution of crimes listed in the Rome Statute of the International Criminal Court, which South Africa has given effect to by virtue of the *Implementation of the Rome Statute of the International Criminal Court Act* 27 of 2002 (ICC Act).

The motivation for submitting the case to the South African authorities was that under the ICC Act South African law enforcement agencies were legally obliged to investigate international crimes and to hold the perpetrators accountable before South African courts. At the time the dossier was submitted, it was also common knowledge that no action was taken by the Zimbabwean authorities to investigate the incidents of torture and to bring those responsible to justice.

Police reaction to the SALC investigation request was sluggish and showed lack of will. Several months passed before an answer of some sort was provided, listing the reasons why the South African Police Service

---

111 *National Commissioner of the South African Police Service v Southern African Human Rights Litigation Centre* (2014) ZACC 30 (30 October 2014).

(SAPS) was unable to initiate an investigation into the matter, namely that the allegations of torture in the statements constituted insufficient evidence of contraventions of the ICC Act and that further investigations will be impractical and legally questionable which could have far-reaching consequences for the country's relations with Zimbabwe. SALC then applied to the High Court for an order reviewing and setting aside the SAPS refusal to investigate. Holding that the refusal was inconsistent with the constitution and South Africa's international obligations, the High Court granted the request for review and ordered the relevant enforcement agencies to reconsider their original decision to decline an investigation into the torture allegations.[112]

This ruling was then appealed by the state[113]) but the Supreme Court of Appeal upheld the ruling of the High Court to the extent that the SAPS is empowered to investigate the alleged offences whether or not the perpetrators are present in South Africa, and are required, by virtue of Act 27 of 2002, to initiate an investigation into the alleged offences.

Still not prepared to accept defeat, the state decided to challenge the Supreme Court of Appeal's judgment in the Constitutional Court. Of specific relevance in dealing with this phase of the legal battle between SALC and the state were section 205 of the constitution and section 4 of the ICC Act. Section 205(3) provides for the constitutional duties of the SAPS and directs the SAPS "to prevent, combat and investigate crime, to maintain public order, to protect and secure the inhabitants of the Republic and their property, and to uphold and enforce the law". This raised the constitutional issue whether section 205 also required the SAPS to investigate crimes against humanity, such as torture, allegedly committed in Zimbabwe, by and against Zimbabwean nationals.

The ICC linked this issue to the *enforcement jurisdiction* of the state seeking to invoke it, which is exercised, inter alia, by means of criminal investigations and prosecutions.[114] As such, the complementarity rule in the ICC Statute (article 17) must be observed.[115] The primary duty of a state party to exercise its criminal jurisdiction under this rule, the CC finds most

112 *Southern African Litigation Centre and Another v National Director of Public Prosecutions and Others,* North Gauteng High Court, case no 77150/09 (8 May 2012).

113 *National Commissioner, South African Police Service and Another v Southern African Rights Litigation Centre and Another* 2014 (2 SA 42 (SCA).

114 paras 25, 29.

115 para 30.

pressing in cases where the territorial state is not a party to the Rome Statute (such as Zimbabwe) and the perpetrators can only be brought to justice under the universal jurisdiction principle.[116] It is at this point that the ICC Act assumes importance, since it has the primary purpose of enabling the South African government to fulfil the country's obligations under the Rome Statute to bring the perpetrators of Rome Statute crimes to justice in its domestic courts pursuant to the principle of complementarity.[117]

The Court's enquiry then focused on the provisions in section 4 of the ICC Act, which regulates the jurisdiction of South African courts in matters of this nature. Of specific relevance is section 4(3)*(c)* which secures the jurisdiction of the South African courts over Rome Statue crimes committed outside the Republic if the perpetrator is present in the territory of the Republic after the commission of the crime. It is this connecting factor – presence on South African territory – that was also seized upon by the SAPS for declining to proceed with an investigation of the torture docket case, since at the time of becoming apprised of the torture allegations the alleged perpetrators were not present in South Africa. The CC rejected this contention as not relevant for purposes of an investigation; the provision only applies to presence as a requirement for the perpetrator's trial under South African law (see sec 35(3)*(e)* of the constitution) and is silent on the circumstances under which the country has a duty to investigate Rome Statute crimes committed beyond the country's borders.[118] Further support for such a reading of the law was found in the absence of state practice requiring presence for purposes of an investigation and the predominant position taken by scholars that there is no such rule in international law and that the presence requirement is limited to the trial phase in criminal proceedings,[119] a position also taken by the Supreme Court of Appeal in the matter. But the Court also alluded to some other valid reasons for distinguishing between investigations and prosecutions with regard to the presence requirement. Requiring presence also for the investigation phase would render obsolete combating international law crimes since it would be impractical to undertake a prosecution if the suspect enters or remains in the country for a brief period and no prior investigation has taken place that could facilitate the prosecution; an anticipatory investigation does not infringe upon due process trial rights;

116 para 32.
117 para 34.
118 para 43.
119 paras 46, 47.

determining presence or anticipated presence requires prior investigation; and any determination of a possible next step, such as whether prosecution is viable, requires an assessment of the facts that can only be achieved on the basis of a prior investigation.[120]

Having found that South Africa's domestic laws, interpreted in the light of the country's international law obligations, placed an obligation on the SAPS to investigate Rome Statute crimes committed outside South Africa, the Court nevertheless alluded to two limitations the exercise of such a duty will be subject to. The first requires respect for non-intervention in the affairs of another country which becomes a matter for consideration only if that country has shown the necessary resolve to pursue an investigation into the alleged crimes, which in the case of Zimbabwe was absent. The second limiting factor relates to practicality which must be decided by taking into consideration all the circumstances of the particular case, such as the prospects of a successful prosecution, the likelihood of arrests, the prospects of gathering evidence, and the resources required for an effective investigation.[121] Apart from fatal misconceptions with regard to their legal duties to investigate further the information provided by SALC, the Court was of the view that the SAPS also acted unreasonably with regard to these considerations by simply declining to proceed with an investigation,[122] an attitude the Court described as a "critical armchair review" of the torture docket and the shortcomings that necessitated further investigation, which "begs the very question that was being asked of them".[123]

By making an order that the SAPS "must investigate the complaint"[124] the CC has certainly brought clarity to South Africa's investigative duties under the Rome Statute in respect of crimes committed elsewhere, especially in future cases. That other states have taken note of the ruling and that it may inspire litigation in other jurisdictions to prevent perpetrators from escaping accountability altogether, are equally significant for strengthening the enforcement of international criminal justice. However, the case has highlighted at least two problematic issues with regard to a remedy for the torture victims. The one is the time element. Six years have lapsed since the torture docket was submitted to the SAPS for investigation – more than enough time for evidence to become unobtainable or tainted and for the

---

120 para 48.
121 paras 63, 64.
122 paras 65 *et seq.*
123 paras 72.
124 paras 84.

prospects of a successful prosecution to become negligible. The other is the monitoring of the SAPS's compliance with the court order. How, by whom and in what measure such monitoring will be executed is perhaps not less significant than the ruling itself.

The issue of the presence of an accused may still raise questions in future. As indicated above, the Court has settled the point that for the exercise of universal jurisdiction for purposes of an investigation, the territorial presence of an accused person is not a requirement; such presence becomes relevant only at a more advanced stage of criminal proceedings, namely when the prosecution and trial phase commences. When exactly this phase begins has not been answered and may still form the subject-matter of future jurisdictional disputes.

A year after the South African government suffered its defeat in the Constitutional Court, a second case involving the country's Rome Statute obligations became the subject-matter of legal proceedings in the courts. The Al Bashir case[125], as it is commonly referred to, has caused significant embarrassment for the South African government and the political storm it created came at a time when tensions between the ICC and the African Union ("AU") on the thorny issue of Head of State immunity was running high. The facts of the case arise from a decision in 2015 by the South African government to host the AU Summit in Johannesburg. On the list of invitees was Sudan's President Al Bashir who has been indicted by the ICC for crimes against humanity, war crimes, and genocide and who has evaded arrest since his indictment in 2009. To facilitate the hosting of the AU Summit the South African government entered into an agreement with the AU which, inter alia, provided for the privileges and immunities of delegates and other representatives to the Summit. The relevant parts of this agreement, whose aims and objectives were sourced from the OAU General Convention on the Privileges and Immunities of the OAU and from the Vienna Convention on Diplomatic Relations (1961), were subsequently published in the *Government Gazette* pursuant to South Africa's Diplomatic Immunities and Privileges Act 37 of 2001. These steps, the South African government believed, would shield Al Bashir from arrest while attending the AU Summit with the result that the government could happily disregard – at least for a while – its obligations under the Rome Statute and the ICC Act.

125 *Southern African Litigation Centre v Minister of Justice and Constitutional Development* 2015 5 SA 1 (GP).

While the Summit was attending to its business, the Southern African Litigation Centre ("SALC"), a human rights NGO, successfully brought an urgent application in the Gauteng Division of the High Court for an order prohibiting Al Bashir from leaving South Africa and instructing the South African government to enforce the order. The court's order was ignored by the government who apparently then also assisted Al Bashir to slip quietly out of the country in clear violation of the order. On being informed of these developments, the court requested the government to explain the circumstances under which Al Bashir had managed to leave the country. It is during this phase of the proceedings that the immunity claims of the government in terms of the agreement with the AU assumed specific importance in the government's explanation of its failure to arrest Al Bashir.

According to the court the immunity claims were ill-considered and ill-conceived and could not trump the international law obligations of the country under the Rome Statute and the ICC Act. In justifying this stance the court pointed out that the OAU Convention on immunities has never been domesticated by law and is therefore not binding on South Africa on the national level; that the agreement between South Africa and the AU did not confer immunity on Heads of State but on members and staff of the AU Commission, and on representatives of inter-governmental organisations; and that Al Bashir could only claim immunity on the basis of customary international law but that this kind of immunity has been expressly excluded by both the Rome Statute and the ICC Act.[126] As far as the obligations of South Africa were concerned, the court relied on the judgements of the Supreme Court of Appeal and the Constitutional Court in the *Torture Docket* case (above) for the conclusion that the obligations South Africa has undertaken to honour in terms of the Rome Statute and the ICC Act enjoy pre-eminence in our constitutional order and cannot be trumped by the immunities the government invoked for not arresting Al Bashir.[127]

In the final analysis, the court, in clear terms, expressed its displeasure at the ostensible link between Al Bashir's secretive departure from South Africa and the apparent disregard for the court's order by the South African government.[128] Referring to "clear indications" that the court order was not complied with, the court remarked critically that "a democratic state based

126 paras 28 et seq.
127 paras 25–27.
128 para 36.

on the rule of law cannot exist or function, if the government ignores its constitutional obligations and fails to abide by court orders".[129]

A further consequence of the government's reckless behavior is that it also owes the ICC an explanation for its failure to arrest Al Bashir. Its appearance in The Hague to settle this account has in the meantime been suspended as a result of a decision to appeal the outcome of the ruling of the High Court. The decision to appeal was not surprising; after all, the outcome of the High Court proceedings were met with acrimonious statements by politicians and members of the ruling party threatening a withdrawal from the ICC and an amendment to the ICC Act to re-introduce absolute sitting Head of State Immunity for Rome Statute Crimes.

Adding insult to injury, the government also lost the appeal.[130] At the outset a brief explanation of why leave to appeal was granted by the Supreme Court of Appeal (SCA) should suffice. In the High Court leave to appeal was denied on two grounds. Firstly, that the matter has become moot in the sense that Al Bashir has left the country with the result that no effect can be given to the order of the High Court; secondly, that an appeal had not reasonable prospect of success. In the SCA the first ground for refusal was dismissed with the argument that the High Court order remained in place and has a continuing effect in the sense that the government remained under a duty to act should Al Bashir again travel to South Africa in future. Of particular interest was the dismissal of the second ground for refusal. In this instance the SCA mentioned two reasons for granting leave to appeal. The one is based on the fact that the government introduced a new argument in the SCA in justifying its opposition to the applicant's claims, namely that under customary international law general Head of State immunity – which is legislated for in section 4(1)*(a)* of the Diplomatic Immunities and Privileges Act 37 of 2001 – qualifies the obligations of South Africa under the Rome Statute and the ICC Act. The second reason the SCA relied upon was that the case raises an issue of public importance with consequences for future matters.[131]

Much of the SCA's judgment centered around the newly introduced argument by the government that under customary international law South Africa was entitled to raise Head of State Immunity in defence of its non-compliance with the High Court order to arrest Al Bashir. In response to

---

129 para 37.2.

130 *Minister of Justice and Constitutional Development v The Southern African Litigation Center* 2016 ZASCA 17 (15 March 2016).

131 paras 19–25.

this issue the SCA dealt extensively with the divided opinions on whether there is an international crimes exception to the customary law principle on immunity and on whether the immunity in the case of Al Bashir was removed by Security Council resolution 1593 (2005) which decided that the government of Sudan shall cooperate fully with the ICC and the prosecutor pursuant to the resolution.[132] In these circumstances, the SCA found that it was "unable to hold that at this stage of the development of customary international law there is an international crimes exception to the immunity and inviolability that heads of state enjoy when visiting foreign countries and before foreign national Courts".[133]

The question that remained was whether the ICC Act removed the immunity Al Bashir would otherwise be entitled to. In seeking to determine the effect of this Act with regard to the immunity issue the SCA first relied on certain settled constitutional principles in determining what would constitute a proper construction of the Act. Of relevance were section 233 of the Constitution and the rights in the Bill of Rights. In terms of the former, courts are instructed, when interpreting any legislation, to prefer any reasonable interpretation that is consistent with international law over any other inconsistent interpretation. As regards the human rights guarantees in the Bill of Rights, the SCA invoked section 39(2) which informs an interpretation of the ICC Act that would promote the spirit, purport and objects of the Bill of Rights. This was relied upon to show that the crimes for which Al Bashir stands accused would have violated several of the rights in the Bill of Rights had those crimes been committed in South Africa.[134]

But the provisions of the ICC Act are even more directly relevant. The long title of the Act, for instance, makes it clear that the purpose of the Act is to ensure effective implementation of the Rome Statute, to ensure that South Africa complies with its obligations under the Statute, and to provide for the prosecution of Rome Statute crimes in South Africa and for the arrest of persons accused of such crimes and their surrender to the ICC. These commitments, the SCA pointed out, provide the context for interpreting a directly relevant provision such as section 4(2) of the Act which removes immunity as a defence to a crime or as a ground for reduction of sentence which could otherwise be claimed by a head of state or government or other government official under customary or conventional international law.

---

132 paras 66–83.

133 para 84.

134 paras 86–87.

This provision, the SCA interpreted as providing a "clear indication that South Africa does not support immunities when people are charged with international crimes".[135] On this point the government introduced the rather disingenuous argument that section 4(2) applies to prosecutions only and leaves arrests unaffected with the result that an arrest will still be inconsistent with immunity.[136]

In the words of the SCA, such an interpretation would create a "serious anomaly" and ignores the ordinary principle of construction that a power given to a functionary includes all ancillary powers necessary to give effect to that power. Put differently, the power to prosecute includes the power to arrest and bring before the courts the person accused of the crimes.[137] Moreover, the government's argument is directly at odds with the provisions in sections 8 to 10 of the ICC Act. These provisions form part of Chapter 4 of the Act which regulates cooperation with the ICC and sections 8 to 10 respectively provides for the endorsement, issuing and execution of warrants of arrest emanating from the ICC or a South African authority in respect of Rome Statute crimes. Section 10(9), in particular, determines that the fact that a person to be surrendered to a court is a head of state or government, or other government official, does not constitute a ground for refusing to issue an order for the surrender of that person.[138]

Given these provisions, the remaining issue in dispute was the relationship between the ICC Act and the Diplomatic Immunities Act, referred to earlier on. Here, the SCA followed the approach that where legislation dealing in general with a topic, exists, and parliament enacts legislation dealing with a specific area, otherwise covered by the general law, the two statutes co-exist, each dealing with its own subject-matter without conflict. This would mean that the reach of the general law, the Diplomatic Immunities Act, will be limited by the ICC Act in the sense that the former continues to regulate diplomatic immunities and privileges in general, but ceases to do so when immunities must be ignored for purposes of giving effect to the ICC Act.[139] Based on the above analysis, the SCA concluded that "when South Africa decided to implement its obligations under the Rome Statute … it did so on the basis that all forms of immunity, including head of state

135 para 93.
136 para 94.
137 para 95.
138 paras 96–100.
139 para 102.

immunity, would not constitute a bar to the prosecution of international crimes in this country or to South Africa's cooperation with the ICC by way of the arrest and surrender of persons charged with such crimes before the ICC, where an arrest warrant had been issued and a request for cooperation made".[140]

One would think that the rather unambiguous provisions of the ICC Act and its overall objective, coupled with the SCA's ruling in the matter would be sufficiently forceful to deter the government to pursue the matter further. That the government thought otherwise became clear when an announcement was made shortly after the SCA's ruling to the effect that an appeal to the constitutional court is being considered. The opportunity seized upon by the government is the SCA's inconclusive response to the divided opinions regarding the customary international law position with regard to sitting head of state immunity. Before it could be heard on 22 November 2016 the government withdrew the appeal. On 19 October 2016, the national executive then took a decision to withdraw officially from the Rome Statute and a notice of withdrawal was deposited subsequently with the Secretary-General of the United Nations in accordance with article 127 of the Statute. This withdrawal was successfully challenged by the official opposition, the Democratic Alliance, before the North Gauteng High Court on the basis that the decision to withdraw was taken without prior parliamentary approval and therefore unconstitutional and invalid.[141] This may not be the end of the government's ICC severance plans and it is not inconceivable that the withdrawal process will be resurrected and steered through parliament as required by the court.

The primary question in this matter is whether the national executive, who by virtue of section 231 of the Constitution has the power to negotiate and sign international treaties, also holds the power to give note of withdrawal from such a treaty without parliamentary approval. In essence the matter goes to the heart of the separation of powers between the executive and the legislature with regard to the conclusion of treaties. In the view of the court, since parliamentary approval is required under section 231 for a treaty to bind the Republic, it is only parliament, and not the executive, that can undo it. In the words of the court:

> "It should also be borne in mind that prior parliamentary approval is required before instruments of ratification may be deposited with the United Nations. From that

140 para 103.

141 *Democratic Alliance v Minister of International Relations and Cooperation* 2017 2 All SA 123 (GP).

perspective, there is a glaring difficulty in accepting that the reverse process of withdrawal should not be subject to the same parliamentary process. The necessary inference, on a proper construction of s 231, is that parliament retains the power to determine whether to remain bound to an international treaty. This is necessary to give expression to the clear separation of powers between the national executive and the legislature embodied in the section. If it is parliament which determines whether an international agreement binds the country, it is constitutionally untenable that the national executive can unilaterally terminate such an agreement."[142]

But there was still the ICC leg of the whole Al Bashir arrest debacle (dealt with above) in terms of which South Africa was required to appear before a chamber of the ICC to explain the country's non compliance with the Court's request for arrest and surrender when Al Bashir was in South Africa for the AU Summity. This matter was concluded on 6 July 2017 when Pre-Trial Chamber II found that South Africa was in breach of its Rome Statute obligations by refusing to arrest and surrender Al Bashir to the Court.[143]

South Africa's main contention was that Heads of State immunity that existed under customary international law prevented it from complying with the Court's request, which, in essence raised the issue of the scope and meaning of article 27(2) of the Rome Statute which reads as follows:

"Immunities or special procedural rules which may attach to the official capacity of a person, whether under national or international law, shall not bar the Court from exercising its jurisdiction over such a person."

The argument put forward by South Africa was that this provision only concerns the court's jurisdiction and has no effect on the rights and obligations of states vis-à-vis the Court, such as a request for arrest and surrender.[144] This narrow interpretation was rejected by the Court since it would place insurmountable obstacles in the Court's attempts to have fugitives from justive to be arraigned before the Court apart from the fact that the meaning ascribed to it by South Africa was clearly not the intention of the drafters of the Statute. The preferable interpretation is that the "effect of article 27(2) of the Statute ... concerns both, vertically, the relationship between a State Party and the Court and, horizontally, the inter-State relationships between States Parties to the Statute".[145]

---

142 *ibid* para 51. See also paras 46–50.

143 See Decision under Article 87(7) of the Rome Statute on the non-compliance by South Africa with the request by the Court for the arrest and surrender of Omar Al- Bashir, Case no ICC-02/05 – 01/09 (6 July 2017).

144 *ibid* para 73.

145 *ibid* para 76.

Following this premise the Court then turned to the Security Council's referral to the Court of the situation in Darfur by means of resolution 1593 (2005) which was adopted under chapter VII of the UN Charter. According to the Court this binding resolution has the effect that the only legal framework that applies to the situation is that of the Statute.[146] Consequently, the result is that both Sudan and South Africa are under an obligation to cooperate fully with the Court in the arrest and surrender of Al Bashir and since article 27(2) renders inapplicable any form of immunity based on official capacity neither state can avoid its obligations under the Statute by invoking Head of State immunity.[147]

The end result of the ICC's finding of non-compliance by South Africa with its Rome Statute obligations and of the domestic law proceedings dealt with above is that South Africa's immunity argument has been rendered inapplicable under both international and domestic law. But this may not bring closure to the issue since South Africa may still decide to pursue the matter further in the ICC's appeals chamber. A request by the UN General Assembly or Security Council for an advisory opinion by the International Court of Justice[148] could be another way of settling the contested customary international law position on immunity in the case of Rome Statute crimes.

3. National enforcement of the SADC Tribunal's judgments

This matter relates to a series of legal challenges to the so-called agrarian reform in Zimbabwe introduced by a constitutional amendment in 2005. The amendment entitled the state to expropriate land identified for resettlement purposes without compensation (except for improvements on the land), barred an affected landowner from challenging the state's decision, and suspended the courts' jurisdiction to entertain a legal challenge.

Without a remedy at the domestic level, a number of landowners, mostly white farmers, who lost their land in this manner, successfully challenged the state's action before the SADC Tribunal entitling them to compensation for the expropriation of their land.[149] Zimbabwe refused to comply with the

146 *ibid* paras 85. 86.
147 *ibid* paras 87–96.
148 UN Charter art 96.
149 *Mike Campbell v Zimbabwe* SADC (T) Case No 2/2007.

ruling which led to contempt proceedings before the Tribunal and a cost order against the Zimbabwean government.[150] When this was also ignored, the applicants approached the High Court in South Africa to have the cost order enforced and obtained from the High Court a writ of execution authorising the attachment and sale of certain properties owned by the Zimbabwean government in Cape Town.[151] This was challenged by Zimbabwe before the Supreme Court of Appeal (SCA) citing immunity against legal proceedings in South Africa's domestic courts and the High Court's lack of jurisdiction because the SADC Treaty and the Tribunal's Protocol were never enacted into law as required by section 231(4) of the South African Constitution. The Zimbabwean government failed on both grounds and the SCA held that South African common law on the enforcement of foreign judgments applied to international tribunals and that the cost order was therefore enforceable in South Africa.[152] The Zimbabwean government then sought leave to appeal to the Constitutional Court against the order made by the SCA. On the basis that a constitutional matter was involved, namely the question about access to courts as well as the human rights and rule of law basis of the dispute between the parties, the majority then granted leave to appeal.[153]

The Constitutional Court (CC) first dealt with the binding effect on South Africa of the amended SADC Treaty which incorporated the Tribunal's Protocol. South Africa acceded to the SADC Treaty on 29 August 1994 and this accession was approved by Parliament in 1995 in accordance with section 231(2) of the South African constitution. This had the effect that the treaty became binding on South Africa at the international level. For the treaty's domestic enforcement parliamentary enactment is required under section 231(4) of the Constitution which did not happen. It is this issue which the Zimbabwean government seized upon in arguing that the Tribunal's cost order was not enforceable in South Africa in a domestic court. The CC rejected the argument that non-compliance with section 231(4) rendered the Tribunal's order unenforceable at the domestic level, accepting

150 *Fick v Republic of Zimbabwe* Case No SADC (T) 01/2010.

151 *Fick v Government of the Republic of Zimbabwe* case no 77881/2009 North Gauteng High Court 25 February 2010 unreported.

152 *Government of the Republic of Zimbabwe v Fick* 2012 ZASCA 122 (20 September 2012).

153 *Government of the Republic of Zimbabwe v Fick* 2013 10 BCLR 1103 (CC).

instead that ratification by parliament alone is sufficient to make it obligatory for South Africa to take steps for giving effect to the Tribunal's decisions in accordance with article 32(2) of the Tribunal's Protocol.[154]

For its claim to immunity in proceedings before domestic courts in South Africa, Zimbabwe relied on section 2(1) of the Foreign States Immunities Act 87 of 1981. However, such immunity, according to section 3(1) of the Act, will be forfeited in proceedings in which the foreign state has *expressly* waived its immunity. Such a waiver, according to the CC, has indeed taken place when Zimbabwe decided to ratify the SADC Treaty and to adopt the Amending Agreement incorporating the Tribunal's Protocol which determines in article 32(3) that decisions of the Tribunal shall be binding upon the parties and enforceable within their territories. By accepting this obligation, Zimbabwe has for all intends and purposes relinquished its claim to sovereign immunity before South Africa courts in respect of the registering and enforcement of decisions made against it by the Tribunal.[155]

The remaining question then was whether South African law provided for the enforcement of the decisions of an international Tribunal in the same manner as for foreign civil orders in accordance with the *Enforcement of Foreign Civil Judgements Act* 32 of 1988. According to this Act, foreign judgements given in countries designated by the Minister for purposes of enforcement in South Africa become enforceable in South Africa but no such designation has been made affecting the Tribunal's decision in the same manner. The second obstacle was that the Act only applied to enforcement by magistrates' courts. Thus, with the applicability of the Act out of the way, the matter had to be dealt with in terms of the common law.

Several common law requirements for enforcement were not in dispute in this matter.[156] The remaining questions were whether the Tribunal had jurisdiction, whether the Tribunal's cost order constituted a "foreign judgement", and, if not, whether the common law needed to be developed as required by the constitution.[157]

With regard to the jurisdictional issue it was pointed out that in the proceedings before the Tribunal Zimbabwe did not object to the jurisdictional capacity of the Tribunal as such, but merely challenged the Tribunal's ju-

154 paras 29–31.
155 paras 32, 35.
156 paras 38, 39.
157 para 39.

risdiction to rule on the alleged human rights violations and the land expropriation without compensation programme. Zimbabwe's argument in this instance was that the SADC instruments did not contain any specific standards against which Zimbabwe's conduct could be measured and that the Tribunal could therefore not invoke norms and standards of other international treaties.[158] This explains, according to the CC, why the Tribunal simply relied on article 4(c) of the SADC Treaty which obliges SADC states to act in accordance with human rights, democratic principles and the rule of law. Moreover, by participating in the proceedings before the Tribunal, Zimbabwe has submitted to the jurisdiction of the Tribunal.[159]

In the proceedings before the CC Zimbabwe raised objections to the jurisdiction of the Tribunal that were different from those raised during the proceedings before the Tribunal. In dealing with this matter the CC held the view that the basis for objecting to the jurisdiction of a foreign court or tribunal whose order is sought to be enforced in South Africa must be materially the same as the objections initially raised before the foreign court or tribunal unless, in exceptional circumstances and at the time, the basis for objection was not available to the objecting party. The analogy the CC used in this instance is the rule that an appeal should be based on the same issues raised in the court a quo.[160] Here, the Court concluded as follows:

> "Once a litigant has submitted to the jurisdiction of a court, ordinarily, it may not in later or appellate proceedings, dispute that jurisdiction. By parity of reasoning, once a litigant has chosen specific grounds for impugning the jurisdiction of a court, it may not in later proceedings attack the jurisdiction of the first Court on new or fresh grounds."[161]

With the jurisdictional question answered, the Court turned to the common law position in South Africa on the enforcement of foreign judgements. In pointing out that the common law only allows for enforcement of judgements or orders by foreign domestic courts, the question then was whether the common law should be developed by the Court (as is required by sections 8(3) and 39(2) of the constitution) to also include judgements and orders by international Tribunals.[162]

158 paras 41, 42.
159 para 42.
160 para 44.
161 para 46.
162 paras 52, 53.

In finding itself obliged to develop the common law to provide for such a solution, the Court took into consideration a number of reasons, including the need to ensure that lawful judgements are not evaded with impunity by any state or person.[163] But the reasons that weighed most heavily with the Court were those enunciated in the constitution itself, namely the right of access to courts and an effective remedy in section 34 of the constitution; the obligation in section 8(3) to develop the common law to give effect to the bill of rights; the obligation in section 39(1)*(b)* to consider international law when interpreting the bill of rights; and the provision in section 233 according to which the courts, when interpreting any legislation, must prefer any reasonable interpretation that is consistent with international law over any other interpretation that is inconsistent with international law.[164]

This constitutional framework the Court read together with the obligation in article 32 of the Tribunal's Protocol which places an obligation on member states to take the measures required for ensuring the execution of the Tribunal's decisions in their domestic legal systems. Consequently, "[s]ection 34 of the Constitution must therefore be interpreted, and the common law developed, so as to grant the right of access to our courts to facilitate the enforcement of the decisions of the Tribunal in this country".[165] This will be achieved, the Court concluded, by regarding the Tribunal as a foreign court, and for that end the "concept of a 'foreign court' will henceforth include the Tribunal".[166]

It must be pointed out that this ruling only affects the position of the SADC Tribunal and does not bring clarity with regard to the domestic enforcement of the judgements of other international tribunals. A legislative amendment to the Enforcement Act addressing this issue is perhaps preferable to *ad hoc* (and costly) judicial interventions.

4. Select extradition issues

The ruling of the Gauteng Local Division of the High Court in the case of *State v Patel*[167] emanates from an extradition request by the United States to have the appellant, a US national, extradited from South Africa to the US

163 para 54.
164 paras 54–69.
165 para 69.
166 para 70.
167 2016 2 SACR 141 (GJ).

to face charges relating to financial crimes associated with the contravention of banking regulations in the US committed between 2005 and 2007. The extradition request was made pursuant to the extradition treaty between South Africa and the USA, and led to the arrest of the appellant and a committal order by a magistrate authorising his extradition on the basis that the offences in question were extraditable offences under the Extradition Act 67 of 1962.

On appeal, one of the main objections raised by the appellant against the ruling by the magistrate was that the double criminality requirement for extradition (sec 2(1) of the Extradition Act) had not been met in the sense that at the time of the alleged commission of the offences in the US, these were not offences under South African law; they only later became so by virtue of the Financial Intelligence Act 38 of 2001, relevant parts of which only took effect in 2010, thus after the commission dates. Consequently, and since the Extradition Act as well as the extradition treaty between South Africa and the US are silent on the matter, the legal question before the court was whether double criminality should be determined with reference to the date of the commission of the alleged offences, or with reference to the date of the extradition request.

This issue remains unsettled in many jurisdictions and scholarly views differ. Even the House of Lords ruling in the *Pinochet No 3* case[168] and in the *Palazollo* case[169] in South Africa, which favoured the time of the commission of the offences for determining double criminality, have met with criticism.[170] It must also be taken into account that in *Pinochet 1*[171] Lord Bingham used the date of the extradition request as the proper date for assessing double criminality, and in *Pinochet 3*, the House of Lords ruling on this issue was based on a specific, and arguably wrong, interpretation of a provision of the UK Extradition Act in force at the time (see for instance the views of Lord Bingham CJ and Lord Loyd). This specific reading also

---

168 *R v Bow Street Magistrate, Ex Parte Pinochet (No 3)* 2000 1 AC 147 169E–G (HL) ("Pinochet 3") per Lord Brown-Wilkinson.

169 *Palazollo v The Minister of Justice and Constitutional Development* (unreported) case no 4731/2010.

170 See Dugard, Du Plessis, Katz et al *International Law: A South African Perspective* (2011) 220; Warbrick "Extradition law aspects of Pinochet 3" 48 (1999) *International and Comparative Law Quarterly (Int'l Comp. L.Q.)* 960 962.

171 *R v Bow Street Metropolitan Stipendiary Magistrate, Ex Parte Pinochet Ugarte* (No 1) 1998 4 All ER 897 (HL).

meant that the bulk of the charges against Pinochet did not qualify as extradition crimes.[172] The approach followed by the House of Lords in this regard has caused one commentator to make the following critical remarks:[173]

> "To apply extradition law retrospectively gives only a chance benefit to a fugitive. There is no violation of the principle of legality (or of the imposition of retrospective criminal liability) because his conduct will have had to have been an offence in the law of the requesting State at the time of its commission if he is to be convicted and the conduct would have been an offence in England if committed here at the time of the extradition request."

The importance of the *Pinochet 3* ruling on double criminality may be further diluted over time in view of the introduction of the 2002 European Council Framework Decision on surrender procedures and the 2004 European Arrest Warrant Scheme. Both these developments have done away with the double criminality requirement for listed crimes. In such instances normal due process guarantees still apply, affording persons to be extradited or surrendered adequate protection against abuse. A note on dual criminality was also published by the Committee of Experts on the Operation of European Conventions on Co-Operation in Criminal Matters on 11 May 2012 (Council of Europe Document PC-OC (2012) 02 Final) where the following conclusion was reached:

> "The PC-OC agreed that the double criminality principle should apply at the moment when the decision to extradite is taken. Other moments, including when the alleged offence took place or when the request for extradition was introduced, are therefore not considered as relevant (at 2)."

In the *Patel* case mentioned in the beginning, and in the context of South African law, Coppin J in the Gauteng High Court ruling, was not prepared to follow the approach in Pinochet in view of differences in context, wording and the laws applicable to interpretation, and rejected *Palazollo* as not binding on this point.[174] In his view the term "punishable offences" in section 2(1) of the Extradition Act does not refer to past conduct which constituted an offence at the time of its commission in a foreign state, but to conduct "which will constitute an offence in this country at least at the time of the extradition request, if not at the time when the enquiry is being conducted by the magistrate".[175] Further support for this interpretation, the

172 Warbrick (n 170) 962.
173 (n 170) 964.
174 Patel (n 167) paras 48, 49.
175 paras 50, 52.

court found in the approach of many European states in respect of the European Convention on Extradition and in section 233 of the Constitution of the Republic of South Africa which enjoins the courts to follow an international law-friendly approach (in casu to the extradition treaty between the two countries) when interpreting legislation.[176] Consequently, an interpretation that will not obstruct the implementation of the treaty must be followed.[177]

One of the underlying principles for the double-criminality rule is the principle of legality – the well-known *nullum crime sine lege* rule. The court has made it clear that this rule is not violated when the time of the extradition request is taken as the decisive moment "because the person's conduct would have had to be an offence in terms of the law of the requesting State at the time of its commission if he is to be convicted and punished for it there".[178] This argument may be further expanded on.

It is commonly accepted that the double criminality rule serves the function of ensuring that a person's liberty is not restricted without a prima facie legal basis in both the requesting and requested state.[179] If this is the rationale for the double criminality requirement, it must follow logically that the question of whether a fugitive from justice may be exposed to a deprivation of liberty without a proper legal basis in extradition proceedings, can only arise at the time of the extradition request. Before that moment, any question of an infringement of the fugitive's rights is premature. The logic of taking the time of the extradition request as decisive for determining double criminality is specifically relevant in the case of statutory offences as the legislative programmes in different states do not follow the same time schedule, with the result that the criminalisation of certain conduct in different countries may be removed in time. To assert, in such circumstances, a double criminality rule based on the time of the commission of an extraditable offence, will create countless safe havens for offenders – a situation that will seriously undermine the current emphasis in the world on mutual legal assistance and cooperation in criminal matters.

176 para 51.
177 para 33.
178 para 53.
179 Shearer *Extradition in International Law* (1971) 137; Bedi *Extradition in International Law and Practice* (1966) 69.

V. Final remarks

Constitutional democracies based on the rule of law and the supremacy of the constitution are characterised by the fact that all state functions derive their legality and legitimacy from the constitutional order and the legal obligations imposed on the state by international law. Hence, there are no constitutionally-free areas within which state organs can perform their typical functions or pursue their political or other objectives. This is equally true for the executive in matters involving foreign relations or when it domestically performs executive functions in accordance with government's political, economic, social, environmental or other policies. Even in politically sensitive cases where the responsible state organ is entitled to a discretionary exercise of its assigned or implied powers, the principle of constitutional circumscription and dependence remains unaffected.

Since judicial review forms an integral part of a constitutional state that respects the supremacy of the law, the judicial arm of government cannot avoid being confronted with political questions when called upon to adjudicate in a dispute that involves the executive's discretion in decision-making. Although the cases are scant, the South African courts have become fully aware of this reality in the first twenty years of an entirely new constitutional reality as the incidents dealt with in this chapter illustrate. That more cases of this kind may end up in the courts in future is something that must be welcomed. It is only through jurisprudential development that a constitution can demonstrate its continuing relevance in the life of a nation apart from being a necessary requirement for bringing legal certainty to contested areas.

In matters of foreign affairs the dilemma for courts under a constitutional democracy is to find the right balance between enforcement of the constitutional principles and values on the one hand and respect for other state organ-specific competencies on the other hand. A guideline worth considering is to first determine the nature of the contested issue.[180] If by its nature it falls within the core functions of the executive, judicial review could be expected to be limited to questions of procedure and rationality. But if the contested issue involves a human rights violation or a constitutional principle of similar gravity, the intervention by the judicial arm of government could focus more on substantive issues and therefore becomes more invasive of the executive's own sphere of competence. In such instances the

180 See also Giegerich (n 21) 556.

responsibility of the judicial branch to protect the integrity of the constitutional state is of a higher order.

The human rights cases dealt with in this chapter indicate that the South African courts are acutely aware of these issues when performing their review powers under the constitution. However, a matter that has thus far escaped proper scrutiny, research and analysis is the potential influence of South Africa's membership of the African Union (AU) and of the South African Development Community (SADC) on the powers and functions of the executive *vis-à-vis* that of parliament and the future role of the national and regional judicial bodies in disputes between different state organs and between state organs and the organs of the AU and/or SADC. As the brief section on the relationship between the EU and its member states has illustrated, this may be a legal and political issue that has become ripe for further consideration.

Bibliography

Bedi SD *Extradition in International Law and Practice* (Dennis & Co., Buffalo New York 1968).

Brand F *Europapolitische Kommunikation zwischen Bundestag und Bundesregierung* (Duncker & Humblot, Berlin 2015).

Corrigan T *South Africa's Foreign Engagement: Whither Human Rights? Workshop Report, South African Institute of International Affairs* (2009), http://www.saiia.org.za/images/stories/research/aprm/2009_hr_workshop/aprm_rpt_corrigan_human_rights_safp_20090827.pdf (15-09-2017).

Department of Foreign Affairs, Press release on end of year report on the activities, 30 December 1996 available at http://www.info.gov.za/speeches/a998/98903_2329810870.htm (21-05-2016).

Department of Foreign Affairs *South African Foreign Policy Discussion Document* http://www.sahistory.org.za/sites/default/files/south_african_foreign_policy.pdf (15-09-2017).

Department of International Relations and Cooperation *2015 – 2020 Strategic Plan* http://www.dirco.gov.za/department/strategic_plan_2015_2018/strategic_plan2015_2020.pdf (15-09-2017).

Dreier H (ed) *Grundgesetz Kommentar, Band II* (3rd Editon, Mohr Siebeck, Tübingen 2015).

Dugard J, Du Plessis M, Katz A et al *International Law: A South African Perspective* (4th Edition, Juta, Cape Town 2011).

Federalist Paper No 75, *George Hamilton commented on the treaty-making power of the executive* http://www.let.rug.nl/usa/documents/1786-1800/the-federalist-papers/the-federalist-75.php (15-09-2017).

Fisher L "Congressional participation in the treaty process" 137 (1989) *University of Pennsylvania Law Review (U. Pa. L. Rev.)* 1511.

Giegerich T "Verfassungsgerichtliche Kontrolle der auswärtigen Gewalt im europaïsch-atlantischen Verfassungsstaat: Vergleichende Bestandsaufnahme mit Ausblick auf die neuen Demokratien in Mittel- und Osteuropa" 57 (1997) *Zeitschrift für ausländisches öffentliches Recht und Völkerrecht (ZaöRV)* 409.

Graham S *South Africa's Voting Behaviour in the United Nations: 1994–2008* (Thesis University of Johannesburg 2013).

Henkin L *Foreign Affairs and the Constitution* (Foundation Press, Mineola, New York 1972).

Hingst U *Auswirkungen der Globalisierung auf das Recht der völkerrechtlichen Verträge* (Duncker & Humblot, Berlin 2001).

Mandela N "South Africa's Future Foreign Policy" 72 (1993) *Foreign Affairs* 85.

Maunz T and Dürig G (eds) *Grundgesetz Kommentar, Band V* (loose-leaf 77th Edition, C.H. Beck, Munich, July 2016).

Shearer IA *Extradition in International Law* (Manchester University Press, Oceana Publications, Manchester, Dobs Ferry, New York 1971).

Tladi D "The right to diplomatic protection, The *Von Abo* decision, and the one big can of worms: Eroding the clarity of *Kaunda*" 20 (2009) *Stellenbosch Law Review (Stellenbosch L Rev)* 14.

UN Watch *Dawn of a New Era: Assessment of the UN Human Rights Council and its Year of Reform* (2007) http://www.unwatch.org/wp-content/uploads/2016/01/DAWN_OF_A_NEW_ERA_HRC-REPORT_FINAL.pdf (15-09-2017).

Von Münch I and Kunig P (eds) *Grundgesetz Kommentar Band I* (6th Edition, C.H.Beck, Munich 2012).

Warbrick "Extradition law aspects of Pinochet 3" 48 (1999) *International and Comparative Law Quarterly (Int'l Comp LQ)* 960.

Wolfrum R "Kontrolle der auswärtigen Gewalt" in *Kontrolle der auswärtigen Gewalt. Veröffentlichungen der Vereinigung der deutschen Staatsrechtlehrer* 56 (1997) 38.

Case Law

Germany

German Constitutional Court (Bundesverfassungsgericht, BVerfG) 29.7.1952 – 2 BvE 2/51 – BVerfGE 1, 372.

German Constitutional Court (BVerfG) 12.7.1994 – 2 BvE 3/92 – BVerfGE 90, 286.

German Constitutional Court (BVerfG) 19.6.2012 – 2 BvE 4/11 – BVerfGE 131, 152.

South Africa

Fick and Others v Government of the Republic of Zimbabwe case no 77881/2009 North Gauteng High Court 25 February 2010 (unreported)

Government of the Republic of Zimbabwe v Fick and Others [2012] ZASC 122 (20 September 2012)

Government of the Republic of Zimbabwe v Fick 2013 10 BCLR 1103 (CC)

Government of the Republic of South Africa v Von Abo 2011 5 SA 262 (SCA)

Kaunda and Others v President of the Republic of South Africa 2005 4 SA 235 (CC)

Minister of Justice and Constitutional Development v The Southern African Litigation Center 2016 ZASCA 17 (15 March 2016)

National Commissioner of the South African Police Service v Southern African Human Rights Litigation Centre 2014 ZACC 30 (30 October 2014)

Palazollo v The Minister of Justice and Constitutional Development case no 4731/2010 (unreported)

Southern African Litigation Centre v Minister of Justice and Constitutional Development 2015 5 SA 1 (GP)

State v Patel 2016 2 SACR 141 (GJ)

Van Zyl v Government of the Republic of South Africa 2008 3 SA 294 (SCA)

Von Abo v Government of the RSA 2009 (2) SA 526 (T)

Von Abo v Government of the Republic of South Africa 2010 3 SA 269 (GNP)

United Kingdom

R v Bow Street Metropolitan Stipendiary Magistrate, Ex Parte Pinochet Ugarte (No 1) 1998 4 All ER 897 (HL).

R v Bow Street Magistrate, Ex Parte Pinochet (No 3) 2000 AC 147 (HL).

United States

United States v Curtiss-Wright 299 US 304 319 (1936).

SADC

Fick v Republic of Zimbabwe SADC (T) case no 1/2010

Mike Campbell v Zimbabwe SADC (T) case no 2/2007

International Court of Justice

Barcelona Traction, Light and Power Company, Ltd (2nd Phase) Judgement ICJ Reports 1970 3.

Permanent Court of International Justice

Mavrommatis Palestine Concessions Case PCIJ Reports Series A No 2 (1924) 12.

European Court of Justice

Case C-70/88 22.5.1990 *European Parliament v Council of the European Communities*, ECLI:EU:C:1990:217.

The German Constitution and international law: some remarks on the comparison with the openness of the South African Constitution

*Stefan Lorenzmeier**

As with the South African Constitution of 1996, the German Constitution of 1949, the "*Grundgesetz*" (Basic Law, GG), is aimed at dealing with the events that lead to its adoption and as part thereof to an openness as to the international forum and its developments. Even the preamble states that the Basic Law is "inspired by the determination to promote world peace as an equal partner in a unified Europe"[1], which underlines Germany aiming at becoming a respected member of the civilized nations once more after the atrocities of the Second World War.

I. Treaty-making: the role of the Parliament

Art. 59 para. 2 GG is the main provision of the German Constitution concerning treaty-making. According to this norm, all

> "treaties that regulate the political relations of the Federation or relate to subjects of federal legislation shall require the consent or participation, in the form of a federal law, of the bodies responsible in such a case for the enactment of federal law. In the

---

* Stefan Lorenzmeier, *Dr. iur., LL.M.*; University of Augsburg, Faculty of Law.

1 Official Translation of the Grundgesetz, available at https://www.bundestag.de/gg (15-09-2016).

> case of executive agreements the provisions concerning the federal administration shall apply mutatis mutandis."

Thus, only two types of treaties require the consent of the federal Parliament: treaties regulating the political relations of the Federation, and those which relate to federal legislation[2]. Executive agreements, on the other hand, can be concluded without the participation of the Parliament[3].

The provisions are rather clear in stating that the German Parliament does not take part in the negotiations of a treaty due to the principle of separation of powers. The foreign competence is a prerogative of the executive branch[4]. Yet, the legislative and executive branches bear a common responsibility for Germany's external powers[5] which stems in essence from the role of the Parliament to control the Government and its right to legislate. In respect of the negotiation of treaties it must be borne in mind that the Government has the personal and technical resources to negotiate these agreements, whereas the Parliament lacks such resources.

Returning to the issue of the required parliamentary approval, which has to be done by the *Bundestag* as well as the *Bundesrat*, it is a part of the principle of checks and balances established by the German Constitution and aims at controlling the Government and is dogmatically a part of the principle of preventive control of the executive branch[6]. It stands next to other means of governmental control laid down in Arts. 43, 44 and 45a para. 1 GG.

The obligation of a parliamentary approval is further elaborated in cases of collective security systems like the United Nations or NATO. Special in these systems is that even after the approval of the treaty, the execution of the treaty might have a direct impact on people, especially German soldiers. This leads to two different legal conclusions by the German Constitutional Court. First, the practice of the respective treaties' execution by the German

---

2 The terms have been defined in numerous judgments of the German Constitutional Court, see e.g. Hans D. Jarass and Bodo Pieroth, *Grundgesetz für die Bundesrepublik Deutschland* (11th Edition, 2011), Art. 59, para. 12 et seqq.

3 A further feature (not addressed in this article) is the competence of the *Länder* to conclude international agreements.

4 Ondolf Rojahn in Ingo v. Münch and Philip Kunig (eds), *Grundgesetz-Kommentar* (6th Edition, 2012), Art. 59 para. 19. The German Constitutional Court addresses this as the operative prerogative of the executive branch, BVerfG 18.12.1984 – 2 BvE 13/83 – BVerfGE 68, 1 (85 et seqq.).

5 Volker Röben, *Außenverfassungsrecht* (2007), 76 et seqq.

6 Ondolf Rojahn in Ingo v. Münch and Philip Kunig (eds), *Grundgesetz-Kommentar* (6th Edition, 2012), Art. 59, para. 30.

Government is under scrutiny by the Bundestag[7]. Second, and in accordance with the jurisprudence of the German Constitutional Court, the German Constitution does contain a reservation for the Parliament if the use of the military is involved as part of a collective security system[8]. Recently, the German Constitutional Court clarified its jurisprudence in this regard and even broadened the right of the federal Parliament. It states explicitly that the parliamentary reservation applies generally in the case of the use of the German military[9] and must be interpreted in a way that is favourable to the federal Parliament[10]. The parliamentary approval is an effective right of co-decision for the federal Parliament, and the Government has usually to acquire it prior to the use of the military forces[11], which entails the qualified expectation that German soldiers might take part in armed conflicts[12]. As a result, the role of the *Bundestag* is strengthened in the stated areas and enjoys a real right to co-determination as created by the Constitutional Court[13].

However, the question remains whether the Government enjoys the power to order the use of the military in cases of urgency. In cases of an urgent threat ("*Gefahr im Verzug*") the Government does have the power to order the use of the military, but it has to inform the federal Parliament as soon as possible with the necessary information needed for a parliamentary decision[14], because only with this information will the *Bundestag* be in a position to control the Government effectively and take a decision on the end of the use of the military. It is not necessary for the Parliament to approve the governmental decision, but the use of the military must cease if the federal Parliament disapproves of it[15].

---

7 BVerfG 22.11.2001 – 2 BvE 6/99 – BVerfGE 104, 151 (195); BVerfG 3.7.2007 – 2 BvE 2/07 – BVerfGE 118, 244, (259 et seq.).

8 BVerfG 12.7.1994 – 2 BvE 3/92 – BVerfGE 90, 286 (357 et seq.); BVerfG 25.3.2003 – 2 BvQ 18/03 – BVerfGE 108, 34 (43); BVerfG 7.5.2008 – 2 BvE 1/03 – BVerfGE 121, 135 (154); BVerfG 4.5.2010 – 2 BvE 5/07 – BVerfGE 126, 55 (69 et seq.).

9 BVerfG 23.9.2015 – 2 BvE 6/11 – BVerfGE 140, 160 (188).

10 BVerfG 7.5.2008 – 2 BvE 1/03 – BVerfGE 121, 135, (162), now restated in BVerfG 23.9.2015 – 2 BvE 6/11 – BVerfGE 140, 160 (187).

11 BVerfG 23.9.2015 – 2 BvE 6/11 – BVerfGE 140, 160 (188).

12 BVerfG 23.9.2015 – 2 BvE 6/11 – BVerfGE 140, 160 (190). Indications can be the carrying of weapons and the authority to use them, BVerfG, ibid.

13 BVerfG 3.7.2007 – 2 BvE 2/07 – BVerfGE 118, 244 (258).

14 BVerfG 23.9.2015 – 2 BvE 6/11 – BVerfGE 140, 160 (202).

15 BVerfG 23.9.2015 – 2 BvE 6/11 – BVerfGE 140, 160 (201).

Rather different, and very special in the course of our analysis of the treaty-making powers of the German Parliament, is Art. 23 GG, the provision on Germany's participation in the European Union. Notably, the federal Parliament has to participate in the decision-making process of the Union (Art. 23 paras. 2 and 3 GG)[16]. For this, it will be informed by the Government and the *Bundestag* shall state its position on a certain manner. The Government has to take these statements into account[17]. The participation is even stronger if the rights of the *Länder* are at stake. In matters which are of special relevance for the *Länder*, the position of the *Bundesrat* does not only have to be respected but shall be given the greatest possible respect for determining the federal position in the EU Council[18]. This provision is due to the special, supranational status of the primary and secondary law of the Union in the national legal order of its Member States, notably Germany.

As scrutiny has shown, in Germany the federal Parliament has not been granted with a treaty-making power, but only with a treaty-approval power, as in South Africa. Moreover, the German Constitutional Court found that the *Bundestag* has a general parliamentary right to take non-binding decisions on external actions of the Government. On the other hand, pursuant to various provisions of the Constitution, the Constitutional Court found a decision-making right in case of the use of the German armed forces outside of the German territory which can only be overridden by the Government in cases of emergency.

II. Constraints of the Constitution

In respect of the treaty-making power, the Government is bound by constitutional constraints, especially the human rights provisions. Art. 1 para. 3 GG states clearly that the "basic rights shall bind the executive (and

16 An in-depth explanation of the provisions is provided by Rupert Scholz in Theodor Maunz and Günter Dürig (eds), *Grundgesetz-Kommentar* (2016), Art. 23 GG, para. 152 et seqq.

17 Details are laid down in the Gesetz über die Zusammenarbeit von Bundesregierung und deutschem Bundestag in Angelegenheiten der Europäischen Union (EUZBBG) from 12 December 1993, BGBl. I 1993, 311; amended 22 September 2009, BGBl. I 2009, 3026.

18 This is further elaborated in the Gesetz über die Zusammenarbeit von Bund und Ländern in Angelegenheiten der Europäischen Union (EUZBLG) of March 1993, BGBl. I 1993, 313; last amended 22 September 2009, BGBl. I 2009, 3031.

the legislative) as directly applicable law". In this context it is generally accepted that the binding nature does not end at the German border but also applies extra-territorially[19]. Consequently, the German forces are also bound by the basic rights of the *Grundgesetz* in their military actions abroad[20].

Human rights treaties concluded by Germany have the status of federal statutory law (Art. 59 para. 2 GG) and do not bind the Government or the *Bundestag* as constitutional law. A long and rather intense argument among scholars and the German Constitutional Court is whether basic human rights treaties, like the European Convention on Human Rights and Fundamental Freedoms (ECHR)[21], could acquire the status of constitutional law[22]. The German Constitutional Court's case law in this respect is accepting of a restricted view. First, international human rights treaties are considered as being treaties and as having the status of federal law, as the Constitution clearly states. Second, fundamental human rights treaties, such as the ECHR, whose provisions are authoritatively interpreted by the European Court of Human Rights, can be used for the interpretation of the basic rights enshrined in the Constitution[23]. As such, it is argued that the provisions of the ECHR enjoy a status similar to a constitutional guarantee.[24] The German Constitutional Court has not accepted this opinion, because the wording of Art. 59 para. 2 GG is not open to such an interpretation[25], but it seems to accept that some very basic human rights enshrined in international documents may be granted a special status if the German Constitution is granting them the status as well[26], such as in the case of the protection of human dignity in Art. 1 GG.

This does also not follow from the unwritten constitutional principle of openness to international law. Recently the German Constitutional Court

---

19 Ondolf Rojahn in Ingo v. Münch and Philip Kunig (eds), *Grundgesetz-Kommentar* (6th Edition, 2012), Art. 1, para. 53.

20 ibid.

21 Of 4 November 1950, UNTS vol. 213, 221.

22 This is, for instance, the case in Austria. For the discussion in Germany see e.g. Ondolf Rojahn in Ingo v. Münch and Philip Kunig (eds), *Grundgesetz-Kommentar* (6th Edition, 2012), Art. 59, para. 45.

23 BVerfG 14.10.2004 – 2 BvR 1481/04 – BVerfGE 111, 307 (323 et seqq.).

24 The arguments brought forward by Martin Nettesheim in Theodor Maunz and Günter Dürig (eds), *Grundgesetz-Kommentar* (2016), Art. 59, para. 184 could lead to such a conclusion.

25 BVerfG 15.12.2015 – 2 BvL 1/12 – NJW 2016, 1295 (1296).

26 BVerfG 15.12.2015 – 2 BvL 1/12 – NJW 2016, 1295 (1301).

had to consider the issue whether national statutes contravening international law are unconstitutional. According to the Court, the principle of openness to international law can derive from the systematic analysis of the BL, namely the provisions of Arts. 23–26 and 59 para. 2 GG, which regulate the relationship between the Federal Republic of Germany and the international community[27]. Yet, as a principle it serves as a guideline for the interpretation of fundamental rights, which means that within the scope of applicable methodical principles an interpretation favourable to international law must always be chosen[28]. Therefore, the Constitutional Court held that Art. 59 para. 2 GG cannot be interpreted in a way that is favourable to international law, which means that the legislature may only in exceptional circumstances override obligations under international law[29].

III. Customary rules on immunity

A further issue addressed in Hennie Strydom's paper was diplomatic immunity. Luckily, until now, Germany has not faced the problems that have arisen under the South African legal regime[30]. The rights of diplomatic immunity are, at least in the context of the scrutiny at bar, part of customary international law. These rules do, compared to treaties, enjoy a special status under German law. According to Art. 25 GG, the general rules of international law are an integral part of federal law and they take precedence over the federal statutory law[31]. However, the rules of immunity are laid down in sections 17 et seqq. GVG[32], which refer in the relevant part to the customary international rules[33].

In Germany, immunity is only granted to the official acts of a state or a person acting for that state, and not for private acts[34]. The nature of the act

27 BVerfG 15.12.2015 – 2 BvL 1/12 – NJW 2016, 1295 (1299).
28 BVerfG 15.12.2015 – 2 BvL 1/12 – NJW 2016, 1295 (1300).
29 BVerfG 15.12.2015 – 2 BvL 1/12 – NJW 2016, 1295 (1300).
30 See the article by Henry Strydom, pp. 249 et seqq. above.
31 See Wolff Heintschel von Heinegg in Volker Epping and Christian Hillgruber (eds), *BeckOK GG* (2015), Art. 25, para. 26 et seqq.
32 *Gerichtsverfassungsgesetz (GVG)*, the general law regulating the jurisprudence of German courts.
33 This is especially so for sec. 20 GVG, see e.g. Christoph Barthe in Rolf Hannich (ed) *KK-StPO* (7th Edition, 2013), § 20 GVG, para. 2.
34 *Acta iure imperii* versus *acta iure gestionis*, see e.g. Stefan Lorenzmeier, *Völkerrecht* (3rd Edition, 2016), 65 et seq.

can be decided upon by the national courts. The International Court of Justice stated in its *Arrest Warrant* decision that certain persons, such as heads of state, enjoy full protection while they are in office because it would otherwise be impossible for them to perform their duties[35]. An exception to this rule can be found in international criminal law, as in the Rome Statute of the International Criminal Court[36]. Unlike South Africa, Germany has until now not been confronted with problems in the regard extraditing criminals to the International Criminal Court, but it is under a statutory obligation to extradite persons to the International Criminal Court if the Court so wishes.

IV. Diplomatic protection

Finally, there is the concept of diplomatic protection. Under international law, diplomatic protection is the right of a state to take care of its individuals and defend their rights in international fora[37]. The German understanding of the doctrine is that any measure taken by Germany for its nationals abroad is at its discretion. Hence, and in general, an individual does not have an enforceable right against Germany that he/she will be protected in another state. The underlying reason is that the state's discretion to take actions on the international stage constitutes a primary right of the executive.

Yet, as stated above[38], the executive is bound by the human rights provisions of the Constitution, and it is a well-established principle of German law that the executive can only exercise its discretion in a lawful manner[39]. As a result, it is possible that in exceptional circumstances the discretionary right might become a full, enforceable right for the individual. This is, in the author's view, particularly so if the violation is a sincere human rights violation due to the absolute character of the right to protect human dignity under German law.

35 International Court of Justice, 14.02.2002, Arrest Warrant (*Democratic Republic of Congo v Belgium*), ICJ-Rep. 2002, 3.

36 Of 17 July 1998, UNTS vol. 2187, 3.

37 Volker Epping in Knut Ipsen (ed), *Völkerrecht* (6th Edition, 2014), § 5, para. 115 et seqq. See also, International Court of Justice, *Barcelona Traction*, ICJ-Rep. 1970, 3 et seqq.

38 See part II. above.

39 This is laid down in sec. 114 VwGO, the German law on procedural rules for the administrative courts. For an analysis see Andreas Decker in Herbert Posser and Heinrich AmadeusWolf (eds), *BeckOK VwGO* (2016), § 114, para. 3 et seqq.

V. Conclusion

The article has shown that the German and the South African legal order are sometimes in close proximity, but they are far from identical. The addressed rules are applicable in both legal systems, but the interpretations of each country's courts appear to be different. The South African legal order does not have to deal with membership in a supranational international organisation, which has a significant impact on the German legal order, as can be seen from Art. 23 GG.

In addition to this peculiarity, the case law of the German Constitutional Court has developed the right to participation of the federal Parliament in the decision-making process if the use of the German military abroad is involved. Moreover, the opinion of the *Bundestag* is decisive for the executive in this respect.

Additionally, the status of international treaties in the German order has been cautiously strengthened by the German Constitutional Court; some treaties not only have the status of federal statutes but can also inform the interpretation of the human rights provisions of the *Grundgesetz*.

The further addressed issues of immunity and diplomatic protection appear to be applied in a very similar manner in the two legal orders. In general, it can be stated that due to the case law of the German Constitutional Court, similar provisions are understood differently in South Africa and Germany, yet it seems to be possible that such decisions may also inform or influence the South African interpretation at some stage.

Bibliography

Beck'scher Onlinekommentar Grundgesetz, Volker Epping and Christian Hillgruber (eds), (30th Edition, C.H. Beck, Munich 2015).

Beck'scher Onlinekommentar VwGO, Herbert Posser and Heinrich Amadeus Wolf (eds), (38th Edition, C.H. Beck, Munich 2016).

Knut Ipsen, *Völkerrecht,* (6th Edition, C.H. Beck, Munich 2014).

Hans D. Jarass and Bodo Pieroth, *Grundgesetz für die Bundesrepublik Deutschland* (11th Edition, C.H. Beck, Munich 2011).

Karlsruher Kommentar zur Strafprozessordnung, Rolf Hannich (ed), (7th Edition, C.H. Beck, Munich 2013).

Stefan Lorenzmeier, *Völkerrecht* (3rd Edition, Springer, Berlin 2016).

Theodor Maunz and Günter Dürig (eds), *Grundgesetz-Kommentar* (loose leaf updated July 2016, C.H. Beck, Munich 2016).

Volker Röben, *Außenverfassungsrecht* (Mohr Siebeck, Tübingen 2007).

Ingo von Münch and Philip Kunig (eds), *Grundgesetz-Kommentar* (6th Edition, C.H. Beck, Munich 2012).

Case Law

BVerfG 18.12.1984 – 2 BvE 13/83 – BVerfGE 68, 1.

BVerfG 12.7.1994 – 2 BvE 3/92 – BVerfGE 90, 286.

BVerfG 22.11.2001 – 2 BvE 6/99 – BVerfGE 104, 151.

BVerfG 25.3.2003 – 2 BvQ 18/03 – BVerfGE 108, 34.

BVerfG 14.10.2004 – 2 BvR 1481/04 – BVerfGE 111, 307.

BVerfG 3.7.2007 – 2 BvE 2/07 – BVerfGE 118, 244.

BVerfG 7.5.2008 – 2 BvE 1/03 – BVerfGE 121, 135.

BVerfG 4.5.2010 – 2 BvE 5/07 – BVerfGE 126, 55.

BVerfG 23.9.2015 – 2 BvE 6/11 – BVerfGE 140, 160.

BVerfG 15.12.2015 – 2 BvL 1/12 – NJW 2016, 1295.

A South African and German perspective on personal information privacy protection in an electronic environment

*Murdoch Watney**
*Robin Cupido***

* Professor of Law, University of Johannesburg, South Africa.
** Lecturer, University of Johannesburg, South Africa.

I. Introduction

Vast amounts of personal information are disclosed on a daily basis by internet and mobile-phone users. This may include personal information pertaining to names, photos, bank details, e-mail addresses, postings on social-networking websites, medical information or computer IP addresses. The growth of internet use for economic purposes such as the selling of goods or for social-media purposes such as Facebook postings, depends to a large extent on the trust that users have that personal information will be protected against unlawful access and that they will retain control over such personal information.

Personal information is not only disclosed, captured and/or processed by means of the internet but huge amounts of personal information are processed electronically as part of our day-to-day existence, for example as part of an employee's work record considerable amounts of personal information are gathered and retained. The same applies in respect of a patient's health records or a client's banking details.

We live in a society of omnipresent watchfulness. George Orwell warned in his book, *1984,* against the government becoming a "big brother" and monitoring our daily activities.[1] This warning reverberated when Edward Snowden, a former United States (US) contractor, revealed in 2013 that the US National Security Agency (NSA) had been collecting vast amounts of personal information in the US and across borders.[2] These allegations sparked outrage throughout Europe. Similar allegations surfaced that the German foreign intelligence agency, the *Bundesnachrichtendienst* (BND) had assisted the NSA to spy on various governmental and industry concerns in the EU, including the European Commission, the French president and Airbus.[3]

It is not only governments, but also businesses and criminals that may potentially gain access to vast amounts of personal information in electronic format. O'Harrow[4] succinctly expressed the concern as follows:

> "You are being watched. Government agencies and private corporations know where you live, how much you earn, what you buy and some even what you read.

1 O'Harrow *No Place to Hide* (2006) 263.

2 Leigh and Harding *Wikileaks* (2013) 279–281.

3 Sykes *Privacy and security: a comparative constitutional law conversation* (2015) 1 http://www.kas.de/wf/doc/kas_41868-544-1-30.pdf?150720180444 (15-09-2017).

4 (n 1) 300; 303–304.

> And increasingly this information is being leaked (or sold) to identity thieves. In a surveillance society, there is no place to hide."

There have been many examples of electronic data breaches.[5] Some of these include the 2014 cyberattacks launched on US Sony Pictures Entertainment and JP Morgan Chase and Company which resulted in the disclosure of employees' personal data and company correspondence which affected 76 million households and 7 million small businesses.[6] In 2016 the Hollywood Presbyterian Medical Centre in Los Angeles was hit by ransomware which allowed the hackers to access and encrypt all data and then demand a ransom to decrypt it. The centre immediately paid the ransom to reduce harm to patients but had no access to e-mail, electronic patient records and some internet-connected medical devices for nearly 2 weeks.[7]

The present-day society has evolved electronically to such an extent that individuals do not have a choice but to divulge personal information to government and businesses. These individuals that disclose personal information have an expectation that their personal information will be protected.[8] It is therefore important to establish the scope of personal privacy protection and to consider the laws governing the collection, processing, accessing and disclosure of personal information.

Much has been written over the years on privacy as the legal protection of personal information is of paramount importance and constitutes a significant concern within an electronic environment. It is therefore not surprising that considerable development in respect of personal information privacy protection has taken place. In this regard South Africa is in the process of implementing the Protection of Personal Information Act (POPI).[9]

---

5 Various examples in this regard are cited in "Paper a refuge in age of cyberattacks" 9 April 2016 *Saturday Star* 17.

6 *Saturday Star* (n 5) 17.

7 *Saturday Star* (n 5) 17.

8 Internet and mobile-phone users increasingly use security technology such as encryption to ensure personal information protection privacy. The consequence is that in many instances the mobile phone messaging application providers in respect of WhatsApp messaging or manufacturers such as Apple (in respect of the iPhone) are unable to decrypt it. The question arises whether businesses should be obliged to decrypt their own security and privacy mechanisms when so requested by law enforcement agencies.

9 Act 4 of 2013. Not all the provisions of POPI are in effect yet. To date (31 July 2017) only sec 1 (the definition), part A of chap 5 (establishing the information regulator), sec 112 (empowering the minister to make regulations) and sec 113 (the procedure for making regulations) have come into effect on 11 April 2014.

Pertaining to the European Union (EU) data protection reform in the format of the Regulation on the Protection of Individuals with regard to the Processing of Personal Data and the Free Movement of such Data (GDPR)[10] had been approved towards the end of 2015. The main legal source of data protection in Germany is the Federal Data Protection Act (*Bundesdatenschutzgesetz*, BDSG).[11] The EU GDPR will have an extensive impact on data protection in Germany and other member states as it will automatically apply to all EU states without the need to pass national legislation.[12]

The discussion consists of 2 parts. Part I entails a comparative synopsis of privacy protection of personal information within the ambit of the South African and German electronic environment whilst Part II considers methods to give practical effect to the online protection of personal information.

The provisions of the South African Constitution pertaining to the interpretation of the Bill of Rights are used as a point of departure when comparing the positions in individual countries. The Constitution provides as follows in this regard:

> "39(1)
> When interpreting the Bill of Rights, a court, tribunal or forum –
> (a) Must promote the values that underlie an open and democratic society based on human dignity, equality and freedom;
> (b) Must consider international law; and
> (c) May consider foreign law."

Individual countries have a different legal, social and moral understanding of privacy rights. It is, however, important that South Africa aligns itself with the global community regarding personal information privacy laws as the internet provides for a borderless world. Germany as part of the EU robustly protects personal information and has the benefit of considerable literature on privacy that has already been referred to in South African case

The rest of the act will come into effect on a date that will be announced by the president in the Government Gazette. Once the commencement date is published businesses will have at least a year to comply with its provisions. The grace period might be extended to a maximum of 3 years (sec 114).

10 See para II.3.a) hereafter for an overview of the GDPR; EU GDPR available at http://ec.europe/eu.justice/data-protection/reform/index_en.htm (04-04-2016).

11 See para II.3.b) hereafter for a brief discussion of German data protection.

12 Art 91 provides that this regulation shall be binding in its entirety and directly applicable in all member states.

law.[13] POPI is modelled on the EU data protection laws.[14] In this regard POPI provides that international guidelines relevant to the protection of individual privacy must be taken into account by the information regulator when exercising its powers.[15] Similarly the privacy policy must reflect international privacy-protection standards as websites and other internet communications can be viewed across borders.

II. A comparative synopsis of personal information privacy protection within the ambit of the South African and German electronic environment

1. International treaty on personal information privacy protection

There is no personal information privacy protection treaty which is binding upon countries on an international level. The EU has taken the lead in this regard and displayed a commitment to data protection as a core value. Most countries have, however, adopted national legislation creating a set of rights (informational or data-protection rights) pertaining to the person to whom personal information relates (the data subject).[16] These rights encompass corresponding obligations restricting the processing of personal information by the persons who control it, including an obligation not to disclose to third parties without the knowledge or consent of the data subject. South Africa is lagging behind other countries in this regard but the position should be addressed once POPI is fully implemented.

---

13 *Bernstein v Bester* 1996 2 SA 751 (CC) para 78–79.

14 De Stadler and Esselaar *A Guide to the Protection of Personal Information Act* (2015) 3; Naude and Papadopoulos "Data protection in South Africa: the Protection of Personal Information Act 4 of 2013 in the light of recent international developments" 2016 *Tydskrif vir Hedendaagse Romeins-Hollandse Reg (THRHR)* 51 52. See para 4.1 for the EU data protection reform.

15 Sec 40(e) provides "to conduct research and to report to Parliament (i) from time to time on the desirability of the acceptance by South Africa on any international instrument relating to the protection of the personal information of a data subject". Sec 44(1)*(d)* provides that the regulator must "consider any developing general international guidelines relevant to the better protection of individual privacy."

16 Currie and De Waal *The Bill of Rights Handbook* (2013) 303.

2. South African privacy protection of personal information

a) South African Constitution

The Constitution provides for the right to privacy as follows

> "14 Everyone has the right to privacy, which includes the right not to have-
> (a) their person or home searched;
> (b) their property searched;
> (c) their possessions seized; or
> (d) the privacy of their communications infringed."

Section 14 consists of two parts. The first part guarantees a general right to privacy whereas the second part protects against specific infringements of privacy and relevant for purposes of this discussion, the violation of communications privacy. This privacy right concerns restricting access to collection and disclosure of personal information.[17]

Currie and De Waal indicate that in other jurisdictions, these two parts are dealt with in separate sections of a bill of rights as for example in Germany art 2(1) of the Basic Law (*Grundgesetz*) is generally viewed as entrenching the right to privacy whereas art 10 explicitly guarantees privacy of correspondence, posts and telecommunications.[18]

The South African constitutional provision does not outline the scope of the privacy right to personal information protection nor the obligations of businesses who collect, process and use personal information in protecting private information. This will have to be addressed by future legislation or developed through case law.

b) Scope of the privacy right to protection of personal information

In the recent decision of *Harley v Niland*[19] the court had to determine whether the admission of unlawfully obtained social-media communications would infringe the respondent's privacy right to personal information protection.

The facts are briefly as follows: Harley and Niland were members in a close corporation which business involved safari and hunting activities. At some stage the respondent (Niland) left Huntershill CC but still remained

17 Currie and De Waal (n 16) 303.
18 Currie and De Waal (n 16) 294–295.
19 2016 2 SA 436 (ECG).

as a member of the close corporation. The applicant (Harley) suspected that Niland was running a safari and hunting business in direct competition with Huntershill and conflicting with the membership agreement which contained a restraint of trade provision. Such conduct would constitute a violation of Niland's fiduciary duties to Huntershill. Niland denied acting contrary to his fiduciary duties. In pursuance of his investigations Harley obtained unlawful access to personal communications on Niland's Facebook which provided proof that Niland was trying to solicit and divert existing clients from Huntershill to his own business. Niland's conduct was clearly in contravention of his fiduciary duties. Harley applied for an interdict to prevent Niland acting contrary to these duties and in support of his application, presented the Facebook messages to court.

The court had to decide whether Niland could rely on his privacy right to personal information protection. In this regard the court stated that the right to privacy must be seen within a specific context. Of specific relevance is the constitutional court's judgment in the *Bernstein* case which provides the "richest and most comprehensive interpretation" of the right to informational privacy.[20] In *Bernstein* the applicant, a company officer, had to disclose books and documents in an enquiry pertaining to the company's insolvency. The applicant was of the opinion that such a disclosure would infringe his right to informational privacy.[21] The court had to decide whether the applicant had a legitimate expectation of privacy. In this regard the court considered the constitutional privacy jurisprudence in the US, Canada and Germany. It established that there was a strong family resemblance in the approaches these jurisdictions followed in respect of privacy. The Constitutional Court determined that a person's privacy extends only to those aspects pertaining to which a legitimate expectation of privacy existed. A legitimate expectation of privacy comprises of a subjective expectation of privacy which must be objectively reasonable. Whether the subjective expectation is objectively reasonable must be seen within a "continuum of privacy interests" whereby stronger protections for privacy are afforded within the home and weaker protections as the individual moves into more public contexts.[22] Privacy therefore exists in a continuum with individuals at different times and in different contexts having either more or

---

20 Currie and De Waal (n 16) 297–300.

21 *Bernstein* case (n 13) para 56; Bilchitz "Privacy, surveillance and the duties of corporations" 2016 *Tydskrif vir die Suid-Afrikaanse Reg (TSAR)* 45 53.

22 *Bernstein* case (n 13) para 67; also see Bilchitz (n 21) 50.

less privacy.[23] In the *Bernstein* case Ackermann J concluded that the applicant as an officer of a public structure had a statutory duty to public disclosure. The applicant may have had a subjective expectation of privacy, but it was not objectively reasonable.[24]

South African law therefore follows a graded approach to privacy protection where the privacy interest of the individual varies within the context he finds himself.[25] This was confirmed by the Constitutional Court in *Gaertner v Minister of Finances*[26] in which the court found:

> "Privacy, like other rights, is not absolute. As a person moves into communal relations and activities such as business and social interaction, the scope of personal space shrinks. This diminished personal space does not mean that once people are involved in social interactions, or business, they no longer have a right to privacy. What it means is that the right is attenuated, nor obliterated. And the attenuation is more or less, depending on how far and into what one has strayed from the inner sanctum of the home."[27]

Privacy rights are therefore not absolute. The South African Constitution provides for the following limitation of rights which includes privacy:

> "36(1)
> The rights in the Bill of Rights may be limited only in terms of law of general application to the extent that the limitation is reasonable and justifiable in an open and democratic society based on human dignity, equality and freedom, taking into account all relevant factors, including-
> (a) the nature of the right;
> (b) the importance of the purpose of the limitation;
> (c) the nature and extent of the limitation;
> (d) the relation between the limitation and its purpose; and
> (e) less restrictive means to achieve the purposes."

The communications of Niland produced information that was relevant to the business operations of Huntershill CC and his fiduciary duties in that regard. It also produced information that was irrelevant to those issues and which was therefore entirely private. In the latter regard, the graded approach to privacy strikes a balance between personal information relating to the "intimate" sphere of an individual's life and information relating to the work of employees and in this instance, a member of a close corporation acting in violation of his fiduciary duties. The court focused only on the

---

23 Haggerty "What's wrong with privacy protections?" in Sarat (ed) *A World without Privacy* (2015) 194.

24 *Bernstein* case (n 13) para 85; Bilchitz (n 21) 53.

25 Currie and De Waal (n 16) 298–299; (n 21) 50–51.

26 *Gaertner v Minister of Finance* 2014 1 SA 442 (CC).

27 *Gaertner* case (n 26) para 49.

communications which served as proof that Niland acted in violation of his fiduciary duties to the close corporation and concluded that he could not evoke his privacy in respect of the said information.

As indicated, rights are not absolute. Niland did not have an objective reasonable expectation of privacy in respect of the communications revealing the wrongdoing. The court did not address the issue of whether an individual who publishes information on a public medium such as the internet and in this regard to a limited audience on Facebook, have an objective reasonable expectation that the personal communications would remain private. A similar situation can present itself regarding Whatsapp messages.

Once the court had established that Niland did not have a right to privacy in respect of the information, it had to decide whether the information was admissible as it had been obtained unlawfully. Harley obtained the password to Niland's Facebook communications and without authorisation gained access to the communications. Such conduct constitutes a crime in terms of section 86(1) of the Electronic Communications and Transactions Act (ECT Act).[28] This section provides that "a person who intentionally accesses or intercepts any data without authority or permission to do so, is guilty of an offence."

The court addressed the admissibility of the communications with reference to *Protea Technology v Wainer*[29] where it was determined that at common law all relevant evidence which was not rendered inadmissible by an exclusionary rule was admissible in a civil court irrespective of how it was obtained. In criminal proceedings the common law was substantially altered with the introduction of section 35(5) of the Constitution.[30] There is no comparable constitutional or statutory provision dealing with the admissibility of unconstitutionally obtained evidence in civil proceedings.[31] In *Waste Products Utilisation v Wilkes*[32] the court referred to the *Protea Technology* case and concluded that "our courts retain a discretion to admit tape record-

28 Act 25 of 2002. It is envisaged that the Cybercrime and Cybersecurity Bill 2015 will in future replace the ECT Act.

29 1979 3 All SA 594 (W) 604b–c.

30 Sec 35(5) provides that "(e)vidence obtained in a manner that violates any right in the Bill of Rights must be excluded if the admission of that evidence would render the trial unfair or otherwise be detrimental to the administration of justice."

31 Currie and De Waal (n 16) 308.

32 2003 2 SA 515 (W) 549J.

ings into evidence notwithstanding the commission of an offence or the infringement of a constitutional right in obtaining the recording".[33] In view of the section 35(5) provision pertaining to criminal cases which requires a court to exclude evidence obtained in a manner which violates a right contained in the Bill of Rights if the admission of the evidence would render the trial unfair or otherwise be detrimental to the administration of justice a court will have no discretion but to exclude the evidence.[34] On the other hand in the *Harley* case the court[35] emphasised the relevance of a discretion in allowing or disallowing unlawfully obtained evidence in a civil matter with reference to *Fedics Group (Pty) Ltd v Matus*[36] in which the court held that it will in the exercise of its discretion have regard to the type of evidence which was in fact obtained.[37]

In respect of the exercise of a discretion in a civil matter the court in *Harley* stated that all relevant factors had to be considered in the exercise of the discretion to exclude unlawfully obtained evidence.[38] The court therefore admitted the unlawfully obtained evidence by stating:

> "...it seems to me that right-thinking members of society would believe that Niland's conduct particularly in the light of his denials and the undertakings that he gave, ought to be exposed and that he ought not to be allowed to hide behind his expectation of privacy; it has only been invoked it seems to me, because he had something to hide."[39]

c) Statutory obligations of businesses in protecting personal information

The provisions of POPI will be applicable to all businesses that deal with personal information.[40] Even if a business does not use personal information in its daily business activities, but still has the personal information of customers, employees and suppliers in its possession it will have a legal duty to protect the personal information of individuals in accordance with POPI.[41]

---

33 (n 32) at 550F.
34 Currie and De Waal (n 16) 309.
35 (n 19) para 46.
36 1989 2 SA 617 (C) paras 90, 92.
37 (n 36) para 92.
38 (n 19) para 47.
39 (n 19) para 52.
40 De Stadler and Esselaar (n 14) 4.
41 De Stadler and Esselaar (n 14) 4.

POPI is applicable to the processing[42] of personal information[43] of an individual (the data subject[44]) which is entered into a record[45] by a business (the responsible party[46]) domiciled in South Africa or makes use of automated[47]

---

42 Sec 1 provides that "processing means any operation or activity or any set of operations, whether or not by automatic means, concerning personal information, including (a) the collection, receipt, recording, organisation, collation, storage, updating or modification, retrieval, alteration, consultation or use; (b) dissemination by means of transmission, distribution or making available in any other form; or (c) merging, linking, as well as restriction, degradation, erasure or destruction of information."

43 Sec 1 defines personal information as "information relating to an identifiable, living, natural person and where it is applicable, an identifiable, existing juristic person, including but not limited to (a) information relating to the race, gender, sex, pregnancy, marital status, national, ethnic or social origin, colour, sexual orientation, age, physical or mental health, well-being, disability, religion, conscience, belief, culture, language and birth of the person; (b) information relating to the education or the medical, financial, criminal or employment history of the person; (c) any identifying number, symbol, e-mail address, physical address, telephone number, location information, online identifier or other particular assignment to the person; (d) the biometric information of the person; (e) the personal opinions, views or preferences of the person; (f) correspondence sent by the person that is implicitly or explicitly of a practical or confidential nature or further correspondence that would reveal the content of the original correspondence; (g) the views or opinions of another individual about the person; and (h) the name of the person if it appears with other personal information relating to the person or if the disclosure of the name itself would reveal information about the person."

44 Sec 1 describes data subject as "the person to whom personal information relates."

45 Sec 1 defines record as "any recorded information (a) regardless of form or medium, including any of the following: (i) Writing on any material; (ii) Information produced, recorded or stored by means of any tape-recorder, computer equipment, whether hardware or software or both, or other device, and any material subsequently derived from information so produced, recorded or stored; (iii) label, marking or other writing that identifies or describes anything of which forms part of or to which it is attached by any means; (iv) book, map, plan graph or drawing; (v) photograph, film, negative, tape or other device in while one or more visual equipment are embodied so as to be capable with or without the aid of some other equipment of being reproduced; (b) in the possession or under the control of a responsible party; (c) whether or not it was created by a responsible party; and (d) regardless of when it came into existence."

46 Sec 1 defines responsible party as "a public or private body or any person which alone or in conjunction with others determines the purpose of and means for processing personal information."

47 Sec 3(4) defines automated as "any equipment capable of operating automatically in response to instruction given for the purposes of processing information."

or non-automated[48] means in South Africa. It is possible that a third person referred to as the operator[49] may process personal information on behalf of the responsible person.

It does not apply where the processing of information:[50] (a) is for personal or household activity; or (b) where the personal information has been sufficiently de-identified; or (c) has been processed by or on behalf of a public body for the purposes of national security or for the prevention of unlawful activities; or (d) relates to the investigation of offences or the prosecution of offenders only to the extent that adequate safeguards have been established in legislation for the protection of such personal information; or (e) relates to the judicial function of a court.

The aim of the act is to give effect to the constitutional right to privacy by safeguarding personal information when processed by a business referred to as a responsible party; to regulate the manner in which personal information may be processed by establishing conditions; to provide the data subject with rights and remedies to protect their personal information from processing that is not in accordance with the act and to establish voluntary and compulsory measures including the establishment of an information regulator to enforce and fulfil the rights protected by the act.[51]

Businesses must comply with certain conditions[52] for the lawful processing of personal information which accord with international standards. These conditions are duties which must be complied with in order for processing activities to be lawful. The duties which are grouped under eight conditions[53] are as follows: accountability, purpose specification, information quality, processing limitation, further processing, openness, security safeguards and data subject participation. A business has an accountability

48 If the processing is taking place by non-automated means, it must form part of a "filing system". Sec 1 defines filing system as "any structured set of personal information, whether centralised, decentralised or dispersed on a functional or geographical basis which is accessible according to specific criteria."

49 Sec 1 defines operator as "a person who processes personal information for a responsible person in terms of a contract or mandate without coming under the direct authority of that party."

50 sec 6(1)*(a)–(e)*.

51 sec 2.

52 secs 8–25.

53 Chap 3 of the act outlines the eight conditions for lawful processing of personal information.

condition[54] which means that the business must ensure that it complies with all conditions briefly discussed hereafter.

The purpose specification condition[55] requires that personal information is collected for a specific, explicitly defined and lawful purpose. A data subject must be aware for which purpose the information is being collected.[56] It must not be retained for any longer than necessary for achieving the purpose for which the information was collected.[57] In accordance with the further processing limitation condition[58] a business may use personal information for similar purposes than the purposes for which it was originally collected but the customer must be aware of it. The condition of openness[59] provides a data subject with the right to be notified that personal information about him is being collected; to establish whether a responsible party holds personal information of that data subject and to request access to his personal information; to object to the processing of his personal information, to submit a complaint to the information regulator and to institute civil proceedings regarding an alleged interference with the protection of his personal information.

Lawful processing requires compliance with the data subject participation condition. A customer has the right to request access to personal information in the possession of a business[60] and the right to request the correction, reduction or deletion of their records.[61] A business must in accordance with the condition of information quality[62] take reasonably practical steps to ensure that the data subject's information is complete, accurate, not misleading and updated where necessary.

Personal information can only be processed if the purpose for which it is being processed is adequate, relevant and not excessive. This condition provides for processing limitation and is referred to as the minimality requirement.[63] This requirement enjoyed a lot of interest and discussion on European level in the context of the right to be forgotten.[64] In 2014 the European

---

54 sec 8.
55 sec 13.
56 sec 13.
57 sec 14.
58 sec 15.
59 secs 5 and 18.
60 sec 23.
61 sec 24.
62 sec 16.
63 sec 10.
64 De Stadler and Esselaar (n 14) 23.

Court of Justice of the European Union (CJEU) came to the conclusion in *Google Spain SL, Google Inc v Agencia Española de Protección de Datos (AEPD), Marios Costeja Gonzáles (Google Spain)* that a search engine is a data controller and as such can only process that which is adequate and relevant. [65] The case involved Costeja Gonzales who was the subject of insolvency proceedings in the late 1990's. The proceedings were published in a newspaper at the time and the article was later made available online. Gonzales requested the newspaper to delete the online article on the basis that it was no longer relevant. The newspaper refused. He then requested Google to delete the link to the article from its search result. The Spanish Data Protection Authority also made this request to Google. Google contested the decision to a national court which referred the question to the CJEU. The CJEU held that the activities of search engines such as Google affect the fundamental right to privacy and to protection of personal data of those subject to searches. The court further held that Google must delete inadequate or irrelevant data from its results on request from members of the public. The court did not find that the information must be deleted from the newspaper's website but that Google had to delete links to the website from the search results for his name. Since the matter was decided under the EU's data protection directive which is similar to POPI, De Stadler and Esselaar[66] are of the opinion that the South African information regulator and courts are likely to act in a similar manner when faced with such an issue.

Data subjects are very vulnerable to unauthorised access pertaining to their personal information and therefore in accordance with the condition of security safeguards a company must secure the integrity and confidentiality of personal information in its possession or under its control to prevent loss of, damage to or unauthorised destruction of personal information and unlawful access to or processing of personal information.[67] Where there are reasonable grounds to believe that personal information has been accessed or acquired by any unauthorised person, the business must notify the information regulator and the customer. Notification to the customer may only

---

65 European Court of Justice Case C-131/12 13.5.2014 *Google Spain SL, Google Inc v Agencia Española de Protección de Datos (AEPD), Marios Costeja Gonzáles (Google Spain)* ECLI:EU:C:2014:317; Laidlaw *Regulating Speech in Cyberspace* (2015) 186–187; (n 21) 61–62.

66 De Stadler and Esselaar (n 14) 23.

67 sec 19.

be delayed if a public body responsible for the prevention, detection or investigation of offences or the regulator determines that notification will impede a criminal investigation.[68]

The abovementioned conditions should be embodied in a privacy policy[69] which is a legal requirement to promote transparency and trust.

The act provides for the establishment of an information regulator[70] in order to enforce compliance.[71] It also provides for offences,[72] penalties[73] and administrative fines.[74]

POPI does not use similar terminology as the EU data-protection laws. It uses the terms "personal information" instead of "personal data", "responsible party" instead of "data controller", "data operator" instead of "data processor" and "conditions" instead of "principles" for lawful processing of personal information.[75]

3. German data protection

a) Impact of EU data protection reform

In 1995 the EU took the lead regarding the protection of personal information. The proposed new reform will result in comprehensive personal information privacy protection which will not only have a huge impact on EU member states but will also have a global reach.

The Protection of Individuals with regard to the Processing of Personal Data and on the Free Movement of such Data (EU Data Directive) was adopted in 1995 with two objectives in mind, namely to protect the fundamental right to data and to guarantee the free flow of personal data between member states. Each Member State could implement their own national data-protection laws which unfortunately resulted in a fragmentation of data protection and legal uncertainty within the EU. The EU Data Directive includes the principle of collection limitation which requires knowledge and

68 sec 21.
69 See para III.1 for the private policy discussion.
70 sec 39.
71 sec 40. See also Naude and Papadopoulos (n 14) 66–67.
72 secs 100 to 106.
73 sec 107.
74 sec 109.
75 Naude and Papadopoulos (n 14) 60.

consent where appropriate but also the principles of data quality, purpose specification, use limitation, security safeguards, openness, individual participation and accountability.[76]

Since the implementation of the EU Data Directive, rapid technological developments brought about challenges for the protection of personal data which necessitated a more comprehensive and coherent policy pertaining to the fundamental right to personal data protection. One of the challenges highlighted was the right to be forgotten as discussed in the *Google Spain*[77] case. Another challenge was the issue of traffic data retention with reference to Snowden's revelations. The development of a surveillance society requires new checks and balances to prevent surveillance overriding the right to personal information privacy.[78] The CJEU[79] was mindful of surveillance practices violating privacy rights when it invalidated the Data Retention Directive[80] in 2014. The CJEU considered that the data-retention obligations under this directive created serious interferences with the fundamental right to privacy and data protection without that interference being limited to what is strictly necessary.

In 2015 the final draft of the regulation[81] on the Protection of Individuals with regard to the Processing of Personal Information and on the Free Movement of such Data was introduced (GDPR).[82] The GDPR will have a major impact on data protection in the EU and globally. It will not only repeal the Data Directive[83] but as it is a regulation instead of a directive it will automatically be applicable to all EU member states without the need for national implementation of legislation.[84] The regulation will serve as a

---

76 Austin "Enough about me: privacy is about power, not consent (or harm)" in Sarat (ed) *A World Without Privacy* (2015) 136–137.

77 De Stadler and Esselaar (n 14) 23.

78 Dubber and Hörne *The Oxford Handbook on Criminal law* (2014) 193.

79 European Court of Justice Case C-293/12 and C-594/12 8.4.2014 *Digital Rights Ireland Ltd (C-293/12) v Minister for Communications, Marine and Natural Resources and Others and Kärntner Landesregierung (C-594/12) and Others* ECLI:EU:C:2014:238.

80 Directive 2006/24/EC of the European parliament and of the Council of 15 March 2006 on the retention of data generated or processed in connection with the provision of publicly available electronic communications services or of pubic communications networks.

81 See n 10.

82 It will come into force after 2 years and twenty days from the date of publication in the official journal.

83 art 88.

84 art 91.

mandate to all EU member states whereas the Data Directive served as a guide to the implementation of national data protection.

In terms of the GDPR a single law and a single data protection board will be applicable to all 28 EU member countries. The GDPR aims at a so-called "one-stop shop" concept and in this regard a company would only be answerable to the data supervisory authority where it has its main establishment.[85] Individuals have the right to refer all cases to their home national data protection supervisory authority where their personal data is processed outside their home country. A company based outside the EU (a non-EU or third country) offering services in the EU must comply with the EU GDPR and therefore the GDPR will have a extra-territorial effect.[86] This means that a South African business offering goods or services to individuals in one or more EU member states will have to comply with the GDPR if it processes personal information.

GDPR regulates the protection of personal data extensively. It lays down rules relating to the protection of individuals with regard to the processing[87] of personal data and rules relating to the free movement of personal data.[88] The definitions of "data subject" and "personal data" are key in determining the scope of the GDPR. A data subject means "any identified natural person who can directly or indirectly be identified by the controller or a third party using reasonably likely means."[89] Personal data[90] is data relating to a data subject but the definition of personal data has been expanded to include data that has the possibility of identifying or singling out an individual directly or indirectly, and will include device identifiers, IP addresses and location

---

85 art 51.

86 Art 3(2)*(a)* stipulates that "(t)his Regulation applies to the processing of personal data of data subjects residing in the Union by a controller not established in the Union where the processing activities are related to: (a) the the offering of goods or services to such data subjects in the Union; or (b) the monitoring of their behaviour". See also art 25.

87 Art 4(2) provides that "processing means any operation or set of operations which is performed upon personal data or sets of personal data whether or not by automated means such as collection recording, organisation, structuring storage, adaptation or alteration, retrieval, consultation, use, disclosure by transmission, dissemination or otherwise making available alignment or combination, erasure or destruction."

88 art 1.

89 art 4(1).

90 art 4(2).

data. The data subject must give explicit consent for the use, processing and storage of personal information.[91]

The regulation is extensive and therefore only certain aspects relevant for purposes of this discussion will be highlighted. It provides that personal data must be processed lawfully, fairly and in a transparent manner.[92] It contains a purpose limitation principle which entails that personal data must be collected for a specific purpose and can only be further processed for a purpose compatible with the purpose of collection, except where the processing of personal data is based on the individual's consent or legal requirement to process data for further purposes. The controller bears the burden of proof to indicate that the data subject has given consent.[93] The data subject must give explicit consent.[94] The data subject must be informed of the storage period and of the rights of rectification, to erasure and to lodge a complaint.[95] It provides to the data subject a right to be forgotten and to erasure.[96] The data controller which made the personal data public must inform third parties on the data subject's request to erase any links to, or copy or replicate that personal data. It also provides for data portability[97] which means that if the data was processed in an electronic format, he can obtain a copy of the data and should be able to take the data when he changes service providers. Processors and controllers of personal data have numerous obligations that they must comply with to ensure the processing is performed in accordance with the regulation.[98] Controllers and processors must implement appropriate security measures for security of processing.[99] They also have a notification obligation regarding personal data breaches.[100] Provision is made that non-compliance with the regulation may result in substantial penalties.[101]

---

91 Art 4(8) determines that "the data subject's consent means any freely given specific informed and explicit indication of his or her wishes by which the data subject, either by a statement or by a clear affirmative action signifies agreement to personal data relating to them being processed."
92 art 5.
93 art 7.
94 art 6.
95 art 15.
96 art 17.
97 art 18.
98 chap IV.
99 art 30.
100 arts 31 and 32.
101 sec 79.

b) Overview of German data protection

The Federal Data Protection Act (*Bundesdatenschutzgesetz*, BDSG)[102] is the main legal source for processing of personal data. The BDSG is based on the Data Directive which will soon be repealed and replaced by the GDPR.

The BDSG provides for the processing of personal data[103] by public authorities and private bodies. It is applicable to the collection, use and processing of personal data.[104] The data subject must give permission for the processing of data.[105] Processing systems must be designed in accordance with the aim of collecting, processing and using as little personal data as possible. In particular personal data should be aliased or rendered anonymous as far as possible.[106]

The strict adherence to data protection is best illustrated with reference to a recent judgment in the so-called "Facebook like button" case.[107] The facts are briefly as follows: a clothing retailer, Peek and Cloppenburg ID Fashion had placed a Facebook like button on its homepage. Facebook uses this button to put cookies on the users' computers with the result that an individual's personal information such as the IP address is automatically forwarded to Facebook. This information is transmitted to Facebook when accessing the page and not only when clicking the button. The social network, Facebook, is funded by advertising and users' data is of enormous value. On the website at the bottom of the website was a privacy policy[108] which was accessible by means of a link. In the privacy policy the company informed the user that personal information may be transmitted to Facebook and also provided a link to the privacy policy of Facebook. The regional court of Düsseldorf found that the personal information had been unlawfully transferred to Facebook in contravention of the BDSG. The court concluded the following: an IP address is personal information, the website acted in the capacity of a data controller and valid consent from the data

---

102 For the BDSG see http://www.gesetze-im-internet.de/englisch_bdsg/ (15-09-2017).

103 which sec 3(1) defines as "any information concerning the personal or material circumstances of an identified or identifiable individual (data subject)".

104 sec 3.

105 sec 4a.

106 sec 3a.

107 LG Düsselfdorf 9.3.2016 – 12 0 151/15 (not yet in force) – 2016 *Zeitschrift für Datenschutz (ZD)* 231.

108 See para III.1 hereafter.

subject was not obtained. Valid consent would, for example, constitute a tick in a checkbox. As a result the clothing retailer had to remove the Facebook like button from its website. The case illustrates that the court interpreted the BDSG strictly in compliance with the envisaged GDPR.

III. Giving practical effect to the online protection of personal information: Privacy policy

1. What is a privacy policy?

The duty to protect the privacy of personal information of consumers and website users takes practical effect in the adoption by websites of online privacy policies,[109] which are documents aimed at informing website users about what the site will do with their personal information. These privacy policies will be explored here, with particular emphasis on the purpose of such a policy, whether or not it constitutes a binding agreement between online service providers and users and which provisions are (and should be) contained therein.

Most online forums normally require internet users to submit personal information before participation in the activities of the forum is allowed. This information is generally referred to as "personally identifiable information" (PII) and includes any information that could be used to identify users, be it public information such as names, addresses or telephone numbers, or more personal information such as credit card details and bank account numbers.[110] Although users may be willing to submit public information without a guarantee of privacy, it is clear that many people upload highly personal information to websites on a daily basis, most notably on social media and networking sites. This personal information may include pictures, communications and financial details for online purchases, and there is thus a need to create an online environment where users may share such information in the knowledge that their privacy will be protected. The method utilised by most online service providers in this regard is a privacy policy.

---

109 These policies are especially important on social-media sites and online shopping sites where a large amount of personal information is uploaded.

110 Tollen *The Tech Contracts Handbook: Cloud Computing Agreements, Software Licenses and other IT Contracts for Lawyers and Businesspeople* (2015) 267.

Although it is not a uniform legislative requirement in all countries,[111] the growing recognition of the importance of data protection has made the existence of a privacy policy part of "best practice" for online businesses. There is, for example, no unified set of laws in the US regarding privacy, with many states having their own applicable statutes. However, the proliferation of regulations in foreign legal systems means that it is more likely than not that online service providers will be affected, and the implementation of privacy policies is thus encouraged.[112] This has become a standard inclusion on international websites, especially with social media sites and online marketplaces, and it has been suggested that "online companies place their privacy policies on their websites to build consumer trust. Online privacy policies are aimed at reducing the fear that personal information will be disclosed."[113] This concept of trust between internet users and online service providers appears to be a main factor in privacy policies becoming a common market practice internationally[114] and it also seems to have influenced the contents and terms of the typical privacy policy.

In keeping with the international trend towards protection of privacy, the majority of websites that require users to divulge personal information have created privacy policies.[115] These documents are usually accessible via links on a website's homepage, typically found at the bottom of the page together with other terms and conditions.[116] Online privacy policies are aimed at explaining to website users how and why their information is collected and what will be done with it. Privacy-policy documents generally

---

111 Tollen (n 110) 266.

112 Custers, Van der Hof and Schermer "Privacy expectations of social media users: the role of informed consent in privacy policies" 2014 *Policy & Internet (P&I)* 268 274: "...while the legislation does not specify how this information must be presented (i.e., having a privacy policy is strictly speaking not a legal requirement), most data controllers present the information via a privacy policy".

113 Wu, Huang, Yen and Popova "The effect of online privacy policy on consumer privacy concern and trust" 2012 *Computers in Human Behavior* 889.

114 Consumer trust and confidence is a big motivator for businesses, as seen on the Michalsons website, where it provides a template for a South African privacy policy which complies with our privacy protection legislation. Amongst the benefits listed by them is that implementing a privacy policy will assist companies in gaining consumer confidence, encourage consumer loyalty and even help to attract new customers. The full list of benefits is accessible at www.michalsons.co.za/privacy-policy-3/2501 (13-04-2016).

115 Custers (n 112) 268 273.

116 This is seen on many social media and online shopping websites, including Facebook, WhatsApp, Instagram, Takealot and Amazon.

include details regarding the type of information collected, the purpose of such collection, how the information will be used and the level of security with which that information will be handled.[117]

However, in practice, privacy policies are not always limited to the inclusion of privacy terms.[118] These policies often include other terms and conditions. It seems, for example, as though privacy policies have become the place where online service providers exempt themselves from liability for sharing information under certain circumstances,[119] which seems to go against the intended purpose of having such a policy in the first place. A good example of this is seen in Takealot.com's privacy policy, which states:

> "Whilst we will do all things reasonably necessary to protect your rights of privacy, we cannot guarantee or accept any liability whatsoever for unauthorised or unlawful disclosures of your personal information, whilst in our possession, made by third parties who are not subject to our control, unless such disclosure is as a result of our gross negligence."[120]

By exempting themselves from liability for anything except gross negligence in sharing users' information, it would appear that online service providers are using the presence of privacy policies to create a sense of security for the user while really not providing much guarantee against any breach of such policy.[121]

Another common occurrence is for online service providers to include guidelines for dispute resolution in the privacy policy.[122] Some online service providers have included mandatory arbitration clauses which users are deemed to have assented to, even if they have not fully read the privacy policy and all of its terms and conditions.

---

117 Haynes "Online privacy policies: contracting away control over personal information?" 111 (2007) *Penn State Law Review (Penn St L Rev)* 587 594; Tollen (n 110) 266.

118 Custers, Van der Hof and Schermer (n 112) 587.

119 Miyazaki and Fernandez "Internet privacy and security: an examination of online retailer disclosures" 2000 *Journal of Public Policy & Marketing (J Pub Pol'y & Marketing)* 54 58.

120 Sec 13(11) of Takealot.com's Terms and Conditions available at http://www.takealot.com/help/terms-and-conditions (15-09-2017).

121 Gindin "Nobody reads your public policy or online contract? Lessons learned and questions raised by the FTC's action against Sears" 2009 *Northwestern Journal of Technology & Intellectual Property (Nw J Tech & Intell Prop)* 1 21.

122 Custers, Van der Hof and Schermer (n 112) 587.

The inclusion of such terms, as well as terms governing any future changes in the policy, links to another problem which arises when considering the nature of these privacy policies. It is unclear to what extent privacy policies are binding on internet users and service providers. Questions regarding information and consent arise when discussing whether or not privacy policies are merely guidelines and principles or whether they are a contract between internet users and service providers.[123]

2. Do privacy policies constitute a binding contractual relationship?

It has been debated whether privacy policies constitute a binding contractual relationship between online service providers and website users. It has been argued by some that internet users must first have the opportunity to read through a privacy policy before assenting to it and submitting their private information.[124] In terms of this view, a privacy policy should only be enforceable once the user has made a positive assent to it, whether by clicking on a button saying "I agree" or by continuing on to a website after being warned that doing so means that they assent to the terms contained in the privacy policy. However, there is no way for online service providers to ensure that website users actually read and understand the contents of privacy policies before they use the website and volunteer their personal information. Tollen states that the law is unclear regarding whether privacy policies are contract clauses,[125] and it seems that the answer lies in practice and how online service providers are currently wording and implementing these policies.

The prevailing view seems to be that "the typical privacy policy purports to bind the consumer, finding consumer consent by the consumer's use of the website or provision of information".[126] This is the approach that appears to have found most support amongst authors[127] and is being expressly incorporated into online service providers' public-policy documents. A

123 Papadopoulos and Snail (eds) *Cyberlaw @SA III: The Law of the Internet in South Africa* (2012) 309.

124 Papadopoulos and Snail (n 123) 309.

125 Tollen (n 110) 267.

126 Custers, Van der Hof and Schermer (n 112) 587 597.

127 Tollen (n 110) 267; Ginden (n 121) 1; Papadopoulos and Snail (n 123) 309.

good example of this is seen in the WhatsApp privacy-policy document, which is incorporated in its terms of service.[128]

In terms of this provision, the mere fact that an individual is using the WhatsApp service is seen as assent to the terms of service and privacy policy. There is no scope for the user to negotiate any of the terms and conditions or the circumstances in which personal information may be divulged to others. The use of the service is seen as acceptance of all the terms and conditions, and it can thus be argued that the privacy policy is a contract between the internet user and the service provider.

The only recourse for users who do not agree with the privacy policy or terms of service is found in the "Your choices" portion of the WhatsApp privacy policy, which states that:

> "If you do not agree with our Privacy Policy or Terms of Service, please delete your account, uninstall the WhatsApp mobile application, and discontinue use of the WhatsApp service."[129]

On the face of it, it would seem that this is an easy decision for consumers to make and any privacy concerns could be accommodated by simply not using the application or website.[130] The challenge with such an approach is that most people want to be connected on social media sites in order to keep abreast with global news, trends and developments all of which are so easily transmitted on the internet. It seems people are generally willing to forego privacy concerns in certain instances, specifically on social-media sites. In this social-media context, studies done on Facebook users have shown that even when users become aware of privacy risks, they ignore them, as it

---

128 The first clause explains the terms of acceptance: "This is an agreement between WhatsApp Inc., a California corporation ("WhatsApp"), the owner and operator of www.whatsapp.com (the "WhatsApp Site"), the WhatsApp software, including WhatsApp Messenger (collectively, including all content provided by WhatsApp through WhatsApp Messenger and the WhatsApp site, the "WhatsApp service", or the "Service") and you ("you" or "You"), a user of the Service. BY USING THE SERVICE, YOU ACKNOWLEDGE AND AGREE TO THESE TERMS OF SERVICE, AND WHATSAPP'S PRIVACY POLICY, WHICH CAN BE FOUND AT http://www.whatsapp.com/legal/#Privacy, AND WHICH ARE INCORPORATED HEREIN BY REFERENCE. If you choose to not agree with any of these terms, you may not use the service." (https://www.whatsapp.com.legal/#Privacy (08-04-2016)).

129 https://www.whatsapp.com.legal/#Privacy (08-04-2016).

130 Papadopoulos and Snail (n 123) 309.

seems that the risk of exposure of personal information is not deemed sufficient for them not to participate in social media.[131] Younger users are especially susceptible to the pressure to be included on these websites, which could be due to a desire to be popular and seen as being "in the loop".[132] In these instances, privacy becomes less of a concern, and people are more willing to agree to the terms included in the privacy policy, regardless of its content.

It is thus accepted in practice that there are two factors that make an online contract and privacy policy enforceable.[133] Firstly, the internet user must be given a reasonable opportunity to read through the terms of the policy and be properly informed.[134] The user must then also indicate assent to the terms, which could be done either by clicking on a button (as seen in clickwrap agreements[135]) or by the mere act of using a website or app, as seen in the WhatsApp policy discussed above. The potential drawback of this approach is that many users fail to read and take notice of the content of the privacy policy and consent to its application, either expressly or by continuing to use the sites.[136]

This issue of informed consent is very important, as it is widely accepted that one cannot fully consent to something if you are not aware of its contents.[137] However, it would not be practical to expect that each internet user

---

131 Gindin (n 121) 22.

132 Miyazaki and Fernandez (n 119) 23: "Facebook users may be aware of privacy risks but provide extensive personal information in order to be popular. Participants reported caring about privacy, but because Facebook is where they experience their social lives, it might be too risky not to participate".

133 Custers, Van der Hof and Schermer (n 112) 268, 274; Gindin (n 121) 1.

134 Custers, Van der Hof and Schermer (n 112) 268, 274.

135 These are electronic agreements that require users to click an icon saying "I agree" or "I accept" before being able to use a product or service.

136 Custers, Van der Hof and Schermer (n 112) 268 270: "When online, it seems that many data subjects simply consent whenever confronted with a consent request…there is therefore a growing scepticism regarding the effectiveness of notice and consent"; Leibowitz *Behavioural Advertising: Tracking, Targeting and Technology* available at http://www.ftc.gov/speeches/leibowitz/071031ehaviour.pdf (07-04-2016) who said "initially, privacy policies seemed like a good idea. But in practice, they often leave a lot to be desired. In many cases consumers don't notice, read or understand the privacy policies. They are often posted inconspicuously via a link at the very bottom of a site's homepage – and filled with fineprint legalese and technotalk."

137 Custers, Van der Hof and Schermer (n 112) 268 270: "In general, the process of providing consent is only considered fair when the person involved is properly

is going to read a privacy policy or even general terms and conditions of use thoroughly. What would be the extent of the online service provider's obligation in this regard? How would they ensure that the user is properly informed of the terms and conditions?

The most practical approach seems to be that there will be informed consent if the internet user is given a reasonable opportunity to access and read the terms of the privacy policy.[138] The online service provider will have fulfilled its duty of disclosure regarding the contents of the privacy policy if it is made available to users on a website, whether as a link or as a separate document. This amounts to providing a reasonable opportunity for the users to familiarise themselves with the content of the policy. Thus, even if users continue to use the site or service without having read the policy, they are still deemed to have assented to it, as it was readily available. The risk then lies with the internet user, and the policy terms and conditions will be enforceable as a contract between the user and the online service provider.

3. Guidelines for creating privacy policies

Privacy policies are an important mechanism that websites may use to assure users that their personal information will be protected in the course of their online transactions. It must be questioned which terms should be included in a model privacy policy in order for it to comply with the provisions in POPI (and the international best practice) to ensure adequate data protection. Although legislation does not set out an exact guideline, it may generally be accepted that certain types of terms must be included in a comprehensive privacy policy.

The document must first specify the audience and purposes of the privacy policy.[139] This will inform users to whom the terms and conditions apply as well as indicate the general scope of the document. It is also prudent to include the terms of acceptance as users will know at which point they are

---

informed of what exactly he or she is consenting to and, to some extent, is (made) aware of the consequences such consent may have".

138 Gindin (n 121) 1.

139 A good example of a comprehensive privacy policy can be found at https://www.cinque.co.za/.../PrivacyPolicy(eCommerce)Cinquev2.0.pdf as drafted by Michalsons Practical Legal Solutions (12-04-2016).

considered bound to the document's provisions.[140] The policy should also specify the categories of personal information that will be collected, especially when the site purports to collect personal and private information.[141] This includes information regarding the manner of information collection.[142] An example of this is seen in the Takealot privacy policy:

> "This website makes use of 'cookies' to automatically collect information and data through the standard operation of the Internet servers. 'Cookies' are small text files a website can use (and which we may use) to recognise repeat users, facilitate the user's on-going access to and use of a website and allow a website to track usage behavior and compile aggregate data that will allow the website operator to improve the functionality of the website and its content. The type of information collected by cookies is not used to personally identify you. If you do not want information collected through the use of cookies, there is a simple procedure in most browsers that allows you to deny or accept the cookie feature." [143]

The policy must also disclose which third parties will receive or have access to the personal information and describe the ways in which the personal information will be used.[144] It is very important that online service providers explain the way in which the information will be protected and what security measures will be taken.[145] The policy should explain what will happen in the event of any changes to the terms and conditions,[146] and should inform users of the proper course of action in the event of a breach of this policy.

The privacy policy should be a flexible document, and must be updated as the law relating to data protection develops.[147] As it is an important tool in online data protection it should thus be reviewed regularly to ensure that it is still compliant with market practices and the applicable legislative framework.

---

140 Seen in both the Cinque privacy policy (accessible at https://www.cinque.co.za/.../PrivacyPolicy(eCommerce)Cinquev2.0.pdf) and the WhatsApp privacy policy (accessible at https://www.whatsapp.com.legal/#Privacy) (12-04-2016).

141 Tollen (n 110) 267.

142 Sec 13.13.4 of Takealot.com's Terms and Conditions available at http://www.takealot.com/help/terms-and-conditions (15-09-2017).

143 ibid.

144 Tollen (n 110) 267.

145 Tollen (n 110) 267.

146 Section 14 of Takealot.com's Terms and Conditions available at http://www.takealot.com/help/terms-and-conditions (15-09-2017).

147 www.michalsons.co.za/privacy-policy-3/2501 (14-04-2016).

IV. Conclusion

Providing for personal information privacy protection in an online environment without a legal framework may tip the scales in favour of government and business. Snowden's 2013 admissions revealed the far reaching extent of clandestine surveillance. His revelations resulted in a heightened awareness of data protection and the threats inherent in living in a surveillance society.

For obvious reasons an individual finds himself in a vulnerable position when he has no choice but to disclose personal information online. It is for this reason that a legal framework must provide for personal information protection. Online businesses should provide a privacy policy which specifies how they endeavour to protect an individual's information. Although not all privacy policies will be perfect and may present challenges, it is a step in the right direction for transparency reflecting the *bona fides* of businesses and affording the user trust and confidence in disclosing information. Evolving technology poses a serious threat worldwide to online privacy protection. The EU recognised the growing technological challenges by implementing the Data Protection Directive in 1995. At the end of 2015 the EU once again took the lead by introducing the GDPR. Over the years the EU has shown a clear commitment to data protection as a core value. German data-protection laws are well-developed and strictly applied. The GDPR will be applicable to Germany once implemented and German data protection will have to comply with the GDPR. The GDPR will also have an indirect impact on South Africa which should align data protection in accordance with international privacy standards especially as the electronic environment has created a world without borders. South Africa will hopefully soon fully implement POPI and in the interpretation of this legislation it may look for guidance to the GDPR, Germany and the CJEU judgments.

Governments, businesses and individuals cannot be complacent in respect of privacy protection, but need to re-visit it continuously to prevent a proliferation in the abuse of data. The alternative will be a sad decline in the advantages of the electronic environment.

Bibliography

Austin L "Enough about me: privacy is about power, not consent (or harm)" in Sarat A (ed) *A World Without Privacy* (Cambridge University Press, New York 2015) 136.

Bilchitz D "Privacy, surveillance and the duties of corporations" 2016 *Tydskrif vir die Suid-Afrikaanse Reg (TSAR)* 53.

Currie I and De Waal J *The Bill of Rights Handbook* (6th Edition, Juta, Cape Town 2013).

Custers B, Van der Hof S and Schermer B "Privacy expectations of social media users: the role of informed consent in privacy policies" 2014 *Policy & Internet (P&I)* 268.

De Stadler E and Esselaar P *A Guide to the Protection of Personal Information Act* (Juta, Cape Town 2015).

Dubber MD and Hörnle T *The Oxford Handbook on Criminal Law* (Oxford University Press, Oxford 2014).

Gindin SE "Nobody reads your public policy or online contract? Lessons learned and questions raised by the FTC's action against Sears" 8 (2009) *Northwestern Journal of Technology and Intellectual Property (Nw J Tech & Intell Prop)* 1.

Haggerty KD "What's wrong with privacy protections?" in Sarat A (ed) *A World Without Privacy* (Cambridge University Press, Cambridge 2015) 194.

Haynes AW "Online privacy policies: contracting away control over personal information?" 111 (2007) *Penn State Law Review (Penn St L Rev)* 587.

Laidlaw EB *Regulating Speech in Cyberspace* (Cambridge University Press, Cambridge 2015).

Leigh D and Harding L *Wikileaks: inside Julian Assange's war on secrecy* (Guardian Books, London 2013).

Miyazaki A and Fernandez A "Internet privacy and security: an examination of online retailer disclosures" 19 (2000) *Journal of Public Policy & Marketing (J Pub Pol'y & Marketing)* 54.

Naude A and Papadopoulos S "Data protection in South Africa: the Protection of Personal Information Act 4 of 2013 in the light of recent international developments" 79 (2016) *Tydskrif vir Hedendaagse Romeins-Hollandse Reg (THRHR)* 52.

O'Harrow R *No Place to Hide* (Free Press, New York 2006).

Papadopoulos S and Snail S (eds) *Cyberlaw@SA III: The Law of the Internet in South Africa* (Van Schaik, Pretoria 2012).

Staff reporter "Paper a refuge in age of cyberattacks" 9 April 2016 *Saturday Star* 17.

Sykes S "Privacy and security: a comparative constitutional law conversation" (2015) *Konrad-Adenauer-Stiftung Publication* 1.

Tollen DW *The Tech Contracts Handbook: Cloud Computing Agreements, Software Licenses and other IT Contracts for Lawyers and Businesspeople* (2nd Edition, American Bar Association, Chicago 2015).

Wu KW, Huang Y, Yen DC and Popova I "The effect of online privacy policy on consumer privacy concern and trust" 28 (2012) *Computers in Human Behavior (Comput Hum Behav)* 889.

Case Law

South Africa

Bernstein v Bester 1996 2 SA 751 (CC)
Fedics Group (Pty) Ltd v Matus 1989 2 SA 617 (C)
Gaertner v Minister of Finance 2014 1 SA 442 (CC)
Harley v Niland 2016 2 SA 436 (ECG)
Protea Technology v Wainer 1979 3 All SA 594 (W)
Waste Products Utilisation v Wilkes 2003 2 SA 515 (W)

European Court of Justice

European Court of Justice Case C-131/12 13.5.2014 *Google Spain SL, Google Inc v Agencia Española de Protección de Datos (AEPD), Marios Costeja Gonzáles (Google Spain)* ECLI:EU:C:2014:317.

European Court of Justice Case C-293/12 and C-594/12 8.4.2014 *Digital Rights Ireland Ltd (C-293/12) v Minister for Communications, Marine and Natural Resources and Others and Kärntner Landesregierung (C-594/12) and Others* ECLI:EU:C:2014:238.

A comparative analysis of the proposed new cyber-crime legislation in South Africa and the situation in Germany and the European Union

*Dawie de Villiers**

---

* Professor of Procedural Law and Criminal Law, University of Johannesburg.

I. Introduction

The current legal framework that combats cybercrime in South Africa is a hybrid of common law and national legislation.

Not less than 20 "new" statutory offences related to cybercrime are proposed in the new Cybercrime and Cybersecurity Bill in chapter 2 and another 21 in the rest of the Bill. A number of these crimes can be linked to some well-known common law crimes such as fraud, theft, forgery, uttering and extortion. Is it really necessary to move towards some form of codification of these crimes where computers are involved and will the important fight against commercial crimes benefit from such a move?

How does the new bill compare to cyber law in Germany and the European Union? Are we not complicating our criminal law with vague and broad definitions of concepts that have already been dealt with over the years by our courts with clear judgments on all the elements of the different crimes? Before discussing these proposals we firstly need to re-visit some of the common law crimes.

II. Cybercrime from a common-law perspective

1. The nature of the common-law crime of fraud

The common-law crime of fraud has an interesting history. It derives from *stellionatus* and *crimina falsi*, two different Roman-law crimes. The reason for the distinction was that harm or prejudice as a result of intentional misrepresentation, had to be involved for *stellionatus,* while it was not a prerequisite for *crimina falsi*. This distinction was, however, not upheld by all the Roman-Dutch authors.[1] Over the years our courts started combining the two concepts and this led to the crime of fraud, as we now know it.

A well-recognised definition of fraud is "the unlawful and intentional making of a misrepresentation which causes actual prejudice or which is potentially prejudicial to another".[2]

The definition does not specify how the misrepresentation should have been made and it is therefore accepted that it can be orally or in writing or through conduct.[3] It also does not exclude any tool, device or instrument like a computer that could have been used to misrepresent facts. There is, however, a debate on whether it is a requirement to make the misrepresentation to a person and whether that excludes computers or machines like a parking meter.[4] In *Mbokazi*[5] the use by the accused of another person's "PIN" number to transfer money was seen as a misrepresentation. Ebersöhn states:

> "When a hacker transfers money from A's account to his account or to someone else's account, he can be charged with fraud (in that he makes a misrepresentation to the bank's system administrator with the intent to defraud the bank) or with theft (in that he stole A's 'money' or more correctly stated: He diminished A's personal rights against the bank)."[6]

Criticism against the definition of fraud based on vagueness and unconstitutionality lead to *Friedman's*[7] judgment: "The present definition of fraud is wide, but that does not make it difficult, much less impossible, to ascertain the type of conduct which falls within it."[8]

---

1 See Snyman *Criminal Law* (2014) 524.

2 (n 1) 523.

3 *MacDonald* 1982 3 SA 220 (A) 239H; *Mdantile* 2011 2 SACR 142 (FB) para 29.

4 See *Myeza* 1985 4 SA 30 (T); Carstens and Trichardt "Computer crime by means of the automated teller-machine – just another face of fraud?" 1987 *South African Journal of Criminal Law and Criminology (SACC)* 132; Botha "Bedrog ten opsigte van die gebruik van tjek en/of kredietkaarte" 1988 *South African Journal of Criminal Justice (SACJ)* 377; Botha "Sogenaamde rekenaarbedrog" 1990 *South African Journal of Criminal Justice (SACJ)* 231 and Ebersöhn "A common law perspective on computer-related crimes" 2004 *Tydskrif vir Hedendaagse Romeins-Hollandse Reg. (THRHR)* 22, 193 and 375.

5 1998 2 All SA 78 (N).

6 Ebersöhn (n 4) 198.

7 1996 1 SACR 181 (W); *Chetty* 2008 2 SACR 157 (W) followed the *Friedman* decision.

8 194b.

2. The nature of the common law crime of theft

The act of theft (*furtum*) was originally described in terms of the carrying away (*auferre*) of the stolen property in Roman law. This later changed to the handling (*contrectatio*) of the stolen property. The Romans, however, adopt a strict interpretation of "handling" as to mean actual handling of the item.[9]

Although the South African criminal law followed Roman and Roman Dutch law and therefore preferred the concept of *contrectatio,* English law influenced it[10] and certain elements like *animus furandi* were imported.

Burchell's definition of theft is: "An unlawful appropriation with intent to steal of a thing capable of being stolen."[11]

Naturally, a strict interpretation of "*contrectatio*" as it was used in Roman Dutch law can no longer suffice. Burchell states:

> "In an age when wealth is increasingly found in physically abstract (incorporeal) things, and where the transfer of property does not necessarily require a handling over of a thing, but can be achieved by instructions to computers and book entries, this concept of the taking of property proves to be highly restrictive and not at all in accordance with the requirements of a modern industrialised capitalist economy".[12]

In *Harper*[13] the court approves Snyman's proposition that "appropriation" should replace *contrectatio* and agrees that a broadened understanding of the concept is necessary. An example of the broadening of the appropriation element can be found in *Van den Berg*[14] where the accused's *contrectatio* was an instruction to a computer to transfer money. The Supreme Court of Appeal also acknowledged "appropriation" as an element of theft in *Visagie*[15] and *Boesak.*[16]

---

9 Snyman (n1) 475.

10 The definition of theft in sec 176 of the *Transkeian Penal Code* 24 of 1886 was copied *verbatim* from English law.

11 Burchell *Principles of Criminal Law* (2016) 689. Snyman (n 1) 475–476 criticised the definition because it does not explain the meaning of "appropriation", "intent to steal" or "thing capable of being stolen".

12 Burchell (n 11) 692.

13 1981 2 SA 638 (D) 665.

14 1991 1 SACR 104 (T).

15 1991 1 SA 177 (A) 181.

16 2000 1 SACR 633 (SCA) para 97.

The Roman Dutch law's contention that only corporeal things are capable of being stolen provided our courts with a number of difficulties.[17] In *Mintoor*[18] it was stated that there could be no theft of electricity[19] or other forms of energy. Copying of computer software programmes would also fall outside the definition of theft.[20] The theft of electricity once again became an issue in *Ndebele.*[21] The court took an opposing view and decided that electricity can actually be stolen.[22]

With regard to the transfer of money the Appellate Division (some 40 years ago) "has come to regard money as being capable of being stolen even where it is not corporeal cash but is represented by a credit entry in books of account".[23]

---

17 Coetzee "Diefstal van onliggaamlike sake" 1970 *Tydskrif vir Hedendaagse Romeins-Hollandse Reg (THRHR)* 369; Van der Merwe "Computer crime" 1983 *Obiter* 124; Skeen "Computers and crime" 1984 *South African Journal of Criminal Law and Criminology (SACC)* 262; Van der Merwe "Diefstal van onliggaamlike sake met spesifieke verwysing na rekenaars" 1985 *South African Journal of Criminal Law and Criminology (SACC)* 129.

18 1996 1 SACR 514 (C).

19 Electricity theft is not only costing South Africa billions each year, it is also costing people their lives. In December 2014, Eskom revealed that as much as 7% of the country's electricity is stolen *via* illegal connections. "We desperately need that revenue … we cannot afford it anymore," said Eskom. Despite efforts like Eskom's Izinyoka campaign, where electricity thieves are portrayed as snakes, the problem has not subsided. City Power's director of engineering operations, Stuart Webb, told Carte Blanche that fighting electricity theft is battle they are losing. He said they often sweep an area and cut off illegal connections – which reappear in a day or two. Webb said they are losing 19% of their revenue because of electricity theft. This amounted to R3 billion in the last financial year, http://mybroadband.co.za/news/energy/137616-how-izinyoka-steal-electricity-worth-billions-each-year-in-south-africa.html (15-09-2017).

20 Skeen (n 17) and Van der Merwe (1985) (n 17).

21 2012 1 SACR 245 (GSJ).

22 Snyman (n 1) 482–483 does not support the decision and Jordaan "Theft – act of appropriation – electricity" 2012 *South African Journal of Criminal Justice (SACJ)* 314–316 is also concerned about the consequences of the decision. For a supporting view of the decision see D'Oliviera "Theft of electricity: a short circuit? – *S v Ndebele* 2012 1 SACR 245 (GSJ)" 2012 *Tydskrif vir Hedendaagse Romeins-Hollandse Reg (THRHR)* 312.

23 *Graham* 1975 3 SA 569 (A) 826; Loubser *The Theft of Money in South African Law* (1977 thesis US) 179; for a strange outcome of why the accused is not guilty of the theft of trust money see *Moolman* 2006 1 SACR 432 (T).

3. The nature of the common law crimes of forgery and uttering

Roman Dutch law did not recognise forgery as a separate crime but the South African courts followed English law where the two crimes of forgery and uttering were acknowledged separately.[24]

An accepted definition of forgery is: "The unlawfully and intentionally making of a false document to the actual or potential prejudice of another".[25]

Because forgery can only be committed in respect of "documents", the lack of a uniform definition of "document" by our courts may cause problems. According to Burchell[26] the following definition should be satisfactory: "A document is any writing in any form, on any material, which communicates to some person or persons a human statement, whether of fact or fiction". It therefore means that the substance on which the writing appears (paper, wood, cloth or computer screen) is irrelevant. The medium used to create the writing also does not matter and may therefore even be a post on social network via a computer or cellphone. The "human statement" part may in some instances be questioned, depending on the way in which new technology can be used to create "documents" on computer.

A definition of uttering is: "The unlawfully and intentionally passing off a false document to the actual or potential prejudice of another."[27]
There is no description of how the communication can be done. It is therefore suggested that it can be done by way of e-mail, SMS or posting on cyber networks.

4. Nature of the common law crime of malicious damage to property

This was not known as a specific offence in Roman or Roman Dutch law and became part of South African law through the influence of English law.[28]

---

24 I cannot agree with Snyman's (n 1) contention (532) that forgery is a species of fraud. The difference between the two crimes, acknowledged by the author, make them separate crimes.

25 Snyman (n 1) 532.

26 Burchell (n 11) 755.

27 Snyman (n 1) 535.

28 Burchell (n 11) 757.

The definition is: "Malicious damage to property consists in unlawfully and intentionally damaging the property of another."[29]

"Damage" is not only the actual destruction or physical damage as was referred to in *Bowden*[30] where a statue was painted.

It is argued that the property must be corporeal and therefore infecting a computer programme with a virus that destroys the data on the disk does not fall within the definition. I believe the same argument for a broadened interpretation of "property" that is used for theft, should also be applied to this crime.[31]

III. Cyber-crime legislation

1. What constitutes cybercrime?

Cyber (computer) crime is defined as "any criminal activity that involves a computer" or "[c]omputer crime encompasses the use of a computer as a tool in the perpetration of a crime as well as situations in which there has been unauthorised access to the victim's computer or data".[32]

Van der Merwe[33] preferred the definition used by the German police: "Computer crime covers all sets of circumstances where electronic data processing forms the means for the commission and/or the object of an offence and represents the basis for the suspicion that an offence has been committed".

As early as in 2000 Van der Merwe[34] had already posed the question whether computer crime was different from ordinary crime and whether computers lead to new categories of specific offences. He also wanted to know whether they affected the general principles of criminal liability in a unique manner. He lastly raised the question "whether the legislature should intervene, as many states in the United States have done, or whether the

29 Burchell (n 11) 757.
30 1957 3 SA 148 (T) 150G.
31 To make provision for this to be punishable the legislature created a statutory offence in sec 87(2) of the Electronic Communications and Transactions Act 25 of 2002.
32 Credo and Michels *Computer Crime in South Africa* (1985) 2.
33 Van der Merwe *Computers and the Law* (2000) 188.
34 Van der Merwe (n 33) 163.

Roman-Dutch common law of South Africa can cope adequately with space-age criminals".[35]

Cybercrime can be divided into at least three categories: The first category deals with situations where well-known common-law crimes that we inherited from Roman Dutch law, for example fraud, theft, forgery and *crimen iniuria,* are committed through the use of a computer. The second deals with situations where statutory commercial crimes like money laundering and racketeering are also committed by using a computer. The last category deals with crimes that can only be committed by means of a computer such as hacking, phishing, cracking or sniffing.

2. Statutory intervention

Before 2002 cybercrime fighters were applying and extending the common law crimes and sometimes even using legislation like the Police Services Act 68 of 1995, the Copyright Act 98 of 1978 and the Prevention of Organised Crime Act 121 of 1998 (POCA) that deal with cyber-related issues.[36]

Very important legislation in the fight against cybercrime was enacted from 2000 to 2002. The Financial Intelligence Centre Act 38 of 2001 (FICA) came into effect on the 1st of July 2003. FICA was introduced to fight financial crime, such as money laundering, tax evasion and terrorist-financing activities. Two others, however, need special mentioning.

a) Regulation of Interception of Communications and Provision of Communication Related Information Act 70 of 2002 (RICA)

Section 2[37] of this act prohibits the unlawful interception or monitoring of any data message and makes it an offence in terms of section 49. This can therefore be used to prosecute hackers and crackers. There are, however, a

35 Van der Merwe (ed) *Information and Communications Technology Law* (2008) 67–69.

36 Crimes applicable to the cyber environment are listed.

37 "Subject to this Act, no person may intentionally intercept or attempt to intercept, or authorize or procure any other person to intercept or attempt to intercept, at any place in the Republic, any communication in the course of its occurrence or transmission."

number of lawful grounds of justification such as lawful interception, consent, directives or being a party to the communication.

Although it seems that section 51(1) covers only one offence this is not the case. Each one of the seven scenarios, dealt with in (i) – (vii), is actually a separate offence. For example (ii)[38] is a form of cyber fraud; (v)[39] a form of cyber forgery; (vi)[40] also a form of cyber fraud and (vii)[41] a form of obstruction and interference as a separate offence.

The offence under section 52[42] reminds us of a rather old statutory offence[43] namely inability to give account of possession of goods suspected of being stolen.

The offence under section 53[44] reminds us of another old statutory offence,[45] namely receiving stolen property without reasonable cause. The constitutionality of this section came under scrutiny in *Manamela*[46] where the court held that the infringement on the right to remain silent was justifiable in terms of the limitations clause[47] in the Constitution. Because the

---

38 "Any person who in any application made in terms of this Act, furnishes information or makes a statement, knowing such information or statement to be false, incorrect or misleading or not believing it to be correct is guilty of an offence."

39 "Any person who forges or, with the intent to deceive, alters or tampers with any direction or entry warrant issued under this Act is guilty of an offence."

40 "Any person who furnishes particulars or information in any affidavit or report referred to in this Act, knowing such particulars or information to be false, incorrect or misleading or not believing it to be correct is guilty of an offence."

41 "Any person who obstructs, hinders or interferes with an authorised person who executes any direction or entry warrant issued under this Act or assists with the execution thereof, in the exercising of his or her powers under that direction or entry warrant is guilty of an offence."

42 "Any person who is found in possession of any cellular phone or SIM-card in regard to which there is reasonable suspicion that it has been stolen and is unable to give a satisfactory account of such possession is guilty of an offence."

43 sec 36 of the General Law Amendment Act 62 of 1955; *Auby* 2007 1 SACR 655 (W).

44 "Any person who in any manner acquires or receives into his or her possession from any other person a stolen cellular phone or SIM-card without having reasonable cause for believing at the time of such acquisition or receipt that such cellular phone or SIM-card is the property of the person from whom he or she acquires or receives it or that such person has been duly authorized by the owner thereof to deal with it or dispose of it, is guilty of an offence."

45 See sec 37 of the General Law Amendment Act 62 of 1955.

46 2000 1 SACR 414 (CC).

47 sec 36 of the Constitution: "(1) The rights in the Bill of Rights may be limited only in terms of law of general application to the extent that the limitation is reasonable and justifiable in an open and democratic society based on human dignity, equality

reverse *onus* provision itself could not be saved by the limitation clause, the court read words into the legislation to replace the invalid reverse *onus*. This resulted in the amendment of this section in 2000.[48]

b) Electronic Communications and Transactions Act 25 of 2002 (ECT)[49]

This act deals comprehensively with cybercrimes in chapter XIII and, I believe, brought some legal certainty as to what constitutes cybercrime. It is important to refer to the interpretation provision (section 3) as well as to section 91, which clearly states that the act does not exclude the application of any other statutory provision or common law and does not affect criminal or civil liability in terms of the common law. These laws, if applicable, are therefore still in force and binding.

Although the Cybercrime and Cybersecurity Bill proposes that the sections[50] in this act that refer to cybercrime should be deleted, I believe a short discussion is still needed to consider the question whether the new cybercrimes are improvements compared to the present ones.

There are nine cybercrime offences in this act, five under section 86 and two each under sections 87 and 88.

Section 86(1)[51] makes it an offence to access or intercept data without authority or permission. Section 87(2)[52] covers the interference with data that results in the modification or destroying thereof. Section 86(3)[53] makes

---

and freedom, taking into account all relevant factors, including— (a) the nature of the right; (b) the importance of the purpose of the limitation; (c) the nature and extent of the limitation; (d) the relation between the limitation and its purpose; and (e) less restrictive means to achieve the purpose."

48 by sec 2 of the Judicial Matters Amendment Act 62 of 2000.

49 See Burchell "Criminal justice at the crossroads" 2002 *South African Law Journal (SALJ)* 579 585.

50 These are secs 85, 86, 87, 88 and 90.

51 "A person who intentionally accesses or intercepts any data without authority or permission to do so is guilty of an offence."

52 "A person who intentionally and without authority to do so, interferes with data in a way which causes such data to be modified, destroyed or otherwise rendered ineffective is guilty of an offence."

53 "A person who unlawfully produces, sells, offers to sell, procures for use, designs, adapts for use, distributes or possesses any device, including a computer program or a component, which is designed primarily to overcome security measures for the protection of data, or performs any of those acts with regard to a password,

it an offence to produce and sell hardware or software that is primarily designed to overcome security measures for the protection of data while section 86(4)[54] criminalises the use of such devices or programmes. These are called anti-cracking or anti-thwarting measures. Section 86(5)[55] makes it an offence to prevent legitimate users from accessing their own service. This should also cover e-mail bombing and spamming.

Section 87 covers what the act refers to as computer-related extortion, fraud and forgery. Section 87(1)[56] makes it an offence to obtain unlawful advantages through performing actions under the act, or threatening to do so. Section 87(2)[57] refers to the obtaining of any unlawful advantage through presenting fake data as if it were authentic.

The two offences under section 88 refer to attempt, aiding and abetting.

The penalties are found under section 89.[58] These criminal sanctions have been criticised by comparison[59] for not being stringent enough.[60]

---

access code or any other similar kind of data with the intent to unlawfully utilise such item to contravene this section, is guilty of an offence."

54 "A person who utilises any device or computer program mentioned in subsection (3) in order to unlawfully overcome security measures designed to protect such data or access thereto, is guilty of an offence."

55 "A person who commits any act described in this section with the intent to interfere with access to an information system so as to constitute a denial, including a partial denial, of service to legitimate users is guilty of an offence."

56 "A person who performs or threatens to perform any of the acts described in section 86, for the purpose of obtaining any unlawful proprietary advantage by undertaking to cease or desist from such action, or by undertaking to restore any damage caused as a result of those actions, is guilty of an offence."

57 "A person who performs any of the acts described in section 86 for the purpose of obtaining any unlawful advantage by causing fake data to be produced with the intent that it be considered or acted upon as if it were authentic, is guilty of an offence."

58 "(1) A person convicted of an offence referred to in sections 37 (3), 40 (2), 58 (2), 80 (5), 82 (2) or 86 (1), (2) or (3) is liable to a fine or imprisonment for a period not exceeding 12 months. (2) A person convicted of an offence referred to in section 86 (4) or (5) or section 87 is liable to a fine or imprisonment for a period not exceeding five years."

59 The Regulation of Interception of Communications and Provision of Communication related Information Act 70 of 2002 makes provision for fines up to R2 m and imprisonment for up to ten years.

60 See Van der Merwe (n 35) 75–78.

IV. Cybercrimes and Cybersecurity Bill, 2016

1. Introduction

The 128 page draft Cybercrimes and Cybersecurity Bill, 2015 was published on 28 August 2015 for public comment in South Africa. A 97 page edited version (now Cybercrimes and Cybersecurity Bill, 2016) was published in June 2016.

In chapter 2 the bill aims to create 20 new offences, which have a bearing on cybercrimes and which impose more stringent penalties. Chapters 3 to 11 mainly deal with jurisdiction, investigative powers, international co-operation and structures that deal with cyber security and evidence. The point of departure of this comparative study, however, is criminal law with the cybercrimes, as created in chapter 2, as focus. The bill criminalises a number of activities relating to: the access to data, computer programs, storage mediums or computer systems; the acquiring of protected data; the possession of protected data; the commitment of various unlawful acts in respect of software or hardware tools; the use of hardware or software tools for purposes of contravening certain sections; the interference with data, computer programs, storage mediums or computer systems; the acquisition, possession, provision or use of passwords, and access codes; computer related fraud, forgery, uttering, extortion and theft; hate speech and incitement of violence; and attempts and participation.

2. Categories of cyber crimes

Chapter 2 with the title "Offences" consists of 17 sections and covers 20 new offences. Sections 2, 3, 4, 5, 6 and 7 can be grouped together: all of them cover various acts that a perpetrator may commit with a computer or data like access, interference and possession. Sections 8, 9, 10, and 15 can be grouped together as offences expanding on the common law crimes of fraud, forgery, uttering, extortion and theft. Section 11 refers to hate speech while section 13 mentions aggravated offences. Sections 12 and 14 refer to incitement, attempting, conspiring and instructing.

There is no space in this article to quote and discuss every single offence comprehensively but at least one or two examples from each of the groups mentioned above are discussed below.

a) Sections 2, 3, 4, 5, 6 and 7: Unlawful securing of access and other unlawful acts

Section 2(1) creates the first offence where a person secures access to data, a computer program, data storage medium or computer system, and section 2(2) explains what constitutes "secures access".

Subsections 3(1) and (2) makes it a crime to unlawfully and intentionally acquire or possess protected data while subsection 3(3) criminalises being found in possession of protected data if there is a reasonable suspicion that such protected data was acquired and the person is unable to give a satisfactory, exculpatory account of such possession.

The constitutionality of subsection 3(3) and the disregard of the principle of innocent until proven guilty may also be challenged where it places a duty on the processor to give a satisfactory exculpatory explanation. See, however, *Osman v Attorney-General, Transvaal*[61] where the court held that a similar provision (section 36 possession) is not incompatible with the Constitution. It concluded that the section does not compel the possessor to do anything. He has a choice whether or not to provide an explanation for the possession of the goods. It is the inability and not the failure or unwillingness to give a satisfactory account of possession that constituted the offence and the burden to prove this rests on the state.

Section 4(1) covers a number of acts[62] related to software or hardware tools and it qualifies the acts with "the purposes of contravening" certain provisions of the Bill. Section 4(2) makes it a separate offence if a person uses the software or hardware for contravening purposes. A wide definition of "software or hardware tool" follows in section 4(3). Section 5(1) refers to the interference with data or a computer program[63] while section 6(1) covers the interference with a data-storage medium or computer system.[64]

The last offence under this group can be found in section 7(1) where it covers the acquiring, possession, providing and use of passwords, access

61 1998 2 SACR 493 (CC).

62 The acts are "manufactures, assembles, obtains, sells, purchases, makes available, possesses or advertises" the software or hardware tools.

63 Sec 5(2) provides a wide meaning of "interference with data or computer program".

64 Sec 6(2) provides a wide meaning of "interference with a computer data storage medium or a computer system".

codes or similar data or devices.[65] Subsection 7(2) is concerned with a person found in possession of an access code, password or similar data or device and can be compared to subsection 3(3) above, where it refers to the reasonable suspicion and the inability to give satisfactory exculpatory account of such possession.

There are many examples of statutory provisions[66] where people are found to be in possession of something and there "is a reasonable suspicion" that leads to certain consequences and expectations of satisfactory explanations. Sometimes the legislature will name the person that must have the reasonable suspicion and sometimes, like in this section, the legislature does not. The issue about the nature of the software or hardware tools as well as the intent of the possessor, is of paramount importance in the forming of the suspicion and if the person who finds the item is not trained in the IT related domain it may create serious problems. The same concern can be raised about "satisfactory exculpatory account" being too wide which may lead to abuse. The same criticism towards the possible "shifting of the onus" mentioned in paragraph II.2.a) above is also applicable here.

b) Sections 8, 9, 10 and 15 expand on the common law crimes like fraud, forgery, uttering, extortion and theft.

The computer related fraud offence in subsection 8(1) is exactly the same as the common law crime of fraud, with the only qualification that the misrepresentation must have been made by means of data or a computer program or through any interference with data, a computer program storage medium or computer system.

---

65 Sec 6(2) provides a wide meaning of "password, access code or similar data or device".

66 Sec 82 of the Third General Law Amendment Act 129 of 1993 provides that any person who possesses any implement or object in respect of which there is a reasonable suspicion that it was used or is intended to be used to commit housebreaking, or to break open a motor vehicle or to gain unlawful entry into a motor vehicle, and who is unable to give a satisfactory account of such possession, is guilty of an offence. Sec 36 of the General Law Amendment Act 62 of 1955 mentions the inability to give account of possession of goods suspected of being stolen.

Is this offense really necessary? The use of a computer[67] or similar device to make the misrepresentation has for many years been recognised as a form of common law fraud. Snyman[68] uses the following example:

> "If X discovers Y's "PIN" number and unlawfully utilises this knowledge to transfer credit which is recorded to Y's advantage in a bank to her (X's) own advantage, or if she succeeds in instructing or manipulating a computer by some underhand method to transfer credit which is not due to her, to her own account, she commits a misrepresentation."

The common law crimes of forgery and uttering are also replicated in subsections 9(1)[69] and 9(2),[70] with the qualification that the offence must have been committed by means of data or a computer program.

Section 10[71] refers to a specific kind of extortion (computer related) that differs from our common law extortion,[72] as well as from statutory extortion.[73] The section 10 extortion clearly refers to offences under the act that have either already been committed or are threatening to another person.

---

67 Carstens and Trichardt (n 4) 134; Botha (1988) (n 4); Botha (1990) (n 4); Ebersöhn (n 4) 2004 and *Nonkonyana* 2008 2 SACR 271 (E).

68 Snyman (n 1) 526.

69 "Any person who unlawfully and intentionally makes false data or a computer program with the intention to deceive, to the actual or potential prejudice of another person is guilty of the offence of computer related forgery."

70 "Any person who unlawfully and intentionally passes off false data or a computer program with the intention to deceive, to the actual or potential prejudice of another person is guilty of the offence of computer related uttering."

71 "Any person who unlawfully and intentionally - (a) threatens to commit any offence under this Act; or (b) commits any offence under this Act, for the purposes of obtaining any advantage from another person, and which induces that person to hand over the advantage is guilty of the offence of computer related extortion.

72 See the definition according to Burchell (n 11) 736: "It consists in taking from another some patrimonial advantage by intentionally and unlawfully subjecting that person to pressure which induces him or her to submit to the taking."

73 sec 1 of the General Law Amendment Act 139 of 1992: "At criminal proceedings at which an accused is charged with extortion it shall with respect to the object of the extortion be sufficient to prove that any advantage was extorted, whether or not such advantage was of a patrimonial nature."

The title of section 15[74] is “Theft of incorporeal” and it only broadens the common law crime of theft to not exclude the theft of an incorporeal. Sections 12[75] and 14 also belong to this group because they relate to the common law crimes of incitement and the role of the accomplice. The incitement in section 12 is, however, limited to violence or damage to property. The only difference in section 14[76] is that the attempt, conspiracy and incitement must be “in terms of this chapter”.

It is common cause that attempts to commit common law crimes and statutory offences are punishable. In *Agliotti*[77] it was held that a person is guilty of attempting to commit a crime if, intending to commit that crime, he unlawfully engages in conduct that is not merely preparatory but has reached at least the commencement of the execution of the intended crime. A statutory provision[78] with general application to all statutory offences also makes attempt punishable. Subsection (2) of the same section covers incitement to commit both common law crimes and statutory offences.[79] An accomplice is a person who does not satisfy all the requirements for liability but furthers the commission of the crime.[80]

74 “The common law offence of theft must be interpreted so as not to exclude the theft of an incorporeal.”

75 “Any person who unlawfully and intentionally distributes to a specific person, group of persons or the general public, through a computer system a data message which incites— (a) violence against; or (b) damage to any property belonging to, a person or a group of persons, is guilty of an offence.”

76 “Any person who unlawfully and intentionally— (a) attempts; (b) conspires with any other person; or (c) aids, abets, induces, incites, instigates, instructs, commands, or procures another person, to commit an offence in terms of this Chapter, is guilty of an offence and is liable on conviction to the punishment to which a person convicted of actually committing that offence would be liable.”

77 2011 2 SACR 437 (GSJ) para 10.2.

78 According to sec 18(1) of the Riotous Assemblies Act “any person: who attempts to commit any offence against a statute or a statutory regulation shall be guilty of an offence”.

79 “Any person who ... incites, instigates, commands or procures any other person to commit any offence, whether at common law or against a statute or statutory regulation, shall be guilty of an offence.”

80 Burchell (n 11) 506.

c) Hate speech and aggravated offences

Subsection 11(1)[81] prohibits the dissemination of a data message, which constitutes hate speech. Since this bill has been published for the first time another bill about hate crime was published[82] and it seems that there may be some overlapping between the two bills. Section 11(1) does not apply if the speech was made in terms of section 11(3) "in good faith in the course of engagement in (a) artistic creativity or performance; (b) any academic or scientific inquiry; or (c) fair and accurate reporting in the public interest". Subsection 11(2) provides a definition of hate speech.

Hate speech is also prohibited in terms of the Promotion of Equality and Prevention of Unfair Discrimination Act.[83] Examples of cases where the Equality Court interpreted "hate speech" include the Julius Malema's "Kill the Boer Case"[84] and the Penny Sparrow Case[85].

Section 13 with the title Aggravated offences created two new categories of serious offences linked in section 13(1)*(a)* to a "restricted computer system" and in section 13(2)*(a)* where a number of scenarios are mentioned which are of a serious nature.

V. Cybercrime in Germany

1. Historical overview

Codified German criminal law is more than 140 years old and began with the promulgation of the 1871 *Strafgesetzbuch für das Deutsche Reich* (RStGB – Criminal Code for the German Reich or German Penal Code). This, together with close to 180 amendments to the law until about 1945, determined criminal law in Germany. It was characterised by the 19th century state directed by the rule of law. In 1949 a Constitution was created as

81 "Any person who unlawfully and intentionally distributes a data message which constitutes hate speech through a computer system which is— (a) accessible by any member of the public; or (b) directed at a specific person who can be considered a victim of hate speech, is, subject to subsection (3), guilty of an offence."

82 The Prevention and Combating of Hate Crimes and Hate Speech Bill 2016. "Communication" in terms of this Bill includes in sec 1(g) "electronic" communication". It also refers to "data" and "data message".

83 Act 4 of 2000.

84 *Afri-Forum v Malema* 2011 4 ALL SA 293 (EqC).

85 *ANC v Sparrow* [2016] ZAEQC 1.

Basic Law (the *Grundgesetz*), which focused on the fundamental rights of the individual as well as the obligation on the state to implement precise laws (for clarity purposes), so that citizens could know what was punishable and what was not. In 1953 an overall process to reform criminal law started with a government draft on criminal law in 1962. It became clear, however, that there was not enough political will for comprehensive codification, but smaller partial reforms could take place. Until 1975 five criminal-reform acts followed with an important part thereof, the decriminalisation of minor offences, the converting of some of them into regulatory offences and a large number deleted without substitution. Since the publication of the new Penal Code in 1975 another more than 70 amendments have followed, which gave the Penal Code a totally different character. As early as 1976 the first Act on the fight against commercial crime was promulgated, which was supported by a second Act, ten years later. Krehl summed up the changes:

> "The classical offences against property had proven insufficient; specific legal elements of economic subsidy fraud and credit fraud were introduced; they are mere endangerment offences, i.e. that no damage need be specified. The second Act on the fight against white-collar crime resulted in a further wave of determining new criminal offences, especially in the sectors of check transactions, computer-related crime and investment fraud." [86]

In 1986 the Criminal Code was amended once again to provide for a large number of information-technology crimes.

The Fight against Organised Crime Acts in 1992 and 1998 introduced money laundering and in 1997 the Fight Against Corruption Act was introduced.

Germany did not escape the developments of the last 20 years that resulted from a Europe growing ever closer together. The "internationalisation of crime" led to criminal law developing beyond national borders. Closer to home the "Europeanisation of criminal law" followed as a reaction to a changed Europe. Germany also had to get used to the framework decisions of the European Union, which would force all members to amend their national law, with the consequence of creating new offences. This tendency towards an increase in criminal law is, however, limited to some extent by

---

86 Krehl "Reforms of the German Criminal Code – stock-taking and perspectives – also from a constitutional point of view" 2003 *German Law Journal (GLJ)* 421 425. For a thorough report on the cybercrime offences in the Penal Code see Weisser *Cyber Crime – The Information Society and Related Crimes – National Report on Germany*, http://www.penal.org/sites/default/files/files/RM-8.pdf (13-01-2016).

guarantees from the Constitution and the Federal Constitutional Court. Examples of these are the requirements that criminal law must be clearly defined so that the citizens can be aware of the consequences. Countries may not retroactively make a specific conduct punishable.

2. Cybercrime in the Penal Code

Although a special code of cybercrimes does not exist in Germany, there are no less than 31 cyber offences specified in the Penal Code. Due to limited space, only a few of these offences will be quoted as examples. Although there is no formal definition of computer or electronic data in German criminal law, section 202a of the Penal Code places a restriction on data "stored or transmitted electronically or magnetically or otherwise in a manner not immediately perceivable".

The Penal Code therefor covers a large number of different actions that can be described as cyber-related offences. What follows is a list of these actions: dissemination of propaganda material of unconstitutional organisations;[87] using symbols of unconstitutional organisations;[88] encouraging the commission of a serious violent offence endangering the state;[89] public incitement to crime;[90] incitement to hatred;[91] attempting to cause the commission of offences by means of publication;[92] dissemination of depictions of violence;[93] child abuse;[94] distribution of pornography;[95] distribution of pornography depicting violence or sodomy;[96] distribution, acquisition and possession of child pornography;[97]distribution, acquisition and possession of juvenile pornography[98]; distribution of pornographic performances by

87 sec 86.
88 sec 86a.
89 sec 91.
90 sec 111.
91 sec 130.
92 sec 130a.
93 sec 131.
94 sec 176.
95 sec 184.
96 sec 184a.
97 sec 184b.
98 sec 184c.

broadcasting, media services or telecommunications services;[99] data espionage;[100] interception of data;[101] acts preparatory to data espionage and phishing;[102] violation of private secrets;[103] violation of the postal and communication secret;[104] stalking;[105] computer fraud;[106] obtaining services by deception;[107] forgery of data intended to provide proof;[108] meaning of deception in the context of data processing;[109] suppression of documents; changing a border mark;[110]organising unlawful gaming[111] and participation

---

99 sec 184d.

100 sec 202a.

101 sec 202b.

102 sec 202c: "(1) Whosoever prepares the commission of an offence under section 202a or section 202b by producing, acquiring for himself or another, selling, supplying to another, disseminating or making otherwise accessible 1. Passwords or other security codes enabling access to data (section 202a(2)), or 2. Software for the purpose of the commission of such an offence shall be liable to imprisonment not exceeding one year or a fine."

103 sec 203.

104 sec 206.

105 sec 238: "(1) Whosoever unlawfully stalks a person by 1. Seeking his proximity, 2. Trying to establish contact with him by means of telecommunications or other means of communication or through third persons, 3. Abusing his personal data for the purpose of ordering goods or services for him or causing third persons to make contact with him, 4. Threatening him or a person close to him with loss of life or limb, damage to health or deprivation of freedom, or 5. Committing similar acts and thereby seriously infringes his lifestyle shall be liable to imprisonment not exceeding three years or a fine."

106 sec 263a: "(1) Whosoever with the intent of obtaining for himself or a third person an unlawful material benefit damages the property of another by influencing the result of a data processing operation through incorrect configuration of a program, use of incorrect or incomplete data, unauthorised use of data or other unauthorised influence on the course of the processing shall be liable to imprisonment not exceeding five years or a fine."

107 sec 265a.

108 sec 269.

109 sec 270.

110 sec 274: "(1) Whosoever 1. Destroys, damages or suppresses a document or a technical record which does not belong to him or not exclusively to him with the intent of causing damage to another; 2. Deletes, suppresses, renders unusable or alters legally relevant data (section 202a(2)), which are not or not exclusively at his disposal, with the intent of causing damage to another; or 3. Takes away, destroys, renders unrecognisable, moves or falsely places a border stone or another sign intended as a designation of a border or water level with the intent of causing damage to another, shall be liable to imprisonment not exceeding five years or a fine."

111 sec 284.

in unlawful gaming;[112] organising an unlawful lottery etc;[113] data tampering;[114] computer sabotage;[115] disruption of telecommunications facilities;[116] breach of official secrets and special duties of confidentiality.[117]

The German legislator aims at amending existing regulations or incorporates new regulations to adapt the law to new developments in computer technology. An example of this was to make provision for hacking[118] (data espionage) and interception of data.[119] These provisions came into force in 2007 in order to comply with the regulations of the Cybercrime Convention (2001) and the European Framework Decision on Attacks Against Information Systems (2005).

Preparatory acts related to computer fraud are punishable where the offence does not require the unlawful access to a computer but covers even the mere preparation of such access.[120]

---

112 sec 285.

113 sec 287.

114 sec 303a: "(1) Whosoever unlawfully deletes, suppresses, renders unusable or alters data (section 202a (2)) shall be liable to imprisonment not exceeding two years or a fine. (2) The attempt shall be punishable."

115 sec 303b: "(1) Whosoever interferes with data processing operations which are of substantial importance to another by 1. Committing an offence under section 303a(1); or 2. Entering or transmitting data (section 202a(2)) with the intention of causing damage to another; or 3. Destroying, damaging, rendering unusable, removing or altering a data processing system or a data carrier, shall be liable to imprisonment not exceeding three years or a fine." It is not required that the damage must be financial.

116 sec 317.

117 sec 353b.

118 sec 202a: "(1) Whosoever unlawfully obtains data for himself or another that were not intended for him and were especially protected against unauthorised access, if he has circumvented the protection, shall be liable to imprisonment not exceeding three years or a fine.

119 sec 202b: "Whosoever unlawfully intercepts data (section 202a(2)) not intended for him, for himself or another by technical means from a non-public data processing facility or from the electromagnetic broadcast of a data processing facility, shall be liable to imprisonment not exceeding two years or a fine, unless the offence incurs a more severe penalty under other provisions."

120 sec 263a(3): "(3) Whosoever prepares an offence under subsection (1) above by writing computer programs the purpose of which is to commit such an act, or procures them for himself or another, offers them for sale, or holds or supplies them to another shall be liable to imprisonment not exceeding three years or a fine."

Forgery of documents under German law does not defend the public's interest in the truthfulness of the contents but focuses on the author's true or false identity.[121]

Although the Penal Code does not specifically criminalise the possession of a hacker's tools it is indirectly criminalised through sections that punish the unlawful acquisition of data. Identity theft is not defined and there is no specific offence covering "phishing". This, however does not mean that that it is not criminalised as criminal or administrative offences. The gathering of data by use of key loggers or Trojans is an offence.[122]

Almost all of the cybercrimes fall under a specific section[123] that requires intent. Intent in the most lenient form of *mens rea* in Germany means that the perpetrator at least must have recognised the risk and acted anyway knowing that the risk might be realised in an infringement. Some offences however require more than this lenient form of intent while in a few instances negligence is sufficient.[124]

More examples are: unauthorised exploitation of copyrighted work;[125] infringement of neighbouring rights;[126] and unlawful exploitation on a commercial basis.[127]

---

121 sec 269: "(1) Whosoever for the purposes of deception in legal commerce stores or modifies data intended to provide proof in such a way that a counterfeit or falsified document would be created upon their retrieval, or uses data stored or modified in such a manner, shall be liable to imprisonment not exceeding five years or a fine."

122 sec 202a (n 112) and 269 (n 115).

123 Sec 15 states: "Unless the law expressly provides for criminal liability based on negligence, only intentional conduct shall attract criminal liability".

124 Sec 317(3) is an example where telecommunications facilities can be disrupted in a negligent manner.

125 sec 106.

126 sec 108.

127 sec 108a.

VI. Cybercrime in the European Union

1. Historical overview

No specific date is known when the European Union first decided to address cybercrime issues.[128] The European Committee on Crime Problems, established under the auspices of the Council of Europe, considered the legal issues raised by computer crime in 1985. The final report was published in 1989 and listed eight cybercrimes.[129]

In an attempt to develop a legal framework to clarify rules and regulations related to service providers, the European Commission circulated a "Communication" on illegal and harmful content on the internet in the late 90's. In 1997 the European Council of Amsterdam requested that experts should conduct a study on the legal issues of cybercrime. The University of Würzburg in Germany was contracted to do the research and came up with a comprehensive report.[130] The European Commission then "issued in 2001 the first 'soft law' instrument to specifically tackle cybercrime: 'creating a safer information society by improving the security of information infrastructures and combating computer-related crimes'".[131]

2. Convention on Cybercrime, 2001

The need to standardise or harmonise criminal laws in Europe led to the adoption of the "Convention on Cybercrime" in Budapest in November 2001. It was signed by 34 of the 44 members of the Council of Europe. Amongst the non-members that were involved in the drafting process, were the United States, Japan, Canada and South Africa.

---

128 Buono "Gearing up the fight against cybercrime in the European Union: a new set of rules and the establishment of the European cybercrime centre" 2012 *New Journal of European Criminal Law (New J Eur Crim L)* 332 334.

129 Computer fraud; computer forgery; damage to computer data or computer programs; computer sabotage; unauthorised access; unauthorised interception; unauthorised reproduction of a computer program; unauthorised reproduction of a topography.

130 Sieber "Legal aspects of computer-related crime in the information society – com crime-study". The full report is available at: http://www.oas.org/juridico/english/COMCRIME%20Study.pdf (15-09-2017).

131 Buono (n 128) 335.

The Convention tackles substantive as well as procedural criminal law and the member states are obliged to implement these measures in their national law. The offences are discussed in three categories: firstly, offences against the confidentiality, integrity and availability of computer data and systems such as illegal access, illegal interception, data interference, systems interference and misuse of devices;[132] secondly, computer-related offences like forgery and fraud;[133] and thirdly, content-related offences like child pornography and infringements of copyright and related rights (articles 9–10).[134]

3. Developments since 2001

An additional protocol to the Convention was agreed to by member states "concerning the criminalisation of acts of a racist and xenophobic nature committed through computer systems" in 2003.

The Framework decision on attacks against information systems was adopted in 2005 and in 2007 the Commission adopted a further communication "towards a general strategy on the fight against cybercrime". In 2009 the "Stockholm programme" was endorsed by the European Council and in 2010 reflected in the European commission's action plan. This plan set out concrete implementing measures and actions, together with a timetable for their implementation.

A number of "Model laws on computer and computer related crimes" were also based on the Convention and subsequent "communications".[135] European countries indicated that they meant business with the addition of a cross-border element in 2009. Article 83(2) of the new Lisbon Treaty classified "computer crime" as a serious crime and put it in the same category as other severe crimes like terrorism, illicit drug trafficking, illicit arms trafficking, money laundering, corruption, counterfeiting of means of payment and organised crime.[136]

132 arts 2–6.
133 arts 7–8.
134 arts 9–10.
135 For an assessment of a number of these "model laws" see the "Discussion paper prepared for the Cybercrime Convention Committee" version 9 December 2014 at https://www.coe.int/t/dghl/cooperation/economiccrime/Source/Cybercrime/TCY/2014/3021_model_law_study_v15.pdf (10-02-2016).
136 Buono (n 128) 337.

The German Constitutional Court, in its judgment on the Lisbon Treaty, held that criminal law and criminal procedure touch the heart of sovereignty and democracy.[137] "Therefore, the 'corresponding foundations of competence in the treaties must be interpreted strictly – on no account extensively –, and their use requires particular justification'".[138] The court also re-emphasised the principle "that it will not review EU secondary law, as long as sufficient and 'essentially similar' protection of fundamental rights is guaranteed at the European level."[139]

Krehl[140] commented on the relationship between member states and the European Union:

> "European states will have to get used to framework decisions of the European Union which will force them to amend their national law and this will also result in the establishment of new offences, in an increase in the threatened measures of punishment, and in the expansion of the authorization to investigate. Whether this, as is feared by some, will go along with a strengthening of European, or certain national interests, or even with the traditions of a state governed by the rule of law being abandoned or undermined, will depend on how decision-making processes in the European framework will proceed in the future, particularly in an ever larger Europe. The Europeanization of criminal law will not become easier with the increasing number of national systems of criminal law that are to be considered in a new 'criminal law with a European character,' because criminal law often, and this becomes particularly evident in the relationship between freedom and security, has strong national traits that can originate in traditional persuasions and concepts of morality, but also in historical experience."

Asp[141] argues: "in spite of the improved legal framework provided by the Lisbon Treaty in relation to EU competences in criminal law, the EU still lacks a criminal law policy".[142] Bergström[143] aims to convince the reader that the express conferral of greater powers to the EU in the field of substantive criminal law has not necessarily restricted EU criminal law to

---

137 German Constitutional Court (Bundesverfassungsgericht, BVerfG) 23.6.2009 –2 BvE 2/08, 2 BvE 5/08, 2 BvR 1010/08, 2 BvR 1022/08, 2 BvR 1259/08, 2 BvR 182/09 – BVerfGE 123, 267 – Lisbon Treaty e.g. at paras 252 and 352. Referred to by Brodowski "Judicial cooperation between the EU and non-members" 2011 *New Journal of European Criminal Law (New J Eur Crim L)* 21 34.

138 Bergström and Cornell (eds) "European Police and Criminal Co-Operation" in Wahl and Cramér (eds) 5 (2014) *Swedish Studies In European Law* 34.

139 http://europeanlawblog.eu/?p=2448#sthash.pxNzmKMv.dpuf (15-09-2017).

140 Krehl (n 86) 429.

141 Bergström and Cornell (n 138) 59.

142 http://europeanlawblog.eu/?p=2448#sthash.pxNzmKMv.dpuf (15-09-2017).

143 Bergström and Cornell (n 138) in the last part of their book.

Chapter 4 of Title V of the Treaty of the Functioning of the European Union (TFEU).

The flagship initiative of the Europe 2020 strategy was the "Digital Agenda for Europe" with its seven pillars. One of these recognised the urgent requirement to speak to the rise of new types of crime, in particular, cybercrime at European level. "Europe must strengthen its policy to combat cybercrime, child pornography and breaches of privacy and personal data security."[144]

4. The European Union's "Area of Freedom, Security and Justice" (AFSJ)

The AFSJ is without a doubt one of the most dynamic EU integration areas. It focuses, amongst other things, on the need to fight financial crime across national borders. It followed up on the Lisbon Treaty and discusses the functioning of the European Union.[145]

Herlin-Karnell[146] states: "The EU has gained increased sanctioning powers that have empowered the EU with state-like features. For example, should a European public prosecutor be established (Article 86 TFEU), such a prosecutor would have far-reaching investigative powers in the area of financial crimes." The author further argues that the AFSJ should not be seen as isolated from the EU's general regulatory framework and one should look at all the policies holistically. The important question, however, is whether member states have the option to pull out of the, for example, antifraud rules. Sub articles 114 (4) and (5)[147] (TFEU) are extremely im-

144 http://eur-lex.europa.eu/legal-content/EN/TXT/?uri=URISERV%3Asi0016 (15-09-2017).

145 In Title V, Treaty of the Functioning of the European Union (TFEU).

146 Herlin-Karnell "Constructing Europe's Area of Freedom, Security and Justice through the framework of 'regulation': a cascade of market-based challenges in the EU's fight against financial crime." 2015 *German Law Journal (GLJ)* 49 51.

147 "4. If, after the adoption of a harmonisation measure by the European Parliament and the Council, by the Council or by the Commission, a Member State deems it necessary to maintain national provisions on grounds of major needs referred to in Article 36, or relating to the protection of the environment or the working environment, it shall notify the Commission of these provisions as well as the grounds for maintaining them. 5. Moreover, without prejudice to paragraph 4, if, after the adoption of a harmonisation measure by the European Parliament and the Council,

portant with respect to the impact on member states. It seems that this article, as well as article 325[148] (TFEU), would not grant member states the "cherry-pick" possibility to opt out[149] if a proposed measure appears to be too sensitive for their national criminal law system. The decision lies with the Commission (article 114 (6)). Contrary to this, it seems that according

---

by the Council or by the Commission, a Member State deems it necessary to introduce national provisions based on new scientific evidence relating to the protection of the environment or the working environment on grounds of a problem specific to that Member State arising after the adoption of the harmonisation measure, it shall notify the Commission of the envisaged provisions as well as the grounds for introducing them. 6. The Commission shall, within six months of the notifications as referred to in paragraphs 4 and 5, approve or reject the national provisions involved after having verified whether or not they are a means of arbitrary discrimination or a disguised restriction on trade between Member States and whether or not they shall constitute an obstacle to the functioning of the internal market."

148 "1. The Union and the Member States shall counter fraud and any other illegal activities affecting the financial interests of the Union through measures to be taken in accordance with this Article, which shall act as a deterrent and be such as to afford effective protection in the Member States, and in all the Union's institutions, bodies, offices and agencies. 2. Member States shall take the same measures to counter fraud affecting the financial interests of the Union as they take to counter fraud affecting their own financial interests. 3. Without prejudice to other provisions of the Treaties, the Member States shall coordinate their action aimed at protecting the financial interests of the Union against fraud. To this end they shall organise, together with the Commission, close and regular cooperation between the competent authorities. 4. The European Parliament and the Council, acting in accordance with the ordinary legislative procedure, after consulting the Court of Auditors, shall adopt the necessary measures in the fields of the prevention of and fight against fraud affecting the financial interests of the Union with a view to affording effective and equivalent protection in the Member States and in all the Union's institutions, bodies, offices and agencies."

149 For a comprehensive discussion on opting out or opting in see Herlin-Karnell "Denmark and the European Area of Freedom, Security and Justice: a Scandinavian arrangement" 2013 *Amsterdam Law Forum (Amsterdam LF)* 95.

to article 83(3)[150] (TFEU), as well as according to protocols 21[151] and 22[152] (AFSJ), the opt-out position is still available.

European cybercrime seems to be at the centre of the latest internet security developments. The European Commission issued a number of directives to ensure a high level of network security.[153] Recently an important proposed directive[154] on attacks against information systems was adopted and aims at getting to a cyber-security policy for the EU. At the same time the European cybercrime center was established by Europol on 11 January 2013 as part of Europol's mission to ensure a cybercrime-free European space.[155]

150 "3. Where a member of the Council considers that a draft directive as referred to in paragraph 1 or 2 would affect fundamental aspects of its criminal justice system, it may request that the draft directive be referred to the European Council. In that case, the ordinary legislative procedure shall be suspended. After discussion, and in case of a consensus, the European Council shall, within four months of this suspension, refer the draft back to the Council, which shall terminate the suspension of the ordinary legislative procedure."

151 Protocol 21 provides that decisions in these areas will not apply to the UK (the default position), but the UK, and separately Ireland, may choose, within three months of a proposal being presented to the Council pursuant to Title V, Part Three TFEU, whether it wishes to participate in the adoption and application of any such proposed measure.

152 "Protocol no 22 grants Denmark a special position by granting it the right to remain outside the project. This protocol means that Denmark participates in Schengen-related measures and Pre-Lisbon third pillar instruments on the basis of international law, which continues to be binding and applicable to Denmark as before, even if these acts are amended. Denmark may however notify the other Member States that it wishes to join the EU criminal law venture. This means that Denmark could decide to opt in to the whole 'thing' unlike the UK and Ireland that need to decide on opting in/or out with respect to each new criminal law measure. So Denmark is out unless it 'buys' the entire concept." Herlin-Karnell (n 149) 100–101.

153 Proposal for a Directive on Attacks Against Information Systems and Repealing Council Framework Decision 205/222/JHA, COM (2010) 517.

154 Directive 2013/40/EU on Attacks Against Information Systems and Repealing Council Framework Decision 2005/222/JHA.

155 Herlin-Karnell (n 146) 66.

VII. Comparative conclusion

From a South African perspective, comparative law has become a source of law.[156] It may offer assistance in the challenges that courts have to face in dealing with new issues. How should we deal with comparative law? Which systems should we compare and in what field of law? Zweigert and Kötz stated: "[i]ncomparables cannot usefully be compared, and in law the only things which are comparable are those which fulfill the same function".[157] The motivation for a comparison between South African and German criminal law is clear. These two systems have a shared Roman history that cannot be ignored. A number of criminal-law scholars included German law in their comparative studies,[158] indicating the influence of "modern" German law on South African law. Academic exchange through universities and funding organisations continue to promote comparative research.[159]

The other field of law that received some attention in this article is constitutional law (human rights). It is common knowledge that the German Basic Law (*Grundgesetz*) together with the American and Canadian constitutions had a huge influence on the South African Constitution. Exchanges between South African and German jurists on constitutional law were followed by a substantial number of references to German law by constitutional court judges, over the last 20 years.[160]

---

156 Sec 39(1) clearly states that foreign law may be considered: "When interpreting the Bill of Rights, a court, tribunal or forum— (a) must promote the values that underlie an open and democratic society based on human dignity, equality and freedom; (b) must consider international law; and (c) may consider foreign law."

157 Zweigert and Kötz *Introduction to Comparative Law* (1998) 34.

158 This was particularly important during the seventies and eighties, of the last century. Some of these scholars became prominent academics (Van der Merwe *Die Leerstuk van Verminderde Strafbaarheid* (1980 thesis SA) and Van Oosten *Oorsaaklikheid by Moord en Strafbare Manslag* (1981 thesis UP); some even became Constitutional Court judges (Van der Westhuizen *Noodtoestand as Regverdigingsgrond in die Strafreg* (1979 thesis UP)).

159 Rabie, Van der Merwe and Labuschagne "The contribution of the Alexander von Humboldt foundation to the development of the South African Legal system and literature" 1993 *Tydskrif vir Hedendaagse Romeins-Hollandse Reg (THRHR)* 608 622.

160 Rautenbach and Du Plessis "In the name of comparative constitutional jurisprudence: the consideration of German precedents by South African constitutional court judges" 2013 *German Law Journal (GLJ)* 1539; Venter "Why should the South African constitutional court consider German sources? Comment on Du Plessis and Rautenbach" 2013 *German Law Journal (GLJ)* 1579.

Due to the fact that the South African criminal law is not codified[161] we also need to compare common law crimes committed by way of computers and the internet to similar crimes in Germany. These crimes are closer to the similar crimes in Germany, compared to for instance the Anglo-American jurisdictions. I only have space for a few examples: the South African definition of fraud[162] can easily be compared to section 263[163] of the German Penal Code. The same can be said for South African theft[164] and German section 242.[165] The resemblance between forgery[166] in South Africa and section 267[167] in Germany is also obvious.

When we start comparing the more specific cybercrimes in the German Penal code to the proposed offences in the South African Cybercrime and Cybersecurity Bill it is clear that there are many similarities but also important differences.

Before the Cybercrime and Cybersecurity Bill came into existence, only a limited number of offences related specifically to cybercrime were created in a few acts. A larger number of offences specifically aimed at cybercrime had by that time already been in the German Penal Code. Is South Africa now moving closer to the German codification of these offences? I believe so, with some important differences.

According to the German Penal Code Germany did not amend "old offences", for example fraud, forgery and theft to make provision for situations where computers are used to commit these offences. They added them

---

161 Snyman *A Draft Criminal Code for South Africa* (1995) already proposed as early as in 1995 how South African criminal law can be codified, but nothing came from his proposal. For an argument that it is the legislature's responsibility to create offences where needed see De Villiers "Parlementêre voete-sleep en uitgediende misdaaddefinisies – is regterlike ingryping die oplossing?" 2007 *Tydskrif vir die Suid-Afrikaanse Reg (TSAR)* 769.

162 para II.1.

163 "(1) Whosoever with the intent of obtaining for himself or a third person an unlawful material benefit damages the property of another by causing or maintaining an error by pretending false facts or by distorting or suppressing true facts shall be liable to imprisonment not exceeding five years or a fine."

164 para II.2.

165 "(1) Whosoever takes chattels belonging to another away from another with the intention of unlawfully appropriating them for himself or a third person shall be liable to imprisonment not exceeding five years or a fine."

166 para II.3.

167 "(1) Whosoever for the purpose of deception in legal commerce produces a counterfeit document, falsifies a genuine document or uses a counterfeit or a falsified document, shall be liable to imprisonment not exceeding five years or a fine."

as new offences, for example where section 263 covers "fraud" and section 263a[168] covers "computer fraud". The Penal Code also makes provision for a number of other varieties of fraud[169] like subsidy fraud, capital investment fraud, insurance fraud, obtaining services by deception, obtaining credit by deception, embezzlement and abuse of trust, non-payment and misuse of wages and salaries and misuse of cheques and credit cards.

Although not to the same extent, the proposed Cybercrime and Cybersecurity Bill also added a number of new fraud-related offences. It is, however, important to note the difference in formulation between these offences and the comparable offences in the German Code. It seems that the authors of this Bill tried to cover as many scenarios as possible with the result that some of the offences may be extremely widely formulated and open to criticism.

Over the years the German Penal Code has done the same with forgery as with fraud, detailing 14 different forgery offences,[170] apart from the 9 counterfeiting offences.[171]

It seems that the Penal Code did not pay the same attention to theft or appropriation-related offences, detailing only 10 offences,[172] without specific mention of something like "computer-theft" or other interference with the intention to appropriate or tamper with data. An interesting added offence in section 248(c)[173] is the "theft of electricity" as a separate offence.

---

168 "(1) Whosoever with the intent of obtaining for himself or a third person an unlawful material benefit damages the property of another by influencing the result of a data processing operation through incorrect configuration of a program, use of incorrect or incomplete data, unauthorised use of data or other unauthorised influence on the course of the processing shall be liable to imprisonment not exceeding five years or a fine."

169 sec 264–266b.

170 sec 267–282.

171 sec 146–152b.

172 sec 242–248(c).

173 "(1) Whosoever taps the electrical energy of another from an electrical facility or installation by means of a conductor which is not intended for the regular withdrawal of energy from the facility or installation, shall, if the offence was committed with the intent of appropriating the electrical energy for himself or a third person, be liable to imprisonment not exceeding five years or a fine."

When comparing the jurisdiction provisions in the German Penal Code to the Cybercrime and Cybersecurity Bill provisions[174] there is a large number of similarities but the German provisions are even more detailed than the South African provision.[175]

On an international front it is obvious that Germany's relationship (as member state) with the European Union should be different from South Africa's situation (as non-member). It should, however, become more similar, once the Cybercrime and Cybersecurity Bill has been promulgated. This is due to the fact that it may then be possible for South Africa to ratify the Convention on Cybercrime 2001, when certain of the required undertakings can be given.

174 sec 2–9.

175 For example see sec 19(2) "If the act or omission alleged to constitute an offence under this Act occurred outside the Republic, a court of the Republic, regardless of whether or not the act or omission constitutes an offence at the place of its commission, has jurisdiction in respect of that offence if the person to be charged— (a) is a citizen of the Republic; (b) is ordinarily resident in the Republic; (c) was arrested in the territory of the Republic, or in its territorial waters or on board a ship or aircraft registered or required to be registered in the Republic at the time the offence was committed; (d) is a company, incorporated or registered as such under any law, in the Republic; or (e) any body of persons, corporate or unincorporated, in the Republic."

Bibliography

Bergström M and Cornell AJ (eds) *European Police and Criminal Co-Operation* in Wahl N and Cramér P (eds) 5 (2014) *Swedish Studies In European Law* (Hard Publishing, Oxford 2014).

Botha CR "Bedrog ten opsigte van die gebruik van tjek en/of kredietkaarte" 1 (1988) *South African Journal of Criminal Justice (SACJ)* 377.

Botha CR "Sogenaamde rekenaarbedrog" 3 (1990) *South African Journal of Criminal Justice (SACJ)* 231.

Buono L "Gearing up the fight against cybercrime in the European Union: a new set of rules and the establishment of the European cybercrime centre" 2012 *New Journal of European Criminal Law (New J Eur Crim L)* 332.

Burchell JM "Criminal justice at the crossroads" 2002 *South African Law Journal (SALJ)* 579.

Burchell JM *Principles of Criminal Law* (5th Edition, Juta Law, Claremont 2016).

Carstens P and Trichardt A "Computer crime by means of the automated teller-machine – just another face of fraud?" 1987 *South African Journal of Criminal Law and Criminology (SACC)* 132.

Coetzee JA "Diefstal van onliggaamlike sake" 1970 *Tydskrif vir Hedendaagse Romeins-Hollandse Reg (THRHR)* 369.

Credo PW and Michels JP *Computer Crime in South Africa* (Data Time 1985).

D'Oliviera JA "Theft of electricity: a short circuit? – *S v Ndebele* 2012 1 SACR 245 (GSJ)" 2012 *Tydskrif vir Hedendaagse Romeins-Hollandse Reg (THRHR)* 312.

De Villiers DS "Parlementêre voete-sleep en uitgediende misdaaddefinisies – is regterlike ingryping die oplossing?" 2007 *Tydskrif vir die Suid-Afrikaanse Reg (TSAR)* 769.

Ebersöhn GJ "A common law perspective on computer-related crimes" 2004 *Tydskrif vir Hedendaagse Romeins-Hollandse Reg (THRHR)* 22, 193 and 375.

Herlin-Karnell E "Constructing Europe's Area of Freedom, Security and Justice through the framework of 'regulation': a cascade of market-based challenges in the EU's fight against financial crime" 16 (2015) *German Law Journal (GLJ)* 49.

Herlin-Karnell E "Denmark and the European Area of Freedom, Security and Justice: a Scandinavian arrangement" 5 (2013) *Amsterdam Law Forum (Amsterdam LF)* 95.

Jordaan L "Theft – act of appropriation – electricity" 2012 *South African Journal of Criminal Justice (SACJ)* 316.

Krehl C "Reforms of the German Criminal Code – stock-taking and perspectives – also from a constitutional point of view" 4 (2003) *German Law Journal (GLJ)* 421.

Rabie A, Van der Merwe S and Labuschagne JMT "The contribution of the Alexander von Humboldt foundation to the development of the South African legal system and literature" 1993 *Tydskrif vir Hedendaagse Romeins-Hollandse Reg (THRHR)* 608.

Rautenbach C and Du Plessis L "In the name of comparative constitutional jurisprudence: the consideration of German precedents by South African constitutional court judges" 14 (2013) *German Law Journal (GLJ)* 1539.

Sieber U "Legal aspects of computer-related crime in the information society – com crime-study", http://www.oas.org/juridico/english/COMCRIME%20Study.pdf (08-12-2016).

Skeen AStQ "Computers and crime" 8 (1984) *South African Journal of Criminal Law and Criminology (SACC)* 262.

Snyman CR *A Draft Criminal Code for South Africa* (Juta Law, Cape Town 1995).

Snyman CR *Criminal Law* (6th Edition, LexisNexis, Durban 2014).

Van der Merwe DP (ed) *Information and Communications Technology Law* (LexiNexis, Durban 2008).

Van der Merwe DP "Computer crime – recent national and international developments" 66 (2003) *Tydskrif vir Hedendaagse Romeins-Hollandse Reg (THRHR)* 30.

Van der Merwe DP "Computer crime" 1983 *Obiter* 124.

Van der Merwe DP "Diefstal van onliggaamlike sake met spesifieke verwysing na rekenaars" 2 (1985) *South African Journal of Criminal Law and Criminology (SACC)* 129.

Van der Merwe DP "Information technology crime – a new paradigm is needed" 70 (2007) *Tydskrif vir Hedendaagse Romeins-Hollandse Reg (THRHR)* 309.

Van der Merwe DP *Computers and the Law* (2nd Edition, Juta Law, Cape Town 2000).

Van der Merwe DP *Die Leerstuk van Verminderde Strafbaarheid* (thesis University of South Africa 1980).

Van der Westhuizen JV *Noodtoestand as Regverdigingsgrond in die Strafreg* (thesis University of Pretoria 1979).

Van Oosten FFW *Oorsaaklikheid by Moord en Strafbare Manslag* (thesis University of Pretoria 1981).

Venter F "Why should the South African Constitutional Court consider German sources? Comment on Du Plessis and Rautenbach" 14 (2013) *German Law Journal (GLJ)* 1579.

Weisser B *Cyber Crime – The Information Society and Related Crimes – National Report on Germany* (2013) http://www.penal.org/sites/default/files/files/RM-8.pdf.

Zweigert K and Kötz H Introduction to Comparative Law (3rd Edition, Oxford University Press, Oxford 1998).

Case Law

South Africa

Bowden 1957 3 SA 148 (T)

Boesak 2000 1 SACR 633 (SCA)

Auby 2007 1 SACR 655 (W)

Agliotti 2011 2 SACR 437 (GSJ)

Chetty 2008 2 SACR 157 (W)

Coetzee 1997 3 SA 527 (CC)
Friedman 1996 1 SACR 181 (W)
Graham 1975 3 SA 569 (A)
Harper 1981 2 SA 638 (D)
MacDonald 1982 3 SA 220 (A)
Manamela 2000 1 SACR 414 (CC)
Mbokazi 1998 2 ALL SA 78 (N)
Mdantile 2011 2 SACR 142 (FB)
Mello 1999 2 SACR 255 (CC)
Mintoor 1996 1 SACR 514 (C)
Moolman 2006 1 SACR 432 (T)
Morgan 1993 2 SACR 134 (A)
Myeza 1985 4 SA 30 (T)
Ndebele 2012 1 SACR 245 (GSJ)
Nonkonyana 2008 2 SACR 271 (E)
Osman v Attorney-General, Transvaal 1998 2 SACR 493 (CC)
Prinsloo 1996 1 SACR 371 CC
Van den Berg 1991 1 SACR 104 (T)
Visagie 1991 1 SA 177 (A)

Germany

German Constitutional Court (BVerfG) 23.6.2009 – 2BvE 2/08, 2 BvE 5/08, 2 BvR 1010/08, 2 BvR 1022/08, 2 BvR 1259/08, 2 BvR 182/09 – BVerfGE 123, 267 *(Lisbon Treaty)*.

Legal and empirical aspects of cybercrime in Germany

*Johannes Kaspar**

I. Introduction

In my contribution, I want to address various legal and empirical aspects of "cybercrime" in Germany. First, it is necessary to clarify what is meant by that term. As yet, there exists no definition that has been agreed upon. What makes things more complicated is that different terms are used in this context – for example, "computer crime" instead of "cybercrime". According to Ulrich Sieber, one of the leading German experts in this field, computer crime is "any illegal, unethical or unauthorised behavior involving automatic data-processing and/or transmission of data"[1]. Cybercrime could then be defined as computer crime that involves the use of the Internet (or "cyberspace"). What is problematic with this approach, however, is the inclusion of "unethical" behaviour, which is a very broad and vague term that reaches beyond the scope of criminal law.

According to the Federal Report on Cybercrime by the German Ministry of the Interior, cybercrime includes all criminal acts which are directed against the Internet, against data networks, against systems of information

---

* Johannes Kaspar, *Dr. iur. habil.*; Professor, University of Augsburg, Faculty of Law. Chair for Criminal Law, Criminal Procedural Law, Criminology and Criminal Sanctions.

1 Ulrich Sieber, *The International Emergence of Criminal Information Law*, 5.

technology or their data or which are committed by making use of this technology.[2] This seems to be a useful and practical definition for the purpose of this paper.

II. Empirical aspects

Hitherto, cybercrime has not been a major subject of criminological research in Germany, so our empirical knowledge about this type of criminality is still rather limited. In a publication in 2006, I described cyberpiracy as a tough challenge for criminological research as it contains various interesting questions – but also methodological difficulties.[3] My colleague Bernd-Dieter Meier recently wrote about the lack of sufficient empirical research in this field and very convincingly emphasised the need for more activities in that area that could be summarised under the label "cybercriminology".[4]

Some information about this type of criminality can be attained from the above-mentioned Federal Report on Cybercrime (*Bundeslagebild*) that was issued by the Government in 2014. According to this report, in 2014 exactly 49,925 cybercrime offences were registered in the German Federal Crime Statistics (PKS) released by the Federal Criminal Police Office (BKA).[5]

---

2 Bundesministerium des Inneren (ed), *Bundeslagebild Cyber-Delinquenz*, 2014.

3 Johannes Kaspar, *Kriminalistik* 2006, 42.

4 Bernd-Dieter Meier, 'Kriminologie und Internet: ein ungeklärtes Verhältnis' in Susanne Beck, Bernd-Dieter Meier and Carsten Momsen (eds), *Cybercrime und Cyberinvestigations* (2015), 93 (115).

5 See Bundesministerium des Inneren (ed), *Bundeslagebild Cyber-Delinquenz* (2014).

As the following diagram shows, we can distinguish between some major types of criminality, computer fraud being the most common offence with a share of 45 %.

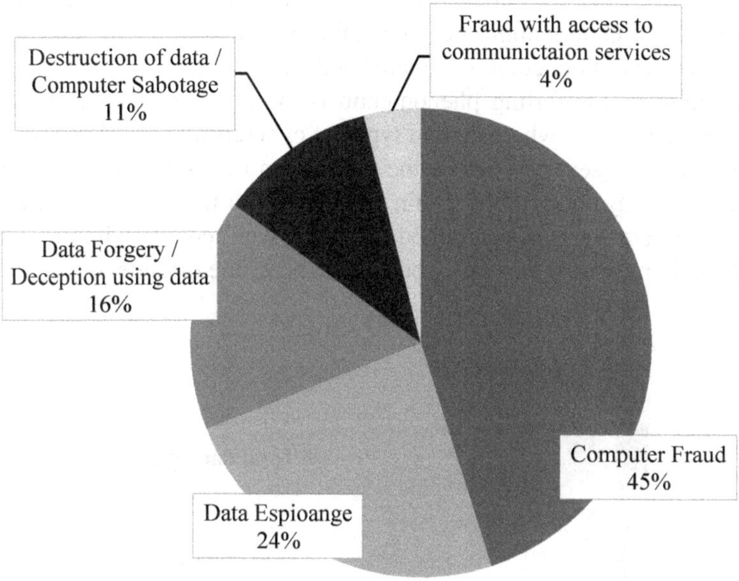

Figure 1 Distribution of types of delinquency[6]

The estimated cost of computer fraud and fraud through access to communication devices alone was 39.4 Mio. Euro.

In 2014, 246,925 offences were committed by making use of the Internet. Of these, 180,826 (74.2%) were cases of fraud, mostly cases of ordering certain goods via the Internet without the intention or ability to pay for them.

Especially with regard to cybercrime, it is a fair assumption that a huge number of offences remain undetected, or at least unreported. We therefore must acknowledge that official statistics probably only show the tip of the iceberg and that a huge "dark area" of cybercrime exists. A study in the State of Lower-Saxony in 2013 estimated that about 91% of cybercrime

6 Bundesministerium des Inneren (ed), *Bundeslagebild Cyber-Delinquenz* (2014), 4.

cases go unreported.[7] There are various reasons for this feature of cybercrime. It is very likely that a large number of cases will remain as attempts, and potential victims will therefore not report these cases to the police as they suffered neither personal harm nor material damage. In many other cases, the offenders might be successful but the crime (e.g. some type of computer fraud) nonetheless remains undetected.

A quite discomforting phenomenon is the development of an "underground economy", where certain types of cybercrime are offered as illegal services. Such services can be the production or distribution of malware, services to stay anonymous within the Internet, or the sale of important and sensitive data such as access codes. In this way, people without in-depth technical know-how can easily become cybercrime offenders.

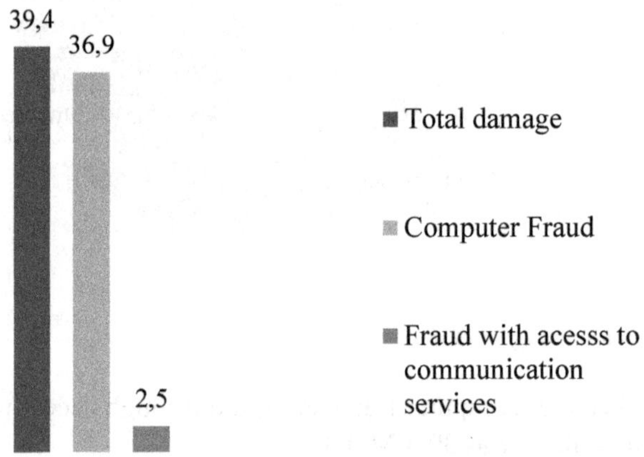

Figure 2 Damage (in Mio. Euro)[8]

A special type of cybercrime is digital identity theft. This includes all possibilities and rights of the single user and his/her personal data and activities within the whole structure of the Internet. Important targets by offenders are all kinds of user accounts, access codes and other information that is important for financial transactions within the Internet. Some examples show the potential danger of this kind of crime: in March 2014, the Public

7 Bundesministerium des Inneren (ed), *Bundeslagebild Cyber-Delinquenz* (2014), 5.

8 Bundesministerium des Inneren (ed), *Bundeslagebild Cyber-Delinquenz* (2014), 4.

Attorney's Office in Verden reported a theft of 16 million e-mail addresses; also in 2014, unknown offenders gained access to a data bank of eBay with 145 million individuals' data sets.[9]

The major motivation for cybercrime offenders seems to be financial gain. By making use of the above-mentioned underground economy with its exchange of know-how and security gaps, offenders can react to new developments quickly and flexibly. Taking a look at group structures, we can see that organised crime seems to have increased in this area. Whereas in 2013 only six organised crime groups were reported, this number doubled in 2014.

III. Cybersecurity and measures of criminal policy

In recent years, cybersecurity has become a much-debated political issue, not least with respect to measures of criminal policy. It is widely agreed that in order to guarantee security within cyberspace, the national states must not only take active measures within their borders but also take part in transnational cooperation, not only within the EU but also worldwide.

The German Ministry of the Interior proposed a report on its "Cybercrime Strategy" in 2011. It states that due to the globalisation of information and communication processes, international coordination of apt measures is essential for reasons of foreign and security policy.[10] In this context, the Ministry not only mentions the United Nations, the EU, the OSCE and other multinational organisations, but also the G8 and even NATO. This shows the strong focus not only on criminal law, but also on matters of foreign or military policy.

With respect to domestic measures, the Ministry mentions two main strategic aims and measures.[11] The first is the introduction of a National Cyberdefence Centre, which started work in 2011. It seeks to optimise cooperation among state agencies in this area and to coordinate all measures of protection and defence against information technology (IT) incidents. Among the institutions and agencies that are named here, we can find the

9 Bundesministerium des Inneren (ed), *Bundeslagebild Cyber-Delinquenz* (2014), 7.

10 Bundesministerium des Inneren (ed), *Cyber-Sicherheitsstrategie für Deutschland* (2011).

11 Bundesministerium des Inneren (ed), *Cyber-Sicherheitsstrategie für Deutschland* (2011).

Federal Criminal Police Office (*Bundeskriminalamt*) as well as military institutions such as the Bundeswehr and the German Intelligence Service (*Bundesnachrichtendienst*).

The second objective set out by the Ministry is the general aim of a stronger and more effective fight against cybercrime. We can find quite vague considerations here, for example the idea that law enforcement agencies should be "strengthened" in their abilities to combat cybercrime (including espionage and sabotage). The exchange of technical know-how should be supported by creating joint ventures with private enterprises.[12] With respect to legal matters, the Ministry proposes a worldwide harmonisation of cybercrime regulations based on the Cybercrime Convention by the European Council[13] mentioned by Mr De Villiers in his contribution. The Ministry also suggests a need for new conventions on cybercrime on the level of the United Nations.

This last point is in relation to criticism against the Cybercrime Convention by some scholars in Germany. They acknowledge that the Convention has served as a useful basis for legislative measures, with a potential influence even beyond the limits of the EU. [14] Mr De Villiers' presentation on this symposium has shown that quite well. Nevertheless, they criticise the Convention, which was introduced in 2001, as a rather old instrument that cannot easily be adapted to new social and technical developments.[15]

IV. Cybercrime in substantive criminal law

Finally, I want to address the role that substantive criminal law might play with regard to cybercrime. The German way of dealing with cybercrime within substantive criminal law has been to create a considerable number of new offences that were introduced step by step into the German Penal Code.

---

12 See also Bundesministerium des Inneren (ed), *Bundeslagebild Cyber-Delinquenz* (2014), 14.

13 The Cybercrime Convention was ratified on 8 November 2001 by the Ministerial Committee of the European Council; for details regarding the signing and ratification, see http://www.coe.int/de/web/conventions/search-on-treaties/-/conventions/treaty/ 185/signatures?p_auth=zD9YQerZ (15-09-2017).

14 Susanne Reindl-Krauskopf, *Zeitschrift für ausländisches öffentliches Recht und Völkerrecht (ZaöRV)* 2014, 563 (566).

15 Susanne Reindl-Krauskopf, *Zeitschrift für ausländisches öffentliches Recht und Völkerrecht (ZaöRV)* 2014, 563 (566 et seq.).

This development started in 1986 when in the course of the First Act to Fight Economic Crime, besides other new provisions the offence of computer fraud (section 263a) was introduced into the German Penal Code. The most recent step was the introduction of section 202d Penal Code in 2015, where data fencing (*Datenhehlerei*) was regulated. It has become a criminal act to buy (or simply acquire) data that has been illegally obtained.

It is true that in the 1980s there existed a clear gap in criminal liability as computers slowly became part of our lives. And this gap is also an important difference in the South African legal situation, where the common law, as Mr De Villiers has shown in his contribution, made it possible to view computer fraud as classic fraud and data theft as classic theft. In Germany, due to the wording of the provisions on fraud and theft, the same was not possible. In terms of fraud, section 263 German Penal Code requires the deception of a human being, so entering false information into a computer system does not fall under this provision. Theft (as per section 242 German Penal Code) only refers to corporeal items, so data (as well as electricity) cannot be an object of classical theft.

Therefore the fact that new regulations were introduced has not attracted criticism, but what has caused problems is the content of these regulations and also the nature of the legislation.[16] In the past the legislature followed the strategy (if we may call it that) of "matching" new cybercrime offences with classic offences, as the example of computer fraud clearly shows.

The new provision on computer fraud was deliberately inserted after the regular offence of fraud in section 263 Penal Code; the structure of both offences is very similar, and they proscribe the same punishment. It is understandable that the legislature makes use of "known" patterns when creating new offences. However, this has also caused problems with the interpretation of computer fraud, as it is – clearly – a different matter if someone tries to deceive a human being or a computer. Whether we interpret computer fraud as simply another type of fraud or whether we should attempt to view it as a very specific computer-related crime remains a topic of debate among German criminal law scholars.[17]

Another example of a problematic "matching" is the provision of section 303a Penal which inhibits the damaging or destruction of data. Its systematic positioning within the Penal Code is right behind the classic damaging

16 For valuable insights in this matter I have to thank my dear colleague Prof. Dr. Tobias Reinbacher (University of Wuerzburg).

17 See, for example, Thomas Fischer, *Strafgesetzbuch* (64th Edition, 2017), § 263a para. 10 et seq.

of corporeal items in section 303 (*Sachbeschädigung*) and, again, the level of punishment is the same. Also in this respect, the question is whether the legislature has neglected the specific features of cybercrime, in this case the very different nature of "data" (being coded information, not a tangible good). If a certain item is destroyed, it is lost forever, and the harm to the owner is clear. If data are destroyed, it might not be a serious matter for the owner if he/she has a copy of such data. I would not doubt that destroying data can be very harmful in some cases and should be a legitimate criminal offence. However, in the light of the principles of equality and proportionality, the same degree of punishment proscribed in sections 303 and 303a seems problematic.

The question to what extent "data" are legitimate legal goods protected by criminal law also arises in the context of section 202a, where data espionage is regulated. All kinds of data are protected in this provision, no matter how important they are in an objective sense. It is sufficient if the owner has installed some form of security mechanism. So if I write down a list of my favourite cooking recipes, save this document on a USB stick and secure this USB stick with an access code, it would be a crime to circumvent this code and take the data (even though the information itself is clearly of no objective worth). This is not only a question of potential over-criminalisation, but also has the strange element that the victim him- or herself can somehow determine the extent of criminal liability simply by adding a security mechanism to otherwise meaningless information not necessarily worthy of protection.[18]

Another very controversial topic is the question whether (or at least to what extent) preparatory acts that take place before an actual violation of legal goods can be punished, as is the case pursuant to section 202c of the German Penal Code. In this provision, mere possession of computer programs that might be used for committing a computer-related crime in the future is deemed a criminal act. Again, there are criticisms in terms of over-criminalisation or, to put it in terms of constitutional law, of unproportionality.[19]

---

18 This problem arises especially in the area of section 202d (Data Fencing), where not even a security mechanism is needed, see Tobias Reinbacher in Werner Leitner and Henning Rosenau (eds), *Wirtschafts- und Steuerstrafrecht* (2017), § 202d para. 3.

19 For the role of the principle of proportionality in substantive criminal law, see Kaspar, *Verhältnismäßigkeit und Grundrechtsschutz im Präventionsstrafrecht* (2014).

To summarise, a problem with German law is that we do have a variety of provisions throughout the Penal Code that seem in some cases too wide and/or too closely connected with ordinary "analogous" crime. We cannot see a clear concept in this area, and general questions relating to the definition of data or the range of legitimate protection remain unanswered.

It would perhaps be better to introduce a coherent and comprehensive new cybercrime Act combining these offences, or at least creating a specific cybercrime section within the Penal Code where also these general questions could be solved. It will be interesting to learn from the experiences in South Africa with its new Cyber Crime Act.

Bibliography

Thomas Fischer, *Strafgesetzbuch* (64th Edition, C.H. Beck, Munich 2017).

Bernd-Dieter Meier, "Kriminologie und Internet: ein ungeklärtes Verhältnis", in Susanne Beck, Bernd-Dieter Meier and Carsten Momsen (eds), *Cybercrime und Cyberinvestigations* (Nomos, Baden-Baden 2015), 93.

Bundesministerium des Inneren (ed), *Cyber-Sicherheitsstrategie für Deutschland* (2011).

Bundesministerium des Inneren (ed), *Bundeslagebild Cyber-Delinquenz* (2014).

Johannes Kaspar, "Cyber-Piraterie als Herausforderung für die kriminologische Forschung", *Kriminalistik* 2006, 42.

Johannes Kaspar, *Grundrechtsschutz und Verhältnismäßigkeit im Präventionsstrafrecht* (Nomos, Baden-Baden 2014).

Werner Leitner and Henning Rosenau (eds), *Wirtschafts- und Steuerstrafrecht*, Commentary (Nomos, Baden-Baden 2017).

Susanne Reindl-Krauskopf, "Cyber-Kriminalität", *Zeitschrift für ausländisches öffentliches Recht und Völkerrecht (ZaöRV)* 2014, 563.

Ulrich Sieber, *The International Emergence of Criminal Information Law* (Carl-Heymanns Verlag, Cologne 1992).

Public participation and reasonableness: exploring the case law and jurisprudential philosophy of the South African Constitutional Court

*David Bilchitz**
*Siyambonga Heleba***

* Professor, Fundamental Rights and Constitutional Law, University of Johannesburg; Director, South African Institute for Advanced Constitutional, Public, Human Rights and International Law; Secretary-General, International Association of Constitutional Law.

** Lecturer, University of Johannesburg, Faculty of Law; Research Associate, South African Institute for Advanced Constitutional, Public, Human Rights and International Law.

I. Introduction

Shaping the nature of South African democracy is a work in progress. The 1993 Interim Constitution ushered in, for the first time, a situation where all adult citizens within the territory of South Africa could vote in a unified polity, after almost a century of minority rule. The establishment of a representative democracy alone thus brought about a major change in the political system.

The Constitutional Court has, however, found that the 1996 Constitution was more ambitious than this. Section 1 which lays out the founding values of the constitutional order includes "[u]niversal adult suffrage, a national common voters' roll, regular elections and a multi-party system of democratic government, to ensure accountability, responsiveness and openness". Section 59 of the Constitution includes a provision that the National Assembly must "facilitate public involvement in the legislative and other processes of the Assembly and its committees". These provisions (and others) have led the Constitutional Court to find a deep principle of participatory democracy in the South African Constitution. Justice Ngcobo, writing for the majority in the landmark case of *Doctors for Life,* expresses the point as follows:

> "[O]ur democracy includes as one of its basic and fundamental principles, the principle of participatory democracy. The democratic government that is contemplated is partly representative and partly participatory, is accountable, responsive and transparent and makes provision for public participation in the law-making processes. Parliament must therefore function in accordance with the principles of our participatory democracy." [1]

This paper seeks to chart the contours of this principle of participatory democracy as it has been developed in the South African courts. There is, we argue, an interesting similarity between the jurisprudence that has developed in three distinct areas which we seek to address in the first part of the paper. First, we consider the context of the parliamentary process, the most obvious instance of law-making which was addressed in the *Doctors for Life* case referred to above and a series of later cases dealing with cross-border municipalities. Secondly, we turn to situations where the government wishes to evict people from their homes, and thus, seriously to impact upon their right to have access to adequate housing. In these circumstances,

1 *Doctors for Life International v Speaker of the National Assembly* 2006 12 BCLR 1399 (CC); 2006 6 SA 416 (CC) para 115 (*Doctors for Life*).

the Constitutional Court has held that the government agency wishing to evict has to engage in a meaningful manner with the individuals or community it is seeking to evict prior to doing so for such an eviction to be lawful.[2] Finally, we consider public participation within the context of administrative law as well as the related doctrine of legality. In this context, participatory requirements are addressed through the notion of procedural fairness.

In each of these areas of the law, the court has held that public participation is an essential component for the validity of legal action in this area. It has, moreover, not simply accepted that the public participation component can be satisfied as a purely formal matter: the court has suggested that it will review the actions taken by the government according to whether they meet substantive standards. The notion of "reasonableness" has been utilised very extensively by the court as the standard of review in this context: in some cases, this has led to a substantive approach being adopted whilst in others a very formalistic approach has been followed.

Having outlined the similarities in these disparate areas of the law in the jurisprudence of the Constitutional Court, we provide in the second part of this paper an account of the deeper theory animating the court in this area. The two key prongs of the court's jurisprudence are the emphasis on participation as well as reasonableness which are rooted in the foundational values of the Constitution related to democratic governance. What unites these two facets of the court's jurisprudence? We draw upon literature on the philosophical underpinnings of procedural justice, to argue that there are three important foundations for the importance of public participation in these contexts: these include an instrumentalist rationale, a dignitarian rationale and a relational rationale. We demonstrate that each of these rationales finds expression in the jurisprudence of the court and provides a particular understanding of the relationship between public participation and reasonableness. In the conclusion, we consider the implications of these deeper jurisprudential substantive rationales for the jurisprudence of the court in each of these three areas. We contend, ultimately, that the procedural innovations of the court should recognise public participation as a component of the doctrine of legality and that the reasonableness standard of review should be constructed in a substantive manner with reference to the underlying values animating the jurisprudence in these areas.

---

2 See, for example, Liebenberg "Engaging the paradoxes of the universal and the particular in human rights adjudication: the possibilities and pitfalls of 'meaningful engagement'" 12 (2012) *African Human Rights Journal (AHRLJ)* 1 4.

II. Public participation and the jurisprudence of the Constitutional Court

As we noted in the introduction, public participation has become of seminal importance in different fields of South African public law. In this section, we seek to investigate three disparate areas where the Constitutional Court has found there to be a requirement of public participation, the review standards that have been articulated, and the legal basis for the court's findings. We also briefly consider the evolution of legal doctrine in these three areas.

1. Participation in parliamentary legislative processes

In *Doctors For Life,*[3] the applicants argued that parliament failed to fulfil its constitutional obligation to facilitate public involvement in the process it adopted when it passed four bills. This was the first opportunity the court had to pronounce on the meaning and content of sections 59(1)*(a)*,[4] 72(1)*(a)*[5] and 118(1)*(a)*[6] of the Constitution, all of which deal with public involvement in the legislative process. The case has become a seminal one in which the majority of the judges outline the basis and scope of the duty of legislatures to facilitate public participation in the legislative process.

Justice Ngcobo, writing for the majority, first engaged with the international context and dealt at length with the nature and scope of the right to political participation that had been developing under international law.[7] The right to public participation under international law, the court finds, provides recognition for the key idea that citizens are sovereign in a political community which is expressed through participation in governmental processes.[8] Ngcobo J then engages the local context rooting public participation in traditional understandings of governance in South African society:

3 *Doctors for Life* (n 1).

4 This section places an obligation on the National Assembly to facilitate public involvement in its legislative processes. It stipulates that the National Assembly must "facilitate public involvement in the legislative and other processes of the Assembly and its committees…"

5 The section places an identical obligation as sec 59(1)*(a)* on the National Council of Provinces.

6 Again an identical obligation as secs 59(1)*(a)* and 72(1)*(a)* is placed by this section on the provincial legislatures.

7 See *Doctors for Life* (n 1) paras 95–129.

8 *Doctors for Life* (n 1) para 110.

> "The idea of allowing the public to participate in the conduct of public affairs is not a new concept. In this country, the traditional means of public participation is imbizo/lekgotla/bosberaad. This is a participatory consultation process that was, and still is, followed within the African communities. It is used as a forum to discuss issues affecting the community. This traditional method of public participation, a tradition which is widely used by the government, is both a practical and symbolic part of our democratic processes. It is a form of participatory democracy."[9]

Of course, this argument needs a constitutional foundation. Ngcobo J thus turns to section 1 of the Constitution which includes reference to the creation of "a multi-party system of democratic government, to ensure accountability, responsiveness and openness". From these words, Justice Ngcobo infers the following: "[c]ommitment to principles of accountability, responsiveness and openness shows that our constitutional democracy is not only representative but also contains participatory elements".[10] The specific provisions requiring legislatures at both the national and provincial levels to facilitate public involvement supported this conclusion.[11] The court further seeks to clarify that the "representative and participatory elements of South Africa's democracy should not be seen as being in tension with each other. They must be seen as mutually supportive. General elections, the foundation of representative democracy, would be meaningless without massive participation by the voters."[12] The court thus concludes that one of the foundational principles of the South African Constitution is a principle of participatory democracy.[13]

Having laid the basis for this idea, the majority of the court then proceeds to consider the practical scope of the duty to facilitate public involvement. It recognises that it was not the court's role to dictate to an elected branch of government what methods to use to meet its constitutional obligation to facilitate public participation in its legislative processes. At the same time, the court could not abdicate its role to exercise scrutiny concerning whether the legislatures had met their constitutional duties in this regard. In giving effect to these dual imperatives, the majority of the court settles on the standard of reasonableness for assessing the actions of legislatures in this

---

9 *Doctors for Life* (n 1) para 101.

10 *Doctors for Life* (n 1) para 111.

11 See sections 59, 72 and 118 of the Constitution.

12 *Doctors for Life* (n 1) para 115. This was largely in response to a dissenting judgment by Yacoob J holding that a complaint of this kind was not suitable for judicial intervention as the solution for the aggrieved communities lay in the electoral booth.

13 *Doctors for Life* (n 1) para 116.

area. This standard is not explicit in the Constitution as a basis for evaluating all legislative action in this area. The court derives the standard from its usage in other contexts which it regards as similar (such as in relation to social and economic rights) as well as from specific provisions relating to public participation (such as the duty on the legislature to take reasonable measures to regulate public access to it in section 72(1)*(b)*).[14] The court recognises that reasonableness is an objective standard but also one that is sensitive to the context of particular matters. In giving effect to reasonableness the court states the following:

> "Whether a legislature has acted reasonably in discharging its duty to facilitate public involvement will depend on a number of factors. The nature and importance of the legislation and the intensity of its impact on the public are especially relevant. Reasonableness also requires that appropriate account be paid to practicalities such as time and expense, which relate to the efficiency of the law-making process. Yet the saving of money and time in itself does not justify inadequate opportunities for public involvement. In addition, in evaluating the reasonableness of Parliament's conduct, this Court will have regard to what Parliament itself considered to be appropriate public involvement in the light of the legislation's content, importance and urgency. Indeed, this Court will pay particular attention to what Parliament considers to be appropriate public involvement".[15]

Having laid out the standard of reasonableness, the court goes further to specify two elements of the obligation to facilitate public involvement (which if not complied with, would not meet the standard of reasonableness). The first element is the "duty to provide meaningful opportunities for public involvement in the law-making process".[16] The second element is the parliament's "duty to take measures to ensure that the people have the ability to take up the opportunities provided".[17] In assessing whether participation was meaningful, a court must consider the time and place arranged for public hearings, for example, and ultimately whether the people had an opportunity to influence the legislative decision.[18] In this case, the Court found that parliament had failed to comply with its constitutional obligation

14 *Doctors for Life* (n 1) para 126. The minority opinion written by Justice Yacoob takes issue with the generality of the majority's findings and finds no general principle of participatory democracy nor a general constitutional basis for reasonableness review of the measures taken by parliament to facilitate public involvement (see paras 246, 249, 313–339).

15 *Doctors for Life* (n 1) para 128.

16 *Doctors for Life* (n 1) para 129.

17 See *Doctors for Life* (n 1) para 129.

18 *Doctors for Life* (n 1) para 171.

to facilitate public involvement in passing some[19] of the bills that were challenged and dismissed the constitutional attack with respect to the others.[20] The majority of the court took the momentous step of declaring legislation invalid that had not adequately involved the public though it suspended the order of invalidity for 18 months in order to enable parliament to enact these statutes in a manner that complied with their constitutional obligations.

Ngcobo J's reasoning in *Doctors for Life* is instructive. It interprets the Constitution to find a principle of participatory democracy and then, on the basis of this foundation, finds that it is duty-bound to review measures taken by parliament for their reasonableness. It also provides some concrete guidance concerning the scope of the obligations upon the legislature. Raboshakga, for instance, has argued that the court here articulates a form of substantive reasonableness which is rooted in a deep vision of democracy in the Constitution[21] and has a set of minimum standards associated with it. As such, it avoids some of the critiques levelled at reasonableness in other settings surrounding its vagueness and lack of content.[22]

Following on the heels of the court's groundbreaking decision in *Doctors for Life* was the *Matatiele* case.[23] Unlike *Doctors for Life*, *Matatiele* marked the beginning of a series of "cross-boundary-municipalities" cases challenging legislative attempts to bring to an end the phenomenon of local municipalities straddling the boundaries of two provinces. The livelihoods as well as the identities, among other things, of the communities who were to be moved from one province into another, were affected by these changes. At issue was also the fact that certain provinces were understood to be governed better than others. In *Matatiele*, the applicants challenged the validity

19 These were the Choice on Termination of Pregnancy Act of 2004 and the Traditional Health Practitioners' Act of 2004.

20 The Dental Technicians Amendment Act of 2004 and the Sterilisation Amendment Act of 2005.

21 Raboshakga "Towards participatory democracy, or not: the reasonableness approach in public involvement cases" 15 (2015) *South African Journal of Human Rights (SAJHR)* 4 20.

22 See the excellent account of Roux "Democracy" in Woolman et al (eds) *Constitutional Law of South Africa* (2nd Edition 2014) vol 1 ch 10 at 63–77 who attempts to formulate the principle that has inspired Raboshakga (n 21) 20. On various models of democracy see among others Held *Models of Democracy* (2nd Edition 1996), Polity press.

23 *Matatiele Municipality v President of the Republic of South Africa (2)* 2007 1 BCLR 47 (CC).

of the Constitution Twelfth Amendment Act[24] and the Cross-boundary Municipalities Repeal and Related Matters Act[25]. The effect of these amendments was to alter the boundaries of the Matatiele municipality and to transfer it from being part of the province of KwaZulu-Natal to being wholly part of the province of the Eastern Cape. The court held that a provincial legislature whose provincial boundary is being altered is required by the Constitution to approve such alteration.[26] Without such approval, the provincial boundary cannot be altered. The court held that, when a provincial legislature makes a decision of this nature, it is clearly involved in a law-making process, and it must therefore, in terms of the Constitution, facilitate public participation in making its decision.[27] Also noteworthy in the judgment were the remarks by the court on the impact the proposed law would have on the affected communities. The court stated that the proposed constitutional amendment

> "would have had the effect of relocating a whole community from one province to another province. Moreover, it had a direct impact on a discreet and identifiable section of the population, the people of Matatiele. It threatened an important and not easily reversible change to the provincial status of a clearly defined section of the population. The consequences of the amendment are of considerable symbolic and practical importance, affecting the identity of the people to be transferred and changing the structures and personnel responsible for welfare payments, health services and education."[28]

The court approved its earlier decision in *Doctors for Life* and raised the question whether the measures taken by the legislatures in question were reasonable? In this case, the Eastern Cape legislature invited submissions and held public hearings on the Acts, and as such, according to the court, acted reasonably in the circumstances. The same could not be said of its counter-part in KwaZulu-Natal as no written submissions were invited on the legislation at issue, nor were public hearings held. As a consequence, KwaZulu-Natal failed to comply with its obligation to facilitate public involvement when approving the two pieces of legislation as required by section 118(1)*(a)* of the Constitution.[29]

---

24 of 2005 (Twelfth Amendment Act).
25 23 of 2005 (Repeal Act).
26 See *Matatiele* (n 23) paras 43–45.
27 *Matatiele* (n 23) para 45.
28 *Matatiele* (n 23) para 81.
29 See *Matatiele* (n 23) paras 78 and 114.

The Matatiele decision follows closely the precedent set in *Doctors for the Life* and the reasoning of the Court was often substantive in having reference to the values of the Constitution and the nature of South African democracy outlined therein. At the same time, it was not clear from the Court's holding how substantive its test of reasonableness would be given that the Kwazulu-Natal legislature had failed completely to provide opportunities for public participation. The court rather lightly scrutinized the efforts of the Eastern Cape legislature. Unfortunately, as is persuasively argued by Raboshakga, the next sequence of cross-boundary municipality cases followed on the tendency in relation to the Eastern Cape legislative process with the Court adopting a "compliance- or process-oriented reasonableness enquiry", where no more will be required than that written submission be invited or that a public hearing be held.[30] In *Merafong,*[31] the provincial legislature in Gauteng had held public hearings but represented to the communities in question that it would vote to keep their municipality within its boundaries. During the national legislative process, it changed its position to allow the municipality to be placed within the boundaries of the North-west province without engaging further with the community. A majority of the court this time held it was sufficient that the community had in the past "had a proper opportunity to air their views".[32]

Poverty Alleviation Network[33] then followed. It once again dealt with the transfer of the Matatiele municipality from KwaZulu-Natal to the Eastern Cape. The applicants argued that the decision to relocate the province had been determined by the party in advance and that the public participation process had simply been conducted for formal compliance but there was no openness on the part of representatives to be persuaded by their submissions. The court refused to consider the motives of legislators and dismissed the case. Once again, the decision here fails to engage with the meaningfulness of the process or to require reasons why the legislators chose to ignore the representations that were made to them.[34]

---

30 Raboshakga (n 21) 28–29.

31 *Merafong Demarcation Forum v President of the Republic of South Africa* 2008 10 BCLR 968 (CC).

32 *Merafong* (n 31) paras 53 and 59.

33 *Poverty Alleviation Network v President of the Republic of South Africa* 2010 6 BCLR 520 (CC).

34 See Bishop "Vampire or prince? The listening constitution and Merafong Demarcation Forum and others 2 (2009) *Constitutional Court Review (CCR)* 313 345.

The last case in the series of the cases challenging the alteration of provincial boundaries is *Moutse*.[35] The applicants contended, among other things, that the provincial legislature had not complied with its obligation to take reasonable measures in facilitating public involvement in the passing of the proposed legislation because, among other things, the report of the Portfolio Committee to the legislatures was minimal and did not reflect in any detail the objections of the community.[36] The worry was that members of the legislature who were not part of the portfolio committee would not have been sufficiently apprised of the opinions of the community. The Constitutional Court rejected the application, holding that the provincial legislature had fulfilled the obligation in question by holding public hearings with the affected communities on the proposed legislation.[37] The court was not entitled to prescribe to the legislature what such a report should contain and the fact that the report was "skeletal" did not mean there was inadequate information before the legislature when making its decision.[38]

We thus see the court begin its engagement in this area with a judgment that articulated a wide-ranging principle of participatory democracy which, on its face, places strong substantive obligations on legislative branches and allows the court to pronounce on their reasonableness with a clear set of standards. Over time, the court, however, moved towards a much less extensive view of what participation is required and the reasonableness standard morphed into something much more formal than substantive in nature. We now turn to consider a different context, that of evictions and the trajectory of the court's decision-making in this area.

2. Participation in eviction cases

As was seen above, the court in *Doctors for Life* references the use of the reasonableness standard in socio-economic rights jurisprudence. We saw how the court in *Doctors for Life* essentially forged this standard out of the constitutional commitment to participatory democracy, existing provisions of the Constitution and the need for some deference to the decisions of other branches. In the socio-economic rights context, we see the reasonableness

35 *Moutse Demarcation Forum v President of the Republic of South Africa* 2011 11 BCLR 1158 (CC).

36 See *Moutse* (n 35) para 56 for the applicants' multi-pronged constitutional challenge.

37 *Moutse* (n 35) paras 75 and 80–82.

38 *Moutse* (n 35) para 8.

standard providing one of the bases for a duty on the government to engage meaningfully with communities.

The right to housing in the South African Constitution is composed of three parts:

> "(1) Everyone has the right to have access to adequate housing.
>
> (2) The State must take reasonable legislative and other measures, within its available resources, to achieve the progressive realisation of this right.
>
> (3) No-one may be evicted from their home, or have their home demolished, without an order of court made after considering all the relevant circumstances. No legislation may permit arbitrary evictions."

Evictions constitute a negative violation of the right to housing as they disturb the existing access an individual has to a home. Under the apartheid government, the main question was whether the occupation was unlawful or not: if it was, unlawful occupiers of land were dealt with harshly and subjected to criminal conviction as well as speedy eviction.[39] A major change was brought about by the Prevention of Illegal Eviction from and Unlawful Occupation of Land Act (PIE), a key piece of legislation that has shifted the law relating to evictions.[40] No longer was unlawful occupation subject to criminal sanction. Moreover, eviction was made the subject of several procedural and substantive requirements which included, for instance, notice needs to be given to the occupiers of the proposed eviction, a court order needs to be obtained for any eviction and courts are given broad discretionary powers based on principles of "justice and equity" to determine whether, and under which circumstances, illegal occupiers may be evicted from public or private land.[41] One important factor courts can take into account if occupiers have been on the land for more than six months is whether or not there is any alternative accommodation for these people. The change PIE has brought about in the law arises as a result of the fact that "property law today cannot simply assume that ownership is deserved and that anyone occupying land has no entitlement to be there".[42] The skewed

---

39 The main piece of legislation in this area was the Prevention of Illegal Squatting Act 52 of 1951.

40 19 of 1998 (PIE).

41 For a comprehensive discussion of the development of evictions law under the influence of section 26(3), see Van Der Walt *Constitutional Property Law* (2006) 410–419; Liebenberg (n 2) 268–311.

42 Bilchitz and Mackintosh "Pie in the sky: where is the constitutional framework in high court eviction proceedings? Marlboro Crisis Committee v City of Johannesburg" 131 (2014) *South African Law Journal (SALJ)* 521 525.

pattern of ownership arising from historical dispossession as well as the fact that many people are simply desperate and have nowhere to go entails that a more humane framework needed to be found to deal with unlawful occupiers.

In *Port Elizabeth Municipality,*[43] one of the early cases dealing with an eviction of a group of 68 people who had lived on private land within the municipality for between two and eight years, the Constitutional Court had an opportunity to outline its approach to the new framework for evictions. Sachs J, writing for a unanimous court, articulated an approach to PIE which, through the requirements of "justice and equity", required there to be a balance struck between the rights of owners to property and those of occupiers to housing. The court went further and found that in trying to diffuse the tension between property and housing rights in eviction cases, "the procedural and substantive aspects of justice and equity cannot always be separated".[44] As such, "justice and equity require that everyone is to be treated as an individual bearer of rights entitled to respect for his or her dignity".[45] In so doing, it was necessary to encourage the parties to engage with one another in an effort to find an equitable solution. The court therefore found that, in establishing the justice and equity of any eviction, one of the important questions for a court to ask was whether, "proper discussions, and where appropriate, mediation have been attempted".[46] These remarks by Sachs J were, however, future-orientated as in the particular case the court found that it needed to decide on the permissibility of the eviction in the absence of the mediation. The direction the court signals in this case has, however, been understood to represent "an affirmation by the Court that the housing rights protected in section 26 of the Constitution, in addition to conferring substantive benefits, entitle unlawful occupiers to participate in the process of finding a just solution to what often appears as an intractable conflict between their housing rights and the property rights of land owners".[47]

---

43 *Port Elizabeth Municipality v Various Occupiers* 2005 1 SA 217 (CC) (*PE Municipality*).

44 *PE Municipality* (n 43) para 39.

45 *PE Municipality* (n 43) para 41.

46 *PE Municipality* (n 43) para 43.

47 Liebenberg (n 2) 14.

These early remarks by the court in *Port Elizabeth Municipality* are taken up in the case of *Olivia Road*[48] to create a new doctrine in which a participatory element is utilised in resolving rights conflicts. The case concerned an attempted eviction by the City of Johannesburg of a number of poor occupiers from buildings that were in a shocking state in the inner city. Occupation of the buildings posed a threat to occupiers' health and safety in terms of, among others, the National Building Regulations and Standards Act[49] (NBRSA). The occupiers of 51 Olivia Road and 197 Main Street were just some of an estimated 67 000 people the City intended to evict from allegedly unsafe properties in the inner City of Johannesburg. This campaign formed part of the Council's Inner City Regeneration Strategy. The occupiers in this case, however, recognised the poor state of the buildings but did not want to be placed in a worse situation, without any housing or in accommodation offered by the City far from their source of livelihood in the inner city. The case was a genuinely difficult one of trying to ensure the safety of individuals whilst not rendering them homeless or destitute.

When the matter reached the Constitutional Court, the court decided to postpone the hearing and ordered the City and the occupiers to:

> "Engage with each other meaningfully…in an effort to resolve the differences and difficulties aired in [court] in the light of the values of the Constitution, the constitutional and statutory duties of the municipality and the rights and duties of the citizens concerned."[50]

The court also instructed the parties to report back on the results of the engagement.[51] The court made it clear that it would have regard to the contents of this report when drafting its judgment or when issuing further directions should this become necessary.[52] The engagement exercise resulted in a detailed settlement agreement between the City and the occupiers, and included steps to be taken to make the building livable and safer to occupy in the interim, with occupiers agreeing to be relocated over time to alternative accommodation in the inner city.

The agreement was submitted to the court and it then issued a final judgment, in which Yacoob J provided the reasons for ordering the parties to engage, as well as the purpose and nature of the engagement. According to

48 *Occupiers of 51 Olivia Road, Berea Township, and 197 Main Street, Johannesburg v City of Johannesburg* 2008 3 SA 208 (CC) (*Olivia Road*).

49 103 of 1977.

50 *Olivia Road* (n 48) para 5 (interim order, para 1).

51 *Olivia Road* (n 48) para 5 (interim order, para 3).

52 *Olivia Road* (n 48) para 5 (interim order, para 4).

Yacoob J, where people face homelessness due to eviction, public authorities should engage seriously and in good faith with the affected occupiers with the view to finding humane and pragmatic solutions to their situation.[53] This approach was grounded in two main arguments. First, the court held that a municipality has a number of obligations to provide services to individuals, improve their quality of life and to encourage involvement in local government. When understood in light of the rights to dignity and life, "a municipality that ejects people from their homes without first meaningfully engaging with them acts in a manner that is broadly at odds with the spirit and purpose"[54] of these constitutional obligations. This argument essentially appears to create an obligation of meaningful engagement from deep principles of the Constitution itself.

Secondly, the court focuses on section 26(2) of the Constitution and the duty upon the state to take "reasonable measures" to achieve the progressive realisation of rights. This provision is interpreted to place an obligation upon a municipality "to engage meaningfully with people who would become homeless before it evicts them".[55] That, in turn, is also used to gloss section 26(3) of the Constitution: the presence or absence of meaningful engagement will be one of the relevant circumstances courts utilise to decide on whether an eviction should be granted or not. [56]

Yacoob J goes on to provide some more detailed understanding of what meaningful engagement requires. The objectives of doing so are outlined in fairly instrumental terms and include understanding:

> "(a)what the consequences of the eviction might be, (b) whether the City could help in alleviating any dire consequences, (c) whether it was possible to render the buildings concerned relatively safe and conducive to health for an interim period, (d) whether the City had any obligations to the occupiers in the prevailing circumstances, and lastly (e) when and how the City could or would fulfil these obligations".[57]

Yacoob J elaborated further on the nature and benefits of meaningful engagement:

> "Engagement has the potential to contribute towards the resolution of disputes and to increased understanding and sympathetic care if both sides are willing to participate in the process. People about to be evicted may be so vulnerable that they may

53 *Olivia Road* (n 48) paras 18–21 and 44.
54 *Olivia Road* (n 48) para 16.
55 *Olivia Road* (n 48) para 18.
56 *Olivia Road* (n 48) para 18.
57 *Olivia Road* (n 48) para 14.

> not be able to understand the importance of engagement and may refuse to take part in the process. If this happens, the municipality cannot walk away without more. It must make reasonable efforts to engage and it is only if these efforts fail that a municipality may proceed without meaningful engagement. It is precisely to ensure that a city is able to engage meaningfully with poor, vulnerable or illiterate people that the engagement process should preferably be managed by careful and sensitive people on its side."[58]

In order to be effective meaningful engagement requires the parties to engage with each other "reasonably" and "in good faith". Thus, inflexible attitudes or the "making of non-negotiable, unreasonable demands" undermines the deliberative process.[59] Furthermore, "proactive solutions" must be pursued and civil society organisations should facilitate the engagement process in every possible way.[60] Moreover, the engagement process should be transparent as secrecy is not only "counter-productive to the engagement process", but also "inimical to the constitutional value of openness".[61] Furthermore, Yacoob J held that in any eviction proceedings, a municipality would be required to produce "a complete and accurate account of engagement including at least the reasonable efforts of the municipality within that process". Any evidence in the record showing that the municipality had failed to engage with the affected community, or had behaved unreasonably during the engagement process, would be "a weighty consideration against the grant of an ejectment order".[62] The importance of this requirement was signaled by Yacoob J's conclusion that the Supreme Court of Appeal should not have granted the ejectment order in the circumstances of the case where there had been an absence of meaningful engagement between the parties.[63]

The court in this case, therefore, has regard both to deep principles of the Constitution and the "reasonableness standard" to derive a clear constitutional obligation of meaningful engagement. That approach provides voice to those who are vulnerable in ensuring that the government is forced to take their views into account in circumstances where eviction is at issue.[64] In this particular case, the settlement agreement between the City of Johan-

---

58 *Olivia Road* (n 48) para 15.
59 *Olivia Road* (n 48) para 20.
60 *Olivia Road* (n 48) para 20.
61 *Olivia Road* (n 48) para 21.
62 *Olivia Road* (n 48) para 21.
63 *Olivia Road* (n 48) para 23.
64 Bilchitz "Are socio-economic rights political rights?" 31 (2015) *South African Hournal on Human Rights (SAJHR)* 86 106–107.

nesburg and the occupiers substantially met all the occupiers' concerns regarding the location, quality and affordability of the alternative accommodation to be provided upon their eviction from the buildings.[65] Liebenberg observes that the order "facilitated a participatory, contextualised solution to the impasse which had developed around the City's concern to avoid habitation of buildings which posed a danger to health and safety, and the residents' interest in having access to adequate alternative accommodation in proximity to the places where they pursued their livelihoods".[66]

Unfortunately, the court also back-tracked to some extent in its *Joe Slovo* decision[67] in holding that meaningful engagement will be a requirement for a reasonable eviction. In that case, an eviction order had been granted despite complaints that there had not been adequate engagement on the nature and implications of the eviction.[68] The majority of the court did not regard this as a basis for vitiating the eviction order. In his separate judgment, Sachs J described how flawed the engagement process between the residents and the authorities was in these terms:

> "There can be no doubt that there were major failures of communication on the part of the authorities. The evidence suggests the frequent employment of a top-down approach where the purpose of reporting back to the community was seen as being to pass on information about decisions already taken rather than to involve the residents as partners in the process of decision making itself."[69]

The top-down approach described above can be contrasted with the "structured and reciprocal deliberative process which the court endorsed in *Olivia Road*".[70] According to McLean, the court "essentially found an eviction to be just and equitable even in the absence of meaningful engagement, and thereby retreating to 'an even narrower conception of reasonableness in section 26(2) of the Constitution'".[71]

---

65 Wilson "Planning for inclusion in South Africa: the state's duty to prevent homelessness and the potential of 'meaningful engagement'" 22 (2011) *Urban Forum* 265 279.

66 Liebenberg (n 2) 17. She goes on to point out a number of concerns with the court's approach in *Olivia Road.*

67 *Residents of Joe Slovo Community, Western Cape v Thubelisha Homes* 2010 3 SA 454 (CC) (*Joe Slovo 1*).

68 See, for instance, *Joe Slovo 1* (n 67) para 166.

69 *Joe Slovo 1* (n 67) para 378.

70 Liebenberg (n 2) 23.

71 McLean "Meaningful engagement: one step forward or two back? Some thoughts on Joe Slovo" 3 (2010) *Constitutional Court Reviw (CCR)* 223 238–239. For a fuller discussion of the implications of the *Joe Slovo* judgment, see Liebenberg (n 2) 22–26.

3. Participation and procedural fairness

A further doctrine which has been developed that has important implications for public participation concerns the requirements of procedural fairness. This idea is of importance in the area of administrative law as well as the wider related principle of legality that has been developed by the Constitutional Court. We shall consider each in turn.

a) Procedural fairness in administrative law

Section 33 of the South African Constitution provides that "[e]veryone has the right to administrative action that is lawful, reasonable and procedurally fair". The Promotion of Administrative Justice Act 3 of 2000 (PAJA) was enacted to give effect to this section of the Constitution. Section 3 of PAJA provides for procedural fairness in relation to decisions that affect individuals. It essentially requires that there be adequate notice of proposed administrative action, and that there be a reasonable opportunity provided to make representations (as well as adequate notice of appeals processes and the right to request reasons).[72] Once again, we see that the notion of reasonableness re-appears in the context of participation in administrative decision-making.

An important decision in this regard was the case of *Joseph v City of Johannesburg*.[73] The case dealt with whether the city had obligations of procedural fairness to a group of lessees of a private building. The city had disconnected the electricity from the building due to the owner not paying the monthly electricity account. The city had notified the owner of the impending disconnection but did not inform the lessees. The lessees claimed that they should have been provided with a notice and an opportunity to make representations. The city argued that it had no contractual relationship with the lessees and, therefore, had no obligations towards them in relation to procedural fairness.

The court found, however, that the city had constitutional and statutory obligations to provide basic municipal services to people.[74] In light thereof, the court found that the government has obligations to treat individuals in a manner that is procedurally fair. That would include, in this instance, a right

72 sec 3(2)*(b)* of PAJA.

73 *Joseph v City of Johannesburg* 2010 4 SA 55 (CC).

74 *Joseph* (n 73) para 39.

to receive a notice about any impending disconnection and, at least, to listen to residents who wished to make representations in this regard. The court regarded the foundations of these duties as lying in broad principles of the constitutional order: it quoted the preamble of PAJA as seeking to "promote an efficient administration and good governance" as well as to "create a culture of openness, transparency and accountability in the public administration".[75] These goals in turn give expression to the founding values of the South African Constitution such as the rule of law and accountability, responsiveness and openness.

Section 195 of the Constitution also gives expression to the need for a responsive and accountable administration. The Court went on to say that these values and principles are central in ensuring the government acts in a way that is responsive, respectful and fair when giving effect to its constitutional and statutory obligations.[76] This was particularly important in the context of local government providing services to people given the fact that it was the level of government closest to citizens. In the *Joseph* case, the court highlighted the fact that government has an enduring constitutional and statutory relationship with citizens which places a duty on it to treat the individuals with respect and, in accordance, with the deepest principles of governance.

In relation to administrative action that affects the public more widely, section 4 of PAJA also outlines various procedural fairness requirements. The procedures in this case do not require one-on-one engagement but rather outline a range of possibilities for public engagement including holding a public inquiry or a notice-and-comment procedure.[77] The standard of "reasonableness" and "justifiability" once again comes up as a basis for departing from these procedures[78] which suggests that, in general, these procedures are considered reasonable methods of realising the right to procedural fairness. It has been argued that these provisions on procedural fairness in matters that affect the public seek to "have a positive effect on the rate and quality of meaningful participation in administrative decision-making which, in turn, has the potential to enhance transparent and accountable public administration".[79]

---

75 *Joseph* (n 73) para 42.

76 *Joseph* (n 73) para 45.

77 sec 4(1)*(a)* and *(b)* respectively.

78 sec 4(4)*(a)* and *(b)*.

79 Brynard "Procedural fairness to the public as a means to enhance public participation in public administration" 2011 *Administratio Publico* 100 115.

b) Legality

Principles which have traditionally only applied within the domain of administrative law have also been extended by courts in post-apartheid South Africa to cover all exercises of public power through what has become known as the principle of "legality". The doctrine of legality is rooted by the Constitutional Court in the foundational principle of the rule of law in section 1 as well as the supremacy of the Constitution in section 2.[80] In *Pharmaceutical Manufacturers Association*, the court had to deal with a mistake made by the President to bring laws regulating medicines into effect before relevant subordinate legislation had been passed which was necessary for the operation of the primary legislation (providing schedules for the various drugs). In reviewing this decision, which the court held was not administrative action, the court stated that the "exercise of all public power must comply with the Constitution which is the supreme law, and the doctrine of legality which is part of that law".[81] The court found that the doctrine of legality requires that all exercise of public power must "be exercised in an objectively rational manner".[82] The decision of the President in that case was found to be objectively irrational and so was declared invalid.

The question has arisen as to whether the doctrine of legality – which has a very wide scope – includes a requirement of procedural fairness and a duty on government when public power is exercised to solicit the participation of members of the public or those affected by the decision in question. Initially, the Constitutional Court seemed wary to develop the doctrine in this way. In the *Masetlha* case,[83] the court dealt with a decision of the President unilaterally to suspend and then terminate the employment of the Director-General of the National Intelligence Agency (Masetlha). Masetlha complained that he was not given a right to be heard prior to his dismissal. The majority of the court held that the power to dismiss, in this instance, was a form of executive action and that the constraints on such action did not include a requirement to act in a procedurally fair manner.[84] This decision was severely criticised as "setting the law of procedural fairness back

80 *Pharmaceutical Manufacturers Association of South Africa: in re Ex parte President of the Republic of South Africa* 2000 2 SA 674 (CC) paras 16–19.

81 *Pharmaceutical Manufacturers Association of South Africa* (n 80) para 20.

82 *Pharmaceutical Manufacturers Association of South Africa* (n 80) para 89.

83 *Masetlhla v President of the Republic of South Africa* 2008 1 SA 566 (CC).

84 *Masetlhla* (n 83) paras 77–78.

twenty years".[85] Two subsequent decisions suggest a significant progression of the court in this regard towards a more expansive conception of the doctrine of legality.

In the *Albutt* decision, [86] the court dealt with the power of the President to grant a pardon to individuals convicted of a criminal offence with a political motive. The question before the court was whether or not the President was required to afford a hearing to the victims of these crimes prior to making a decision. The court held that the power of President required ascertaining whether, on the facts, the crime was committed with a political motive. In order to determine that, the President had to hear from both perpetrators and victims. As a result, the court held, in the context of this particular case, that the right of victims to participate in the process is an incident of the requirement of rationality on executive decision-making (which is part of the doctrine of legality).[87] The court, once again, in reaching its decision references the principles of accountability, responsiveness and openness in section 1 of the Constitution.[88] The court was though quite specific about limiting its finding to the context of the case and thus it remained unclear the extent to which procedural fairness could be seen to flow from the principle of legality.[89]

The court has, however, in the case of *Minister of Defence* v *Motau*[90] in obiter remarks sought to limit the effect of its decision in *Masetlha* and, possibly, expand the content of the doctrine of legality. The case concerned a decision by the Minister of Defence to remove members from the board of a state-owned corporation Armscor. One of the questions that arose concerned whether there was a duty to act in a procedurally fair manner. The court found that the Minister had violated the Companies Act by failing to afford the members of the board the opportunity to make representations prior to dismissing them. It, however, went beyond what was required for

85 Hoexter "Clearing the intersection? Administrative and labour Law in the Constitutional Court" 1 (2008) *Constitutional Court Review (CCR)* 209.
86 *Albutt v Centre for the Study of Violence and Reconciliation* 2010 5 BCLR 391 (CC).
87 *Albutt* (n 86) paras 70–74.
88 *Albutt* (n 86) para 71.
89 See Murcott "Procedural fairness as a requirement of legality: is a reconciliation between Albutt and Masetlha possible?" 130 (2013) *South African Law Journal (SALJ)* 260.
90 *Minister of Defence and Military Veterans v Motau* 2014 5 SA 69 (CC).

the decision to consider whether or not there would be a duty to act in a procedurally fair manner in the absence of a statutory duty to do so.

The court held that its statements in the *Masetlha* case should be read only to apply in the specific context which dealt with the special relationship between the President and the head of the intelligence services.[91] The court rejected the notion that the statements in *Masetlha* meant that the doctrine of legality did not include a requirement of procedural fairness more generally.[92] It suggested it was minded to rule in that direction by referencing the long tradition of the courts in South Africa of upholding the *audi alteram partem* principle (that the other side should generally be heard) particularly where prejudicial allegations are levelled against an individual.[93] As a result, dismissal from service would generally attract requirements of procedural fairness. The line of cases we just described in relation to the doctrine of legality is important as we see a progression in which the court increasingly appears to regard procedural fairness and participation in government decision-making as, possibly, being required by the doctrine of legality which governs all exercises of public power. The key standard is what is regarded as procedurally fair, though even here, the court has regard to the notion of reasonableness in constructing this standard.[94] We discuss what we regard as the logical next step in this development when we consider the implications of the deeper philosophical foundations for procedural fairness that we address in the next section.

III. Exploring the deeper foundations of the public participation jurisprudence

1. Common themes in public participation jurisprudence

We have seen, through an analysis of the case law, thus far in the three distinct areas we have considered, that the court is insistent on the importance of public participation in wide-ranging areas where individuals interact with the government. Mere participation is also not regarded as sufficient: the participation must be meaningful and the standard of reasonableness is used to review actions taken by the government in this area.

---

91 *Minister of Defence and Military Veterans* (n 90) para 81.
92 *Minister of Defence and Military Veterans* (n 90) para 81.
93 *Minister of Defence and Military Veterans* (n 90) para 83.
94 The court appears to accept this notion in *Joseph* (n 73) paras 59 and 62.

The case law also suggests that there is a two-way relationship between the requirement of public participation and the notion of reasonableness. In some of the cases such as *Doctors for Life*, the court first finds a jurisprudential basis for the requirement of public participation and then, largely for reasons relating to the separation of powers and deference, forges a reasonableness standard to allow for judicial review but maintain an appropriate relationship of respect for the powers of other branches. In *Olivia Road*, on the other hand, we see the court forge a public participation requirement partially out of the requirement of reasonableness: an action or decision would not be regarded as reasonable without taking into account the views of those affected. *Albutt*, similarly, finds – in the limited context of that decision – that a duty to hear the voices of victims of the crimes in question flowed from a requirement of rationality.[95]

The relationship we see in the case law between these two requirements raises a number of questions. Reasonableness relates to the idea that the new constitutional order in South Africa sought to develop a culture of justification: all exercises of public power must be capable of being justified with reasons that are at least plausible (even if not the best available).[96] Public participation is essentially an important requirement about processes: that they must involve members of the public or individuals where they are affected by a decision. As we saw in the case law, these two ideas have been brought together in the case law of the Constitutional Court in at least these three areas. What then is the deeper explanation we can give of the relationship between the reasonableness standard and the requirement of public participation?

In answering this question, it is instructive to note as we have emphasised in the account above, that in its case law in this area, we have seen that the Constitutional Court often references as a basis for its doctrines not only specific provisions in the Constitution but also specific founding values in section 1. In particular, the court places great emphasis on the key values of democratic governance outlined there, namely, accountability, responsiveness and openness. Its reference to these founding values is often cursory without explaining in more detail the manner in which they connect with

95 Rationality in South African law is regarded as a lesser standard of review than reasonableness. Nevertheless, the decision connects public participation and notions of the reasonable nature of a decision.

96 Mureinik "A Bridge to where? Introducing the Interim Bill of Rights" 10 (1994) *South African Journal on Human Rights (SAJHR)* 31 32.

public participation and the review standard of reasonableness. In trying to draw out a deeper understanding of its jurisprudence in this area, it is clear though from the identification of these values that the court's work in this area falls within the realm of developing the nature of South African democracy[97] and establishing a particular kind of relationship between the government and those it governs.[98] In attempting to understand its approach in this area, we now turn to an examination of the literature on some of the deeper philosophical underpinnings of requirements for public participation and the possible links these suggest with the notion of reasonableness.

2. Three rationales connecting public participation and reasonableness

A recent impressive article by Denise Meyerson has identified three types of rationales that can underpin requirements for procedural justice such as participation in hearings that affect one.[99] We consider each in turn and show how the Constitutional Court has, in its case law on public participation, utilised each of these.

a) Instrumentalist rationales

The first set of reasons is what we might call "utilitarian" or "instrumentalist" in nature. These reasons essentially involve the notion that public participation is valuable as a means to achieve other ends that are important. Thus, Yacoob J in *Olivia Road*, for instance, regards some of the objectives of engagement as essentially helping the municipality to gain information

---

97 See Roux (n 22) 62–65.

98 This work can thus be seen to build on the work of Bilchitz "Citizenship and community: exploring the right to receive basic municipal services in Joseph" 3 (2010) *Constitutional Court Review (CCR)* 45.

99 We are influenced and draw on the categorisations offered by Meyerson "The moral justification for the right to make full answer and defence" 35 (2015) *Oxford Journal of Legal Studies (OJLS)* 237. Meyerson's article focuses on the basis for the criminal law right of a defendant to participate in his or her trial and to be heard. The approaches she considers, however, are applicable to the philosophical underpinnings of procedural justice more generally than we are concerned with here.

concerning "the consequences" of the eviction and thus enabling it to alleviate some of those dire consequences.[100] *Albutt* provides a good example of an instrumental justification as well: without the participation of victims of the crimes in question, the President could make the wrong decision about granting pardons.[101] Clearly, public participation can help improve decision-making by providing a greater range of perspectives and information as inputs to the decisions. It can also enhance good governance. A government which encourages wide-ranging participation in its decisions would not be able to claim it did not know about potential consequences of a decision and thus enhances both accountability and responsiveness in decision-making. The court has also, at various points, indicated the importance of openness to prevent decisions being made on the basis of "secret lobbying and influence peddling".[102] Secrecy the court holds is also "counter-productive to the process of engagement".[103] Openness is thus essential to gain the instrumental benefits of public participation.

Instrumental justifications also provide a basis for the link between public participation and reasonableness: a decision that fails to take account of crucial information and that does not take account of a range of perspectives in the community is not adequately capable of being justified to all in the community. Public participation thus is essential to the very ability of decisions to be justified in an instrumental manner.

Instrumental justifications, however, only take one so far: it is entirely conceivable that there will be circumstances in which there are no major instrumental benefits to be gained by participation. For instance, if the consequences of a decision are relatively predictable and there seems to be virtually unassailable support for a particular outcome, does participation still remain of importance?[104] We also suggest below that the case law of the Constitutional Court does not support a purely instrumentalist approach to public participation.

100 *Olivia Road* (n 48) para 14.
101 See, for example, *Albutt* (n 86) paras 63–68.
102 *Doctors for Life* (n 1) para 115.
103 *Olivia Road* (n 48) para 21.
104 Meyerson (n 99) 241 (in the context of the problems with error reduction accounts as justifications for hearings for defendants).

b) Dignitarian rationales

The second approach that we consider is what we might call "dignitarian". This approach roots the value of public participation in the notion of dignity or worth: the idea is usually developed in a Kantian manner requiring individuals to be treated as ends in themselves and not merely as means (as is required by his second formulation of the categorical imperative). That, in turn, is understood to require respect for the rational agency of another human being.[105] Such an approach requires treating individuals "as active subjects, not passive objects – ends not means – which involves respecting them as people who can reason, explain themselves and enter into a dialogue with the state".[106] Waldron expresses this idea as follows:

> "[a]pplying a norm to a human individual is not like deciding what to do about a rabid animal or a dilapidated house. It involves paying attention to a point of view and respecting the personality of the entity one is dealing with. As such, it embodies a crucial dignatarian idea – respecting the dignity of those to whom the norms are applied as being capable of explaining themselves".[107]

This idea is clearly embraced by the Constitutional Court of South Africa in its jurisprudence on public participation. In *Doctors for Life*, Ngcobo J states that public participation:

> "encourages citizens of the country to be actively involved in public affairs, identify themselves with the institutions of government and become familiar with the laws as they are made. It enhances the civic dignity of those who participate by enabling their voices to be heard and taken account of."[108]

In *Olivia Road*, Yacoob J specifically references his statement in *Grootboom* that the reasonableness of state action in relation to socio-economic rights had to be constructed in relation to the fundamental value of human dignity.[109] He also states expressly that a "municipality that ejects people from their homes without first meaningfully engaging with them acts in a

105 See, for instance, Hill "Humanity as an end in itself" 1980 *Ethics* 84.

106 Meyerson (n 99) 249.

107 Waldron "The rule of law and the importance of procedure" in Fleming (ed) *Getting to the Rule of Law* (2011) 16.

108 *Doctors for Life* (n 1) para 115.

109 *Olivia Road* (n 48) para 10.

manner that is broadly at odds with the spirit and purpose of the constitutional obligations set out in this paragraph taken together".[110] The most important sources of these obligations referred to by Yacoob J are the right to life and the right to dignity. Furthermore, he states that:

> "People in need of housing are not, and must not be regarded as a disempowered mass. They must be encouraged to be pro-active and not purely defensive."[111]

In *Albutt*, the court also references the Truth and Reconciliation Commission report which speaks about the commission as restoring the "human and civic dignity of victims by granting them an opportunity to relate their own accounts of the violations of which they were a victim".[112]

Public participation and reasonableness on this view are connected in a different manner. This rationale begins with a central conception of the human being as an individual who is capable of reasoning and having his or her own point of view. Public participation thus flows not from the instrumental benefits that will be achieved but as a requirement flowing from what is required to show respect to a being of this kind. By failing to engage the views of individuals, one disrespects their rational natures. Any decision that results would also therefore be unreasonable in two senses: firstly, it would usually fail to take account of the full range of reasons available (public participation, on this view, helps to facilitate an understanding of the various reasons for and against a decision); and secondly, it would undermine the very practice of reason-giving which assumes a community of rational actors whose views and arguments matter.[113]

c) Relational rationales

The third and final approach we consider is what we might call the "relational" approach. This approach is concerned with the relationships between individuals in society and between those individuals and the government. Requiring public participation in government processes is ultimately about establishing particularly valuable forms of democratic relationships

---

110 *Olivia Road* (n 48) para 16.

111 *Olivia Road* (n 48) para 20.

112 *Albutt* (n 86) para 60, referencing the Truth and Reconciliation Commission *Truth and Reconciliation Report Vol 1* (1998) 128.

113 This could perhaps relate to the idea of Kant's Kingdom of Ends.

in the society which also impacts on the ways individuals perceive themselves. Meyerson examines recent empirical evidence surrounding the value of fair processes[114] and summarises the upshot as follows:

> "[t]he opportunity to present one's own perspective is perceived as a symbolic marker of inclusion within the larger community, conveying the information that one is a valued member of the group, whose views are worthy of being heard. Conversely, not to be allowed to present one's own side would be experienced as an expression of contempt, which in turn would detrimentally affect one's sense of self-worth or self-respect".[115]

This account is different from the dignatarian account which is focused very much on ensuring respect for individuals as rational agents. The relational account focuses on the quality of the relationships between individuals (as well as individuals and the state) as a primary matter of concern. Botha argues, for instance, for a relational account of rights that is "not rooted in abstract individualism. They are, rather, an expression of connectedness among the self and others. On this understanding, the language of individual rights is fully compatible with the insight that the self is forged within a network of social relations, that the self is always situated within a concrete context".[116]

This relational account of the value of public participation is also deeply connected in the South African context to the African value of ubuntu. Mokgoro J has stated that the notion of ubuntu can be understood metaphorically through the statement umuntu ngumuntu ngabantu (a person is a person because of other people).[117] Ubuntu gives expression to the importance of a relational ethic which prises such values as hospitality, friendliness, care and compassion. Desmond Tutu has stated in light of this that "[s]ocial harmony is for us the summum bonum – the greatest good".[118] Metz has sought to develop a moral theory out of these ideas which he regards as being based on the following principle:

---

114 Tyler has done a number of studies on the psychology relating to procedural justice: see, for instance, Tyler "Procedural justice research" 1 (1987) *Social Justice Research* 41.

115 Meyerson (n 99) 259.

116 Botha "Metaphoric reasoning and transformative constitutionalism Part 2" 1 (2003) *Tydskrif vir die Suid-Afrikaanse Reg (TSAR)* 20 23.

117 *S v Makwanyane* 1995 3 SA 391 (CC) para 308.

118 Tutu *No Future without Forgiveness* (1999) 31 35.

> "An act is right/just insofar as it is a way of living harmoniously or prising communal relationships, ones in which people identify with each other and exhibit solidarity with one another; otherwise, an act is wrong".[119]

The Constitutional Court has, in many of its statements around public participation, suggested it is influenced by such a relational view. In *Doctors for Life*, the Constitutional Court references the legacy of apartheid where

> "[a] majority of people had, for many years, been denied the right to influence those who have ruled over them. They had been discriminated against in almost every sphere of life. The result was gross inequality in education, financial resources, access to knowledge and other areas that are crucial for effective participation in the law-making process".[120]

Recognising these problems that affected the relationships between citizens and the state, the court recognised the need of the government to take active duties to develop the capacity of individuals to participate. The court also holds that public access to parliament is a central part of public involvement in law-making processes given that "it allows the public to present when laws are debated and made".[121] Presence is clearly important as it enables a relationship to develop between the public and their institutions.

In the evictions context, the court in *Port Elizabeth Municipality* writes that "wherever possible, respectful face-to-face engagement or mediation through a third-party should replace arm's length combat by intransigent opponents".[122] The court is concerned on the one hand with how government views the people involved in an eviction. Thus, "those seeking eviction should be encouraged not to rely on concepts of faceless and anonymous squatters automatically to be expelled as obnoxious social nuisances".[123] On the other hand, the court is also concerned about how the relationships of unlawful occupiers affect their own self-conception. Sachs J writes:

> "At the same time those who find themselves compelled by poverty and landlessness to live in shacks on the land of others, should be discouraged from regarding

119 Metz "Human Dignity, Capital Punishment, and an African Moral Theory: Toward a New Philosophy of Human Rights" 9 (2010) *Journal of Human Rights* 81 84.

120 *Doctors for Life* (n 1) para 130.

121 *Doctors for Life* (n 1) para 137.

122 *PE Municipality* (n 43) para 39.

123 *PE Municipality* (n 43) para 41.

themselves as helpless victims, lacking the possibilities of personal moral agency."[124]

The court is also concerned with the manner in which relationships in the community are formed and suggests that the mediation process "enables parties to relate to each other in pragmatic and sensible ways, building up prospects of good neighbourliness for the future".[125] Unsurprisingly, in *Olivia Road*, where the court develops the doctrine of meaningful engagement, it continues this line of thinking when it writes that "[e]ngagement has the potential to contribute towards the resolution of disputes and to increased understanding and sympathetic care if both sides are willing to participate in the process".[126]

In the administrative law context, we see the "relational" approach being expressly referred to by the court in the *Joseph* case. Essentially, in that case, the government denied it had a legal relationship with the lessees which could form the basis of duties of procedural fairness. After finding that there was indeed a public law legal relationship between government and its citizens to provide basic services, the court said the following:

> "Municipalities are, after all, at the forefront of government interaction with citizens. Compliance by local government with its procedural fairness obligations is crucial therefore, not only for the protection of citizens' rights, but also to facilitate trust in the public administration and in our participatory democracy".[127]

Clearly, here the court was concerned about the interactions between the municipality and its citizens and to establish the relationship on the basis of trust. In an important footnote, the court references the government policy of "Batho Pele" (people first) which clearly articulates an obligation upon government to provide public services to all citizens and prescribes the manner in which that is to take place. The court states that "Batho Pele gives practical expression to the constitutional value of ubuntu which embraces the relational nature of rights. Courts must move beyond the common law conception of rights as strict boundaries of individual entitlement".[128] Bilchitz has argued that the court in this case articulates a particular understanding of the relationship between the government and its citizens

124 *PE Municipality* (n 43) para 41.
125 *PE Municipality* (n 43) para 43.
126 *Olivia Road* (n 48) para 15.
127 *Joseph* (n 72) para 45.
128 *Joseph* (n 72) footnote 39.

founded in a more African communal ethic that "prises the creation of harmonious relationships between individuals and the government".[129]

The relational ethic provides us with another insight into the relationship between public participation and reasonableness. Including the public in decision-making reflects a trust in individuals as well as an ethic of friendliness and warmth towards the public. Including the public in decision-making is also the foundation for establishing harmonious relationships between people. Those relational values in turn encourage a form of relationship that is in good faith and where decisions are taken in a reasonable manner. Reasonableness, as it is rooted in the notion of reason-giving, creates and presupposes an ability of individuals to engage with one another in a framework of mutuality and respect. Through not imposing on individuals an outcome simply by fiat but by engaging them, the very process instantiates a relationship based on give-and-take and mutual understanding.

IV. Conclusion: implications for doctrinal law

In this chapter we have explored the court's jurisprudence on public participation in three distinct areas of law and illustrated how the court has utilised the notion of reasonableness both as a standard for reviewing the actions taken by the government in this regard as well as a jurisprudential foundation for the duty to involve the public. The court has linked these requirements to the foundational values of the Constitution and we have developed a deeper understanding of the connection between these two facets of its jurisprudence through considering recent literature on the philosophical foundations of procedural justice.

We have shown that all three of the philosophical strands we identify – instrumentalist, dignitarian and relational – co-exist in the jurisprudence of the Constitutional Court. This pluralist approach is not incoherent in our view but adds depth to its jurisprudence and enables a more holistic understanding to be developed of the values that lie behind the requirement of public participation. We have also illustrated through exploring these different rationales, the multi-faceted relationship that exists between the requirement of public participation and the doctrine of reasonableness developed by the Constitutional Court. We consider now briefly in conclusion some of the implications of this deeper understanding of the court's reasoning for legal doctrine in these three areas.

129 Bilchitz (n 98) 66.

In relation to public involvement in legislative processes, we have seen how the court began very promisingly in *Doctors for Life* to provide a deeply substantive understanding of reasonableness and thus what was required to fulfill the government's duties in this regard. Gradually, we saw how the court has increasingly weakened this understanding of reasonableness such that public participation has become a formal requirement that must be complied with. Given the court's linkage of public participation to the foundational values of the Constitution, we suggest that these developments are regrettable and, hopefully, can be reversed.[130] Understanding the philosophical foundations of public participation, also suggest that there is a range of substantive goals which must be met through such a process. A purely formal public participation process will not, in general, achieve the instrumental goals that are aimed at; it definitely, however, will not establish deep respect for the dignity of citizens or develop relationships upon a foundation of trust, and harmony. The court should thus require public participation to reflect the substantive values it aims at and be prepared to scrutinise and overturn actions by other branches of government when they do not.

In the context of evictions, the court has, as we saw, developed the important doctrine of meaningful engagement. Yet there has also been some back-tracking in the *Joe Slovo* case from the full implications of its progressive holdings in *Olivia Road*. There have also been some worries about the meaningful engagement doctrine. First, it has been argued that there is a danger that meaningful engagement may "descend into unprincipled, normatively-empty process of local dispute settlement".[131] This is because the court held in this case that meaningful engagement should take place before litigation starts unless it is not possible or reasonable to do so because of urgency or some other compelling reason.[132] Liebenberg sees a danger with this approach and makes these remarks:

> "The implication is that not all engagement processes will be subjected to the judicial scrutiny and approval which took place in Olivia Road. There is no guarantee that the process or outcome of engagement between the communities and the authorities will respect and vindicate relevant constitutional rights. This is a particular concern given the power imbalance which exists between deeply disadvantaged groups facing homelessness in an eviction situation, and local authorities or private

130 In this we concur with Raboshakga (n 21) 21–22.

131 See Ray "Proceduralisation's triumph and engagement's promise in socio-economic rights litigation" 27 (2011) *South African Journal on Human Rights (SAJHR)* 111 112; Liebenberg (n 2) 19.

132 *Olivia Road* (n 48) para 30.

> landowners. Communities who lack the support of non-governmental organisations or public interest lawyers are particularly vulnerable in this context, and may not be in a position to secure the effective protection of their housing and other rights in an engagement process."[133]

We wish to add that deep divisions as to the way forward which sometimes exist amongst a community could frustrate the engagement process, thus entitling the authorities to proceed with evictions without meaningful engagement.[134] All these concerns suggest the need to understand the notion of meaningful engagement in light of what it seeks to achieve substantively. We have sought to show that it has a base in instrumental, dignatarian and relational justifications. As such, all these substantive goals need to be considered by courts in understanding whether any engagement process has truly been meaningful. This approach also would help address some of the worries about the notion of reasonableness in the socio-economic rights context – namely, that it is inherently vague and lacking in content. These problems can partially be addressed if, in making judgments of reasonableness, there is a more transparent engagement with and reference to the deeper values that underpin its use in in the rights context.[135]

Finally, in the context of administrative law, we saw the manner in which requirements of procedural fairness must now infuse all interactions between the bureaucracy of the state and citizens. The *Joseph* case illustrated the manner in which the government is required to interact with citizens. The philosophical underpinnings we have provided could help strengthen the duty of procedural fairness to ensure that it meets the instrumental, dignitarian and relational justifications.

This reasoning, though, has clear implications for the direction in which the jurisprudence on the doctrine of legality should head. We have seen that the courts have attempted to limit its problematic holding in *Masetlha* to that context. We have also seen how participation in decision-making is linked to the founding values of the Constitution. As such, we suggest that it would make sense for the court to take the next logical step and recognise

133 Liebenberg (n 2) 19.

134 Arguably, many of these worries were in evidence in the recent case of *Occupiers of Erven 87 88 Berea v Christiaan Frederick De Wet NO* 2017 ZACC 18 (8 June 2017) where the community did not appear to be adequately informed of its rights in relation to evictions and individuals claimed to be representatives of the occupiers where they did not have a mandate from the community.

135 Liebenberg *Socio-Economic Rights: Adjudication under a Transformative Constitution* (2010) 183 suggests a need to adopt a more substantive approach to reasonableness more generally in the socio-economic rights context.

that legality – which is a requirement of all law and exercise of public power – places a requirement of procedural fairness on the government. Exercises of public power must always be understood to be in the public interest and thus are required to take into account the perspectives of those whom they affect. As is true of all such duties, there is a high level of flexibility as to exactly what that procedural fairness requires which can prevent this requirement from becoming unmanageable. Understanding the philosophical foundations of public participation, can provide the basis for determining what procedural fairness requires in any particular circumstance. The doctrine of legality, nevertheless, is the most general of doctrines we have considered: given the importance the court has placed on public participation and its rootedness in the foundational values of the Constitution, we are of the view that it should be developed to require that, in all cases where public power is exercised, each branch of government, at least, provides a reasonable opportunity for public participation.

Bibliography

Bilchitz D "Are socio-economic rights a form of political rights?" 31 (2015) *South African Journal on Human Rights (SAJHR)* 86.

Bilchitz D and Mackintosh D "Pie in the sky: where is the constitutional framework in high court eviction proceedings? Marlboro Crisis Committee v City of Johannesburg" 131 (2014) *South African Law Journal (SALJ)* 521.

Bishop M "Vampire or prince? The listening constitution and Merafong Demarcation Forum and Others" 2 (2009) *Constitutional Court Review (CCR)* 313.

Botha H "Metaphoric reasoning and transformative constitutionalism Part 2" 1 (2003) *Tydskrif vir die Suid-Afrikaanse Reg (TSAR)* 20.

Brynard DJ "Procedural fairness to the public as a means to enhance public participation in public administration" 19 (2011) *Administratio Publica* 100.

Held D *Models of democracy* (2nd Edition, Polity press, Cambridge 1996).

Hoexter C "Clearing the intersection? Administrative and labour Law in the Constitutional Court" 1 (2008) *Constitutional Court Review (CCR)* 209.

Liebenberg S "Engaging the paradoxes of the universal and the particular in human rights adjudication: the possibilities and pitfalls of 'meaningful engagement'" 12 (2012) *African Human Rights Law Journal (AHRLJ)* 1.

Liebenberg S *Socio-Economic Rights: Adjudication under a Transformative Constitution* (Juta Law, Claremont 2010).

McLean K "Meaningful engagement: one step forward or two back? Some thoughts on *Joe Slovo*" 3 (2010) *Constitutional Court Review (CCR)* 223.

Metz T "Human dignity, capital punishment and African moral theory: towards a new philosophy of human rights" 9 (2010) *Journal of Human Rights* 81.

Meyerson D "The moral justification for the right to make full answer and defence" 35 (2015) *Oxford Journal of Legal Studies (OJLS)* 237.

Murcott M "Procedural fairness as a requirement of legality: is a reconciliation between Albutt and Masetlha possible?" 130 (2013) *South African Law Journal (SALJ)* 260.

Mureinik E "A bridge to where? Introducing the Interim Bill of Rights" 10 (1994) *South African Journal on Human Rights (SAJHR)* 31.

Raboshakga N "Towards participatory democracy, or not: the reasonableness approach in public involvement cases" 31 (2015) *South African Journal on Human Rights (SAJHR)* 4.

Ray B "Proceduralisation's triumph and engagement's promise in socio-economic rights litigation" 27 (2011) *South African Journal on Human Rights (SAJHR)* 107.

Roux T "Democracy" in Woolman S, Bishop M, Roux T et al (eds) *Constitutional Law of South Africa* (2nd Edition, Juta Law, Landsdowne 2014) vol 1 ch 10 1–77.

Tutu D *No Future without Forgiveness* (Doubleday, New York 1999).

Tyler TR "Procedural justice research" 1 (1987) *Social Justice Research* 41.

Van der Walt AJ *Constitutional Property Law* (Juta Law, Cape Town 2006).

Waldron J "The rule of law and the importance of procedure" in Fleming JE (ed) *Getting to the Rule of Law* (New York University Press, New York 2011).

Wilson S "Planning for inclusion in South Africa: the state's duty to prevent homelessness and the potential of 'meaningful engagement'" 22 (2011) *Urban Forum* 265.

Case Law

Albutt v Centre for the Study of Violence and Reconciliation and Others 2010 5 BCLR 391 (CC)

Doctors for Life International v Speaker of the National Assembly 2006 12 BCLR 1399 (CC); 2006 6 SA 416 (CC)

Masetlhla v President of the Republic of South Africa 2008 1 SA 566 (CC)

Matatiele Municipality and Others v President of the Republic of South Africa and Others (2) 2007 1 BCLR 47 (CC)

Merafong Demarcation Forum and Others v President of the Republic of South Africa and Others 2008 10 BCLR 968 (CC)

Minister of Defence and Military Veterans v Motau and Others 2014 5 SA 69 (CC)

Moutse Demarcation Forum v President of the Republic of South Africa and Others 2011 11 BCLR 1158 (CC)

Occupiers of 51 Olivia Road, Berea Township, and 197 Main Street, Johannesburg v City of Johannesburg 2008 3 SA 208 (CC)

Occupiers of Erven 87 88 Berea v Christiaan Frederick De Wet NO 2017 ZACC 18 (8 June 2017)

Port Elizabeth Municipality v Various Occupiers 2005 1 SA 217 (CC)

Pharmaceutical Manufacturers Association of South Africa and Another: In re Ex parte President of the Republic of South Africa and Others 2000 2 SA 674 (CC)

Poverty Alleviation Network and Others v President of the Republic of South Africa and Others 2010 6 BCLR 520 (CC)

Residents of Joe Slovo Community, Western Cape v Thubelisha Homes 2010 3 SA 454 (CC)

S v Makwanyane 1995 3 SA 391 (CC)

Comment on "Public Participation and Reasonableness: Exploring the Case Law and Jurisprudential Philosophy of the South African Constitutional Court"

*Ferdinand Wollenschläger**

The extremely rich paper entitled above explores two fundamental concepts of constitutional law: public participation and reasonableness. It sketches the development of the principle of public participation, notably in the jurisprudence of the South African Constitutional Court with regard to the legislative process, eviction cases and procedural fairness in administrative law. Moreover, it identifies three rationales underlying public participation, namely an instrumentalist, a dignitarian and a relational approach. Finally it explores links between the concepts of public participation and reasonableness.

The paper offers much food for thought, comparison and debate. In view of limitations on content, however, my observations and discussion will focus on three points. First, I propose a contextualisation within the debate on the constitutionalisation of administrative law (part I.). Second, I will seek to address the relationship between the concepts of public participation and reasonableness (part II.). Third, I will highlight the increasing significance of participation in administrative procedure as a recent phenomenon of German administrative law (part III.).

* Ferdinand Wollenschläger, *Dr. iur. habil.* The commentator holds a chair for Public Law, European Law and Public Economic Law at the Faculty of Law, University of Augsburg, Germany.

I. A Contextualisation within the debate on the constitutionalisation of administrative law

In large parts, the paper demonstrates how the constitutional law concepts of public participation and reasonableness, notably as interpreted by the South African Constitutional Court, have influenced the development of administrative law by requiring a certain standard of public participation in decision-making, such as in eviction cases. Hence, it may be understood as a piece on constitutionalisation of administrative law. Here we see a parallel development between South Africa and Germany worth exploring further. In Germany, the *Grundgesetz* and its interpretation by the German Constitutional Court has been exercising a profound influence on the development of administrative law since the former came into force. This is why administrative law is conceived as "concretised constitutional law"[1]. Issues for further comparative research and debate may comprise an analysis of the degree of constitutionalisation of administrative law, its reasons, its actors (courts, academia) or conflicting processes – like Europeanisation in Germany.[2]

II. Relationship between public participation and reasonableness

The paper argues for and gives evidence of understanding the concept of reasonableness as a foundation for public participation – not only against the German constitutional law background. I wonder, however, whether a distinction should be maintained between reasonableness as a substantive standard for assessing actions of public authorities and the procedural requirement of involving the public in decision-making.

It is true that such a distinction is also made in parts of the paper (cf. Bilchitz/Heleba, p. 402 above): "reasonableness" is defined as relating "to the idea that the new constitutional order in South Africa sought to develop a culture of justification: all exercises of public power must be capable of being justified with reasons that are at least plausible (even if not the best available)", whereas "public participation" is regarded as "essentially an important requirement about processes: that they must involve members of

1 Fritz Werner, *Deutsches Verwaltungsblatt (DVBl.)* 1959, 527 (528 et seq.).

2 Cf. on all this Ferdinand Wollenschläger, 'Verfassung im Allgemeinen Verwaltungsrecht: Bedeutungsverlust durch Europäisierung und Emanzipation?' *Veröffentlichungen der Vereinigung der Deutschen Staatsrechtslehrer 75* (2016), 187.

the public or individuals where they are affected by a decision." Such a distinction would also correspond to the situation under German constitutional law. A substantive requirement of reasonable decisions – in the sense of justified decisions – follows from the requirement that interferences with fundamental rights must be proportionate, that is, pursue a legitimate aim, be suitable and necessary to realise this aim and be appropriate when balancing all interests at stake; the principle of proportionality is, moreover, also rooted in the rule of law. In contrast, a duty to involve the public in decision-making follows from the principle of democracy (Art. 20 para. 2 GG), the rule of law and positive obligations comprised by fundamental rights (procedural dimension of fundamental rights – *Grundrechtsschutz durch Verfahren*).

When linked to the instrumentalist rationale of public participation (Bilchitz/Heleba, pp. 403 et seq. above), the substantive understanding of the principle of reasonableness is maintained since input from the public is necessary to have a sound factual basis for reaching justifiable decisions. In the paper, reasonableness is, however, also understood as a broader foundation for public participation. First, it is linked to the dignitarian rationale of public participation: "By failing to engage the views of such an individual, one disrespects their rational nature. Any decision that results would also therefore be unreasonable, in the sense, not only of failing to take account of the full range of reasons available but also undermining the very practice of reason-giving which assumes a community of rational actors" (Bilchitz/Heleba, p. 406 above). Second, it is linked to the relational rationale of public participation: "Including the public in decision-making reflects a trust in individuals as well as an ethic of friendliness and warmth towards the public. Including public in decision-making is also the foundation for establishing harmonious relationships between people. Those relational values in turn encourage a form of relationship that is reasonable and in good faith. Reasonableness, as it is rooted in the notion of reason-giving, creates and presupposes an ability of individuals to engage with one another in a framework of mutuality and respect" (Bilchitz/Heleba, p. 410 above).

While not questioning these rationales as sound reasons for involving the public in decision-making, I wonder whether it is necessary to develop such a broad concept of reasonableness. For, as a consequence, it might lose its contours and become open for political preferences. It might be preferable to deduce procedural requirements of public participation from more specific and established constitutional principles like the procedural dimension of fundamental rights, the principle of democracy and the rule of law.

Finally, the same applies to the concept of legality as proposed to be understood in the paper. The authors "suggest that it would make sense for the court to take the next logical step and recognise that legality – which is a requirement of all law and exercise of public power – places a requirement of procedural fairness on the government" (Bilchitz/Heleba, p. 413 above). According to the German understanding, the principle of legality (*Vorrang des Gesetzes*) requires public authorities to act in line with the law (cf. Art. 20 para. 3 GG). It does, however, not comprise substantive or procedural standards.

III. Stressing the importance of involving the public in administrative decision-making

The paper underlines the importance of involving the public in administrative decision-making. Reflecting the role of procedure in German administrative law, it is fair to say, though, that producing administrative decisions in line with substantive requirements has been superordinated over procedural correctness. The consequences of not hearing a person concerned by an administrative decision before issuing that decision illustrate this. Even if the right to a hearing is guaranteed by sec. 28 *Verwaltungsverfahrensgesetz* (Administrative Procedure Act) and does also constitute a standard following from the procedural dimension of fundamental rights, an infringement of the right to a hearing does not necessarily entail the illegality of the administrative decision; rather, illegality supposes an effect of this procedural error on the content of the decision. sec. 46 *Verwaltungsverfahrensgesetz*– in line with the interpretation of the fundamental rights[3] – stipulates in this respect:

> "Application for annulment of an administrative act which is not invalid under section 44 cannot be made solely on the ground that the act came into being through the infringement of regulations governing procedure, form or local competence, where it is evident that the infringement has not influenced the decision on the matter."[4]

---

3 Cf. from a fundamental right perspective: BVerfG 18.06.1986 – 1 BvR 787/80 – BVerfGE 73, 280 (299); BVerfG 22.03.2000 – 1 BvR 1370/93 – NVwZ-RR 2000, 487 (488); Ferdinand Wollenschläger, *Verteilungsverfahren* (2010), 82 et seqq.

4 Translation taken from http://www.migrationsrecht.net/german-act-of-administrative-procedure-vwvfg.html?catid=78 (15-09-2017).

Moreover, sec. 45 Verwaltungsverfahrensgesetz allows for making good defects in procedure or form at later stages of the procedure, even during the court procedure (cf. sec. 45 para. 2 *Verwaltungsverfahrensgesetz*).

Reflecting this approach from the instrumentalist perspective developed in the paper, the result is not to be criticised since a hearing would not have changed the outcome of the procedure. However, adopting the dignitarian perspective (stressing the individual's role as subject of the procedure) and the relational perspective (emphasising the significance of interaction) the irrelevance of procedural defects has to be seen more critically. Hence, reflecting the deeper foundations of public participation, as undertaken in the paper, might lead to a strengthening of procedural law, as do, by the way, influences coming from EU law[5].[6] The question has to be raised, though, what weight is to be attributed to the principle of effectiveness – is it convincing to oblige the administration to repeat a procedure if the result will be the same?[7]

The paper also underlines the democratic importance of involving the public in administrative decision-making. Reflecting the role of the citizen in German administrative law, it has to be said that for a long time a rule of law-based approach prevailed. Far-reaching fundamental rights standards

---

5 See only Peter M. Huber, 'Grundzüge des Verwaltungsrechts in Europa – Problemaufriss und Synthese' in Armin von Bogdandy, Sabino Cassese and Peter M. Huber (eds), *Verwaltungsrecht in Europa: Grundzüge, IPE V* (2014), § 73, paras. 28, 130; Wolfgang Kahl, *Die Verwaltung* 42 (2009), 463 (472 et seqq.); Wolfgang Kahl, 'Grundzüge des Verwaltungsrechts in gemeineuropäischer Perspektive: Deutschland' in Armin von Bogdandy, Sabino Cassese and Peter M. Huber (eds), *Verwaltungsrecht in Europa: Grundzüge, IPE V* (2014), § 74, paras. 66 et seq.; Eberhard Schmidt-Aßmann, 'Verfassungsprinzipien für den Europäischen Verwaltungsverbund' in Wolfgang Hoffmann-Riem, Eberhard Schmidt-Aßmann and Andreas Voßkuhle (eds), *Grundlagen des Verwaltungsrechts Vol. 1* (2nd Edition, 2012), § 5, paras. 88 et seq.; Angela Schwerdtfeger, *Der deutsche Verwaltungsrechtsschutz unter dem Einfluss der Aarhus-Konvention* (2010), 92 et seqq.

6 Cf. Klaus F. Gärditz, *Hochschulorganisation und verwaltungsrechtliche Systembildung* (2009), 151 et seq. with n 406; Oliver Lepsius, *Die Verwaltung Beiheft 10* (2010), 179 (184 et seqq.); Markus Ludwigs, *Neue Zeitschrift für Verwaltungsrecht (NVwZ)* 2015, 1327 (1334).

7 Markus Ludwigs, *Neue Zeitschrift für Verwaltungsrecht (NVwZ)* 2015, 1327 (1334); Eberhard Schmidt-Aßmann, 'Grundrechtswirkungen im Verwaltungsrecht' in Bernd Bender, Rüdiger Breuer, Fritz Ossenbühl and Horst Sendler (eds), *Rechtsstaat zwischen Sozialgestaltung und Rechtsschutz: Festschrift für Konrad Redeker zum 70. Geburtstag* (1993), 225 (231); Ferdinand Wollenschläger, *Verteilungsverfahren* (2010), 82 et seqq., 601 et seq., 692 et seqq.

including a strict understanding of the guarantee of effective legal protection had a profound influence on the development of German administrative law; the insight into the democratic (participatory) role of the citizen in administrative procedures is a rather new development.[8] An example of this is the reluctance to grant citizens access to information irrespective of a legitimate interest; here, it needed EU law obligations to trigger the introduction of such claims into national law.

8 Armin von Bogdandy, 'Grundprinzipien' in Armin von Bogdandy and Jürgen Bast (eds), *Europäisches Verfassungsrecht* (2nd Edition, 2009), 13 (66 et seqq.); Armin von Bogdandy and Peter M. Huber, 'Staat, Verwaltung und Verwaltungsrecht: Deutschland' in Armin von Bogdandy, Sabino Cassese and Peter M. Huber (eds), *Verwaltungsrecht in Europa: Grundlagen, IPE III* (2010), § 42, paras. 92 et seqq.; Peter M. Huber, 'Grundzüge des Verwaltungsrechts in Europa – Problemaufriss und Synthese'in Armin von Bogdandy, Sabino Cassese and Peter M. Huber (eds), *Verwaltungsrecht in Europa: Grundzüge, IPE V* (2014), § 73, paras. 154 et seq.; Johannes Masing, 'Der Rechtsstatus des Einzelnen im Verwaltungsrecht' in Wolfgang Hoffmann-Riem, Eberhard Schmidt-Aßmann and Andreas Voßkuhle (eds), *Grundlagen des Verwaltungsrechts Vol. 1* (2nd Edition, 2012), § 7, paras. 95 et seq.

Bibliography

Armin von Bogdandy, 'Grundprinzipien' in Armin von Bogdandy and Jürgen Bast (eds), *Europäisches Verfassungsrecht* (2nd Edition, Springer, Berlin 2009), 13.

Armin von Bogdandy and Peter M. Huber, 'Staat, Verwaltung und Verwaltungsrecht: Deutschland' in Armin von Bogdandy, Sabino Cassese and Peter M. Huber (eds), *Verwaltungsrecht in Europa: Grundlagen, IPE III* (C.F. Müller, Heidelberg 2010), § 42.

Klaus F. Gärditz, *Hochschulorganisation und verwaltungsrechtliche Systembildung* (Mohr Siebeck, Tübingen 2009).

Peter M. Huber, 'Grundzüge des Verwaltungsrechts in Europa – Problemaufriss und Synthese' in Armin von Bogdandy, Sabino Cassese and Peter M. Huber (eds), *Verwaltungsrecht in Europa: Grundzüge, IPE V* (C.F. Müller, Heidelberg 2014), § 73.

Wolfgang Kahl, 'Grundzüge des Verwaltungsrechts in gemeineuropäischer Perspektive: Deutschland' in Armin von Bogdandy, Sabino Cassese and Peter M. Huber (eds), *Verwaltungsrecht in Europa: Grundzüge, IPE V* (C.F. Müller, Heidelberg 2014), § 74.

Wolfgang Kahl, Über einige Pfade und Tendenzen in Verwaltungsrecht und Verwaltungsrechtswissenschaft – ein Zwischenbericht, *Die Verwaltung* 42 (2009), 463.

Oliver Lepsius, Hat die Europäisierung des Verwaltungsrechts Methode? Oder: Die zwei Phasen der Europäisierung des Verwaltungsrechts, *Die Verwaltung Beiheft 10* (2010), 179.

Markus Ludwigs, Verfassung im Allgemeinen Verwaltungsrecht – Bedeutungsverlust durch Europäisierung und Emanzipation?, *Neue Zeitschrift für Verwaltungsrecht (NVwZ)* 2015, 1327.

Johannes Masing, 'Der Rechtsstatus des Einzelnen im Verwaltungsrecht' in Wolfgang Hoffmann-Riem, Eberhard Schmidt-Aßmann and Andreas Voßkuhle (eds), *Grundlagen des Verwaltungsrechts Vol. 1* (2nd Edition, C.H. Beck, Munich 2012), § 7.

Eberhard Schmidt-Aßmann, 'Grundrechtswirkungen im Verwaltungsrecht' in Bernd Bender, Rüdiger Breuer, Fritz Ossenbühl and Horst Sendler (eds), *Rechtsstaat zwischen Sozialgestaltung und Rechtsschutz: Festschrift für Konrad Redeker zum 70. Geburtstag* (C.H. Beck, Munich 1993), 225.

Eberhard Schmidt-Aßmann, 'Verfassungsprinzipien für den Europäischen Verwaltungsverbund' in Wolfgang Hoffmann-Riem, Eberhard Schmidt-Aßmann and Andreas Voßkuhle (eds), *Grundlagen des Verwaltungsrechts Vol. 1* (2nd Edition, C.H. Beck, Munich 2012), § 5.

Angela Schwerdtfeger, *Der deutsche Verwaltungsrechtsschutz unter dem Einfluss der Aarhus-Konvention. Zugleich ein Beitrag zur Fortentwicklung der subjektiven öffentlichen Rechte unter besonderer Berücksichtigung des Gemeinschaftsrechts* (Mohr Siebeck, Tübingen 2010).

Fritz Werner, Verwaltungsrecht als konkretisiertes Verfassungsrecht, *Deutsches Verwaltungsblatt (DVBl.)* 1959, 527.

Ferdinand Wollenschläger, 'Verfassung im Allgemeinen Verwaltungsrecht: Bedeutungsverlust durch Europäisierung und Emanzipation?' *Veröffentlichungen der Vereinigung der Deutschen Staatsrechtslehrer 75,* (2016), 187.

Ferdinand Wollenschläger, *Verteilungsverfahren* (Mohr Siebeck, Tübingen 2010).

Case Law

BVerfG 18.6.1986 – 1 BvR 787/80 – BVerfGE 73, 280.

BVerfG 22.3.2000 – 1 BvR 1370/93 – NVwZ-RR 2000, 487.

Transconstitutionalism and democratic legitimacy as dilemmas of regionalism in Germany and South Africa

*Jentley Lenong**

I. Introduction

The democratic legitimacy of the nation-state at the end of the twentieth century has almost entirely been dependent on its constitutional status. Constitutional democracy brought with it the rise of the constitutional state as well as the development of international law. The proliferation of constitutional democracy seemed to bring about a synergy of both functional and structural order between different states' municipal legal systems. In turn, this provides for the development of international law based on the common realities of the democratic nation-state. International law embraced the greater conceptual alignments between states through its contemporary

* BA (Law) LLB LLM; lecturer at the University of Johannesburg and researcher with the South African Research Chair in International Law (SARCIL).

foundational principles.[1] These foundational principles were developed into rights for both states and individuals.[2] Holmes argues that "the emergence of new instruments of global governance has developed a legal dimension of its own, setting free the expansive dynamic of functional social sectors that are not limited by political or territorial boundaries."[3] Constitutionalism and international law functioned well under the traditional monist and dualist regime for the incorporation of international law into municipal law. However, the development of international law and globalisation has revealed a deficit of democracy, particularly within international law institutions.

The rise of regional institutions like the European Union (EU) and the Southern African Development Community (SADC) anchored in international law, increased the pressure for the further democratisation of international law. The traditional legitimacy of international law premised on state consent has come under pressure due to the undemocratic structural nature of this international system, particularly within the United Nations (UN). It could be argued that as a consequence of this tension or impasse within broader international law refuge was sought within closer regional establishments to resolve this. The confidence which states had built within municipal constitutionalism was exported into treaties, establishing these regional organs. However, constitutionalism suffers inherently from sovereign autonomy or jurisdictional exceptionalism. More narrowly one can refer to it as constitutional exceptionalism. This leads to fragmentation in the interpretation and application of regional or international law between states, primarily, because different states seek to rationalise legal concepts in line with the comprehension of their municipal law. Whether this happens through ratifications or judicial application, the approach is always the domestication of international law through the rationalisation provided by the local legal system.

---

1 For a further reading on the general foundational principles on International Law see Brownlie, *Principles of Public International Law* (2012); Evans (ed) *International Law* (2006) and Shaw *International Law* (2008).

2 These rights refer to the generational rights as developed through instruments like the United Nations General Assembly – International Convention on Civil and Political Rights (ICCPR) 6 ILM 368 (1967) and the United Nations General Assembly – International Covenant on Economic, Social and Cultural Rights (ICESCR) 6 ILM 360 (1967).

3 Holmes "The politics of law and the laws of politics: the political paradoxes of transnational constitutionalism" 21 (2014) *Indiana Journal of Global Legal Studies (Ind J Global Legal Stud)* 553 561.

Thus, the concept of constitutional exceptionalism resides at the heart of constitutionalism as a discourse: this idea that the operation of laws should be confined to their jurisdictional demarcation. Together with constitutional exceptionalism is the notion of legislative hegemony or the bottom-upward supremacy of legislation and courts. This finds expression within the principle of subsidiarity. A traditional interpretation of constitutionalism favours this paradigm which secures the constitution of a state at the very top of the legislative totem pole. Municipal constitutional exceptionalism consequently is promoted through the principle of subsidiarity which serves as a guard against overt lower judicial intrusion. This defensive posture of municipal constitutional exceptionalism presents a dilemma when exported to a regional or international context. The judiciary is burdened with the responsibility to protect and promote the constitution but also holds the potential to subvert the spirit of the legislative endeavour on a regional or international level. So when Mark Tushnet introduces the idea of "the inevitable globalisation of constitutional law"[4], naturally the concept of municipal constitutional exceptionalism undermines his thesis. Tushnet, however, admits that "[t]o speak of the globalisation of domestic constitutional law is to suggest that these and other traditions of exceptionalism are likely to weaken over time."[5] Consequently, for a constitution to have transboundary impact, the system within which it will operate will need to resolve the fact of constitutional exceptionalism.

The concept of transconstitutionalism as proposed by Marcelo Neves is a model for resolving these and other constitutional impasses.[6] This chapter will accept and submit that "transconstitutionalism appears to be the most promising alternative for the strengthening of its (world society) normative dimensions"[7]. Neves employs systems theory to make the case for the traversal nature of constitutions when scaling between legal order or social systems, predicated through the entanglement of politics and law. Neves argues that:

> "As far as the connection between classical international law and state law is concerned, under the Treaty of Westphalia (1648) the incorporation of international norms into internal law is effected by means of ratification, just as a reproduction

4 Tushnet "The inevitable globalization of constitutional law" 50 (2008) *Virginia Journal of International Law (Va J Int'l L)* 985.

5 Tushnet (n 4) 987.

6 Neves *Transconstitutionalism* (2013) 74.

7 Neves (n 6) 83.

> of the international legal order depends on the presence of state representatives legitimated by the same order."[8]

In the specific context of transconstitutionalism, he proposes that one delineate the different forms of relationships between legal orders. This study limits its focus in terms of legal orders to the legislative and judicial scales of municipal constitutions and regional organisations, thus seeking to test transconstitutionalism within a more restrictive context on the plurality of legal orders. This will be demonstrated by employing the municipal constitutions of South Africa in relations to SADC and Germany in the contexts of the EU respectively. Neves suggest that there is a need for structural coupling as "fundamental mechanisms of concentrated and lasting interpenetration between social systems".[9] For example, he argues that in the external relationship between society and consciousness, languages become that structural coupling. However, what needs to precede the inquiry into structural coupling between systems is the traversal reasoning of constitutional imperatives. In the South African context, we will make use of transformative constitutionalism to address the requirement of the transversal reasoning of constitutional imperatives for transconstitutional exchange and learning. This is not to suggest that there are no other salient features of the South African constitution through which this can be achieved. There are features like the justiciability of rights and developments around socio-economic rights. However, transformative constitutionalism presents the most researched feature to demonstrate and analyse transconstitutionalism. In the German context, the theory of multilevel constitutionalism is employed together with the principle of subsidiarity to demonstrate the traversal reasoning of constitutional imperatives between the regional and municipal legal systems.

This chapter will start by presenting the concept of transconstitutionalism. It will then interrogate the legal concepts of transformative constitutionalism and multilevel constitutionalism in the contexts of South Africa and Germany respectively. The chapter will conclude by answering the question whether democratic legitimacy is compromised through regionalism and if transconstitutionalism can provide solutions. The chapter essentially needs to address the following: in its assertion to resolve or treat constitutional problems between legal orders, transconstitutionalism is burdened with two constitutional challenges emanating from the cross-scaling of constitutions. The first is the functional traversal rationalities between

8 (n 6) 75.
9 (n 6) 27.

the two jurisdictions in relation to democratic legitimacy. The second is the potential for externalising their constitutionalism and resolving cross-scale constitutional paradoxes and challenges through the structural coupling.

II. The case for transconstitutionalism

There is no universal concept or definition of what a constitution is, but rather it has come to capture different interpretations within different societies. Transconstitutionalism rejects the view of a constitution as a metaphorical concept, capable of flexible application in accordance to whichever semantics is resorted to. Neves argues that a "constitution cannot be considered a mere metaphor with no link to certain structural implications".[10] Consequently, he argues against the indiscriminate use of "constitution" as a term which is infinitely arbitrary. "Constitution" holds both functional and descriptive value within a legal, social and political context. It is for this reason that Neves makes the statement that:

> "[a] discussion of transconstitutionalism presupposes semantic delimitation of the concept of the constitution with which notions of constitutionalism and constitutionalisation are associated."[11]

The preceding quote seeks to warn against the inherent vagueness on a denotative level. These words also hold the potential for the reader to commit fallacies of ambiguity. The words of Patrick Henry ring eerily relevant now where he states:

> "What right had they to say, We the people? My political curiosity, exclusive of my anxious solicitude for the public welfare, leads me to ask, who authorised them to speak the language of We, the people, instead of We, the States?"[12]

These potential fallacies don't only lie within the ambiguity of the actual words, but also within their interpretation, a challenge which is further exacerbated through the departure of a document from its original intended purpose. The discourse that informs its origin operates with liberty within the structural fibre of such a document. Thus, reconciling its rationality with a new purpose requires an adjustment of both the rationality and the structural operative link between systems. Ignorance of this allows for the potential of fragmented interpretation and application within a new system.

10 (n 6) 6.
11 (n 6) 5.
12 Hamilton, Madison, Jay, Kramnick and Hamilton *The Federalist Papers* (1987) 32.

Consequently, in the functioning of a constitution outside of its jurisdiction, it needs to be structurally linked to the new system and has an identity to export. An alternative perspective is proposed by Marcelo Neves to better comprehend the relationship tensions between legal orders in his theory on *transconstitutionalism.* This theory seeks to realign the challenges of the legal relationships between political organisations.

Neves argues that his proposal of transconstitutionalism "is not international, transnational, supranational, national, or local constitutionalism",[13] but rather a traversal reasoning of constitutional imperatives amongst jurisdictions. Transconstitutionalism finds no point of departure in any higher system of legal norms and does not profess that any legal order or our particular focus – constitution, holds the *ultima ratio.* It further "rejects nation-statism, internationalism, supranationalism, transnationalism, and localism as privileged spaces for solving constitutional problems".[14] Neve's proposal is premised on limiting the notion of a constitution to two basic constitutional characteristics. This premise relies on a two-tiered model of a constitution as one, an articulation of basic human rights and two, a representation of the structural and functional limitation of state or public power. So what are the primary characteristics that inform the structure of transconstitutionalism?

Transconstitutionalism seeks to resolve constitutional impasses or problems via cross-scale dialogue or conversations amongst, for example, courts at different levels. The actors being judges and/or courts being the sources of interpenetration between legal orders to form "bridges of transition". In its rejection of any legal orders' claim of autonomy, Neves stresses the point that:

> "This situation entails relations of mutual observation, in the context of which there develop forms of learning and exchange without any possibility of supremacy for one of the orders as legal ultima ratio."[15]

What transconstitutionalism consequently postulates is the transversal movement of ideas between legal orders. It still seems to recognise scaling between constitutional dispensations. Neves argues that:

---

13 Neves "Comparing transconstitutionalism in an asymmetric world society: Conceptual background and self-critical remarks" 2015 *Adam Smith Research Foundation Working Papers Series* 1 5.

14 (n 13) 5.

15 (n 6) 75.

> "The orders involved in solving a specific constitutional problem continuously reconstruct their identity at the level of their self-referential foundations by means of transconstitutional entanglement with another order or with other orders: identity is rearticulated on the basis of alterity."[16]

Consequently, the entanglement produces constitutional otherness or new constitutional identities, separate from their original. In doing so, constitutions presents themselves as coupling constructs between law and politics. Not only do they hold the potential for traversal reasoning between states, but also between states and international organisations. Transconstitutionalism moves from the perspective of a constitution as only a mechanism to resolve or avoid structural paradoxes and tensions to a norm-based evolution of constitutions. Neves' thesis on transconstitutionalism challenges the fundamental core of what is conventionally understood to be the nature and function of constitutions.

With the focus on the South African and German constitutions, what can then be said to be the constitutional imperatives for traversal rationality possessed by these two constitutions? In other words, which primary characteristic of these constitutions holds the potential to be that "bridge of transition" between regional and municipal interchange? Importantly which characteristic is capable of cross-scale learning and exchange according to the theory of transconstitutionalism? In the context of the German Constitution and the EU, it can be argued that the principle of subsidiarity holds this potential. However, this chapter will first look at the South African Constitution which has been famously described as a transformative constitution. The notion of transformative constitutionalism consequently holds the greatest potential for exporting a progressive constitutional imperative to other SADC jurisdictions. Transconstitutionalism provides a manner of application to resolve constitutional transnational challenges without compromising sovereignty or democratic legitimacy.

III. South African transformative constitutionalism

The old apartheid South African dispensation was marred by a totalitarian and authoritarian relationship between state and the populace. The poverty of democratic legitimacy is a well-documented historical fact. Consequently, within the new democratic South African context the role of

16 (n 6) 75.

the Constitution was to address the injustices of the past and assist in building a non-racial, non-sexist and politically free society. The Constitution was employed as a mechanism to transform the society. This objective was expressed by Chief Justice Arthur Chaskelson in the case *Soobramoney v Minister of Health, KwaZulu-Natal*[17] where he vigorously argued that as a society our "commitment ... to transform our society... lies at the heart of the new constitutional order"[18].

A society or community's relationship with law, politics or economics is premised on the structural independence and dependence of that system. Neves employs the terms "structural coupling" to illustrate the multilevel exchange between systems. He postulates that "[s]tructural coupling are fundamental mechanisms of concentrated and lasting interpenetration between social systems".[19] The South African constitutional dispensation operates internally on the premise of constitutional supremacy. Section 2 of the titled "*Supremacy of Constitution*" states "This Constitution is the supreme law of the Republic; law or conduct inconsistent with it is invalid, and the obligations imposed by it must be fulfilled."[20] This perspective of the South African constitutional structure is consistent with the operation of the principle of subsidiarity. In the case of *My Vote Counts NPC v Speaker of the National Assembly,*[21] Cameron J brings clarity to this principle when he states that:

> "Parliament's argument brings to the fore the principle of subsidiarity in our constitutional law. Subsidiarity denotes a hierarchical ordering of institutions, of norms, of principles, or of remedies, and signifies that the central institution, or higher norm, should be invoked only where the more local institution, or concrete norm, or detailed principle or remedy, does not avail."[22]

Accordingly the South African constitutional dispensation subscribes to the structural legislative hegemony of the principles of subsidiarity. One can thus accept that in the entanglement of systems, the South African Constitution would enjoy sufficient autonomy for external structural coupling. Can it be argued that this principle curtails the potential of the Constitution for external exchange? The rationale would be that the presence of the prin-

17 1998 1 SA 765 (CC).
18 (n 17) 8.
19 (n 6) 27.
20 The Constitution of South Africa Act 108 of 1996.
21 2015 (12) BCLR 1407 (CC).
22 (n 21) 45.

ciple postulates either constitutional dominance or subservience when coupling with an external system. In terms of the traversal rationality of a constitutional imperative to build "bridges of transition", the characteristic of transformative constitutionalism needs to be interrogated with this reality in mind. The notion of the transformative nature of the South African Constitution gained prominence in an article by Karl Klare in 1998.[23] Klare defines transformative constitutionalism as:

> "[A] long-term project of constitutional enactment, interpretation, and enforcement committed (not in isolation, of course, but in the historical context of conducive political developments) to transforming a country's political and social institutions and power relations in a democratic, participatory, and egalitarian direction."[24]

Klare examines the South African Constitution within six themes to reflect its contrast with classical liberal constitutions. He characterises the Constitution as social, redistributive, caring, positive, at least partly horizontal, participatory, multicultural, and self-conscious.[25] Through his examination of these themes Klare deliberately refrains from a reading of the Constitution as a "social democratic" document, but rather advises on a reading of it as possibly "postliberal", a position for which he is criticised by Roux, who sees no rational justification for a postliberal reading of the constitution. Roux remarks that "this proposition makes no logical sense unless it is understood to mean that the post-liberal reading is somehow able to better interpretative justice..."[26]

Theunis Roux takes Klare's view of the transformative nature of the South African Constitution a step further and argues that the Constitution does not represent an "empowered model of democracy".[27] He dismisses Klare's contentions together with the six themes as 'uncontroversial'. With the benefit of the passing of time, Roux further criticises the proposition of Klare that any correct reading of the Constitution "requires a particular form of an interpretative method consistent with its commitment to social transformation through law".[28] Whichever side of the debate one follows it has

---

23 Klare "Legal culture and transformative constitutionalism" 14 (1998) *South African Journal of Human Rights* (*SAJHR*) 146.

24 (n 23) 150.

25 (n 23) 153.

26 Roux "Transformative constitutionalism and the best interpretation of the South African Constitution: Distinction without a difference?" 2009 *Stellenbosch Law Review (Stellenbosch L Rev)* 263 285.

27 (n 26) 262.

28 (n 26) 263.

to be in line with a reading of section 39 of the Constitution. This section entitled "Interpretation of Bill of Rights," reads that:

> "When interpreting the Bill of Rights, a court, tribunal or forum-
> (a) must promote the values that underlie an open and democratic society based on human dignity, equality and freedom;
> (b) must consider international law, and
> (c) may consider foreign law."

One can conclude then that the traversal rationality available as constitutional imperatives within the South African Constitution are informed by its transformative nature. The potential for traversal seems to be built into the interpretative justice sought through the Constitution. It could be argued, that an extraterritorial reading or application of the Constitution would be possible where the traversal rationality is the constitutional imperative of democratically transforming a society. This does not mean that the constitutional project is without paradoxes and challenges. Henk Botha reflects on the paradoxes which breed a series of tensions as part of the character of the South African Constitution as "conflicting constitutional visions".[29] He argues that:

> "Firstly, the Constitution views the state both as a threat to and as a protector of fundamental rights. Second, the private sphere is conceived as a space characterised both by individual freedom and fulfilment and by social subordination and inequality. And third, the Constitution is committed both to the protection and the restitution of property."[30]

Within the two-tiered hypothesis of a constitution presented above, it is evident that both in the limitation of state power and the provision of rights, the constitution experiences paradoxes and challenges. However, these paradoxes and challenges seem to be internal matters. Transconstitutionalism would resolve these through its normative approach in bridging internal constitutional rationalities. The South African Constitution does hold the potential for entanglements with external systems and functioning without the natural hegemony, even though in recent times it could be argued that this has brought a tension between the executive and judiciary.[31]

---

29 Botha "Transforming state and society: From the public/private dichotomy to mutual cooperation and destabilisation" in van der Schyff (ed) *Constitutionalism in the Netherlands and South Africa: A Comparative Study* (2008) 208.

30 Botha (n 29) 209.

31 *Minister of Justice and Constitutional Development v Southern African Litigation Centre* 2016 2 All SA 365 (SCA). See also *Southern Africa Litigation Centre v Minister of Justice and Constitutional Development* 2015 3 All SA 505 (GP) and

Although the SADC has been established, the regional integration project has not sufficiently developed to provide one with observable evidence to test transconstitutionalism beyond the potential of the South African Constitution. In the context of the SADC, the objective is clear – deeper regional integration. This is reflected in the Regional Indicative Strategic Development Plan (RISDP).[32] However following the failed SADC tribunal, it would be near impossible to test this hypothesis currently. The tribunal was suspended after it pronounced against the Zimbabwean government in the case *Fick v Republic of Zimbabwe*.[33] Furthermore, none of the regional integration themes within RISDP deals directly with the formation of an integrated legal system. The approach as it relates to financial and socio-economic integration is only policy-based and the imperative is on the Member States to implement within their jurisdiction.

IV. German multilevel constitutionalism and subsidiarity

The German constitutional dispensation's potential for traversal rationality finds the best application from the perspective of multilevel constitutionalism. This concept stems from the academic work by the German scholar Ingolf Pernice and his colleagues. The notion of multilevel constitutionalism "emerged in the mid to late 1990s in response to the dominant *Staatsrecht* tradition in German public law and as an alternative way of conceiving constitutional authority in the face of the exponential growth of the

---

Democratic Alliance v Minister of International Relations and Cooperation (Council for the Advancement of the South African Constitution Intervening) 2017 2 All SA 123 (GP).

32 See http://www.sadc.int/about-sadc/overview/strategic-pl/regional-indicative-strategic-development-plan/ (15-09-2017).

33 (SADC (T) 01/2010) 2010 SADCT 8 (16 July 2010). See also *Campbell v Republic of Zimbabwe* (SADC (T) 03/2009) 2009 SADCT 1 (5 June 2009). For greater insight into the burden the court held in addressing Zimbabwean human-rights problems see further *Zimbabwe Human Rights NGO Forum v Republic of Zimbabwe* (SADC (T) 05/2008) 2009 SADCT 2 (1 January 2009); *Tembani v Republic of Zimbabwe* (SADC (T) 07/2008) 2009 SADCT 3 (14 August 2009); *United Peoples' Party of Zimbabwe v SADC* (SADC (T) 12/2008) [2009] SADCT 4 (14 August 2009).

supranational European Union".[34] The position of multilevel constitutionalism is that within a union, no union or regional organisational constitution is needed. The collective constitutions of the union serve as one multilevel constitution. Pernice responded that "[t]his concept treats European integration as a dynamic process of constitution-making instead of a sequence of international treaties which establishes and develop [sic] of international cooperation"[35].

The position of the former European Community (EC) in relation to the nation-state was best describe in the case of *N V Algemene Transport- en Expeditie Onderneming Van Gend & Loos and Nederlandse administratie der belastingen*,[36] where it was stated that:

> "The European Economic Community constitutes a new legal order of international law for the benefit of which the States have limited their sovereign rights, albeit within limited fields, and the subjects of which comprise not only the Member States but also their nationals."[37]

It could be argued that this rationale was continued from the EC through to the EU. From the German constitutional perspective, this position was confirmed in 1967 by the German Federal Constitutional Court where it confirmed that the European Economic Community treaty functions almost like a constitution.[38] Through the popularly known *Solange II* judgement[39], the German Constitutional Court concluded that the "European Court is a lawful adjudicator within the meaning of Article 101, section I, Sentence 2 of the Basic Law; this question, until now undecided by the Federal Constitutional Court, ... must receive an affirmative answer".[40] The problem with

34 Walker *Multilevel constitutionalism: looking beyond the German debate* (LEQS Paper No 08/2009) 1.

35 Pernice "Multilevel constitutionalism and the Treaty of Amsterdam: European constitution-making revisited?" 36 (1999) *Common Market Law Review (CML Rev)* 707. Contextually it is clear that Pernice means that this dynamic process establishes and develops international cooperation.

36 (ECJ) Case C.26/62 5.3.1963.

37 This was the court's response to the first question on the applicability of Article 12 of the European Economic Community (EEC) Treaty to domestic law, particularly the rights of citizens of member states to assert their rights in accordance to their respective domestic law.

38 German Constitutional Court (*Bundesverfassungsgericht, BVerfG*) 18.10.1967 – 1 BvR 248/63, 1 BvR 216/67 – BVerfGE 22, 293, 296.

39 These two popular judgements were the judgments BVerfG 29.5.1974 – 2 BvL 52/71 – BVerfGE 37, 271 *(Solange I)* and BVerfG 22.10.1986 – 2 BvR 197/83 – BVerfGE 73, 339 *–(Solange II)*.

40 BVerfG 22.10.1986 – 2 BvR 197/83 – BVerfGE 73, 339, 366.

this position premised on the principle of subsidiarity is that it seems to undermine German sovereignty, without the application of the constitutional procedure to dispose of sovereignty in accordance with section 23 of the Basic Law. Even in the absence of a union constitution as postulated through multilevel constitutionalism, this potential threat to democratic legitimacy seems to flow from the German Constitution self. Pernice sheds light on the position of multilevel constitutionals in this regard when he states that:

> "[W]hat the concept of multilevel constitutionalism focuses on is the correlation of national and European law from the perspective not only of the states but also of the citizens. On the assumption that in modern democracies the citizens are the basis and origin of whatever public authority and decision-making power, whether vested with national or with European…"[41]

The structural reality of the German constitutional dispensation in relation to the EU was best articulated under the old Article 24 of the Basic Law. It provided that "[t]he Federation may by legislation transfer sovereign powers to an international organisation". This was the precursor to the creation of the EU through the Treaty of Maastricht, which led to an amendment which was articulated under Article 23 of the new Basic Law. The new Article 23 reads:

> "With a view to establish a united Europe the Federal Republic of Germany shall participate in the development of the European Union, which is committed to the rule of law, democracy, social and federal principles as well as the principle of subsidiarity, and ensures protection of basic rights comparable in substance to that afforded by the Basic Law. To this end, the Federation may transfer sovereign powers by law with the consent of the Bundesrat."

Solange II had the implication that the principle of subsidiarity allows for the subverting of the constitutional procedure in the disposing of German sovereignty. The principle of subsidiarity as articulated under Article 3 of the Treaty of Maastricht recognises the shared competence between Member States and the EU and is a departure from the state-centred approach during the EC. The Treaty of Lisbon[42] and other EU treaties have perverted a principle which enjoyed legitimate constitutional purpose internally in Germany. Adam Cygan concurs that "[w]ithin the context of the German

---

41 Pernice "The Treaty of Lisbon: multilevel constitutionalism in action" Walter Hallstein-Institut (WHI) *Paper 2/09* 24 http://www.whi-berlin.de/documents/whi-paper0209.pdf (15-09-2017).

42 *Treaty of Lisbon Amending the Treaty on European Union and the Treaty Establishing the European. Community* Brussels CIG 14/07.

Constitution, this arrangement provides an important contribution to the overall system of constitutional checks and balances in the Federal Republic".[43] The same principle is now being interpreted as a supranational obligation, an approach which Cygan warns against because "this form of sophisticated accountability mechanism does not exist within the EU's supranational Treaty framework where there is an absence of specific regional competences".[44] Effectively, the German constitution allows for the potential of disposing of its sovereignty to the regional organ unconstitutionally. In *Costa v ENEL*[45] the European Court stated that "[t]he executive force of Community Law cannot vary from one state to another in deference to subsequent domestic law, without jeopardising the attainment of the objectives of the Treaty."[46] This position informs the current spirit of the German constitutional adjudication in relation to the EU and the European Court of Justice (ECJ). The subverting of the constitutions applies in concert with the principle of subsidiarity that holds, judicial matter would be considered inadmissible to a higher court where it could be reasonably expected that for such a matter relief could have been sought by bringing the case before the regular courts.[47] Critically in a collective judgement[48] the German Constitutional Court attempted to make a case for a safeguard when it stated that "the Federal Constitutional Court must review the applicability and binding effect of acts of institutions and other agencies of the European Union in Germany insofar as these acts provide the basis of actions taken by German authorities".[49]

In terms of the impact of Article 23 and a German citizen's right to elect the members of the *Bundestag* the German Constitutional Court made it clear that:

> "Article 38 of the Grundgesetz excludes the possibility that, in the area of application of Article 23 of the Grundgesetz, the legitimation of state authority and the influence on its exercise which an election provides is depleted by a transfer of the

---

43 Cygan "Regional governance, subsidiarity and accountability within the EU's multi-level polity" 19 (2013) *European Public Law (EPL)* 161 163.

44 (n 43) 163.

45 (ECJ) C 6-64 15.7.1964.

46 (n 45) 593–594.

47 See BVerfG 25.6.2015 – 1 BvR 555/15 – NJW 2015, 2242.

48 BVerfG 14.1.2014 – 2 BvR 13/13, 2 BvR 2728/13, 2 BvR 2729/13, 2 BvR 2730/13, 2 BvR 2731/13 – BVerfGE 134, 366 (*OMT*).

49 (n 48) para 23.

Bundestag's responsibilities and powers to such a degree, that the democratic principle is violated to the extent that Article 79 section 3 of the Grundgesetz in conjunction with Article 20 section 1 and 2 of the Grundgesetz declares it inviolable."[50]

In this context, even the powers of the electorate are compromised in that the decision never serves in front of their elected officials. The German Constitutional Court has been clear that "[t]he actions of the institutions and agencies of the European Union are democratically legitimated – as far as Germany is concerned".[51] This piercing statement of the court is premised on the statutory Acts of Assent and the Treaty establishing the EU as well as the functioning of the EU. In the same breath, the court remarked that "[a]n essential element of this programme of integration is the principle of conferral".[52] A breach of this principle will only be recognised by the German courts where there has been an overreach on the part of the EU and its structures.[53] The test which the German Constitutional court seems to have developed relates to the impact on their constitutional identity where acts of the EU could be regarded as *ultra vires*. Traversal rationality for the exchange of constitutional imperative becomes difficult where the imperative is the dominance of one system over the other. The potential for cross-scale exchange and learning becomes impossible. Consequently, under such legal conditions transconstitutionalism would not find application.

Other theories have been formulated to address Germany's constitutional dilemma, like "epistemic meta-constitutionalism"[54] and "harmonious discursive constitutionalism"[55]. However it is only with multilevel constitutionalism "that sovereignty retains its unitary character and it rests with the peoples of Europe".[56] Matej Avbelj further makes the case for multilevel constitutionalism in that:

"The masters of the Treaties, if any, can only be the citizens, not the Member States, and given the obligations of homogeneity, it is even doubtful whether the latter still remains the sovereign masters of their own constitutions. Since the real sovereign

50 BVerfG 12.10.1993 – 2 BvR 2134/92, 2 BvR 2159/92 – BVerfGE 89, 155, 171 et seq.

51 (n 48) para 20.

52 (n 48) para 20.

53 See BVerfG 30.6.2009 – 2 BvE 2/08 et al – BVerfGE 123, 267, 353 and 400 (*Lissabon*).

54 Avbelj 'Questioning EU constitutionalisms' 9 (2008) *German Law Journal (GLJ)* 5. See also Walker 'The idea of constitutional pluralism' 65 (2002) *The Modern Law Review (MLR)* 317 320.

55 Avbelj (n 54) 9.

56 Avbelj (n 54) 9.

> is the peoples, they are those who hold the key to Kompetenz-Kompetenz and subsequently there is even no room for consideration of the Member States to leave the European Union by unilateral action."[57]

The focus of what one can call German multilevel constitutionalism is the effective functioning of its regional legal institutional structures. The potential for cross-scale learning and exchange is curtailed by the higher order law to which the EU subjects Germany and other Member States. Attila Vincze comes to a similar conclusion that "[s]upremacy, direct effect and pre-emption of EU law made the preeminent role of national constitutions, and, by the same token, also the role of the national constitutional courts somewhat insecure".[58]

V. Regionalism as a threat to democratic legitimacy?

Within the world that is increasingly operating as a singular political sphere, fragmentation within legal orders is a reality. This is particularly pernicious with the influence of a dominant legal system over another. The very notion that an external constitutional dispensation can find application within a local system undermines democratic legitimacy as a fundamental of the constitutional enterprise. Democratic legitimacy relies on the notion of "the will of the people" and the constitution being the supreme expression of this assertion. In essence, the constitutional enterprise within a democratic society emanates from the collective legal and political consciousness and subscription of the majority of the citizenry. The consequence of the intimacy of a constitution with the constituency in producing a constitution, in theory, restricts its function and operation within the sovereign territory of such constituency – that which has been described herein as constitutional exceptionalism. However, even if a particular legal order is functioning so as not to impact others, this does not restrict other legal orders from fragmenting it.

One of the primary principles of constitutional theory holds that a constitution is dependent on the reality of its constitutional authority. It is from this authority that a constitution also draws its constitutional legitimacy. Linked with an elementary comprehension of democracy theory, constitutional legitimacy is premised on the legitimacy of the democratic authority.

---

57 Avbelj(n 54) 9.

58 Vincze "What role for constitutional courts in a multi-level constitutionalism?" 55 (2012) *Annales University of Science Budapestinensis Rolando Eotvos* 60.

However, such Aristotle-like denotive logic demonstrates the basic necessity of democratic legitimacy between constitutional systems.

The proliferation of regional organisations has seen the amalgamation of states on political, economic and legal spheres. Multilateral treaties have been employed to bring these organisations and their structural agencies about. However, as argued above, regional organisations, and more particularly for the purposes of this chapter, the SADC and the EU, suffer from a deficiency of democracy. Particularly in the case of the EU much has been written on its democratic deficiency.[59]

These regional treaties have been elevated to have constitution-like characteristics. In the EU context Nico Krisch argues that the EU constitutional project might have been stalled, "but constitution and constitutionalisation have become indispensable terms of reference in the debate on the European project".[60] This chapter does not seek to test the legitimacy of any theory of democracy;[61] rather it accepts democracy as a viable indicator to reflect on the legitimacy of a system during legal and socio-political entanglements.

---

59 See Peters "European democracy after the 2003 Convention" 41 (2004) *Common Market Law Review (CML Rev.)* 37; Lord "Assessing democracy in a contested polity" 2001 *Journal of Common Market Studies (JCMS)* 641; Siedentop *Democracy in Europe* (2001); Schmitter How to Democratize the European Union... and Why Bother? (2000); Coultrap "From parliamentarism to pluralism: models of democracy and the European Union's 'democratic deficit' 11 (1999) *Journal of Theoretical Politics (IJTP)* 107; Weiler *The Constitution of Europe* (1999); MacCormick *Questioning Sovereignty: Law, State and Nation in the European Commonwealth* (1999); Weiler *The Constitution of Europe "Do the New Clothes Have an Emperor?" and other Essays on European Integration* (1999); Follesdal and Koslowski (eds) *Democracy and the European Union* (1998); Beetham and Lord *Legitimacy and the European Union* (1998); Lord *Democracy in the European Union* (1998); Abromeit *Democracy in Europe* (1998); Newman *Democracy, Sovereignty and the European Union* (1996); and Bellamy et al (eds) *Democracy and Constitutional Culture in the Union of Europe* (1995).

60 Kirsch *Beyond Constitutionalism: The Pluralist Structure of Postnational Law* (2010) 29.

61 See Dixon and Landau "Transnational constitutionalism and a limited doctrine of unconstitutional constitutional amendment" 13 (2015) *International Journal of Constitutional Law (ICON)* 606; here the authors make the case that even in the contexts of unconstitutional constitutional amendments it still finds democratic legitimacy because it is "a way of defending popular sovereignty, because it limits the amendment power wielded by political institutions while preserving certain fundamental changes amounting to replacement of the constitution to 'the people' acting as constituent power" (612).

In contrast to the EU, the majority of SADC Member States account for some of the poorest countries in the world, with the notable exception of South Africa. The SADC has key structural hurdles still to overcome. However, there are lessons to be learnt from the EU and German constitutional relationship, in bringing integration ambitions into the constitution.

The deficiency of democratic legitimacy was best evidenced in the SADC context through the failure of the SADC tribunal.[62] Regional integration did not serve as a bridge to transport or export progressive constitutional traits into other jurisdictions within the region. The traversal rationality that transconstitutionalism encapsulates serves as a potential vehicle through which the progressive potential of a notion such as transformative constitutionalism could find application within other SADC jurisdictions.

How can Germany then overcome the issues discussed above, to return to a more plausible position as to its democratic legitimacy *vis-à-vis* the EU? A novel approach is followed by Martin Nettesheim by departing from the democratic deficit argument and rather arguing for a "theory of democracy for the European Union".[63] He argues that "the process of European integration may itself lead to a modernisation, supra-nationalisation or 'Europeanisation' of democratic theory".[64] Nettesheim criticises the proposition that the EU suffers from a democratic deficiency. He argues:

> "Such analyses frequently lead to the conclusion, if not the demand, that the EU ought to acquire the attributes and characteristics of a nation-state democracy – be it by transforming the decision-making system into a parliamentary democracy, by creating a 'European people,' a 'European identity' or via other steps – in order to gain democratic 'dignity'."[65]

Even though other theories[66] have been formulated in the German contexts, transconstitutionalism presents a viable option to resolve constitutional impasses. A critical distinctive characteristic of transconstitutionalism from these other theories is that it does not challenge sovereignty or the principle of sovereign equality. Rather, it deconstructs the hegemony of supranational

---

62 See further Ruppel and Bangamwabo "The SADC Tribunal: a legal analysis of its mandate and role in regional integration" 8 (2008) *Monitoring Regional Integration in Southern Africa Yearbook* 187 and Nathan "The disbanding of the SADC Tribunal: a cautionary tale" 35 (2013) *Human Rights Quarterly* 870. https://muse.jhu.edu/ (20-05-2017).

63 Nettesheim "Developing a theory of democracy for the European Union" 23 (2005) *Berkeley Journal of International Law (Berkeley J Int'l L)* 358.

64 (n 63) 359–360.

65 (n 63) 359.

66 Avbelj (n 54).

or transnational (constitutional) law. Together with this deconstruction it allows for the filtering through of superior constitutional thought without compromising the democratic legitimacy of the State.

VI. Conclusion

The interpretation of the traversal nature of contemporary constitutionalism should not seek to produce structural hegemony. Except for constitutional exceptionalism, internal paradoxes and challenges would normally bar the externalisation of a constitution beyond its jurisdiction. Transconstitutionalism overcomes this by advocating for a norm-based focus in establishing the traversal rationality of the constitutional imperatives.

The ultimate departure of municipal constitutional law in exposing itself to international, regional or other municipal laws cannot be ignorant of democratic legitimacy. Alessandro Passerin d'Entrèves reminds us that "[t]he greater the consensus on the ends to be pursued, the sounder is that authority".[67] In following this rationality, democratic legitimacy remains the pivotal norm which virtue needs to remain sacred in the externalisation of a constitution. How then can one answer the question as to our concern for what we can call the contraction of international law and the expansion of constitutional law into regionalism? Here one would have to concur with Holmes when he proposes "that questions regarding the fragmentation of world law and its so-called creeping constitutionalisation can only be deemed to be problematic due to its relations to a very particular perception of the phenomenon of social inclusion in world society."[68] This is no different from when the German constitutional court refers to the protection of its constitutional identity.

Transconstitutionalism is not the silver bullet to resolve theories on externalising constitutional norms; it is itself not without teething problems. Alexandre De Carvalho identifies two dilemmas which transconstitutionalism needs to deal with. The first is the question on "whether there is any competent body for the appraisal of issues involving the entanglement of

---

67 Passerin d'Entrèves *The Notion of the State: An Introduction to Political Theory* (1967) 228.

68 Holmes "The rhetoric of 'legal fragmentation' and its discontents" 7 (2011) *Utrecht Law Review (Utrecht LR)* 114.

the legal systems on multiple levels".[69] However, transconstitutionalism rejects this institutionalist approach of establishing new structures to address new conflicts. Instead, it relies on negotiation to bring about the legitimacy of outcome through learning and dialogue. The second dilemma is "the challenge of finding a legitimate way for the internal reading of decisions taken with reference to external elements when constitutional theory and legal doctrine keep asserting national sovereignty".[70] Here again, transnationalism provides a solution in that it follows the assumption that the different legal orders all function within a singular global system. The need to rely on national sovereignty becomes moot where interaction or communication is premised on the structural coupling. Consequently, the method through which democratic legitimacy was originally acquired becomes irrelevant for transconstitutionalism. It is through this knowledge that the democratic constituents of both states need to be more vigorous in defending their democracy through the process of integration.

69 de Carvalho "Transconstitutionalism or cosmopolitanism: perspectives for a dialogical semantics in contemporary constitutionalism" 2015 *Social Science Research Network SSRN* http://papers.ssrn.com/sol3/papers.cfm?abstract_id=2474144 (15-09-2017) 26.

70 (n 69) 10.

Bibliography

Abromeit H *Democracy in Europe* (Berghahn Books, New York 1998).

Avbelj M "Questioning EU constitutionalisms" 9 (2008) *German Law Journal (GLJ)* 1.

Beetham D and Lord C *Legitimacy and the EU* (Longman, Essex, England 1998).

Bellamy R, Bufacchi V and Castiglione D *Democracy and Constitutional Culture in the Union of Europe* (Lothian Foundation Press, London 1995).

Botha H "Transforming state and society: from the public/private dichotomy to mutual cooperation and destabilisation" in van der Schyff G (ed) *Constitutionalism in the Netherlands and South Africa: A Comparative Study* (Wolf Legal Publishers, Nijmegen 2008).

Brownlie I and Crawford J *Principles of Public International Law* (Oxford University Press, Oxford 2012).

Buchanan AE *Justice, Legitimacy, and Self-determination: Moral Foundations for International Law* (Oxford University Press, Oxford 2004).

Collier JG *Conflicts of Law* (Cambridge University Press, Cambridge 2001).

Coultrap J "From parliamentarism to pluralism: Models of democracy and the European Union's 'democratic deficit'" 11 (1999) *Journal of Theoretical Politics (IJTP)* 107.

Cygan A "Regional governance, subsidiarity and accountability within the EU's multilevel polity" 19 (2013) *European Public Law (EPL)* 161.

De Carvalho A "Transconstitutionalism or cosmopolitanism: Perspectives for a dialogical semantics in contemporary constitutionalism" 2015 *Social Science Research Network (SSRN)* https://papers.ssrn.com/sol3/papers.cfm?abstract_id=2474144 (14-04-2016).

Dixon R and Landau D "Transnational constitutionalism and a limited doctrine of unconstitutional constitutional amendment" 13 (2015) *International Journal of Constitutional Law* 606.

Dugard J et al *International Law: a South African perspective* (4th Edition, Juta, Cape Town 2012).

Evans M *International law* (2nd Edition, Oxford University Press, Oxford 2006).

Follesdal A and Koslowski P *Democracy and the European Union* (Springer, Berlin/ New York 1998).

Fontanelli F and Biondi Dal Monte F "The decisions nr. 348 and 349/2007 of the Italian Constitutional Court: The efficacy of the European Convention in the Italian legal system" 9 (2008) *German Law Journal (GLJ)* 890.

Fuller L *The Morality of Law* (2nd Edition, Yale University Press, New Haven 1969).

Grimm D "The role of fundamental rights after sixty-five years of constitutional jurisprudence in Germany" 13 (2015) *International Journal of Constitutional Law (ICON)* 9.

Hart H *Law, Liberty, and Morality* (Stanford University Press, Stanford 1963).

Holmes O "The rhetoric of 'legal fragmentation' and its discontents: Evolutionary dilemmas in the constitutional semantics of global law" 7 (2011) *Utrecht Law Review (Utrecht LR)* 113.

Holmes P "The politics of law and the laws of politics: The political paradoxes of transnational constitutionalism" 21 (2014) *Indiana Journal of Global Legal Studies (Ind J Global Legal Studies)* 553.

Iyi J-M *Humanitarian Intervention and the AU-ECOWAS Intervention Treaties under International Law: Towards a Theory of Regional Responsibility to Protect* (Springer, Cham 2016).

Klare K "Legal culture and transformative constitutionalism" 14 (1998) *South African Journal of Human Rights (SAJHR)* 146.

Krisch N *Beyond Constitutionalism: the Pluralist Structure of Postnational Law* (Oxford University Press, Oxford/New York 2010).

Langa PN *Transformative Constitutionalism* Stellenbosch 9 October 2006 (Unpublished Prestige Lecture).

Lanier, ER "Solange, farewell: The Federal German Constitutional Court and the recognition of the Court of Justice of the European Communities as lawful judge" 11 (1988) *Boston College International and Comparative Law Review (B.C. Int'l & Comp L Rev)* 1.

Lopes C "Law globalization and judicial pluralism: Cooperation limits in the magistrates dialogue"9 (2012) *Brazilian Journal of International Law* 229.

Lord C "Assessing democracy in a contested polity" 39 (2001) *Journal of Common Market Studies (JCMS)* 641.

Lord C *Democracy in the European Union* (4th Edition, Sheffield Academic Press, Sheffield, 1998).

MacCormick N *Questioning Sovereignty: Law, State, and Nation in the European Commonwealth* (Oxford University Press, Oxford/New York 1999).

Madison J, Hamilton A, Jay J et al. *The Federalist papers* (5th Edition, Penguin, London 1987).

Michalowski S and Woods L *German Constitutional Law: The Protection of Civil Liberties* (Aldershot, Ashgate/Dartmouth 1999).

Nathan L 'The disbanding of the SADC Tribunal: a cautionary tale' 35 (2013) *Human Rights Quarterly* 870. https://muse.jhu.edu/ (20.05.2017).

Nettesheim M "Developing a theory of democracy for the European Union" 23 (2005) *Berkeley Journal of International Law (Berkeley J Int'l L)* 358.

Neves M "Comparing transconstitutionalism in an asymmetric world society: Conceptual background and self-critical remarks" 2015 *Adam Smith Research Foundation Working Papers Series* 13.

Newman M *Democracy, Sovereignty and the European Union* (St. Martin's Press, New York 1996).

Okowa P *State Responsibility for Transboundary Air Pollution in International Law* (Oxford University Press, Oxford/New York 2000).

Passerin d'Entrèves A *The Notion of the State: An Introduction to Political Theory* (Oxford University Press, London 1967).

Pernice I "Multilevel constitutionalism and the Treaty of Amsterdam: European constitution-making revisited" 36 (1999) *Common Market Law Review (CML Rev.)* 703.

Pernice I "The Treaty of Lisbon: Multilevel constitutionalism in action" Walter Hallstein-Institut für Europäisches Verfassungsrecht Humbold-Universität zu Berlin (WHI) Paper 2/09, http://www.whi-berlin.de/documents/whi-paper0209.pdfhttp://www.whi-berlin.de/documents/whi-paper0209.pdf (01-12-2016).

Peters A "European democracy after the 2003 Convention" 41 (2004) *Common Market Law Review (CML Rev.)* 37.

Rapatsa M "Transformative constitutionalism in South Africa: 20 years of democracy" 5 (2014) *Mediterranean Journal of Social Sciences* 887.

Reisman W *The Quest for World Order and Human Dignity in the Twenty-First Century: Constitutive Process and Individual Commitment* (Martinus Nijhoff, Leiden 2012).

Roux T "Transformative constitutionalism and the best interpretation of the South African Constitution: Distinction without a difference?" 2009 *Stellenbosch Law Review (Stellenbosch L. Rev.)* 263.

Ruppel OC and Bangamwabo FX "The SADC Tribunal: a legal analysis of its mandate and role in regional integration" 8 (2008) *Monitoring Regional Integration in Southern Africa Yearbook* 187.

Saurombe A "Flexible integration: a viable technique for the process of deeper integration in the Southern African Development Community (SADC)" 45 (2012) *The Comparative and International Law Journal of Southern Africa* 91.

Schmitter P *How to democratize the European Union...and why bother?* (Rowman & Littlefield, Lanham 2000).

Sen A *Development as Freedom* (Knopf, New York 1999).

Shaw M *International Law* (6th Edition, Cambridge University Press, Cambridge/New York 2008).

Siedentop L *Democracy in Europe* (Columbia University Press, New York 2001).

Stiglitz J *Globalization and Its Discontents* (W.W. Norton, New York 2002).

Tushnet M "The inevitable globalization of constitutional law" 50 (2008) *Virginia Journal of International Law (Va J Int'l L)* 985.

Van Marle K "Transformative constitutionalism as/and critique" 2009 *Stellenbosch Law Review (Stellenbosch L. Rev.)* 286.

Vincze A "What role for constitutional courts in a multi-level constitutionalism?" 2012 *Annales University of Science Budapestinensis Rolando Eötvös* 55.

Walker N "Multilevel constitutionalism: Looking beyond the German debate" 2009 *London School of Economics 'Europe in Question' (LEQS) Discussion Paper* Series No 8.

Weiler JHH. *The Constitution of Europe* (Cambridge University Press, Cambridge/New York 1999).

Weiler JHH. *The Constitution of Europe : "Do the New Clothes have an Emperor?" and Other Essays on European Integration* (Cambridge University Press, Cambridge/New York 1999).

Yusuf A *Pan-Africanism and International Law* (Hague Academy of International Law, Hague 2014).

Case Law

South Africa

Democratic Alliance v Minister of International Relations and Cooperation (Council for the Advancement of the South African Constitution Intervening) 2017 2 All SA 123 (GP)

Minister of Justice and Constitutional Development v Southern African Litigation Centre 2016 2 All SA 365 (SCA)

My Vote Counts NPC v Speaker of the National Assembly 2015 12 BCLR 1407 (CC)

Soobramoney v Minister of Health, KwaZulu-Natal 1998 1 SA 765 (CC)

Southern Africa Litigation Centre v Minister of Justice and Constitutional Development 2015 3 All SA 505 (GP)

Germany

BVerfG 18.10.1967 – 1 BvR 248/63, 1 BvR 216/67 – BVerfGE 22, 293.

BVerfG 29.5.1974 – 2 BvL 52/71 – BVerfGE 37, 271 *(Solange I)*.

BVerfG 22.10.1986 – 2 BvR 197/83 – BVerfGE 73, 339 *(Solange II)*.

BVerfG 21.6.2016 – 2 BvR 2728/13, 2 BvR 2729/13, 2 BvR 2730/13, 2 BvR 2731/13 – NJW 2016, 2473 *(OMT)*.

European Court of Justice

Costa v ENEL (ECJ) Case C6-64 15.7.1964 *N V Algemene Transport- en Expeditie Onderneming Van Gend & Loos and Nederlandse administatie der belastingen* (ECJ) Case C-25/62 5.2.1963

Social insurance in South Africa: are there lessons to be learnt from the German experience?

*Letlhokwa George Mpedi**
*Mathias Nyenti***

I. Introduction

Social insurance is a part and parcel of the three main social security strategies found in the Republic of South Africa. These strategies comprise of social assistance, social insurance and social allowance.

---

* Professor (Executive Dean) and Director: Centre for International and Comparative Labour and Social Security Law (CICLASS), University of Johannesburg, Faculty of Law.

** Senior Lecturer: Department of Mercantile Law and Research Associate: Centre for International and Comparative Labour and Social Security Law (CICLASS), University of Johannesburg, Faculty of Law.

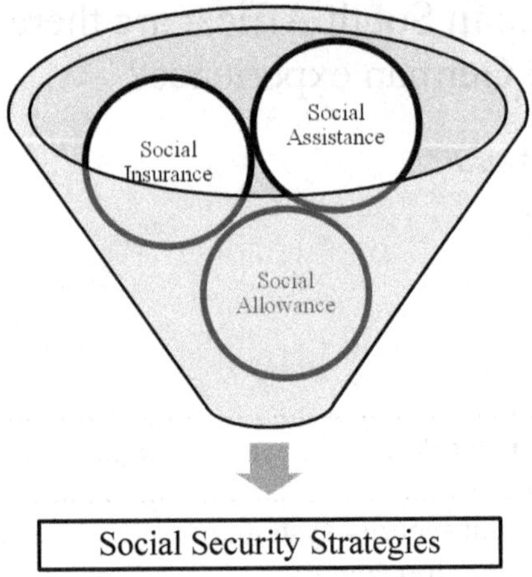

Figure 1: Main social security strategies in South Africa

In reality, social assistance and social insurance feature more prominently in the South African social security system than social allowance. It should be pointed out from the onset that the South African social security system is well developed for an emerging economy. This view is informed by, among others, the fact that the system covers all the social risks articulated in the International Labour Organization Social Security (Minimum Standards) Convention 102 of 1952, ie sickness, maternity, employment injury, unemployment, invalidity, old age, death, medical care and family. All these risks are covered through the social insurance system. It should also be mentioned that some of the risks are catered for directly and, in some instances, indirectly, through one of the largest social assistance programmes on the African continent. Such contingencies include old age, invalidity and family.

However well the South African social security system may be, particularly when one looks at the social insurance scheme, it should be cautioned that the system is far from perfect. This can, to a large extent, be attributed to the colonial and apartheid heritage of the entire South African social-security system. Laws and policies of that time had a profound adverse impact on the design and reach of the programme. Many of the negative effects of such laws and policies (eg social exclusion) are still being felt today. The post-apartheid South Africa wasgreatly influenced by the current Constitution, which is the supreme law of the country and recognises social security rights as human rights. The country embarked on a journey of transforming the social security system inclusive of the social insurance scheme. While much has been achieved, it is clear that South Africa is not yet out of the woods.

This chapter seeks to explore the lessons that could be drawn from the German social insurance experience. Germany is renowned for its long social insurance history. Nonetheless, the foregoing observation should not be understood as implying that the German experience is wholly transferable – particularly to the South African context. There are social and economic factors that make such a thought to be a fallacy. Notwithstanding that, there are – as shown in this chapter – social insurance principles and approaches that could be taken into account by South Africa in its ongoing endeavour to craft a comprehensive social security system. Accordingly, this chapter does not seek to cover all the various aspects of social security. It is hoped that the approaches and principles covered will lay the foundation for future research on the transnational impact of social security. The approaches and principles examined in this contribution are discussed under the following themes: the legislative framework, scope of coverage, financing, adjudication and enforcement. This discussion is then followed by some thoughts on lessons to be learnt and some concluding observations.

II. Legislative framework

The South African social security legislative framework is set out, as shown in Table 1 below, in a variety of social security laws.

CONSTITUTION OF THE REPUBLIC OF SOUTH AFRICA, 1996			
PUBLIC SCHEMES		PRIVATE SCHEMES	
Social Assistance	**Social Insurance**		**Informal Social Security**
	Statutory Funds	Voluntary Funds	
Social Assistance Act 13 of 2004 South African Social Security Agency Act 9 of 2004 Military Pensions Act 84 of 1976. Special Pensions Act 69 of 1996	Compensation Fund: Compensation for Occupational Injuries and Diseases Act 130 of 1993. Unemployment Insurance Fund: Unemployment Insurance Act 63 of 2001 and Unemployment Insurance Contributions Act 4 of 2002. Road Accident Fund: Road Accident Fund Act 56 of 1996.	Medical Schemes: Medical Schemes Act 131 of 1998. Pension Funds: Pension Funds Act 24 of 1956.	Informal Social Security: Friendly Societies Act 25 of 1956.

Table 1 South African Social Security Legislative Framework

In addition, there are other laws that are not social security laws as such which are nonetheless pertinent to the efficient administration of social security. These laws cover areas such as access to information,[1] administrative justice,[2] labour relations[3] and basic conditions of employment.[4] As apparent from the preceding, the South African social security system is based on a variety of laws. These laws are designed to facilitate the smooth administration of social security and, most importantly, the provision of access to social security. Nonetheless, a number of problems have emerged. Firstly, the current legislative framework is complex.[5] The problem is compounded by the fact that a number of social security laws, rules and regulations have been adopted since the demise of apartheid. This was done predominantly to align social security laws with the new political and constitutional dispensation. As a result of this, in most instances a majority of persons who should benefit from the protection afforded by the various social security laws are invariably prevented from doing so due to ignorance. In some cases, social security laws are simply unknown to the general populace. This problem invariably leads to the exclusion and marginalisation of the vulnerable members of the society of which the majority have limited education.

South Africa needs to systematise its social security laws so as to make them accessible to all. It seriously needs to consider consolidating its social security laws under one code. Such a step is desirable for the reason that it generally renders social security law accessible. This is the case albeit it is

1 Promotion of Access to Information Act 2 of 2000.
2 Promotion of Administrative Justice Act 3 of 2000.
3 Labour Relations Act 66 of 1995.
4 Basic Conditions of Employment Act 75 of 1997.
5 It is for this reason that the court remarked in *Cele v South African Social Security Agency and 22 Related Cases* 2008 BCLR 734 (D) para 11 that: "...in the field of social assistance in South Africa the primary and secondary legislation is as labyrinthine as it apparently is in the United Kingdom and the entitlement of any applicant to relief flowing from a failure on the part of the Minister of Social Development or SASSA [South African Social Security Agency] may well be complex. All this can only serve to emphasise the necessity for those lawyers who practise in this area of the law to be thoroughly familiar with the applicable legislation, both primary and secondary and to ensure that it is properly placed before the Court in a coherent form when the need for litigation arises."

sometimes argued that codification cannot bring the law within the comprehension of laymen.[6] Needless to say, codification makes the law more accessible to those (ie, paralegals, non-governmental organisations or even trade unions) who advise on or aid ordinary people in legal matters. In addition, codification of social security laws does not mean that social security institutions (particularly those that deal with social assistance) do not have the duty of generating public awareness about the services and benefits they provide. Furthermore, codification, depending on the type of codification adopted,[7] will improve several aspects of social- security law due to greater certainty in the legal system. Reforming codification provides an opportune moment for, among others, addressing inconsistent concepts; reconceptualising social security; harmonising social security dispute resolution, enforcement mechanisms and procedures; and identifying lacunae in current social security law.

Unlike South Africa, Germany has a Social Code (*Sozialgesetzbuch* (SGB)). The SGB is divided into twelve separate books as follows:

Book	**Titel**	**In force since**
SGB I	General Part (*Allgemeiner Teil*)	1 January 1976
SGB II	Basic Insurance for Employment Seekers (*Grundsicherung für Arbeitsuchende*)	1 January 2005
SGB III	Employment Promotion (*Arbeitsförderung*)	1 January 1998

6 Hahlo "Here lies the common law: rest in peace" 30 (1967) *Modern Law Review (Mod L Rev)* 241 245.

7 As pointed in *Law Drafting Manual in Albania: Guide to the Legislative Process in Albania* (2006) 27 (accessed at http://www.legislationline.org/download/action/download/id/2029/file/Albania_Law_Drafting_Manual_2006.pdf (15-09-2017)) codification has two purposes: "One is to reform the law as well as organising it systematically. This is attractive because it is innovative. It consists of redrafting and reformulating a legal domain with the integration of new concepts and the creation of new norms. This ambitious codification requires a great deal of time and application, and it is not always successful. Secondly, there is codification of the existing law by simply consolidating the texts. This is more modest in its aims, consisting of gathering and structuring the law in force as it stands and not as it should be. It does not involve creating new rules, but a stocktaking that paves the way for any necessary reform. This type of codification certainly has the advantage of simplifying access to law."

SGB IV	Common Social Insurance Provisions (*Gemeinsame Vorschriften für die Sozialversicherung*)	1 January 1977
SGB V	Statutory Health Insurance (*Gesetzliche Krankenversicherung*)	1 January 1989
SGB VI	Statutory Retirement Insurance (*Gesetzliche Rentenversicherung*)	1 January 1992
SGB VII	Statutory Accident Insurance (*Gesetzliche Unfallversicherung*)	1 January 1997
SGB VIII	Assistance for Children and Adolescents (*Kinder- und Jugendhilfe*)	3 October 1990 (States of the Former East Germany)
		1 January 1991 (States of the former West Germany
SGB IX	Rehabilitation and Participation of Disabled People (*Rehabilitation und Teilhabe behinderter Menschen*)	1 July 2001
SGB X	Social Administrative Procedure and Social Data Protection (*Sozialverwaltungsverfahren und Sozialdatenschutz*)	1 January 1981
		1 January 1995
SGB XI	Social Care Insurance (*Sozial Pflegeversicherung*)	1 January 1995
SGB XII	Social Assistance (*Sozialhilfe*)	1 January 2005

Table 2 Social Code Framework

What is notable about the SGB is that it makes provision for both social assistance and social insurance benefits. Furthermore, it is not fixated with compensation. The payment of benefits is underpinned by measures aimed at preventing social risks and those that are aimed at (re)integration. These measures are weak and in some cases lacking in the South African social security system.

III. Scope of coverage

South Africa's Constitution provides everyone with the right to have access to social security, including social assistance for persons who are unable to support themselves and their dependants.[8] The Constitution further guarantees other social security related rights, such as housing, health, food and water.[9] In order to give effect to these rights, the state is required to adopt reasonable legislative and other measures, within its available resources, to achieve their realisation.[10] Therefore, there is an obligation on the state to establish a comprehensive social security system.[11]

As pointed out earlier, the South African social security system consists of social insurance and social assistance schemes. Social insurance is made up of mandatory contributory social insurance and voluntary private insurance. Mandatory contributory social insurance schemes exist for unemployment (the Unemployment Insurance Fund), occupational injury and disease protection (the Compensation Fund and the Compensation Commissioner for Occupational Diseases) and for motor vehicle accident insurance (the Road Accident Fund); while voluntary private insurance is made up of medical insurance schemes and retirement funds. Social assistance consists of the social grants system and the provision of various social welfare services.

However, there are gaps in the personal scope of coverage of the South African social security system. Social insurance coverage is limited by the labour market context and the eligibility conditions of the various schemes. In relation to the labour market context, Statistics South Africa reveals that out of a population of about 52 million, the working age population in the fourth quarter of 2015 was 36.3 million.[12] The labour force was just over 21.2 million, with 16 million employed. Out of this total, 11.2 million were employed in the formal (non-agricultural) sector, 2.7 million were employed in the informal (non-agricultural) sector, 860 000 were employed in

---

8 sec 27(1)*(c)* of the Constitution of South Africa, 1996.

9 secs 26(1) and 27(1)*(a)* and *(b)* of the Constitution of South Africa.

10 secs 26(2) and 27(2) of the Constitution of South Africa.

11 See Committee of Inquiry into a Comprehensive System of Social Security for South Africa *Transforming the Present – Protecting the Future* (Draft Consolidated Report) (March 2002) http://www.ci.org.za/depts/ci/pubs/pdf/poverty/news/report_release_of_coi.pdf (16-11-2016).

12 Statistics South Africa *Quarterly Labour Force Survey, Quarter 4 2015* iv http://www.statssa.gov.za/publications/P0211/P02114thQuarter2015.pdf (15-09-2017).

agriculture and 1.3 million were employed in private households.[13] Just over 15 million were not economically active and 5.2 million were unemployed.

The mandatory social insurance schemes are restricted to persons who are employed in the formal sector (employees).[14] The restriction of access to these schemes to persons in an employee-employer relationship means that the self-employed and other informally-employed persons have no social insurance coverage. Moreover, some categories of employees are excluded from the scope of coverage of some of these schemes.[15] As a result of this, only 8.75 million workers were contributors to the Unemployment Insurance Fund as of March 2015.[16]

Furthermore, private insurance schemes (medical aid schemes and pension funds) are voluntary schemes which entail a lack of compulsory affiliation.[17] This has led to low levels of membership in these schemes. As an example, there were 8.81 million members of medical aid schemes in 2014.[18] Therefore, a vast majority of South Africans have no health insurance protection and depend on the public health sector. In addition, National Treasury estimates the retirement insurance coverage rate for formal sector employees at 60 per cent.[19]

---

13 Statistics South Africa (n 12) iv.

14 See secs 1 and 23 of Compensation for Occupational Injuries and Diseases Act (COIDA) 130 of 1993; and secs 1 and 3 of the Unemployment Insurance Act (UIA) 63 of 2001.

15 Sec 3(1) of the UIA states that the Act applies to all employers and employees, other than employees employed for less than 24 hours a month with a particular employer, and their employers; employees who receive remuneration under a learnership agreement registered in terms of the Skills Development Act 97 of 1998, and their employers; employers and employees in the national and provincial spheres of government; and temporary foreign workers and their employers. COIDA also excludes some categories of employees, including domestic employees employed as such in a private household (sec 1 of COIDA).

16 Unemployment Insurance Fund *Annual Report 2015*, 56 http://www.labour.gov.za/DOL/downloads/documents/annual-reports/unemployment-insurance-fund/2015/uifannualreport2015.pdf (16-11-2016).

17 See Medical Schemes Act 131 of 1998 and Pension Funds Act 24 of 1956.

18 Council for Medical Schemes *Annual Report 2014–2015*, 138 https://www.medicalschemes.com/files/Annual%20Reports/AR2014_2015.pdf (15-09-2017).

19 National Treasury *Social Security and Retirement Reform* (2007) 5, http://www.treasury.gov.za/documents/national%20budget/2007/Social%20security%20and%20retirement%20reform%20paper.pdf (15-09-2017).

The social assistance system is limited to children, persons with disabilities and persons over the age of 60.[20] During the 2016–2017 financial year, the social grants will cover 17.4 million people (about 33 per cent of the population). The figures for the various grants were as follows:

Social Grant	Total Number of Recipients
Child Support Grant	12.349 million
Foster Care Grant	461,000
Care Dependency Grant	148,000
Disability Grant	1.086 million
Old Age and War Veterans Grants	3.3 million

Table 3 Social grants and total number of recipients[21]

The limitation of access to mandatory social insurance to selected categories of employees, the lack of compulsion for private social insurance and the absence of social assistance for unemployed able-bodied persons between the ages of 18 and 59 means that a large proportion of the working-age population is without any social security coverage. There is thus a need to extend the social security scope of coverage. This requires getting as many people as possible into the labour market; and ensuring their participation in social insurance schemes (including the self-employed and other informally-employed persons).

This is supported by the basic formula for social security, which provides that every adult (who is not yet elderly or occupied by family responsibilities) must earn an income in the labour market and meet his own and society's needs.[22] This formula finds expression in the South African Constitution as well as the German Constitution and Social Code.[23]

20 See the Social Assistance Act 13 of 2004.

21 National Treasury *2016 Budget Review* 64 http://www.treasury.gov.za/documents/national%20budget/2016/review/FullReview.pdf (15-09-2017).

22 Zacher *Social Policy in the Federal Republic of Germany: The Constitution of the Social* (2013) 355.

23 It must be noted that sec 27(1)*(c)* of the South African Constitution states that everyone with the right to have access to social security, including social assistance for persons who are unable to support themselves and their dependants. This means the state's duty to realise the right differs according to a person's ability to realise the right themselves; see *Government of the Republic of South Africa v Grootboom* 2000 11 BCLR 1169 (CC); 2001 1 SA 46 (CC) 36. On its part, art

With its comprehensive social security system, Germany presents a benchmark for South Africa in its current reform initiatives aimed at developing a comprehensive social security system.[24] The comprehensiveness of Germany's social security system is made possible by a well-functioning labour market that ensures stable employment. As at August 2015 the labour force was 42.2 million out of a population of about 81 million, with about 2.8 million people unemployed and the unemployment rate at 6.4 per cent.[25] This promotes access to social insurance for a large number of people of working age.

The German social security system is made up of various statutory social insurance and social assistance schemes which are aimed at providing comprehensive life-cycle support.[26] The system has a greater reliance on social insurance coverage than on social assistance, with about 31 million people employed in jobs subject to social security deductions.[27] The social insurance system is based on 5 pillars: health insurance, retirement insurance, unemployment insurance; occupational injury or disease insurance and nursing care insurance.[28]

20(1) of the German Constitution states that the Federal Republic of Germany is a democratic and social federal state. According to sec 1 of the German Social Code *(Sozialgesetzbuch I, SGB I)*, the Code's objectives are the achievement of social justice and social security benefits, including social and educational aids. It is intended to (amongst others) help secure a dignified existence, to protect and promote the family, to enable the acquisition of livelihood through freely chosen activity; and prevent or compensate special burdens of life by helping people help themselves.

24 Social Security Administration *Social Security Programs Throughout the World: Europe* (2014) 114, https://www.ssa.gov/policy/docs/progdesc/ssptw/2014-2015/europe/ssptw14europe.pdf (15-09-2017).

25 European Job Mobility Portal (EURES) *Labour Market Information: Germany*: https://ec.europa.eu/eures/main.jsp?acro=lmi&lang=en&parentId=0&countryId=DE (15-09-2017); and World Bank *World Development Indicators; Labor Force Structure*: http://wdi.worldbank.org/table/2.2. (18-04-2016).

26 Hong Kong Legislative Council Secretariat *Fact Sheet: Social security System in Germany* (2015) 1, http://www.legco.gov.hk/research-publications/english/1415fsc11-social-security-system-in-germany-20150225-e.pdf (15-09-2017).

27 The European Job Mobility Portal (n 25).

28 Hong Kong Legislative Council Secretariat (n 26) 1.

The statutory health insurance scheme *(gesetzliche Krankenversicherung)* is compulsory for employees earning up to a defined limit.[29] Employees earning above the defined threshold may opt either to be insured voluntarily under the statutory scheme or participate in the private health insurance system. There is full health insurance coverage of the population, with about 70 million people (85 per cent) covered by the statutory health insurance scheme.[30]

Membership in the statutory retirement insurance scheme (*Rentenversicherung*) is also compulsory for employed persons (including apprentices), certain self-employed persons (such as tradespeople and freelance artists), persons on paternity leave, and military personnel. There is voluntary coverage for certain categories of people who are not required to participate, such as German citizens who are resident abroad, foreign residents in Germany and housewives. Special retirement insurance schemes have been established for certain self-employed persons, miners, public sector employees and farmers.[31]

Participation in the unemployment insurance scheme (*Arbeitslosenversicherung*) is mandatory for employed persons, including household workers, apprentices, and trainees; and other groups, including recipients of sickness benefits and persons raising a child. Coverage for self-employed persons, caregivers, and foreign workers from outside of the European Union is voluntary. However, persons in irregular employment are excluded.[32]

The occupational injury and disease insurance scheme (*Berufsunfallversicherung*) protects all employed persons; some categories of self-employed

---

29 Obermann et al (eds) *Understanding the German Health Care System* Mannheim Institute of Public Health (2013) 20, https://www.goinginternational.eu/newsletter/2013/nl_03/SpecialDE_EN_Understanding_the_German.pdf (15-09-2017); Espoo, Amanjani, Zanjani et al "A comparative study on social security systems in Iran, Germany, France, and Turkey" 5 (2015) *Journal of Applied Environmental and Biological Sciences (J. Appl. Environ. Biol. Sci.)*174 177; Deutsche Bundesbank *Germany's Statutory Health Insurance Scheme: Past Developments and Future Challenges* (Monthly Report: July 2014) 29, https://www.bundesbank.de/Redaktion/EN/Downloads/Publications/Monthly_Report_Articles/2014/2014_07_health.pdf?__blob=publicationFile (15-09-2017).

30 Ellis et al "Comparisons of health insurance systems in developed countries" in Culyer (ed) *Encyclopedia of Health Economics* (vol 1) (2014) 396; and Deutsche Bundesbank (n 29) 30.

31 Social Security Administration (n 24) 114; and Hong Kong Legislative Council Secretariat (n 26) 2.

32 Social Security Administration (n 24) 119; and Hong Kong Legislative Council Secretariat (n 26) 2.

persons; persons engaged in specified voluntary activities; apprentices; and students. There is a possibility for voluntary coverage. However, most categories of self-employed persons are excluded.[33]

Long-term nursing care insurance (*Pflegeversicherung*), for those in need of care and the assistance of other people, is available for persons covered by the statutory sickness insurance system. Persons who are covered by private health insurance schemes must also get private long-term care insurance.[34] As a result there is also complete coverage of the long-term nursing care insurance scheme.[35]

Reliance on social insurance has given social assistance a residual function, with only about 7.57 million people (9.3 per cent of the population) dependent on social assistance in 2014.[36] Social assistance consists of an unemployment benefit scheme (for persons between the ages of 15 and 64 who are fit for employment, cannot get a job, or are not earning enough income to meet their basic needs); the social assistance scheme (for persons falling outside the unemployment benefit scheme but who cannot meet their basic needs and are not eligible for social insurance and other social assistance schemes that enable them to live in dignity); child benefits (as a tax refund for persons with children and in some cases for young people over 18); and parental benefits (for loss or reduction of earnings due to family responsibilities).[37]

However, it must be noted that Germany's social security system, with its focus on stable employment and participation in social insurance, is currently being threatened by the rising number of "mini jobs".[38] Since workers in such work earn below the threshold for inclusion in the statutory social

---

33 Social Security Administration (n 24) 118; and Hong Kong Legislative Council Secretariat (n 26) 4.

34 Social Security Administration (n 24) 116; and Hong Kong Legislative Council Secretariat (n 26) 4.

35 Schulz *The Long-term Care System in Germany* (2010) 6 http://www.diw.de/documents/publikationen/73/diw_01.c.359024.de/dp1039.pdf (15-09-2017).

36 See *Statistiches Bundesamt* (German Statistics Office) *Statistisches Jahrbuch 2015*, https://www.destatis.de/DE/Publikationen/StatistischesJahrbuch/StatistischesJahrbuch2015.pdf?__blob=publicationFile (15-09-2017).

37 Hong Kong Legislative Council Secretariat (n 26) 5–6.

38 These are part-time jobs paying below the threshold for social security contributions, see Weinkopf "Germany: precarious employment and the rise of mini-jobs" in Vosko et al *Gender and the Contours of Precarious Employment* (2010) 177.

insurance schemes, they are marginalised or excluded from social security.[39]

IV. Financing of social security system

There are different modalities for financing the various aspects of a social-security system. Social insurance schemes are funded through employer and employee (and sometimes state) contributions, while social assistance schemes are mostly funded though taxes. The same applies to the South African and German systems.

In South Africa, unemployment insurance is funded by the employer and employee each paying 1 per cent of the employee's remuneration (2 per cent in total).[40] Health and retirement insurance is financed through premiums from employees, with contributions by employers. Occupational injuries and diseases insurance is financed from levies paid by employers in the form of annual assessments on a basis of a percentage or fixed rate of the annual earnings of their employees.[41] The social assistance system is funded through allocations from the national budget.[42] Due to South Africa's reliance on public health care and on the social assistance grants, a sizeable proportion of its budget is spent on these. In the 2016–2017 financial year, government plans to spend 13.1 per cent of the national budget on health and 12.9 per cent on social protection (with social grants making up 84.2 per cent of the social protection budget and 3.2 per cent of GDP).[43]

Germany spends about 25.5 per cent of GDP on social security expenditure.[44] Its reliance on social insurance has ensured that a large part of its

---

39 Weinkopf (n 38) 177.

40 sec 6 of the Unemployment Insurance Contribution Act 6 of 2002.

41 See Compensation Fund *Annual Report 2014–2015* 18 http://www.labour.gov.za/DOL/downloads/documents/annual-reports/compensation-for-occupational-injuries-and-diseases/2015/cfannualreport2015.pdf (16-11-2016).

42 See National Treasury *2016 Budget Review* (n 21) 64.

43 *Ibid.*

44 Kirkegaard *The True Levels of Government and Social Expenditures in Advanced Economies* Peterson Institute for International Economics Policy Brief (March 2015) 5, https://piie.com/publications/pb/pb15-4.pdf (15-09-2017); and OECD *Social Spending is Falling in Some Countries, but in Many Others it Remains at Historically High Levels: Insights from the OECD Social Expenditure Database (SOCX)* (November 2014) 1, https://www.oecd.org/els/soc/OECD2014-SocialExpenditure_Update19Nov_Rev.pdf (15-09-2017).

social security system is financed from contributions by employees and employers. As a result of this, only about 20 per cent of social security expenditure comes from general taxes.[45] The country spends approximately $4218 annually per capita on health care, representing 11.5 per cent of Gross Domestic Product. Public health care expenditures are 77 per cent of health spending, with the primary health insurance accounting for 58 per cent.[46]

Employers and employees pay contributions for sickness insurance, long-term care insurance, unemployment insurance and pension insurance; while employers pay the premiums for occupational injury and disease insurance.[47] An employee's level of statutory insurance contributions is a fixed percentage of his or her earnings.[48]

V. Adjudication and enforcement

Both the South African and German Constitution guarantee the right of access to justice or a fair trial. In terms of section 34 of the South African Constitution, everyone has the right to have any dispute that can be resolved by the application of law decided in a fair public hearing before a court or, where appropriate, another independent and impartial tribunal or forum.

---

45 Espoo, Amanjani, Zanjani et al (n 29) 175.

46 Ellis et al (n 30) 400.

47 Employers and employees contribute on an equal basis to the statutory health insurance scheme. In 2015, this was set at 14.6 % employee's gross income. Employees are further required to contribute an additional premium of 0.9 % on average. The contribution rate for retirement insurance was 18.7 % in 2015 (subject to contribution assessment limits) which is also equally shared by employees and employers. The unemployment insurance scheme is funded by equal contributions by employees and employers, with the rate set in 2015 at 3 % of an employee's gross earning (up to a defined contribution assessment limit). Long-term nursing care insurance is also financed through equal employer and employee contributions. The 2015 rate of contribution was 2.35 % (subject to a defined contribution assessment limit) with childless contributors paying a 0.25 % supplement. An employer's contribution rate for occupational injury and disease insurance depends on the total annual wage bill and risk assessment, see European Commission *Your Social Security Rights in Germany* (2013) 8 http://ec.europa.eu/employment_social/empl_portal/SSRinEU/Your%20social%20security%20rights%20in%20Germany_en.pdf (15-09-2017); and Hong Kong Legislative Council Secretariat (n 26) 2–4.

48 European Commission (n 47) 8.

The right of access to justice in the Constitution requires that dispute resolution institutions must be accessible, that these institutions must be independent and impartial in the execution of their duties, and that disputes must be resolved in a fair and public hearing.

Regarding the German Constitution, article 19(s) provides that a person whose rights are violated by public authority may have recourse to the courts. Article 19(4) further states that if a court with specific jurisdiction in respect to the dispute has not been established, the aggrieved person will have recourse to the ordinary courts. The German Federal Constitutional Court's jurisprudence reveals that the right of access to justice in the Constitution requires an effective and coherent system of remedies against all acts of state that affect the citizens. It is for this reason that the Constitution envisages independent ordinary as well as special courts.[49]

In addition to constitutional courts, the German judicial system consists of five jurisdictions, namely ordinary (civil and criminal), labour, administrative, financial and social jurisdictions[50]

In South Africa, each of the statutes regulating social insurance schemes provides for dispute resolution mechanisms and institutions.[51] Appeal

---

49 See arts 93, 95, 96 and 97 of the German Constitution.

50 Gärditz *Judicial Review and Remedies in a Nutshell: Annual Report 2010 – Germany* (May 2011) 2 and 5 http://www.ius-publicum.com/repository/uploads/05_07_2011_9_42_Gaerditz.pdf (15-09-2017); Bundessozialgericht *Das Bundessozialgericht und die deutsche Sozialgerichtsbarkeit – eine Information* (English Summary) (August 2015) 39 http://www.bsg.bund.de/SharedDocs/Publikationen/Broschuere/Das_Bundessozialgericht_und_die_deutsche_Sozialgerichtsbarkeit_Broschuere_2015_2016.pdf?__blob=publicationFile (15-09-2017); European Union Agency for Fundamental Rights (FRA) *Access to Justice in Europe: An Overview of Challenges and Opportunities* (National Thematic Study – Germany) (2010) 1 http://fra.europa.eu/sites/default/files/fra_uploads/1526-access-to-justice-2011-country-DE.pdf (15-09-2017); and Jaeger and Broß *The Relations between the Constitutional Courts and the Other National Courts, including the Interference in this Area of the Action of the European Courts* (Report of the Constitutional Court of the Federal Republic of Germany) paper presented at the Conference of European Constitutional Courts XIIth Congress (Karlsruhe, August 28, 2001) 2 http://www.confeuconstco.org/reports/rep-xii/Duitsland-EN.pdf (16-11-2016).

51 The adjudication system consists of the Compensation Court in terms of the COIDA; Certification Committee of the Medical Bureau for Occupational Diseases and Medical Reviewing Authority for Occupational Diseases under the Occupational Diseases in Mines and Works Act 78 of 1973 (ODMWA); the Regional Appeals Committees and National Appeals Committee of the Board of the Unemployment Insurance Fund in terms of the UIA; the Road Accident Fund Appeal

mechanisms are also fragmented across the social- security system, at times involving specially-constituted appeal bodies and at times the Labour or High Court. Therefore, the social security dispute resolution system is fragmented and uncoordinated due to the absence of a uniform framework.

Tribunal in terms of the Road Accident Fund Act 56 of 1996; the Office of the Pension Funds Adjudicator established by the Pension Funds Act; and the Registrar and Appeal Board of the Council for Medical Schemes regulated by the Medical Schemes Act. A Financial Services Tribunal is envisaged in the Financial Sector Regulation Bill (2014) to adjudicate appeals in terms of a financial sector law (secs 153 and 154 of the Financial Sector Regulation Bill). The Tribunal will hear appeals against decisions of the Pension Funds Adjudicator, with the decisions of the Tribunal reviewable by the High Court (see para 2.2.9.5 of the Memorandum on the Objects of the Financial Sector Regulation Bill of 10 December 2014).

Some of the other challenges include the inaccessibility of some social security institutions,[52] inappropriateness of some current appeal institutions,[53]

52 Their accessibility is not always appropriately ensured. Some forums are geographically spread across the Republic, while legislation also empowers some of the adjudication forums to be convened at any determined place. However, others are centrally located. Accessibility is also facilitated through multiple application lodgement options and reasonable timeframes. The relevant documentation for the lodging of applications and consideration of disputes are in English and the hearings (where applicable) are also conducted in English. However, interpreters are provided where necessary. In addition, the Road Accident Fund provides for the travel and accommodation needs of persons required to attend a hearing. The parties to a dispute are also notified of the dispute resolution outcome. However, the speedy resolution of disputes is not guaranteed, as timeframes for finalisation have not been stated in many statutes. In addition no power is granted to the adjudication forums to reconsider their original decision. Furthermore, avenues for alternative (speedier, more flexible) dispute resolution are not available for most disputes. Adjudication forums adopt a variety of dispute resolution procedures (convening of a hearing or simply consideration of documentary evidence). External dispute resolution avenues are only through litigation in the High Court (at times the Labour Court) (see sec 50(1) of ODMWA; the Regulations under COIDA (GN 16 in GG No 30646 of 11 January 2008); Regulation 8(1) of the Regulations to the Unemployment Insurance Act (GN 400 in GG 23283 of 28 March 2002); Regulation 3(4)*(a)* of the Regulations to the Road Accident Fund Act of 21 July 2008; the Compensation Fund's *Objection Against a Decision Form* (Form WG 29); ODMWA's "Objection Against a Decision Form" WG 29; the RAF Objection Form; Compensation Fund *Annual Report 2009* 34 http://www.labour.gov.za/DOL/downloads/documents/annual-reports/compensation-for-occupational-injuries-and-diseases/2009/CFund%20Annual%20Report%2009%20for %20web.pdf (15-09-2017); Rule 18 of the *Rules for the Conduct of Hearings before the Compensation Court in Section 91 Hearings of COIDA*; sec 66 of the UIA; sec 92 of COIDA; sec 15(2) Road Accident Fund Act; Committee of Inquiry (n 11) 124; *Cele* case (n 5); and *The Permanent Secretary, Department of Welfare, Eastern Cape Provincial Government v Ngxuza* 2001 4 SA 1184 (SCA)).

53 Some social security statutes provide for reviews by and appeals to the ordinary courts (especially the High Court). However, the ordinary courts are not always the appropriate forums to deal with social security appeals. The powers of these courts to deal with the matters are unsatisfactory as the courts mostly have review powers with little appeal powers. They are also apparently not specialised enough to deal effectively with social security matters. Appeals to such courts may also pose difficulties for aggrieved persons, due *inter alia* to limited access to the courts especially for indigent persons (also due to costs in the absence of legal aid), undue delays that characterise court proceedings, and the technical and legalistic basis on which cases are considered (with little regard to broader fairness considerations) (see, for example, Kanyane "Exploring and developing a culture of good governance" in Olivier and Kuhnle (eds) *Norms and Institutional Design: Social Security in Norway and South Africa* (2008) 104).

the lack of a systematic approach in establishing appeal institutions,[54] the limited scope of jurisdiction and powers of adjudication institutions,[55] inconsistencies in review and/or appeal provisions in various laws,[56] the unavailability of alternative dispute resolution procedures,[57] and the absence of

---

54 While some laws specifically provide for the establishment and functioning of appeal institutions and mechanisms other laws leave such issues to the discretion of the relevant Minister. It is inappropriate to establish an appeal tribunal purely on the basis of Ministerial or Registrar direction/regulation, also due to the gravity and importance of the issues at stake (see Regulation 3(8)*(a)* of the Regulations to the Road Accident Fund Act of 21 July 2008; and Olivier et al *Commentary on the Regulations to the Social Assistance Act, Act 13 of 2004 (A Report to the Department of Social Development)* (October 2005).

55 The scope of jurisdiction and powers of the social security adjudication institutions/forums is limited as they can only exercise the powers and functions as circumscribed in legislation. The scope of jurisdiction and powers of appeal institutions is also sometimes limited, particularly in relation to the types of cases or issues that it can decide. Possible remedies that can be provided are also limited due to circumscription. Most of the adjudication forums are also not afforded the power and mechanisms to enforce their rulings. The effectiveness of some of the institutions is also restricted due to the provision of multiple dispute resolution avenues in some statutes (see, for example, sec 30H(2) of the Pension Funds Act and sec 91 of COIDA).

56 Most statutes fail to make an appropriate distinction between (internal) reviews and (external) appeal procedures. Social security adjudication standards require that the administrative organs/institutions that undertake the determination of applicants' rights to social security benefits should also undertake internal review procedures (first-level adjudication procedures) (see secs 50 and 52 of ODMWA; and Wiles "Compensation for occupational Diseases" 1987 *South African Medical Journal (SAMJ)* 416 417). There is a lack of consistency in the provisions relating to reviews and appeals in the various laws. Some laws make provision for appeals to appeal bodies established in terms of the relevant laws, while other laws provide for appeals to other adjudication bodies (see, for example, the case of the UIA and ODMWA).

57 Social security disputes are resolved mainly by resort to litigation. Few social security statutes provide for other external dispute resolution avenues other than litigation in the normal court system (see Rule 13 of the *Rules for the Conduct of Hearings before the Compensation Court in Section 91 Hearings of COIDA* and sec 30E(1)*(b)* of the Pension Funds Act). The absence of alternative dispute resolution avenues in South African social security statutes implies that persons not satisfied with the internal adjudication processes can only have their right of access to social security in the ordinary courts of law. However, the various problems plaguing the current court structure indicate that the courts are not the most appropriate forum for the resolution of social security disputes.

institutional independence.[58] These challenges require reforms to the social security system.

In Germany, courts in the social security jurisdiction (as is the case in the other four major jurisditions) are organised in three levels. The social courts (*Sozialgerichte*) are at the first level, with the regional or higher social courts (*Landessozialgerichte*) at the second level and the federal social court (*Bundessozialgericht*) at the final level.[59] Social courts decide disputes on the merits of the case as well as on points of law.[60] Appeals from social courts are decided by higher social courts, where the courts review factual and legal aspects of the case. The federal social court decides appeals on points of law only.[61]

The adjudication system is made accessible through a range of appeal options, including internal review, court action and constitutional challenge.[62] A person who is dissatisfied with a social- security administrative

58 Most adjudication forums can effectively be regarded as internal organs of the social security institutions and therefore not independent of these institutions. In the first place, the Ministers or Directors-General of the relevant Departments are in most instances responsible for the appointment of members of the adjudication. The relevant Ministers or Directors-General also determine the length and conditions of employment of members, including remuneration. Ministers or Directors-General can further discipline the members and terminate their appointment. In addition, most adjudications institutions/ do not have independent funding through direct appropriations from parliament but are mostly funded by the relevant Departments as part of the Departments' annual budget allocations (see sec 30T(1) of the Pension Funds Act and sec 13 of the Medical Schemes Act; regulation 6 of the Regulations to COIDA of 11 January 2008; sec 41(1) of ODMWA; sec 51 of the UIA; and regulation 3(8)*(a)* of the Regulations to the Road Accident Fund Act of 21 July 2008). The institutions are also not independent accountable institutions in terms of the Public Finance Management Act. Management, governance, oversight and supervision are also undertaken by the departmental or institutional heads; and the adjudication forums are also required to report to departmental or institutional heads. Human resource and administrative support is mostly provided by the social security administration institutions (see, for example, regulation 3(8)*(a)* of the Regulations to the Road Accident Fund Act of 21 July 2008; sec 2(1)*(b)* read with the definition of presiding officer in sec 1 in COIDA; sec 40(2)*(b)* of ODMWA; sec 47 of the UIA; and secs 12, 14 and 50 of the Medical Schemes Act).

59 Federal Ministry of Labour and Social Affairs *Social Security at a Glance – Total Summary* Bonn (January 2011) 162.

60 Federal Ministry of Labour and Social Affairs (n 59) 164.

61 Federal Ministry of Labour and Social Affairs (n 59) 163–164.

62 OECD *Better Regulation in Europe: Germany* (2010) 130, http://www.oecd.org/gov/regulatory-policy/45079989.pdf (15-09-2017).

decision is required first to lodge an application for reconsideration of the decision with the relevant authority or institution that made the decision, unless a law provides for an exception to this.[63] After reconsideration, a person can lodge an appeal with a social court with further appeals or applications for review to the higher social courts and then to the federal social court. Germany's multi-tiered social courts system with sequential and complementary internal review and external appeal processes ensure the resolution of disputes quickly and easily at the most appropriate level, thereby promoting the right of access to courts or a fair trial for social security beneficiaries. Accessibility is also ensured through multiple dispute-lodgement options and reasonable timeframes,[64] the non-payment of application fees and availability of legal aid.[65] A wide scope of persons can bring disputes to the courts (such as unemployment insurance beneficiaries, recipients of basic security benefits for job-seekers, social assistance claimants and asylum seekers). In addition, the scope of disputes covered by the

---

63 See sec 78 of the Code of Social Court Procedure *(Sozialgerichtsgesetz, SGG)*.

64 A complainant can lodge the complaint with a social court in writing or by describing the dispute to a clerk of the social court, who puts the complaint in writing (see Federal Ministry of Labour and Social Affairs (n 59) 162). Where a complaint does not have the proper form or is incomplete, the presiding judge of the panel has to take steps to have such deficiencies repaired (sec 92(2) of the Code of Social Court Procedure). Where a decision includes information as to the available avenues of appeal, an appeal must be made to the social court within a month of notification of the decision or rejection of the review application. If this was not the case, the time is one year (sec 66 of the Code of Social Court Procedure). If the complaint is lodged in time with any domestic public authority or with any German consulate, it will be regarded as being filed in proper time (sec 91 of the Code of Social Court Procedure).

65 Bringing a dispute to the social courts is free of charge to insured persons in the statutory insurance system, social assistance applicants and beneficiaries and persons with disabilities (Federal Ministry of Labour and Social Affairs (n 59) 164). In terms of the Legal Advice Assistance Act, the State is required to establish a framework for the provision of legal assistance either through legal advice centres or by reimbursement of private lawyers who assist needy persons (see European Union Agency for Fundamental Rights (n 50) 12; Herbert *Administrative Justice in Europe: Report for Germany* (2005) 6–7; and Küsters *Social Partnership: Basic Aspects of Labour Relations in Germany* (2007) 14 http://library.fes.de/pdf-files/iez/06632.pdf (15-09-2017)).

courts is wide, with limited circumscription. The social courts are also afforded wide powers enabling them to provide an array of possible remedies.[66]

Procedures and the organisation of the social courts lead to effective running of court proceedings, thereby guaranteeing their fairness.[67] The effectiveness of the German social courts' system is further promoted through the guarantee of independence and impartiality. The Constitution states that judges are independent and subject only to the law.[68] The courts are thus required to be independent and impartial, and to have the necessary expertise to perform their duties. Such independence, impartiality and expertise enable them to provide effective redress to applicants. The independence and impartiality of courts is protected through procedures for appointment and the conditions of service of judges. The appointment of members of the

---

66 The jurisdiction of Social Courts consists of statutory pension insurance for employees; craftsmen insurance; pension for farmers; statutory accident insurance; compulsory health insurance; social long term care insurance; artists' social security; the law (regulating the practice) of panel doctors; tasks undertaken by the Federal Labour Agency (which comprises unemployment insurance and support in case of insolvency; basic financial security for the unemployed; social compensation for damage to health (such as care for war victims, soldiers, compensation for injuries from immunisation, compensation for victims of violence, and certain aspects of the Severely Handicapped Persons Act)); issues of social aid and issues arising under the Asylum Seekers' Benefit Act; and other welfare benefits (such as basic security benefits for job-seekers and social assistance) (see secs 54, 55 and 131 of the Code of Social Court Procedure; Gärditz (n 50) 7; Böckenförde, Wiesner and Nora *Max Planck Manual on the Judicial Systems in Germany and the Sudan* (2006) 37–38; Bundessozialgericht (n 50) 39; and Federal Ministry of Labour and Social Affairs (n 59) (162).

67 Proceedings generally include one oral hearing. Before the oral hearing, the presiding judge can request papers, electronic documents and health records. The presiding judge can also request information, hear witnesses, including expert witnesses, commission written opinions from expert witnesses, summons others to appear at the hearing, and discuss the matter in person at a meeting with the parties so that the dispute can be dealt with if possible in a single hearing (see secs 103, 106, 106a and 110 of the Code of Social Court Procedure; sec 139 of the Civil Procedure Code *(Zivilprozessordnung, ZPO)*; sec 86(1) of the Code of Administrative Court Procedure *(Verwaltungsgerichtsordnung, VwGO)*; Hueck *The Justice System of the Federal Republic of Germany: Lessons for Developing and Transition Countries* (May 2002) 9 and 11 http://siteresources.worldbank.org/INTLAWJUSTINST/Resources/GermanWorkshopTalks.pdf (15-09-2017); Gärditz (n 50) 5; Federal Ministry of Labour and Social Affairs (n 59) 163; Küsters (n 65) 14; and Böckenförde et al (n 66) 39.

68 art 97(1) of the German Constitution.

institutions promotes their effectiveness. Judges in Germany's social courts are appointed by multi-stakeholder committees.[69] Their conditions of service of the members of these institutions are also prescribed by statute.[70] Judges are also protected from arbitrary discipline and termination.[71]

The social courts (as is the case with the other German courts) are specialised courts with specific and exclusive jurisdiction.[72] Efforts are also made to promote the effectiveness of the institutions by stating minimum academic qualifications and relevant professional and other experience.[73] This ensures that only suitably qualified persons are appointed as members of these institutions. The expertise and specialisation of social courts also ensures their competence.

VI. Lessons to be learnt

South Africa is currently in the process of reforming its social security system.[74] In undertaking this process, there are several lessons that can be learnt from the German experience. Some of these include the following:

---

69 See art 95(2) and 98(4) of the German Constitution.

70 See the German Judiciary Act *(Deutsches Richtergesetz, DRiG)* of 19 April 1972 as amended.

71 art 97(2) of the German Constitution.

72 Damle "Specialize the judge, not the court: a lesson from the German Constitutional Court" 91 (2005) *Virginia Law Review (Va. L. Rev.)* 1267 1289.

73 A person can only be appointed as a judge if he/she satisfies the legal training requirements (see secs 5–7 of the German Judiciary Act (n 70)).

74 See, for example, Department of Health *National Health Insurance for South Africa: Towards Universal Health Coverage* (National Health Insurance White Paper) (2015) https://www.health-e.org.za/wp-content/uploads/2015/12/National-Health-Insurance-for-South-Africa-White-Paper.pdf (15-09-2017); Olivier et al *Developing a Policy Framework for the South African Social Security Adjudication System: Final (Research) Report* (Report prepared for the Department of Social Development, South Africa (October 2011)); Olivier et al *Developing a Policy Framework for the South African Social Security Adjudication System* (Policy prepared for the Department of Social Development, South Africa (December 2011)); Inter-Departmental Task Team on Social Security (IDTT) *Comprehensive Social Protection: Overview (A Consultation Document Prepared for the Inter-Ministerial Committee on Social Security, Retirement Reform and National Health Insurance)* (2010); and National Treasury (n 19) 5.

1. Establishment of national social insurance schemes

In South Africa, health and retirement insurance are only protected by means of private or occupational schemes. This has an impact on the development of social insurance. As National Treasury has remarked:

> "There are more than 13 500 private pension funds, including occupational pension funds, provident funds and retirement annuity (personal plan) funds. Approximately 80 per cent of funds have less than 100 members, which adds considerably to the regulatory workload and raises challenges relating to administration costs, risk-pooling and governance arrangements..."[75]

In the area of heath care, the two-tiered system of healthcare provision (medical aid for the well-off and the public healthcare system for the rest of the population) fails to embrace the principles of equity and access.[76] South Africa thus aims to establish a more comprehensive and inclusive framework for retirement insurance in which saving, risk-pooling, self-reliance and social solidarity will be more firmly rooted. [77] A national health insurance scheme is also planned, which will create a unified health system (through the improvement of equity in financing, reduction of fragmentation in funding pools, and making health care delivery more affordable and accessible for the population). Here, too, the German framework provides lessons. The creation of compulsory national social insurance schemes with a large number of members (about 31 million people subject to social security deductions) guarantees risk-pooling on a national scale, lower administration costs and social solidarity.

2. Comprehensiveness of scope of coverage

South Africa should endeavour to extend social insurance coverage to every employed person. This will require the inclusion of all workers (employees and self-employed persons). Current social security and retirement reform proposals envisage compulsory participation of employees and the self-employed in the formal sector, and encouragement of voluntary participation by those in the informal sector.[78] In addition, there is a need to prioritise labour market participation of the over 20 million people of working age

75 National Treasury (n 19) 5.
76 Department of Health (n 74) 6.
77 National Treasury (n 19) 5.
78 National Treasury (n 19) 6.

who were out of the labour market in the fourth quarter of 2015 (15 million not economically active and 5.2 million unemployed). This will guarantee access to social security (social insurance) for this category of persons. It will also promote the basic formula of social security (that every adult who is not yet elderly or occupied by family responsibilities must earn an income in the labour market and meet his own and society's needs). It will also allocate a residual function for the social grants system, which will cater only for persons who are unable to enter the labour market.

3. Adoption of a coherent legislative framework

In its quest to systematise its social security legislative framework, South Africa could learn from the German experience as regards the adoption of the Social Code (*Sozialgesetzbuch*). Such an endeavour will need to be approached with an understanding that the codification process does not happen overnight. This is abundantly clear from the German experience where the various books of the Social Code, for example, came into force in different years over a long period of time.[79]

4. Reduced budgetary allocation for social security

Improvement of the labour market context and the extension of social insurance coverage will enable a large part of the social security system to be financed through contributions from employers and employees. This will lead to a reduction of the allocation for social security in the national budget.

5. Efficient and effective dispute resolution framework

An efficient and effective dispute resolution framework is necessary for the South African social security system. To achieve this, there must be properly-functioning internal review or revision mechanisms within the various institutions. In addition, a uniform, external appeals framework

---

79 See, for example, Von Maydell "The codification of social law in Germany" in Kremalis (ed) *Simplification and Systematisation of Social Protection Rules* (1996) 125–135.

should be created to hear appeals from the decisions of social security institutions on the basis of law and fairness.[80] Germany's multi-tiered social-courts system, with sequential and complementary review and appeal processes that facilitate the speedy resolution of disputes at an appropriate level is instructive.

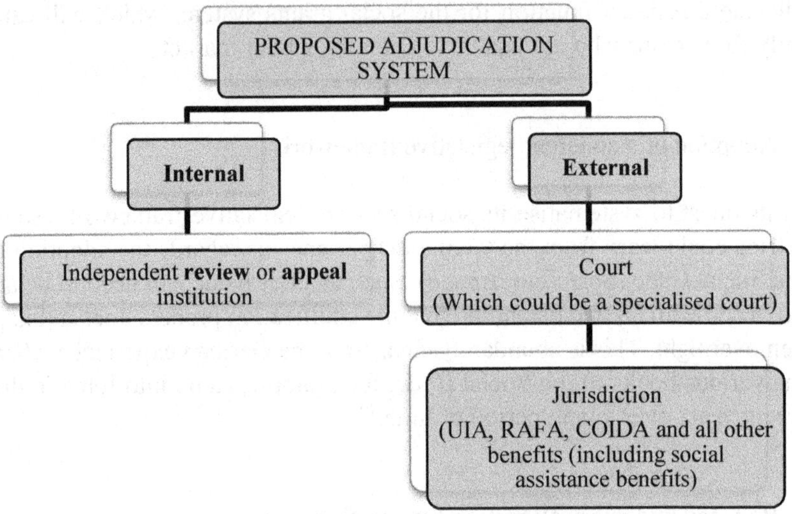

Figure 2 Proposed uniform adjudication social-security system for South Africa[81]

VII. Conclusion

Both the South African and German Constitution guarantee the right to social security. In realising this right, each country has established a social security system. South Africa is currently reforming its system to ensure comprehensive coverage. Germany's comprehensive social security system presents several lessons that are useful for South Africa in this endeavour.

However, it must be noted that Germany's social security system, with its focus on stable employment and participation in social insurance, is currently being threatened by the rising number of "mini jobs". Workers in

80 Committee of Inquiry (n 11) 124.

81 Mpedi "Social security dispute resolution and the need for a coherent adjudication system" in Tokiso/Juta *The Dispute Resolution Digest* (2013) 92.

these jobs earn below the threshold for inclusion in the statutory social insurance schemes, leading to their marginalisation or exclusion from social security. South Africa also faces a similar situation with rising informal employment[82] with the result that more people may be without social security coverage in the future.

82 Cohen and Moodley "Achieving 'decent work' in South Africa?" 2012 *Potchefstroomse Elektroniese Regsblad (PER)* 320 322; and Statistics South Africa (n 12) vi.

Bibliography

Böckenförde M, Wiesner V and Nora I *Max Planck Manual on the Judicial Systems in Germany and the Sudan* (2006).

Bundessozialgericht *Bundessozialgericht und Sozialgerichtsbarkeit – eine Information*, http://www.bsg.bund.de/SharedDocs/Publikationen/Broschuere/Das_Bundessozialgericht_und_die_deutsche_Sozialgerichtsbarkeit_Broschuere_2015_2016.pdf?__blob= publicationFile (15-09-2017).

Cohen T and Moodley L "Achieving 'decent work' in South Africa?" 2012 *Potchefstroomse Elektroniese Regsblad* (*PER)* 320.

Committee of Inquiry into a Comprehensive System of Social Security for South Africa *Transforming the Present – Protecting the Future* (Draft Consolidated Report March 2002) http://www.ci.org.za/depts/ci/pubs/pdf/poverty/news/report_release_of_coi.pdf (16-11-2016).

Compensation Fund *Annual Report 2014–2015*, http://www.labour.gov.za/DOL/downloads/documents/annual-reports/compensation-for-occupational-injuries-and-diseases/2015/cfannualreport2015.pdf (16-11-2016).

Council for Medical Schemes *Annual Report 2014–2015*, https://www.medicalschemes.com/files/Annual%20Reports/AR2014_2015.pdf (15-09-2017).

Damle SV "Specialize the judge, not the court: a lesson from the German Constitutional Court" (2005) 91 *Virginia Law Review* 1267.

Department of Health *National Health Insurance for South Africa: Towards Universal Health Coverage* (National Health Insurance White Paper 2015), https://www.health-e.org.za/wp-content/uploads/2015/12/National-Health-Insurance-for-South-Africa-White-Paper.pdf (15-09-2017).

Department of Labour *Rules for the Conduct of Hearings before the Compensation Court in Section 91 Hearings of COIDA*, accessed at http://www.labour.gov.za/DOL/downloads/documents/useful-documents/compensation-for-occupational-injuries-and-diseases/Conduct%20of%20hearings_CF_PamphletR.pdf (15-09-2017).

Deutsche Bundesbank *Germany's Statutory Health Insurance Scheme: Past Developments and Future Challenges (Monthly Report: July 2014)*, https://www.bundesbank.de/Redaktion/EN/Downloads/Publications/Monthly_Report_Articles/2014/2014_07_health.pdf?__blob=publicationFile (15-09-2017).

Ellis RP, Chen T and Luscombeet CE "Comparisons of health insurance systems in developed countries" in Culyer A (ed) *Encyclopedia of Health Economics* (Vol 1) (Elsevier Press, Waltham 2014).

Espoo P, Amanjani AM, Zanjani H et al "A comparative study on social security systems in Iran, Germany, France, and Turkey" 5 (2015) *Journal of Applied Environmental and Biological Sciences (J Appl Environ Biol Sci)* 174.

European Commission *Your Social Security Rights in Germany* (2013) http://ec.europa.eu/employment_social/empl_portal/SSRinEU/Your%20social%20security%20rights%20in%20Germany_en.pdf (15-09-2017).

European Job Mobility Portal (EURES) *Labour Market Information: Germany* https://ec.europa.eu/eures/main.jsp?acro=lmi&lang=en&parentId=0&countryId=DE (15-09-2017).

European Union Agency for Fundamental Rights *Access to justice in Europe: An Overview of Challenges and Opportunities* (National Thematic Study – Germany 2010), http://fra.europa.eu/sites/default/files/fra_uploads/1526-access-to-justice-2011-country-DE.pdf (15-09-2017).

Federal Ministry of Labour and Social Affairs *Social Security at a Glance – Total Summary* (January 2011).

Gärditz FK *Judicial Review and Remedies in a Nutshell: Annual Report 2010 – Germany* (May 2011), http://www.ius-publicum.com/repository/uploads/05_07_2011_9_42_Gaerditz.pdf (15-09-2017).

Hahlo HR "Here lies the common law: rest in peace" 3 (1967) *Modern Law Review (Mod L Rev)* 241.

Herbert G *Administrative Justice in Europe: Report for Germany* (Questionnaire presented to the Association of the Councils of State and Supreme Administrative Jurisdictions of the European Union Seminar on Administrative Justice in Europe held in Trier on 12 December 2005), http://www.juradmin.eu/en/eurtour/i/countries/germany/germany_en.pdf (16-11-2016).

Hong Kong Legislative Council Secretariat *Fact Sheet: Social Security System in Germany* (2015), http://www.legco.gov.hk/research-publications/english/ 1415fsc11-social-security-system-in-germany-20150225-e.pdf (15-09-2017).

Hueck C *The Justice System of the Federal Republic of Germany: Lessons for Developing and Transition Countries* (May 2002), http://siteresources.worldbank.org/INTLAWJUSTINST/Resources/GermanWorkshopTalks.pdf (15-09-2017).

Inter-Departmental Task Team on Social Security *Comprehensive Social Protection: Overview (A Consultation Document Prepared for the Inter-Ministerial Committee on Social Security, Retirement Reform and National Health Insurance)* (2010), http://www.gov.za/sites/www.gov.za/files/Comprehensive_Social_Security_in_South_Africa_a.pdf (15-09-2017).

Jaeger R and Broß S *The Relations between the Constitutional Courts and the Other National Courts, Including the Interference in this Area of the Action of the European Courts* (Report of the Constitutional Court of the Federal Republic of Germany) paper presented at the Conference of European Constitutional Courts XIIth Congress (Karlsruhe, August 28, 2001), http://www.confeuconstco.org/reports/rep-xii/Duitsland-EN.pdf (15-09-2017).

Kanyane H "Exploring and developing a culture of good governance" in Olivier M and Kuhnle S (eds) *Norms and Institutional Design: Social Security in Norway and South Africa* (Sun Press, Stellenbosch 2008).

Kirkegaard JF *The True Levels of Government and Social Expenditures in Advanced Economies* Peterson Institute for International Economics Policy Brief (March 2015), https://piie.com/publications/pb/pb15-4.pdf (15-09-2017).

Küsters H *Social Partnership: Basic Aspects of Labour Relations in Germany* (Friedrich Ebert Stiftung, Bonn 2007), http://library.fes.de/pdf-files/iez/06632.pdf (15-09-2017).

Mpedi "Social security dispute resolution and the need for a coherent adjudication system" in Bosch C (ed) *Tokiso Dispute Settlements Staff – The Dispute Resolution Digest* (Juta, Cape Town 2013) 76.

National Treasury *2016 Budget Review*, http://www.treasury.gov.za/documents/national%20budget/2016/review/FullReview.pdf (15-09-2017).

National Treasury *Social Security and Retirement Reform* (2007), http://www.treasury.gov.za/documents/national%20budget/2007/Social%20security%20and%20retirement%20reform%20paper.pdf (15-09-2017).

Obermann K, Müller P, Müller HH et al (eds) *Understanding the German Health Care System* (2013), https://www.goinginternational.eu/newsletter/2013/nl_03/SpecialDE_EN_Understanding_the_German.pdf (15-09-2017).

OECD *Better Regulation in Europe: Germany* (2010), http://www.oecd.org/gov/regulatory-policy/45079989.pdf (15-09-2017).

OECD *Social Spending is Falling in Some Countries, but in Many Others it Remains at Historically High Levels: Insights from the OECD Social Expenditure Database (SOCX)* (November 2014), https://www.oecd.org/els/soc/OECD2014-SocialExpenditure_Update19Nov_Rev.pdf (15-09-2017).

Olivier M, Fourie E and Nyenti MAT *Commentary on the Regulations to the Social Assistance Act, Act 13 of 2004 (A Report to the Department of Social Development)* (October 2005) [unpublished].

Olivier M, Govindjee A and Nyenti MAT *Developing a Policy Framework for the South African Social Security Adjudication System: Final (Research) Report (Report Prepared for the Department of Social Development, South Africa)* (October 2011) [unpublished].

Olivier M, Govindjee A and Nyenti MAT *Developing a Policy Framework for the South African Social Security Adjudication System (Policy Prepared for the Department of Social Development, South Africa)* (December 2011) [unpublished].

Schulz E "The long-term care system in Germany" German Institute for Economic Research (DIW) Berlin Discussion Paper No 1039 (2010), https://www.diw.de/documents/publikationen/73/diw_01.c.359024.de/dp1039.pdf (15-09-2017).

Social Security Administration *Social Security Programs throughout the World: Europe 2014*, https://www.ssa.gov/policy/docs/progdesc/ssptw/2014-2015/europe/ssptw14europe.pdf (15-09-2017).

Statistiches Bundesamt (German Statistics Office) *Statistisches Jahrbuch 2015*, https://www.destatis.de/DE/Publikationen/StatistischesJahrbuch/StatistischesJahrbuch2015.pdf?__blob=publicationFile (15-09-2017).

Statistics South Africa *Quarterly Labour Force Survey, Quarter 4 2015*, http://www.statssa.gov.za/publications/P0211/P02114thQuarter2015.pdf (15-09-2017).

Unemployment Insurance Fund *Annual Report 2015*, http://www.labour.gov.za/DOL/downloads/documents/annual-reports/unemployment-insurance-fund/2015/uifannualreport2015.pdf (15-09-2017).

Von Maydell B "The codification of social law in Germany" in Kremalis KD (ed) *Simplification and Systematisation of Social Protection Rules* (Ant. N. Sakkoulas, Athens 1996).

Weinkopf C "Germany: precarious employment and the rise of mini-jobs" in Vosko L, MacDonald M and Campbell I (ed) *Gender and the Contours of Precarious Employment* (Routlege, London, New York, 2009).

Wiles FJ "Compensation for occupational diseases" 71 (1987) *South African Medical Journal (SAMJ)* 416.

Zacher HF *Social Policy in the Federal Republic of Germany: The Constitution of the Social* (Springer, Heidelberg 2013).

Case Law

Cele v the South African Social Security Agency 2009 5 SA 105 (D)

Government of the Republic of South Africa v Grootboom 2000 11 BCLR 1169 (CC); 2001 1 SA 46 (CC)

The Permanent Secretary, Department of Welfare, Eastern Cape Provincial Government v Ngxuza 2001 4 SA 1184 (SCA)

Comment on: "Social insurance in South Africa: are there lessons to be learnt from the German experience?"

*Ulrich M. Gassner**

I. Introduction

As Letlhokwa George Mpedi and Mathias Nyenti correctly pointed out in their paper[1], a cautious view seems to be appropriate when analysing the issue whether and to what extent the German social insurance system may serve as a model for South Africa.

Yet, at least at first sight, a pretty striking similarity between the two systems can be observed. There is a three-fold social strategy mainly comprising of social assistance, social insurance and social allowance in South Africa. Similarly, in Germany the common concept of the social security system is that it is based on the three pillars: social insurance, social allow-

* Ulrich M. Gassner, *Dr. iur., Mag. rer. publ., M. Jur. (Oxon.)*; Professor, University of Augsburg, Faculty of Law. Founder-Director of the Center for Medical Device Law and the Center for E-Health Law. Professor for Public Law.

1 See pp. 451 et seqq. in this book.

ance and social assistance. Accordingly, there is a three-fold classical definition of social law[2] that is presumed by Articles 74, No 7, 10 and 12 of the German Constitution.

Admittedly, the concepts of social insurance, social allowance and social assistance may differ between South Africa and Germany, at least when applying the scholarly definitions relating to the structure of social law that have been developed in Germany over the years. The term "social insurance" is commonly understood as financial coverage for life's vicissitudes and old age in a reciprocal relationship of contributions and benefits. The main differentiating feature of social insurance in comparison to social assistance is that the granting of benefits does not depend on the individual's neediness. This is also true with respect to the second pillar of social law regulating the area of social allowance. Unlike social insurance social allowance is funded by the taxpayers and granted for the reason that the recipients have made sacrifices for the public good. One prominent example is the civil servant's pension. The third pillar of social law relates to social assistance. It is also financed by taxes and will only be granted on a subsidiary basis in case of indigence. The most important examples of statutes regulating this branch of social law are set out in two books of the Social Code (*Sozialgesetzbuch,* SGB), the SGB II[3] and the SGB XII[4].

II. Legislative framework

The social security legislative framework in Germany has a rather long tradition of codification. The Reich Insurance Code (*Reichsversicherungsordnung,* RVO) was adopted in 1911 and consolidated statutes concerning the health insurance of blue-collar workers, work accident insurance and disability and old-age disability. It consisted of six books with

2 With respect to a modern function-based classification that can be traced back to Hans F. Zacher see Axel Kokemoor, *Sozialrecht* (5th Edition, 2013), 10 et seq.; Gerhard Igl and Felix Welti, *Sozialrecht* (8th Edition, 2007), § 2 para. 2; Raimund Waltermann, *Sozialrecht* (11th Edition, 2015), para. 62 et seqq.

3 Federal Ministry of Labour and Social Affairs, *Social security at a glance 2015* (2015), 33 et seqq.

4 ibid, 114 et seqq.

originally 1,805 sections. A legal historian once called it a paramount example of the high level of the art of legislation in the early 20th century.[5]

In the second half of the 20th century it became more and more apparent that the RVO has been cluttered with many additions and amendments. Therefore, the Social Code was gradually developed from 1975. It replaced the RVO in many areas. However, even nowadays, some provisions of the RVO are in force.[6] Furthermore, the codification of the German social law by the Social Code is far from being complete and conclusive as it does not embrace all the relevant statutes. Some important benefit statutes such as the Federal Act on Family Allowances (*Bundeskindergeldgesetz,* BKGG) and the Federal Education and Training Allowance Act (*Bundesausbildungsförderungsgesetz,* BAföG) have not yet been incorporated into the Social Code. This also holds true with respect to insurance schemes for whole groups of people such as farmers and artists.

In addition, it is to be borne in mind that in Germany, just as in South Africa, private insurance schemes play an important role. For example, currently only about 85 % of the workforce is enrolled in the Mandatory Public Retirement Insurance scheme (*Gesetzliche Rentenversicherung,* GRV). Civil servants, who make up about 9 % of the workforce, have their own pension system and the self-employed, who also make up about 9 % of the workforce, are mostly self-insured but are also allowed to participate in the GRV.

In addition to the government-run systems of Mandatory Retirement Insurance and the pension scheme for civil servants there are two other pillars to the German retirement system: private company plans and private individual retirement investments. Occupational pension schemes are designed to supplement Public Retirement Insurance. Government tax breaks and subsidies encourage companies and employees to invest in private plans. Though company plans are not compulsory, they cover about three-fifths of the working population, a percentage that is expected to grow. The third pillar of the German retirement system, individual retirement investments, has to date been very significant, but since 2002 has been getting even more attention as supplements to the Public Retirement Insurance. Those private

5 Michael Stolleis, 'Das Maschinenhaus des Sozialstaats', *Frankfurter Allgemeine Zeitung (FAZ)*, 14 July 2011, 6.

6 Secs. 349–360 of the RVO concerning a special kind of employee of the social insurance agencies.

plans include, but are not limited to, the so-called Riester and Rürup insurance schemes. Workers and other participants are entitled to certain tax advantages and benefits from government subsidies for those plans. As of 30 May 2016 more than 16 mio. Riester agreements have been concluded.[7]

III. Scope of coverage

Unlike South Africa's Constitution, the German Basic Law (*Grundgesetz*, GG*)* does not provide for individual social rights, save for one exception for mothers.[8] Instead, only the Social State principle is set out as a state aim.[9] It follows that the current social system is not constitutionally guaranteed. Consequently, it may be abolished. However, due to the so-called guarantee of permanence[10] there is a limit of legislation in so far as even the *pouvoir constituant* is not allowed to abolish the Social State principle and to enact a law that infringes upon the guarantee of human dignity.[11] In that respect, Germany's constitutional court has held that pursuant to Article 1(1) in conjunction with Article 20(1) of the Basic Law at least a dignified existential minimum is to be guaranteed by the State[12] (the so-called *Existenzminimum* doctrine[13]).

Above this basic level, Germany owns, as *Letlhokwa George Mpedi* and *Mathias Nyenti* correctly observed, a rather comprehensive system of social security that has even been extended in recent years. Thus, for example, a general obligation to insure oneself against health risks was implemented in

7 Federal Ministry of Labour and Social Affairs, *Statistik zur privaten Altersvorsorge* (2016).

8 See Art. 6 para. 4 of the Basic Law.

9 See Art. 20 para 1 of the Basic Law.

10 See Art. 79 para. 3 of the Basic Law.

11 See Art. 1 para. 1 of the Basic Law.

12 See BVerfG 9.2.2010 – 1 BvL 1/09; 1 BvL 3/09; 1 BvL 4/09 – BVerfGE 125, 175, 222 et seqq. para. 133 et seqq.; BVerfG 18.7.2012 – 1 BvL 10/10; 1 BvL 2/11 – BVerfGE 132, 134, 162 et seq. para. 70; BVerfG 23.7.2014 – 1 BvL 10/12; 1 BvL 12/12; 1 BvR 1691/13 – BVerfGE 137, 34, 73 et seq. para. 77.

13 For more details see Jeff King, 'Direitos sociais, constitucionalismo, e o princípio do estado social Alemão (Social rights, constitutionalism, and the German Social State Principle)' 3 (2014) *e-Pública – Revista Eletrónica de Direito Público*, 1 (16 et seqq).

2007.[14] Consequently, even a billionaire must be insured “voluntarily” under the statutory health scheme or participate in the private health insurance system.

On the other hand there has been a deliberate tendency to expand the exemptions from compulsory statutory health and long-term care insurance for so-called mini-jobs, a specific form of marginal employment that could be generally characterised as part time with low wage. The socio-economic idea behind this concept is to promote employment by making the workforce cheaper. The employer pays only a lump sum of approximately 3 % (including health insurance: 13 %, retirement insurance: 15 %, wage tax: 2 %, levies: max. 1.42 %, individual occupational injury and disease) whereas the employee is exempt from income tax and only charged a retirement insurance contribution of 3.9 %. As mentioned before, everybody including a mini-job worker must have health insurance. Since the compulsory health insurance offers a non-contributory family insurance in case of students and married persons earning a moderate income, for the majority of mini-jobbers this obligation bears neither additional cost nor a restricted access to health insurance. The latter holds also true for pensioners and non-working persons who do mini-jobs. Notwithstanding that, there are some minor disadvantages for mini-jobbers. For example, they are not entitled to sickness pay after six weeks of illness when they have a non-contributory family insurance. Moreover, the occupation as a mini-jobber does not establish any entitlements to unemployment benefits as no contributions to the unemployment insurance are to be paid. In summary, however, the conclusion drawn by some German observers that mini-jobbers have been marginalised or even excluded from social security[15] sounds grossly exaggerated.

IV. Financing of the social security system

German social insurances are often used to pay for things they have not been originally designed to cover (so-called extraneous benefits). This relates, inter alia, to pensions based on the minimum wage to make up for

---

14 Federal Ministry of Labour and Social Affairs (n 2), 76 et seq.

15 Claudia Weinkopf, 'Germany: precarious employment and the rise of mini-jobs' in Leah F.Vosko, Martha MacDonald and Iain Campbell (eds), *Gender and the Contours of Precarious Employment* (2009), 17 (181 et seqq).

lower salaries in the past or terminations of pregnancy and the free co-insurance of spouses.

As non-insurance benefits place a burden on labour-intensive small and medium-sized companies and, of course, on employee contributions, it seems to be appropriate to finance the social security system partly through tax subsidies. Thereby a legitimate exception to the traditional principle of contribution parity between employer and employee is created.

V. Adjudication and enforcement

When it comes to the efficiency of the German courts system, it is to be noted that it may well be ranked in the midfield of European states. This holds especially true for the length of proceedings.[16] In that respect, it seems to be characteristic that the European Court of Human Rights (ECtHR) has held several times that the length of the proceedings before the German social courts was excessive and that Germany therefore failed to meet the "reasonable time" requirement of Article 6(1) of the European Convention on Human Rights (ECHR).[17]

VI. Conclusions and observations

Notwithstanding the provisos set out above, the planned reforms of the South African insurance system may be at least partly inspired by the long-lasting German experience, especially with respect to the adoption of a coherent legal framework and an effective and efficient dispute resolution framework.

This also holds true for the establishment of national social insurance schemes. A better-structured and organised retirement insurance scheme may lead to a reduction of administrative costs and bureaucracy and can

---

16 See European Commisssion, *The 2016 EU Justice Scoreboard* (2016), 6 et seqq.

17 See, e.g., ECHR 25.03.2010 – 901/05, *Petermann v Germany,* ECLI:CE:ECHR:2010:0325JUD000090105; ECHR 18.11.2010 – 38187/08, *Wagner v Germany,* ECLI:CE:ECHR:2010:1118JUD003818708; ECHR 16.12.2010 – 39778/07, 11171/08, 43336/08, 52719/08, 15895/09, 16123/09, 16127/09, 16129/09, 27529/09, 27533/09 and 27596/09, *Dudek v Germany,* ECLI:CE:ECHR:2010:1216JUD003977807; ECHR 20.10.2011 – 53550/09, *Kurczveil v Germany,* ECLI:CE:ECHR:2011:1020JUD005355009.

contribute to the overall sound management of pensions. However, a one-size-fits-all path to a totally comprehensive retirement social insurance would probably end up in even more red tape. As in Germany, a more flexible approach dependent on the special needs of single social groups seems to be preferable. In addition, the risk of corruption may be enhanced by national insurance schemes.[18] Furthermore, a policy of incentives based on consent is always a better choice than pure coercion by means of a compulsory insurance.

With respect to health insurance a lesson to be learnt from the German scheme may be its bottom-up structure including social elections by the insured persons[19] (so-called self-government). This marks a major difference to the top-down schemes of Beveridgean systems. Furthermore, even in the area of mandatory health insurance there is an individual right to choose between over 100 health insurance agencies.

Ultimately, from a German perspective there are some doubts as to the extension of social insurance coverage to self-employed persons. In fact, in Germany there are no compulsory retirement insurance schemes that embrace this group of persons with, to some extent, the exception of farmers or artists who are deemed to be in need of special social protection. Then again, those who earn more than EUR 4,687.50 (ZAR 76,000) may opt to obtain health insurance from private companies.

At the end of the day, at least in principle, in a free country[20] it should be left to the single individual to choose his or her preferred insurance. Otherwise, there is the risk of creating a paternalistic "nanny state" invading the autonomy of the individuals concerned and potentially infantilising them. A much less worse reform strategy would embrace a guarantee of access to any insurance fund independent of the individual's circumstances in combination with a capped contribution and, if necessary, with additional monetary incentives. Such a concept may be considered as being principally flawed with Eurocentric thought but would probably even succeed in a situation such as in South Africa where there are many vulnerable members of society, the majority of whom have limited education and whose inclusion and integration is at the top of the social agenda.

---

18 E.g. there is an estimated percentage of between 3 and 10% corruption-related misallocations in the German healthcore sector: Transparency International, *Transparenzmängel, Korruption und Betrug im deutschen Gesundheitswesen – Kontrolle und Prävention als gesellschaftliche Aufgabe* (2015), 5.

19 See Axel Kokemoor (n 1), 58; Hans F. Zacher, *Social policy in the Federal Republic of Germany: The Constitution of the Social* (2013), 106 et seq.

20 See sections 1(a), 12(1)*(a)*, *(c)* of the South African Constitution.

Bibliography

European Commission, *The 2016 EU Justice Scoreboard* (2016), http://ec.europa.eu/justice/effective-justice/files/justice_scoreboard_2016_en. pdf (02-09-2017).

Federal Ministry of Labour and Social Affairs, *Sozialbudget 2014* (2015), http://www.bmas.de/SharedDocs/Downloads/DE/PDF-Publikationen/a230-14-sozialbudget-2014.pdf?__blob=publicationFile (15-09-2017).

Federal Ministry of Labour and Social Affairs, *Statistik zur privaten Altersvorsorge*, http://www.bmas.de/DE/Themen/Rente/Zusaetzliche-Altersvorsorge/statistik-zusaetzliche-altersvorsorge.html (2 July 2016).

Federal Ministry of Labour and Social Affairs, *Social security at a glance 2015* (2015), https://www.bmas.de/SharedDocs/Downloads/DE/PDF-Publikationen/a998-social-security-at-a-glance-total-summary.pdf?__blob=publicatio nFile (15-09-2017).

Gerhard Igl and Felix Welti, *Sozialrecht* (8th Edition, Werner Verlag, Baden-Baden 2007).

Jeff King, 'Direitos sociais, constitucionalismo, e o princípio do estado social Alemão (Social rights, constitutionalism, and the German Social State Principle)' 3 (2014) *e-Pública – Revista Eletrónica de Direito Público*, 1 (http://e-publica.pt/pdf/artigos/Vol.%201-%20N%C2%BA%203-Art.03.pdf (15-09-2016)).

Axel Kokemoor, *Sozialrecht* (5th Edition, Verlag Franz Vahlen, Munich 2013).

Michael Stolleis, 'Das Maschinenhaus des Sozialstaats', *Frankfurter Allgemeine Zeitung (FAZ)*, 14 July 2011, 6.

Transparency International, Transparenzmängel, Korruption und Betrug im deutschen Gesundheitswesen – Kontrolle und Prävention als gesellschaftliche Aufgabe (5th Edition 2015), https://www.transparency.de/fileadmin/pdfs/Themen/Gesundheitspapier_Stand_2008_Auflage_5_08-08-18.pdf (15-09-2017).

Raimund Waltermann, *Sozialrecht* (11th Edition, C.F. Müller Verlag, Heidelberg 2015).

Claudia Weinkopf 'Germany: precarious employment and the rise of mini-jobs' in Leah F. Vosko, Martha MacDonald and Iain Campbell (eds), *Gender and the Contours of Precarious Employment* (Routledge, London 2009), 177.

Hans F. Zacher, *Social policy in the Federal Republic of Germany: The Constitution of the Social* (Springer-Verlag, Berlin 2013).

Case Law

Germany

BVerfG 9.2.2010 – 1 BvL 1/09; 1 BvL 3/09; 1 BvL 4/09 – BVerfGE 125, 175.

BVerfG 18.7.2012 – 1 BvL 10/10; 1 BvL 2/11 – BVerfGE 132, 134.

BVerfG 23.7.2014 – 1 BvL 10/12; 1 BvL 12/12; 1 BvR 1691/13 – BVerfGE 137, 34.

European Court of Human Rights

ECHR 25.03.2010 – 901/05 – *Petermann v. Germany,* ECLI:CE:ECHR:2010:0325 JUD000090105.

ECHR 18.11.2010 – 38187/08 – *Wagner v. Germany,* ECLI:CE:ECHR:2010:1118 JUD003818708.

ECHR 16.12.2010 – 39778/07, 11171/08, 43336/08, 52719/08, 15895/09, 16123/09, 16127/09, 16129/09, 27529/09, 27533/09 and 27596/09 – *Dudek v. Germany,* ECLI:CE:ECHR:2010:1216JUD003977807.

ECHR 20.10.2011 – 53550/09 – *Kurczveil v. Germany,* ECLI:CE:ECHR:2011:1020 JUD005355009.

Labour and social protection for migrant domestic workers in South Africa

*Elmarie Fourie**
*Warren Bowles***

---

* Senior Lecturer, Department of Procedural Law, University of Johannesburg.
** Lecturer, Department of Procedural Law, University of Johannesburg.

I. Introduction

> "Throughout human history, migration has been a courageous expression of the individual's will to overcome adversity to live a better life."[1]

Migration is not a new occurrence; it affects most countries in the world and is currently the focus of the global, national and regional policy agenda. Migrant workers account for 150 million of the world's 244 million international migrants.[2] According to the International Labour Organization (hereafter ILO), women represent approximately half of the total population of international migrants worldwide and one in every five domestic workers is an international migrant.[3] Migration has increased as a result of globalisation, conflicts, demographic change, income inequalities, socio-economic and political crises as well as climate change.[4] In Europe, many migrant workers enjoy labour and social protection. Germany provides a good example of how migrant workers are entitled to and enjoy the same rights as German citizens, in that there are work councils that ensure they are not discriminated against and they are fully integrated into the German workforce.[5] However, the position in our region, the Southern African Development Community (hereafter SADC), is different in a variety of areas that affect migrant workers.

It must be noted that there are various categories of non-citizens. In South Africa, permanent residents, temporary residents (this category includes migrant workers), asylum seekers, refugees and undocumented migrants are

---

1 United Nations *International Migration and Development: High-level dialogue of the general assembly* (2006) 1, http://www.un.org/esa/desa/desaNews/DESANewsSepOct2006.pdf (11-01-2017).

2 International Labour Organization (ILO) *International Labour Office Global Estimates on Migrant Workers: Results and Methodology* Labour Migration Branch (2015) xi, http://www.ilo.org/wcmsp5/groups/public/---dgreports/---dcomm/documents/publication/wcms_436343.pdf (15-09-2017).

3 International Labour Organization (ILO) *Protection of Migrant Domestic Workers in Destination Countries* ILO human rights training manual for consular officials and labour attaches (2006) 2, http://www.ilo.org/wcmsp5/groups/public/---asia/---ro-bangkok/---ilo-jakarta/documents/publication/wcms_122313.pdf (15-09-2017).

4 ILO (n 2) 1.

5 Gyo "Migrant workers in Germany" 31 (2009–2010) *Comparative Labor Law and Policy Journal (Comp. Lab. L. & Pol'y J.)* 47 57.

classified as non-citizens. Labour and social protection[6] of these workers is often directly linked to their legal status in the host country and irregular or undocumented migrant workers[7] are a particularly vulnerable group. In Germany, migrant workers who enter for employment purposes usually fall into one of two categories, namely those workers who have access to employment and are obliged to leave Germany, usually citizens of the so-called EU15, EFTA, Cyprus and Malta, and the second category are foreign nationals of the ten Central Eastern European countries that joined the EU in 2004 and 2007.[8] It is interesting to note that the largest group of migrants living in Germany are Turkish citizens.[9]

Although migration can be a positive experience for some migrants, others are particularly vulnerable and face many challenges such as discrimination, poor working conditions, harassment and a lack of social and labour protection.[10] Positive aspects of migration include a contribution to growth and development in the host country and the countries of origin benefit from their remittance and skills development while in the country of destination.[11] Women workers usually move to more developed countries in search of a better life for themselves and for their families. However, these workers face specific problems including trafficking as well as severe human rights abuses. Unfortunately patterns of gender inequality are reproduced and these workers find themselves once again in female-dominated employment

---

6 Social protection encompasses the traditional measures of social insurance, social assistance and social services; however it extends beyond that to focus on causality through an integrated policy approach. See Guthrie *Transforming the Present – Protecting the Future: Report of the Committee of Inquiry into a Comprehensive System of Social Security for South Africa* (2002) 40 41.

7 The concept "irregular migrants" provides for a variety of irregular movements and "undocumented migrants" provide for migrants that enter the country without the required documentation. Excluded from this concept are migrants who enter the country with the required documentation but become irregular at a later stage.

8 Gyo (n 5) 48–49. EU15 refers to fifteen countries that were part of the European Union before it expanded to include eight Central and Eastern European countries. Cyprus and Malta were included in 2004 as well as Romania and Bulgaria in 2007. EFTA refers to the European Free Trade Association, founded on 3 May 1960, that was comprised of countries that were unable or unwilling to join the European Union or what was the European Economic Community (EEC) back then.

9 Gyo (n 5) 49.

10 Fourie and Smit "Labour market flexibility, migration and inflexible labour and social protection in the SADC region" 27 (2011) *International Journal of Comparative Labour Law and Industrial Relations (IJCCLIR)* 41 43.

11 Fourie and Smit (n 10) 42.

such as domestic work. Domestic workers and specifically migrant domestic workers are one of the least protected groups of workers in respect of labour and social security legislation, and specific statistics are problematic as migrant domestic workers work mostly in the informal economy.[12] Countries like Germany,[13] Italy, and France have explicit coverage for these workers in, for example, workers' compensation schemes, general health care schemes and retirement schemes. Within Europe, France, Italy and Spain employ the highest number of domestic workers.[14]

The links between domestic work and female international labour migration is well established.[15] The growing demand of households for domestic services due to the "care crisis" is considered to be one of the main triggers of the feminisation of labour migration.

II. The nature of domestic work

In general the domestic worker's relationship with her employer was often founded on a paternalistic model, without a clearly defined contract regulating rights and obligations.[16] In the United Kingdom, employers employing migrant domestic workers describe themselves as benefactors hosting migrants. Similarly, in South Africa, employers have described the employment of domestic workers as an act of charity.[17] This perspective contrib-

12 For the purpose of this paper, informal economy refers to all economic activities by workers and economic units not covered or inadequately covered by formal arrangements. International Labour Organisation Recommendation 204 of 2015 defines the term as to include all economic activities by workers and economic units that are in law or in practice not covered by formal arrangements. The informal economy, according to this definition, excludes any illicit activities.

13 In 2013 domestic work in Germany accounted for only 0.5 percent of total employment. See International Labour Office *Domestic Workers across the World: Global and Regional Statistics and the Extent of Legal Protection* (2013) 37, http://www.ilo.org/wcmsp5/groups/public/---dgreports/---dcomm/---publ/documents/publication/wcms_173363.pdf (15-09-2017).

14 International Labour Office *Domestic Workers across the World: Global and Regional Statistics and the Extent of Legal Protection* (2013) 35, http://www.ilo.org/wcmsp5/groups/public/---dgreports/---dcomm/---publ/documents/publication/wcms_173363.pdf (15-09-2017).

15 ILO (n 2) xiii.

16 International Labour Office (n 14) 44.

17 International Labour Office (n 14) 44.

utes to a precarious legal system and an extreme dependency on the employer for migrant workers, whose legal status combined with a lack of knowledge of the language and laws increase their vulnerability. General complaints from migrant domestic workers include verbal and sexual assault, confinement, isolation and restrictions on freedom of movement that resulted in forced labour.[18] The feminisation of domestic work, the informal nature and the fact that domestic work is not valued pose many challenges in respect of policy implementation and proper regulation.[19]

A definition of domestic work remains problematic as these workers do not represent a homogenous group with reference to the nature of their job and their demographic profile.[20] To overcome the problematic nature of a single definition, the Domestic Workers Convention's[21] definitions provide for common characteristics of these workers. Article 1 defines "domestic work" as "work performed in or for a household or households", and a "domestic worker" as "any person engaged in domestic work within an employment relationship". It further provides that "a person who performs domestic work only occasionally or sporadically and not on an occupational basis is not a domestic worker".

The definition is limited in its scope as it excludes institutional care services. The exclusion of workers who perform occasionally is problematic for countries such as South Africa where many domestic workers only perform these duties occasionally and for different employers. Migrant domestic workers provide indispensable services to the countries that they enter, contributing to the wealth of ageing societies and to the sustainability of these countries' welfare and employment systems, but the value of their work is often unrecognised.[22] The value of domestic work must not be underestimated and it must be highlighted that these workers allow their employers to earn their own living.

---

18 International Labour Office (n 14) 45.

19 Du Toit (ed) *Exploited, Undervalued – and Essential: Domestic Work and the Realisation of Rights* (2013) 222.

20 International Labour Office Report (n 14) 7. Their demographic profile includes age, gender and migration status. Domestic workers perform a variety of daily tasks, such as cleaning, cooking, gardening and care duties for elderly people and children.

21 2011 (No 189).

22 Galotti *The Gender Dimension of Domestic Work in Western Europe* International Migration Programme (2009) ix, http://www.ilo.org/wcmsp5/groups/public/---ed_protect/---protrav/---migrant/documents/publication/wcms_178149.pdf (15-09-2017).

The nature of their work is often seen as their everyday duties. Feminisation of poverty and gender discrimination, such as lack of access to education, health care and economic resources mean that these female workers are particularly vulnerable. Employers often prefer migrant domestic workers, and specifically, irregular and undocumented workers as these workers accept longer hours, lower wages and in general less favourable working conditions as a result of their legal status, and these precarious situations also make them more dependent on the employer.[23]

An ILO report in 2016 estimated that there is a minimum of 67 million domestic workers worldwide but accurate data on domestic workers is uncommon and the real number may be higher.[24] It is reported that one in every five domestic workers is an international migrant.[25] Accurate data in respect of migrant domestic workers is also affected by undocumented migrants who are reluctant to divulge information. In Germany, for example, domestic work is often part of the "shadowy economy" and accurate statistics are problematic. Domestic work accounts for 1.7 per cent of total employment worldwide and 3.6 per cent of all wage employment.[26] These statistics illustrate the significant extent of domestic work and the importance of setting international standards for these workers as promoted by the Domestic Workers Convention.[27] Establishing a framework or benchmark and promoting decent work would have an impact on the lives of millions of workers. This convention aims at improving the living and working conditions of domestic workers and advancing decent work for these workers.

In Africa, there are currently more than 5.2 million domestic workers and 74 per cent of these workers are women. Nonetheless, domestic work is

23 International Labour Office (n 14) 23.

24 International Labour Office *Social Protection for Domestic Workers: Key Policiy Trends and Statistics* Social protection paper (2016) ix, http://www.ilo.org/wcmsp5/groups/public/---ed_protect/---soc_sec/documents/publication/wcms_458933.pdf (15-09-2017).

25 International Labour Office (n 24) x.

26 International Labour Organisation (ILO) *Extension of Social Protection of Migrant Domestic Workers in Europe* (2013) 1, http://www.ilo.org/wcmsp5/groups/public/@ed_protect/@protrav/@migrant/documents/publication/wcms_232552.pdf (15-09-2017).

27 2011 (No 189).

often described as invisible and accurate data collection also remains problematic.[28] Domestic migrant workers often face additional vulnerabilities, leading to violations of their human and labour rights. Their vulnerabilities are often linked to precarious recruitment processes (including passport and contract substitution as well as charging of excessive fees), exclusion from social security legislation, discrimination resulting from lack of equal treatment with other workers, lack of representation and the absence of adapted assistance and protection mechanisms. These workers are also confronted with social and cultural isolation in the destination country due to language and cultural differences, lack of advanced and accurate information on terms and conditions of employment and restrictions on freedom of movement.[29] They often have to balance various responsibilities such as being sole providers, child care, domestic duties and care for the elderly. Although theoretically domestic workers in South Africa should be covered by national labour laws, their effective enforcement remains a key challenge. Currently, Mauritius and South Africa are the only SADC countries that have ratified the Domestic Workers Convention. Progress has been made in other countries such as Angola, where the Angolan Union of Domestic Workers has initiated a campaign for ratification of the abovementioned convention.[30]

Factors that influence the low wages of domestic workers include unequal bargaining power, isolation and the perception that the ability to perform domestic work is innate.[31] Internationally and nationally, an increased awareness of the economic and social value of domestic work exists as well as a need to improve their living and working conditions.[32] Domestic work

---

28 International Labour Office *An overview of domestic work in Africa* (2013) 1–2, http://www.ilo.org/wcmsp5/groups/public/---africa/documents/meetingdocument/wcms_213683.pdf (15-09-2017). On page 4 of this briefing note, it is indicated that limited data from only 20 countries on the African continent demonstrate how domestic work accounts for 62% of the region's total employment.

29 Gallotti *Making Decent Work a Reality for Migrant Domestic Workers* Domestic Work Programme (2015) 5, http://www.ilo.org/wcmsp5/groups/public/---ed_protect/---protrav/---travail/documents/publication/wcms_436974.pdf (15-09-2017).

30 International Labour Organisation Report (n 24) 16. In Zambia and Tanzania, surveys and campaigns have been launched to promote awareness of the rights of these workers.

31 International Labour Office (ILO) *Measuring the Economic and Social Value of Domestic Work* (2011) 4, http://www.ilo.org/wcmsp5/groups/public/---ed_protect/---protrav/---travail/documents/publication/wcms_156071.pdf (15-09-2017).

32 International Labour Office (ILO) (n 31) 1.

across the world is characterised by marginalisation and exclusion. Employers of these workers often disregard existing legislative provisions, such as hours of work and leave, due to the intimate nature of the place of employment, being the employer's residence. This provides the employer with unlimited access to the employee's time and the intimate nature of the workplace can leave these workers lacking power to challenge employers.[33]

It is important for governments, civil society and others not to disregard the economic and social value of domestic work. The diverse nature of domestic work requires an innovative approach to protection of these workers while responding to the needs of the employer (households and families) in this intimate employment relationship.

III. Legal and Economic Empowerment of Migrant Domestic Workers

The legal and economic empowerment of migrant domestic workers is essential to the extension of labour and social protection of these vulnerable women workers. In line with an integrated approach to the extension of protection of these workers is a sustainable approach of empowerment.

The process of legal empowerment[34] means that the poor have the ability to exercise their human rights as individuals within a community, and live and work with dignity.[35] The Commission on Legal Empowerment (CLEP) defines legal empowerment as a process of systemic change, whereby the poor and excluded become able to use the law, legal system and legal services to protect and advance their rights and interests, both as citizens and economic actors.[36] This includes the effective recognition and protection of

---

33 Bonner and Spooner "Organising the informal economy: a challenge for trade unions" 2011 *International Politics and Society Journal* 87 89–90.

34 This is a process that increases access to justice and the legal rights of the poor. See Banik (ed) *The Legal Empowerment Agenda: Poverty, Labour and the Informal Economy in Africa* (2011) 2.

35 Banik (ed) (n 34) 2.

36 Commission on Legal Empowerment of the Poor *Making the Law Work for Everyone* (2008) 3 http://www.undp.org/content/dam/aplaws/publication/en/publications/democratic-governance/legal-empowerment/reports-of-the-commission-on-legal-empowerment-of-the-poor/making-the-law-work-for-everyone---vol-ii---english-only/making_the_law_work_II.pdf (15-09-2017).

their labour and human capital. Legal empowerment is an important and sustainable tool in reducing poverty for workers in the informal economy.[37]

Role players in any empowerment strategy must include the government and those responsible for legal reform.[38] A successful strategy requires commitment from state and public institutions to take positive measures to ensure that the legal system is sensitive to the needs and circumstances of those most vulnerable in a society. Civil-society organisations can play a vital role in creating awareness amongst these workers about their legal rights.[39] Through legal empowerment, vulnerable and precarious workers could gain opportunities to participate and compete on equal terms.[40] The achievement of social justice and long-term social change require that these workers are aware of their rights and can actively campaign for legal reform.

Women in Informal Employment: Globalising and Organising (WIEGO) defines economic empowerment as "increased access to and control over resources and markets, increased agency and improvements in and control over specific outcomes".[41] Economic empowerment symbolises change whereby vulnerable female workers have the ability to gain access to resources, and the means to influence wider policy, thereby enabling them to

---

37 Banik (ed) (n 34) 2. This entails the enforcement of the minimum core labour rights as set out in the ILO's Declaration on the Fundamental Principles and Rights at Work of 1998, the promotion of the Decent Work Agenda, measures to protect and promote the rights of workers in the informal economy and that the poor are entitled to rights when developing their own business.

38 Von Broembsen "Poverty, legal empowerment and informal business in South Africa" in Banik (ed) (n 34) 46.

39 The mission of the Women on Farms Project (WFP) in South Africa is to empower and strengthen the capacity of female farm workers. They address their specific socio-economic needs by providing rights-based education. The project aims to create a "rural landscape" where these women workers are organised, confident and assertive when representing their own interests. See Solomon "Understanding the dynamics of and NGO/MBO partnership: organizing and working with farm women in South Africa" in Kabeer, Sudarshan and Milward (eds) *Organizing women workers in the informal economy: beyond the weapons of the weak* (2013) 74.

40 Banik (ed) (n 34) 46.

41 These outcomes include improved wellbeing and dignity, better work-life balance and improved economic opportunities. See WIEGO *Women's Economic Empowerment: WIEGO position and approach* (no date) 1, http://wiego.org/sites/wiego.org/files/resources/files/Chen_Economic%20Empowerment_WIEGO_Position.pdf (15-09-2017).

shape their livelihood and lives.[42] When considering the challenges in providing decent work and adequate social protection to precarious women workers, role players must consider an integrated approach. An integrated approach would consider factors such as access to water, maternal health, improved sanitation and addressing the disparities in school enrolment between boys and girls.[43] Governments should strive to create an enabling legal environment and a framework at national and local level to support women workers and ensure basic rights, such as a healthy and safe workplace. An enabling legal environment will promote work and economic opportunities, labour rights, benefits and protection.[44] Inclusion in existing social security programmes would require wider coverage and lowering barriers to access.

Member-based organisations (MBOs), cooperatives and non-governmental organisations (NGOs) can provide links with government institutions at both national and international levels and can ensure political pressure when promoting the interests of these workers. Legal and economic empowerment together with decent work agendas have the potential to provide sustainable solutions for such workers and this integrated approach may have a considerable impact in the reduction of poverty and improving their lives.[45]

IV. The international framework

The ILO director recently stated:

> "[T]he ILO's mandate requires it to reach out to those who are most vulnerable, who face great insecurities and for whom the denial of social justice is most cruel.[46] This is certainly true for domestic workers across the world and even more so for migrant domestic workers."

---

42 WIEGO (n 41).

43 Globally, 748 million people still rely on unsafe drinking water from different sources. Water is often not easily accessible and women and young girls often have to walk long distances to gain access to safe water. See UNESCO *The United Nations World Water Development Report: Water for a sustainable world* (2015) 19, http://unesdoc.unesco.org/images/0023/002318/231823E.pdf (15-09-2017).

44 Sankaran and Madhav "Legal and policy tools to meet informal workers' demands: lessons from India" WIEGO *Legal Brief* 1 (2013) 1.

45 Banik (ed) (n 34) 43.

46 International Labour Office (n 14) iii.

Most core labour standards apply to all workers or contain provisions for extension to other categories of workers. Furthermore, the ILO has adopted the Declaration on Fundamental Principles and Rights at Work[47] and in terms of this declaration, member states are required to adopt at least the core rights conventions. Internationally, the trend is to extend coverage to include non-standard workers, but the number of countries that have ratified the relevant conventions remains low and often the ratifying countries do not have a high prevalence of non-standard workers. Therefore the effectiveness of these conventions in protecting non-standard workers is limited.[48]

The ILO Declaration on Fundamental Principles and Rights at Work requires member states to adopt at least the core conventions containing certain core rights.[49] South Africa has ratified all 8 core conventions. These conventions are:

- the Forced Labour Convention 29 of 1930;[50]
- the Freedom of Association and the Protection of the Right to Organise Convention 87 of 1948;[51]
- the Right to Organise and Collective Bargaining Convention 98 of 1949;[52]
- the Equal Remuneration Convention 100 of 1951;[53]
- the Abolition of Forced Labour Convention 105 of 1957;[54]
- the Discrimination (Employment and Occupation) Convention 111 of 1958;[55]
- the Minimum Age Convention 138 of 1973;[56] and
- the Worst Forms of Child Labour Convention 182 of 1999.[57]

47 Adopted by the International Labour Organisation in 1998.
48 Important conventions and recommendations include the Social Security Convention 102 of 1952 and the Social Protection Recommendation 202 of 2012.
49 Art 2 in the Preamble to the Declaration.
50 South Africa ratified this Convention on 5 March 1997.
51 South Africa ratified this Convention on 19 February 1996.
52 South Africa ratified this Convention on 19 February 1996.
53 South Africa ratified this Convention on 30 March 2000.
54 South Africa ratified this Convention on 5 March 1997.
55 South Africa ratified this Convention on 5 March 1997.
56 South Africa ratified this Convention on 30 March 2000.
57 South Africa ratified this Convention on 7 June 2000.

The Domestic Workers Convention[58] and Recommendation 201 of 2011, concerning decent work for domestic workers, specifically recognises the precarious position of migrant domestic workers and the importance of extending protection to these workers through improved regulation, policies and labour laws and specific regulation to provide them with the required protection.[59] The adoption of this convention and recommendation endeavours to make decent work a reality for the precarious workers. Since its adoption in 2013, only 22 countries have ratified this convention, including Germany and South Africa.[60] This convention extends labour and social protection to domestic workers, while recognising the specific characteristics of domestic work. It is important to note that the convention applies to all domestic workers, including migrant workers and that member states are required to promote and protect the human rights of all domestic workers.[61] To provide decent work for these workers, the convention requires member states to respect, promote and realise the fundamental principles at work.[62] Article 15 specifically provides protection for workers, including migrant workers, recruited by private employment agencies through national regulation of these agencies to avoid abusive practices. This convention aims at improving the living and working conditions of domestic workers and advancing decent work for these workers and because of the large percentage of female domestic workers, the convention is an important vehicle in the quest for gender equality. Specific provision is made for migrant domestic workers. They must be provided with a written employment contract and conditions and provisions under which they will be entitled to repatriation, and private employment agencies should be regulated and monitored to

---

58 2011 (No 189).

59 The preamble of this convention highlights important factors of domestic work, such as the significant contribution to the global economy, that the work is often undervalued and carried out mostly by female workers, of whom a large number are migrants or part of disadvantaged groups and that many of these factors contribute to the precarious nature of their employment.

60 See International Labour Organisation *Information System on International Labour Standards* http://www.ilo.org/dyn/normlex/en/f?p=NORMLEXPUB:11300:0::NO::P11300_INSTRUMENT_ID:2551460 (19-01-2017). Germany ratified this convention in 2013.

61 See arts 2 and 3 of the convention.

62 Art 3 provides for freedom of association of these workers, elimination of all forms of forced labour, abolition of child labour and the elimination of discrimination in respect of employment and occupation.

avoid abusive practices.[63] Member states are obliged to take measures to cooperate with each other to ensure the effective application of this convention to migrant domestic workers.[64]

Regulations and policies should be formulated through social dialogue with all role players. The regulation of these workers at international level can only be effective if member states include the provisions in national legislation and ensure effective enforcement thereof. The enactment of these standards can be more problematic for developing countries but the ILO provides support through their various national offices. However, governments can start by removing all obstacles to the free organisation of these workers. Furthermore, platforms where the social partners may debate and consult on ways to extend protection should be effectively established.

The Maternity Protection Convention 103 of 1952 (revised) includes domestic workers and applies to all women, including those in atypical forms of dependent work.[65] In South Africa, four months maternity leave is provided for by the Basic Conditions of Employment Act (hereafter BCEA)[66] and maternity benefits are paid by the Unemployment Insurance Fund established by the Unemployment Insurance Act (hereafter UIA),[67] a compulsory contributory social insurance scheme. Migrant domestic workers should, without qualification, benefit from this but migrant workers who do not have a work permit or permanent residency status will be excluded and will be in a particularly vulnerable position.[68]

Apart from this convention there are other instruments that specifically regulate the position of migrant workers. They are highlighted below. Since the recent migration crisis in Europe it is interesting to note that as from 2011, there have been no ratifications by countries of these migrant-specific conventions:

---

63 art 8(1).
64 art 8(3).
65 See art 2(1).
66 75 of 1997.
67 63 of 2001.
68 In *Khosa v The Minister of Social Development & Others; Mahlaule v The Minister of Social Development* 2004 (6) BCLR 569 (CC), the court stated that temporary workers and illegal residents have only a tenuous link with the country and it is reasonable to exclude them from certain legislative provisions. In this case specific reference was made to social-assistance provisions.

1. Migration for Employment Convention (as revised) no 97 of 1949 and Recommendation no 86

This convention has been ratified by forty nine countries, including Germany. South Africa has not ratified this convention.[69] In terms of this convention "migrant for employment" means "a person who migrates from one country to another with the view of being employed otherwise than for his own account".[70] Although self-employed persons are excluded from the scope, domestic workers are included. This convention provides for member states to undertake medical services responsible for migrants during arrival and departures in host countries,[71] prevention of discrimination in respect of employment conditions, freedom of association, accommodation and social security.[72]

2. Migrant Workers (Supplementary) Convention no 143 of 1975 and Recommendation no 151

This convention has been ratified by twenty three countries.[73] Neither South Africa nor Germany have ratified this convention and the last ratification by a member state was in 2007. This convention provides for the promotion of equality, opportunity and treatment of migrant workers. This convention requires member states to respect basic human rights of all migrants, despite their status.[74]

---

69 SADC countries that have ratified this convention include Malawi, Mauritius, Zambia and Tanzania. See International Labour Organization *Information System on International Labour Standards* http://www.ilo.org/dyn/normlex/en/f?p=NORMLEXPUB:11300:0::NO:11300:P11300_INSTRUMENT_ID:312242:NO (19-01-2017).

70 See art 11.

71 See art 5.

72 See art 6.

73 International Labour Organisation *Information System on International Labour Standards* http://www.ilo.org/dyn/normlex/en/f?p=NORMLEX-PUB:11300:0::NO:11300:P11300_INSTRUMENT_ID:312288:NO (19-01-2017).

74 See art 1.

3. The Private Employment Agencies Convention no 180 of 1997

This convention has been ratified by thirty one countries. This convention applies to all private employment agencies. The convention aims to ensure that workers are not denied their fundamental rights such as freedom of association and collective bargaining[75] and the prohibition of discrimination, and places an obligation on member states to provide adequate protection as well as prevent abuse of migrant workers recruited by private employment agencies.[76] This convention should provide protection through member states to domestic migrant workers with the assistance of agencies.

The ILO Multilateral Framework on labour migration provides for non-binding principles and guidelines in support of a rights-based approach to migrations. Important guidelines for migrant domestic workers include the implementation of policies that address the specific vulnerabilities of certain groups. Policies should be gender sensitive and address specific problems and abuses these female workers face.[77]

Principles of equal treatment, non-discrimination and protection of non-citizens can also be found in the International Convention on the Protection of the Rights of all Migrant Workers and Members of their Families,[78] the International Covenant on Civil and Political Rights,[79] the International Covenant on Economic, Social and Cultural Rights,[80] the International Covenant on the Elimination of all forms of Racial Discrimination,[81] the Convention on the Elimination of all forms of Discrimination against Women,[82]

75 See arts 4 and 5.

76 See art 8. Member states should include provisions in national legislation which provides for penalties for abusive practices by these agencies.

77 See guidelines 4.4 and 4.5.

78 South Africa has not ratified this convention. Germany has not ratified this convention.

79 South Africa ratified this convention in 1998. Germany ratified this convention in 1973.

80 South Africa ratified this convention in 2015. Germany ratified this convention in 1973.

81 South Africa ratified this convention in 1998. Germany ratified this convention in 1969.

82 South Africa ratified this convention in 1995. Germany ratified this convention in 1985.

the Convention against Torture and other Cruel, Inhuman or Degrading Treatment or Punishment[83] and the Convention on the Rights of the Child.[84]

Extending the required labour and social protection to these precarious workers must include an integrated and comprehensive approach by all role players. This approach must include awareness campaigns, more regulation of recruitment actors, promotion of social dialogue to develop comprehensive policies, skills training for these workers and effective labour market integration.[85]

In Germany, migrant workers enjoy protection under international, European and German Law. Just like in South Africa, Germany has a constitution that is the supreme law of the country and this means that all laws, especially labour and immigration laws, must coincide with its principles and values.[86] Various directives and regulations also govern different categories of migrant workers in Germany, for example: Turkish citizens are governed by regulations of Council Decision No 1/80 of the Association Council EEC – Turkey; the right to free movement and residency of EU and EFTA nationals is governed by Directive 2004/38/EC; and Directive 96/71/EC, concerning the allocation of workers, seeks to protect employers in high wage countries against unfair competition of companies from low wage countries seeking to operate their businesses with low paid native staff in their home markets.[87] Entering the labour market and seeking residence in Germany is regulated in terms of federal German legislation (namely, the German Residency Act) and ordinances governing residency and admission procedures for foreigners that are issued by the German Department of Labour and Social Affairs.[88]

---

83 South Africa ratified this convention in 1998. Germany ratified this convention in 1990.

84 South Africa ratified this convention in 1995. Germany ratified this convention in 1992.

85 International Labour Organisation (n 24) iii.

86 Gyo (n 5) 51.

87 Gyo (n 5) 50–51.

88 Gyo (n 5) 51.

V. The SADC regional framework

Regional instruments are also applicable to the position of migrant workers in South Africa.[89] The vision, based on common values and principles, is one of a regional community, improved standards of living, freedom and social justice, and peace and security for all people.[90] Instruments that impact on the social and labour protection of workers include the SADC treaty, Charter of Fundamental Social Rights,[91] the Code on Social Security,[92] the Draft Protocol on the Facilitation of Movement of Persons and the Protocol on Gender and Development.

VI. South Africa

In Southern Africa, people are constantly moving across borders and they often migrate to improve their current situation. Migration can be seen as an important tool in the alleviation of poverty as these workers are constantly seeking better working and living conditions. In the SADC region, persons are migrating among low and middle income countries and South Africa is seen as a host country. In this region, and more specifically in Botswana, Lesotho, Namibia, South Africa[93] and Zimbabwe, domestic

---

89 The SADC was formed in 1980, http://www.sadc.int/about-sadc/overview/history-and-treaty/ (15-09-2017).

90 SADC treaty, http://www.sadc.int/files/5314/4559/5701/Consolidated_Text_of_the_SADC_Treaty_-_scanned_21_October_2015.pdf (08-12-2016). Article 3 of the SADC treaty affords the SADC legal personality. Signatories of the treaty undertake to harmonise policies, take initiatives to develop ties across the region and to join in the implementation of all programmes and projects of the community. Areas of cooperation in the area include social welfare, social and human development and special programmes that are crucial for the extension of social protection to vulnerable workers.

91 A key objective of the charter is the harmonisation of legal, economic and social policies and programmes and the establishment and harmonisation of social security schemes. The charter recognises basic human rights, equality for all, and that specific vulnerable groups need protection. Article 10 of this charter requires member states to create an enabling environment to provide every worker with adequate social protection, regardless of their status.

92 This code refers to lawfully employed immigrants and requires their protection. The scope is extended to self-employed migrants. This code also provides guidelines for the development, coordination and consolidation of social security.

93 South Africa has the highest number of domestic workers.

workers are more prevalent and the prevalence of domestic work is often ascribed to the common colonial history of these countries. In Sub-Saharan Africa, poverty, conflicts and HIV/AIDS impact on migration flows.[94] The perception exists in the SADC region that South Africa offers a better quality of life.[95] This means that South Africa appears to be a beacon of economic prosperity and hope for migrant workers.

In 2011, it was reported that South Africa was estimated to have 2.2 million immigrants and in 2015 it was estimated that there were between five hundred thousand and one million undocumented migrants.[96] According to the UN Refugee Agency's 2015 country report, there were approximately 65 000 recognised refugees and 230 000 applications for asylum at the end of 2013.[97] There are multiple reasons that have been given for why a great number of foreign migrants enter South Africa, most emphatically because these migrants seek better work opportunities for themselves and their families by finding work in South Africa as well as to escape dire poverty and social unrest in their countries of origin on the African continent.[98] Globalisation and the motivation to find work that provides one with a good living and improved work conditions also drives millions of migrant workers to leave their homes in their mother countries to pursue better work opportunities in more developed countries like South Africa.[99]

The difficulty for foreign migrant workers lies not only in the lengthy and treacherous journey that they sometimes have to make across the African continent to reach South African borders, but their entry into the South African labour market is also fraught with risks and challenges. Migrant

94 Du Toit (n 19) 224.

95 Du Toit (n 19) 226.

96 International Labour Office (n 14) 23.

97 It must be noted that the figure concerning recognised refugees in South Africa is only in relation to Somali refugees (41 500) and refugees from the Democratic Republic of Congo (32 600). The figure in relation to pending applications for asylum is the result of updated statistical information that also accounted for pending applications that were subject to a review and appeal process. See UNHRC Report *Global Trends: Forced Displacement in 2015* (2015) 17 and 44, http://www.unhcr.org/statistics/unhcrstats/576408cd7/unhcr-global-trends-2015.html (15-09-2017). South Africa has not yet ratified the Convention relating to the status of Refugees.

98 See Southern Africa Trust *Crossing the Threshold of Regionalism: Can We Meet the Social Cost of Integration in Southern Africa?* (2008) 5 http://www.southernafricatrust.org/wp-content/uploads/2014/09/crossing-the-threshold-of-regionalism.pdf (15-09-2017) for a comprehensive exposition on causes of migration.

99 Fourie and Smit (n 10) 41–43.

workers usually have to settle for informal protection measures, for example, where employers provide accommodation for undocumented migrant workers, and informal schemes provided by burial societies and churches, which would provide presumably lesser social protection to these migrant workers than social security measures in their mother countries.[100] This results in migrant workers taking on what is described as employment of a precarious nature and such workers usually fall into a category that regards them as being vulnerable, for example, women (usually domestic workers), workers in the informal economy, children and youth, temporary migrant workers or migrant workers with irregular status.[101] A significant majority of migrant workers are women and this makes them a vulnerable category of migrant workers as they are susceptible to abuse, transmission of HIV/AIDS at border posts and in informal settlements, exploitation and they can even be victims of sexual offences like rape.[102] In addition, the entry of both male and women migrant workers into South Africa is also determined based on their immigration status and their reasons for entering the country based on its own immigration laws and regulations.[103] Such immigration laws take into account that foreign nationals may be classified as permanent residents, temporary residents (the category into which migrant workers usually fall), refugees, asylum seekers and irregular or undocumented non-citizens.[104]

The fall of Apartheid in South Africa heralded a mass continental and regional migration into the country on a scale so great that government policy could not regulate it efficiently.[105] In this regard, legislation concerning

---

100 Fourie and Smit (n 10) 43.

101 Fourie and Smit (n 10) 45–46.

102 Fourie and Smit (n 10) 46.

103 Fourie and Smit (n 10) 44.

104 Fourie and Smit (n 10) 44. It is interesting to note that there are no definitions for "irregular" or "undocumented" foreigners in the Immigration Act 13 of 2002 but it is submitted that there are provisions in the Act that provide for sanctions against such foreigners in the event that they cannot provide documentation to substantiate their status or stay in the Republic, for example, section 48 (dealing with foreigners erroneously allowed into the Republic) and section 49 (offences that can be committed in terms of the Act, in the context of those that can be committed by illegal foreigners).

105 See Department of Labour RSA *Labour Migration and South Africa: Towards a Fairer Deal for Migrants in the South African Economy* (Labour Market Review 2007) 6, http://www.labour.gov.za/DOL/downloads/documents/annual-reports/labour-market-review-report/2007/labourmigration2007part1.pdf (15-09-2017).

social protection for migrant workers has not been as progressive in relation to giving certain groups of workers social protection in recent years, for example, in the case of South African domestic workers. It is submitted that Germany experienced a similar influx of migrants after the end of the Second World War that was welcomed as a way for Germany to rebuild its economy. A substantial contingent of Germany's workforce had perished on the battlefields during the war and surviving German workers could not engage in the country's economic restructuring alone. It was during the 1950s that Germany was rebuilding its economy at a rapid rate (the so-called *Wirtschaftswunder* or "economic miracle") and this paved the way through a variety of treaties for so-called "guest workers" (or *Gastarbeiter*) to do work in Germany on what was supposed to be a rotating scale, in other words, such workers would work in Germany for three years and then return to their mother countries to give other migrant workers an opportunity to help build the German economy.[106] There also came a point eventually when the German government had to limit migration into Germany, especially due to increases in unemployment rates, but the European Economic Community (or EEC) made it possible for migrant workers to move freely within the community so this inhibited Germany in restricting migrants into the country, except in the case of non-EEC nationals and asylum seekers.[107] What this demonstrates is that both South Africa and Germany have had to re-evaluate their approaches to migrant domestic workers, and in South Africa, there is still much to be done in this regard as will be explained with reference to different pieces of legislation, and, to some degree, South African case law.

1. The position of domestic workers in South Africa

During the apartheid era, domestic workers were excluded from labour and social protection. However, this changed in 1994 with a new democracy and a rights-based constitutional dispensation. The Constitution of the Republic of South Africa, 1996 (hereafter, the Constitution) is the supreme

106 Gyo (n 5) 47–48.
107 Gyo (n 5) 48.

law of the country and provides standards against which all laws are measured.[108] Chapter 2 of the Constitution contains the Bill of Rights and has formed a basis for the construction of a regulatory framework for domestic work in line with the underlying values of the Constitution, the international obligations in terms of the Domestic Workers Convention and the promotion of decent work for all.[109]

Domestic workers, in most instances, enjoy the same protection as all employees in South Africa. Since 2002, domestic workers in South Africa have been covered by a designated Sectoral Determination 7 of 2002 (hereafter, sectoral determination) providing terms and conditions of employment.[110] The scope of the determination is wide and includes workers employed by an employment agency, independent contractors and workers who perform care services in a private home, but domestic workers employed on farms are specifically excluded. The inclusion of independent contractors who are engaged in domestic work widens the scope as these workers are excluded from the Labour Relations Act (hereafter the LRA).[111] This exclusion means that independent contractors performing domestic work covered by the sectoral determination will be excluded from dismissal protection in terms of the LRA. The sectoral determination has certainly improved the working conditions of these workers but enforcement remains problematic and although principles of equal treatment are found in the Domestic Workers Convention that South Africa has ratified and in national legislation, this is not a reality yet in practice. The sectoral approach to setting minimum standards is not always ideal, as there is a risk that domestic work is undervalued and that the minimum wages for domestic workers are lower than other female or male dominated sectors with similar skills.[112]

---

108 Sec 2. Section 23 of the Constitution provides for the labour rights, and, especially, the right to fair labour practices.

109 Du Toit (n 19) 81.

110 The sectoral determination provides for prescribed minimum wages and it regulates hours of work, leave and termination of employment. Regulation by a sectoral determination highlights the uniqueness of the nature of domestic work and the need for specific regulation. The sectoral determination was issued in terms of section 51(1) of the BCEA.

111 66 of 1995.

112 In Tanzania the 2011 Wage Order set a very low wage for domestic workers, mostly women, and a much higher rate for mine workers, mostly male workers. The setting of minimum wages in this instance had the unintended consequence of reinforcing gender wage inequalities and undervalued domestic work. International Labour Office (n 14) 76.

Once again the intimate nature of the workplace allows the employer unlimited access to the working time of the domestic worker. These workers often enjoy legislative protection in respect of working hours; however exceptions are made as they are expected to work longer hours.[113]

The sectoral determination excludes all workers who work for less than twenty-four hours a month for an employer, except for the minimum wage provisions. The justification for this exclusion was the avoidance of an administrative burden on the employer where employment is "casual". A similar exclusion can be found in the convention where workers who perform domestic work do so occasionally or sporadically. The exclusion, however, will leave the most vulnerable workers without protection. It must also be noted that the nature of domestic work is often on an occasional basis for more than one employer.

Apart from sectoral determination, domestic workers are protected by a number of statutes. The LRA provides various labour rights to employees who are covered by the definition in section 213 and domestic workers are included. In chapter 2 of the LRA the right to freedom of association of both employees and employers is protected and in section 5 the protection is extended to persons seeking employment. Chapter 3 regulates collective bargaining, including organisational rights, collective agreements, bargaining councils and statutory councils. The right to strike is protected in chapter IV and protection against unfair dismissal and unfair labour practices are covered in chapter VIII. The act does not define a domestic worker, but it defines an employee in section 213 as:

> "(a) [A]ny person, excluding an independent contractor, who works for another person or for the State and who receives, or is entitled to receive, any remuneration; and
>
> (b) any other person who in any manner assists in the carrying on or conducting the business of the employer."

The LRA excludes independent contractors from its scope and to overcome evasion by employers in this respect a presumption was created in the LRA[114] and the BCEA,[115] whereby a worker meeting one of the criteria, shifts the onus on the employer to prove that the worker is not an employee. The sectoral determination includes independent contractors in its scope, thereby providing minimum terms and conditions to these domestic workers. This is also in line with the wording in section 23 of the Constitution,

113 International Labour Office (n 14) 60.
114 See section 200A of the LRA.
115 See section 83A of the BCEA.

namely "every worker". Although legislation in South Africa and international standards grant these workers the right to organise, they face many administrative and other barriers in their quest to mobilise. The traditional concept of a trade union is not always effective for mobilisation of these workers, because the diverse nature of their employment and the unique workplace pose difficulties. Trade unions face a number of challenges, including conceptual challenges, lack of resources and perhaps the political will. As these workers often work in private dwellings, it is particularly difficult to recruit and contact them. The different social, cultural and religious context of migrant workers can also impact on their mobilisation. Voice and representation of these workers is vital in extending labour and social protection to them. Workers' organisations, such as MBOs, cooperatives, NGOs and community-based organisations can provide a suitable vehicle for mobilisation of these workers as they are often in a better position to address the specific needs of these workers and to address these through innovative solutions.[116] To ensure political pressure, it is important to link these networks at both national and international levels.

The BCEA regulates hours of work, various types of leave, including maternity leave, severance pay, notice pay and sectoral determinations.[117] In Germany, the law in respect of decent working conditions is similar to the BCEA, in that the hours of work are limited to a total duration of a 48 hour week; thus normal and overtime hours cannot exceed the threshold.[118]

The purpose of the Employment Equity Act[119] (hereafter EEA) is to achieve equity in the workplace by promoting equal opportunities and fair treatment by eliminating unfair discrimination and implementing affirmative action measures. The Act's scope extends to the same categories of workers as for the LRA and BCEA. Domestic workers will be protected against unfair discrimination. Before the 2014 amendments, a claim based

116 In South Africa, a non-governmental organisation, The Women of Farms Project (WFP) assisted women workers through specific programmes addressing health, labour and social security rights, empowerment and access to land and housing. These programmes undertook rights-based capacity building. See Banik (n 34) 164.

117 Section 1 defines a domestic worker as: "[A]n employee who performs domestic work in the home of his or her employer and includes – (a) a gardener; (b) a person employed by a household as a driver of a motor vehicle; and (c) a person who takes care of children, the aged, the sick, frail or disabled, but does not include a farm worker." Similar definitions appear in the UIA and the UICA.

118 International Labour Office (n 14) 60.

119 55 of 1998.

on discrimination in the EEA would have been referred to the Labour Court after unresolved conciliation at the CCMA. Litigation in the Labour Court is expensive and unaffordable for many workers. These matters can now be referred to the CCMA, where referrals are free of charge.

Section 27(1)*(c)* of the Constitution provides that everyone has the right to have access to social security. From 2003, domestic workers were included in the scope of the Unemployment Insurance Act[120] (that is, the UIA) and the Unemployment Insurance Contributions Act[121] (hereafter UICA). These are two pieces of legislation that have as their essence the economic support of employees who are unemployed as a result of not being able to work for a variety of reasons. This essence is summarily explained as the purpose of the UIA in the following terms:[122]

> "The purpose of this Act is to establish an unemployment insurance fund to which employers and employees contribute and from which employees who become unemployed and their beneficiaries, as the case may be, are entitled to benefits and in so doing to alleviate the harmful economic and social effects of unemployment."

The UIA and the UICA provide legal provisions on contributions to be made to the Fund by employers and employees, therefore demonstrating a most straight-forward form of social protection for workers, in that when they become unemployed, through dismissal, disease or disability, these Acts ensure that they are able to receive in sum the contributions they have made to the Fund. Employers and employees are mandated to make contributions and the determination of the contribution to be made is one per cent of the remuneration that an employee receives on a monthly basis.[123] By contributing, employees who become unemployed are entitled to a range of benefits which are listed in section 12 of the UIA, namely unemployment benefits,[124] illness benefits,[125] maternity benefits,[126] adoption benefits,[127] and dependent's benefits.[128]

---

120 63 of 2001.
121 4 of 2002.
122 sec 2.
123 sec 6 in the UICA.
124 sec 12(1)*(a)*.
125 sec 12(1)*(b)*.
126 sec 12(1)*(c)*.
127 sec 12(1)*(d)*.
128 sec 12(1)*(e)*.

In terms of the Occupational Health and Safety Act (hereafter OHSA)[129] domestic workers have protection in the context of the employer providing them with a safe environment, where they would not be susceptible to, for example, injuries sustained from family pets, harm caused by criminal acts like break-ins at the private home and occupational diseases caused in the scope of their work.[130] In terms of South African common law employers must ensure healthy and safe working conditions for their employees. Employers of domestic workers will have a common-law and statutory duty to take reasonable precautions to prevent accidents in the home. The Act focuses primarily on the employer and employee relationship providing that an employer must fulfil duties towards employees in terms of providing a safe and secure work environment,[131] a duty on the part of employers and employees to inform one another of safety and risk hazards in the workplace,[132] and the general duties of employees in the workplace.[133] In Germany, the situation concerning occupational safety for workers is the same but it also goes so far as to include migrant workers in their occupational health and safety laws by ensuring that employers not only speak to employees about occupational health and safety but do so in a variety of languages to ensure that they are able to understand what the employers' duties are and what their duties are.[134]

All domestic workers in South Africa are excluded from the scope of the Compensation for Occupational Injuries and Diseases Act[135] (hereafter COIDA). Just as in the OHSA, there is no mention of provisions made for migrant workers. It is also interesting to note that domestic workers are not included within the ambit of this Act in the definition of "employee".[136]

---

129 85 of 1993.

130 Smit and Mpedi "Decent Work and Domestic Workers in South Africa" 27 (2011) *International Journal of Comparative Labour Law and Industrial Relations (IJCCLIR)* 315 329–330.

131 sec 8.

132 sec 13.

133 sec 14.

134 Gyo (n 5) 57.

135 130 of 1993.

136 Section 1(v) of COIDA reads as follows: "'employee' means a person who has entered into or works under a contract of service or of apprenticeship or learnership, with an employer, whether the contract is express or implied, oral or in writing, and whether the remuneration is calculated by time or by work done, or is in cash or in kind, and includes - … but does not include – *a domestic employee employed as such in a private household.*" (emphasis added).

This essentially means that migrant workers, even in the position of domestic workers, are excluded from obtaining a range of benefits in terms of this Act as a result of accidents occurring in the workplace,[137] accidents occurring outside the Republic,[138] and occupational diseases.[139] Although domestic workers are protected in terms of OHSA, they are not protected in terms of COIDA which makes it difficult for a domestic worker who suffers a severe injury or contracts an occupational disease in the workplace to get compensation, as the way forward for such an employee would be to sue his or her employer in civil proceedings, which has its advantages but also presents challenges to domestic workers who generally do not have the resources to pursue civil litigation against their employers.[140]

Domestic workers are a particularly vulnerable group of workers and a claim against the employer due to an occupational injury based at common law will often not be possible due to the lack of financial resources. Is this limitation of their right to social security in section 27 of the Constitution reasonable and justifiable? Justifications such as the intimate workplace and difficulties in the enforcement of compliance do not seem reasonable as these workers are covered by labour legislation and unemployment insurance. The expressed exclusion of domestic workers from COIDA is also contrary to article 14 of the Domestic Workers Convention that requires member states to ensure that these workers enjoy conditions that are not less favourable than those applicable to workers generally in respect of social security protection. This leaves South Africa in breach of its international obligations.

There are a number of grants in terms of the Social Assistance Act[141] (hereafter SAA) available to domestic workers, namely, the child support grant, foster child grant, care dependency grant, disability grant and the older person's grant. In *Khosa v Minister of Social Development; Mahlaule v Minister of Social Development,*[142] the court had to decide whether permanent residents like the applicants in this matter were entitled to the social grants in question despite the fact that they were not South African citizens

137 sec 22.

138 sec 23, where in terms of section 23(1)*(a)*, such accidents would be deemed to have occurred within the Republic.

139 sec 65.

140 See Smit and Mpedi (n 130) 330–331.

141 13 of 2004.

142 2004 (6) BCLR 569 (CC).

as required in the provisions of both the SAA and the Welfare Laws Amendment Act[143](hereafter WLAA). The court adopted this interpretation as part of its purposive approach to interpreting the rights, which essentially entails that the court seeks to determine "the core values that underpin the listed fundamental rights in an open and democratic society based on human dignity, equality and freedom, and then to prefer the interpretation of a provision that best supports and protects those values."[144]

The court held further that the right of access to social security, including social assistance for those unable to support themselves and their dependents is entrenched because human beings are to be valued and to have their basic needs in society met in order for such a society to be regarded as one built on the cornerstones of human dignity, freedom and equality.[145] The court held further that permanent residents also contribute to the welfare system and taxes of the country just as much as normal citizens do, so to deny them social benefits makes them seem inferior to citizens as a result of what the legal provisions in question encompass.[146] This creates the situation where permanent residents may have to seek assistance from friends, family and their communities who may need social assistance themselves, placing an undue burden on them and affecting the dignity of permanent residents as a result.[147] The court held that such a denial of social assistance to permanent residents was unfair as it marginalised permanent residents in a great way.[148] Mokgoro J stated:

> "I accept that the concern that non-citizens may become a financial burden on the country is a legitimate one. And I accept that there are compelling reasons why social benefits should not be made available to all who were in South Africa irrespective of their immigration status. The exclusion of all non-citizens who are destitute, however, irrespective of their immigration status fails to distinguish between those who become part of our society and have made their homes in South Africa and those who have not. It may be reasonable to exclude from the legislative scheme workers who are citizens of other countries, visitors and illegal residents, who have only a tenuous link with this country."[149]

---

143 106 of 1997.

144 para 47. The brief definition for the purposive approach is taken from Currie and de Waal *The Bill of Rights Handbook* (2013) 136.

145 para 52.

146 para 74.

147 para 76.

148 para 77.

149 paras 58–59.

2. The position of migrant domestic workers in South Africa

The Immigration Act[150] (hereafter IA) states in its preamble its aim as enabling the South African economy to have access to the full measure of required contributions by foreigners. However, it then states that the contribution must not adversely impact on existing labour standards and the rights and expectations of South African workers. To obtain permanent residency or temporary residency status entails a complicated process and in the case of work permits, employers of migrant workers must indicate that they are unable to employ a South African citizen with the same qualifications or skills.[151] This requirement poses an unsurmountable barrier to low-skilled and semi-skilled migrant workers in obtaining work permits.

In South Africa, refugees enjoy full legal protection, including the rights in chapter 2 of the Constitution. Although refugees are not allowed to seek employment in the private security industry, they are allowed to seek employment as domestic workers.[152] Refugees who work as domestic workers will be entitled to the same labour protection as South African domestic workers and they will also have access to basic health care and primary education.[153] Undocumented migrant workers will not be entitled to the same rights as refugees or migrant domestic workers, but they will have access to emergency health care.[154]

The position of undocumented migrant domestic workers is more precarious as they may fear that reporting their employer may affect their legal status and deportation is a real threat. This does not mean that these workers will be without any protection. In *Lawyers for Human Rights v Minister of Home Affairs*[155] the court stated that an illegal foreigner is a foreigner who is in the Republic in contravention of the IA but the court also confirmed that the rights contained in the Constitution, specifically section 12 and section 35 rights, are integral to the constitutional values and that to deny these

---

150 13 of 2002.

151 See sec 19(2)*(a)* of the Immigration Act 13 of 2002.

152 *Union of Refugee Women v Private Security Industry Regulating Authority* 2007 4 BCLR 339 (CC).

153 Mpedi and Smit (eds) *Access to Social Services for Non-citizens and the Portability of Social Benefits within the Southern African Development Community* (2011) 14.

154 Mpedi and Smit (n 153) 16.

155 2004 7 BCLR 775 (CC) 3.

illegal foreigners these rights would constitute a negation of our constitutional values.[156] In *Discovery Health Limited v Commission for Conciliation, Mediation and Arbitration*[157] the overall question that had to be addressed was whether "a foreign national who works for another person without a work permit issued under the Immigration Act is an 'employee' as defined by the Labour Relations Act?" and entitled to dismissal protection.[158] In respect hereof, the court analysed relevant legislative provisions, starting with section 38(1) and section 49(3) in the Immigration Act.[159] Section 38(1) reads as follows:

> "Employment – (1) No person shall employ –
>
> (a) An illegal foreigner;
> (b) A foreigner whose status does not authorise him or her to be employed by such person; or
> (c) A foreigner on terms, conditions or in a capacity different from those contemplated in such foreigner's status."

Section 49(3) reads as follows:

> "Anyone who knowingly employs an illegal foreigner or a foreigner in violation of this Act shall be guilty of an offence and liable on conviction to a fine or to imprisonment not exceeding one year, provided that such person's second conviction of such an offence shall be punishable by imprisonment not exceeding two years or a fine, and the third or subsequent convictions of such offences by imprisonment not exceeding three years without the option of a fine."

These provisions only emphasise prohibition of employing a migrant worker who does not have a valid work permit and what the consequences of employing such a migrant worker might be.[160] At the outset, the focus of these provisions in the Act does not seem to militate against a contract of employment between an illegal migrant worker and employer, as much as it enforces the notion that an employer must be guarded against employing an illegal migrant worker or face the consequences of doing so.[161] It is further submitted that by criminalising the action of the employer who employs

---

156 para 26.

157 [2008] ZALC 24. See also *Kylie v Commission for Conciliation, Mediation and Arbitration* [2008] ZALC 86.

158 para 1.

159 paras 21–22.

160 para 24.

161 Bosch "Can unauthorized workers be regarded as employees for the purposes of the Labour Relations Act?" 35 (2006) *Industrial Law Journal (ILJ)* 1342 1348–1349. In Germany, where an illicit worker is employed intentionally or negligently

an illegal migrant worker, the legislature could not have intended that these provisions in the IA were to deprive employees of legal recourse under the employment contract.[162]

The court highlighted that the right to "fair labour practices" as it appears in section 23 of the Constitution is a right that these provisions in the IA aims to limit.[163] The court then emphasised what the drastic social consequences would be if the limitation imposed on the right by section 38 were allowed to limit the right to "fair labour practices".[164] It was further held that criminalising the conduct of an employer who employs foreign nationals without valid work permits does not make the contract of employment void in the circumstances. Therefore, the contract between Mr. German Lanzetta (the third respondent in the matter and an Argentinian citizen who was lawfully resident in South Africa but had an invalid work permit) and Discovery Health Limited was valid and this made him an employee in terms of the LRA.[165] The court observed in making this decision that it provides legal recourse to illegal migrant workers that are not given to them in terms of the law, but the court argued that the effect of doing this would make employers more savvy when it comes to not hiring illegal migrant workers as required by section 38(1) of the IA because such workers have legal recourse.[166]

With regard to the contract of employment, the court held that there are other factors that extend beyond a contract of employment and the protection afforded to "everyone" in terms of section 23 in the Bill of Rights means that this right to "fair labour practices" does not only depend on the contract of employment but on other factors that are relevant to an employee's working relationship with the employer, such as other contracts, relationships and arrangements.[167] Taking this and a variety of international standards into consideration (specifically the ILO Migrant Workers (Supplementary Provisions) Convention), the court held that the contract of employment is not the only determining aspect that makes one an employee in

---

by an employer who has not checked that foreign national's residence status, that employer commits an administrative offence. This means that illegal or illicit migrant workers will very seldom work as regular employees. See Gyo (n 5) 63.

162 See Bosch (n 161) 1342 1349.
163 paras 28–29.
164 para 31.
165 para 32.
166 para 33.
167 para 41. See also Bosch (n 161) 1351.

terms of section 213 of the LRA, so Mr Lanzetta's contract was not invalid just because he did not have a valid work permit.[168] The case concerning Mr Lanzetta is ground-breaking in the sense that it brought an end to the notion that illegal migrant workers had no rights or remedies under any laws in the Republic when it came to employment disputes (a notion that was exploited by employers thinking that such workers had no legal recourse).[169] The infringement upon the rights of undocumented migrants also impairs their right to dignity.

Domestic migrant workers, categorised as temporary residents, will not have access to public health care (except emergency health care) and will have access to benefits from the Road Accident Fund. In South Africa it is compulsory for employers of domestic workers to register under the UIA and these workers are entitled to certain benefits, such as illness, maternity, adoption and other benefits when the employment is terminated. With regard to migrant workers, it is observed in section 3(1)*(d)* in the UIA and section 4(1)*(d)* in the UICA that they are not entitled to benefits as contemplated above. These sections are the same in their wording in both Acts and they read as follows:

> "This Act applies to all employers and employees, other than –Persons who enter the Republic for the purpose of carrying out a contract of service, apprenticeship or

168 para 49.

169 In *Kylie v Commission for Conciliation, Mediation and Arbitration* [2008] ZALCCT 14, similar to the reasons for decision in *Discovery Health*, the court took into consideration the definition of "everyone" as it appears in sec 23 and it held that sex workers are included in this word and are therefore afforded protection as employees under the LRA. What was also key in the Labour Appeal Court's decision to reverse the court *a quo*'s decision was that sex workers form part of a vulnerable group of employees who are susceptible to exploitation and abuse in the society, and this motivates the notion further that they should be afforded constitutional protection that accords with their dignity and the constitutional principles that ground provisions in the LRA. This case therefore lends credence to the judgment by the court in *Discovery Health*, in that employees who need constitutional protection, whether they are South African or foreign migrant workers, and who may be involved in employment and contracts of employment tainted by some illegality, are granted such protection and implied protection in terms of labour legislation like the LRA. It has been observed that the locus of such quandaries considering illegal workers and illegal contracts of employment should not focus on those contracts themselves but on the individuals that require the necessary constitutional protection and whether the severity of their illegal acts would cause more harm to the applicants if they are denied their remedies under labour legislation. See Bosch (n 161) 1348–1349.

> learnership within the Republic if upon the termination thereof the employer is required by law or by the contract of service, apprenticeship or learnership, as the case may be, or by any other agreement or undertaking, to repatriate that person, or that person is so required to leave the Republic, and their employers."

Migrant domestic workers who are performing duties in terms of a fixed-term contract and must at the end of the period return to their home country will be excluded from the scope of the UIA and will be in a particularly vulnerable position should they become pregnant, sustain injuries or if their services be terminated.[170] This provision in the act is contrary to article 54(1)*(b)* of the UN International Convention on the Protection of the Rights of all Migrant Workers and their Families in that this article requires the equal treatment of migrant workers in respect of unemployment benefits.

With reference to the statement of Justice Mokgoro in the *Khosa* judgment, undocumented migrant workers will have no right of access to social assistance. Refugees, however, enjoy the right in the Bill of Rights, and this will include the right to access to social security. Refugees further qualify for the disability grant and foster child grant. Asylum seekers will only qualify once they receive refugee status. The overall assessment of South African legislation in regard to social protection that could be provided to migrant domestic workers does not bode well for them, for although there is some protection for local domestic workers, migrant domestic workers are generally excluded from social protection in the different pieces of legislation considered above. This may change in the near future as a result of the ground-breaking cases heard in the South African courts as discussed above.

Asylum seekers are entitled to work in South Africa.[171] Formal requirements such as work permits and identity documents pose barriers to their entry into the labour market. In practice they seek low-paid employment that does not require the above documentation.[172] Asylum seekers are thus often employed as domestic workers and are in a particularly precarious position as they do not have the required documentation and may be reluctant to alert authorities to abusive and unfair labour practices.

---

170 See sec 3(d).

171 *Minister of Home Affairs v Watchenuka* 2004 4 SA 326 (SCA).

172 Mpedi and Smit (n 153) 22.

Portability of social security benefits in the SADC region remains problematic. Bilateral agreements between South Africa and neighbouring countries do exist. However, there is no multi-lateral agreement in place.[173] It is important that these agreements include principles of equality between nationals and migrant workers in respect of social security benefits. In the case of migrant domestic workers it relates to the portability of the benefits of the Unemployment Insurance Fund (or UIF). This means that the worker may return home without any of the benefits, and in particular, a migrant domestic worker during maternity may return home without receiving maternity benefits. The European Union (EU) is one of the best examples of portability of social benefits and EU regulation (EC) 883/2004 can be used as an example for the SADC region to illustrate the use of one source to provide a common standard and to limit administrative burdens imposed on countries in respect of the portability of benefits. However the challenges faced by the European Union and the SADC may differ immensely. The European Social Charter excludes undocumented migrants, however, minimum core rights do apply to undocumented migrants, including social protection.[174] It must be highlighted that multilateral agreements only provide for minimum standards for the purpose of coordinating social security schemes.[175] The European Court of Justice has confirmed that coordination rules do not affect national schemes and only supersede these rules when they are to the disadvantage of migrant workers.[176] Thus EU regulations coordinating the social security systems of member states do not impact on the freedom of member states to determine the content of their own social security schemes.[177] The EU-initiated dialogue with non-EU countries in respect of

---

173 The bilateral agreements regulate migrant labour between countries, however social security measures remain secondary. Bilateral agreements exist between Lesotho and South Africa and South Africa and Mozambique.

174 It provides that persons covered by arts 1 to 17 include foreigners only insofar as they are nationals of other contracting parties, lawfully resident or working regularly within the territory of the contracting party concerned. European Social Charter http://www.*polis.osce.org/library* (10-04-2016).

175 Olivier and Govindjee *Labour rights and social protection of migrant workers: in search of a co-ordinated legal response* (2013) 10.

176 Cornelissen "50 Years of European social security coordination" 2009 *European Journal of Social Security (Eur J Soc Sec)* 17.

177 Cornelissen (n 176).

coordination highlights three goals, namely, facilitating and organising legal migration, preventing and reducing irregular migration and maximising the development impact of migration and mobility.[178]

Recently the first ever ministerial level Migration Dialogue for Southern Africa (MIDSA) adopted the following key recommendations for managing migration in the region, namely, strengthening coordination in the region, encouraging ratification of the protocol of the Facilitation of the Movement of Persons[179] and promoting legal labour mobility and opportunities.

Although migrant domestic workers are covered by national legislation, they might not have the protection in practice. The extreme dependency on the employer, specifically in the case of migrant workers, renders them particularly vulnerable to exploitation. Where migrant domestic workers are recruited through private employment agencies, they have little opportunity to negotiate with the employer in respect of their working conditions, and language is often an additional barrier, rendering these workers even more vulnerable. These workers might be reluctant to alert authorities to abusive labour practices as this might affect their residency status. It has also been indicated that obtaining more accurate statistics about the number of migrant workers in Germany has proven to be difficult because this would put such workers' stay in Germany at risk.[180]

VII. Conclusions

The courts in South Africa have taken a totally different stance to improving the social security and labour protection of migrant workers in different categories. The courts have done this generally based on not only the nature of the employer-employee relationship and the contract of employment, but by taking into consideration the values, rights and imperatives that are laid down by the Constitution to protect all who are on South African soil and to give them the peace of mind that they need in order to live as dignified citizens in South African society, even though they themselves may not be South African citizens or the nature of their work is questionable in terms of other legislation. There have been measures put into place by the government to address the plight of domestic workers, via a so-called sectoral

---

178 Van Ginneken "Social protection for migrant workers: national and international policy challenges" 2013 *European Journal of Social Security (Eur J Soc Sec)* 215.

179 This Protocol is aimed at eliminating obstacles to free movement in the region.

180 Gyo (n 5) 49.

determination. However, how this sectoral determination will later be enforced by legislation is something for parliament to decide and the courts to adjudicate when matters concerning migrant workers from different backgrounds bring their disputes to dispute resolution agents like the CCMA and the courts.

In order to extend labour and social protection to migrant domestic workers across the globe, certain key issues must be addressed. Public and private role-players must not disregard the social and economic value of domestic work; the economic contribution to productivity, economic growth and human development in host countries and remittance in countries of origin must not be underestimated. Policy makers must consider the challenges that these workers face in respect of harassment, discrimination,[181] their vulnerability to exploitation and abuse. Ratification of relevant ILO instruments remains important in the quest for decent work for all. The intimate nature of the workplace can isolate these workers and integration programmes are essential for them.[182] Through the legal empowerment of these workers they must be informed of their legal rights and empowered to use the law to ensure protection.

International and regional cooperation between countries is of the utmost importance in the regulation of migration as the challenges facing these workers when migrating across borders cannot be addressed adequately by countries in isolation.[183]

---

181 Migrant domestic workers face discrimination on different levels, as women, as migrants and as domestic workers.

182 International Federation of Red Cross and Red Crescent Societies (IFRC) *Domestic Workers: Protection and support for migrant workers – The IFRC Perspective* (no date) http://www.ifrc.org/Global/Documents/MENA/201405/Fact%20sheet%20on%20migrant%20domestic%20workers.pdf (15-09-2017).

183 International Labour Organisation (ILO) *Non- binding Principles and Guidelines for a Rights-based Approach to Labour Migration* Multilateral Framework on Labour Migration (2006) 3 http://www.ilo.org/wcmsp5/groups/public/---ed_protect/---protrav/---migrant/documents/publication/wcms_178672.pdf (15-09-2017).

Bibliography

Banik D (ed) *The Legal Empowerment Agenda: Poverty, Labour and the Informal Economy in Africa* (Ashgate, Farnham, Burlington 2011).

Bonner C and Spooner D "Organising the informal economy: a challenge for trade unions" 2011 *International Politics and Society Journal* 87.

Bosch C "Can unauthorized workers be regarded as employees for the purposes of the Labour Relations Act?" 35 (2006) *Industrial Law Journal (ILJ)* 1342.

Commission on Legal Empowerment of the Poor *Making the Law Work for Everyone* (2008), http://www.undp.org/content/dam/aplaws/publication/en/publications/democratic-governance/legal-empowerment/reports-of-the-commission-on-legal-empowerment-of-the-poor/making-the-law-work-for-everyone---vol-ii---english-only/making_the_law_work_II.pdf (15-09-2017).

Cornelissen R "50 Years of European social security coordination" 2009 *European Journal of Social Security (Eur J Soc Sec)* 17.

Currie I and de Waal J *The Bill of Rights Handbook* (6th Edition, Juta, Cape Town 2013).

Department of Labour RSA *Labour migration and South Africa: towards a fairer deal for migrants in the South African economy* (*Labour Market Review* 2007), http://www.labour.gov.za/DOL/downloads/documents/annual-reports/labour-market-review-report/2007/labourmigration2007part1.pdf (15-09-2017).

Du Toit D (eds) *Exploited, Undervaluedand Essential: Domestic Workers and the Realisation of their Rights* (Pretoria University Press, Pretoria 2013).

Fourie E and Smit N "Labour market flexibility, migration and inflexible social protection in the SADC Region" 27 (2011) *International Journal of Comparative Labour Law & Industrial Relations (IJCCLIR)* 41.

Galotti M *The Gender Dimension of Domestic Work in Western Europe* International Migration Programme (2009) ix, http://www.ilo.org/wcmsp5/groups/public/---ed_protect/---protrav/---migrant/documents/publication/wcms_178149.pdf (15-09-2017).

Guthrie T *Transforming the Present – Protecting the Future: Report of the Committee of Inquiry into a Comprehensive System of Social Security for South Africa* (2002), http://www.ci.org.za/depts/ci/pubs/pdf/poverty/news/report_release_of_coi.pdf (01-12-2016).

Gyo C "Migrant workers in Germany" 31 (2009–2010) *Comparative Labor Law and Policy Journal (Comp Lab L & Pol'y J)* 47.

International Federation of Red Cross and Red Crescent Societies (IFRC) *Domestic Workers: Protection and support for migrant workers – The IFRC Perspective* (no date), http://www.ifrc.org/Global/Documents/MENA/201405/Fact%20sheet%20on%20migrant%20domestic%20workers.pdf (23-04-2016).

International Labour Office (ILO) *An overview of domestic work in Africa* (2013) 1 – 2, http://www.ilo.org/wcmsp5/groups/public/---africa/documents/meetingdocument/wcms_213683.pdf (15-09-2017).

International Labour Office (ILO) *Measuring the Economic and Social Value of Domestic Work 2011*, http://www.ilo.org/wcmsp5/groups/public/---ed_protect/---protrav/---travail/documents/publication/wcms_156071.pdf (15-09-2017).

International Labour Office (ILO) *Domestic Workers across the World: Global and Regional Statistics and the Extent of Legal Protection* (2013), http://www.ilo.org/wcmsp5/groups/public/---dgreports/---dcomm/---publ/documents/publication/wcms_173363.pdf (15-09-2017).

International Labour Organization (ILO) *Information System on International Labour Standards*, http://www.ilo.org/dyn/normlex/en/f?p=NORMLEXPUB:11300:0::NO::P11300_INSTRUMENT_ID:2551460 (19- 01-2017).

International Labour Organization (ILO) *Information System on International Labour Standards*, http://www.ilo.org/dyn/normlex/en/f?p=NORMLEXPUB:11300:0::NO:11300:P11300_INSTRUMENT_ID:312242:NO (19-01-2017).

International Labour Organization (ILO) *Information System on International Labour Standards*, http://www.ilo.org/dyn/normlex/en/f?p=NORMLEXPUB:11300:0::NO:11300:P11300_INSTRUMENT_ID:312288:NO (19- 01-2017).

International Labour Organization (ILO) (2013) *Extension of Social Protection of Migrant Domestic Workers in Europe*, http://www.ilo.org/wcmsp5/groups/public/@ed_protect/@protrav/@migrant/documents/publication/wcms_232552.pdf (15-09-2017).

International Labour Organization (ILO) *Protection of Migrant Domestic Workers in Destination Countries* ILO Human Rights Training Manual for Consular Officials and Labour Attaches (2006) 2, http://www.ilo.org/wcmsp5/groups/public/---asia/---ro-bangkok/---ilo-jakarta/documents/publication/wcms_122313.pdf (15-09-2017).

International Labour Organization (ILO) *International Labour Office Global Estimates on Migrant Workers: Results and Methodology* Labour Migration Branch (2015), http://www.ilo.org/wcmsp5/groups/public/---dgreports/---dcomm/documents/publication/wcms_436343.pdf (15-09-2017).

Mpedi LG and Smit N (eds) *Access to Social Services for Non-citizens and the Portability of Social Benefits within the Southern African Development Community* (Sun Press, Stellenbosch 2011).

Olivier M and Govindjee A *Labour rights and social protection of migrant workers: in search of a co-ordinated legal response* (2013) 10.

Sankaran K and Madhav R "Legal and policy tools to meet informal workers' demands: lessons from India" 1 (2013) *WIEGO Legal Brief* 1.

Smit N and Mpedi LG "Decent work and domestic workers in South Africa" 27 (2011) *International Journal of Comparative Labour Law & Industrial Relations (IJCCLIR)* 315.

Solomon C "Understanding the Dynamics of an NGO/MBO Partnership: Organizing and Working with Farm Women in South Africa" in Kabeer N, Milward K and Sudarshan RM (eds) *Organizing women workers in the informal economy: Beyond the Weapons of the Weak* (Zed Books, London 2013).

Southern Africa Trust *Crossing the Threshold of Regionalism: Can We Meet the Social Cost of Integration in Southern Africa?* (2008), http://www.southernafricatrust.org/wp-content/uploads/2014/09/crossing-the-threshold-of-regionalism.pdf (15-09-2017).

Statistics South Africa *Quarterly Labour Force Survey, Quarter 4 2015* iv, http://www.statssa.gov.za/publications/P0211/P02114thQuarter2015.pdf (15-09-2017).

United Nations (UN) *International Migration and Development: High-level dialogue of the general assembly* (2006) 1, http://www.un.org/esa/desa/desaNews/DESANews-SepOct2006.pdf (11-01-2017).

United Nations Educational, Scientific and Cultural Organization (UNESCO) *The United Nations World Water Development Report: Water for a sustainable world* (2015) 19, http://unesdoc.unesco.org/images/0023/002318/231823E.pdf (15-09-2017).

United Nations Human Rights Council (UNHRC) Report *Global Trends: Forced Displacement in 2015* (2015) 17 and 44, http://www.unhcr.org/statistics/unhcr-stats/576408cd7/unhcr-global-trends-2015.html (15-09-2017).

Van Ginneken W "Social protection for migrant workers: national and international policy challenges" 15 (2013) *European Journal of Social Security (Eur J Soc Sec)* 215.

Von Broembsen M "Poverty, legal empowerment and informal business in South Africa" in Banik D (ed) *The Legal Empowerment Agenda: Poverty, Labour and the Informal Economy in Africa* (Ashgate, Farnham 2011) 46.

Women in Informal Employment: Globalizing and Organizing (WIEGO) *Women's Economic Empowerment: WIEGO position and approach* (no date) 1, http://wiego.org/sites/wiego.org/files/resources/files/Chen_Economic%20Empowerment_WIEGO_Position.pdf (15-09-2017).

Case Law

Discovery Health Limited v Commission for Conciliation, Mediation and Arbitration 2008 ZALC 24

Kylie v Commission for Conciliation, Mediation and Arbitration 2010 ZALAC 8

Kylie v Commission for Conciliation, Mediation and Arbitration 2008 ZALCCT 14

Lawyers for Human Rights v Minister of Home Affairs 2004 7 BCLR 775 (CC) 3

Minister of Home Affairs v Watchenuka 2004 4 SA 326 (SCA)

Union of Refugee Women v Private Security Industry Regulating Authority 2007 4 BCLR 339 (C)

Labour and social protection for migrant workers in South Africa and in Germany: a comparative study

*Martina Benecke**

I. Differences between the situation in South Africa and Germany

The study of Bowles and Fourie contains a great deal of praise for Germany: they pointed out that in Germany migrant workers enjoy the benefits of legislation, which essentially protects from dangerous situations, from sexual and economic abuse and from discrimination. Of course such benefits are not to be credited to the German lawyers but the differences in legal background and legal practice between Germany and Europe, and South Africa.

Indeed, the position of migrant workers and domestic workers in Germany is far less problematic, dangerous and vulnerable than in South Africa and many other parts of the world. This is, first, due to the legislation of Germany and – more importantly – of the EU. Most migrant workers in Europe are citizens of EU member states and therefore enjoy the privileges of the principle of freedom of movement for such citizens. Consequently, the employment conditions in the EU member states are similar – with the major exception of salaries, which depend on the spending power of the

* Martina Benecke, *Dr. iur. habil.*; Professor, University of Augsburg, Faculty of Law. Chair for Civil Law, Commercial Law, Labor Law and Economic Law.

individual countries. Of course, the situation of the recent and current waves of refugees is different – they are not classified as migrant workers.

The second reason for the privileged situation of migrant domestic workers in Germany is the nature of the work. In Germany, workers who perform traditional housekeeping work – particularly cleaning and washing – do not usually live with their employers. Accordingly they are not in any situation of dependence; on the contrary, if they are good at their jobs and reliable in their work, they can be highly sought after and in a position to choose their employers. Very few families in Germany employ domestic workers and have them living with them and they maybe rather are a kind of British butlers – wealthy and even more desirable.

Notwithstanding the above, domestic workers or cleaners may have what is nowadays called "a migration background"; they themselves or their ancestors will have often come from Turkey, Russia or other Eastern Europe states. Pursuant to Article 8 of the Rome I Regulation[1], German law is applied to their employment contract and working conditions because they are

---

1 Council Regulation (EC) No 593/2008 of the European Parliament and of the Council of 17 June 2008 on the law applicable to contractual obligations (Rome I) (OJ 2008 L 177, p. 6) has replaced the Rome Convention. This regulation applies to contracts concluded after 17 December 2009. Article 8 of Regulation No 593/2008, entitled 'Individual employment contracts', provides:

> "1. An individual employment contract shall be governed by the law chosen by the parties in accordance with Article 3. Such a choice of law may not, however, have the result of depriving the employee of the protection afforded to him by provisions that cannot be derogated from by agreement under the law that, in the absence of choice, would have been applicable pursuant to paragraphs 2, 3 and 4 of this Article.
> 2. To the extent that the law applicable to the individual employment contract has not been chosen by the parties, the contract shall be governed by the law of the country in which or, failing that, from which the employee habitually carries out his work in performance of the contract. The country where the work is habitually carried out shall not be deemed to have changed if he is temporarily employed in another country.
> 3. Where the law applicable cannot be determined pursuant to paragraph 2, the contract shall be governed by the law of the country where the place of business through which the employee was engaged is situated.
> 4. Where it appears from the circumstances as a whole that the contract is more closely connected with a country other than that indicated in paragraphs 2 or 3, the law of that other country shall apply."

living and working in Germany.[2] Therefore, even if they are not German citizens, they are treated in the same way as German employees.

II. Similar problems: women in nursing business

The study of *Bowles* and *Fourie* reveals a group of workers who face very similar and parallel problems. Many European societies are ageing societies, with a growing group of people needing care and help in their daily lives. As a result of the German social system, the cheapest solution is care by members of the family; the alternative solution is care in a nursing home. A large number of families with elderly and infirm family members suffer a serious dilemma. They are unable to care for their relatives at home, either because they live far away, have to go to work and/or have to care for small children. Moreover, they lack the expertise and knowledge to provide home care. On the other hand, nursing homes are not the most pleasant place to live and elderly people will usually wish to remain in their homes.

Therefore many families employ a special kind of domestic worker: women who provide care for elderly, infirm (who may also be suffering from mental illness) persons in their own homes. Most of such workers come from Eastern Europe, especially Poland and Romania, and they usually live in the home of their employers. Working in Germany, their salary and working conditions are attractive compared with Eastern Europe. Legally, they enjoy the working conditions and the protection of EU citizens, as highlighted by *Bowles* and *Fourie*.

However, in reality, a substantial number of them experience poor working conditions and accordingly there are serious parallel problems of vulnerability and lack of social insurance. Perhaps this is symptomatic of many female migrant workers. So is Germany a country of criminal, non-compliant and unscrupulous families and old people? I think that there are two sectors of German and European legislation which may be necessary and reasonable for "normal" employer-employee relations but which make

2 For interpretation of the regulation and its protective aim, see European Court of Justice (Grand Chamber), Case C-29/10, 15.3.2011, *Heiko Koelzsch v État du Grand Duchy of Luxemburg*, ECLI:EU:C:2011:151.

home care for the elderly vulnerable to illegal practices because it is simply too expensive for most families.[3]

III. Maximum working time and minimum wage as reasons for the problems

The problem is caused by the nature of care required for infirm and mentally ill people. While they do not need care and supervision every minute of every day (there are times of sleep, watching television and so on), they do need care and help 24 hours a day, 7 days a week. So in practice, the carers usually live in a room in the same home, provide care when they are needed and attend to their own affairs when they are not needed. This sounds quite a comfortable arrangement, so why the legal problems?

The first reason is the German *Arbeitszeitgesetz* (ArbZG)[4], which can be translated as "the law on maximum working time", and the second reason is the *Mindestlohngesetz* (MiLoG)[5], which launched a minimum wage of EUR 8.50/hour two years ago – EUR 8,84/hour since 1 January 2017. The ArbZG introduced a maximum working time of 8 hours a day and 48 hours a week (with Saturday counting as a working day). A specific problem is created by the definition of "working time" by the European Court of Justice (ECJ). Since 2000 its interpretation has led, in the sector of working time legislation, to stand-by duty counting as working time.[6] In 2003 the German law has been changed in accordance with European case law.

---

3 See also Bernhard Emunds and Uwe Schacher, *Ausländische Pflegekräfte in Privathaushalten – Abschlussbericht zum Forschungsprojekt*, http://nbi.sankt-georgen.de/fileadmin/redakteure/Dokumente/FAgsFs/Pflege_HBS_Endfassung.pdf (17 February 2017); Eva Kocher, *Neue Zeitschrift für Arbeitsrecht (NZA)* 2013, 929; Deirdre McCann and Jill Murray, *The Legal Regulation of Working Time in Domestic Work* (2010), http://www.ilo.org/wcmsp5/groups/public/---ed_protect/---protrav/---travail/documents/publication/wcms_150650.pdf (15-09-2017).

4 Act on Working Hours (Arbeitszeitgesetz) from 6 June 1994 (BGBl. I, S. 1170, 1171) implementing Directive 2003/88/EC of the European Parliament and of the Council of 4 November 2003 concerning certain aspects of the organisation of working time.

5 Minimum Wage Act (Mindestlohngesetz) from 11 August 2014 (BGBl. I, S. 1348).

6 European Court of Justice, Case C-303/98, 3.10.2000, *Sindicato de Médicos de Asistencia Pública (Simap) v Conselleria de Sanidad y Consumo de la Generalidad Valenciana*, ECLI:EU:C:2000:528 with the keywords: Social policy – Protection of the safety and health of workers – Directives 89/391/EEC and 93/104/EC

However, an important exception in the ArbZG has sparked debate among commentators. According to section 18 subsection 1 No 3 ArbZG the limitations on working hours do not apply to employees who live in a common household with people entrusted to care for them and educate them.[7] However, as the term "educate" suggests, this exception does not apply to carers for the elderly but rather to people who look after children, especially orphans, and live with them. This kind of employment is based on living together; the real "work" is of far less importance. Therefore most commentators believe that the exception does not apply to domestic workers.[8]

In terms of working hours and to comply with the ArbZG, one would need three workers working in shifts to take care of an elderly or mentally ill or disabled person – a huge financial burden for a family. The mathematic solution may be a very low wage. But of course, this would be illegal. On the contrary, as mentioned above, after much consideration Germany introduced a legal minimum wage of now EUR 8.84 per working hour. This ended the long discussion on the application of a minimum wage in the area of domestic care.[9]

The probing question is whether hours of stand-by duty have to be paid as working hours.[10] Most authors and commentators in Germany do not think so[11] but recently – a short time after our conference in June 2016 – the German Federal Labour Court decided that stand-by duty is suitable for the minimum wage to be applied.[12] The next problem is to divide working time in the provision of domestic care into usual work, stand-by duty and social interaction. For example, when the carer asks how the patient is, should this be categorised as care or just kindness? Moreover, the law places many du-

– Scope – Doctors in primary health care teams – Average period of work – Inclusion of time on call – Night workers and shift workers.

7 German text: Dieses Gesetz ist nicht anzuwenden auf [...] 3. Arbeitnehmer, die in häuslicher Gemeinschaft mit den ihnen anvertrauten Personen zusammenleben und sie eigenverantwortlich erziehen, pflegen oder betreuen [...].

8 Christiane Brors and Marta Böning, *Neue Zeitschrift für Arbeitsrecht (NZA)* 2015, 846 (847); Ingrid Heinlein, *Arbeit und Recht (AuR)* 2013, 469 (473).

9 BAG 19.11.2014 – 5 AZR 1101/12, BeckRS 2014, 74316; Christiane Brors and Marta Böning, *Neue Zeitschrift für Arbeitsrecht (NZA)* 2015, 846; further particulars Ingrid Heinlein, *Arbeit und Recht (AuR)* 2013, 469.

10 See further Ingrid Heinlein, *Arbeit und Recht (AuR)* 2013, 469 (472).

11 Rolf Wank, *Recht der Arbeit (RdA)* 2015, 88 (91); Ivo Natzel, *Betriebs-Berater (BB)* 2015, 2938 (2940).

12 BAG 29.06.2016 – 5 AZR 716/15, NZA 2016, 1332, 1334.

ties on employers, especially duties relating to the documentation of working hours and of supervision. If the employee's working hours exceed the limits prescribed in law, punishment and compensation will be the consequence.

With the cost of full care amounting to a financial burden of up to EUR 6,000 per month, it will be beyond the reach of most families. Of course, there are alternatives (e.g. special agencies[13] or a contract for services instead of an employment contract[14]), but many migrant domestic workers work illegally – mostly because even working long hours in a strange home without any social protection for a very low wage is better than life in Eastern Europe. There is therefore a small but growing group of people in wealthy, safe and compliant Germany with very similar vulnerability to migrant domestic workers in South Africa.

13 For details, see Lothar Knopp, *Neue Zeitschrift für Arbeitsrecht (NZA)* 2015, 851 and Christiane Brors and Marta Böning, *Neue Zeitschrift für Arbeitsrecht (NZA)* 2015, 846 (849).

14 There is controversial debate on this possibility; see Maximilian Fuchs, *Neue Zeitschrift für Arbeitsrecht (NZA)* 2010, 980.

Bibliography

Christiane Brors and Marta Böning, Rechtliche Rahmenbedingungen für 24-Stunden-Pflegekräfte aus Polen in Deutschland, *Neue Zeitschrift für Arbeitsrecht (NZA)* 2015, 846.

Bernhard Emunds and Uwe Schacher, *Ausländische Pflegekräfte in Privathaushalten – Abschlussbericht zum Forschungsprojekt*, http://nbi.sankt-georgen.de/fileadmin/redakteure/Dokumente/FAgsFs/Pflege_HBS_Endfassung.pdf (17 February 2017).

Maximilian Fuchs, Der rechtliche Status von Pflegekräften aus den neuen EU-Staaten, *Neue Zeitschrift für Arbeitsrecht (NZA)* 2010, 980.

Ingrid Heinlein, Kein Mindestlohn und unbegrenzte Arbeitszeit für häusliche Pflege, *Arbeit und Recht (AuR)* 2013, 469.

Lothar Knopp, Gesetzlicher Mindestlohn auch für osteuropäische Pflegehilfen – legale Modelle versus Schwarzmarkt, *Neue Zeitschrift für Arbeitsrecht (NZA)* 2015, 851.

Eva Kocher, Hausangestellte im deutschen Arbeitsrecht – Ratifikation der ILO-Konvention 189, *Neue Zeitschrift für Arbeitsrecht (NZA)* 2013, 929.

Deirdre McCann and Jill Murray, *The Legal Regulation of Working Time in Domestic Work* (2010), http://www.ilo.org/wcmsp5/groups/public/---ed_protect/---protrav/---travail/documents/publication/wcms_150650.pdf (15-09-2017).

Ivo Natzel, Bereitschaftsdienste – nicht nur eine Frage der Arbeitszeit, *Betriebs-Berater (BB)* 2015, 2938.

Kirsten Scheiwe and Verena Schwach, Das Arbeitszeitrecht für Hausangestellte nach Ratifizierung der ILO-Konvention 189, *Neue Zeitschrift für Arbeitsrecht (NZA)* 2013, 1116.

Rolf Wank, Der Mindestlohn, *Recht der Arbeit (RdA)* 2015, 88.

Case Law

European Court of Justice

European Court of Justice, Case C-303/98, 3.10.2000, Sindicato de Médicos de Asistencia Pública (Simap) v Conselleria de Sanidad y Consumo de la Generalidad Valenciana, ECLI:EU:C:2000:528.

European Court of Justice (Grand Chamber), Case C-29/10, 15.3.2011, *Heiko Koelzsch v État du Grand Duchy of Luxemburg*, ECLI:EU:C:2011:151.

Germany

BAG 19.11.2014 – 5 AZR 1101/12, BeckRS 2014, 74316.

BAG 29.6.2016 – 5 AZR 716/15, NZA 2016, 1332, 1334.

Index